Funding Public Schools in the United States and Indian Country

Funding Public Schools in the United States and Indian Country

edited by

David C. Thompson
Kansas State University

R. Craig Wood
University of Florida

S. Craig Neuenswander
Kansas State Department of Education

John M. Heim
Kansas Association of School Boards

Randy D. Watson
Commissioner of Education, State of Kansas

INFORMATION AGE PUBLISHING, INC.
Charlotte, NC • www.infoagepub.com

Library of Congress Cataloging-in-Publication Data

A CIP record for this book is available from the Library of Congress
http://www.loc.gov

ISBN: 978-1-64113-676-1 (Paperback)
  978-1-64113-677-8 (Hardcover)
  978-1-64113-678-5 (ebook)

Disclaimer

While this book has been meticulously reviewed by multiple national experts in school finance, all chapters, content, and opinions represent the individual and collective work and professional judgments of the individual chapter authors.

Copyright © 2019 Information Age Publishing Inc.

All rights reserved. No part of this publication may be reproduced, stored in a retrieval system, or transmitted, in any form or by any means, electronic, mechanical, photocopying, microfilming, recording or otherwise, without written permission from the publisher.

Printed in the United States of America

Contents

	Foreword ix	
	Acknowledgments xi	
1	Alabama .... 1 *Philip Westbrook*	
2	Alaska .... 15 *Amy Lujan*	
3	Arizona .... 27 *Daniel W. Eadens*	
4	Arkansas .... 39 *Kevin P. Brady and Steve Bounds*	
5	California .... 57 *Ann E. Blankenship-Knox, Paul C. Jessup, and Robert W. Blattner*	
6	Colorado .... 77 *Spencer C. Weiler*	
7	Connecticut .... 91 *Lesley A. DeNardis*	
8	Delaware .... 101 *Staff Writer*	
9	District of Columbia .... 113 *Michael C. Petko*	
10	Florida .... 127 *R. Craig Wood and Robert C. Knoeppel*	
11	Georgia .... 143 *Marvin L. Dereef Jr. and Larry O. Jackson*	

12	Hawai'i .... 151 *Staff Writer*	
13	Idaho .... 163 *Staff Writer*	
14	Illinois.. 177 *Michael A. Jacoby, Benjamin Boer, and Melissa Figueira*	
15	Indiana .... 193 *Marilyn A. Hirth*	
16	Indian Country... 211 *Alex RedCorn, Meredith L. McCoy, and Hollie J. Mackey*	
17	Iowa .... 249 *Patti Schroeder and Shawn Snyder*	
18	Kansas .... 265 *David C. Thompson, S. Craig Neuenswander, John M. Heim, and Randy D. Watson*	
19	Kentucky.. 283 *William E. Thro*	
20	Louisiana.. 295 *Janet M. Pope, Dannie P. Garrett, III, and Markey W. Pierré*	
21	Maine...311 *Staff Writer*	
22	Maryland .... 325 *Laura Checovich and Jennifer King Rice*	
23	Massachusetts .... 339 *Glenn Koocher*	
24	Michigan .... 351 *Brett Geier*	
25	Minnesota .... 365 *Nicola Alexander*	
26	Mississippi .... 383 *Judy Rhodes*	
27	Missouri... 391 *Staff Writer*	
28	Montana .... 407 *Christiana Stoddard*	

29 Nebraska 417
   Joel Applegate, Bryce Wilson, and Jeffrey Zacharakis

30 Nevada 431
   Staff Writer

31 New Hampshire 443
   Staff Writer

32 New Jersey 455
   Luke J. Stedrak

33 New Mexico 477
   Staff Writer

34 New York 487
   Brian O. Brent and Karen J. DeAngelis

35 North Carolina 505
   Eric A. Houck and Kyle Abbott

36 North Dakota 517
   Jerry Coleman

37 Ohio 531
   Barbara M. De Luca

38 Oklahoma 543
   Jeffrey Maiden and Shawn Hime

39 Oregon 555
   Angie Peterman

40 Pennsylvania 575
   Andrew L. Armagost and Timothy J. Shrom

41 Rhode Island 599
   Ken Wagner

42 South Carolina 613
   Henry Tran and Mazen Aziz

43 South Dakota 633
   Wade Pogany, Matt Flett, and Tyler Pickner

44 Tennessee 647
   Lisa G. Driscoll

45 Texas 671
   Lynn M. Moak and Mary P. McKeown-Moak

46 Utah 691
    W. Bryan Bowles and Robert W. Smith

47 Vermont 717
    Susan B. Holson and Nicole Mace

48 Virginia 729
    William Owings and Leslie S. Kaplan

49 Washington 747
    Staff Writer

50 West Virginia 763
    Keith A. Butcher

51 Wisconsin 777
    Faith E. Crampton

52 Wyoming 797
    Brian Farmer

Foreword

American public education is a massive undertaking. In 2016 nearly 51 million students enrolled in publicly funded schools at a total cost of over $678 billion. Yet the entirety of these costs only tells part of the story. Exclusive to the finance of public education in the United States is that individual states comprise the locus of funding rather than any central government. A major strength in the American system is the complex allocation formulae that use a mix of local, state and federal revenue to direct money to school districts in response to children's needs, policy aspirations and legislative prerogative.

Like a tapestry of different fibers, colors, and weave patterns, American public education is an eclectic patchwork of programs whose statutory and financial support is documented through expedient, albeit unexpected, sources. In other words, information related to the funding of public elementary and secondary education is published and archived in excess of hundreds of local, state and federal venues; most of which are unknown except to finance experts. It is nearly impossible to locate highly current accurate information on funding that is comparable across states using a single source.

With recent increases in negative sentiment toward funding public schools, fueled in part by inaccurate school funding information presented in the general press, it behooves the education finance profession to address this issue. In response, the National Education Finance Academy is pleased to endorse this 2019 compendium of state and tribal school finance systems. This volume, *Funding Public Schools in the United States and Indian Country,* provides current and verifiable information on the funding of public schools in a format that enhances comparability among states. To ensure the credibility of each entry, recognized school finance leaders were invited to become contributors to the volume. Especially inimitable to this volume is the inaugural inclusion of school funding systems impacting Native American Tribal Governments.

This volume is the most current effort to gather and broadly disseminate information about the status of public school finance across the United States. Editors and authors David C. Thompson, R. Craig Wood, S. Craig Neuenswander, John M. Heim, and Randy D. Watson represent an impressive cadre of scholars and state education officials who have brought many valuable projects to fruition in the field of education finance.

Lisa G. Driscoll, Ph.D.

Lisa G. Driscoll

President, 2018–2019
National Education Finance Academy

Acknowledgments

A book of this tremendous size, scope, and complexity of content is an impossible undertaking without an army of experts and supporters whose loyalty to the profession and to each other is unmatched. Such was the case with this current book, as all the people and organizations acknowledged below came together to produce this extraordinary volume.

Simply said, *Funding Public Schools in the United States and Indian Country* is an unprecedented achievement. Many years ago the American Education Finance Association (AEFA) infrequently published a bulky two-volume set of brief descriptions of state K–12 fiscal programs. In contrast, this new volume provides concise descriptions under a single cover and represents the first time that Native American Nations and affiliated bureaucracies have been embraced as active stakeholders in the field of education finance. These sovereign entities possess unique legal rights to self-determination while operating alongside local, state, and federal agencies with overlapping jurisdictions, contributing to the diverse quilt of agencies that manage schoolchildren's lives today. In the end, *Funding Public Schools in the United States and Indian Country* is at once an unequaled celebration of progress and a reminder that much still needs to be done to sustain and grow the dream of absolute equality in 21st century public schools.

The editorial team cannot sufficiently thank everyone who contributed to this volume. We have acknowledged in endnote various contributors and reviewers and resources—we are truly indebted for their service. Those who have been closest to the book have included the following persons and organizations—we are especially indebted for their dedication, support and contributions.

The National Education Finance Academy (NEFA)—the origin and inspiration for this volume, along with its many members whose high skills as chapter authors and in-state experts made this book a reality;

Members of state affiliates of the Association of School Business Officials International (ASBOI)—particularly Dr. Rob Balsters (Kansas), Dr. Deborah Cunningham (New York), and Dr. Traci Ginsburg (Texas) who provided valuable and ongoing assistance in securing various chapter authors;

Members of state affiliates of the National School Boards Association (NSBA)—their willingness and expertise in authoring chapters provided the book with unique expertise and policy credentials;

All authors and coauthors of all 52 chapters in this book—all hail from high offices throughout the school finance world—in all, more than 70 experts whose knowledge came together for the sole purpose of informing the field, the profession, and the policy arena.

The editors also express deep gratitude to the Elvon G. and Lydia E. Skeen Education Fund for financial support of this first edition. The Skeen Family's generous backing made possible selected complimentary distribution.

The editors also owe an enormous debt of gratitude for the unbounded support of Dr. Debbie Mercer, Dean of Education at Kansas State University. Her enthusiasm and support for this daunting project made possible the Skeen Family contribution. Of equal value was the requisite and enduring encouragement she provided—an exceedingly rare talent and gift that only comes from a true advocate's vision of a better world for children.

Finally, the editors are indebted to the expert skills and production capabilities of those who take the work of content experts and make it all appear in print. Particularly, the editors thank Karen Low, Skeen Graduate Assistant and Ph.D. candidate—her copyediting skills were timely, insightful and indispensable. And the editors particularly salute IAP—a respected publishing house well known to these editors and throughout the education profession for its lightning speed and quality of product and service.

—**The Editors**

CHAPTER 1

Alabama

Philip Westbrook Ed.D.
Clinical Professor
University of Alabama

GENERAL BACKGROUND

Alabama has had six constitutions since the state was first established in 1819. The first, the Constitution of 1819, known as the Frontier Constitution, established public schools in Alabama.[1] Based on the principles of the Northwest Ordinances of 1787, the sixteenth section of each township was set aside for public schools. From 1819 to 1828, the individual townships owned these lands. In 1828 the Public School Fund was established, with the state legislature providing for the sale of these lands with the proceeds deposited into the State Bank. The State Bank funded the operations of state government. In 1843 the State Bank failed, and the state went bankrupt. The Public Education Act of 1854 created the first statewide system of public schools, the position of state superintendent, and the 'Education Fund,' with certain revenue and endowments to be distributed by the State Superintendent.[2]

The Constitution of 1861, known as the Secession Constitution, repeated basic philosophies of the 1819 Constitution regarding public education. Education languished in the devastation of the Civil War.[3]

The Constitution of 1865, known as the Reorganization Constitution, preserved the sixteenth section land endowment for public schools. However, with the state struggling to provide basic services little attention could be provided to public education.[4]

Funding Public Schools in the United States and Indian Country, pages 1–13
Copyright © 2019 by Information Age Publishing
All rights of reproduction in any form reserved.

The Constitution of 1868, known as the Reconstruction Constitution, encouraged and strengthened public education by calling for a free education for children "... between the ages of five and twenty-one years," including both white and black children, created a state board of education, preserved the sixteenth section lands for public schools, empowered local school boards to levy taxes for schools, and appropriated one-fifth of state revenue for public education.[5]

The Constitution of 1875, known as the Conservative Constitution, abolished the state board of education, consolidated power in the hands of an elected state superintendent, required separate schools for white and "children of citizens of African descent," reduced expenditures, and limited taxes.[6]

The Constitution of 1901, the current state constitution known as the Disenfranchising Constitution, returned White rule to the state, disenfranchised black citizens, and consolidated power in the state legislature by greatly limiting the local control of counties and municipalities. This constitution, the longest in the United States and believed to be longest in the world, has been amended over 900 times and maintains Alabama in a post-Civil War and emerging industrial economy mindset. The constitution still contains outdated language on segregated schools stating that "... separate schools shall be provided for white and colored children, and no child of either race shall be permitted to attend a school of the other race."[7]

BASIC SUPPORT PROGRAM

Alabama operates with two different budgets: The Education Trust Fund (ETF) which funds public schools, higher education, and other education-related agencies; and the General Fund (GF) which funds all other state functions. Only two other states, Michigan and Utah, have separate education and general fund budgets. The ETF is the largest operating fund of the state.

The Education Trust Fund

The Education Trust Fund was created in 1927 'for educational purposes only' and 'for the support, maintenance, and development of public education and capital improvements relating to educational facilities.' It levied revenue sources for education and set them apart as a special fund for education.[8] The ETF receives funds generated by state income tax, state sales tax, state utility tax, and a state use tax. Monies on deposit in the ETF are annually appropriated by the state legislature. Ten tax sources are earmarked for the ETF, but its major sources of revenue are (1) state income tax, (2) state sales tax, (3) state utility tax, and (4) state use tax. Table 1.1 provides a description of ETF receipts for the Fiscal Years 2015–2017.

Income tax is the largest source of revenue for the Education Trust Fund. Income tax was first established in Alabama in 1935.[9] Current individual income tax rates are described in Table 1.2.

The corporate income tax rate is 6.5%. Corporations doing business in more than one state must determine the income generated in Alabama.[10] Individual income tax receipts are the single largest contribution to the ETF. Individual income tax receipts for the fiscal years 2013–2017 are listed in Table 1.3.

For FY 2019 the total state budget for public K–12 schools is $4,597,282,016. Public school spending represents 69% of the ETF, with the remaining allocations going to higher education which receives 25% and other education-related agencies which receive 6%.[12]

TABLE 1.1 Education Trust Fund Receipts, 2015–2017			
	FY 2015	FY 2016	FY 2017
Income Tax	$3,725,299,372	$3,722,129,992	$3,892,525,501
Sales Tax	$1,623,588,330	$1,744,468,414	$1,811,657,811
Utility Tax	$401,700,962	$376,625,096	$387,966,309
Use Tax	$222,096,692	$157,068,198	$165,057,908
Insurance Premium Tax	$30,993,296	$40,993,346	$30,993,296
Beer Tax	$22,838,290	$22,909,170	$22,231,590
Mobile Telecommunications Tax	$19,991,675	$17,700,484	$15,904,023
All Other	$1,832,455	$1,041,361	$9,907,780
Grand Total	$6,048,341,072	$6,072,936,061	$6,327,327,218

Source: Alabama Legislative Services Agency (2019).

TABLE 1.2 Income Tax Rates	
Household	Rate
Single Persons, Head of Family, and Married Persons Filing Separate Returns	
First $500 of taxable income	2%
Next $2,500 of taxable income	4%
All taxable income over $3,000	5%
Married Persons Filing Joint Return	
First $1,000 of taxable income	2%
Next $5,000 of taxable income	4%
All taxable income over $6,000	5%

Source: Alabama Legislative Fiscal Office (2019).

TABLE 1.3 Individual Income Tax Receipts, FY 2013–2017

Year	Gross Collections	Refunds	Net Collections	Percent Change
2017	$4,206,789,721	$582,246,928	$3,624,542,793	3.77%
2016	$4,072,002,891	$579,098,369	$3,492,904,520	4.68%
2015	$3,929,550,713	$592,963,468	$3,336,587,245	4.05%
2014	$3,752,015,058	$545,431,933	$3,206,583,125	0.13%
2013	$3,753,387,566	$550,867,831	$3,202,519,735	6.13%

Source: Alabama Legislative Fiscal Office (2018).[i]

ROLLING RESERVE ACT

The Rolling Reserve Act (Act 2011-3 as amended by Act 2015-538) establishes the maximum amount that may be legislatively appropriated in any fiscal year. This maximum amount, known as a 'Fiscal Year Appropriation Cap,' is calculated by taking the sum of the total amount of revenue deposited into the ETF for the highest 14 years out of the last 15 years. The cap may be adjusted if the legislature passes legislation adding revenue to the ETF, but by no more than 95% of anticipated new revenue as described by the fiscal note attached to the legislative act.

The Act further requires that revenues in excess of the appropriation cap be placed in an account known as the ETF Rainy Day Fund Account. The EFT Rainy Day Fund has two different subaccounts: (1) The ETF Budget Stabilization Fund, and (2) the ETF Advancement and Technology Fund. The Budget Stabilization Fund is first funded at a rate of 1% of the previous year's ETF appropriations until the fund reaches 7.5% of the previous year's appropriation to be used in times in which there is a shortfall in the revenue needed to meet budget allocations. The ETF Advancement and Technology Fund is the excess over the required funds for the Budget Stabilization Fund and is to be appropriated in an independent supplemental appropriation bill once the balance of this fund is at $10 million. These funds are to be used for (1) repairs or deferred maintenance of facilities, (2) classroom instruction support, (3) insurance for facilities, (4) transportation, or (5) technology.[13]

FOUNDATION PROGRAM DISTRIBUTION MODEL

Alabama's current funding distribution model for public K–12 schools is known as the Foundation Program. This Foundation Program was created in 1995 by the state legislature to replace the old 1935 Foundation Program that was commonly referred to as the 'State Minimum Program,' which was considered both inadequate and inequitable.[14]

The Foundation Program is an equalization grant in that state funds are disbursed based on the needs and ability of local school systems to generate funding for schools. Each local school system is required to contribute the equivalent of ten mills ad valorem tax based on local millage rate yield. This amount is considered a chargeback to the system and requires each system to participate at a basic level of support according to the fiscal capacity of each community.

Foundation Program funds are distributed to school systems based two main sources of data: (1) the Average Daily Membership (ADM) of a school system, and (2) the Local Education Agency Personnel Report System (LEAPS Report).

System ADM is the average daily enrollment for a system during the first twenty days after Labor Day. ADM is collected by the State Department of Education through the system's student database. ADM is calculated for each school in the system using the formula:

Pupil Days for the 20 School Days after Labor Day/20 = ADM

Each school system is required to file a report on personnel called the Local Education Agency Personnel System Report (LEAPS Report) which lists all personnel, their highest degree, years of experience, salary, and work assignments. This report ensures that Foundation Program-funded personnel are (1) properly certified to teach in the fields assigned, and (2) personnel are assigned to complete work as funded by the legislature. The LEAPS Report is submitted annually to the Alabama State Department of Education by each school system. School systems report all personnel, including staff funded by local or federal funds. All Foundation Program units must be employed in the school in which they are earned, or Foundation Funds must be returned to the state. Districts may add personnel using local funds as determined by the local board of education.

The Foundation Program funds teacher units and other personnel. Funds are distributed to support teacher units using a formula with divisors for each grade level (See Table 1.4). In addition, teacher units are funded based on the state's Minimum Salary Schedule for Teachers, which is based on the highest degree earned and years of experience. Additional funds are provided to support administrators, counselors, and career and technical education administrators. For FY 2019, the Foundation Program funding included a 2.5% raise for all employees.[15]

In 2018, Alabama had 138 school systems, including 67 county school systems, 69 city school systems, and one charter school system. An additional city system began operation in 2019 by separating from the Mobile

TABLE 1.4 Grade Divisors for FY 2019[a]

Grade	Divisors
Grade K	14.25
Grade 1	14.25
Grade 2	14.25
Grade 3	14.25
Grade 4	21.03
Grade 5	21.03
Grade 6	21.03
Grade 7	19.70
Grade 8	19.70
Grade 9	17.95
Grade 10	17.95
Grade 11	17.95
Grade 12	17.95

[a] Alabama State Department of Education, FY 2019 State Totals (2019).

County Schools, and one additional charter opened in fall 2018. In that same year, there were 1,473 total public schools, 742,444 students, 46,715 teachers and a total of 91,797 education employees.[16]

FISCAL YEAR CALENDAR

Alabama's fiscal year runs October 1 through September 30 which makes budgeting more complex since it matches neither the academic year nor the employee contract year. Alabama is one of only four states that do not use a July 1–June 30 fiscal year.[17]

EMPLOYEE FRINGE BENEFITS

Fringe benefits funded by the state of Alabama include retirement, healthcare, Social Security, Medicare, unemployment compensation, and sick and personal leave. All full-time employees are required to participate in the Teachers Retirement System of Alabama (TRS), a defined benefit plan established in 1941.[18] There are currently two tiers of membership: Members who were employed prior to January 1, 2013, known as Tier 1 members, and members employed on or after January 1, 2013, known as Tier 2 members. These plans provide both disability and service retirement to members and qualified survivor beneficiaries. The Tier 1 member contribution rate is 7.5% of total salary, and the employer rate is set annually by the legislature based on recommended actuarial valuation of participating agencies. For 2019, the employer contribution for Tier 1 employees is 12.41%. Tier 1 members may retire with 25 years of service at any age or ten years of service at age 60. The Tier 2 member contribution rate is 6% of total salary, and the employer rate is 11.01%. Tier 2 members are not eligible for 25-year retirement and cannot collect retirement until age 62 after a minimum of ten years of service credit. Table 1.5 details and compares the tiers affecting TRS member retirement.

Education employees may elect to participate in the Public Education Employees' Health Insurance Plan (PEEHIP) which was established in 1983. The employer contributes $800 per month per employee, for a total of $9,600 per year toward health insurance. The Teachers' Retirement System and Public Education Employees' Health Insurance Plan Boards of Control set monthly premiums, which are an additional source of funding for the insurance program. The PEEHIP Board is composed of 15 members who are elected or hold office ex officio. Board members serve as the trustees of the funds and are responsible for administration of the retirement system.[19]

Education employees participate in Social Security and Medicare; the employer contribution rate is 6.20% and 1.45% respectively. The employer

TABLE 1.5 TRS Member Retirement Comparison

TRS Member Retirement Comparison

	Tier 1 Employee	Tier 2 Employee
Date of Employment	Prior to January 1, 2013	On or after January 1, 2013
Member Contribution Rate	7.5% for Regular Employees 8.5% for FLC* Employees	6.0% for Regular Employees 7.0% for FLC* Employees
Employer Contribution Rate	12.41%	11.01%
Retirement Eligibility	25 years of service at any age 10 years of service at the age of 60	No 25 year retirement 10 years of service at the age of 62
Retirement Factor	2.0125%	1.6500%
Average Final Salary	Average of the highest three years of the last ten years	Average of the highest five years of the last ten years
Benefit Cap	None	80% of Average Final Salary
Retirement Contributions on Overtime Pay	Earnable Compensation cannot exceed 120% of base pay	Earnable Compensation cannot exceed 125% of base pay
Sick Leave Conversion	Yes	No

Source: University of North Alabama. Teachers Retirement System of Alabama. Adapted from https://www.una.edu/humanresources/benefits/teachers-retirement.html

contribution to unemployment compensation for 2019 is 0.1250%.[20] The state funds five sick leave days and two personal days per year for each employee, although many local districts elect to provide more. The state provides compensation for substitutes for certified employees at a rate of $70.00 per day.

TRANSPORTATION

Alabama has a funding formula for transportation of public school pupils that provides funding for (1) a fleet of buses; (2) fuel; (3) bus driver and other employee salaries; (4) employee benefits including healthcare and pension; and (5) maintenance. Transportation is funded by a cost reimbursement formula for students who live more than two miles from the local school; however, most school systems provide optional transportation to children living closer than two miles at the expense of the local system.

The Alabama Fleet Renewal program provides school systems with funding for each bus that is ten years old or less. For FY 2019 this amount is $7,109 per bus. Districts may use the funds to purchase or lease new school buses. Currently, 92% of Alabama's school buses are ten years old or newer. School systems are reimbursed for fuel based on the actual number of miles driven as calculated in the system's Route Report. Consideration is given for the type of route driven (general transportation, special education transport, choice transport, midday transport to special schools and career centers, etc.) and the number of students transported. The cost of employees including bus drivers, supervisors, support workers, bus aides for special needs students, and maintenance, is calculated in the plan.[21]

For FY 2019 the total amount of state funding for Fleet Renewal is $40,571,063 and the total amount for Transportation Operations is $307,385,994—both increased above FY 2018.[22] In 2018 there were 9,908 school buses covering 520,452 daily route miles transporting 382,824 students at an annual rate of $958.68 per child. Approximately 71,248 gallons of fuel were consumed per day, and approximately 53% of public school students were transported via public school buses.[23]

CAPITAL OUTLAY AND DEBT SERVICE

Alabama provides support for capital outlay and debt service through an allocation in the ETF. For FY 2019 the Capital Purchase is $185,000,000 and the Debt Service is $532,864. Each school system is required to contribute 0.860704 mills to receive the Capital Purchase allocation from the state. For FY 2019 this amount is $50,222,764.[24] Capital Outlay funds are distributed based on a complex formula that considers the system's yield of three mills ad valorem tax divided by the system's ADM to determine the millage yield per pupil. Systems are ranked, and funds are distributed by an equalization grant that considers the differences in capacity of each system.

SPECIAL EDUCATION

The Alabama Foundation Program funds teacher units earned by school systems which may be used to employ special education teachers. The Foundation Program does not provide weighted per-pupil funding for special needs children; however, the ETF includes special allocation for (1) preschool special education, and (2) a catastrophic fund for the support of individual special education students to which the system may apply for additional funding for unbudgeted expenses related to severe needs of a special education child.

Preschool Special Education

Alabama funds preschool for special education services for children with disabilities in an amount determined annually by the state legislature per Act No. 1991-474. School systems report the number of children ages 3–5 with special needs who attend preschool, and the allocation is divided per school system by ADM. The preschool special education program is a specific line item in the ETF allocation.

Catastrophic Fund Allocation

Alabama provides a catastrophic fund allocation that serves as a pool of money to which school systems can apply based on extreme expenses related to individual special education students who were not considered in the regular school budget. This fund is limited, and systems must justify an exceptional case supporting additional state funding. The funds are distributed by the SDE until the pool of money is exhausted. The catastrophic fund allocation is a specific line item in the ETF allocation.[25]

CAREER AND TECHNICAL EDUCATION

The Foundation Program funds teacher units earned by school systems and may be used to employ career and technical education certified teachers. In addition, a weighted formula provides career tech administrators and counselors for school systems having career tech schools.[26] Other career tech funds are provided by the federal government or local school system funds. In 2017, 72% of high school students were enrolled in at least one CTE class. These students took 391,601 career tech classes in 515 different courses.[27]

CLASSROOM INSTRUCTIONAL SUPPORT

For FY 2019 Alabama provides classroom instructional support for the following:

- *Student Materials* for the purchase of classroom supplies at a total allocation of $25,359,298 or $536.07 per teaching unit;
- *Library Enhancement* for the purchase of school library books and materials at a total allocation of $4,547,871 or $96.14 per teaching unit;
- *Professional Development* at a total allocation of $4,257,638 or $90.00 per teaching unit;
- *Textbooks* at a total allocation of $1,164,998 or $70 per student ADM.[28]

TECHNOLOGY

Alabama provides a technology coordinator for each school district with a special line item of $7,775,573. In addition, FY 2018 provides $300 per teacher unit for the purchase of technology.[29]

FOOD SERVICES AND OTHER NONTRANSPORTATION SUPPORT STAFF

Alabama's Child Nutrition Program (CNP) workers are included in the Foundation Program in a category called 'Other Current Expenses' which is a catch-all for non-transportation support employees (all employees related to transportation are funded in a separate allocation). This includes school secretarial and bookkeeping staff, custodial staff, teacher aides, and other noncertified employees who are not specifically allocated in a separate line item in the Foundation Program. This allocation is based on the number of teacher units. For FY 2019 the allocation is $17,950 per certified unit for a total of $849,147,372.

SCHOOL NURSES

Alabama provides school nurses with an appropriation allocated for each system to receive one school nurse at a base salary determined by the legislature plus additional funding based on the ADM of the school system. For 2019 the total allocation is $31,964,511. This allocation was created in 1998 by Act No. 1998-672.[30]

STATE FUNDING FOR CHARTER SCHOOLS

The state legislature passed the Alabama School Choice and Student Opportunity Act (Alabama Act 2015-13) in 2015. The act (1) created the Alabama Public Charter School Commission; (2) established a process for the formation of a charter school and the conversion of a currently existing public school to a charter school; (3) created standards and a process for the renewal, revocation, and nonrenewal of charters; and (4) addressed funding and facilities for charter schools. The first charter school opened in Mobile in 2017, and a unique public charter school opened in August 2018 in affiliation with The University of West Alabama, a public university located in rural Sumter County. Critics noted the irony in the timing of the announcement, in that the largest private school in the county (Sumter Academy) which was established in 1970 as one of many Christian academies created following federal desegregation orders in the years after *Brown v Board of Education*, announced it would be closing its doors.[31]

STATE FUNDING FOR NONPUBLIC SCHOOLS

Alabama provides a line-item appropriation for two nonpublic schools: Lyman Ward Military Academy, and Talladega College, one of the Historically Black Colleges and Universities (HBCUs). For FY 2019 the allocation for Lyman Ward Military Academy is $1,000,000 and the allocation for Talladega College is $971,296.[32]

VIRTUAL EDUCATION

Alabama requires each school system to adopt a policy for providing virtual school options for students in grades 9 through 12 (Alabama Act 2015-89). Systems may contract with a vendor or operate their own virtual school programs.

SUMMARY

Alabama saw a decline in education funding since the Great Recession. FY 2019 saw the largest budget since FY 2008, but it was still slightly less.[33] More than a decade of reduced funding drastically impacted Alabama's public schools. As a result, student achievement declined compared to national norms, and Alabama's students fell farther behind their peers in other states. Teacher salaries failed to match inflation, drastic changes to retirement and healthcare benefits made a career in education less appealing, and enrollment in teacher education programs declined.[34] School employees received only two raises since FY 2009 (2% in FY 2014 which was consumed for most employees by a corresponding increase in healthcare premiums, and either 2% or 4% in FY 2017 based on whether an employee earned more or less than $75,000 respectively). Still, the 2.5% raise granted by the legislature for FY 2019 was welcomed by employees.

NOTES

1. Alabama Legislature. Constitution of 1819. Retrieved from http://www.legislature.state.al.us/aliswww/history/constitutions/1819/1819.html
2. Ira Harvey. "School Finance for the Alabama Superintendent. Alabama State Department of Education (2015). Retrieved from http://uasa.ua.edu/uploads/3/0/1/2/30128295/finance_reference_2015_122115.pdf
3. Alabama Legislature. Constitution of 1861. Retrieved from http://www.legislature.state.al.us/aliswww/history/constitutions/1861/1861.html
4. Alabama Legislature. Constitution of 1865. Retrieved from http://www.legislature.state.al.us/aliswww/history/constitutions/1865/1865.html
5. Alabama Legislature. Constitution of 1868. Retrieved from http://www.legislature.state.al.us/aliswww/history/constitutions/1868/1868all.html
6. Alabama Legislature. Constitution of 1875. Retrieved from http://www.legislature.state.al.us/aliswww/history/constitutions/1875/1875.html
7. Alabama Legislature. Constitution of 1901. Retrieved from http://alisondb.legislature.state.al.us/alison/codeofalabama/constitution/1901/toc.htm
8. Ibid, Harvey (2015).
9. Ibid.
10. Alabama Code Title 40. Revenue and Taxation § 40-27-1. Retrieved from https://codes.findlaw.com/al/title-40-revenue-and-taxation/al-code-sect-40-27-1.html
11. Alabama Legislative Services Agency, Fiscal Division. *Tax Guide 2018.* (2018). Retrieved from http://lsa.state.al.us/PDF/LFO/TaxGuide/2018_Tax_Guide.pdf
12. Alabama State Department of Education. *FY2019 State Totals.* (2019). Retrieved from http://www.alsde.edu/dept/data/Foundation%20Reports%20Tabbed/FY%202019%20State%20Allocation.pdf

13. Alabama Legislative Services Agency, Fiscal Division. *Budget Fact Book 2018* (2018). Retrieved from http://lsa.alabama.gov/PDF/LFO/BudgetFactBook/2018_Budget_Fact_Book.pdf
14. Ibid, Harvey (2015).
15. Ibid, Alabama State Department of Education, *FY 2019 State Totals* (2019).
16. Alabama State Department of Education, *Quick Facts* (2018). Retrieved from https://www.alsde.edu/sec/comm/Quick%20Facts/QF-2018-Online.pdf
17. National Conference of State Legislatures. *FY 2019 State Budget Status* (2019). Retrieved from http://www.ncsl.org/research/fiscal-policy/fy-2019-budget-status.aspx
18. Retirement Systems of Alabama. *Teachers Retirement System.* Retrieved from http://www.rsa-al.gov/index.php/members/trs
19. Retirement Systems of Alabama. *Public Education Employees' Health Insurance Plan.* Retrieved from http://www.rsa-al.gov/index.php/members/peehip/
20. Ibid, Alabama State Department of Education, *FY 2019 State Totals* (2019).
21. Alabama State Department of Education, *Pupil Transportation* (2019). Retrieved from https://www.alsde.edu/sec/pt/Pages/home.aspx
22. Ibid, Alabama State Department of Education, *FY 2019 State Totals* (2019).
23. Ibid, Alabama State Department of Education, *Quick Facts* (2018).
24. Ibid, Alabama State Department of Education, *FY 2019 State Totals I* (2019).
25. State of Alabama, *Executive Budget, Fiscal Year 2019* (2019). Retrieved from http://budget.alabama.gov/wp-content/uploads/sites/9/2018/01/BudDoc20192.pdf
26. Ibid, Alabama State Department of Education, *FY 2019 State Totals I* (2019).
27. Ibid, Alabama State Department of Education, *Quick Facts* (2018).
28. Ibid, Alabama State Department of Education, *FY 2019 State Totals* (2019).
29. Ibid.
30. Alabama State Department of Education. *A Guide to State Allocation Calculations 2017–2018* (2018). Retrieved from http://www.alsde.edu/sec/leafa/State%20Allocations/State%20Guide%20to%20Allocations%202017-18.pdf
31. Trisha Powell Crain, *AL.COM.* "Alabama Commission Approves Two New Public Charter Schools. (June 27, 2017). Retrieved from http://www.al.com/news/index.ssf/2017/06/alabama_commission_approves_tw.html
32. Ibid, State of Alabama *Executive Budget* (2019.
33. Trisha Powell Crain, *AL.COM.* "A Closer Look at Alabama's $6.63 Billion Education Budget, Largest in a Decade." (April 3, 2018). Retrieved from https://www.al.com/news/index.ssf/2018/04/a_closer_look_at_alabamas_663.html
34. Trisha Powell Crain, *AL.COM.* "Alabama Teacher Salaries Worth Less Than a Decade Ago." Retrieved from https://www.al.com/news/index.ssf/2018/05/alabama_teacher_salaries_worth.html

CHAPTER 2

Alaska

Amy Lujan, MBA, SFO
Executive Director
Alaska Association of School Business Officials

GENERAL BACKGROUND

Alaska is the geographically largest state in the country, making up nearly 20% of the United States. It is larger than the next three largest states combined: Texas, California, and Montana. Yet in population, Alaska is among the smallest states, with just less than 740,000 estimated in 2017, and with over 40% of the population concentrated in the Anchorage area. Alaska's geographic size and sparse population have created challenges for funding public education.

Alaska's K–12 funding formula must fund 53 school districts, ranging from single-site districts to districts with sprawling geography. For example, an area slightly larger than the state of Minnesota is served by a single school district, the North Slope Borough School District. For FY 2018, district size ranged from just eight students in the Pelican School District to 47,624 in the Anchorage School District. More than half of all districts (29) had a total enrollment of fewer than 500 students, and just four districts had enrollments greater than 5,000.[1]

Logistics and transportation are an extreme challenge in Alaska, with many communities in the state accessible only by air and perhaps seasonally by water. Several school districts own airplanes. Pupil transportation by small, chartered planes to sporting events and other school activities is common. Some students regularly travel to school by boat or snow machine.

Funding Public Schools in the United States and Indian Country, pages 15–25
Copyright © 2019 by Information Age Publishing
All rights of reproduction in any form reserved.

The Alaska state constitution has a unique provision:

Article VII—Section 1–Public Education—The legislature shall by general law establish and maintain a system of public schools open to all children of the State, and may provide for other public education institutions. Schools and institutions so established shall be free from sectarian control. No money shall be paid from public funds for the direct benefit of any religious or other private educational institution.[2]

When Alaska achieved statehood in 1959, there were municipal and territorial schools serving the urban population, while federal Bureau of Indian Affairs (BIA) schools served the Native population in rural communities. The above constitutional provision signaled a desire for a single statewide system, but it took several decades to reach this goal.

In 1962, the Alaska State Legislature established Alaska's first foundation program.[3] Under this plan, the state departed from the past practice of reimbursing school districts for expenses and instead funded districts based on 'basic need.' A local contribution was also required; area cost differentials were factored in; and there was a deduction for federal impact aid funds[4] received by districts. These characteristics carry through to the current state K–12 foundation formula funding program.

During the 1970s and 1980s, foundation programs based on instructional units were implemented. In rural areas, Regional Education Attendance Areas (REAAs) were formed in 1975, which provided for locally elected school boards. The REAAs received funding through the foundation program so that public schools across the state were finally funded through one program.

The passage of Senate Bill 36 in 1998 moved the state to a school aid formula based on the number of students per school. The use of funding communities and instructional units in the prior formula was abandoned. To ease the transition, approximately $21 million in new funding was injected into the formula, and a supplemental funding floor was implemented which would erode over time.[5]

The 1998 formula was adjusted in subsequent years in various ways. The most significant adjustments were following the recommendations of the Joint Legislative Education Funding Task Force (JLEFT), which issued its report in 2007.[6] Again, the legislature was able to inject new funding into the formula to ease the transition. The resulting formula currently in use is reviewed in the following section.

FOUNDATION FORMULA

The current funding formula[7] is student-based and covers K–12, plus prekindergarten special education. The process begins with an annual 20-day student count, ending on the fourth Friday in October. The State Department of Education and Early Development tightly controls the count procedure and subsequent verification of data.

Next, there are six calculations required to reach the District Adjusted Average Daily Membership (ADM):[8]

- Step 1—Adjust: ADM for School Size;
- Step 2—Apply: District Cost Factor;
- Step 3—Apply: Special Needs Factor;
- Step 4—Apply: Vocational & Technical Funding;
- Step 5—Add: Intensive Services Count;
- Step 6—Add: Correspondence Student Counts.

Step 1—School Size Adjustment

This step is the most complex adjustment. The purpose is to adjust for cost differences based on school size so that the smaller schools receive additional operational funds and larger schools are adjusted downward, assuming economies of scale.

First, correspondence students are subtracted from a school's ADM. Next, there are guidelines for determining how school districts with enrollments less than 425 will be accounted for within the calculation. There are also special provisions for alternative and charter schools. Finally, ADM is adjusted as shown in Table 2.1.

Next, a hold-harmless provision may apply if ADM adjusted for school size has decreased 5% or more compared to the prior year. If so, the drop in ADM is phased in over three years.

Step 2—District Cost Factors

Cost factors are specific to each school district and range from 1.000 to 2.116, with the Anchorage School District currently set at 1.000. At this step

TABLE 2.1	ADM Adjustment
School Size	Formula
10–19.99	39.60
20–29.99	$39.60 + (1.62 \times (ADM - 20))$
30–74.99	$55.80 + (1.49 \times (ADM - 30))$
75–149.99	$122.85 + (1.27 \times (ADM - 75))$
150–249.99	$218.10 + (1.08 \times (ADM - 150))$
250–399.99	$326.10 + (0.97 \times (ADM - 250))$
400–749.99	$471.60 + (0.92 \times (ADM - 400))$
Over 750	$793.60 + (0.84 \times (ADM - 750))$

of the formula, the district's school size adjusted ADM is multiplied by the district's cost factor. The difficulty of updating the district cost factors is further discussed in the last section of this chapter.

Step 3—Special Needs Funding

Vocational, special education (except intensive special education), gifted/talented education, and bilingual/bicultural education are block-funded. At this step of the formula, the previously adjusted ADM is now multiplied by the Special Needs factor of 1.2. The block funding approach is a departure from the method in prior formulas of calculating special needs entitlement based on individual student counts in these programs. Currently, only prekindergarten special needs students must be specifically identified for inclusion in the regular count, along with identification of intensive needs students (see Step 5 below).

Step 4—Vocational and Technical Funding

Funding at this step is also referred to as Career & Technical Education (CTE) funding. These funds are intended to assist districts in providing CTE instruction to students in grades 7 through 12. At this step of the formula, the previously adjusted ADM is now multiplied by the CTE factor of 1.015. Again, this is a departure from prior formulas which relied on individual student counts for this type of funding.

Step 5—Intensive Services Funding

In the case of Intensive Services Funding, the basis for calculation is an actual count of students receiving intensive services who are enrolled on the last day of the 20-day student count period and who have an Individual Education Plan (IEP) in place. State regulations strictly define the qualification of students for the Intensive Services, high-needs classification. At this step of the formula, the district's intensive student count is multiplied by 13. This calculation is added to the previously adjusted ADM.

Step 6—Correspondence Programs

Funding for correspondence programs is calculated by multiplying the correspondence ADM by 90%. Note that correspondence student counts were excluded from the preceding calculations beginning in Step 1. At this step of the formula, the correspondence calculation is now added to the previously adjusted ADM to arrive at the Final Adjusted ADM.

Basic Need

The next step is to multiply the Final Adjusted ADM by the Base Student Allocation (BSA) to determine Basic Need. For FY 2019, the BSA is $5,930.

The BSA is the figure that is debated each year in the state legislature. However, due to the calculations in Steps 1–6, the effect of a change to the BSA will vary widely among districts, even those with a similar number of students enrolled. For the FY 2019 projection, the total Basic Need for the Alaska K–12 Foundation Funding program is $1.5 billion.

Other Formula Funding Elements

City and borough school districts have taxing authority, whereas Regional Education Attendance Areas (REAAs) do not. City and borough districts are required to contribute the equivalent of a 2.65 mill tax levy on the full and true value of the taxable real and personal property in the district, not to exceed 45% of the district's basic need for the preceding fiscal year. Taxable value is established by the state assessor and may differ from the valuations determined at the local level.

The required contribution is subtracted from Basic Need for city and borough school districts. For the FY 2019 projection, the total required local contribution statewide is $256 million. Boroughs and municipalities may also choose to fund their local districts an additional amount above the required local contribution, up to the level of 23% of basic need. However, once they reach 23% of basic need, they are funding 'to the cap,' an issue discussed later in the 'Persistent Questions' section.

As referenced previously, the federal Title VIII Impact Aid program provides funds to school districts for children of parents living and/or working on federal property in-lieu of local tax revenues. After deductions, 90% of the eligible funds are subtracted from Basic Need. For the FY 2019 projection, the total eligible federal Impact Aid received in the state was $111 million, of which $77 million was subtracted from Basic Need. A Quality School Grant in the amount of Adjusted ADM x $16 is added as a final step.

To summarize the final calculations in the Alaska K–12 Foundation Funding Formula:

Basic Need – Required Local Contribution – Deductible Impact Aid + Quality Schools Grant = Total State Entitlement

For the FY 2019 projection, the Total State Entitlement across all 53 school districts plus the Mt. Edgecumbe state-operated boarding school is $1.2 billion. This funds services for an unadjusted projected count of 116,814 students. Of this total, the largest district in the state (Anchorage School District) was projected to receive $325 million (27%) based on an unadjusted projected student count of nearly 46,000 (39%). The five largest districts in the state combined (Anchorage, Matsu, Fairbanks, Kenai, and

Juneau) were projected to receive $726 million (60%) based on an unadjusted projected student count of just over 88,000 (76%). These statistics reflect a large number of small schools in the remaining 48 districts, plus Mt. Edgecumbe. In total, state funding for FY 2018 supported 506 schools, 75 of which had enrollments of less than 25 students as of October 1, 2017.[9]

Additional detail on these calculations, including projected funding by the school district, can be found in the excellent *Public School Funding Program Overview* which is updated annually by the Alaska Department of Education and Early Development and was referenced earlier in this section.

OTHER K–12 STATE FUNDING

In addition to the K–12 Foundation Funding Formula, the state provides funding to school districts through other funding mechanisms. Most notably, this funding includes pupil transportation, capital projects, and retirement system funding.

For pupil transportation, districts receive funding on a per-pupil basis, with the per-pupil amount based on a calculation of actual district transportation expenses. For FY 2018, the total amount of pupil transportation funding to 48 districts was $78 million.[10]

There are three mechanisms for state funding of capital projects: (1) School Construction and Major Maintenance Grants; (2) State Aid for School Construction in REAAs, and the Small Municipal School District Grant Program; and (3) the Debt Reimbursement Program. For the period FY 2011–FY 2018, the state-funded nearly $1 billion in school construction and $388 million in major maintenance through the first two programs. However, the state funding crisis due to low oil prices resulted in significant reductions in funding over the past few years, with just $46 million in construction funding in FY 2018 and no funding for major maintenance in FY 2017 and FY 2018.[11] Furthermore, the legislature placed a complete moratorium on approving projects for the Debt Reimbursement Program for January 1, 2015, through July 1, 2020. Due to the declining condition of school facilities over time, these program reductions are a major concern for school district administrators.

The state administers two retirement funding systems that serve school district employees, the Teacher Retirement System (TRS) and the Public Employees Retirement System (PERS). Benefits in both systems have been reduced significantly for new employees over the past three decades, with different tiers implemented. Most significantly, as of July 2006, all new employees are enrolled in a defined contribution system, as opposed to the previously defined benefit plans. Due in part to miscalculations by actuarial consultants, the state is now faced with a multibillion-dollar pension shortfall. However, it was decided that school districts and municipalities would not be required to pay escalating amounts toward this shortfall; rather, district rates for the pension plans would be fixed and the state would make 'on-behalf' payments toward the pension plans. In FY 2017 pension payments made on behalf of school districts totaled $125 million.[12] Note that these pension payments are in addition to the contributions by school districts and individuals toward the pension system, which are calculated as a percentage of payroll expense.

Several times in recent years, legislators have wanted to increase K–12 funding but have not wanted to make the increase 'permanent' by increasing the Base Student Allocation in the funding formula. This has resulted in special funding allocations outside the formula. In some cases, this made good sense, such as when energy costs spiked and the impact was thought to be temporary. However, education advocates are unified in calling for increases to the Base Student Allocation to support the bulk of K–12 expenditures, since the funding formula is seen as the fair way to allocate funding across the K–12 system as a whole.

PERSISTENT QUESTIONS

It is not surprising that the K–12 Foundation Funding Formula is periodically criticized by legislators, particularly when they feel the schools in their districts are disadvantaged by the calculations. Also, the state funding crisis in recent years has made the relatively high percentage of the state budget devoted to K–12 education a target for funding reductions. However, when the legislature commissioned a review of Alaska's school funding program, the report released in July 2015 was very complimentary of the Alaska Foundation Funding Formula program.[13] At the conclusion of a study that included extensive interviews with Alaska's education stakeholders as well as a comparison of the details of Alaska's funding program with programs in other states, the consultants found that "The variations in school size, district size and location create unique challenges for districts across the state." But "(o)verall, the study team believes Alaska's current funding system has the right elements in place to address the variations described above."[14] It should be noted, however, that the study was not intended to address adequacy. Also, the consultants identified numerous recommendations for review of components in the formula, some of which have been studied in subsequent legislative sessions, but none of which pointed to a need to extensively modify the formula itself.

Within the formula, it has been suggested that there may be a need to review and revise the District Cost Factors set for each district, which may become outdated over time. Currently, it has been more than ten years since the last update, which was based on an analysis by the Institute of Social and Economic Research (ISER) at the University of Alaska.[15] Just prior to ISER's 2005 study, the American Institutes for Research (AIR) completed another study in 2003 that was widely thought to be inadequate and was replaced by the ISER study, though it too was the subject of controversy.[16] Also, it is important to note that in the past when new cost factors were implemented, winners and losers were appeased by the injection of additional funds into the formula, which is a difficult challenge when state budgets are tight.

Another point of controversy surrounds local contribution. Since the REAAs cannot tax by law, they are not required to make a local contribution based on a mill rate. Some say that REAAs do not make a contribution, but in fact, most of them contribute up to 90% of eligible federal Impact Aid funding. As noted previously, the $77 million in Impact Aid that figures into the funding formula is not an insignificant amount, particularly in relation to the size of these districts. Contribution of Impact Aid funds by the REAAs, while the municipalities and boroughs provide a local contribution based on mill rates, provides an equalization mechanism in the funding formula within the parameters of federal law.

On the other side of the debate, city and borough school districts are restricted in the amount they can contribute to their local districts above the required minimum contribution. The calculation of a maximum contribution is directly related to the ability of the state to deduct eligible Impact Aid within the state formula. The federal government mandates this 'disparity testing.' The result is frustration by residents of city and borough districts when they fund their local districts 'to the cap' and are unable to increase funding unless state funding is also increased. However, if the maximum contribution caps were removed, the state would no longer be able to deduct eligible Impact Aid in the funding calculations.

Instructional advocates have pointed out that Alaska is falling behind in its funding for prekindergarten, which research has shown is highly beneficial for future educational achievement.[17] To date, the state has funded prekindergarten only through very limited grant programs and for prekindergarten special needs services. Some local districts have chosen to fund prekindergarten programs with their own resources.

Another issue that may affect the ability to deliver effective instruction is the lack of any funding adjustment for at-risk or low-income students. This was noted as atypical, compared to other states with student-centered funding formulas.[18] The APA researchers also documented significant variation among Alaskan districts with regard to percentages of low-income students.[19] High rates of suicide and adverse childhood experiences (ACES) in Alaska clearly indicate the challenges to educators from at-risk student populations.[20]

Viewed from a local level, one of the greatest difficulties posed by the current funding system is that the state legislature typically does not finalize the base student allocation funding amount for the next school year until the end of the legislative session, which ends in April but is sometimes extended into the late spring or summer. Consequently, districts often must proceed with hiring and planning for the next fiscal year without knowing the final state funding level. The other significant planning variable is the student count, which is not known until October when the 20-day count is taken. After all the reconciliations from the fall student count are completed, a district's funding for the fiscal year ending in June may not be finalized until as late as March of that same year. School district administrators have advocated for an earlier commitment to the base student allocation and for changes in the timing of the student count that is figured into the funding formula. Notably, the legislature committed to a three-year base student allocation funding plan for FY 2009-FY 2011. Although the plan was nonbinding on the legislature, it was fully implemented and district administrators found this commitment extremely helpful for longer-term planning. In most years, however, legislators fall back on using education funding as an end-of-session bargaining chip, since it is one of the largest components of the state budget.

Finally, the size and diversity of Alaska will continue to create challenges for the school funding system. Like other states with large, rural areas, the population has been migrating to the urban centers. Can the state continue to afford hundreds of schools with very small enrollments? Currently, the minimum enrollment is ten; is this sustainable? Is it in the best interest of students? Due to the expansive geography of Alaska, the alternative to village schools is either distance delivery education or boarding schools in most cases.

When considering these questions, one must inevitably return to the seminal ruling in *Molly Hootch*[21] decided in 1976, which mandated the system of K–12 schools across the state, replacing a system that relied on boarding schools for older students. More recently, *Kasayulie* and *Moore*,[22] settled by consent decrees in 2011 and 2012 respectively, have focused on the adequacy of capital funding and funding for improving educational outcomes for students in rural districts. In the future, policymakers will also turn to understanding how other states have handled K–12 funding, including the examples found in this volume.

NOTES

1. Alaska Department of Education and Early Development (2017). District Enrollment by Grade as of October 1, 2017. Retrieved from https://education.alaska.gov/stats/DistrictEnrollment/2018DistrictEnrollment.pdf

2. G. Harrison (2012). Alaska's Constitution—A Citizen's Guide. *Alaska Legislative Affairs Agency*. Retrieved from http://w3.legis.state.ak.us/docs/pdf/citizens_guide.pdf
3. J. Livey. G. and Keiser (1987). Public School Financing in Alaska. *House Research Agency – Alaska State Legislature*. Retrieved from http://archives2.legis.state.ak.us/PublicImageServer.cgi?lra/SAC_86-87/87-400001M.pdf
4. Title VIII of the Elementary and Secondary Education Act authorizes the federal government to compensate school districts for any impact on either the district's revenue or expenditures resulting from federal presence in the district. In Alaska, this includes Native lands, military bases, low rent housing and other federal facilities.
5. Alaska Department of Education and Early Development (2001). Alaska's Public School Funding Formula: A Report to the Alaska State Legislature. Retrieved from https://education.alaska.gov/publications/fundingformulasb36report.pdf
6. Joint Legislative Education Funding Task Force Report to the Governor and Legislature (2007). Retrieved from https://library.alaska.gov/asp/edocs/2007/09/ocn173495965.pdf
7. Alaska Statute 14.17.410.
8. Alaska Department of Education and Early Development (2018). Public School Funding Program Overview. Retrieved from https://education.alaska.gov/SchoolFinance/pdf/FundingOverview.pdf
9. Alaska Department of Education and Early Development (2018). School Enrollment by Grade as of October 1, 2017. Retrieved from https://education.alaska.gov/data-center
10. Alaska Department of Education and Early Development (2018). Pupil Transportation Grants by District FY05–FY18. Retrieved from https://education.alaska.gov/schoolfinance/pupiltransport
11. Alaska Department of Education and Early Development (2018). School Capital Project Funding Under SB237—A Report to the Legislature. Retrieved from https://education.alaska.gov/facilities/pdf/Final_SB237_Report2018.pdf
12. Alaska Department of Education and Early Development (2017). Audited FY17 Revenues. Retrieved from https://education.alaska.gov/schoolfinance/budgetsactual
13. Augenblick, Palaich and Associates (2015). Review of Alaska's School Funding Program. Retrieved from http://lba.akleg.gov/download/publications/school2015.pdf
14. Ibid, p. 106.
15. Institute of Social and Economic Research (2005). Alaska School District Cost Study Update. Retrieved from http://lba.akleg.gov/download/publications/school2005.pdf
16. Joint Legislative Education Funding Task Force Report to the Governor and Legislature (2007). Retrieved from https://library.alaska.gov/asp/edocs/2007/09/ocn173495965.pdf
17. Brookings Institution Pre-Kindergarten Task Force (2017), The Current State of Scientific Knowledge on Pre-Kindergarten Effects. Retrieved from

https://www.brookings.edu/wp-content/uploads/2017/04/duke_prekstudy_final_4-4-17_hires.pdf
18. Augenblick, et. al (2015), p. 38.
19. Ibid, p. 42.
20. Alaska Department of Health and Social Services (2014), Adverse Childhood Experiences—Overcoming ACEs in Alaska. Retrieved from http://dhss.alaska.gov/abada/ace-ak/
21. *Tobeluk v. Lind*, consent decree signed in October 1976. Molly Hootch was the first of 27 plaintiffs named in the case.
22. *Kasayulie v. State of Alaska*, consent decree signed September 2011, and *Moore v. State of Alaska*, consent decree signed January 2012.

CHAPTER 3

Arizona

Daniel W. Eadens, Ed.D.
*Associate Professor
Northern Arizona University*

GENERAL BACKGROUND

The Arizona constitution requires the state legislature to establish a general and uniform public school system.[1] Section 10 of that same article further requires:

> The revenue for the maintenance of the respective state educational institutions shall be derived from the investment of the proceeds of the sale, and from the rental of such lands as have been set aside by the enabling act approved June 20, 1910, or other legislative enactment of the United States, for the use and benefit of the respective state educational institutions. In addition to such income, the legislature shall make such appropriations, to be met by taxation, as shall ensure the proper maintenance of all state educational institutions, and shall make such special appropriations as shall provide for their development and improvement.

The language of the constitution's education article is mostly clear. However, the words in the last sentence have been subjected to wide interpretation. Arizona has had an equalization formula since the 1970s, but prior to 1980[2] there were unlimited overrides with no time limits, no limit on transportation spending, no limit on county-paid employer retirement and social security for certified employees, 7% annual increases for regular education and special education, separate budgets for regular and special education transportation, and districts were allowed wide levy discretion. Beginning in 1980, revenue control limits were set and equalization of budget limits occurred from 1981–1986. In 1994, open enrollment was mandated.

In 2016, the Arizona state senate wrote that due to the plethora of court cases in other states, "... Arizona began reforming its school finance system to address the potential unconstitutionality of its system and to reestablish a 'general and uniform' public school system..." It continued, saying that the statutory formula from 1980 (modified in 1985 to eliminate district funding disparities and to increase state funding) is the current system which is designed to "... equalize per-pupil spending among school districts, taking into account student enrollment and property values."[3] Under these conditions, Arizona today is a system where spending is capped and each district gets approximately the same amount of base funding for each of its students.

BASIC SUPPORT PROGRAM

General Fund Formula Operation

While some wealthy school districts in Arizona with high property values are able to independently generate sufficient funding, "most school districts require revenues in the form of Basic State Aid in order to receive full funding under the statutory formula."[4] The current school district funding formula[5] is seen later in Figure 3.1 and is expressed as:

Equalization Base − Qualifying Tax Rate = Equalization Assistance
Equalization Assistance − State Equalization Tax Rate = Basic State Aid

The first part of the formula is the Equalization Base. Essentially, the base is the limit of each school district's spending and is derived by adding the Base Support Level (BSL), Transportation Support Level (TSL), and District Additional Assistance (DAA), expressed as:

Equalization Base = BSL + TSL+ DAA

The BSL includes capital and program weights. The BSL contains weights for special education (SPED), high school students, English Language Learners (ELL), K–3 students, and small and isolated school districts. In Fiscal Year 2010, SPED weights were calculated by multiplying the number of diagnoses times the BSL. For example, students with multiple disabilities with severe sensory impairment were weighted 7.947; Orthopedic Impairment was weighted at 6.773; Visual Impairment was weighted at 4.806; Hearing Impairment was weighted at 4.771; Moderate Mental Retardation was weighted at 4.421; while Developmental Delay, Mild Retardation, Speech and Language Impairment, and Other Health Impaired were all weighted at 0.003.

In contrast, district unweighted enrollment for particular ranges of grades had student counts times a specified legislated amount in order to yield the DAA. In particular, student counts were < 100, 100–600, and > 600 expressed as:

$$DAA = \text{Unweighted Count} \times \text{Per Pupil Amount}$$

The legislative set amount, adjusted annually for inflation, multiplied by daily mileage of bus routes, tokens, and passes, generates the Transportation Support Level (TSL), not to be confused with the Transportation Revenue Control Limit option, to assess additional amounts to the property tax for costs greater than the TSL expressed as:

$$TSL = \$ \text{ Amount} \times \text{Route Miles} + \text{Tokens/Passes}$$

The BSL is a school district's total Weighted Student Count (WSC) multiplied by the Base Level Amount (BLA) multiplied by the Teacher Experience Index (TEI). District size and location (rural, urban, suburban), certain grade levels (Group A) and student characteristics (Group B) determine the WSC. The per-student amount set by the legislature and adjusted for inflation is the Base Level Amount (BLA) expressed as:

$$BSL = WSC \times BLA \times 1.0125 \times TEI$$

The Qualifying Tax Rate (QTR), adjusted annually, is the primary property tax rate set by the legislature to determine how much funding districts receive from the state. The QTR is multiplied by the Net Assessed Value (NAV) of local property to determine the amount of state aid. In small, rural communities where there are typically fewer businesses and lower property taxes, basic state aid from the state's General Fund often makes up the difference that local property taxes cannot generate due to the equalization base funding being greater than the QTR times the NAV. The reverse is true in wealthier communities and cities, where QTR times NAV is more than the equalization base. Additionally, property owners are assessed a State Equalization Tax Rate (SETR). Yields from the primary property tax and minimum qualifying tax rate levied and collected by each county, goes directly into Arizona's State General Fund. Districts are thereby eligible for equalization assistance if the revenue from the QTR does not exceed the district's equalization base according to the following sequence:

$$\text{Equalization Assistance} > SETR = \text{Basic State Aid}$$
$$QTR > \text{Equalization Base} = \text{No Equalization Assistance}$$
$$\text{Equalization Base} > QTR = \text{Equalization Assistance}$$

Arizona's school finance formula is therefore driven by pupil needs and tied to local fiscal capacity to generate enough local resources. Its operation is complex, with the above elements illustrated in flowchart form in Figure 3.1 at the end of this chapter. Selected impactful elements affecting formula operation round out the chapter discussion.

SCHOOL FACILITIES AND CAPITAL OUTLAY

In 1994, the Arizona supreme court declared the state's capital funding system unconstitutional based on *Roosevelt v. Bishop*.[6] Essentially, the issue arose from severely unequalized funding disparities among school districts relating to school facilities. As briefed to the state Senate, Arizona's system of school capital finance was declared unconstitutional because it failed to conform to the state constitution's 'general and uniform' clause because it relied too heavily on property tax revenue. Subsequent litigation in *Hull v. Albrecht*[7] failed to produce a solution, as the state high court rejected proposals and imposed a deadline to develop a constitutional system of school capital finance or risk closure of K–12 public schools. In July 1998 during a special session, legislation was passed reforming the way traditional K–12 public schools (not including charter schools) finance capital investment and construction, called Students Fair and Immediate Resources for Students (Students FIRST). Since 1998, the Students FIRST program has served as Arizona's school capital finance system, funded partly by Proposition 301 revenues dedicated from the state transaction privilege tax, state trust land revenues, and annual legislative appropriations to the School Facilities Board (SFB).[8]

Presently, there are three programs in Students FIRST dealing with emergency deficiency corrections, building renewals, and new school construction. While the emergency deficiency fund has gone dry, the building renewal program was funded via formula during Fiscal Years 1999 – 2008 and was replaced by an appropriated amount in FY 2009. From FY 2009 through FY 2013, the state legislature placed a moratorium on all new school construction but exempted lease-to purchase authority and land acquisition. The moratorium was lifted in FY 2014.

FOOD SERVICE

School districts are permitted to operate school meal programs on a nonprofit basis for children in attendance at each school. All revenue collected in the operation of a district's school meal program must be deposited to the district's school meal program fund.

TEACHER RETIREMENT

The Arizona State Retirement System (ASRS) contribution rate is 11.80% for retirement, long-term disability, and health insurance. Public education's total share of ASRS is 66%, and as of FY 2017, it held $37.8 billion in asset investment.

SPECIAL EDUCATION

Funding for special education in Arizona was mandated in 1973, but the mandate did not become effective until the 1976–77 school year. Originally, 90% of excess costs were placed in the 1974 state funding formula, although the formula changed one year later. In the 1980–81 school year, a 'Group A' component was added, and a provision was put in place to fund 85% of special education student costs. Current operation provides 11 weights, including those described earlier under the Base Support Level.

BILINGUAL EDUCATION

A state General Fund special line item funds Arizona's structured English immersion program which was initiated in 2006. It is designed to improve the English proficiency of English language learners. Programs may include individual or small group instruction, extended day classes, summer school, or intercession school. A weighting of .115 is included in the BSL calculation.

EARLY CHILDHOOD AND GIFTED EDUCATION

The state also funds special projects in addition to formula-based funding of the equalization system. State projects, however, are significantly less expensive than the ESEA Title I and IDEA Part B grants. A few of these special projects are grants for vocational education, early childhood education, adult education, dropout prevention, gifted, and family literacy.

OTHER CATEGORICAL PROGRAMS

Assistance to School Districts for Children of State Employees, Certificates of Educational Convenience, and the Special Education Fund are three examples of Other State Aid programs.[9] The latter fund covers special education student costs at schools for deaf and blind, state hospitals, disabled programs, and residential facilities when placed by the state.

CHARTER SCHOOLS[10]

A proposed voucher law became Arizona's charter school law in 1994, with charters surging thereafter. By 1998, charters had captured 4.3% of average daily membership of Arizona pupils while school districts held 95.7%. Projections indicate that by FY 2021 charters will enroll 20.1% of all Arizona pupils compared to school districts' share at 79.9%.

In 2017, charter schools' share of state revenue was $1.3 billion with 170,000 students, while school districts' revenue share was $3.4 billion serving 928,000 pupils. Both regular and charter school students share in transportation funding; in FY 1997 a transportation aid formula was set at $174 per pupil—that amount has since risen to $261 and is a permanent part of additional assistance for charter schools.

Since charter schools do not have taxing authority and have no other revenue from local tax sources, charters are eligible for state aid from the state's General Fund. The charter school formula operates separately and is comprised of two parts. Under these conditions, charter schools are eligible for the BSL identically with regular school districts (minus TEI), plus Charter Additional Assistance (CAA) which is similar to the earlier discussion of the DAA.

$$\text{Charter School Funding} = \text{BSL} + \text{CAA}$$
$$\text{where}$$
$$\text{CAA} = \text{unweighted count} \times \text{per pupil amount}$$

PRIVATE SCHOOLS, TAX CREDITS, DEDUCTIONS, AND EXEMPTIONS

Private school tuition income tax credits for individuals were launched in Arizona in 1998. Corporate tax credits were added in 2006. Beginning in 2011, public school monies became available to provide Empowerment Scholarship Accounts (ESAs) and Student Tuition Organizations (STOs), both of which allowed payment for private school tuition. Both ESAs and STOs are ways to opt out of public schools at taxpayer expense. Currently, there are 65 STOs, and donations are allowed by corporations. While families are limited in annual donation amounts, corporations can donate up to their entire tax liability. The fiscal impact on the state is that state revenues are reduced as individuals and corporations earn income tax credits. In

2006, the corporate credit cap was increased to $10 million per year plus a 20% annual increase.[11]

In FY 2018, approximately 5,000 ESAs were accessed at a state cost of about $75 million. Statute restricts uses to private school tuition, textbooks, curricular materials, and tutoring, with ESA contracts renewed annually. The Arizona Department of Education disburses funds quarterly to applicants' parents on a prepaid debit card, with amounts ranging annually from $3,00–$30,000. These amounts are about 90% of what the state would normally pay a regular school district for the same educational purpose.[12]

The ESA is subject to an expansion cap that is limited to .5% (about 5,000 students) until 2020. Additional cost to the Arizona state General Fund for annual ESA expansion is substantial, reaching $2.1 million for 2018. Under current law, any awarded ESA funds unused by a recipient (up to $2,000 annually) may be converted to a Coverdell Education Savings Account for college. Students may not use an ESA while simultaneously receiving an STO scholarship or tax credit scholarship.

EARMARKED STATE REVENUES

Whenever designated Arizona state trust lands are sold, the funds are placed in the Permanent State School Fund (investment earnings, lease proceeds, and interest on land purchases) to offset the state General Fund costs for Basic State Aid. Proposition 123, initiated in 2010, required the state to increase the base level tied to inflation. A 2015 settlement, approved by voters in 2016, increased the land trust distribution from 2.5% to 6.9% through FY 2025. Additionally, an automatic homeowner's rebate helps provide additional state aid to school districts.[13]

LOCAL SCHOOL REVENUE

Neighborhood elections are opportunities for citizens to supplement local school funding through voted overrides, bonds, and line-item property taxes such as adjacent ways, desegregation, transportation, and prevention. Bonds and overrides, pending voter approval, can increase district funding, although this avenue is unavailable to charter schools. Voter overrides are typically for seven years, but at the end of the fifth year, they begin decreasing. Maintenance and operations (M & O) overrides, commonly used for staff positions and salaries, can be approved up to a cap of 15% of the local M & O budget. Also, capital overrides can be approved up to 5%. Bond funding amounts and usage are restricted specifically for individual projects such as school buses and new buildings and renovations and must be audited on an annual basis. The use of bonds for capital expenditures is restricted to the information on the ballot and the voter information guide, and proceeds of bonds must be spent within three years. Additionally, some school districts can obtain Indian Gaming funds. Finally, Proposition 301 was approved by Arizona voters in the year 2000 to require the state to provide extra educational funds.

SUMMARY

Arizona school funding is based on an equalization formula. While the base support level of funding for each student is initially the same, funds are added to school district budgets to compensate for cost differences among certain students such as English language learners and those with special needs. Those cost differences are redressed through additional weighted funding. New and growing school districts are also allowed additional funding for facilities; voters have opportunity to increase property taxes for schools; and voters can supplement property taxes to create additional support at the local level. Finally, the equalization formula provides state aid to school districts that fail to raise enough local tax base funding.

The proliferation and coexistence of charter schools in Arizona meaningfully impacts state and local funding. Table 3.1 identifies a six-year expenditure pattern for the state. Figure 3.1 provides an overall visual of the Arizona school funding scheme. The Arizona Department of Education also provides a brief walk-through of basic calculations for equalization assistance.[14]

TABLE 3.1 Education General Fund Annual Expenditure FY 2014–2019

Education	2014	2015	2016	2017	2018	2019
Arts, Arizona Commission on the	$0	$0	$0	$0	$0	$0
Charter Schools, State Boards for	$786,900	$896,400	$1,024,300	$997,300	$1,200,600	$1,209,800
Community Colleges, Arizona (36)	$69,508,700	$71,906,400	$54,373,200	$54,312,700	$55,086,500	$57,205,500
Deaf and the Blind, School for the	$21,418,500	$21,921,300	$21,378,100	$21,616,900	$21,932,000	$21,659,300
Education, State Board of (58)	$0	$0	$1,139,100	$921,700	$1,153,600	$1,146,300
Education, Department of (7) (58)	$3,661,757,100	$3,831,124,100	$3,939,909,800	$4,079,045,400	$4,422,725,400	$4,704,652,000
Historical Society, Arizona (64)	$3,155,000	$3,156,000	$3,157,000	$2,723,100	$3,179,800	$3,195,000
Historical Society, Prescott	$826,000	$809,000	$825,800	$824,500	$840,200	$832,700
Medical Student Loans Boards	$0	$0	$0	$0	$0	$0
Postsecondary Education, Commission for (23)	$1,396,800	$1,396,800	$1,396,800	$1,396,800	$1,881,800	$1,646,800
School capital Facilities, State Board for	$0	$0	$0	$0	$0	$0
School Facilities Board (30)	$191,646,800	$178,355,700	$230,378,000	$227,889,600	$302,286,600	$274,700,300
Universities/Board of Regents						
Board of Regents (23)	$21,902,600	$24,928,400	$21,928,400	$21,928,400	$6,909,300	$6,898,100
Arizona State University (68)	$0	$0	$0	$0	$0	$0
Arizona State University–Tempe/DPC (68)	$270,228,200	$290,102,200	$315,844,800	$305,397,600	$320,259,000	$328,775,800
Arizona State University–East Campus (68)	$22,704,200	$25,853,400	$28,095,600	$0	$0	$0
Arizona State University–West Campus (68)	$33,328,100	$33,328,100	$39,024,400	$0	$0	$0
Arizona State University–Other	$0	$0	$0	$0	$0	$0
Northern Arizona State University	$109,245,000	$118,281,200	$131,452,600	$105,227,000	$108,612,800	$112,095,700
University of Arizona–Main Campus (5) (64)	$208,501,000	$209,341,200	$241,652,500	$197,059,600	$199,600,900	$208,836,400
University of Arizona–Health Sciences Center (18)	$69,585,300	$69,585,300	$85,170,200	$68,859,800	$69,437,700	$68,897,700
University of Arizona–Other	$0	$0	$0	$0	$0	$0
University Medical Center/Post Secondary Education Board	$0	$0	$0	$0	$0	$0
Subtotal Universities/Regents	$735,494,400	$771,419,800	$863,168,500	$698,472,400	$704,819,700	$725,503,700
Total Education	$4,685,990,200	$4,880,985,500	$5,116,750,600	$5,088,200,400	$5,319,639,200	$5,791,751,400

Note: Joint Legislative Budget Committee. Education General Fund Annual Expenditure. FY 2014–2019. (2018) Excerpted from https://www.azleg.gov/jbc/gfhistoricalspending.pdf

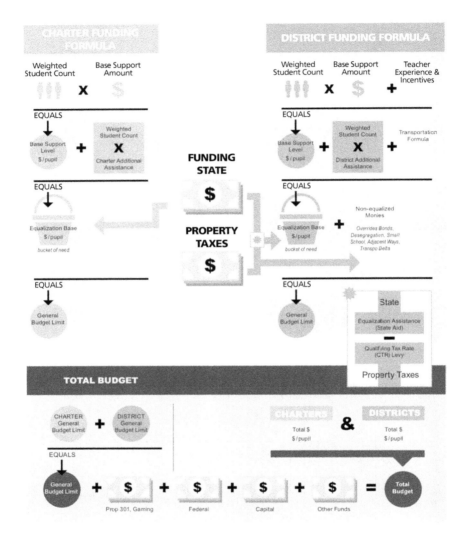

Figure 3.1 Arizona School Funding Flowchart 2019. *Source:* Greater Phoenix Chamber of Commerce. "Arizona School Finance: A Brief Introduction." Phoenix, AZ: Phoenix Center for Community Development (2014), p6. Used by express permission. Available at http://www.arizonatax.org/sites/default/files/publications/special_reports/file/pccd_2014_educationfinance_policybrief.pdf

NOTES

1. Article 11, §1. Retrieved from https://www.azleg.gov/viewDocument/?docName=http://www.azleg.gov/const/11/11.htm
2. Laws 1980, 2nd S.S., Ch. 9. Retrieved from: http://azmemory.azlibrary.gov/digital/collection/azsession/id/2/
3. Arizona State Senate Issue Brief (October 20, 2016). "Arizona's School Finance System." Retrieved from https://www.azleg.gov/briefs/Senate/ARIZONA'S%20SCHOOL%20FINANCE%20SYSTEM.pdf
4. Ibid. p. 1.
5. Ibid. pp. 2–5.
6. 179 Ariz. 233; 877 P.2d 806 (1994).
7. 190 Ariz. 520 950 P.2nd 1141 (1997).
8. Arizona State Senate Issue Brief (2016).
9. Ibid.
10. C. Essigs. "How Things Got This Way: A Brief History of Recent Arizona School Finance." PowerPoint at the Arizona School Boards Association 42nd Annual Law Conference, Phoenix Arizona. (September 5, 2018). Unpublished.
11. S. Laux and L. Jensen. "Student Tuition Organizations: What Are They, Who Do They Benefit, and What Is the True Cost?" PowerPoint at the Arizona School Boards Association 42nd Annual Law Conference, Phoenix Arizona. (September 5, 2018). Unpublished.
12. J. Ellen, M. Lozano, and C. O'Brien. "Empowerment Scholarship Accounts." PowerPoint at the Arizona School Boards Association 42nd Annual Law Conference, Phoenix Arizona. (September 5, 2018). Unpublished.
13. Arizona State Senate Issue Brief (2016).
14. Arizona Department of Education. "Formula Overview." (January 17, 2018). Presentation to the Education Subcommittee. Retrieved from: https://www.azleg.gov/jlbc/19adefundingformulasjlbcpres.pdf

CHAPTER 4

Arkansas

Kevin P. Brady, Ph.D.
Associate Professor
University of Arkansas

Steve Bounds, Ed.D.
Professor
Arkansas Tech University

GENERAL OVERVIEW

In 1983, the Arkansas Supreme Court ruled in *Dupree v. Alma School District*[1] that the state's funding formula was unconstitutional. While this specific ruling did not address the level of financial support that was legally mandated, it made clear that the state of Arkansas' duty is to distribute educational funds in an equitable manner. The *Dupree* ruling as well as the federal government's *A Nation at Risk*[2] report gave definite momentum to then-Governor Bill Clinton's education agenda during his second presidential term. The Education Standards Committee, which was headed by then-state first lady Hillary Rodham Clinton, concentrated on achieving better teacher quality, a more rigorous curriculum, a longer school year, and smaller class sizes in the state of Arkansas. Governor Clinton connected school consolidation to these new standards and was able to raise the state sales tax by 1% to fund public P–12 education reforms.

In 1992, the Lakeview School District filed suit alleging that the state's formula for distributing education funds to public schools remained inequitable. The trial court found that the school finance distribution formula violated the state's constitutional provisions but stayed its order to give the Arkansas General Assembly additional time to enact a constitutional school funding system. After several unsuccessful attempts to resolve the issue, a compliance trial was held in 2000. Other public school districts throughout the state joined the suit, alleging that Arkansas' school funding system was both inequitable and inadequate. The court agreed but left the choice of legal remedy to the legislative and executive branches.

In 2001, ongoing education reform was impacted by the school funding lawsuit *Lake View School District*[3] and the federal education reform initiative of *The No Child Left Behind Act*.[4] The state legislature enacted comprehensive legislation to modify the state's school funding formula, increasing teacher pay, improving school facilities, and imposing an extensive standardized testing program. These reforms significantly improved the condition of public education in the state and the *Lakeview* case was finally decided in the Arkansas Supreme Court in 2004.[5]

The focus of state policymakers on reforming public education and enhancing funding continued during the years 2007–2015. For example, during the Eighty-sixth General Assembly, the state approved the largest single capital expenditure for public P–12 education in Arkansas history by committing $456 million to improve school facilities. The Arkansas Constitution provides that the state "shall ever maintain a general, suitable and efficient system of free public schools and shall adopt all suitable means to secure to the people the advantages and opportunities of education."[6] Thus, the two primary Arkansas Supreme Court decisions interpreting the state's constitutional school funding provisions are the *Dupree* and *Lake View* decisions. In order to comply, the Arkansas General Assembly created the Joint Committee on Educational Adequacy during the 2003 regular legislative session and charged it with conducting an adequacy study.[7] Based on the consultants' recommendations and additional information, the subcommittee refined the funding levels established in the state's foundation funding matrix, and in 2006, the Arkansas General Assembly increased Arkansas' foundation funding rate.[8]

BASIC SUPPORT PROGRAM

Arkansas public P–12 schools receive many different types of funding. Table 4.1 displays a current classification of Arkansas public P–12 school districts organized by district size, poverty, and student achievement. In Fiscal Year 2017, Arkansas school districts and open-enrollment charter schools received approximately $5.7 billion in total revenue.[9] Currently, foundation funding is the primary method of public education funding in Arkansas.[10] Foundation funding is based on a district's average daily membership

TABLE 4.1 Classification of Arkansas Public K–12 Districts					
	# of Districts	District Avg. ADM	Total ADM	District Avg. FRPL %	District Avg. Achievement
District Size					
Small (750 or Fewer)	79	520	41,107	71.5%	44.9%
Medium (751–5,000)	140	1,738	243,343	64.4%	48.1%
Large (5,001+)	16	10,967	175,468	56.9%	52.2%
Poverty					
Low Poverty (<70%)	120	2,223	266,748	56.2%	53.2%
Medium Poverty (70%–<90%)	105	1,772	186,013	75.3%	42.9%
High Poverty (90%+)	10	716	7,156	93.3%	23.6%
Student Achievement					
Top Quartile	59	2,712	159,995	54.4%	61.1%
2nd Quartile	58	1,909	110,715	64.0%	51.0%
3rd Quartile	59	1,288	76,004	69.0%	44.5%
Bottom Quartile	59	1,919	113,204	77.8%	32.7%

Source: Arkansas Department of Education, State Aid Notice; Child Nutrition Unit, Audited Free and Reduced Price Lunch; Office of Innovation for Education (2018).

(ADM). Each year, the state distributes foundation funding to each of its 235 school districts on a per-pupil basis.

State Funding

Arkansas school foundation funding is unrestricted, meaning that Arkansas does not specify what school districts may or may not purchase with state appropriated monies. The policy is intended to provide flexibility for the specific financial needs of each school district, allowing some districts the fiscal discretion to spend more on teacher salaries, for example, while other districts may have higher transportation funding needs. Foundation funding is comprised of two main sources: the uniform rate of tax (URT) and the state foundation funding aid. The URT is a constitutionally mandated minimum millage rate, or property tax rate that school districts must levy at the local level. This rate is set at 25 mills and the revenue generated is used specifically for school operations. State foundation funding aid is provided to make up the difference between the amount of money raised through the URT and the foundation funding rate set by the Arkansas legislature. The two smaller components of foundation funding are the 98% URT Actual Collection

Adjustment and other types of funding collectively considered miscellaneous funds. The 98% URT adjustment funding is state money used to supplement districts, whereas actual URT collections are less than 98% of what was anticipated based on assessments. This funding ensures that districts receive at least 98% of their total URT funding when the county is unable to collect the full amount from its citizens. Miscellaneous funds are monies school districts receive from "federal forest reserves, federal grazing rights, federal mineral rights, federal impact aid, federal flood control, wildlife refuge funds, and severance taxes," that are "in lieu of taxes and local sales and use taxes dedicated to education."[11] Among districts statewide in FY 2017, the URT made up approximately 35% of the state's total foundation funding, while state foundation funding aid covered about 64%. However, these percentages varied greatly among individual school districts. For the state's charter schools, which currently have no tax base from which to collect funds, the entire foundation funding amount is covered by state foundation funding aid. Table 4.2 reflects foundation funding levels per pupil from FY 2016 and projected to FY 2019. The current foundation funding per pupil amount is $6,713.

The primary revenue types for funding Arkansas public K–12 schools include five main sources:

- *Foundation Funding* primarily consists of property tax revenues (uniform rate of tax, or URT) and the state aid portion of foundation funding (the components of foundation funding are described later in this chapter);
- *Other Unrestricted Funds* including state funding such as enrollment growth, declining enrollment, and isolated school funding and local revenue sources in excess of URT. School districts have broad authority to spend these funds for their educational needs without limitation;
- *State Restricted Funds* including state categorical funds, as well as funding for magnet school programs, early childhood education, adult education, career education, special education, academic facilities, and other grants for specific programs;
- *Federal Revenues* including Title I funding, the Individuals with Disabilities Education Act (IDEA), Part B funding, school lunch and breakfast grant funds and other federal grant funding;

TABLE 4.2 Foundation Funding Per Pupil

Fiscal Year	Per Student
2016	$6,584
2017	$6,646
2018	$6,713
2019	$6,781

Source: State of Arkansas, Bureau of Legislative Research (2018).

- *Other Funding Sources* including the sale of bonds for construction activities, loans, insurance compensation for loss of assets, other gains from disposals of assets and other miscellaneous funding.

Arkansas' K–12 education foundation funding formula, often referred to as 'the matrix,' is used to determine the per-pupil level of foundation funding disbursed to each school district in the state. Each year, Arkansas legislators involved in the state's adequacy study determine the dollar amount necessary to fund each line item of the foundation funding formula (matrix) based on the money needed to adequately fund school districts' educational needs. The state's matrix formula is not intended to reimburse schools for actual expenditures but rather provide a methodology for determining an adequate funding level allowing schools to meet state accreditation standards as well as to adequately educate the state's students. The matrix calculates per-pupil funding based on the cost of personnel and other resources needed to operate a prototypical school of 500 students. Unlike the foundation funding rate, the matrix is not established in state statute: instead, it is used as a tool to set the state's foundation funding rate. The matrix is divided into two basic sections: (1) the number of people needed for funding a prototypical school of 500 students; and (2) costs associated with all needed resources for a school district. Table 4.3 displays the four components that comprise foundation funding in Arkansas. Since 2011, state foundation aid has consistently made up 64–65% of foundation funding, while URT has made up 34–35%. Table 4.4 illustrates the first section of the state's matrix formula, the number of people needed for the prototypical school of 500 students. Table 4.5 illustrates the second component of the state's matrix formula, which specifies the cost of the staff described in the first section of the matrix, as well as the cost of all other needed resources. The matrix is divided into three cost categories, including (1) school-level salaries of teachers and other pupil support staff, (2) school-level resources, including instructional materials and technology-related

TABLE 4.3 Arkansas Formula Foundation Funding Components

Foundation Funding Components	District Total	% of Total	Charter Total	% of Total
URT	$1,112,682,647	36.3%	$0	0%
State Foundation Funding Aid	$1,924,159,757	62.8%	$84,318,554	100%
98% Adjustment	$17,583,692	0.6%	$0	0%
Miscellaneous	$9,809,489	0.3%	$0	0%
Total	$3,064,235,755		$84,318,554	

Source: State of Arkansas, Bureau of Legislative Research (2018).

TABLE 4.4 Matrix Formula: Personnel Needed for Sample Prototypical School of 500 Students

	Matrix Item	2016–17 FTEs per 500 students
Classroom Teachers	Kindergarten	2.00
	Grades 1–3	5.00
	Grades 4–12	13.80
	Non-Core	4.14
	Subtotal	**24.94**
Pupil Support Staff	Special Education	2.90
	Instructional Facilitators	2.50
	Library Media Specialist	0.85
	Counselors & Nurses	2.50
	Subtotal	**8.75**
Administration	Principal	1.00
	Secretary	1.00
	Total	**35.69**

Source: State of Arkansas, Bureau of Legislative Research (2018).

TABLE 4.5 Funding Needed for School-Level Salaries, School-Level Resources, and District-Level Resources

School-Level Salaries	Salary & Benefits	Per-Student Funding Amt.
Classroom Teachers	$64,196	$3,202.10
Pupil Support Staff	$64,196	$1,123.43
Principal	$99,012	$198.10
School-Level Resources		**Per-Student Funding Amt.**
Technology		$250.00
Instructional Materials		$183.10
Extra Duty Funds		$64.90
Supervisory Aides		$50.00
District-Level Resources		**Per-Student Funding Amt.**
Operation & Maintenance		$664.90
Central Office		$438.80

Source: State of Arkansas, Bureau of Legislative Research (2018).

expenses, and (3) district-level resources, including funding for operations and maintenance and transportation expenses.

Table 4.6 details the level of state funding made available to the Arkansas Department of Education (ADE) from FY 2005 through 2018, specifically for P–12 education.

TABLE 4.6 State Funding for the Arkansas Department of Education

Fiscal Year	Dept. of Education Public School Fund Amount	General Education Fund Dept. Education Fund Account	Educational Excellence Trust Fund		Educational Facilities Partnership Fund Account and Dept. of Public School Academic Facilities & Transp. Fund Account	Educational Adequacy Fund	Total All Selected Funds
			Dept. of Education Public School Fund Account	Dept. of Education Fund Account			
2005	$1,587,868,208	$11,841,192	$165,146,201	$809,075	$20,439,774	$442,872,886	$2,228,977,336
2006	$1,664,928,944	$13,536,267	$178,219,239	$873,122	$54,214,982	$426,505,888	$2,338,278,442
2007	$1,722,737,993	$13,433,942	$191,219,957	$936,815	$90,976,326	$448,450,030	$2,467,755,062
2008	$1,830,265,989	$15,799,231	$200,422,877	$981,901	$502,643,292	$438,730,903	$2,988,844,395
2009	$1,843,274,503	$14,769,806	$193,587,342	$948,413	$51,585,902	$433,090,041	$2,537,256,006
2010	$1,790,947,911	$17,529,999	$190,786,665	$934,692	$36,916,527	$411,286,403	$2,448,402,197
2011	$1,829,267,307	$15,167,661	$180,391,694	$883,765	$57,704,295	$451,110,054	$2,534,524,776
2012	$1,882,316,142	$15,701,088	$188,051,836	$921,294	$58,528,882	$438,147,425	$2,583,666,667
2013	$1,936,432,524	$15,471,687	$193,026,506	$945,665	$62,465,585	$444,832,631	$2,653,174,598
2014	$1,980,965,210	$16,578,345	$195,093,479	$955,792	$84,858,082	$456,647,180	$2,735,098,088
2015	$2,072,170,259	$16,587,878	$199,766,427	$978,685	$51,071,087	$460,221,761	$2,800,796,088
2016	$2,113,356,522	$16,162,434	$202,031,412	$989,781	$98,785,465	$477,029,412	$2,908,355,026
2017	$2,136,234,690	$16,162,434	$210,504,218	$1,031,291	$59,633,327	$488,716,784	$2,912,282,744
2018	$2,110,560,691	$16,162,434	$215,134,282	$1,053,974	$150,579,640	$504,750,501	$2,998,241,522

Source: State of Arkansas, Bureau of Legislative Research (2018).

Local Funding

In Arkansas, local taxes are collected through eight local revenue sources including *property taxes-current* (received July-December); *property relief sales tax*; *property tax by 6/30* (Received January-June); *property relief tax 6/30*; *property tax-delinquent*; *excess commission*; *land redemption in state sales*; *penalties/interest on tax.*

Real, personal and *utility* taxes comprise three main categories. Real, personal and utility assessments are added together to create the Total Assessment for a school district, reflected in the following formula:

$$\text{Real} + \text{Personal} + \text{Utility} = \text{Total Assessment}$$

Based on Article 14 of the Arkansas Constitution, a public school district is required to charge a minimum of 25 mills, known as the Uniform Rate of Tax (URT), dedicated to maintenance and operation.[12] The local school district has the option to increase its millage rate by having voters within the district vote on additional mills. To estimate the amount of taxes a district could receive, the amount of Total Assessment is multiplied by the millage rate.

SPECIAL EDUCATION FUNDING

Special needs, or categorical, funding is pursuant to state statute.[13] During FY 2017 school year, Arkansas public school districts spent $436.8 million on special education services, or approximately $7,481 per pupil with a classified disability. The state's open-enrollment charter schools spent $5.8 million on special education services, or approximately $4,523 per pupil with a disability. Those figures should not be mistaken to reflect the total cost of educating students with disabilities because they do not include all expenditures districts incurred behalf of all students, such as the cost of principal salaries or utilities. These figures represent only the expenditures specific to special education services or students. Arkansas primarily uses monies obtained through the local millage and foundation funding matrix for special education funding purposes. Local and state aid monies are deposited to the general fund and coded to special education expenditures as needed. In addition to local and foundation funds being used to support special education, monies from other categorical funds are also used, including the following specific school fund categories: Isolated, Student Growth and/or Declining Enrollment funds, state National School Lunch, English Language Learner, and Professional Development funds, Special Education Services funds which are designed to help districts and charters pay for special education supervisors and extended-year services for students with disabilities, Residential Treatment funds for special education provided to students in residential treatment centers, youth shelters, juvenile detention centers, and other minor state special education funding sources such as the Arkansas School Recognition Program and Professional Quality Enhancement Teacher & Administrator Induction Program (PATHWISE).

In Arkansas, some students are classified as high-cost special education pupils. Nationally, approximately 5% of special education students are classified as high-cost. Once a school district spends more than $15,000 on specialized resources for a student, the district may apply for catastrophic loss funding. The state of Arkansas pays 80% of special education costs beyond $15,000 up to $50,000 and 50% of costs over $50,000 up to $100,000.[14] Table 4.7 lists the special education expenditures from various state funding sources for FY 2018 for public K–12 districts in Arkansas.

Alternative Learning Environment (ALE), English Language Learners (ELL), National School Lunch State Categorical (NSL) and Professional Development (PD) are considered state categorical funds. The expenditure of funds from each of these categories is restricted. Allowable expenditures for each category are specified in law and/or rules. A school district may transfer funds received from any categorical fund source to another categorical fund source. Per-pupil state categorical funding is provided in addition to per-pupil foundation funding. There is a limit to the amount of categorical funds a district can carry over in a fiscal year. Districts carrying over balances larger than allowed may be required to surrender those unspent excess funds. Districts must expend a minimum of 85% of the current NSL of the current year NSL funding. The total aggregate balance of categorical funds at year-end may not exceed 20%.

TABLE 4.7   Special Education Spending: By Source of Funds FY 2018

Source	Public K–12 Schools	Public Charter Schools
Foundation and Local Funds	$270,476,393	$3,091,394
Isolated, Student Growth, Declining Enrollment	$870,360	$13,462
Categorical Funds	$3,031,885	$38,810
Special Education Services	$2,656,613	$15,420
Residential Treatment	$5,675,123	$0
Catastrophic Loss	$11,506,253	$34,201
Other State Special Ed Funding	$23,577	$0
Early Childhood Special Education	$3,264,783	$11,519
Desegregation	$2,065,749	$0

TABLE 4.8 Special Education Funds Distributed to Arkansas K–12 Public Schools

School Year	Funds Distributed
2013–14	$33,715,146
2014–15	$33,441,371
2015–16	$34,050,823
2016–17	$33,652,335
2017–18	$29,245,658

In addition to these funds, Arkansas public schools can apply for Medicaid and Arkansas Medicaid Administrative Claiming (ARMAC) reimbursement. Medicaid is a federally funded program allowing districts to be reimbursed for medical services provided as part of an Individualized Education Plan (IEP). ARMAC is a federally funded program that helps school districts cover the cost of administrative activities related to Medicaid or other health services. Other special education funds are restricted accounts to be used only for special education purposes. Two major sources of federal special education funds provided to the state to be distributed to school districts include the Special Education School Age—Section 611 Allocations and the Special Education Federal Preschool—Section 619 Allocations accounts. During the 2017–18 school year, approximately $117,332,895 and $5,372,923 of Section 611 and Section 619 funds, respectively, were available to the state of Arkansas. Local allocations to LEAs are based on a formula that determines the amount per special education pupil for each individual district. Key elements of the formula include a base amount from the previous year, a population component based on the number of eligible students, and a poverty component based on free/reduced lunch status. Table 4.8 lists funds distributed to Arkansas public schools over a five-year period.

ALTERNATIVE LEARNING ENVIRONMENT

An Alternative Learning Environment (ALE) program must comply with state law and relevant Arkansas Department of Education (ADE) rules.[15] It is important to point out that for ALE funding eligibility, a student must be enrolled in an eligible ALE program for a minimum of 20 consecutive days per school year. Beginning in FY 2018, ALE funding for each school year was $4,640 multiplied by the district's eligible ALE students' full-time equivalence (FTE) in the previous year[16] as defined in 4.06 of the ADE Rules Governing the Distribution of Student Special Needs Funding and the Determination of Allowable Expenditures of Those Funds—May 2016. The FTE is calculated by dividing the number of days each student was enrolled in the ALE by the total number of days in the school year (typically 178) and multiplying the result by the number of enrolled course minutes divided by the number of minutes in a day. Examples are as follows:

Student "B" FTE = (89/178) × (216/360) = .30
Student "C" FTE (178/178) × (360/360) = 1.0

To calculate ALE funding, multiply the total full-time equivalent (FTE) (1.3) by the per-student ALE funding amount ($4,640). 1.3 × $4,640 = $6,032.

ENGLISH LANGUAGE LEARNERS

English Language Learners (ELL) are students identified as not proficient in the English language based on approved English proficiency assessment instruments which measure proficiency in and comprehension of English in reading, writing, speaking, and listening.[17] The ELL funding amount is the amount authorized by law multiplied by the district's identified ELL pupil population in the current school year. In FY 2018, ELL funding for each school year was $338 multiplied by the number of identified ELL students, with the pupil count verified on October 1.

STUDENT GROWTH FUNDING

To help ease the potential financial burden resulting from rapid increases in student populations, a school district with enrollment growth in quarterly average daily membership (ADM) compared to its prior-year three-quarter average daily membership may be eligible for student growth funding.[18] For example, to calculate student growth funding for FY 2018, the following formula would be used:

(12.95 × $1,678.25) + (12.4 × $1,78.25) + (8.89 × $1,678.25)
+ (0 × $1,678.25) = $57,027

Arkansas school districts may expend student growth funding on any eligible school purpose while maintaining the student growth revenue code. No district can receive both declining enrollment and student growth funding, and no district can receive both declining enrollment and special needs isolated funding. Therefore, a district will receive the larger amount of either declining enrollment funding or the sum of Student Growth Funding and Special Needs Isolated Funding.

DECLINING STUDENT ENROLLMENT FUNDING

Declining enrollment funding is defined as the amount of state financial aid provided to an eligible school district from funds made available for the decline in the average daily membership of the school district in the preceding school year compared to the school year before the preceding school year.[19] Declining enrollment funding is equal to the three-quarter ADM of the prior year, subtracted from the average of the three-quarter ADMs of the prior fiscal year and the fiscal year prior to the prior fiscal year, multiplied by the current per-student foundation funding amount. For example, to calculate declining student enrollment funding for FY 2018, the formula would be calculated:

$$(870.28 + 851.34) \div - 851.34 = 9.47$$
$$9.47 \times \text{FY18 per student foundation funding}$$
$$9.47 \times \$6,713 = /463,572 \text{ declining enrollment funding}$$

ISOLATED FUNDING

Isolated Funding is addressed in Arkansas law and specifically states that (a) undistributed funds under this section and §§ 6-20-601 and 6-20- 603 shall be distributed on an equal basis per school district to each school district that is eligible to receive funds under subsections; or (b) funds distributed under subdivision shall be used by the school district only for transportation costs of the isolated school areas in the school district.[20]

GENERAL TRANSPORTATION

Similar to special education funding, Arkansas mainly uses monies obtained through the local millage and foundation funding matrix for transportation-related expenses. Local and state aid monies are deposited to the general fund and coded to transportation expenditures as needed. In the foundation funding matrix, transportation is funded at $321.20 per pupil for FY18 and FY19. This money, although considered transportation aid in the funding matrix, is not restricted money and can be spent for other purposes. Senate Bill 303 (now Act 445) provides enhanced transportation funding to school districts facing higher than normal costs to provide transportation for students to and from school. Enhanced transportation funding is not restricted money and can be spent for other purposes. The method utilized to determine and allocate the enhanced funding is based

TABLE 4.9 Transportation Expenses		
Fiscal Years	Enhanced Transportation Funds	Transportation Expenses
2013	N/A	$199,822,772
2014	N/A	$203,025,960
2015	N/A	$197,320,327
2016	N/A	$198,542,601
2017	$3,088,374	$199,531,255

on a relatively secret statistical analysis of transportation behavior of all school districts in Arkansas and incorporates ADM, daily route miles, and the number of actual bus riders. For FY 2018, $3 million was appropriated for enhanced transportation funding. That amount increased to $5 million projected in FY 2019. Superintendents must wait for the state to determine how much each school district receives since they have no way to predict an amount. For example, District 1 and District 2 are neighboring rural districts consisting of 235 and 298 square miles, respectively, and an ADM of 1,363 and 601, respectively. District 1 received $5,112 while District 2 received $50,512 in enhanced transportation funding. Table 4.9 illustrates transportation expenses for Arkansas public school districts from FY 2013 to 2017.

SCHOOL FACILITIES AND CAPITAL OUTLAY

Bonded debt assistance is restricted funding to be used exclusively for the payment of bonded debt. The calculation of bonded debt assistance is based on a school district's principal and interest payment schedule in effect and on file with the Department of Education (ADE).[21] ACA § 6-20-2503 attributes 90% of each school district's outstanding bonded debt to the financing of academic facilities. However, the law provides for a school district to submit documentation if more than 90% of its outstanding bonded debt was issued in support of academic facilities. This established percentage of 90% or more is applied to each district's fiscal year principal and interest bonded debt payment from the January 1, 2005 debt schedule. The resulting 'adjusted 1/1/05 scheduled debt payment' is divided by the total assessed value of the district multiplied by 1,000 to calculate the required debt service mills. This product is multiplied by the state wealth index[22] and is different from the facilities wealth index[23] multiplied by the prior year three-quarter average daily membership (ADM) and multiplied by a funding factor of $18.03.

PROFESSIONAL DEVELOPMENT

During FY 2018 and subsequent years, the professional development funding per-student is an amount up to $32.40 multiplied by the school district's prior-year three-quarter average daily membership (ADM). A portion of the $32.40 is used to fund statewide professional development programs each year. The funding amount per-pupil provided directly to a school district is calculated after removing the portion corresponding to statewide programs. For FY 2018, the amount of per-student professional development funding excluding statewide programs was $26.05. This amount is provided on the preliminary state aid notice each year.

To calculate professional development funding, the state multiplies prior-year three-quarter ADM by the per-pupil professional development funding amount. For example, for a school district with FY 2017 three-quarter ADM of $629.17 and a per-student professional development funding rate for FY 2018 of $26.05, the professional development funding amount would be calculated as follows:

$$\$629.17 \times \$26.05 = \$16,390$$

SUMMARY

Table 4.10 summarizes Arkansas' foundation matrix funding formula trends for FY 2005 through projected FY 2019. Table 4.10 shows expenditures including school-level salaries as well as district and school-level resources. Finally, and overall, Arkansas P–12 school districts and open-enrollment charter schools received about $5.7 billion in total revenue during FY 2017. Foundation funding clearly made up the largest percentage of that revenue (56%) followed by federal revenue (11%) and state restricted funds (10%). One measure of the adequacy of Arkansas' education funding system is its total per-pupil spending, whereby nationally Arkansas ranks 34th and its per-pupil expenditure is more than $1,600 below the national average.[24]

Arkansas • 53

TABLE 4.10 Arkansas' Foundation Matrix Funding Formula Trends Fiscal Years 2005 Through Projected 2019

	FY05	FY06	FY07	FY08	FY09	FY10	FY11	FY12	FY13	FY14	FY15	FY16	FY17	FY18	FY19
Matrix Calculations															
School Size	500.0	599.0	500.0	500.0	500.0	500.0	500.0	500.0	500.0	500.0	500.0	500.0	500.0	500.0	500.0
K = 8% of students	40.0	49.0	40.0	40.0	40.0	40.0	40.0	40.0	40.0	40.0	40.0	40.0	40.0	40.0	40.0
Grades 1–3 = 23% of students	115.0	115.0	115.0	115.0	115.0	115.0	115.0	115.0	115.0	115.0	115.0	115.0	115.0	115.0	115.0
Grades 4–12 = 69% of students	345.0	345.0	345.0	345.0	345.0	345.0	345.0	345.0	345.0	345.0	345.0	345.0	345.0	345.0	345.0
Staffing Ratios															
K P:T ratio = 20:1	2.0	2.0	2.0	2.0	2.0	2.0	2.0	2.0	2.0	2.0	2.0	2.0	2.0	2.0	2.0
Grades 1–3 P:T ratio = 23.1	5.0	5.0	5.0	5.0	5.0	2.0	5.0	5.0	5.0	5.0	5.0	5.0	5.0	5.0	5.0
Grades 4–12 P:T ratio = 25.1	13.8	13.8	13.8	13.8	13.8	13.8	13.8	13.8	13.8	13.8	13.8	13.8	13.8	13.8	13.8
PAM = 20% of classroom	4.2	4.2	4.2	4.1	4.14	4.14	4.1	4.1	4.1	4.14	4.14	4.1	4.14	4.1	4.14
Total Classroom Teachers	25.0	25.0	25.0	24.94	24.94	24.94	24.94	24.94	24.94	24.94	24.94	24.94	24.94	24.94	24.94
Special Ed Teachers	2.9	2.9	2.9	2.9	2.9	2.9	2.9	2.9	2.9	2.9	2.9	2.9	2.9	2.9	2.9
Instructional Facilitators	2.5	2.5	2.5	2.5	2.5	2.5	2.5	2.5	2.5	2.5	2.5	2.5	2.5	2.5	2.5
Librarian/Media Specialist	0.7	0.7	0.7	0.825	0.825	0.825	0.825	0.825	0.825	0.825	0.825	0.85	0.85	0.85	0.85
Guidance Counselor & Nurse	2.5	2.5	2.5	2.5	2.5	2.5	2.5	2.5	2.5	2.5	2.5	2.5	2.5	2.5	2.5
Total Pupil Support Personnel	8.6	8.6	8.6	8.725	8.725	8.725	8.725	8.725	8.725	8.725	8.725	8.75	8.75	8.75	8.75
Subtotal	33.6	33.6	33.665	33.665	33.665	33.665	33.665	33.665	33.665	33.665	33.665	33.69	33.69	33.69	33.69
Principal	1.0	1.0	1.0	1.0	1.0	1.0	1.0	1.0	1.0	1	1.0	1.0	1	1	1
Secretary	0.0	0.0	0.0	1.0	1.0	1.0	1.0	1.0	1.0	1	1.0	1.0	1	1	1
Total School-Level Personnel	34.6	35.6	34.6	35.665	35.665	35.665	35.665	35.665	35.665	35.665	35.665	35.69	35.96	35.69	35.69

NOTES

1. 651 S.W.2d 90 (1983).
2. United States. National Commission on Excellence in Education. *A Nation at Risk: The Imperative for Educational Reform: A Report to the Nation and the Secretary of Education,* United States Department of Education. Washington, DC: The Commission: [Supt. of Docs., U.S. G.P.O. distributor], 1983.
3. 351 Ark. 31 SW3d 472 (2002).
4. P.L. 107-110 (2001).
5. *Lake View School District No. 25 v. Huckabee,* 189 S.W.3d 1 (Ark. 2004).
6. Ark. Const. art. 14, § 1.
7. Allen Odden, Lawrence Picus, and Mark Fermanich (2003). *An Evidence-based Approach to School Finance Adequacy in Arkansas. Report* prepared for the Arkansas Joint Committee on Education Adequacy. Retrieved from http://www.arkleg.state.ar.us/education/K12/AdequacyReportYears/2003%20Final%20Arkansas%20Report%2009_01_2 003.pdf
8. Adequacy Study Oversight Subcommittee, A Report on Legislative Hearings For the 2006 Interim Study on Educational Adequacy, Final Report and Recommendations, January 22, 2007.
9. State of Arkansas, Bureau of Legislative Research (2018).
10. A.C.A. § 6-20-2301 et seq.
11. Ark. § 6-20-2303(12)(A).
12. Ark. Cont. Art 14.
13. A.C.A. §6-20-2301 et seq. *See*: "Rules Governing the Distribution of Student Special Needs Funding and the Determination of Allowable Expenditures of Those Funds" (May 2016).
14. Michael Griffith, *State Funding Programs for High-Cost Special Education Students* (May 2008). Retrieved from: https://www.ecs.org/clearinghouse/78/10/7810.pdf
15. A.C.A §6-48-101 et seq.
16. Rule 4.06 of the ADE "Rules Governing the Distribution of Student Special Needs Funding and the Determination of Allowable Expenditures of Those Funds" (May 2016).
17. Ibid, Rule 3.11 of the ADE (2016).
18. Arkansas Department of Education (ADE) Act 741, "Rules Governing the Calculation Methods for Declining Enrollment and Student Growth Funding for Public School Districts" (2017). Retrieved from: http://adecm.arkansas.gov/ViewApprovedMemo.aspx?Id=3304
19. Arkansas Department of Education (ADE), "Rules Governing the Calculation Methods for Declining Enrollment and Student Growth Funding for Public School Districts" (2009). Retrieved from: http://www.arkansased.org/public/userfiles/Legal/LegalCurrent%20Rules/ade_296_declining_1009_current.pdf
20. A.C.A. §6-20-601 et seq.
21. A.C.A. § 6-20-2503.
22. A.C.A. § 6-20-2503(a)(6).
23. A.C.A. § 6-20-2502.

24. National Center for Education Statistics, Revenues and Expenditures for Public Elementary and Secondary Education: School Year 2014–15 (Fiscal Year 2015). Retrieved from: https://nces.ed.gov/pubs2018/2018301.pdf

CHAPTER 5

California

Ann E. Blankenship-Knox, JD, Ph.D.
*Assistant Professor
Program Coordinator
University of Redlands*

Paul C. Jessup, MS
*Deputy Superintendent
Riverside County Office of Education
Visiting Professor
University of Redlands*

Robert W. Blattner, MJ
*Partner, Blattner & Associates
Northern California*

GENERAL BACKGROUND

California's role in school funding has been infamous since the 1970s. The 1971 *Serrano v. Priest*[1] state supreme court decision placed California on the map in terms of school funding debates and constitutional supports. The *Serrano* decision shifted the focus of school finance reform from federal courts to state-level constitutional provisions, effectively proving that strict interpretation of state education articles could substitute for elusive federal protections. Indeed, the *Serrano* ruling launched a national reform wave that persists today, so that states' school aid plans are typically first subjected to judicial scrutiny on the basis of strength of education article language, albeit still with varying outcomes. Under these conditions, California led the way in defining the tensions and disputes surrounding state responsibility for funding public schools, so much so that today's legal arguments still echo the challenge that a child's education may not depend on the accident of residence.[2]

Today, California public school funding is the largest single portion of the state's budget, capturing more than 40% of the state's general fund resources. The 2017–18 state budget included more than $54 billion in general fund resources for K–12 education and child development.[3] Overall spending for California public schools is about $92.5 billion when federal funds and other funding sources, including local property taxes, are added.[4]

In a grand overview, the annual state budget is put in place by the state legislature and the governor. The budget cycle begins when the governor submits to the legislature an itemized proposed budget on or before each January 10.[5] The Senate Budget and Fiscal Review Committee and the Assembly Budget Committee conduct hearings on the governor's proposed budget bill in late February.[6] The governor proposes budget revisions in May based on updated information about state revenues. After considering the governor's initial and revised budget proposals, the two houses of the state legislature work through a Conference Committee to finalize a version of the budget bill that can pass in each house by a simple majority vote.[7] The legislature must pass a budget bill on or before June 15 and send it to the governor for signature.[8] The governor can reduce spending items before approving the final budget.[9]

Overall, the state budget directs how education funds are appropriated. At the local level, budgets are approved by local school boards after public hearings.[10] But the impact of *Serrano*, combined with the emaciated yields of local property taxes (now capped at 1%) after passage of Proposition 13[11] in 1978, has given local school boards very little control over revenues. California's funding system is extraordinarily centralized at the state level, and at the heart of it beats Proposition 98,[12] a constitutional amendment narrowly passed by voters 30 years ago to protect funding levels for K–14 public schools.[13]

Proposition 98 calculates a minimum funding guarantee for K–14 schools based on various 'tests' that weigh the impact of fiscal and demographic inputs (state tax revenues, per capita personal income, local property taxes, public school enrollment, and more).[14] The three tests that determine K–14 funding are:[15]

> **Test 1**: K–14 education must receive a minimum percentage of General Fund revenues (currently about 38%);

Test 2: K–14 education must receive at least the same amount of state aid and local property tax dollars as received in the prior year (adjusted for changes in K–12 attendance and per capita personal income); or

Test 3: K–14 education must receive at least the same amount of state aid and local property tax dollars as received in the prior year (adjusted for changes in K–12 attendance and per capita General Fund revenue plus .5% of the prior year Proposition 98 spending amount).[16] The three tests are graphically shown in Figure 5.1.

As a fiscal safety net, Proposition 98 has shortcomings. Just two years after passage, another constitutional amendment (Proposition 111) severely weakened its provisions by adding a third 'test' basically allowing automatic suspension of the minimum guarantee if state tax growth could not support it.[17] Now, however, because of Test 3, because it is based on year-to-year changes rather than longer-term trends and because state tax collections are increasingly volatile, the minimum guarantee is subject to enormous swings—usually negative. There is a constitutional promise—the 'Maintenance Factor'—to eventually get funding back on track.[18] But correction can take years, with billions lost in the meantime never recovered.[19] Proposition 98 almost always determines the funding ceiling these days, i.e., it is

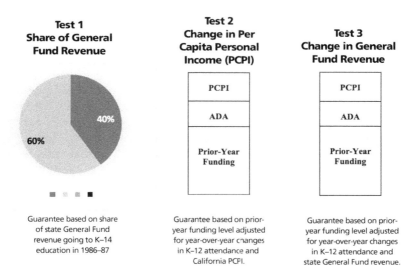

Figure 5.1 Three Proposition 98 "Tests." *Source:* https://lao.ca.gov/Publications/Report/3526#Formulas

not the floor as was intended. Its stated goal of pushing California into a top 10 state in terms of high funding and low class size is almost forgotten. But maligned as Proposition 98 often is, and while it only defines the size of the funding pot (not how that pot is spent), it still looms over budgeting for public schools in California.

BASIC SUPPORT PROGRAM[20]

In 2013–14, California implemented a new public education finance system called Local Control Funding Formula (LCFF), replacing a system that had been in place for approximately 40 years.[21] Prior to 2013, schools were funded through a mixture of general purpose grants and more than 50 categorical grants.[22] LCFF greatly simplified the school finance system while attempting to improve equity, transparency, and performance in public schools.[23] For school districts and charter schools, LCFF provided local education agencies (LEAs) with uniform base grants and with supplemental and concentration grants based on student demographic profiles.[24]

Base Grants for School Districts and Charter Schools Under LCFF

Base grants are distributed to school districts and charter schools to cover recurring general operational costs, such as teacher and administrator salaries, books, supplies, etc.[25] Base grants are calculated based on average daily attendance[26] (ADA) based on the grade span of pupils.[27] Base grant amounts for each grade span were initially set for the 2013–14 school year as follows: grades K–3 ($6,845); grades 4–6 ($6,947); grades 7–8 ($7,154); and grades 9–12 ($8,289). The base grant is determined each year by adding cost of living adjustments (COLA) to the prior year's base grant (before grade span adjustments).[28] For grades K–3 and 9–12, base grants are further augmented by applying grade span adjustments of 10.4% and 2.6% respectively.[29] Table 5.1 shows how the 2018–19 base grants (and adjusted base grants) were calculated based on the 2017–18 base grants, the COLA, and the grade span adjustments.

Supplemental and Concentration Grants for School Districts and Charter Schools Under LCFF

In addition to base grants calculated based on the ADA of all students, school districts and charter schools may also receive additional program

TABLE 5.1 Base Grant Funding, Education Code (EC) Section 42238.02(d)

Grade Span	2017–18 Base Grant per ADA	2018–19 'Super COLA' (3.70%)	Grade Span Adjustments (K–3: 10.4% 9–12: 2.6%)	2018–19 Base Grant/Adjusted Base Grant per ADA
K–3	$7,193	$266	$776	$8,235
4–6	$7,301	$270	N/A	$7,571
7–8	$7,518	$278	N/A	$7,796
9–12	$8,712	$322	$235	$9,269

Source: California Department of Education. Funding Rates and Information, Fiscal Year 2018–19: Principal Apportionment Funding Rates and Other Fiscal Information for Fiscal Year 2018–19.

funds for distribution to districts to support populations of students who are in the foster care system or who are classified as homeless, students who are classified as English learners, and students who are classified as low-income based on their qualification for free or reduced-price meals.[30] These students, referred to as "unduplicated pupils," are counted only once, even if they may be classified in more than one of the covered categories.[31] The number of unduplicated pupils, collectively referred to as the "unduplicated count," entitles a school district to supplemental grants, and potentially concentration grants, if the count reaches a certain threshold.[32]

School districts receive supplemental grants for all unduplicated pupils. The supplemental grant is calculated by multiplying 20% of the adjusted base grant multiplied by the unduplicated count (as a percent of the total school district population). For example, if a high school district having a population of 1,200 students (based on ADA) for the 2018–19 school year had an unduplicated count amounting to 17% of that population, the supplemental grant would be calculated as seen in Table 5.2.

If a school district has a significant unduplicated count (in excess of 55% of student population) meaning it has a high concentration of students who may need additional supports to be successful in the public school system, it will also receive concentration funding. Concentration funding is calculated by multiplying 50% of the adjusted base grant by the unduplicated count (as a percent of the total school district population) that exceeds 55%.[33]

TABLE 5.2 Example Calculation of Supplemental Grant

Grade Level	Adjusted Base Grant (see Table 5.1)	20% of Adjusted Base Grant	Unduplicated Count (17% of district population)	Supplemental Grant
9–12	$9,269	$1,853.80	204	$378,012

TABLE 5.3 Example Calculation of Concentration Grant

Grade Level	Adjusted Base Grant (see Table)	50% of Adjusted Base Grant	Unduplicated Count in Excess of 55% (12% of district population)	Supplemental Grant
9–12	$9,269	$4,634.50	144	$667,368

TABLE 5.4 Example Calculation of Total Local Control Funding Formula Grant (Based on 67% Unduplicated Count)

Funding Source	Adjusted Base Grant (see Table 5.1)	Portion of Adjusted Base Grant	Total Number of Students	Number of Unduplicated Pupils	Supplemental Grant
Adjusted Base Grant	$9,269	N/A	1,200	N/A	$11,122,800
Supplemental Grant	N/A	$1,853.80	N/A	804	$1,490,455.20
Concentration Grant	N/A	$4,634.50	N/A	144	$667,368
Total					$13,280,623.20

For example, if the same high school district in the example above had an unduplicated count amounting to 67% of its population (rather than 17%), the concentration grant would be calculated as seen in Table 5.3.

Table 5.4 provides a clear picture of how the base grant and the supplemental and concentration grants work together to provide the calculation of total education grant funding for the high school district mentioned above, with 67% of its students classified as unduplicated pupils.

Local Control Accountability Plan

The Local Control Accountability Plan (LCAP) is a three-year plan that describes how the school district will support positive student outcomes for state and local priorities, particularly for unduplicated pupils.[34] Using a template provided by the state,[35] each school district provides a full accounting of how LCFF funds are spent and how each expenditure supports the state's eight educational priorities:

1. Appropriate basic educational supports in the form of appropriately credentialed teachers, standards-aligned instructional materials, and school facilities that are maintained in good repair;[36]

2. Implementation of academic content and performance standards;[37]
3. Parental involvement and family engagement;[38]
4. Academic achievement for all students;[39]
5. Student engagement;[40]
6. Positive school climate;[41]
7. Access to and enrollment in a broad course of study;[42]
8. Other student outcomes.[43]

Priorities 1, 2, and 7 address the basic conditions of learning. Priorities 4 and 8 address student outcomes. Priorities 3, 5, and 6 address community engagement.

Each LCAP is intended to tell the story of where a school district has been, where it is, and where it is trying to go. It includes a narrative statement, school district progress and goals, identification of performance gaps, plans of action, identification of services, and planned expenditures.[44] At the beginning of the three-year LCAP process, the school district, in consultation with members of the community,[45] establishes a set of goals on which it wants to focus for that period. Each goal is aligned to state and local priorities, and the district identifies annual measurable outcomes on which to evaluate progress.[46] The plan is modified and updated in the two years between LCAP drafting years.[47] Every year, the LCAP or a modification/revision of the LCAP must be approved by the governing district board of education on or before July 1.[48] Within five days of adoption, the LCAP and the budget are then sent to the county superintendent of schools for final approval.[49]

California School Dashboard and Statewide System of Support

State funding for education is tied to the California School Dashboard,[50] an accountability system aimed at continuous improvement for the purpose of providing information about how well local education agencies and schools are meeting the needs of the state's diverse student population.[51] The California School Dashboard provides educators, parents, and community members open access to aggregated education data on schools and districts.[52] Building on the Dashboard, the budget provides funds to support school districts identified with consistently low performing student subgroups and connects them to a network of resources available through the companion Statewide System of Support.[53]

Revenue Sources

While the LCFF represents a dramatic departure from previous California education spending plans, the funding mechanism is not new. Once the LCFF amount is calculated, an LEA is first funded using local property taxes. If local property tax revenues are insufficient to reach the LCFF level, as is the case for more than 90% of the state's LEAs, then the state provides additional funds up to the LCFF funding level.[54] If property taxes raised in a particular community exceed the LCFF funding level, the LEA does not receive any LCFF funds from the state but is permitted to keep the overage of property tax revenues generated.[55]

Gap Appropriations

The LCFF itself did not create a new source of revenue; it only regulates how state revenue is distributed and managed.[56] And it directs the distribution of additional monies for students classified as high need; in 2014–15, 63% of California's students qualified as high need according to LCFF.[57] When the LCFF passed, the governor estimated that it would cost approximately $60 billion to fully fund the system, about $21 billion more than was previously allocated for education.[58] This dramatic increase in funding required a transition period, during which time LEAs received their pre-LCFF funding plus a portion of the difference toward the full-funding target.[59] The gap funding transition period was predicted to take seven years. However, as a result of strong growth in tax receipts, the governor was able to ensure that the LCFF was fully funded before he left office in 2018.[60]

Economic Recovery Target Funding

For a small number of California school districts and charter schools, LCFF actually generates less money than the previous funding system. Under LCFF, these districts are entitled to Economic Recovery Target (ERT) funds through 2020–21, calculated based on the difference between the amount the district or charter school would have received under the old funding system and the estimated amount it would receive under LCFF.[61] School districts and charter schools at, or below, the 90th percentile of per-pupil funding rates (2013–14) of school districts under the old funding system were eligible to receive ERT.[62] ERT funding was calculated in 2013–14 and then eligibility was closed to new participants.[63]

BUDGET ACT OF 2018–19

As the largest program funded by the state's General Fund, California public school funding is a significant focus in every budget.[64] In June 2018, the governor signed the Budget Act for the 2018–19 school (and fiscal) year.[65] The budget package included $97.2 billion for TK–12 education,[66] with per-pupil spending of $16,352 for 2018–19.[67] In addition to fully funding LCFF two years ahead of the estimated time frame, the 2018–19 Budget Act also included the following allocations:

- **Fire-Related Funding Relief** In 2017, California experienced the most destructive fire season to that point in history. The fires destroyed thousands of properties. The 2018–19 budget sought to address some of the damages of the fires by backfilling wildfire-related property tax revenue loss and providing additional financial support to LEAs that suffered fire damage.[68] The budget included $15.9 million to assist LEAs that sustained damage in the 2017 fires to reopen schools and $3.7 million to provide basic aid and special education programs for LEAs that lost local property tax revenue.[69] The 2018 California wildfires surpassed the 2017 wildfires as the most deadly and destructive fires in California's history.[70] Burning nearly two million acres, killing 92 people, and leveling over 20,000 structures, the 2018 wildfires will certainly necessitate continued fire-related funding relief in future education budgets.[71]
- **Early Childhood Education and Child Care** The 2018–19 budget continued to build early childhood programs with over $3.6 billion in funding, up $288 million from the previous year.[72] The funding included $1.2 billion for the state preschool program, $588 million for child care, and $427 million for alternative payment programs.[73] The budget also included funding for LEAs to retrofit or construct facilities to provide full-day kindergarten, professional development for early care and education in inclusive settings,[74] and additional funding for Early Head Start Child Care Partnership Grants.[75] The new governor, who took office in January 2019, is a strong proponent of early childhood education programs and proposed a $1.8 billion increase in funding to boost enrollment in early childhood education and child-care programs in his first proposed budget.[76]
- **Career Technical Education** The 2018–19 budget included a $150 million allocation for competitive matching grants to continue the Career Technical Education Incentive Grant Program.[77] The budget gives the California Department of Education, in collaboration with the State Board of Education, the power to determine how these funds will be used.[78] The budget also includes $164 million in competitive grants with a matching requirement for LEAs to expand and align career technical education programs with programs offered by higher education institutions and with regional labor markets.[79]

- **Low Performing Students** The 2018–19 budget allocates a one-time sum of $300 million for the Low Performing Students Block Grant, to be distributed equally during the 2018–19 fiscal year to LEAs for students who perform at the lowest levels of the state's academic assessments and who do not generate supplemental LCFF funds or special education funds (from state or federal governments).[80]
- **Special Education** The 2018–19 budget included supplemental special education funding to improve student performance and to address the shortage of special education teachers.[81] It allocated $10 million for Special Education Local Plan Areas[82] to help county offices of education in providing technical assistance to school districts that need additional support and/or training specific to students with disabilities.[83] It also included a one-time allotment of $100 million to the Commission on Teacher Credentialing to increase and retain special education teachers through a teacher residency grant program and a competitive grant for LEAs to implement local solutions.[84] Increases to special education funding will likely continue under the leadership of the new governor, as in his 2019 budget proposal he proposed a budget allocation of more than $576 million for special education funding to account for the increasing cost of services and greater concentrations of students with exceptional needs.[85]
- **Facilities and Transportation** The 2018–19 budget package included $640 million in bond authority[86] for new construction and modernization of education facilities, particularly for career technical education and charter facility projects.[87]
- **One-Time Discretionary Funding/Mandates** The Budget Act of 2018–19 included a number of one-time appropriations, including a teacher residency grant program, a grant for the After School Kids Code Grant Pilot Program, suicide prevention, history and social science curriculum, and an incentive for schools to purchase California-grown food for school meal programs.[88]

SUMMARY

California's school finance system is complex and accounts for nearly half of the state's annual general fund spending. The funding reforms of 2014 sought to improve resources for the state's most vulnerable students and to provide LEAs with more control and accountability for education's resources. Longitudinal data for recent past years show increasing education revenue from multiple sources. Figure 5.2 graphically demonstrates how

Figure 5.2 California School Revenue Sources, Amounts and Trends, Fiscal Years 2013–2017. *Source:* https://www.ed-data.org/state/CA

the LCFF has steadily increased education funding across Fiscal Years 2013–2017. Figure 5.3 parses those same data to a per-pupil view.

Still, funding for California's approximately 6.2 million students is the subject of considerable criticism. Despite decades of nearly continuous school finance litigation and significant increases in funding levels, critics

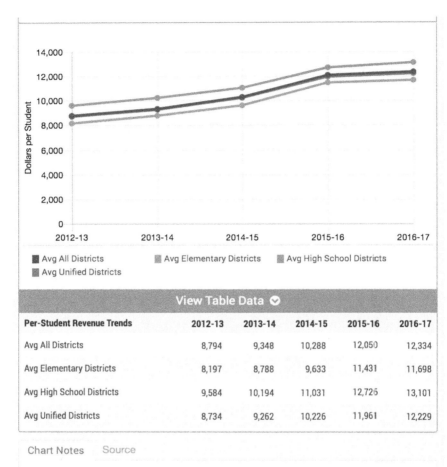

Figure 5.3 California Per-Student Revenue Trends Fiscal Years 2013–2017. *Source:* https://www.ed-data.org/state/CA

argue that schools are at least standing still if not regressing in terms of pupil performance.[89] A 2018 survey[90] of school superintendents across the state found general support for the LCFF, but with considerable dissatisfaction relating to numerous elements of state support. More specifically, the insider view strongly favored the tenets of the LCFF, but concerns focused on administrative burden, inadequate base funding, and lack of flexibility regarding use of supplemental and concentration funds.[91] Superintendents expressed concern regarding stakeholder engagement and the timeliness of the Dashboard. Unsurprisingly, school district context played a huge role in relative satisfaction with the LCFF, with favorability increasing as school district size increased—conversely, the smaller the district, the greater the dissatisfaction with perceptions involving administrative burden and losses perceived by elimination of categorical programs. Overall, a large majority (78%) regarded the LCFF as underfunded related to its goals and expectations, despite acknowledgment (69%) that LCFF's increased funding had been essential to successes so far.[92]

Outsider criticism of California school finance reform has been strong as well. While all sides generally regard the state as having made progress through increased focus and spending, critics argue that LCFF funding does not necessarily help unduplicated pupils as intended.[93] Critics also argue that there is still a lack of transparency, understandability, and disparities when micro-analyzing equal access to high-quality resources under the LCFF.[94]

At the core, all sides appear to agree in recognizing the complexity and size of California's school funding system[95]—a system containing over 6 million children, with 59% coming from low-income backgrounds, 21% classified as English Language Learners, and another 12% with special needs.[96] Above all, large achievement gaps exist which the LCFF intends to redress. What happens next is yet to be seen.

NOTES

1. 5 Cal.3d 584 (1971) (*Serrano I*); subsequent litigation followed in *Serrano v. Priest*, 18 Cal.3d 728 (1976) (*Serrano II*); and *Serrano v. Priest*, 20 Cal.3d 25 (1977) (*Serrano III*). For a more complete synopsis of subsequent California finance litigation through 2018, see *California*, SCHOOLFUNDING.INFO: A PROJECT OF THE CENTER FOR EDUCATIONAL EQUITY AT TEACHERS COLLEGE, http://schoolfunding.info/litigation-map/california/#1484003321788-7f4cb732-5834 (last visited January 31, 2019).
2. Ibid, *Serrano I*, 5 Cal.3d at 589, stating "... makes the quality of education for school-age children in California, including Plaintiff Children, a function of the wealth of the children's parents and neighbors, as measured by the tax base of the school district in which said children reside."
3. *K Thru 12 Education Budget Summary*, 2017–18 GOVERNOR'S BUDGET, (Jan. 10, 2018), http://www.ebudget.ca.gov/2017–18/pdf/Enacted/BudgetSummary/Kthru12Education.pdf
4. Ibid.
5. CAL. CONST., art. IV, § 12(a). If the governor's budget includes proposed expenditures that exceed anticipated revenues, the governor must recommend sources of additional revenue.

6. Committee hearings generally begin soon after they receive the "Analysis of the Budget Bill" from the Legislative Analyst. The Legislative Analyst is appointed by the Joint Legislative Budget Committee and is charged with providing a nonpartisan analysis and recommendations for changes to the governor's proposed budget. *California's Budget Process*, STATE OF CAL. DEP'T OF FIN., http://www.dof.ca.gov/budget/Budget_Process/index.html (last visited Jan. 19, 2019).
7. Ibid.
8. CAL. CONST., art. IV, § 12(b)(3).
9. *Education Budget*, CAL. DEP'T OF EDUC., https://www.cde.ca.gov/fg/fr/eb/ (last visited Jan. 19, 2019).
10. CAL. EDUC. CODE § 42127 (a)(1) (West 2019).
11. CAL. CONST., art. XIIIA. On June 6, 1978, voters passed Proposition 13, reducing property tax rates on homes, businesses, and farms. Proposition 13 limits increases in assessed property value and caps property tax and ad valorem property tax rates to 1% of the full cash value at the time of acquisition. "What is Proposition 13?" California Tax Data, https://www.californiataxdata.com/pdf/Prop13.pdf (last visited Jan. 31, 2019); *A Historical Review of Proposition 98*, LEGISLATIVE ANALYST'S OFFICE (Jan. 18, 2017), https://lao.ca.gov/Publications/Report/3526#Formulas.
12. CAL. EDUC. CODE § 41206 (West 2019).
13. CAL. CONST., art. XIIIB; CAL. CONST., art. XVI.
14. *Proposition 98 Primer*, LEGISLATIVE ANALYST'S OFFICE (Feb. 2005), https://lao.ca.gov/2005/prop_98_primer/prop_98_primer_020805.htm.
15. Ibid. The test used depends on how the economy and General Fund revenues grow annually.
16. *Proposition 98 Sets a Minimum Funding Guarantee for Education* (Policy Brief), EDSOURCE (Mar. 2009), https://edsource.org/wp-content/publications/PolicyBriefR3.pdf.
17. The original version allowed political suspension, but only by a two-thirds vote of the legislature and a governor's signature.
18. CAL. CONST., art. XVI; CAL. EDUC. CODE § 41207.2 (West 2019).
19. During the Great Recession, for instance, the Maintenance Factor exceeded $10 billion per year.
20. See generally, *Education Budget*, CAL. DEP'T OF EDUC. (Dec. 4, 2018), https://www.cde.ca.gov/fg/fr/eb/; also, *Local Control Funding Formula Overview*, CAL. DEP'T OF EDUC (Jan. 9, 2019) https://www.cde.ca.gov/fg/aa/lc/.
21. *Local Control Funding Formula Overview*, CAL. DEP'T OF EDUC. (Jan. 9, 2019) https://www.cde.ca.gov/fg/aa/lc/.
22. Ibid.
23. *Local Control Funding Formula*, WESTED, https://lcff.wested.org (last visited Jan. 31, 2019).
24. CAL. EDUC. CODE § 42238.02 (West 2019).
25. *Local Control Funding Formula Overview*, CAL. DEP'T OF EDUC. (Jan. 9, 2019) https://www.cde.ca.gov/fg/aa/lc/; CAL. EDUC. CODE § 42238.03 (West 2019) (setting forth how base entitlement rates are calculated).

26. *Local Control Funding Formula Overview*, CAL. DEP'T OF EDUC. (Jan. 9, 2019) https://www.cde.ca.gov/fg/aa/lc/.
27. CAL. EDUC. CODE § 42238.02(d) (West 2019).
28. Cost-of-living adjustments (COLA) rates are set each year as part of the budget negotiation process. The governor presents an estimated COLA in the budget he or she submits in January. *LCFF Gap and COLA*, CAL. DEP'T OF EDUC. (July 16, 2018), https://www.cde.ca.gov/fg/aa/pa/lcffgapfunding.asp. Under California law, the COLA is linked to the national price index developed by the Bureau of Economic Analysis for the U.S. Department of Commerce. *2018–19 COLA for K–14 Education Programs*, LEGISLATIVE ANALYST'S OFFICE (Apr. 30, 2018), https://lao.ca.gov/Publications/Report/3816. The legislature makes adjustments to the COLA based on updated information from the Bureau of Economic Analysis, generally released in late April. For the 2018–19 budget, the updated COLA was 2.71%, higher than it had been in several years. The 2018–19 Budget Act overfunded the statutory COLA of 2.71% by $570 million, creating a one-time 'Super COLA' rate of 3.70%. This results in a permanent increase in base grant funding across grade levels and increases supplemental and concentration grants where applicable. *Letter to County and District Superintendents Regarding Budget Act for 2018–19* (Revised), CAL. DEP'T OF EDUC. (Oct. 8, 2018), https://www.cde.ca.gov/fg/fr/eb/yr18l-tr1008.asp.
29. CAL. EDUC. CODE § 42238.02(d)(2)-(3) (West 2019). The adjustment of 10.4% for K–3 grades is to help reduce class size and the 2.6% adjustment for high school grades is to help offset the cost of career-technical education.
30. CAL. EDUC. CODE § 42238.02 (West 2019).
31. Ibid.
32. Ibid at (e).
33. Ibid at (f).
34. CAL. EDUC. CODE § 52060 et seq. (West 2019); *Local Control Accountability Plan (LCAP)*, CAL. DEP'T OF EDUC. (Jan. 30, 2019), https://www.cde.ca.gov/re/lc/.
35. CAL. EDUC. CODE § 52060(a) (West 2019).
36. Ibid at (d)(1).
37. Ibid. Specifically, this goal relates to the implementation of Common Core State Standards for all students, including English learners. *See LCFF and LCAP State Priority Areas*, SAN JUAN UNIFIED SCH. DIST., https://www.sanjuan.edu/Page/23613 (last visited Jan. 24, 2019).
38. Ibid at (d)(3).
39. Ibid at (d)(4). Measures of this include standardized test scores, Academic Performance Index (API) scores, percent of student population who are college and career ready, ELs who become English proficient, and Advance Placement (AP) test passage rates. *LCFF and LCAP State Priority Areas*, SAN JUAN UNIFIED SCH. DIST., https://www.sanjuan.edu/Page/23613 (last visited Jan. 24, 2019).
40. Ibid at (d)(5). Measures of this include student attendance rates, chronic absenteeism rates, and dropout rates. *LCFF and LCAP State Priority Areas*, SAN

JUAN UNIFIED SCH. DIST., https://www.sanjuan.edu/Page/23613 (last visited Jan. 24, 2019).

41. Ibid at (d)(6). Measures of this include student suspension and expulsion rates and other local measures of climate, such as student feedback and climate survey results.
42. Ibid at (d)(7). The broad course of study includes all subject areas described in CAL. EDUC. CODE § 51210, 51220(a)-(i) (West 2019).
43. Ibid at (d)(8). Specifically, this refers to pupil outcomes in the broad course of study described in the previous endnote.
44. *Local Control Accountability Plan (LCAP)*, CAL. DEP'T OF EDUC. (Jan. 30, 2019), https://www.cde.ca.gov/re/lc/.
45. The superintendent, with the support and help of their staff, drafts the LCAP. CAL. EDUC. CODE § 52062(a)(1) (West 2019). The superintendent presents the LCAP to the parent advisory committee (established pursuant to Cal. Educ. Code § 52063) and the English learner parent advisory committee (also established pursuant to CAL. EDUC. CODE § 52063) for review and comment. The superintendent is also required to give members of the community an opportunity to give feedback on the LCAP (CAL. EDUC. CODE § 52062(a)(3)) before submitting the LCAP to the governing board of the school district for adoption. (CAL. EDUC. CODE § 52062(a)). In an effort to ensure that additional funding is used to benefit the unduplicated pupils, school districts often seek out more extensive community feedback on the programming funded by supplemental and concentration grants. They may solicit participation of a large group of parents, teachers, classified employees, and community members to serve on LCAP advisory committees.
46. Ibid. The district measures outcomes using both state and local matrices.
47. CAL. EDUC. CODE § 52062 (West 2019).
48. CAL. EDUC. CODE § 52061 (West 2019). The school board must hold at least one public hearing to allow the public to review the LCAP and make recommendations or comments before it is adopted. CAL. EDUC. CODE § 52062(b)(1) (West 2019). The school board adopts the LCAP in a public meeting (after and not on the same day as the public comment meeting) during which they also adopt the school district budget. CAL. EDUC. CODE § 52062(b)(2) (West 2019).
49. CAL. EDUC. CODE § 52070 (West 2019). A school district's budget cannot be approved and funded until the county superintendent of schools reviews the school district LCAP and confirms that it complies with the LCAP requirements.
50. *California School Dashboard and System of Support*, CAL. DEP'T OF EDUC. (Jan. 24, 2019), https://www.cde.ca.gov/ta/ac/cm/.
51. *Letter to County and District Superintendents Regarding Budget Act for 2018–19* (Revised), CAL. DEP'T OF EDUC. (Oct. 8, 2018), https://www.cde.ca.gov/fg/fr/eb/yr18ltr1008.asp.
52. CALIFORNIA SCHOOL DASHBOARD, https://www.caschooldashboard.org (last visited Jan. 31, 2019). The Dashboard provides information on student achievement scores, student discipline, absenteeism rates, graduation rates, and college and career readiness. The Dashboard also allows these statistics to

be further broken down by race and for English learners, special education, foster/homeless students, and low-income students.

53. *California's System of Support*, CAL. DEP'T OF EDUC. (Jan. 11, 2019), https://www.cde.ca.gov/sp/sw/tl/csss.asp.
54. *Local Control Funding Formula: LCFF Dictates How State Funds Flow to School Districts*, ED100, https://ed100.org/lessons/lcff (last visited Jan. 26, 2019).
55. Ibid.
56. *Local Control Funding Formula Guide*, EDSOURCE, 5 (Mar. 1, 2016), https://edsource.org/wp-content/uploads/2016/02/lcff-guide-print-version.pdf.
57. Ibid at 6.
58. Ibid at 7. Proposition 30 (The Schools and Local Public Safety Protection Act of 2012) was approved by voters the same year LCFF passed. It temporarily increased personal income tax and sales and use tax rates to provide additional revenue for public elementary and secondary schools and community colleges. It expired in 2016, at which time Proposition 55 (The California Children's Education and Health Care Protection Act of 2016) was approved to extend the increases to personal income tax rates on earnings over $250,000 to provide continued revenue for elementary and secondary schools and community colleges through fiscal year 2030-31. A.B.1808, 2017–18 Reg. Sess. (Cal. 2018).
59. *Local Control Funding Formula Guide*, EDSOURCE, 8 (Mar. 1, 2016), https://edsource.org/wp-content/uploads/2016/02/lcff-guide-print-version.pdf.
60. *Letter to County and District Superintendents Regarding Budget Act for 2018–19* (Revised), CAL. DEP'T OF EDUC. (Oct. 8, 2018), https://www.cde.ca.gov/fg/fr/eb/yr18ltr1008.asp.
61. CAL. EDUC. CODE § 42238.025 (West 2019).
62. *LCFF Frequently Asked Questions*, CAL. DEP'T OF EDUC. (June 1, 2018), https://www.cde.ca.gov/fg/aa/lc/lcfffaq.asp.
63. Ibid.
64. *Education Budget*, CAL. DEP'T OF EDUC. (Dec. 4, 2018), https://www.cde.ca.gov/fg/fr/eb/index.asp.
65. *Letter to County and District Superintendents Regarding Budget Act for 2018–19* (Revised), CAL. DEP'T OF EDUC. (Oct. 8, 2018), https://www.cde.ca.gov/fg/fr/eb/yr18ltr1008.asp.
66. Inclusive of all public funding sources (federal, state, and local).
67. Ibid. Per pupil spending indicated here is an average rate, across grade spans. The comparable 2017–18 per pupil spending rate was $15,775.
68. Ibid.
69. Ibid.
70. Jack Nicas & Thomas Fuller, *Wildfire Becomes Deadliest in California History*, THE NEW YORK TIMES (Nov. 12, 2018), https://www.nytimes.com/2018/11/12/us/california-fires-camp-fire.html.
71. Ibid.
72. *Letter to County and District Superintendents Regarding Budget Act for 2018–19* (Revised), CAL. DEP'T OF EDUC. (Oct. 8, 2018), https://www.cde.ca.gov/fg/fr/eb/yr18ltr1008.asp.
73. Ibid.

74. Cal. Educ. Code § 8492 (West 2019).
75. Ibid.
76. *Proposed Budget Summary, 2019–20* Governor's Budget (Jan. 10, 2019), http://www.ebudget.ca.gov/budget/2019-20/#/BudgetSummary.
77. Ibid. *See also*, Cal. Educ. Code § 53070(c) (West 2017); Cal. Educ. Code § 53070.1 et seq. (West 2019).
78. Cal. Educ. Code § 53070(d) (West 2017).
79. *Letter to County and District Superintendents Regarding Budget Act for 2018–19* (Revised), Cal. Dep't of Educ. (Oct. 8, 2018), https://www.cde.ca.gov/fg/fr/eb/yr18ltr1008.asp; Cal. Educ. Code § 88820 et seq. (West 2019); Cal. Educ. Code § 88833 (West 2019); Cal. Educ. Code § 53076.4 (West 2019);
80. Ibid. Cal. Educ. Code § 41570 (West 2019).
81. Ibid.
82. In 1977, California school districts and county school offices formed regional consortiums to better meet the special education service needs of the students residing in the region boundaries. Each Special Education Local Plan Area develop plans for providing special education services in their region. *California Special Education Local Plan Areas*, Cal. Dep't of Educ. (Jan. 8, 2018), https://www.cde.ca.gov/sp/se/as/caselpas.asp; Cal. Educ. Code §§ 56205, 56206, 56208, 56211, 56213, 56241, 56243, 56244, & 56245 (West 2019).
83. *Letter to County and District Superintendents Regarding Budget Act for 2018–19* (Revised), Cal. Dep't of Educ. (Oct. 8, 2018), https://www.cde.ca.gov/fg/fr/eb/yr18ltr1008.asp.
84. Ibid; Cal. Educ. Code § 44416 (West 2019).
85. *Proposed Budget Summary, 2019–20* Governor's Budget (Jan. 10, 2019), http://www.ebudget.ca.gov/budget/2019-20/#/BudgetSummary.
86. Cal. Educ. Code § 101110 (West 2019)
87. *Letter to County and District Superintendents Regarding Budget Act for 2018–19* (Revised), Cal. Dep't of Educ. (Oct. 8, 2018), https://www.cde.ca.gov/fg/fr/eb/yr18ltr1008.asp. The budget also provided a one-time allocation of $21.1 million to support the Charter Facility Grant Program.
88. *Letter to County and District Superintendents Regarding Budget Act for 2018–19* (Revised), Cal. Dep't of Educ. (Oct. 8, 2018), https://www.cde.ca.gov/fg/fr/eb/yr18ltr1008.asp. The total funds allocated for one-time appropriations was $43.2 million.
89. John Affeldt, *California Needs a New Master Plan to Close the Education Equity Gap*, EdSource (Oct. 31, 2018), https://edsource.org/2018/california-needs-another-master-plan-to-close-the-education-equity-gap/604068.
90. Julie A. Marsh & Julia E. Koppich, *Superintendents Speak: Implementing the Local Control Funding Formula (LCFF)*, PACE (June 27, 2018), https://www.documentcloud.org/documents/4561241-LCFF-Supt-Survey-2018.html.
91. Ibid.
92. Ibid.
93. Nadra Kareem Nittle, *Why School Funding Will Always Be Imperfect*, The Atlantic (Aug. 24, 2016), https://www.theatlantic.com/education/archive/2016/08/will-there-ever-be-a-perfect-way-to-fund-schools/497069/

94. *See, e.g.*, Matt Barnum, *How New Evidence Bolsters the Case for California's Education Policy Rebellion*, CHALKBEAT (Feb. 8, 2018), https://www.chalkbeat.org/posts/us/2018/02/08/how-new-evidence-bolsters-the-case-for-californias-education-policy-rebellion/; *see also*, Susan Ferriss, *Will New Funding Formula Move Schools Toward Education Equity?* KQED (Feb. 8, 2017), https://www.kqed.org/news/11305666/will-new-funding-formula-move-schools-towards-education-equity.
95. *The 2018–19 Budget: K–12 Education in Context*, LEGISLATIVE ANALYST'S OFFICE (Jan. 26, 2018), https://lao.ca.gov/Publications/Report/3736
96. CalFacts 2018, Legislative Analyst's Office, https://lao.ca.gov/reports/2018/3905/calfacts-2018.pdf (last visited Jan. 31, 2019).

CHAPTER 6

Colorado

Spencer C. Weiler, Ph.D.
Professor
University of Northern Colorado

GENERAL BACKGROUND

Colorado enacted its first constitution and was granted statehood in 1876.[1] However, public schools began to dot the territory as early as 1861, and funding for these early schools was exclusively based on local revenue.[2] By the turn of the twentieth century, public schools had increased services provided for pupils to include a high school curriculum; with these increases in overall quality of the educational experience for school-aged children, state aid was initiated to augment local efforts to fund schools.[3] Eventually, state sales and income tax revenues were used to supplement the overall funding for public education.[4] By the time Colorado entered the twenty-first century, state aid accounted for roughly 60% of total funding for public education, despite efforts to equally distribute the tax burden between state and local taxes. Two anti-tax constitutional amendments have contributed to the overall overreliance on state aid to fund public education.[5]

The primary focus of this chapter is to provide a thorough understanding of Colorado's funding formula for public education. The discussion touches on an array of topics, including the general fund, special education, transportation, the marijuana tax, school facilities, virtual/online schools, special levies, and the state retirement system. The discussion then moves to summarize the major school finance lawsuits originating in Colorado.

BASIC SUPPORT PROGRAM

The current funding formula for Colorado was first enacted in 1994.[6] Recently, advocates for public schools have contended that the current state aid formula is antiquated and needs revision to reflect the current fiscal realities of providing all students 'a thorough and uniform'[7] educational experience. During the 2018 legislative session, there was a bill that, if passed, would have completely altered funding for public schools. The new funding formula would have included a $1.6 billion tax increase, pending voter approval. However, the author of the bill pulled the proposed legislation in committee because it may have lacked enough bipartisan support. The bill's author pledged to try again in 2019.[8] Implicit, then, is that the current funding formula detailed below could change in the near future.

GENERAL FUND

The state funding formula, titled the Public School Finance Act of Colorado, determines per-pupil funding for the state's 178 school districts. Charter schools that are chartered by the Charter School Institute[9] are included in the funding law. The amount of money school districts and charter schools receive is referred to as the total program. A school district's or charter school's total program is determined by a pupil count formula tied to a count date on or around October 1 each year.[10] The formula for the total program is expressed in the following equation:

(Funded Pupil Count × Total Per-pupil Funding) + At-risk Funding + Online Funding + Budget Stabilization Factor = TOTAL PROGRAM[11]

Several terms in this equation require explanation in order to make sense of the total program formula. First, the total per-pupil funding is, in effect, the base funding level for each full-time equivalency (FTE) pupil.[12] For the 2017–2018 school year, the base funding was $6,546.20.[13] The state funding formula includes weights that add to the base per-pupil funding. These weights include:

- *Cost of Living*: This weight provides additional revenue to school districts located in regions of the state with above-average cost of living indices. The state cost of living factor is based on mean scores from the Denver and Boulder communities.[14] The cost of living factor ranges from 1.012 to 1.650 in Colorado.[15]
- *Personnel Costs*: Certain school districts have a more veteran workforce and, as a result, the percentage of a school district's total

program allocated to personnel costs may exceed the state average. The state funding formula, therefore, provides additional monies to districts where personnel costs amount to more than 80% of the district's total program.[16] The personnel cost factor ranges from 1.010 to 2.243.[17]
- *Size*: Rural Colorado contains small and inefficient school districts serving fewer than 100 pupils. These districts are required to fully staff a building despite the fact that there may be fewer than ten students in any particular classroom. The state's funding formula allocates additional resources to smaller school districts to ensure they can properly serve children living in these geographically isolated areas.[18] The size factor ranges from 1.0297 to 2.3958.[19]

As a result of these weights, the base per-pupil funding varies across school districts based on cost of living, personnel, and size.

The Colorado school funding formula also provides additional resources to school districts with higher percentages of students who qualify for free and reduced meals. The statewide average of pupils qualifying for free and reduced meals is roughly 37%. School districts exceeding that percentage receive additional at-risk funding.[20]

Finally, a budget stabilization factor (BS) serves to reduce the overall impact of the weights on the state funding formula. In essence, the BS factor reduces state aid for public education to ensure that the state's funding commitment does not exceed state revenues. The formula for budget stabilization is:

$$(\text{Total program after BS}/\text{Total program before BS}) - 1 = \text{BS Factor reduction}$$

The minimum total program funding per-pupil for the 2017–2018 school year was $8,187.76.[21] It should be noted that the BS factor does not negatively impact school districts that do not rely on state aid to meet the total program.

EXTERNAL FORCES ON THE GENERAL FUND

Colorado voters approved two state constitutional amendments that have worked to drive down the local contribution to public education, with negative impacts on the general fund for public schools. Consequently, state aid has been forced to backfill lost local revenue instead of supplementing local funds in pursuit of an adequate education. The end result of these two constitutional amendments is that the legislatively desired balance between state and local contributions[22] to public education has proved unattainable.

The Gallagher Amendment was adopted in 1982 in an effort to stabilize property tax rates by establishing a static relationship between the overall revenues generated from residential and nonresidential properties.[23] The purpose of the Gallagher Amendment (to stabilize residential property rates) was a commendable goal, but the actual implementation resulted in unintended consequences. Specifically, after Gallagher was passed, the overall number and value of each residential property increased at a faster rate than nonresidential properties. As a result, the taxable portion for residential properties fell from 21% in 1982 to 7.96% today, while taxation rates on nonresidential properties remained constant over this same period of time, a rate of 29%.[24]

From Gallagher in 1982 until 1992 when Colorado voters approved the Taxpayer Bill of Rights (TABOR),[25] school districts were able to increase the millage levied on property owners as the taxable portion of residential property fell, thus ensuring that the local contribution to public schools did not decrease over time. However, TABOR ended that practice because a key component of the amendment was that all proposed tax increases must be approved by voters. Thus, county commissioners and school district officials could no longer increase mill levies without first obtaining voter permission. As a result, starting in 1992 the local contribution to the total program in Colorado's schools has slowly decreased, and state revenues have been required to supplant lost local revenue. Research suggests that TABOR and Gallagher, together, are annually depriving public schools of more than $2 billion.[26]

LOCAL CONTRIBUTION

The local contribution to Colorado's school funding formula is derived from two primary sources: property taxes and specific ownership taxes.[27] Property tax rates are based on two key factors: (1) the net assessed value of all properties within a given school district, and (2) the local share, as mandated by the state, to the district's total program. The net assessed value of each school district in the state varies greatly, and these variances may result in inequities in the funding formula. In an effort to stabilize declining property tax rates throughout the state, legislation was enacted in 2007 that capped the maximum mill rate at 27 mills and froze all mill levy rates below 27. As a result, the range of mill rates in Colorado school districts is currently from 1.68 to 27 mills. For the 2016–2017 school year, local property tax revenues for public schools accounted for $2.24 billion, or 34% of the state's $6.612 billion budget for public schools.[28]

The specific ownership tax refers to vehicle registration tax.[29] These taxes are collected at the county level and then disbursed to local school districts. The specific ownership tax only generated $172 million for the 2016–2017 school year or $199 per pupil.[30]

In brief, the local contribution to a school district's total program ranges from 0% to 95%. The reason for this variation stems from the progressive nature of the state's funding formula. In essence, the state recognizes school districts in Colorado that are property-poor, as well as districts having inadequate net assessed valuation. In response, the state provides property-poor school districts with a greater percentage of state aid.

COMPENSATORY EDUCATION

In addition to the factors detailed regarding the general fund, Colorado's school funding formula recognizes that certain pupils require additional resources to be successful in school. Specifically, Colorado provides school districts with added resources for each child who is classified as:

- *A student with a disability*—Colorado allocates $167 million to meet the unique educational needs of pupils with disabilities. These funds are distributed to local school districts based on the needs of children served. Typically, districts receive $1,250 for each student who qualified for special education services during the previous year;[31]
- *A student who qualifies for gifted and talented services*—the state funding formula provides school districts with $12.1 million to help with the identification process of potential gifted and talented students, and to assist with curriculum enrichment;[32]
- *Non-native English-speaking students*—English language learners make up roughly 14% of the entire pupil population in Colorado. The state annually allocates $45 million to support ELL programs;[33]
- *Students at risk of dropping out of school*—proxying free and reduced meal counts to define at-risk pupils, the state provides school districts with $340 million. Districts receive an additional 12% of the base per-pupil funding for each student classified as at-risk.[34]

SPECIAL EDUCATION

Under Colorado's Exceptional Children's Education Act (ECEA), school districts must provide appropriate educational opportunities in the least restrictive environment.[35] Districts are required to provide services to students with disabilities between the ages of three to 21 years. Such services may be provided by school districts, specialized day programs, residential programs, and private programs. The appropriate services for an individual student are dictated by the child's academic or emotional needs and the ability of the local school district to meet those needs.

On or around December 1 of each year, school districts report to the state the number of pupils receiving special education services and the percent of services each student receives. These data are used by state officials to generate a special education budget for each school district for the following school year. Once district officials receive the special education budget from the state, a budget is developed for each school within the district. This school-specific budget for special education services includes personnel costs for both teachers and paraprofessionals, as well as funding for specific and specialized programs.

GENERAL TRANSPORTATION

On average, roughly 42% of Colorado's schoolchildren rely on transportation services to get to and from school each day. School districts throughout the state own over 6,000 buses that annually travel over 58 million miles. To help offset the costs associated with transporting pupils to and from school, the state established the Public School Transportation Fund.[36] These funds are not meant to cover costs of purchasing new buses;[37] rather, the funds provide school districts with a $0.37 reimbursement per mile traveled. The $0.37 reimbursement amounts to 40% of the total travel expense. School district efforts to fund the remaining 60% of the transportation expense include drawing funds from the total program, charging families a transportation fee, or building into a mill levy override a line for transportation.

Transportation is required by state law for children who are forced to cross dangerous intersections or who live beyond a reasonable walking distance from a school. It should be noted that charter schools are not required to provide pupil transportation; however, if charter school officials decide to provide transportation, all rules and regulations placed on traditional public schools apply.[38]

SCHOOL FACILITIES/MARIJUANA TAX

The majority of school districts needing to remodel an existing building or to build a new facility find it necessary to approach voters with a request to approve a bond initiative. However, there are several school districts in Colorado where the tax base is insufficient to generate the necessary local resources needed to construct a new facility. As a result, the state established the Building Excellent Schools Today (B.E.S.T.) Grant program.[39] The B.E.S.T. Grant was created when a lawsuit was filed against the state, contending the state funding formula was unconstitutional as a result of the inequities related to replacing or remodeling school facilities.[40] As part of the settlement, the state agreed to put $190 million aside in a matching fund for school districts needing assistance related to facility expenses. The B.E.S.T. Grant also receives resources from the state's land trust funds, the state's lottery, marijuana taxes, and earned interest each year.

School districts with facility projects apply to the state for B.E.S.T. funds, and state officials determine (based on the fiscal needs of the district) the percentage of the proposed project that will be covered by B.E.S.T. dollars. Since its inception in 2000, the B.E.S.T. Grant has received over $2.8 billion in requests and has been able to fund $1.2 billion in capital construction projects.

Beginning in 2014, the state of Colorado commenced collecting sales tax on recreational marijuana products. In 2017, marijuana tax revenues amounted to $247 million, with $100 million going to public schools.[41] The first $40 million in marijuana sales tax goes to the B.E.S.T. Grant program, with the remaining tax revenues from marijuana sales allocated to the Public School Permanent Fund and the State Public School Fund.

CAREER AND TECHNICAL EDUCATION

Funding for Career and Technical Education (CTE) is provided to Colorado school districts on a per-pupil basis, and the funds are used to provide instruction, materials, equipment, and related services.[42] Specifically, the state provides school districts with up to 80% of the first $1,250 spent on CTE needs on a per-pupil basis and 50% of any costs that exceed the initial $1,250.

VIRTUAL EDUCATION

There are over 17,000 pupils in Colorado enrolled in online educational programs. The two most common options are online charter schools which typically span multiple school districts and online options offered through local school districts. Funding for online programs differs based on the services being provided.[43] For cross-school district charter schools, the state's funding formula provides a reduced per-pupil amount, which on average is 10% less than the minimum per-pupil funding by the state.[44] Students enrolled in online schools sponsored by a local school district generate the same per-pupil funding as traditional students.

SPECIAL LEVIES

Colorado school districts are authorized to approach voters to approve a mill levy override, but the maximum amount a district may seek in a mill levy override is 25% of the district's total program.[45] To date, 119 of the 178 school districts have voter-approved mill levy overrides. School districts may also seek voter approval to secure Special Building and Technology Funds in the form of ten additional mills for up to three years.[46] These funds are specifically designated for the purchase of land, construction expense, purchasing facilities, maintaining existing facilities, security expense, and expenses related to technology.

CAPITAL OUTLAY

Colorado school districts have several options for funding capital projects. One option, no longer required in state law, is to set aside a per-pupil portion of the total program to cover capital projects. For large-scale capital projects, school districts have these options:

- *Bonded indebtedness.*[47] School districts seeking a bond may hold an election in which local voters approve or reject a ballot initiative to raise funds for extensive capital needs. Bonds include a loan amount with principal and interest payments. The state imposes a cap on the total amount of bond indebtedness for school districts; the cap is 20% (25% for districts with rapidly increasing student populations) of the net assessed value for the district.[48]
- *Loan Program for Capital Improvements.*[49] Reserved for school districts deemed as growth districts, the loan program allows eligible districts to apply for loans from the state treasurer, pending approval by local voters. These funds are then used to address immediate capital improvement needs in the school district, such as the purchase of portable classrooms.
- *Supplemental Capital Construction, Technology and Maintenance Fund.*[50] School district officials can choose to approach voters seeking permission to levy additional mills for technology (upgrade and replacement) and maintenance needs. These monies represent an ongoing cash fund for the district to address technology and facility needs.

CAPITAL IMPROVEMENT

Prior to fully appreciating the effects of the Great Recession in Colorado, state law required school districts to take a portion of the total program, on a per-pupil basis and set these funds aside for capital improvement projects. However, in 2009 this requirement was eliminated; school districts could continue the practice or could roll the funds that would have been designated for capital improvement projects into the total program for instructional needs. The long-term impact of this decision remains to be seen, but potentially alarming trends are already surfacing throughout the state. Some school districts are opting to roll traditional capital improvement projects, such as reroofing or recarpeting a school building, into bond initiatives. As a result, voters are being asked to pay interest on top of the cost of these capital improvement expenditures. In addition, over the last few years, two school districts have sought bonds in excess of $500 million and it is expected that this trend of large bond amounts will continue.

FOOD SERVICES

The state requires school districts to provide an array of food services, including after-school snack program; emergency feeding; fresh fruit and vegetables program; National School Lunch Program; School Breakfast Program; seamless summer option; and summer food service program.[51] The state reimburses districts based on the number of students served in each of the programs. Reimbursement rates vary by program. School districts receive $0.37 per pupil who participates in the National School Lunch Program each day, $0.30 per pupil in the School Breakfast Program, $0.20 per eligible pupil in the Special Milk Program, and $0.08 per pupil in the after-school snack program.

STATE FUNDING FOR NONPUBLIC SCHOOLS

The Colorado Constitution specifically states, "Neither the general assembly, nor any county, city, town, township, school district or other public corporation, shall ever make any appropriation, or pay from any public fund or moneys whatsoever, anything in aid of any church or sectarian society, or for any sectarian purpose."[52] In short, state law specifically prohibits the allocation of public funds to any nonpublic school.

OTHER STATE AID

As discussed earlier, the state funding formula recognizes the need to provide school districts with additional support for students who are at-risk, gifted and talented, non-English speaking, and students with disabilities.

The state provides financial support to school districts to provide these students with the educational support they require.[53]

RETIREMENT

Colorado's retirement system, titled the Public Employee Retirement Association (PERA),[54] is a pre-funded retirement program, or a retirement program where employees and employers contribute a percentage of each employee's monthly income into the plan. Currently, the employee contributes 8% and the employer contributes 20%.[55] The monthly funds are used to make payouts to retired individuals who are drawing from PERA, and the fund's income is invested to generate interest for PERA. The process is overseen by PERA's Board of Trustees.[56]

There are over 560,000 people, or one in every ten people in Colorado, who are either contributing to or drawing retirement from PERA. When a PERA-eligible employee retires, that person's actual monthly payment is based on a number of factors, including the highest average salary of the employee (currently based on the average of the three highest annual salaries), and the total number of years the employee contributed to PERA.

In 2010 after the Great Recession hit Colorado, PERA's overall value fell by $11 billion, or 26%. In response, the state increased the minimum required contribution for employees and employers. In addition, the overall benefits that employees would receive were reduced. However, despite the assurance that these measures would fix PERA, in 2018 PERA had over $32 billion in unfunded liability. The unfunded liability is a source of concern throughout the state since it is assumed that another economic downturn could bankrupt PERA. In an effort to ensure that PERA remains fiscally viable, the state's General Assembly is exploring remedies that would ensure PERA is completely solvent. Solutions for fixing PERA include: reducing the annual cost of living adjustment from 2% to 1.5%, increasing the employee contribution from 8% to 11%, increasing the employer contribution from 20% to 22%, and increasing the eligible retirement window from 30 years in the system to age 65. It is anticipated that these changes would make PERA fiscally solvent in 30 years.

REVENUE

Revenues for public education in Colorado are derived from three sources: local taxes, state taxes, and federal title funds. Local revenues for public schools are generated through property and specific ownership taxes, or vehicle registration. The local revenue sources generate $2.41 billion, or 34.1% of the total funding for public education in Colorado.

State revenues are generated from an array of taxes: Sales, Insurance Premium, Income, Corporate, and Cigarette. Sales and Income Taxes generate over 91% of state revenues.[57] State revenues account for $4.2 billion, or 59.4% of the total funding for public education in Colorado.

The federal contribution to public education in Colorado is primarily generated from federal income tax, and federal dollars are aimed at providing historically disadvantaged pupils with the necessary support to be successful in school. Federal funds are rolled into different federal programs, such as the Every Student Succeeds Act, and Title services. Title funds are specifically designed to support students at risk of dropping out of school, English language learners, and rural school districts. Federal dollars amount to $456 million, or 6.5%, of the total funding for public education in Colorado.

SCHOOL FINANCE LITIGATION IN COLORADO

Colorado has had several lawsuits filed over the years, contending that the state's funding formula fails to properly fund public education. Some cases were adjudicated, while others were settled. Two landmark decisions help to illustrate the overall landscape in Colorado related to the state's role in funding public education in a 'thorough and uniform'[58] fashion.

In 1977 a group of plaintiffs filed a lawsuit titled *Lujan v. Colorado State Board of Education*[59] against the state Board of Education, contending that the state's funding formula at the time perpetuated disparities in school district funding that ultimately deprived certain students of equal access to education. The trial court ruled in favor of plaintiffs, but the state supreme court reversed that ruling. In its ruling, the state supreme court held that the state's education clause of 'thorough and uniform' did not guarantee students "absolute equality in educational services or expenditures." The ruling also upheld local control as a constitutional justification for funding disparities between districts.

As stated earlier, in 1994 the state enacted a new funding formula for public education. In 2005, the School Finance Act of 1994 was challenged in the *Lobato v. State*[60] lawsuit. In *Lobato*, plaintiffs' claim centered on evidence that the state funding formula failed to provide all students with a 'thorough and uniform' educational experience. Specifically, the plaintiffs' arguments centered on the educational needs of students with disabilities, English language learners, and the need for preschool and full-day kindergarten, along with transportation services for all students. The claim was initially dismissed by the district court, and that decision was appealed.

The appellate ruling sided with plaintiffs, claiming that the state's funding formula was irrational and unconstitutional.

The appellate ruling was subsequently appealed to the state supreme court. The state supreme court first set out to define the educational clause standard of 'thorough and uniform.' The state supreme court defined thorough and uniform as "a free public school system that is of a quality marked by completeness, is comprehensive, and is consistent across the state" and then applied the claims in *Lobato* to this definition. The state supreme court ruled that the current funding formula is constitutional since the array of statutes governing public education are applied uniformly to all 178 school districts.

SUMMARY

Public education is the single greatest item in the state's general fund, as illustrated in Table 6.1. The state of Colorado spends 47% of its general fund on P–20 education services. However, the current trajectory for the state's general fund does not appear to be sustainable under the anti-tax amendments. The state cannot continue to allocate 47% of the general fund to P–20 education's needs and, at the same time, address the transportation, health care, and correctional needs throughout the state.

TABLE 6.1 State Operating Budget, General Fund, Fiscal Year 2018[a]

Program	General Fund Appropriation	Percent of Total General Fund
Human Services/Health Care	$3,689,800,000	34.7%
Higher Education	$894,900,000	8.4%
Correctional/Judicial	$1,282,200,000	12.1%
Education (K–12)	$4,201,200,000	38.6%
Transportation[b]	$0	0.0%
General Government	$96,100,000	0.9%
Other	$554,700,000	5.2%
Total	**$10,619,800,000**	**100.0%**

[a] Joint Budget Committee, *Budget in Brief Fiscal Year 2017–18*, at 5.
[b] Currently, transportation expenditures are covered through cash funds, re-appropriated funds, and federal funds. None of the general funds are allocated toward transportation needs.

NOTES

1. Carl Abbott, Colorado: A History of the Centennial State 114-116 (Colorado Associated University Press, 1976).
2. Wilbur Fisk Stone (ed.), History of Colorado: Illustrated 586 (The S. J. Clarke Publishing Company, 1918).
3. LeRoy R. Hafen and Ann Hafen, The Colorado Story: A History of Your State and Mine 436 (The Old West Publishing Company, 1953).
4. Ibid.
5. Spencer C. Weiler and Gabriel R. Serna, "Colorado," *Journal of Education Finance* 40, no. 3 (2015): 307.
6. C.R.S. 22-54-101.
7. Colo. Const. (1876), Article IX, §2.
8. Erica Meltzer, "Sponsor Pulls Bill that Would Change how Colorado Distributes Money to Schools," *Colorado Chalkbeat* (April 26, 2018). Retrieved from https://www.chalkbeat.org/posts/co/2018/04/26/sponsor-pulls-bill-that-would-change-how-colorado-distributes-money-to-schools/
9. C.R.S. 22-54-101.
10. C.R.S. 22-54-104.3.
11. Colorado Department of Education (CDE), *Understanding Colorado School Finance and Categorical Program Funding* (July 2017).
12. C.R.S. 22-54-104.3.
13. CDE (2017), p. 3.
14. C.R.S. 22-54.5-208.
15. CDE (2017), p. 3.
16. C.R.S. 22-54.5- 205.
17. CDE (2017), p. 3.
18. C.R.S. 22-54-122.
19. CDE (2017), p. 4.
20. C.R.S. 22-54-136.
21. CDE (2017), p. 5.
22. The desired balance between state and local aid used to support public education is 50/50.
23. Colo. Const. Art. X, §3.
24. Colorado Department of Treasury (n.d.), *Constitutional Provisions*. Retrieved from http://www.colorado.gov/cs/Satellite/Treasury/TR/1196935260080
25. Colo. Const. Art. X, §20.
26. Gabriel R. Serna and Spencer C. Weiler, "Tempered Optimism in Colorado: 2015 State-of-the-States." *Journal of Education Finance*, 387–390, at 389.
27. C.R.S. 22-54-106.
28. CDE (2017) p. 2.
29. C.R.S. 22-54-106.
30. CDE (2017) p. 8.
31. C.R.S. 22-20-101.
32. C.R.S. 22-20-104.5.
33. C.R.S. 22-24-101.
34. C.R.S. 22-20 through C.R.S. 22-29.

35. C.R.S. 22-20-102.
36. C.R.S. 22-51-101.
37. Bus purchases are typically added to a bond proposal.
38. C.R.S. 22-30.5-103.
39. C.R.S. 22-43.7-101.
40. *Giardino v. Colorado Board of Education*, No. 98-CV-0246 (Denver Dist. Ct. 1998).
41. Colorado Department of Revenue, *Marijuana Tax Data*. Retrieved from https://www.colorado.gov/pacific/revenue/colorado-marijuana-tax-data
42. C.R.S. 23-8-101.
43. C.R.S. 22-30.7-107.
44. C.R.S. 22-54-104 (4.5).
45. C.R.S. 22-54-108.
46. C.R.S. 22-45-103(1)(d).
47. C.R.S. 22-42-102.
48. C.R.S. 22-42-104.
49. C.R.S. 22-2-125.
50. C.R.S. 22-54-108.7.
51. C.R.S. 22-54-123.
52. Colo. Const. Article IX, § 7.
53. C.R.S. 22-24-101.
54. C.R.S. 24-51-101.
55. C.R.S. 24-51-401.
56. C.R.S. 24-51-202.
57. Joint Budget Committee, *Appropriations Report Fiscal Year 2017–18*, at 10.
58. Colo. Const. (1876), Article IX, §2.
59. *Lujan v. Colorado State Board of Education*, 649 P.2d 1005 (1982).
60. *Lobato v. State*, 304 P.3d 1132 (2013).

CHAPTER 7

Connecticut

Lesley A. DeNardis, Ph.D.
Associate Professor
Sacred Heart University

GENERAL BACKGROUND

While Connecticut has had a longstanding practice of supporting public education dating back to colonial times, it was not until the state constitution was amended in 1965 that this relationship was formalized as a primary responsibility of state government. According to the constitutional provision added in 1965:

> There shall always be free public elementary and secondary schools in the state. The general assembly shall implement this principle by appropriate legislation.[1]

Due to strong traditions of local control, Connecticut school districts were long funded primarily by local property taxes. Until the 1970s, the state's sole support to local districts was a flat grant of $250 per pupil based on Average Daily Membership (ADM). In 1977, as the result of a legal challenge to Connecticut's heavy reliance on the property tax, the state supreme court ruled in *Horton v. Meskill*[2] that the state's financing mechanism for schools violated the education rights clause and the equal protection clause of the state constitution. The court also held that public education is a fundamental right.[3] In anticipation of the court decision, the Connecticut General Assembly had enacted a Guaranteed Tax Base (GTB) plan in 1975 which distributed funds to local school districts through a system that rewarded local tax effort.[4] However, delays and phased-in spending meant that the GTB was never fully implemented. Meanwhile, the flat grant system remained in place until 1985, fueling another legal challenge which resulted in adoption of the 'Education Cost Sharing' (ECS) plan in 1988 which was designed to equalize funding across school districts. The original formula included the following elements: a foundation, resident students, poverty weighting, mastery weighting, town wealth, and State Guaranteed Wealth Level (SWGL).[5] The ECS formula was since modified twice; once in 1995, and again 2007. Continual capping and phased-in spending plans brought a renewed legal challenge in an adequacy case *CCJEF v. Rell* (2005).[6] In 2016, the trial court declared the entire K–12 education system in violation of students' constitutional right to adequate education and ordered the legislature to develop a plan within 180 days.[7] On appeal, the state supreme court reversed the superior court's decision and found that Connecticut does provide a minimally adequate education sufficient to satisfy the constitution. The court held:

> Although Connecticut has 'an imperfect public educational system,' [i]t is not the function of the courts... to create educational policy or to attempt by judicial fiat to eliminate all of the societal deficiencies that continue to frustrate the state's educational efforts... [T]he function of the courts is to determine whether the narrow and specific criteria for a minimally adequate educational system under [Connecticut's] state constitution have been satisfied.[8]

SCHOOL PROFILE[9]

The state of Connecticut educates approximately 535,000 students, an amount that has declined by approximately 6.3% over the past ten years. Simultaneously, the number of low-income students increased by about 7% to a total of 196,247. English language learner population increased statewide by around 7% during the same time period. Special education enrollments also increased by about 15%. Total spending from all sources was nearly $11.2 billion in the most recent year of record. Proportions of revenues to Connecticut schools was 39.5% state, 56.3% local, and 4.2% federal. Spending per pupil in that same timeframe varied, with a low $12,742 to a high $36,176 with an average $16,592 across all costs.

BASIC SUPPORT PROGRAM

Basic support for public education in Connecticut is subject to annual legislative appropriation during the biennial budget process. As the agency overseeing K–12 public education, the Connecticut State Department of Education receives and distributes all General Assembly appropriations. For Fiscal Year 2018, $1.985 billion was allocated in ECS grants and $2.016 billion for FY 2019.[10] The Education Cost Sharing (ECS) grant is the major mechanism through which state aid is distributed to local school districts. Based on a task force's recommendations, the ECS grant formula was modified in 2017 to include the following components: (1) resident student count; (2) foundation amount; (3) concentrated poverty weight; (4) low-income student weight; (5) English Learner weight; and (6) base aid ratio.

The new formula is scheduled for implementation in 2019.[11] The state uses a total of ten different funding formulas to distribute aid. In addition to the ECS grant, there are five funding formulas for magnet schools, two for charter schools, one for Connecticut's technical education system, and one for the state's open choice program.

The structure and operation of the new ECS are illustrated in Table 7.1.

SPECIAL EDUCATION

Connecticut has no separate budget for special education. A majority of funding comes from the state through the ECS grant. To help offset costs that exceed net current revenues, the state makes available an excess cost grant which is subject to a statutory cap of $140 million.[12] While the old ECS grant reduced funding to $139 million, the new ECS grant increases to $140.6 million for FY 19.[13]

GIFTED AND TALENTED EDUCATION

Although gifted and talented programs have been available in Connecticut public schools since the 1970s via a statute calling for the identification of gifted students, there was no enabling legislation to implement the law. A new law took effect July 1, 2017, requiring the Commissioner of Education to designate an employee of the State Department of Education to assist local and regional boards of education and parents or guardians with awareness and identification of services for gifted and talented students.[14] The law called for the State Department of Education to develop guidelines for provision of services to be made available to local and regional school boards by January 1, 2018.[15]

TABLE 7.1 What's in the New ECS Formula?

The Education Cost Sharing (ECS) formula is the formula the Connecticut state legislature has established to distribute approximately $2 billion in state education funding to local public school districts. After several years of not faithfully using an ECS formula and instead funding local public schools through block grants, in October 2017, the Connecticut General Assembly passed a new ECS formula as part of the state's biennial budget for fiscal years 2018 and 2019. The new formula is scheduled to be implemented beginning in FY 2019. Below is a table comparing the components of the new ECS formula to those of the most recent formula.

Comparing Education Cost Sharing Formulas

Formula Component	Previous ECS Formula[a]	New ECS Formula[b]
Foundation[c]	$11,525 per student	$11,525 per student
State Aid for Special Education Incorporated in Foundation[d]	Yes	Yes
Low-income Student Weight[e]	*Weight per Student:* 30% *Identification Method:* Eligibility for Free and Reduced Price Lunch	*Weight per Student:* 30% *Identification Method:* Eligibility for Free and Reduced Price Lunch
Concentrated Poverty Weight[f]	N/A	*Weight per Student:* 5% *Identification Method:* Low-income student residing in district where low-income students account for over 75% of the district's enrollment
English Learner Weight[g]	N/A	*Weight per Student:* 15%
Best Aid Ratio[h]	90% Property Wealth Factor • Determined by town's Equalized Net Grand per Capita (ENGLPC), compared to state median town ENGLPC[i] *10% Income Wealth Factor* • Determined by a town's Median Household Income (MHI), compared to state median MHI[j]	70% Property Wealth Factor • Determined by town's Equalized Net Grand per Capita (ENGLPC), compared to state median town ENGLPC[k] *30% Income Wealth Factor* • Determined by a town's Median Household Income (MHI), compared to state median MHI[l]
Base Aid Ratio Bonus for Higher-Need Towns	N/A	Adds a bonus of 3–6 percentage points to the Base Aid Ratio of communities with scores over 300 according to the Public Investment Communities (PIC) index[m]
State Guaranteed Wealth Level[n]	1.5	1.35
Minimum Aid Ratio[o]	*Alliance Districts:* 10% *Non-Alliance Districts:* 2%	*Alliance Districts:* 10% *Non-Alliance Districts:* 1%

(continued)

TABLE 7.1 What's in the New ECS Formula? (continued)

Comparing Education Cost Sharing Formulas

Formula Component	Previous ECS Formula[a]	New ECS Formula[b]
Hold Harmless	All towns were "held harmless" and could not receive less ECS funding than they did the previous fiscal year.	Applies only to Alliance Districts.[p] If, according to the formula, an Alliance District would receive less that its FY 2017 ECS grant, it is "held harmless" and will receive its FY 2017 grant amount instead.
Includes Public School Choice Programs	No	No
Phase-in Plan	For the first year of the formula, all towns were guaranteed a percentage of their fully funded grant amount (according to the fomula).[q] • Educational Reform Districts (the state's 10 lowest performing districts) were guaranteed 12% • Alliance Districts were guaranteed 8% • Non-Alliance Districts were guaranteed 1%	Formula is phased in over 10 years with the phase-in schedule differing between towns receiving, according to the formula, an increase in ECS funding over their FY 2017 grants and those receiving a decrease. **Towns Receiving an Increase** *FY 2019:* Increase phased in by 4.1% *FY 2020–2027:* Increase phased in by 10.66% per year *FY2028:* Grant fully funded **Towns Receiving a Decrease** *FY 2019:* Decrease phased out by 25% *FY 2020–2027:* Decrease phased out by 8.33% per year *FY 2028:* Grant fully funded
Estimated Total Cost When Fully Funded (based on FY 2018 data)	$2.66 billion	$2.36 billion

Source: Reprinted by permission. Connecticut School Finance Project. "What's in the New ECS Formula?" (2018). Retrieved from http://ctschoolfinance.org/assets/uploads/files/ECS-Comparison-One-Pager.pdf

[a] Conn. Acts 13–247
[b] Conn. Acts 17–2 (June Special Session).
[c] Amount that is intended to represent the estimated cost of educating a Connecticut general education student who does not have any additional learning needs.
[d] Approximately 22% of the ECS foundation amount is attributable to special education. Connecticut General Assembly, Office of Fiscal Analysis and the Office of Legislative Research. (2014). *CT Special Education Funding.* Retrieved from http://www2.housedems.ct.gov/MORE/SPED/pubs/OFA-OLR_Presentation_2013-01-23.pdf

(continued)

TABLE 7.1 What's in the New ECS Formula? (continued)

Comparing Education Cost Sharing Formulas

Formula Component	Previous ECS Formula[a]	New ECS Formula[b]

[e] Increases foundation amount by a certain percent for students in low-income households as identified by a designated eligibility metric.

[f] Increases foundation amount by a certain percentage for students who reside in a district where the percentage of the district's enrollment of low-income students is above a designated threshold.

[g] Increases foundation amount by a certain percentage for students who are identified as needing additional English-language skills.

[h] Variable in the ECS formula that determines each community's ability to financially support its public schools.

[i] Amount of taxable property (at 100 percent of fair market value) per person in a city or town. Each town's ENGLPC, along with the state median town ENGLPC, is calculated annually by Connecticut's Office of Policy and Management.

[j] Refers to the income level earned by a given household where half of the homes in the area earn more and half earn less. The ECS formula uses the MHI for each town, as well as the state medial MHI, as calculated by the U.S. Census Bureau's American Community Survey.

[k] Amount of taxable property (at 100 percent of fair market value) per person in a city or town. Each town's ENGLPC, along with the state median town ENGLPC, is calculated annually by Connecticut's Office of Policy and Management.

[l] Refers to the income level earned by a given household where half of the homes in the area earn more and half earn less. The ECS formula uses the MHI for each town, as well as the state median MHI, as calculated by the U.S. Census Bureau's American Community Survey.

[m] Calculated annually by Connecticut's Office of Policy and Management, the PIC index measures the relative wealth and need of Connecticut's towns by ranking them in descending order by their cumulative point allocations based on: per capita income; adjusted equalized net grand list per capita; equalized mill rate; per capita aid to children receiving Temporary Family Assistance benefits; and unemployment rate. The below chart outlines the additional percentage point bonus towns with a PIC index score over 300 will see added to their Base Aid Ratio.

Town's PIC Index Rank	Additional % Points Added to Base Aid Ratio
1–5	6 percentage points
6–10	5 percentage points
11–15	4 percentage points
16–19	3 percentage points

[n] Commonly referred to as the threshold factor, the Statewide Guaranteed Wealth Level (SGWL) determines each town's ECS aid percentage. Each town's ability to support its public schools (as determined by the Base Aid Ratio) is compared to the SGWL to determine what percentage of the per-student funding amount the town will receive from ECS and what will have to come from local tax dollars. As the SGWL is lowered, and all other formula factors remail constant, the formula distributes education aid more equitably.

[o] Ensures every town receives some amount of ECS funding, even when the result of the ECS formula calculation would be that the town would be ineligible to receive ECS grant funding.

[p] The 33 lowest-performing school districts in Connecticut as designed by the commissioner of the Connecticut State Department of Education and determined by various measures of student performance.

[q] The most recent ECS formula was never fully funded and the Connecticut General Assembly ceased faithfully following the formula beginning with the 2013–14 school year.

EARLY CHILDHOOD

As of 2015, 94% of all kindergarten programs in Connecticut operated on a full-day basis.[16]

BILINGUAL EDUCATION

Connecticut statute provides that "any local or regional board of education may establish at any level of instruction a bilingual and bicultural program of study involving a culture in which a language other than English is predominantly spoken, provided the purpose of such program shall be to enable children to become proficient in English. A private school may, with approval of the State Board of Education, establish a program of bilingual education."[17]

STATE AID FOR PRIVATE SCHOOLS

Connecticut provides transportation for nonpublic schools. It also loans authorized textbooks and learning aids to private schools. It allows municipalities to loan money for capital construction.[18]

CHARTER SCHOOL FUNDING

Connecticut's charter school law was passed by the state General Assembly in 1996 in the wake of the *Sheff v. O'Neill*[19] desegregation case and was designed to address racial isolation in Connecticut's urban schools. The legislation stipulated that charter schools must serve at-risk populations that are subject to racial and economic isolation. In the 20 years since the charter school law was adopted, the state has opened 24 charters with a total enrollment of 9,700 students which represents approximately 1.5% of the total school population in Connecticut. Charter schools receive roughly 70% of the total per-pupil revenue received by traditional public schools.[20] On average, charter schools receive $4,000 less per pupil than traditional public schools, with an allocation of $11,000 for FY 2018 and a per-pupil increase of $250 for FY 2019. In addition, Connecticut is one of only two states in the nation that disallows state and local education funding to follow students to charter schools. In the 2019 budget biennium, state funds for charter schools were $108,526,000 for FY 2018 and $109,788,500 for FY 2019.[21]

TRANSPORTATION

Connecticut's local and regional boards of education are required to provide transportation to children ages 5–20 years who attend public and private schools whenever it is "reasonable and desirable."[22] Until 2016, the state reimbursed school districts on a sliding scale of 0–60% based on local wealth tied to legislative appropriations. Transportation reimbursements are capped at the amount appropriated by the General Assembly in the annual budget.[23] No funds were appropriated for transportation in the 2017–2019 biennial budget.[24]

TEACHER RETIREMENT

The Teacher Retirement System (TRS) in Connecticut figured prominently in General Assembly budget deliberations for the 2017–2019 budget biennium. Escalating teacher pension costs are the single largest driver in Connecticut's overall budget deficit of nearly $5 billion over the next two budget biennial cycles. Ranked 48th among the states by Fitch in unfunded pension obligations, the state has a $13 billion unfunded pension liability to the TRS account.[25] The unfunded pension liability is attributed to legacy costs, inadequate contributions, and low investment returns.[26] During the budget deliberations for the 2017–2019 biennial budget, the governor proposed moving one-third of TRS costs to municipalities. The proposal was rejected by the General Assembly, and in 2018 the legislature established the Connecticut Pension Sustainability Commission. A report with recommendations was due in 2019.

CONCLUSION

Compared to the national average of $13,474 per-pupil revenue, Connecticut allocates $21,745.[27] The state also relies more heavily than other states on local revenue sources—primarily the property tax—to fund public schools. Local revenue sources comprise over 60% of local school funding compared to a national average of 45%.

At the same time, Connecticut is one of 25 states that place constitutional and statutory limits on expenditures.[28] In 1991, the General Assembly passed legislation to cap spending, and voters approved a 1992 constitutional amendment capping state spending. However, the General Assembly has yet to adopt a statutory spending cap reflecting updated data concerning inflation and personal income.[29] The state's attorney general issued an opinion saying that the lack of legislative agreement to define terms has rendered the spending cap useless. Certain categories of public education spending, such as special education excess cost grants, are affected by the spending cap.

NOTES

1. Conn. Constitution, Article Eight, Sec. 1. Retrieved from: https://www.cga.ct.gov/asp/Content/constitutions/CTConstitution.htm
2. 376 A2d 359 Ct. (1977).
3. Leslie DeNardis (2010). "Horton's Odyssey: The Politics of School Finance Reform in Connecticut." *New England Journal of Political Science,* 4(2), 237–281.
4. Ibid.
5. John Moran. *Education Cost Sharing Formula.* Office of Legislative Research, 202-R-0101 (n.d.).
6. First filed in 2005. Amended complaint, *Conn. Coal. For Justice in Educ. Funding, Inc. v. Rell,* No. HHD-CV-05-4019406-S (Conn. Super. Ct. Jan 20, 2006).
7. Leslie DeNardis (2018) "Connecticut," *Journal of Education Finance,* University of Illinois Press. Volume 43, Number 3, Winter 2018.
8. *Connecticut Coalition for Justice in Education Funding, Inc. v. Rell,* 327 Conn. 650 (2018).
9. This section relies generally on the Connecticut School Finance Project (2018). Data Library. Retrieved from: http://ctschoolfinance.org/data
10. Office of the State Comptroller, Operating Expenses, State Education Budget. Retrieved from: https://openbudget.ct.gov/#!/year/2018/operating/0/fund_type/General/0/service/Education++Libraries+%2526+Museums/0/department
11. Office of Legislative Research Report, Task Force to Study State Education Funding Final Report, January 2013. Retrieved from: https://www.cga.ct.gov/2013/rpt/2013-R-0064.html
12. Connecticut State Department of Education (2016). *LEA Special Education Expenditures.*
13. Connecticut School Finance Project. "Comparison Table of School Funding Formulas." Retrieved from: http://ctschoolfinance.org/assets/uploads / files/Formula-Comparison-Table-May-10-2018.pdf
14. Public Act No. 17-82 An Act Concerning Services for Gifted and Talented Students.
15. Ibid, Section 2.
16. Connecticut Office of Early Childhood Education, "Connecticut Enrollment by School 2014–2015.
17. Connecticut General Statutes (1971, P.A. 432, S. 2; P.A. 78-218, S. 14).
18. Education Commission of the States, "Non Public Schools," February 2012. Retrieved from https://www.ecs.org/clearinghouse/01/00/97/10097.pdf
19. 238 Conn. 1, 678 A.2d 1267 (1996).

20. Charter schools are authorized by the State Board of Education. Local charter schools are funded by local or regional boards of education; state charter schools are funded by the state.
21. Connecticut Office of the State Comptroller, Office of the State Comptroller, Operating Expenses, State Education Budget. Retrieved from: https://openbudget.ct.gov/#!/year/2018/operating/0/fund_type/General/0/service/Education++Libraries+%2526+Museums/0/department
22. Connecticut General Statutes (CGS § 10-220(a).
23. Judith Lohman. (October 8, 2009). OLR Research Report, 2009-R-0358, "State Assistance to Private Schools."
24. Marybeth Sullivan. Office of Legislative Research, Research Report (September 2, 2016).
25. Fitch's Ratings, State of Connecticut. Retrieved from: https://www.fitchratings.com/site/pr/982869
26. J. Aubry and A. Munnell. (2015) "Final Report on Connecticut's State Employees Retirement System and Teachers' Retirement System." Center for Retirement Research at Boston College.
27. S. Cornman, M. Howell, L. Zhou, and J. Young. "Revenues and Expenditures for Public Elementary and Secondary Education School Year 2015–2016," National Center on Education Statistics. Retrieved from: https://nces.ed.gov/pubs2019/2019301.pdf
28. J. Rappa. (2016) Office of Legislative Research, Research Report 2016-R-0040, "Tax and Expenditure Limits and Revenue Volatility." Retrieved from: http:/www.cga.ct.gov.olr
29. State of Connecticut, Spending Cap Commission, section 24 of PA 15-1, January 20, 2017.

CHAPTER 8

Delaware

Staff Writer[1]

GENERAL BACKGROUND

Delaware's constitution was first created in 1776. P–12 education today in Delaware is governed by the constitution's education article, requiring the state General Assembly to "provide for the establishment and maintenance of a general and efficient system of free public schools, and may require by law that every child not physically or mentally disabled shall attend the public school, unless educated by other means."[2] Article X of the state constitution further elaborates that "the General Assembly shall make provision for the annual payment of not less than one hundred thousand dollars for the benefit of the free public schools which, with the income of the investments of the Public School Fund, shall be equitably apportioned among the school districts of the State."[3] The language of the Delaware education article has been judged to be among the more moderate legal obligations placed upon states to provide equitable and adequate resources, rated as Category II (on a scale I–IV) defined as a mandate that the system of public schools must meet a certain minimum standard of quality, such as 'thorough and efficient.'[4]

Litigation Overview

Until recently, Delaware was among those rare states having never experienced school finance litigation. However, in 2018 the American Civil Liberties Union (ACLU) sued the state of Delaware on grounds of educational inadequacy. In *Delawareans for Educational Opportunity v. Carney*,[5] the suit alleged failure by the legislature to fairly and adequately fund education across schools in the state and that the state constitution guarantees all children an adequate education and substantially equal educational opportunity. More particularly, plaintiffs alleged that the state had failed to provide for students from low-income families, students with disabilities, and English language learners. Finally, plaintiffs charged that state funding provides more support to economically advantaged children. In October 2018, a chancery court denied the state's motion to dismiss. In late 2018, the same court held that the substantive educational adequacy aspects of the complaint would stand because (among other examples in a 133-page ruling), unlike 35 other states, Delaware provides no additional support for educating low-income students and, unlike 46 other states, Delaware provides almost no additional support for English language learners. The court noted that Delaware schools enrolling the most disadvantaged students tend to have larger class sizes, fewer specialists and counselors, and insufficient dual language resources and that Delaware's schools might be perceived as segregated by race and class.[6] While plaintiffs would have much to prove at trial, the court said:

> In my view, the plain language of the Education Clause mandates that the State establish a system of free public schools, and it uses the term 'schools' in accordance with its ordinary and commonly understood meaning—as a place where students obtain an education. The adjectives 'general and efficient' relate to and function in the service of this noun. Consequently, when the Delaware Constitution mandates that the State create and maintain 'a general and efficient system of free public schools,' it contemplates a system that educates students and produces educated citizens. The system of public schools must actually provide schooling.[7]

The court also went to the issue of equity, remarking that decisions in 31 other states' courts had taken interest in qualitative dimensions of equity and adequacy and that 13 other states having constitutional provisions similar to Delaware's had considered that same qualitative interest. Ultimately, the Delaware court related the current case to the historic 1954 *Brown v. Board of Education*[8] ruling in context of drawing parallels between segregation and inadequate and ineffective schooling.[9] Reasonably, more litigation is expected, both for development and compliance.

Current Directions[10]

The 2018 Delaware legislative session was marked by gubernatorial proposals for public school policy and funding. Proposals focused on school finance equity, economic/workforce development and career/technical education (CTE), policy additions and reorganization, health and equity for children, teacher recruitment and retention, and targeted funding for selected programs. More particularly, the governor's state of the state address called for:

- *Finance equity:* creating opportunity grants, adding resources to schools in support of low-income students, English language learners, and trauma-based supports. Proposed funding would at least triple the number of schools receiving grants;
- *Finance equity* (continued): calling for monies to reduce class size, expand professional development, engage capital upgrades, and provide supports for early learning and parental support in the neediest district(s);
- *Economic workforce development and CTE:* calling for strengthening programs having externships and on the job training, including investment in related higher education;
- *Policy changes:* including the creation of an Office of Innovation and Improvement housed in the Delaware Department of Education (DDOE) to support high needs schools, along with reorganizing the DDOE to provide expanded classroom supports;
- *Health equity:* calling for basic needs closets in schools to support underserved children; and
- *Targeted Funding:* calling for additional funding for P–3 early invention; hiring 200 new teachers in response to enrollment growth; expanding access to math instruction in middle schools; and enacting a student loan forgiveness program for teachers agreeing to serve in high need schools and high demand subject areas.

Many of these proposals appeared to parallel the 2018 court case. The legislature ultimately passed an FY 2019 budget[11] totaling $4.2 billion, along with a $49 million supplemental appropriation.[12] Selected details[13] relating to public schools were:

- $20.9 million for school enrollment growth;
- $8.8 million for child care serving more children;
- $5 million through savings in energy, fleet services, and DDOE restructuring;
- $10.2 million for annual salary step increases for teachers, plus a 2% general salary increase;
- $3.8 million for early learning centers;
- $6 million for expanded opportunity grants, largely aimed at schools with high poverty and ELL levels;
- $1.5 million earmarked for schools in the Wilmington school district.

Current Profiles

An overhead view of Delaware's P–12 schools across all three counties[14] is seen in table form. Table 8.1 identifies all types of schools, followed by the nature and prevalence of public choice schools; i.e., Table 8.1 enumerates the state's 225 public schools and 33 choice options. Table 8.2 reveals enrollment data by level and organization for the 2017–2018 school year. Table 8.3 lays out revenue receipts from state appropriations for 2016–2017. Table 8.4 provides insight into state allocations to current expenses in the same year. Table 8.5 indicates average per-pupil expenditures by a school district, charter school, and county-average. Finally, Table 8.6 reveals the proportions of school revenues from federal, state, and local sources.

TABLE 8.1 Delaware Public School and Choice School Types 2017–2018

All Public Schools				
Type of School	New Castle	Kent	Sussex	Total
Elementary School	62	28	20	110
Middle School	17	7	8	32
High School	22	8	8	38
Pre-kindergarten/kindergarten[a]	5	2	0	7
Special, alternative, and other	21	10	7	38
Total	127	55	43	225
Public Choice Schools[b]				
Vocational technical (Vo-tech schools)	4	1	1	6
Public Charter Schools	17	6	1	24
Magnet Schools	2	0	1	3
Total	23	7	3	33

[a] Most pre-kindergarten/kindergarten students are served within elementary schools and not included in this count.
[b] Public choice schools are counted above in elementary, middle, and high school rows. Public choice schools refer to public school choice options without a designated feeder pattern such as: vo-tech, public charter, and magnet schools.
Note: Totals reflect the public school totals reported for the 2016–17 school year and have been adjusted to reflect public charter schools that closed and opened in the 2017–18 school year.
Sources: Delaware Department of Education (2017). Online School and District Profiles: Delaware Public Schools by Type and County. In 2017–18 Delaware Public Education at a Glance. Rodel Foundation of Delaware. http://www.rodelfoundationde.org/ataglance/

TABLE 8.2 Delaware Public/Non-Public Enrollment 2017–2018

	Public School Enrollment	Home Schools	Private Schools	Total by County	Percent NonPublic
Kent	31,372	1,031	17,521	34,155	8%
New Castle	79,113	1,566	11,443	92,122	14%
Sussex	27,886	859	855	29,600	6%
Total	138,371	3,544	16,631	158,546	13%
Percentage	87%	2%	10%	100%	
Out of State		88	2,581	2,669	100%

Source: http://profiles.doe.k12.de.us/SchoolProfiles/State/Finance.aspx

TABLE 8.3 Delaware School Finance Revenue Receipts—State Appropriations 2016–2017

School Finances	Revenue Receipts
Division I	65.75%
Division II	3.91%
Division III	6.90%
Transportation	5.47%
Debt Service	0.00%
Major Instructional Programs	0.395%
Other Funds	13.55%

Note: see "Funding Formula" later for explanation of school divisions relating to revenue/expense categories.
Source: http://profiles.doe.k12.de.us/SchoolProfiles/State/Finance.aspx

TABLE 8.4 Delaware Percent State Allocation Current Expenses Public Schools 2016–2017

Category	2016–17	Percentage
Others	$204,956,798	9.17%
Instructional Service	$1,272,194,517	56.94%
Food Services	$144,711,674	6.48%
Instructional Support	$37,247,813	1.67%
Support Services Student Transportation	$105,391,357	4.72%
Supports Services Operations and Maintenance	$217,240,540	9.72%
Administrative Costs	$160,592,535	7.19%
Support Services/Students	$91,944,649	4.12%

Source: http://profiles.doe.k12.de.us/SchoolProfiles/State/Finance.aspx

TABLE 8.5 Delaware Average Per-Pupil Expenditure by School Type 2016–2017

	School Districts	Charter Schools	County Average
Kent	$12,954	$12,368	$12,914
New Castle	$14,839	$12,227	$14,477
Sussex	$13,618	$10,441	$13,538
State Average	$14,132	$12,157	$13,935

Source: http://profiles.doe.k12.de.us/SchoolProfiles/State/Finance.aspx

TABLE 8.6 Delaware State Revenue Source 2016–2017

Category	2016–17	Percentage
Federal	$187,335,947	8.55%
State	$1,300,818,500	59.36%
Local	$703,311,992	32.09%

Source: http://profiles.doe.k12.de.us/SchoolProfiles/State/Finance.aspx

FUNDING FORMULA

Current Formula

Delaware school funding in FY 2017 was directed by a total state budget of $4.09 billion, with about $1.4 billion (34%) appropriated to public schools. The state's 19 school districts added around $700 million from local funds, along with about $187 million in federal monies. Total education in Delaware, inclusive of its 19 school districts and 25 charter schools, brought FY 2017's total to nearly $2.2 billion. Those amounts were spent in support of the state's 138,000 students. As a result, Delaware ranked 13th in the nation in 2014 expenditure per pupil. Fully 84% of expenditures were for salaries—more than half of all state employees in Delaware relate to education in some direct fashion.[15]

Like most states, Delaware receives federal, state, and local monies for public schools. In Delaware's case, state funds must be used to match the state's contribution in a 70/30 state-local ratio. Within limits, state and local funds may be used for local priorities. Almost all local funds are raised from property taxes on residential and commercial property.[16] Local school districts set tax rates, although there has been criticism of assessment practices that lag due to reappraisal issues. In addition to the 19 local school districts,

TABLE 8.7 Delaware Base School Aid Formula 2018	
Preschool	1 unit for 12.8 students
Kindergarten through 3rd grade	1 unit for 16.2 students
Grades 4–12 Regular Education	1 unit for 20 students
Grades 4–12 Basic Special Education	1 unit for 8.4 students; preK–12 Intensive Special Education 1 unit for 6 students
PreK–12 Complex Special Education	1 unit for 2.6 students

Source: Osborne and Ratledge, "Demystifying Delaware's Public Education Funding." *Delaware Business* (May/June 2017).

Delaware has three countywide vocational-technical school districts that have access to county property tax revenue—these latter are exempt from the voter approval constraints placed on regular public school districts.[17]

The state aid formula for Delaware is generally regarded as originating 70 years ago.[18] The aid formula is pupil-driven based on academic grade and classification. The formula calls for the ratios shown in Table 8.7.

Major Formula Elements

State formula support to public schools in Delaware is provided in five components.[19] School district costs reference formula units, so that:

- *Division I costs* include salary and other employment costs. Division I support is allocated through the state aid formula (i.e., driven by the student-based unit system);
- *Division II costs* relate to All Other Costs (AOC). Division II support follows the pupil-based unit system using a flat statewide rate per unit earned. AOC funds can be used for operational costs other than personnel costs, transportation, or debt service;
- *Division II AOC costs* relate to vocational education. This support is allocated based on pupils in vocational classes. Funds are used in support of operations costs of vocational programs;
- *Division II Energy costs* are allocated on a pupil-based unit system using a flat statewide rate per unit earned. Energy funds may be used for heating oil, gas, or electricity;
- *Division III Equalization costs.* Division III costs are equalized based on school district wealth on a per-unit basis. Equalization funds seek to balance monies for schools between poorer and wealthier districts. Division III funds may be used for either positions or operations.

SPECIAL OR CATEGORICAL SUPPORTS

Special Education Supports

Special education funding is provided by the instructional unit. Delaware uses a needs-based funding system involving categories of basic, intensive, and complex need. Fiscal detail was provided earlier in Tables 8.1 and 8.7.

Academic Enhancement Supports

Block grant monies are provided through a program known as Academic Excellence. Instruction units are provided on the basis of one unit per 250 pupils enrolled, and funds are provided for use by districts to address areas of need. Also available are Educational Sustainment Fund monies which may be used in the same manner as equalization dollars. Academic Excellence recently appropriated $38.7 million which, along with the Education Sustainment Fund, provided an additional $28.1 million. Gifted and Talented Education can be regarded as addressed under these programs, along with English Language Learner/Bilingual education.

Career and Technical Education

See earlier discussion and tables in this chapter.

Preschool Education

The state of Delaware provides a range of programs and services relating to preschool education. A fuller description is available at the state Department of Education's website.[20]

Capital Outlay and/or Debt Service

The state of Delaware pays 60–80% of approved major capital projects, defined as projects exceeding $750,000. The state pays 100% for special schools and vocational schools. Bond issues are subject to referendum at the local level. Bonded indebtedness is limited to 10% of assessed valuation in each district. Additionally, minor capital projects (up to $750,000) are supported by the state, although school districts and charter schools must match the state contribution with a 40% local match.

Transportation

The state of Delaware provides transportation for eligible public school students. The state pays 90% of costs. Transportation benefits are provided for grades K–6 when students reside one mile or more from school. The state also pays for pupils in grades 7–12 residing two miles or more from school. Public charter schools are eligible for transportation funding based on 70% of the average cost per student of transportation within the vocational district in which the charter school is located.

SCHOOL CHOICE[21]

The Delaware School Choice Program began in 1996. No regulations exist for School Choice Programs. Statutory authority and enabling descriptions are encoded in legislation.[22] Briefly said:

> Each receiving local education agency shall adopt and make available a policy regarding the order in which applications for enrollment shall be considered and the criteria by which such applications shall be evaluated for approval or disapproval pursuant to Title 14 §405. The receiving district's policy shall seek to eliminate discrimination against choice students by: (1) allowing the receiving district to request supplemental application information from choice students only to the extent it requires the same information from attendance zone (resident school) students; (2) limiting the supplemental criteria a receiving district may use to evaluate choice applications—after that, receiving local education agencies must use a lottery system; and (3) removing the provision that allows a receiving local education agency to reject applications of students with special needs.

Under these limitations, education agencies must accept the standard application form provided by the Delaware Department of Education. The application form resides on the DDOE's website and receiving local education agency websites. Data on school choice profiles, application, and practice can be found on the Delaware Department of Education website.[23] Figure 8.1 graphically illustrates how Delaware pupils variously choose among schooling options, while Table 8.8 provides revenue data on choice schools.

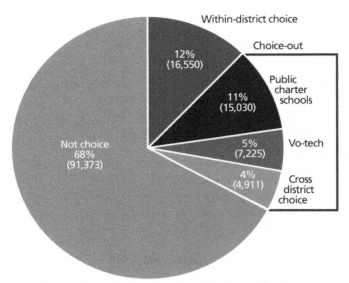

Note: "Not choice" refers to students that attend designated feeder-pattern school. Choice to enroll in magnet schools may be categorized as either within-district choice or cross-district choice. Percentages may not total 100 due to rounding

Source: Delaware Department of Education. (2017). 2016–17 Charter School and Across District Choice: Statistics and Maps

Figure 8.1 Distribution of Fiscal Support Percentages for Delaware Choice Schools 2016–17.

TABLE 8.8 Delaware Charter School Revenue Source 2016–2017		
Category	2016–17	Percentage
Federal	$7,965,611	4.16%
State	$116,828,254	61.07%
Local	$66,499,711	34.76%

Source: Rodel Foundation of Delaware. http://www.rodelfoundationde.org/ataglance/

CONCLUSION

In a state notoriously having escaped the contentious litigation surrounding most other states' school funding schemes, Delaware now finds itself in the real world—due both to legal challenge and to the dilemma of keeping up with regional and national data. With a formula aging by decades and with a recent court ruling indicating improvements must be pending, the state finds itself on the threshold of a new era that has yet to be determined.

NOTES

1. No state-based expert was available to author this chapter at the time of publication. The chapter is drawn from multiple sources as footnoted and represents the editorial staff's best interpretation of issues, trends, and findings regarding the state of Delaware. For additional information and updates and detail, contact the Delaware Department of Education.
2. Del. Const. art X, §1.
3. Education Commission of the States, "50 State Review" (2016). Retrieved from https://www.ecs.org/wp-content/uploads/2016-Constitutional-obligations-for-public-education-1.pdf
4. National Conference of State Legislatures, "The State Role in Education Finance." Referencing a system for evaluating and cataloging of state education articles by William Thro. Retrieved from http://www.ncsl.org/research/education/state-role-in-education-finance.aspx
5. Civil Action No. 2018-0029-VCL. Memorandum Opinion. Court of Chancery of the State of Delaware (October 5, 2018).
6. SchoolFunding.Info. "Delaware Judge Issues Strong Ruling." (December 3, 2018). Retrieved from http://schoolfunding.info/news/delaware-judge-issues-strong-adequacy-ruling/
7. *Delawareans* Motion to dismiss. Case No. 2018-0029-JTL. Filed November 27, 2018. Retrieved from https://aclu-de.org/wp-content/uploads/2018/10/70478217_Motion-to-Dismiss-I-II-FINAL.pdf
8. 347 U.S. 483 (1954).
9. SchoolFunding.Info (2018).
10. This section borrows and follows National Conference of State Legislatures, "2018 State of the State Addresses Education-Related Proposals." Denver, CO: NCES. Retrieved from https://b5.caspio.com/dp.asp?AppKey=b7f930000b022f77936f47ef9886&yr=2018
11. Senate Bill 235 (2018).
12. Senate Bill 236 (2018).
13. Delaware.gov "Governor Signs Fiscal Year 2019 Budget and Supplemental Appropriation." Dover, DE (June 28, 2018). Retrieved from https://news.delaware.gov/2018/06/28/governor-carney-signs-budget/
14. Delaware has only three counties, the least of any state in the nation.
15. Bill Osborne and Ed Ratledge, "Demystifying Delaware's Public Education Funding." *Delaware Business* (May/June 2017).
16. Ibid.
17. Ibid.
18. Ibid.
19. Formula description and related elements borrow from Deborah Verstegen, "A Quick Glance at School Finance: A 50-State Survey of School Finance

Policies and Programs." (2018). Retrieved from https://schoolfinancesdav.wordpress.com
20. Delaware Department of Education. https://www.doe.k12.de.us/domain/534
21. For more information about Delaware school choice, see https://www.doe.k12.de.us/domain/81
22. Delaware Department of Education. http://delcode.delaware.gov/title14/c004/index.shtml
23. Delaware Department of Education. https://www.doe.k12.de.us/domain/81

CHAPTER 9

District of Columbia

Michael C. Petko, Ed.D.
Senior Researcher
National Education Association

GENERAL BACKGROUND

The District of Columbia basically operates two public school districts. The DC Public School System (DCPS) operates what would be considered more traditional public schools, while the DC Public Charter School District (DCPCS) provides funding to public charter schools. Although charter schools are required to be managed by private nonprofits, they are considered public for purposes of funding. Although both the DCPS and DCPCS are fiscally dependent on the District for funding and both budgets are set by the mayor and city council, they function as two separate Local Education Agencies (LEAs) with separate budgets, boards, and accounting standards. The Deputy Mayor for Education's (DME) office contains the State Education Agency (SEA) and has a separate office of the State Superintendent. DCPCS was created with the enactment of the DC *School Reform Act* of 1995, which was later amended in 1996 to create the DCPCS School Board, acting as an independent school board and as sole authorizer of charter schools.[1] The Act also required that the District provide a uniform dollar amount per resident pupil for both the DCPS and DCPCS.[2]

Funding for DCPS and DCPCS comes from the Uniform Per Student Funding Formula (UPSFF), which was originally passed in 1998 and became effective in 1999.[3] The UPSFF provides a minimum allocation per resident pupil and uses weightings to provide additional funding percentages for grade levels and special categories. The UPSFF also requires that the DCPS provide tuition for special education students who are placed in nonpublic schools and for SEA functions for teacher certification and grant administration.[4]

Governance

The mayor and DC city council are ultimately responsible for the function of the two public school systems, and budgets are appropriated from the mayor's annual budget. The Office of the Deputy Mayor for Education is charged with implementing the mayor's vision, and it monitors the Office of the State Superintendent for Education (OSSE) and the DCPS. The DCPCS's board is appointed by the mayor and charged with overseeing the charter schools. The DCPCS Board is also the sole authorizer of charter schools.

There is a total of six different entities that control public education funds in the District:[5]

1. The Office of the State Superintendent manages the disbursement of federal funds to the two systems and also provides placement of special education systems into nonpublic schools as well as any loan guarantees to charter schools.
2. The Department of General Services (DGS) manages maintenance and repairs for DCPS.
3. DCPS is the public system for traditional public schools.
4. DCPCS is considered a public school system but all charter schools are required to be private, nonprofit.
5. DCPCS School Board (PCSB) acts as the sole authorizer for charter schools and also monitors legal compliance and fiscal management of all charter schools.
6. District of Columbia Retirement Board (DCRB) is the teacher pension for DCPS staff and has a separate funding system outside of the DCPS budget. Teachers pay into the system in two tiers.
The DC government provides additional funding to keep the fund sound when necessary. Currently, charter schools must provide for separate retirement plans.

Basic Facts

Student population in DC has grown since the Great Recession. In 2011, enrollment was 45,191. By 2017, enrollment had grown to over 48,000. The District has one of the highest per-pupil funding in the nation: approximately $21,299 in 2016.[6] Over 77% of students attending the District's public school system (both DCPS and DCPCS) are classified as economically disadvantaged; 14% are ELL; and another 14% receive special education services. DCPS also lists its starting teacher salary as $55,209 for 2017, and the average teacher salary as $84,765. These numbers are for ten-month employees. Twelve-month employees receive $65,427 as a starting salary and the average salary is $96,176.[7]

BASIC SUPPORT PROGRAM

General Fund

The UPSFF is contained in the DC Code and is updated every year as needed to reflect changes in the base and weights.[8] The UPSFF provides funding only for students who are considered residents of the District. Nonresident students are required to pay tuition to attend any District public school or charter school. The formula also does not apply to students enrolled in private institutions that provide special education services, which is paid directly by the District. The formula applies only to operating budget appropriations and does not consider funds from federal or other sources. Charter schools are funded equally by law from the UPSFF. The only limit to the UPSFF for charter schools occurs after the DCPS enrollment count is verified by an independent contractor. Once the count is verified, additional enrollment in a charter school will not count for that school year.[9]

Base Funding

Base funding is established in the code and updated periodically by need. For Fiscal Year 2018, the foundation level was $9,972 per student. According to the code, this amount is set for subsequent years with adjustments made for inflation, any potential revenue losses, or revisions required by law.[10] Such revisions are adjusted by code and established in law. Previous years' USPFF allocations were as shown in Table 9.1.

Weighting

The base funding amount is not the total amount provided to schools by the District. Additional weights are applied to the base according to grade level and need.[11] Weighting is applied to adjust for different educational services required at different grade levels. Table 9.2 reflects the weights applied in the 2018 formula. For example, the allocation for a three-year-old prekindergarten pupil was 34% above the base or $13,363 for the 2017–18 school year.

TABLE 9.1 UPSFF History

Fiscal Year	USPFF Base Funding	Law
2003	$6,555 adjusted to $6,419	D.C. Law 14-190; 14-307
2004	$6,551	D.C. Law 15-39
2005	$6,904	D.C. Law 13-205
2006	$7,307	D.C. Law 16-33
2007	$8,002	D.C. Law 16-192
2008	$8,322	D.C. Law 17-20
2009	$8,770	D.C. Law 17-219
2010	$8,945	D.C. Law 18-223
2011	$8,770	D.C. Law 18-370
2012	$8,945	D.C. Law 19-21
2013	$9,124	D.C. Law 19-168
2014	$9,306	D.C. Law 20-61
2015	$9,492	D.C. Law 20-155
2016	No Change	No Change
2017	$9,682	D.C. Law 21-36

Note: Numbers are rounded to the nearest dollar amount.

TABLE 9.2 Weighting System

Grade Level	Weighting	Per-Pupil Allocation
Prekindergarten 3	1.34	$13,363
Prekindergarten 4	1.30	$12,964
Kindergarten	1.30	$12,964
Grades 1–5	1.00	$9,972
Grades 6–8	1.08	$10,770
Grades 9–12	1.22	$12,166
Alternative program	1.44	$14,360
Special education school	1.17	$11,668
Adult	0.89	$8,875

The total foundation then is found by applying the additional percentage for grade level to the base. The formula expressed as an equation is:

$$\text{Base} \times \text{Weight} = \text{PPA (or the USPFF foundation for each student)}[12]$$

Per-School Totals

Appropriations for DCPS are based on the verified enrollment of the previous year.[13] Adjustments are then made after the current year's official count is completed during the fall of the new school year. For DCPCS, appropriations are derived from projected enrollment of resident students in all public charter schools plus the total estimated per-pupil cost for facilities allotment.[14] Adjustments are also made after the verified count is completed. Budget planning for the DCPS and DCPCS is governed by the Office of the Chief Financial Officer (CFO) through the Annual Operating Budget and Capital Plan.[15] The CFO provides guidance through its annual Proposed Budget and Financial Plan.[16] Each department is presented with budget plan guidance for the following year. Also, the CFO requires that each department provides monthly financial reports and quarterly capital budget reports.

SUPPLEMENTAL GENERAL FUND

The UPSFF also provides supplemental allocations to the foundation level via weighting factors. These supplemental revenues are available in addition to the base counts and are applied to pupils who are entitled or receive special education, English as a second language or bilingual education services, summer school instruction,[17] LEP/NEP, summer school, and residential school support.

Supplemental allocations are applied to four areas: special education; English as a second language or bilingual education services; summer school instruction; and extended school days for at-risk or full-time residence students. Allocation of supplemental funding is calculated by applying weightings to the foundation level. Table 9.3 details the 2018 Code for supplemental weights for DCPS and DCPCS.[18]

The supplemental allocation is a full amount added to the USPFF. For example, a student in grades 6–8 who is listed as a Special Education 2 would receive an allocation totaling $22,736.76. The formula would be applied as follows:

Base × Weight + Level 2, Sped, or $9,972 × 1.08 + $11,967 = $22,736.76

Special Weighting for At-Risk Students

There is an additional amount provided through the USPFF for pupils considered at-risk. Weighting is determined by the mayor and applied after other weights are considered. The additional amount is then added to the total. For example, a student who attends grades 6–8 and is classified as a Special Education 2 student would receive the $22,736.76 plus at-risk weighting. At-risk weighting is only applied to the Base but is added to the total. For example, if the at-risk weight is determined to be 0.15 of Base, that would be an additional $1,495 added to the $22,736.76 for a total of $24,232.56 for that child.

TABLE 9.3 Supplemental Weights

Level/Program	Definition	Weighting	Per-Pupil Supplemental Allocation FY 2018
Special Education Add-ons			
Level 1: Special Education	Eight hours or less per week of specialized services	0.970	$9,673
Level 2: Special Education	More than 8 hours and less that or equal to 16 hours per school week of specialized services	1.200	$11,967
Level 3: Special Education	More than 16 hours and less than or equal to 24 hours per school week of specialized services	1.970	$19,646
Level 4: Special Education	More than 24 hours per week of specialized services which may include instruction in a self-contained (dedicated) special education school other than residential placement	3.490	$34,804
Blackman Jones Compliance	Weighting provided in addition to special education level add-on weightings on a per-student basis for Blackman Jones Compliance	0.069	$688
Attorney's Fees Supplement	Weighting provided in addition to special education level add-on weightings on a per-student basis for attorney's fees.	0.089	$888
Residential	DC public school or public charter school that provides students with room and board in a residential students with room and board in a residential setting, in addition to their instructional program	1.670	$16,654
General Education Add-ons			
ELL	Additional funding for English Language Learners.	0.490	$4,887
At-risk	Additional funding for students in foster care, who are homeless, on TANF or SNAP, or behind grade level.	0.219	$2,184
Residential Add-ons			
Level 1: Special Education–Residential	Additional funding to support the after-hours level 1 special education needs of students living in a DC public school or public charter school that provides students with room and board in a residential setting	0.368	$3,670

(*continued*)

District of Columbia ■ 119

TABLE 9.3 Supplemental Weights (continued)

Level/Program	Definition	Weighting	Per-Pupil Supplemental Allocation FY 2018
Level 2: Special Education–Residential	Additional funding to support the after-hours level 2 special education needs of students living in a DC public school or public charter school that provides students with room and board in a residential setting	1.337	$13,333
Level 3: Special Education–Residential	Additional funding to support the after-hours level 3 special education needs of students living in a DC public school or pubic charter school that provides students with room and board in a residential setting	2.891	$28,830
Level 4: Special Education–Residential	Additional funding to support the after-hours level 4 special education needs of students living in a DC public school or public charter school that provides students with room and board in a residential setting	2.891	$28,830
LEP/NEP–Residential	Additional funding to support the afterhours limited and non-English proficiency needs of students living in a DC public school or public charter school that provides students with room and board in a residential setting	0.668	$6,662
Special Education Add-ons for Students with Extended School Year (ESY) Indicated in Their Individualized Education Programs (IEPs)			
Special Education Level 1 ESY	Additional funding to support the summer school or programs need for students who require extended school year (ESY) services in their IEPs.	0.063	$628
Special Education Level 2 ESY	Additional funding to support the summer school or programs need for students who require extended school year (ESY) services in their IEPs.	0.227	$2,264
Special Education Level 3 ESY	Additional funding to support the summer school or programs need for students who require extended school year (ESY) services in their IEPs.	0.491	$4,896
Special Education Level 4 ESY	Additional funding to support the summer school or programs need for students who require extended school year (ESY) services in their IEPs.	0.491	$4,896
Special Education Level 1 ESY	Additional funding to support the summer school or programs need for students who require extended school year (ESY) services in their IEPs.	0.063	$628

Excluded Education Costs

Certain costs are excluded from the USPFF. Costs for transportation for pupils with disabilities covered by the Office of the State Superintendent of Education's Division of Student Transportation[19] (OSSE DOT) are excluded, as are tuition payments for private placements for students with disabilities and any costs associated with the performance of any function of the state education office of the District. Such costs are allocated by the mayor and council of the District directly to the Office of the State Superintendent of Education (OSSE) or to a credited agency that performs a special function.[20] Other functions such as school resource officers and nurses are covered outside of the DCPS and are funded through outside departments. Legal services arising from special education lawsuits are covered by the Office of the Attorney General (OAG). Construction costs (only DCPS; charter schools are covered under another provision in the law) are covered by the Department of General Services (DGS). The Metropolitan Police Department (MPD) provides school resource officers. The Departments of Health (DOH) and Behavioral Health (DBH) provide nurses and mental health professionals. The Department of Transportation provides crossing guards.[21]

Adjustment to the USPFF

There is a provision in the code to allow for adjustments to the per-pupil allotment during years of economic downturn. However, the amount cannot go below 95% of the previous year's funding.[22]

COMPENSATORY EDUCATION

Compensatory education costs are covered outside the normal DCPS and DCPCS budgets. The OSSE manages all compensatory education requests through its Special Education office. Disputes are handled through a special Dispute Resolution office. The expense is covered by OSSE, with the process managed by the Office of Specialized Instruction. Expenses are covered by the OSSE budget.

GENERAL TRANSPORTATION

Transportation in the District for public and charter school students is not generally provided by the District. However, under special conditions, transportation may be provided through various District offices. Transportation would be provided for students requiring Special Education Services; those who are temporarily moved to a different location (swing space); those attending extracurricular activities outside the regular school day; and those attending field trips.[23]

Students who are eligible for transportation due to special education needs can receive transportation services through the OSSE's Department of Transportation. The District provides transportation for pupils who are temporarily moved from their primary school and makes arrangements with the individual schools. Field trips and outside activities are also provided by the District and managed by the individual school through approved vendors.

As part of the *School Transit Subsidy Act* of 1978,[24] The District Department of Transportation (DDOT) arranged with the Washington Metropolitan Area Transit Authority (WMATA) to provide free rides to students on city services and discounted fares on the subway. The subsidy is managed and paid through the DDOT.[25]

SCHOOL FACILITIES

The District provides funding for DCPS and DCPCS schools, but such funding varies considerably. Funding for DCPS facilities comes directly from the District's budget as part of the Master Facilities Plan (MFP), which is required to be updated every year.[26] The MFP is a ten-year plan that covers all buildings and construction in the District. The Deputy Mayor for Education is responsible for providing the MFP for DCPS, which was originally managed by the Office of Public Education Facilities Planning (OPEFP) and was responsible for facilities maintenance and construction. Starting in 2012, the OPEFP's functions were assigned to the DGS.[27] Part of the OPEFP's original charge was to also establish a Public Charter School Registry to assist charter schools with planning and technical support, although charter schools are not funded directly through the DME.

Capital Improvement

The MFP is connected to the District's budget process through the District's Capital Improvement Plan (CIP), a six-year plan for capital construction, which includes schools. The CIP includes information on specific projects' funding and construction schedule. It includes information on modernization and replacement of school facilities; small capital projects like upgrades, replacements for areas like roofs, and any federally required changes or improvements.[28] Financing for the capital plan comes from general obligation municipal bonds issued by the District, which are paid in 20- to 30-year cycles.

Facilities Funding for Charter Schools

Charter schools do not receive direct funds for facilities from the District. Rather, funding is provided annually through the UPSFF on a per-pupil basis, with additional funding provided for residency programs.[29] The annual allotment provides charter schools with funds to rent or acquire school space. No additional money is provided by the District for charter facilities, but charters have complete discretion over how the additional allotted funds are spent. Charters also have access to additional federal facilities programs through the OSSE's Office of Public Charter School Financing and Support.[30] In 2014, the District Council enacted a law allowing the mayor to designate DCPS buildings as surplus; those buildings may then be bought or leased by charter schools.

CAREER AND TECHNICAL TRAINING

Programs for career and technical education (CTE) are managed through the DCPS's Career and Technical Education Office (CTTO). The program is a three- or four-year course which supplements the high school core classes. The CTE programs include participation for certification exams and provide work-based learning experiences. There are approximately 17 schools providing over 19 CTE programs. There is no supplemental funding provided through the USPFF at this time.

FOOD SERVICES

The Food and Nutrition Services (FNS) of DCPS provides guidance to all DCPS schools. Currently, all DCPS students are provided a free breakfast. In 2017–18, 87 schools were certified for the Community Eligibility Provision (CEP), allowing students to receive lunch at no charge. All DCPS students are required to fill out a Free and Reduced-price Meal application regardless of eligibility.[31]

STATE FUNDING FOR NONPUBLIC SCHOOLS

The District does not provide funding for nonpublic schools through the USPFF except for authorized charter schools, which are considered public for USPFF purposes but are to be managed by private nonprofit organizations. There is a provision in the code for the District to provide funding to a private school which serves a special-needs student. Such funding is provided at cost. There is no provision for travel to such schools for the student.

Appropriations to charter schools are paid directly to the charter school by the mayor and sent to a bank selected by the charter school. Payments are made quarterly based on each charter school's quarterly report. Payments are made on the 15th of July, October, January, and April. Amounts are determined by the USPFF based on charter student counts.[32]

RETIREMENT[33]

The Teachers' Retirement System is a separate entity from the District Public School System, with resources provided through a combination of teacher participation and the government of the District. In 1998, the federal government passed the *Police Officers, Firefighters, and Teachers Retirement Benefit Replacement Plan Act* (Act 1998). Under this act, the federal government assumed the District's unfunded pension liabilities for teachers, police officers, firefighters, and judges. Under Act 1998, the federal government pays the retirement, death benefits, and any disability benefits for employees for any service accrued prior to July 1, 1997. Cost for benefits after that date falls on the District government. The plan is available to all DCPS teachers, but not to DCPCS teachers. Funding for the plan by the District government is governed by law[34] whereby the District is to contribute an amount equal to or greater than that certified by the District of Columbia Retirement Board (DCRB). The District contribution for 2018 was $59,046,000, a 4% increase from 2017.

REVENUE

Besides the funds provided by the USPFF, District schools receive additional funding from various sources. The DGS provides funding directly for school facilities, while the DOT provides resources for crossing guards. Additionally, funding for school nurses is provided by the Department of Health, and mental health professionals are funded by the Department of Behavioral Health. The Metropolitan Police Department funds school resource officers, and the District's Office of Attorney General provides support for any lawsuit the DCPS might face.[35] The OSSE receives all federal funds for both the DCPS and DCPCS and distributes the funds to each LEA, which then allocates accordingly. In the event that a special-needs child requires outside placement, the LEA is required to provide funding.

The OSSE also has a special source of funding for such placement. Monitoring of the child is still the responsibility of whichever school he or she is attached to for public funds.

Private Funding

Both the DCPS and DCPCS are allowed to seek private funding. The DC Public Education Fund connects the DCPS with philanthropic sources. Parent organizations also help raise resources, and there are currently no restrictions on how funds may be used.[36]

SUMMARY

Tables 9.4 and 9.5 summarize the DCPS and DCPCS budgets for FY 2016 through FY 2018. Total funds for DCPS have grown by 3.5% since 2016. The budget for DCPCS has grown substantially since 2016, with funding for 2018 expected to be an additional $90 million over 2017 (an increase of over 12.4%).

TABLE 9.4 Budget for DCPS 2016–2017

Appropriated Fund	Dollars in Thousands				
	Actual FY 2016	Approved FY 2017	Proposed FY 2018	Change From FY 2017	%
General Fund Local Funds	$728,787	$756,389	$789,566	$33,177	4.4
Special Purpose Revenue Funds	$5,980	$5,901	$9,263	$3,363	57.0
Total For General Fund	$734,766	$762,290	$798,830	$36,540	4.8
Federal Resources Federal Payments	$0	$20,000	$15,000	–$5,000	–25.0
Federal Grant Funds	$41,096	$21,648	$14,712	–$6,936	–32.0
Total For Federal Resources	$41,096	$41,648	$29,712	–$11,936	–28.7
Private Funds Private Grant Funds	$2,615	$220	$1,411	$1,192	542.8
Private Donations	$138	$0	$0	$0	N/A
Total For Private Funds	$2,753	$220	$1,411	$1,192	542.8
Intradistrict Funds	$126,149	$101,516	$107,050	$5,533	5.5
Total For Intradistrict Funds	$126,149	$101,516	$107,050	$5,533	5.5
Gross Funds	$904,764	$905,673	$937,002	$31,329	3.5

*Percent change is based on whole dollars.
Source: Proposed Budget and Financial Plan-Congressional Submission; District of Columbia Public Schools (2018).

TABLE 9.5 Budget for DCPS 2016–2018

Appropriated Fund	Actual FY 2016	Approved FY 2017	Proposed FY 2018	Change From FY 2017	Percentage Change[a]
General Fund Local Fund	$738,844	$723,717	$813,738	$90,021	12.4
Total for General Fund	$738,844	$723,717	$813,738	$90,021	12.4
Gross Funds	$738,844	$723,717	$813,738	$90,021	12.4

[a] Percent change is based on whole dollars.
Source: 2 Proposed Budget and Financial Plan-Congressional Submission; District of Columbia Public Charter Schools (2018).

The increase in charter schools in the District has brought changes to the way the District allocates resources to public education and to the sharing of resources with private entities. Since charter schools are governed by private nonprofits, they are traditionally private schools. However, under the District's rule for funding, they are considered public and are beginning to receive a larger and larger share of public monies. The budget for charter schools for FY 2018 was approximately 86% of DCPS. At the current rate of growth, the DCPCS will soon require a larger budget than for the DCPS.

NOTES

1. About the District of Columbia Public Charter School Board. Retrieved from: http://dcpubliccharter.com/About-the-Board.aspx.
2. DC Code § 31-2853.41.
3. DC Code § 31-2901.
4. DC Code § 31-2907.
5. Soumya Bhat, *Investing in Our Kids: District of Columbia School Finance Primer*. Fiscal Policy Institute. Retrieved from: https://www.dcfpi.org/wp-content/uploads/2015/03/Revised-School-Primer-March2015-FINAL.pdf>
6. Rankings & Estimates: Rankings of the States 2016 and Estimates of School Statistics 2017. May 2017. National Education Association. Table H-9. NEA Rankings estimates that per-student spending will be $25,025 for 2017 and $25,323 for 2018.
7. DCPS Fast Facts 2017–2018. Retrieved from: https://dcps.dc.gov/sites/default/files/dc/sites/dcps/publication/attachments/DCPS%20Fast%20Facts%202017-18.pdf
8. See, DC Code, Title 38, Chapter 29, Subchapter 1 §§ 38-2901 – 38-2914.
9. DC Code, § 38-2902.
10. DC Code § 38-2903 (see also, §§ 38-2909, 2910, and 2911).
11. DC Code § 38-2904.
12. DC Code § 38-2904.
13. DC Code § 38-2906(a).

14. DC Code § 38-2906(b)(1)(2).
15. Retrieved from: https://cfo.dc.gov/node/289642.
16. Ibid.
17. DC Code § 38-2905.
18. Ibid.
19. See, OSSE, Special Education Transportation Services Policy. Online: ttps://osse.dc.gov/publication/special-education-transportation-services-policy.
20. DC Code § 38-2907.
21. Soumya Bhat, *Investing in Our Kids: District of Columbia School Finance Primer.* Fiscal Policy Institute. Retrieved from: https://www.dcfpi.org/wp-content/uploads/2015/03/Revised-School-Primer-March2015-FINAL.pdf>
22. DC Code § 38-2910.
23. Student Transportation Policy: Chancellor's Directive #301. November 2017.
24. D.C.Law 2-152.
25. Ibid. *See also,* Finance & Administration Committee, Action Item III-A, July 10, 2014, DC Student Transit Subsidy Agreement. Retrieved from: https://www.wmata.com/about/board/meetings/board-pdfs/upload/071014_3ADCStudentTransitSubsidyCOMBINED.pdf
26. DC Code § 38-2803.
27. Soumya Bhat, *Investing in Our Kids: District of Columbia School Finance Primer.* https://www.dcfpi.org/wp-content/uploads/2015/03/Revised-School-Primer-March2015-FINAL.pdf>
28. Ibid.
29. DC Code § 38-2908.
30. Soumya Bhat, *Investing in Our Kids: District of Columbia School Finance Primer.* Fiscal Policy Institute. Retrieved from: https://www.dcfpi.org/wp-content/uploads/2015/03/Revised-School-Primer-March2015-FINAL.pdf>.
31. About School Meals. Retrieved from: https://dcps.dc.gov/food
32. DC Code § 38-2906.02
33. Information provided by the District of Columbia's FY 2018 Proposed Budget and Financial Plan, Vol. 3, Agency budget Chapters, Part II, Public Education system. P. D-21.
34. DC Code § 1-907.03(b).
35. Soumya Bhat, *Investing in Our Kids: District of Columbia School Finance Primer.* Fiscal Policy Institute. Retrieved from: https://www.dcfpi.org/wp-content/uploads/2015/03/Revised-School-Primer-March2015-FINAL.pdf>.
36. Ibid.

CHAPTER 10

Florida

R. Craig Wood, Ed.D.
Professor
University of Florida

Robert C. Knoeppel, Ph.D.
Dean of Education
University of South Florida

GENERAL BACKGROUND

The Florida Constitution states, "The education of children is a fundamental value of the people of the State of Florida. It is, therefore, a paramount duty of the state to make adequate provision for the education of all children residing within its borders. Adequate provision shall be made by law for a uniform, efficient, safe, secure and high-quality system of free public schools that allows students to obtain a high-quality education."[1]

In 1973, the Florida legislature enacted the Florida Education Finance Program (FEFP) and established state policy regarding equalized funding to guarantee to each student in the public education system the availability of programs and services appropriate to his or her educational needs that are substantially equal to those available to any similar student, notwithstanding geographic difference and varying local economic factors.[2] To equalize educational opportunities, the FEFP formula recognized: (1) varying local property tax bases; (2) varying education program costs; (3) varying costs of living; and (4) varying costs of equivalent educational programs due to sparsity and dispersion of student populations.

The current FEFP is the primary mechanism for funding the operating costs of Florida school districts. FEFP funds are primarily generated by multiplying the number of full-time equivalent (FTE) students in each of the funded education programs by cost factors to obtain a weighted FTE. Weighted FTE is then multiplied by a base student allocation and by a district cost differential to determine the base funding from state and local FEFP funds. Program cost factors represent relative cost differences among the FEFP programs.

BASIC SUPPORT PROGRAM

Source of Funds for School Districts

School districts receive approximately 40% of financial support from state sources, 48% from local sources, and 12% from federal sources.

State Support
The major portion of state support is distributed through the FEFP. Taxes from multiple sources are deposited in the state's General Revenue Fund. The predominant tax source is the 6% sales tax on goods and services.

In 2018, the Florida legislature established the Education Enhancement Trust Fund, which includes net proceeds of the Florida lottery and the tax proceeds from slot machines in Broward and Miami-Dade counties. Lottery proceeds are also used to fund the cash and debt service requirements of the Classrooms First and 1997 School Capital Outlay Bond Program, debt service for the Class Size Reduction program, and the Educational Facilities Lottery Revenue Bond Program and school district workforce education.[3]

The Florida constitution authorizes certain revenues to be used by school districts for capital outlay purposes. The state constitution guarantees a stated annual amount for each district from proceeds of licensing motor vehicles, referred to as Capital Outlay and Debt Service (CO&DS) funds. The constitution provides that school districts may share in the proceeds from gross receipts taxes referred to as Public Education Capital Outlay (PECO) funds as provided by legislative appropriation.[4]

Local Support
Local revenue for school support is derived almost entirely from property taxes levied by Florida's 67 counties, each of which constitutes a school district. Each district must levy a required local effort millage against its assessed valuation. The state legislature sets the required local effort. Each district's share of the state-required local effort is determined by a statutory procedure that is initiated by certification of the property tax valuation of

each district. Millage rates are also adjusted because required local effort may not exceed 90% of a district's total FEFP entitlement.

Based on the specified tax roll provided by the Florida Department of Revenue, the Commissioner certifies the required millage for each school district. The state average millage was set at 4.308 and certifications for the 67 school districts varies from 4.501 mills (Osceola) to 1.608 mills (Monroe) due to the assessment ratio adjustment and the 90% limitation. The 90% limitation reduced the required local effort of six school districts. Those districts and adjusted millage rates were: Collier (2.892), Franklin (3.609), Monroe (1.608), Sarasota (3.961), Sumter (3.485) and Walton (2.456).

The Department of Revenue is required to calculate the Prior Period Funding Adjustment Millage (PPFAM) which is levied by school districts if in a prior year, the full amount of required local effort funds was not collected due to changes in property values or if a prior year's final taxable value was not certified.[5] The Commissioner calculates the amount of unrealized required local effort funds from the prior period and the millage required to generate that amount. This levy is in addition to the required local effort millage certified by the Commissioner, but it does not affect the calculation of the current year's required local effort. Funds generated by this levy are not included in the district's FEFP allocation.

School boards may set discretionary tax levies of the following types:

- *Current operation.* The legislature set the maximum discretionary current operating millage for 2017–2018 at 0.748 mills.[6] If revenues from 1.5 mills were insufficient to meet the payments due under a lease-purchase agreement entered into before June 30, 2009, or to meet other critical district fixed capital outlay needs, the board may levy an additional 0.25 mill for fixed capital outlay in lieu of levying an equivalent amount of discretionary mills for operations.[7]
- *Capital outlay and maintenance.* School boards may levy up to 1.5 mills[8] and are required to share a portion of the levy with eligible charter schools.[9] Eligible charter schools receive 1.5 mill capital outlay funding based on the per-student value of 1.5 mills for the entire school district. Charter schools serving 75% or more free or reduced price school lunch students or 25% or more students with disabilities are eligible for additional capital outlay funds.[10] Charter school funds are received through the state-funded Charter School Capital Outlay Allocation, with remaining funds are provided from the district's 1.5 mills revenue.

School boards are authorized to expend the funds raised by the 1.5 mill capital outlay levy for the following:

- *The educational plant*. Costs of construction, renovation, remodeling, maintenance and repair of the educational plant, including maintenance, renovation, and repair of leased facilities to correct deficiencies;
- *Expenditures directly related to the delivery of student instruction*. Purchase, lease or lease-purchase of equipment, educational plants and construction materials directly related to the delivery of student instruction;[11] additionally, school boards are authorized to expend up to $100 per unweighted FTE from revenue generated by the 1.5 mill capital outlay millage levy for specific purposes.[12]

If revenues from the 1.5 mill levy were insufficient to meet payments under a lease-purchase agreement entered into prior to June 30, 2009, an amount up to 0.25 mill of the taxable value for school purposes within the school district is legally available, notwithstanding other restrictions on the use of such revenue imposed by law. The additional levy must be made in lieu of levying an equivalent amount of the 0.748 discretionary operating millage for operations authorized in section.[13]

Levies established by the local school board, subject to qualified electors, may vote an additional millage levy for operations and/or capital outlay purposes for a period not to exceed two years.[14] In addition to levies

TABLE 10.1 Florida Schedule of Millages			
Type of Millage	Statutory Authority	Established by	Uses
Required Local Effort	FRS §1011.62(4)	Commissioner	Operating
Prior Period Funding Adjustment	FRS §1-011.62(4)(e)	Commissioner	Operating
Current Operating Discretionary– Max .748 Mills	FRS §1011.71(1)	School Board	Operating
Local Capital Improvement–Max 1.5 Mills	FRS §1011.71(2)	School Board	Capital Improvements
Capital Improvement Discretionary–Max .25 Mills	FRS §1011.71(3)	School Board	Lease = purchase payments/meet fixed capital outlay in lieu of operating discretionary millage
Operating or Capital (Not to exceed 2 yrs)	FRS §1011.73(1)	Voter Referendum	Not specified
Additional Millage (Not to exceed 4 yrs)	FRS §1011.73(2)	Voter Referendum	Not specified
Debt Service	Fl. Const. art. VII, sec 12, FRS §200.001(3)(e)	Voter Referendum	Not specified

established by the school board and the previously voted millage levy for operations and/or capital outlay for two years, qualified electors may also vote an additional levy for voter-approved purposes not to exceed four years.[15] An additional levy for operational purposes, not to exceed four years, may be authorized by the electorate through a local referendum. This voted levy and levies established by the school board may not exceed a total of 10 mills. This levy is distinguished from the constitutional authority for voted millage because it is only for operations; may be approved for up to four years instead of two years; and is included in the 10 mill limit established by the state constitution.

School districts are authorized to sell bonds for capital outlay projects to be repaid from local property taxes.[16] Budgeted revenues from local taxes are determined by applying millage levies to 96% of the school taxable value of property.[17] Additionally, school boards/county commissioners are authorized, via voter referendum, to levy a sales surtax of up to 0.5 or 1% for purposes as defined by statute.[18]

Federal Support

School districts receive funds directly from the federal government and through the state as an administering agency. Districts may receive federal funds from various agencies such as the Department of Labor, Veterans Administration, Department of the Interior, Department of Education, Department of Defense, and Department of Agriculture. Federal funding also supports the Every Student Succeeds program; Individuals with Disabilities Education Act programs; Workforce Investment Act entitlement programs. and Perkins Career and Technical Education Act programs.

Requirements for FEFP Participation

Each school district participating in state appropriations for the FEFP must provide evidence of effort to maintain an adequate school program throughout the district and must meet at least the following requirements:

- *Maintain* adequate and accurate records, including a system of internal accounts for individual schools and file with the Department, in correct and proper form, on or before the date due, each annual or periodic report that is required by the Florida Administrative Code;
- *Operate* all schools for a term of 180 actual teaching days or the equivalent on an hourly basis. Upon written application, the Florida State Board of Education may prescribe procedures for altering this requirement;
- *Provide* written contracts for all instructional personnel;

- *Expend* funds for salaries in accordance with a salary schedule or schedules adopted by the school board in accordance with Florida Statutes and the Florida Administrative Code;
- *Observe* all requirements of the Florida State Board of Education relating to the preparation, adoption, and execution of budgets for the district school system;
- *Levy* the required local effort millage rate on the taxable value for school purposes of the district;
- *Maintain* an ongoing systematic evaluation of the education program needs of the district and develop a comprehensive annual and long-range plan for meeting those needs.

DISTRIBUTING STATE DOLLARS

The amount of Gross State and Local FEFP Dollars for each school district is defined in Table 10.2.[19] Each formula element is explained in subsequent sections of the chapter.

For purposes of calculating the FTE student membership, a student is considered in membership until withdrawn or until the eleventh consecutive school day of absence. A student is eligible for FTE membership reporting under controlling statutes regarding exceptions, year-round schools, dual enrollments, home-schooled, and so on. The FTE generated by a student for purposes of FEFP funding is limited to 1.0 FTE during the 180-day school year. At least four FTE student membership surveys must be conducted under the administrative direction of, and on the schedule provided by, the Commissioner.[20]

Program Cost Factors and Weighted FTE

The cost per-FTE student in each FEFP program is used to produce an index of relative costs, with the cost per-FTE of Basic, Grades 4–8, established as 1.000. In order to minimize fluctuation in program cost factors, the legislature typically uses a three-year average in computing cost factors. Multiplying the FTE students in a program by its cost factor produces a 'weighted FTE.' This calculation weights the FTE to reflect the relative costs of programs as represented by program cost factors. Program cost factors established for use in 2017–18 are shown in Table 10.3.

Florida ■ 133

TABLE 10.2 Determining Gross State and Local FEFP for Florida School Districts

FTE Students × Program Cost Factors = Weighted FTE Students
WFTE Pupils × Base Student Allocation × District Cost Differential = Base Funding $12.9 billion
+
Department of Juvenile Justice Supplement $7.5 Million
+
Declining Enrollment Supplement $2.2 Million
+
Sparsity Supplement $52.8 Million
+
State Funding Discretionary Contribution $8.6 Million
+
0.748 Mills Discretionary Compression $226.5 Million
+
Safe Schools $64.5 Million
+
Reading Program $130 Million
+
Supplemental Academic Instruction $712.2 Million
+
ESE Guaranteed Allocation $1.1 Billion
+
Instructional Materials $231 Million
+
Teachers Classroom Supply Assistance $45.3 Million
+
Student Transportation $438.9 Million
+
Virtual Education Contribution $12.2 Million
+
Digital Classrooms Allocation $80 Million
=
Gross State and Local FEFP Dollars
−
Required Local Effort 7.6 Billion
=
Gross State FEFP $16 Billion
+/−
Adjustments
=
Net State FEFP Allocation $8.4 Billion
+
Class Size Reductions $3.1 Billion
+
Discretionary Lottery $135 Million
=
Total State Funding $11.7 Billion
+
Required Local Effort $7.6 Billion
=
.0748 Discretionary Local Effort $1.4 Billion
=
Total Local Funding $9 Billion
=
Total State & Local Funding $20.6 Billion

TABLE 10.3 Determining Gross State and Local FEFP for Florida School Districts

Programs	Current Cost Factors
K–Grades 1, 2, 3	1.107
Grades 4, 5, 6, 7, 8	1.000
Grades 9, 10, 11, 12	1.001
K, Grades 1, 2, 3 with ESE Services	1.107
Grades 4, 5, 6, 7, 8, with ESE Services	1.000
Grades 9, 10, 11, 12 with ESE Services	1.001
ESE Support Level 4	3.619
ESE Support Level 5	5.526
English for Speakers of Other Languages	1.212
Programs for Grades 9–12 Career Education	1.001

Exceptional Student Education Guaranteed Allocation

Florida provides supplemental funding, called the Exceptional Student Education (ESE) supplement. ESE services for students whose level of service is less than Support Levels 4 and 5 are funded through the ESE Guaranteed Allocation. This allocation provides for additional services needed for exceptional students.

Small District Exceptional Student Education Supplement

This supplement is provided to districts having fewer than 10,000 FTE and fewer than three FTE students in ESE Support Levels 4 and 5. This supplement is limited to the statewide value of 43.35 weighted FTE.

Small, Isolated High School Supplement

High schools with at least 28 students and no more than 100 students in grades 9–12 and that are no closer than 28 miles to the nearest high school may qualify for an isolated school supplement. A district elementary school may also qualify under certain conditions.[21]

School districts may also qualify for certain Bonus FTE Programs under a variety of programs such as Advanced Placement, International Baccalaureate, and Advanced International Certificate of Education. From funding generated by the bonus FTE of these programs, school districts distribute bonuses to certain classroom teachers.[22] Additionally, certain specified Career and Professional Education Act provisions can generate additional FTE.[23]

Base Student Allocation

The base student allocation from state and local funds is determined annually by the legislature. For Fiscal Year 2018, the base student allocation was set at $4,203.95.

District Cost Differential

The District Cost Differential (DCD) is annually determined by adding each school district's Florida Price Level Index for the most recent three years and dividing the sum by three (3). The result is multiplied by 0.800 and divided by 100, and 0.200 is added to the product to obtain the DCD. This serves to limit the factor's adjustment to 80% of the index (i.e., the approximate percentage of district salary costs to total operating costs).

Base Funding

Base Funding is derived from the product of the weighted FTE students multiplied by the Base Student Allocation and the District Cost Differential.

Florida Department of Juvenile Justice Supplement

The total K–12 weighted FTE student membership in juvenile justice education programs in each school district is multiplied by the amount of the state average class-size reduction factor multiplied by the district's cost differential.

Declining Enrollment Supplement

The declining enrollment supplement is determined by comparing the unweighted FTE for the current year to the unweighted FTE of the prior year. In those districts where there was a loss in unweighted FTE, 25% of the decline is multiplied by the prior-year base funding per unweighted FTE.

Sparsity Supplement

A sparsity supplement index is computed by dividing the FTE of the district by the number of permanent senior high school centers. By General Appropriations Act proviso, participation is limited to districts of 24,000 or fewer FTE students. This supplement was limited to $52.8 million statewide for FY 2018.

State-Funded Discretionary Contribution

Laboratory schools and the Florida Virtual School (FLVS) were established as separate school districts for purposes of FEFP funding. Calculation and allocation of funds for lab schools, in lieu of discretionary local tax revenue, is the same as that generated for district students by the tax base of the district where the school is located.[24] The FLVS discretionary contribution is calculated by (1) multiplying the maximum allowable nonvoted discretionary millage for operations[25] by the value of 96% of the current year's taxable value for school purposes for the state; (2) dividing this product by the total FTE student membership of the state; and (3) multiplying this quotient by the FTE student membership of the school. Funds for the discretionary contribution are appropriated from state funds in the General Appropriations Act.

0.748 Mills Discretionary Compression

If any school district levies the full 0.748 mill levy and generates an amount of funds per unweighted FTE student that is less than the state average amount per unweighted FTE student, the district receives a discretionary millage compression supplement that, when added to the funds generated by the district's 0.748 mill levy, makes it equal to the state average.[26]

Safe Schools

Funds are allocated so that each district is guaranteed a minimum of $62,660. From the remaining appropriation, 67% is allocated based on the latest official Florida Crime Index and 33% is allocated based on each district's share of the state's total unweighted student enrollment.[27]

Reading Program

Funds are provided for a K–12 comprehensive districtwide system of research-based reading instruction. The amount of $115,000 is allocated to each district, and the remaining balance is allocated based on each district's proportion of the total K–12 base funding.[28]

Supplemental Academic Instruction

The Supplemental Academic Instruction (SAI) component of the FEFP formula provides funding of $712,207,631. From these funds, at least $75 million is earmarked to provide additional reading support to the 300 lowest performing elementary schools.[29]

Instructional Materials

Funds are provided to purchase instructional materials. This includes instructional content, as well as electronic devices, technology equipment, and infrastructure. The remainder is for core subject instructional materials. Instructional materials funding also provides for library media materials, science lab materials and supplies, dual enrollment instructional materials, and digital instructional materials for students with disabilities.[30]

Florida Teachers Classroom Supply Assistance Program

This appropriation provides an allocation to each school district based on the prorated total of each district's share of the total grades K–12 unweighted FTE student enrollment.[31]

Student Transportation

Student Transportation[32] contains the following provisions in the state allocation: (1) students with special transportation needs earn a higher rate of funding than base students; (2) base funding for each school district is established by the district's proportionate share of total statewide students eligible for transportation; and (3) indices are applied that modify the base funding amount to reward more efficient bus utilization, compensate for rural population density, and adjust funding based on the cost of living.

Virtual Education Contribution

The virtual education contribution is allocated pursuant to the formula which generated $5,230 per FTE.[33]

Digital Classrooms Allocation

Funds are provided to school districts to support efforts to integrate technology. The amount of $500,000 is allocated to each district, and the remaining balance is allocated based on each district's share of the total unweighted FTE.[34]

Federally Connected Student Supplement

The Federally Connected Student Supplement provides additional funding for school districts to support the education of students connected with federally owned military installations, National Aeronautics and Space Administration property, and Indian lands.[35]

Required Local Effort

The school district's required local effort is subtracted from the district's total FEFP dollars. Required local effort from ad valorem taxes is adjusted using the certified tax roll from the Florida Department of Revenue. The Commissioner computes and certifies the required local effort millage rate for each district. Each district's contribution for required local effort is the product of the certified mills multiplied by 96% of taxable value.[36] The Commissioner must adjust the required local effort millage rates if the millage would produce more than 90% of a district's total FEFP entitlement. The amount produced by applying the average computed required local effort millage rate to the certified tax roll is adjusted by an equalization factor.[37] A millage rate is computed based on the positive or negative variation of each district from the state average assessment level. This equalization factor is added to the state average required local effort millage. The sum of these two rates becomes each district's certified required local effort millage.

Adjustments

The Department of Revenue is authorized to make prior-year adjustments in the allocation of funds to a school district for adjudication of litigation, arithmetical errors, or assessment roll change.

Categorical Program Funds

Categorical program funds are added to the FEFP allocation that is distributed to school districts. Categorical programs include the Class Size Reduction Program[38] and the District Discretionary Lottery and Florida School Recognition Programs.[39]

PUBLIC EDUCATION CAPITAL OUTLAY FUND

The Public Education Capital Outlay (PECO) and Debt Service Trust Fund consists of revenues derived from the collection of gross receipts tax on utilities, including transfers from the Communications Services Tax and through the issuance of bonds supported by these revenues.[40] School districts receive PECO funds to construct new facilities or to perform maintenance, renovation, and/or repairs on facilities. Funds are also used for site acquisitions and improvements. Charter schools also receive PECO funds.[41] During the 2018 budget year, $50 million was appropriated to charter schools and $50 million appropriated to public schools. PECO funds may be appropriated to districts lacking sufficient resources to meet urgent construction needs.[42]

CAPITAL OUTLAY AND DEBT SERVICE FUNDS

Tax on motor vehicle licenses is available for school district capital outlay purposes.[43] The number of instruction units determines the annual allocation of these funds to each school district. Each instruction unit for the base year equals $600 and each growth unit, or the increase in instruction units of the current year over the base year is valued at $800. A district may elect to bond its allocation or receive the funds as cash, in which case it is commonly referred to as 'flow-through' funds. Capital Outlay and Debt Service (CO&DS) funds may be used for capital outlay projects.

WORKFORCE DEVELOPMENT EDUCATION FUND

Workforce Development Education Fund programs are administered by the Division of Career and Adult Education. The distribution of funds for 2017–18 was identified with a specific appropriation for each school district. Lifelong Learning may be offered at the discretion of the district, but is not to be reported for funding under the Workforce Development Education Fund or under the FEFP.

FUNDS FOR STUDENT TRANSPORTATION

The student transportation funding formula provides funds to the state's 67 school districts based on each district's pro-rata share of eligible state-transported students. Eligible transported charter school students are reported in the student membership surveys.[44] The formula includes an additional weighting for transportation of students with disabilities requiring specialized transportation services. In addition. the funding formula includes students transported on local public transit. The formula also includes students transported in private passenger cars and boats when the transportation is for certain isolated students or for students with disabilities when the need is documented in the student's Individual Education Plan (IEP). Adjustments to each district's share of state transportation funds are made for cost of living differences, the percentage of the population outside urban centers, and efficiency (as defined by average bus occupancy or the average number of students transported per day, per bus).[45]

SUMMARY

The state of Florida is projected to have nearly 22 million residents by year-end 2019. As such, Florida is projected to be the third most populous state. The state has 67 school districts organized along county lines; additionally, Florida has the largest virtual school in the nation as well as growing numbers of charter schools. The legislature also has a number of tax credit programs for parents choosing private schools. The primary mechanism for funding public schools is the Florida Education Finance Program, first created in the early 1970s. Although heavily amended in the ensuing years, the formula's basic conceptual framework has remained the same and has withstood numerous constitutional challenges. However, with the election of a new governor and appointment of a new Commissioner of Education, it is anticipated that charters, vouchers, tax credit programs, and various options increasing parental choice will be expanded.

NOTES

1. Florida Constitution, Art. IX, sec. 1.
2. This section, as well as other sections, are largely adapted from various Florida Department of Education documents most notably, in large part, *2017–18 Funding for Florida School Districts*, Florida Deptartment of Education. Retrieved from http://www.fldoe.org/fefp
3. FRS §1004.02(25).
4. FL Const. Art. XII sec. 9(d) and sec. 9(a)(2).

5. FRS §1011.62(4)(e).
6. FRS §1011.71(1).
7. FRS §1011.71(3).
8. FRS §1011.71(2),
9. FRS §1013.62(3)(4).
10. FRS §1013.62(2)(b).
11. FRS §1011.71(2)(a)-(k); for permissible items see FRS § 1011.62.
12. FRS §1011.71(5).
13. FRS §1011.71(1)(3).
14. Florida Const. Art. VII, sec. 9 and FRS §1011.73(1).
15. FRS. §1011.71(9) and §1011.73(2).
16. Fl. Const. Art. VII, sec. 12 Article VII, FRS §200.001(3)(e), §1010.40-1010.55.
17. School board adoption of millage levies is governed by the advertising and public meeting requirements of FRS Chap. 200.
18. FRS §212.055(2)(6).
19. All figures are approximate appropriations rounded to the nearest $100,000.
20. Florida Administrative Code, Rule 6A-1.0451(4).
21. FRS §1011.62(1)(h),
22. FRS §1011.62(1)(l), (m),(n),(o).
23. FRS §1011.62(1)(o).
24. FRS §1002.32(9).
25. FRS §1011.71(1).
26. FRS §1011.62(5).
27. School funds are to be utilized to comply with sections FRS.§1006.07-1006.148, with priority given to establishing a school resources officers FRS §1006.12.
28. FRS §1008.22(3), §1008.32, §1011.62(9).
29. See FRS §1008.32.
30. FRS §1011.67.
31. FRS §1012.71.
32. The formula for allocating the funds is outlined in FRS §1011.68.
33. FRS §1011.62(11).
34. FRS §1001.20(4)(a)1.b.
35. See, Title VIII of the Elementary and Secondary Education Act of 1965 §7003; FRS §1011.62(13) and §1011.71(2).
36. FRS §1011.62(4).
37. FRS §1011.62(4)(b).
38. FL Const. Art. IX, sect. 1
39. FRS §008.36, see also §24.121(5)(c), §1001.452, §1001.42(18).
40. FL Const. Art. XII, sec. 9(a)(2). See FRS §1002.32(9)(e), §1013.64(3).
41. FRS §1013.62(1)(a)(b) and §1013.64(1).
42. FRS §1013.64(2)
43. FL Const. Art. XII, sec. 9(d).
44. F.A.C. 6A-1.0451(4).
45. FRS §1011.68, 1006.21-1006.27.

CHAPTER 11

Georgia

Marvin L. Dereef Jr., SFO
Deputy Chief Financial Officer
Fulton County Schools
ASBO International Board of Directors

Larry O. Jackson
Chief Financial Officer
Savannah-Chatham County Public Schools

GENERAL BACKGROUND

In 1985 the Georgia General Assembly[1] passed the *Quality Basic Education Act*[2] (QBE) that became effective July 1, 1986. Since that time there have been several attempts to replace the QBE, but those efforts have resulted in only minor revisions.

The main components[3] of QBE now consist of weighted funding for 18 programs addressing personnel and non-personnel costs. Allocations are driven by full-time equivalent (FTE) pupil counts conducted in October and March of each year. Dollars are said to be 'earned' in the allotment to each school district. Earning of personnel dollars is determined by the state salary schedule. School districts can pay teachers more and can acquire more teachers than the state itself will fund, but local dollars are required to cover the additional costs.

As part of the QBE calculation, the state also includes a local funding requirement that school districts must contribute as added support to the basic educational program. The local tax effort is currently set at five mills,

TABLE 11.1 Austerity Reduction			
Year	Austerity Reduction	Year	Austerity Reduction
2003	$(134,933,642.00)	2011	$(1,089,521,696.00)
2004	$(283,478,659.00)	2012	$(1,147,859,436.00)
2005	$(332,838,099.00)	2013	$(1,143,762,797.00)
2006	$(332,835,092.00)	2014	$(1,061,127,407.00)
2007	$(169,745,895.00)	2015	$(746,769,852.00)
2008	$(142,959,810.00)	2016	$(466,769,852.00)
2009	$(495,723,830.00)	2017	$(167,243,775.00)
2010	$(1,355,168,599.00)	2018	$(166,769,847.00)

Source: GaDoe.org website QBE State allotment Sheets FY 2003–2018 (2018).

called the local five mill share. A reduction to QBE earnings that began in 2003 was known as austerity,[4] more accurately titled the Amended Formula Adjustment. The cost of the austerity provision across the period 2003–2018 was impactful as shown in Table 11.1. However, this reduction was eliminated beginning Fiscal Year 2019.

BASIC SUPPORT PROGRAM

The current QBE formula consists of categories known as Direct Instructional Cost, Indirect Cost, and Categorical Grants. Direct instructional cost funds 18 programs across two broad program areas. One such group of programs, titled Special Programs, is intended to support students with special needs. QBE is additionally intended to support other programs under the General and Career Education headings. The basic support formula is expressed in the following equation:

QBE Earnings + Categorical Grants + Equalization

Program support is calculated in a series of steps for the various components in order to determine the total school district allotment,[5] such as salary and benefits for classroom teachers; cost of textbooks and instructional materials; cost of utilities and maintenance; and allocations for specialists, instructional support, and administrative expenses at the school and system levels. Salaries for teachers and other certificated positions are based on the state's minimum salary schedule,[6] with adjustments for training and experience of each school system's certificated employees in each field, with allowance for health insurance[7] and pension benefits. The formula amount per pupil depends on the number of students in each class (i.e., the 'Funding Ratio'), as well as staffing ratios for other positions. The resulting cost per student is then multiplied by the FTE pupils in each program, i.e., taking into account the portion of the school day that each student spends in each program. Technology specialists, psychologists, and social workers are also earned through the QBE. Middle and high school counselors are also earned. Secretaries and media specialists are earned at the rate of one per 'base-size school.' A base-size school may vary by program, and the pupil/teacher ratio may also vary. The school district earns the beginning salary for a principal at each school through a 'principal of record' for the preceding year. Finally, at the central office level, the district is funded for one superintendent, six assistant superintendents, one secretary, and one accountant. The school district must use other funding sources for positions not funded by the QBE.

Briefly said, the QBE is comprised of multiple steps by which each school district determines its QBE Formula Earnings. As an enrollment-driven state aid plan, the QBE follows a defined sequence:

1. The first step is to count pupils in FTE attendance.
2. The second step adds adjustments through educational program weights and training and experience factors.
3. The third step multiplies these variables.
4. The fourth step finds the state adding funding for indirect costs.
5. The fifth step deducts the local five mill share.
6. Historically, the sixth step involved deducting austerity cuts (eliminated for FY 2019).

Table 11.2 identifies Georgia's FY 2018 program weights under the QBE and Table 11.3 details the state's Education Department Financial Summary for FY 2016 through FY 2019.

TABLE 11.2 Fiscal Year 2018 Program Weights			
Program	Weight	Program	Weight
Kindergarten	1.6532	Special Education Category I	2.3828
Kindergarten—Early Intervention	2.0382	Special Education Category II	2.7933
Primary Grades 1–3	1.2859	Special Education Category III	3.5559
Primary Grades 1–3 Early Intervention	1.7955	Special Education Category IV	5.7624
Upper Elementary 4–5	1.0358	Special Education Category V	2.4532
Upper Elementary 4–5—Early Intervention	1.7892	Special Education Category VI	1.6609
Middle Grades 6–8	1.1317	Remedial Education	1.3099
Grades 9–12 (Base)	1.0000	Alternative Education	1.4727
Vocational Labs Grades 9–12	1.1907	English Speakers of Other Languages	2.5096

Source: Georgia Department of Education Financial Management for Georgia Local Units of Administration Manual (2018).

TABLE 11.3 Georgia Education Department Financial Summary for Fiscal Years 2016–2019

Program/Funding Sources	FY 2016 Expenditures	FY 2017 Expenditures	FY 2018 Original Budget	Amended FY 2018 Budget	FY 2019 Budget
Agricultural Education	$10,895,215	$11,346,098	$11,820,623	$11,820,529	$12,344,708
Audio-Video Technology and Film Grants		$1,990,000	$2,500,000	$2,500,000	$2,500,000
Business and Finance Administration	$37,654,871	$24,635,043	$28,611,662	$44,359,875	$28,603,015
Central Office	$14,073,002	$14,633,780	$22,940,113	$22,864,337	$21,982,047
Charter Schools	$2,151,203	$2,215,800	$2,598,135	$2,597,999	$2,596,386
Chief Turnaround Officer					$2,193,941
Communities in Schools	$1,053,100	$1,203,100	$1,228,100	$1,228,100	$1,228,100
Curriculum Development	$5,595,087	$5,381,239	$6,808,642	$6,807,919	$6,840,677
Federal Programs	$1,156,050,230	$1,111,800,843	$993,010,318	$993,010,318	$993,010,318
Georgia Network for Educational and Therapeutic Support (GNETS)	$74,238,367	$76,309,493	$14,402,830	$74,402,785	$72,081,380
Georgia Virtual School	$10,958,753	$10,645,398	$10,181,528	$10,180,714	$10,247,065
Information Technology Services	$23,864,329	$22,393,208	$22,441,583	$22,438,739	$22,439,828
Non Quality Basic Education Formula Grants	$10,644,109	$11,158,091	$11,744,265	$11,568,686	$11,733,752
Nutrition	$752,314,829	$762,832,285	$854,370,145	$854,370,052	$854,374,123
Preschool Disabilities Services	$31,446,339	$33,698,294	$35,563,123	$35,563,132	$37,355,426
Quality Basic Education Equalization	$507,107,607	$498,726,526	$584,562,416	$584,562,416	$615,316,420
Quality Basic Education Local Five Mill Share	($1,774,571,231)	($1,703,956,027)	($1,777,164,321)	($1,777,164,321)	($1,872,395,263)

(continued)

TABLE 11.3 Georgia Education Department Financial Summary for Fiscal Years 2016–2019 (continued)

Program/Funding Sources	FY 2016 Expenditures	FY 2017 Expenditures	FY 2018 Original Budget	FY 2018 Amended Budget	FY 2019 Budget
Quality Basic Education Program	$9,503,905,669	$9,944,181,009	$10,330,098,597	$10,431,482,043	$10,769,680,035
Regional Education Service Agencies (RESAs)	$10,223,951	$10,810,026	$12,233,109	$12,233,109	$13,968,093
School Improvement	$13,246,851	$13,694,649	$16,469,937	$16,467,772	$15,821,670
State Charter School Commission Administration	$3,549,483	$3,943,510	$4,156,309	$4,156,309	$4,156,309
State Interagency Transfers	$29,449,954	—	—	—	—
State Schools	$30,648,330	$29,002,659	$30,045,887	$30,040,057	$31,144,703
Technology/Career Education	$39,995,005	$70,593,209	$68,337,903	$68,837,464	$68,628,403
Testing	$38,957,664	$47,379,960	$42,783,501	$42,282,855	$41,239,261
Tuition for Multiple Disability Students	$1,322,403	$1,551,946	$1,551,946	$1,551,946	$1,551,946
Pupil Transportation	$0	—	—	—	$132,884,118
Federal Funds	–$1,964,260,355	–$1,937,705,176	–$1,917,274,955	–$1,917,274,955	–$1,917,274,955
Federal Recovery Funds	($2,499,857)	($1,882,850)	($2,333,773)	($2,333,773)	($2,333,773)
Other Funds	($54,756,271)	($39,439,792)	($44,329,264)	($44,329,264)	($44,479,264)
Prior Year State Funds	($9,117,759)				
Total State Funds	$8,614,133,878	$9,027,142,321	$9,427,358,368	$9,544,224,843	$9,937,438,469
State General Funds	$8,409,786,446	$9,027,142,322	$9,427,358,368	$9,544,224,843	$9,937,438,469
RSR for K12	$204,347,430				
Total State Funds	$8,614,133,876	$9,027,142,322	$9,427,358,368	$9,544,224,843	$9,937,438,469

STATE FUNDING FOR NON-PUBLIC SCHOOLS

Charter schools in Georgia are funded in the same manner as traditional public schools through the QBE formula. While differences exist in governance, there are no significant differences in funding. In 2012 the state legislature created the State Charter Schools Commission, granting it full power to approve or deny charter contracts. Currently, 83,000 (5%) pupils are enrolled in Georgia's 99 charter schools.[8] More funding detail can be found on the state's website.[9]

OTHER PROGRAMS OF NOTICE

Food Service

The state of Georgia participates fully in national school food service programs.[10] This includes AfterSchool Snack Care, National School Breakfast, National School Lunch, Fresh Fruit and Vegetable, Farm to School, Healthy Meal Pattern, Seamless Summer Option, Smart Snacks in Schools, Shake It Up, Student Chef Competition, and USDA Healthy School Meals programs.

Retirement[11]

The Teachers' Retirement System[12] (TRS) is the retirement fund for public school teachers, state university employees, and others in educational environments. The TRS was established in 1943 by the state legislature to provide retirement security for educational system servants. The TRS is the largest public retirement system in the state of Georgia and is a governmentally defined benefit plan—meaning retirement benefits are determined by a formula rather than directly related to contributions made to the TRS.

Other school employees participate in the Public School Employees Retirement Plan[13] (PSERS). The purpose of PSERS is to provide a supplemental retirement plan for school employees who do not belong to the TRS. Members include bus drivers, food service workers, and maintenance or custodial personnel. Some managers in these positions are members of TRS. PSERS was established in 1970 to provide school employees with a supplemental retirement plan. Member and state contributions are paid to PSERS for the exclusive benefit of members of system employees and beneficiaries. PSERS is administered by a Board of Trustees plus two additional members appointed by the governor, and the ability of the fund to meet future obligations is examined each year.

Transportation

State aid is provided according to a schedule of standard transportation costs and a schedule of variable transportation costs.[14]

SUMMARY

The QBE is a comprehensive funding formula, meaning most state aids are included in the basic scheme. Other categorical programs exist and may be largely described as categorical grants made by the state for activities, including pupil transportation and nursing, which are earned on a system-wide basis instead of a per-student basis. Since the QBE has not changed greatly since inception, a useful primer on Georgia school finance can be synopsized.[15]

NOTES

1. "The provision of an adequate public education for the citizens shall be a primary obligation of the State of Georgia. Public education for the citizens prior to the college or postsecondary level shall be free and shall be provided for by taxation." (Georgia Constitution 8-1-1).
2. Act 770, *The Quality Basic Education Act* (1986).
3. See Georgia Department of Education Budget Services for explaining links. Available at http://www.gadoe.org/Finance-and-Business-Operations/Budget-Services/Pages/default.aspx
4. In 2003, the Georgia legislature was unable to fully fund public K–12 education. To address the shortfall, the Department of Education added a line to the QBE allotment sheet called 'austerity.' The amount of austerity varied from year to year until it was finally removed for FY 2019 (July 1, 2018–June 30, 2019). During its tenure, austerity was proportionately distributed to all school systems in Georgia, so that the larger a system's QBE amount, the larger its share of the austerity measure.
5. Operation of the QBE can be seen in state allotment sheets. Retrieved from https://app.doe.k12.ga.us/ows-bin/owa/qbe_reports.public_menu?p_fy=2000
6. Past years are available. For FY 2019 setting the base at $34,092 see http://www.gadoe.org/Finance-and-Business-Operations/Budget-Services/Documents/FY19-TeacherSalaryScheduleReport.pdf
7. The Georgia Department of Education via QBE funds the employer contribution for the certified school employees' health premiums. The health premium rates are set and billed by the Georgia Department of Community Health. The current rate is $945 per member per month.
8. R. Craig Wood, David C. Thompson, and Faith E. Crampton. *Money and Schools 7th Edition*. New York, NY: Routledge (2019).

9. https://scsc.georgia.gov/state-charter-funding
10. http://snp.wpgadoe.org
11. This section relies on Employees' Retirement System of Georgia. (2019). Retrieved from https://www.ers.ga.gov
12. https://www.trsga.com
13. Georgia Laws 1969 (O.C.G.A. Title 47, Chapter 4).
14. Deborah Verstegen, "A Quick Glance at School Finance: A 50-State Survey of School Finance Policies and Programs—Georgia." (2018). Retrieved from https://schoolfinancesdav.files.wordpress.com/2018/09/10-georgia.pdf
15. Georgia Department of Education, "Financing Georgia's Schools: A Primer." Ross Rubenstein and David L. Sjoquist (2003). Retrieved from https://cslf.gsu.edu/files/2014/06/financing_georgias_schools_a_primer.pdf

CHAPTER 12

Hawai'i

Staff Writer[1]

GENERAL BACKGROUND

Hawai'i's educational history and operation are unique among the 50 states. As the last state to join the Union in 1959, Hawai'i is also among those rare states never having experienced school finance litigation. A major reason for such uniqueness is that Hawai'i is the only state in the nation to have only one school district within its borders, making inter-district fiscal equity a moot point. Since traditional school finance equity is not a topic for dispute in Hawai'i apart from intra-system equity, only issues of adequate funding remain as a point of contention.

The constitution[2] of the state of Hawai'i specifically provides for public education. Article 10 §1 says:

> The State shall provide for the establishment, support, and control of a statewide system of public schools free from sectarian control, a state university, public libraries, and such other educational institutions as may be deemed desirable, including physical facilities therefore.

Hawai'i is also unique in that property taxes form no part of its true school funding base, making funding for schools almost entirely reliant on the state legislature. As a result, the state's single school district has no independent tax authority. Fiscal support for public schools comes from the state's general fund—a source primarily characterizable as funded by general excise taxes, personal income taxes, corporate income taxes, and other special taxes on use and consumption.[3]

Funding Public Schools in the United States and Indian Country, pages 151–161
Copyright © 2019 by Information Age Publishing
All rights of reproduction in any form reserved.

Hawai'i's basic school fiscal support program entails a $1.99 billion budget funded by state, federal, trust fund, and special fund sources (see Table 12.1). Hawai'i runs the entire state's budget on a biennium with a supplemental budget in the alternating years. The state board of education makes annual requests each October, with submission for review each January. The current biennium is comprised of the budgetary years 2019–2021.

In 2004, the state engaged in sweeping school system redesign. Act 51[4] provided reforms in 13 areas, chief among which was establishment of a new weighted student formula meant to reflect the costs of educational needs. Hawai'i's Department of Education (DOE) has continued to focus on system design, most recently advancing for legislative review a budgetary request containing four priorities for the 2019–2021 biennium: (1) reprogram existing funds to align with strategic priorities; (2) focus on significant Capital Improvements Program [CIP] needs; (3) address Title IX in athletic concerns; and (4) pursue targeted advancements in strategic priority areas.[5] Stated priorities were tied to the DOE's goals of Student Success, Staff Success, and Successful Systems of Support. More specifically, the DOE's targets[6] for 2019–2021 included:

- *Reprogramming:* $0 cost, i.e., reprogramming existing funds to align with strategic priorities to include student supports, information technology, talent management, facilities and school supports, fiscal services, and strategy, innovation and performance;
- *CIP Needs:* $1.46 billion, i.e., focusing on providing facilities to reflect 21st-century instructional spaces supporting innovation and discovery learning;
- *Title IX:* $10.7 million directed to finishing upgrades of athletic facilities and to particularly begin addressing under-resourced high schools having no athletic facilities;
- *Targeted Investments:* $28.8 million to continue implementing the state board's strategic plan via high impact strategies involving school design, teacher collaboration and student voice, Medicaid supports, additional Pre-K classes; and adding monies to the school aid formula in support of new academic standards.

In total, Hawai'i's school funding system currently supports about 180,000 students across 292 schools, 15 complex areas, and the state office. Nearly all appropriated funds go to schools, with monies distributed by program categories known as EDNs.[7]

BASIC SUPPORT PROGRAM[8]

As indicated, Hawai'i's single school district covers a diverse range of educational needs and services. In 2019, the state legislature funded public schools through a $1.6 billion appropriation from the state's General Fund. These monies combined with $270 million in federal funding, $84.3 million in special funds, and $15.9 million in trust funds to reach a combined total of $1.99 billion as shown in Table 12.1. A five-year history of funding is seen in Table 12.2.

State funds in Table 12.1 and Table 12.2 are derived from the state's General Fund and comprise the bulk of DOE monies. Federal funds are comprised of various federal grants from sources including the U.S. Department

TABLE 12.1 Hawai'i DOE Operating Budget FY 2019

Total Operating Budget	$1,999,403,622	100%
State Funds	$1,629,121,724	81.5%
EDN 100 School Based Budgeting	$948.3 million	58.2%
EDN 150: Special Education	$367.7 million	22.6%
EDN 200: Instructional Support	$56.1 million	3.4%
EDN 300: State Administration	$51.7 million	3.2%
EDN 400: School Support	$197.6 million	12.1%
EDN 500: School Community Services	$4 million	<1%
EDN 700: Early Learning	$3.8 million	<1%
Federal Funds (authorized ceiling)	$270,081,479	13.5%
Special Funds (authorized ceiling)	$84,300,419	4.0%
Trust Funds (authored ceiling)	$15,900,000	1.0%

Source: Excerpted and condensed from Hawai'i State Department of Education Briefing to the Senate Committee on Ways and Means and Senate Committee on Education. "Fiscal Biennium 2019–2021 Budget Briefing FB 2019–2021." (January 14, 2019), p. 34. http://www.hawaiipublicschools.org/DOE%20Forms/budget/FB1921-briefing.pdf

TABLE 12.2 FY 2015–2019 P–12 DOE Operating Budget, All Sources

	State	Federal	Special	Trust	Total	% Change
FY 2019	$1,629,121,724	$270,081,479	$84,300,419	$15,900,000	$1,999,403,622	1.0081
FY 2018	$1,610,321,050	$272,881,479	$84,150,419	$15,900,000	$1,983,252,948	1.0253
FY 2017	$1,567,678,982	$265,034,049	$83,954,451	$17,640,000	$1,903,063,554	1.0164
FY 2016	$1,530,655,758	$258,012,049	$96,755,747	$17,640,000	$1,903,063,554	1.0730
FY 2015	$1,402,889,559	$250,994,824	$95,339,367	$24,290,000	$1,773,513,750	0.9970

Source: Executive Biennium and Supplemental Budget Bills. Modified from http://www.hawaiipublicschools.org/ConnectWithUs/Organization/Budget/Pages/home.aspx

of Education, the U.S. Department of Agriculture, the U.S. Department of Defense, and the U.S. Department of Health and Human Services. Special funds are derived from income-generating activities such as food service, transportation, summer school, driver education, and more. Trust fund revenues are broadly sourced to include foundations, donations, grants, developer fees, and more.[9]

Weighted Student Formula

Most state funds are distributed to Hawai'i's individual schools through the Weighted Student Formula (WSF). The WSF ties money to pupils' educational needs through a system of program weights. Weights are based on (1) student characteristics, (2) school characteristics, and (3) a non-weighted lump sum.

Student Characteristics

Student characteristics are those typically associated with vertical equity considerations in school finance, including primary grades (K–2); English Language Learner (including breakouts of Fully English Proficient, Limited English Proficient, and Non-English Proficient); Economically Disadvantaged; Transiency; Gifted and Talented, and Grade Levels.

School Characteristics

School characteristics relate to Multi-track and Neighbor Island variables.

Non-Weighted Lump Sum

The non-weighted lump sum is based on school type such as elementary, middle/high, and combinations.[10]

Committee on Weights

The actual weights applied in the WSF are established and evaluated by a Committee on Weights (COW). Pupil counts related to weights are conducted three times annually.

Table 12.2 earlier also detailed operation of the WSF/COW by yielding a funding profile for Hawai'i's schools by each weight's proportion and function. The EDNs identified in Table 12.2 showed relative amounts of money associated by use through the WSF. More specifically, Table 12.2 showed that money meant for school-based budgeting (EDN 100) is almost entirely distributed through the WSF and accounts for 48.2% of the $1.63 billion in state funding for FY 2019—i.e., the majority of state money goes to student characteristic formula elements.

The other EDNs in Table 12.2 can be read in the same way: e.g., money meant for special education services (EDN 150) accounts for 22.6% of available WSF funds; EDN 400 (12.1%) pays operations costs; EDN 500 (0.2%) pays for adult learner programs in schools; and EDN 700 (0.2%) provides prekindergarten programs.

The effect of the WSF is to assign 93% of state funds to direct-to-school support and the remaining 7% to school, district, and state levels.[11] Table 12.3 accumulates the details of the WSF.

Capital Improvements Program Budget

Capital improvements are part of the basic support program for public schools in Hawai'i. The state heavily supports the Capital Improvements Program (CIP), funding it at nearly 100%. The CIP budget is set by the state as part of a comprehensive program to manage all state facilities. The CIP includes development and improvements, renovation, repair and major maintenance to facilities, landscaping, new construction, land acquisition, and utility modifications.[12]

State facilities staff work directly with school site principals to prioritize school-level needs. Like EDNs, CIP appropriations are added into planning categories to direct funds to needs resolution. Those categories include:

- *Condition:* including maintenance and repair, technology infrastructure, hazardous materials, health and safety, and structural improvements;
- *Program Support:* gender equity, restrooms, ADA compliance, support program spaces, and playgrounds;
- *Capacity:* new facilities and additions, temporary facilities, repurposing for capacity;
- *Equity:* science spaces, special education, energy, right-sizing, physical education, abatements.

Earlier discussion indicated the CIP as a priority, seeking to allocate $1.46 billion focused on providing facilities to reflect 21st-century instructional spaces supporting innovation and discovery learning.

Table 12.4 reveals the scope and amount of CIP support at the DOE as presented to the state legislature. As in all appropriations for entire state governments' resource competition, Table 12.4 identifies the consonance and dissonance between agency requests and legislative enactment.[13]

TABLE 12.3 FY 2019–2020 Statewide Weighted Student Formula Calculation

		Total Projected Enrollment[a]	Weighting Factor	Weighted Projected Enrollment	$ per Student	Total Allocation
1	Pre-K (SpEd)	1,610	1.000	1,610.00	$4,465.25	$7,189,055
2	K–2	41,514	1.000	41,514.00	$4,465.25	$185,370,452
3	Other Elem	44,029	1.000	44,029.00	$4,465.25	$196,600,559
4	Middle	33,767	1.000	33,767.00	$4,465.25	$150,778,148
5	High	49,353	1.000	49,353.00	$4,465.25	$220,373,559
6	**Subtotal**	**170,273**		**170,273.00**		**$760,311,773**
	Student Characteristics					
7	Grade Level Adjustment					
8	Middle	33,767	0.034	1,134.33	$150.00	$5,065,050
9	K–2 Class Size	41,514	0.150	6,227.10	$669.79	$27,805,568
10	English Language Learners (Aggregate)	17,563	0.2506	4,400.70	$1,118.84	$19,650,217
11	Fully English Proficient (FEP)	1,091	0.065	70.70	$289.35	$315,715
12	Limited English Proficiency (LEP)	10,670	0.194	2,074.27	$868.04	$9,262,155
13	Non-English Proficient (NEP)	5,802	0.389	2,255.72	$1,736.09	$10,072,347
14	Economically Disadvantaged	84,429	0.100	8,442.90	$446.53	$37,699,672
15	Gifted & Talented	5,037	0.265	1,334.85	$1,183.29	$5,960,453
16	Transiency	6,167	0.050	308.35	$223.26	$1,376,872
17	**Subtotal**			**21,848.23**		**$97,557,83**

(*continued*)

TABLE 12.3 FY 2019–2020 Statewide Weighted Student Formula Calculation (continued)

		Total Projected Enrollment[a]	Weighting Factor	Weighted Projected Enrollment	$ per Student	Total Allocation
	School Characteristics					
18	Neighbor Island	54,415	0.004	217.66	$17.86	$971,907
19	**Subtotal**			**217.66**		**$971,907**
20	**Total Weighted Allocation**	170,273		192,338.89		**$858,841,512**
	Non-Weighted School Characteristics					
	Base Funding—per school based on school type	Number of Schools				
21	Elem	167			$307,000	$51,269,000
22	Elem–Multi-Track	1			$402,000	$402,000
23	Middle	36			$461,000	$16,596,000
24	Middle–Multi-Track	2			$556,000	$1,112,000
25	High	33			$472,000	$15,576,000
26	Combination Schools					
27	K–12	5			$750,000	$3,750,000
28	K–8	4			$525,000	$2,100,000
29	6–12	5			$537,000	$2,685,000
30	**Subtotal**	**253**				**$93,490,000**
31	Total WSF Funds Available for Tentative Enrollment Allocation					$952,331,512

[a] Total Enrollment includes General Education, Special Education and Pre-K (SpEd) at a rate of 1.00 per student.

Disclaimer: Projected allocations are tentative and are subject to change based on the Department's final appropriation for Weighted Student Formula and statewide enrollment figures. Final allocations will be determined based on Official Enrollment Count, taken August 2019.

Source: Hawai'i Department of Education. "Details of WSF Tentative Allocation Calculation Based on FY2019–20 Preliminary Appropriation and Projected Enrollment." http://www.hawaiipublicschools.org/Reports/FY20WSFWeights.pdf

TABLE 12.4 CIP Budget Requests and Appropriations FY 2018 Biennium and FY 2019 Supplemental (in millions)

	FY 2018 (Biennium Budget)		FY 2019 (Supplemental Budget)	
	Requested	Approved	Requested	Approved
Condition	$159.3	$90.0	$213.3	$54.5
Capacity	$259.6	—	$247.0	—
Equity	$146.0	$33.0	$199.4	$10.0
Program Support	$100.7	$33.0	$123.9	$17.0
Lump Sums (project completion, Title IX, equipment)	$9.0	—	—	$33.0
Total	$674.6	$156.0	$783.6	$114.5
Legislative Add-Ons		$118.5		$166.9
Special: Act 57, energy efficiency and/ heat abatement	$30.8	$46.4	—	—
Total	$705.4	$320.9	$783.6	$281.4

Source: http://www.hawaiipublicschools.org/ConnectWithUs/Organization/Budget/Pages/home.aspx

CHARTER SCHOOLS[14]

Hawai'i's 36 public charter schools are run by independent governing boards operating under performance contracts with the State Public Charter School Commission. In Hawaii, charter schools are public schools, funded on a per-pupil allocation separate from the Department of Education.

Funding for charter schools in Hawai'i should be carefully parsed to provide an accurate comparison to traditional public schools. The best parsing explanation is found in the statute as footnoted below.[15] In general, the Hawai'i Department of Education cautions that comparisons should be made on the basis of recognizing that reporting differences in fiscal data can produce inaccurate comparisons that give the appearance of substantial differences in per-pupil funding between traditional and charter schools.

OTHER PROGRAMS OF NOTICE

Food Service

Foodservice operates in the much same manner as other states. For more information, see the state's explanation.[16]

Retirement

Hawai'i operates the Employee Retirement System[17] (ERS) containing contributory, non-contributory, and hybrid plans.

Contributory Plan

Employees hired after July 1, 1945, through June 30, 1984, are members of the Employee Retirement System (ERS) contributory plan. Employees in this group contribute 7.8% of gross monthly salary to the ERS.

On resignation, employees with less than five years of service must within four years of date of resignation withdraw contributions made to the retirement fund. Employees in this plan may retire at age 55 with a minimum of five years' service or with 25 years of service regardless of age. Benefits calculation is expressed as

$$\text{Service} \times \text{Average Final Compensation (AFC)}.$$

Non-Contributory Plan

Employees hired July 1, 1984, through June 30, 2006, are members of the ERS non-contributory plan. Employees make no contributions to the ERS. Employees in this plan are eligible to retire at age 62 with a minimum of 10 years' service or at age 55 with a minimum 30 years service. Normal retirement benefit is calculated as

$$1.25\% \times \text{Years of Credited Service} \times \text{AFC}.$$

Hybrid Plan

Employees hired on or after July 1, 2006 through June 30, 2012 are members of the ERS hybrid plan. Members of the contributory and non-contributory retirement plans were provided with the option to join the new hybrid plan or to remain in a current plan. Employees contribute 6% of gross monthly salary to the ERS. Normal retirement benefit is calculated as

$$2\% \times \text{Years of Credited Hybrid Service} \times \text{AFC}.$$

On June 23, 2011, the governor signed into law Act 163.[18] The new law provided for retirement benefit changes under the hybrid plan for employees who became members of the ERS after June 30, 2012. Employees hired on or after July 1, 2012, became eligible to retire at age 65 with a minimum of 10 years service or at age 60 with a minimum 30 years service.

Transportation

Transportation to and from school is offered to students enrolled in Hawai'i's public schools. The Student Transportation Services Branch works with private vendors to set transportation and route agreements, with a focus on effectiveness, efficiency, and safety.

SUMMARY

Although the state of Hawai'i has been immune from school finance litigation and its unique organizational structure prevents the traditional interdistrict disparity common to state legislative debates, it has not been free of criticism. Critics argue Hawai'i's public schools are severely underfunded, a message weighing on state legislators facing upcoming legislative sessions.[19] Agreement on the need for a fiscal adequacy study to assess the amount of state underfunding seems certain. The governor's 2019 state-of-the-state address[20] echoed many similar themes, reciting issues relating to the DOE's priorities (see discussion at the beginning of this chapter—e.g., restructuring based on academic and learning standards, preschool, teacher supply, and more). Data comparisons abound, citing Hawai'i's rankings in areas such as test scores, graduation rates, post-secondary completion, teaching conditions, and national expenditure ranking. The state's educators were pinning hopes on a constitutional amendment to institute a tax on investment properties having a value of $1 million or more—but before it could reach the polls, it was struck down over ballot language by the state supreme court. In this context, the DOE's funding targets discussed at the chapter's outset are challenging.

NOTES

1. No state-based expert was available to author this chapter at the time of publication. The chapter is drawn from multiple sources as footnoted and represents the editorial staff's interpretation of issues, trends, and findings regarding the state of Hawai'i. For additional information and detail, contact the Hawai'i State Department of Education.
2. Constitution, State of Hawaii. Retrieved from http://lrbhawaii.org/con/
3. Deborah Verstegen, "A Quick Glance at School Finance: A 50 State Survey of School Finance Policies." (2019). Retrieved from https://schoolfinancesdav.wordpress.com
4. Act 51: Reinventing Education Act of 2004. SB3238, SD2, HD2, CD1. As amended. Retrieved from http://www.hawaiipublicschools.org/DOE%20Forms/State%20Reports/Act51.pdf

5. Hawai'i State Department of Education, "2019–2021 Fiscal Biennium Budget Priorities. (2019). Retrieved from http://www.hawaiipublicschools.org/DOE%20Forms/budget/FBbudgetpriorities.pdf
6. Ibid.
7. EDN = acronym for "Education." A Budget Program Structure Designation for the Department of Education. Retrieved from http://www.hawaiipublicschools.org/ConnectWithUs/FAQ/Pages/Acronyms.aspx#W
8. Formula description herein generally follows the Hawai'i State Department of Education's self-explanation entitled "The Department's Budget." (2019). Retrieved from http://www.hawaiipublicschools.org/ConnectWithUs/Organization/Budget/Pages/home.aspx. The current chapter also follows the state department's website description at "The Department's Budget." (2019). Retrieved from http://www.hawaiipublicschools.org/ConnectWithUs/Organization/Budget/Pages/home.aspx
9. Ibid.
10. State of Hawai'i, Department of Education. "Factsheet: WS/COW: Weighted Student Formula and the Committee on Weights." (2019). Retrieved from http://www.hawaiipublicschools.org/DOE%20Forms/WSF/WSFCOW.pdf
11. State of Hawai'i, Department of Education. "Factsheet: The Budget FY 2019." Retrieved from http://www.hawaiipublicschools.org/DOE%20Forms/budget/Budget1sheet.pdf
12. Ibid.
13. Detail on CIP requests and approvals are found at these addresses respectively: Retrieved from http://www.hawaiipublicschools.org/DOE%20Forms/budget/BOEFY19CIP.pdf and https://www.capitol.hawaii.gov/session2018/worksheets/HB1900-EXEC-CD1-CIP-SPREADSHEET.pdf
14. This section draws generally on the Hawai'i Department of Education webpage at http://www.hawaiipublicschools.org/TeachingAndLearning/EducationInnovation/CharterSchools/Pages/home.aspx
15. §302D-28 Funding and Finance. Retrieved from https://www.capitol.hawaii.gov/hrscurrent/Vol05_Ch0261-0319/HRS0302D/HRS_0302D-0028.htm
16. http://www.hawaiipublicschools.org/TeachingAndLearning/HealthAndNutrition/StudentHealthResources/Pages/FreeReducedLunch.aspx
17. http://www.hawaiipublicschools.org/ConnectWithUs/Employment/WorkingInHawaii/Pages/ERS.aspx
18. 2011 Hawaii Code DIVISION 1. GOVERNMENT TITLE 7. PUBLIC OFFICERS AND EMPLOYEES 88. Pension and Retirement Systems CHAPTER 88 PENSION AND RETIREMENT SYSTEMS. Retrieved from https://law.justia.com/codes/hawaii/2011/division1/title7/chapter88/.
19. "Hawaii Lawmakers Address Education on Opening Day of 2019 Legislative Session." *Hawaii State Teachers Association* (January 16, 2019). Retrieved from https://www.hsta.org/News/Recent-Stories/hawaii-lawmakers-address-education-on-opening-day-of-2019-legislative-session
20. Hawaii Governor State of the State Address 2019. Retrieved from https://governor.hawaii.gov/wp-content/uploads/2019/01/2019-State-of-the-State-Address-by-Governor-David-Ige.pdf

CHAPTER 13

Idaho

Staff Writer[1]

GENERAL BACKGROUND

Idaho's constitution was approved in 1890. Article IX, Section I contained the new state's education clause, placing a duty on the state legislature for the oversight of public education. Article IX has remained unchanged since adoption. The education provision requires the legislature to establish a system of free schools, saying:

> The stability of a republican form of government depending mainly upon the intelligence of the people, it shall be the duty of the legislature of Idaho, to establish and maintain a general, uniform and thorough system of public, free common schools.[2]

Idaho has 115 public school districts, ten district-sponsored charter schools, 40 LEA charter schools, and educates nearly 300,000 schoolchildren across school organizations that include a range from one-teacher schools to more urban settings.

Like many states, Idaho has experienced variable fortunes related to economic and other conditions. Since Fiscal Year 2000 the state engaged reductions in the share of total state spending going to public schools, with reduction blamed on tax cuts and health and human services primarily in the form of Medicaid.[3] While dollars were said to track closely according to that pattern, it was additionally said that changes to tax structure also contributed, as beginning in 2000 Idaho's legislature began reducing taxes. Tax changes included a reduction in the corporate income tax rate, indexing individual income tax brackets for inflation, increasing the income tax

---

Funding Public Schools in the United States and Indian Country, pages 163–175
Copyright © 2019 by Information Age Publishing
All rights of reproduction in any form reserved.

grocery credit, and exchanging a sales tax rate increase for an elimination of the public school maintenance and operations property tax levy, resulting in tens of millions of dollars in lost net revenue. Each of these changes reduced the state's capacity to fund public services and contributed to the slowing of state spending after FY 2000. Among other changes, these events had the effect of elimination of equalized levies for M&O funding and increased activity surrounding voter approval of supplemental tax override levies.[4]

Fast-forwarding to 2018, the recent legislative session represented forward progress, with the state approving a 5.9% increase in state funding for FY 2019. The new budget for public schools totaled $1.785 billion, including an increase in discretionary funding. Monies in the new budget reflected a long road over the past few years to reach accord on a five-year plan for improvement, tied in part to full funding for the career ladder plan; new monies for technology; increased funding for health insurance costs; increases for funding literacy, proficiency, professional development and more—in total, approximately $100 million in new funds for public schools.[5]

BASIC SUPPORT PROGRAM

Idaho Public Schools are funded primarily from state general funds and are supplemented by state dedicated funds, federal funds, and local funds. Table 13.1 indicates that the legislature appropriated approximately $2.7 billion for FY 2019 from a mix of these sources.

Idaho uses a foundation program to fund schools based on Support (instructional) Units. Pupil count defined as Average Daily Attendance (ADA) is the basis for determining Support Units. School districts and charter schools are included in the state's funding formula. As indicated earlier, the 2006 legislature replaced local tax revenues for M&O with state general fund

TABLE 13.1   Idaho Legislative Appropriation for Schools FY 2019

	Public Schools	IESDB	Total
General Funds	$1,774,811,000	$10,454,900	$1,785,265,900
State Dedicated Funds	$90,709,700	$301,000	$91,010,700
Federal Funds	$264,115,000	$233,500	$264,338,500
Total Revenues Appropriated	$2,129,635,700	$10,979,400	$2,140,615,100
Local Funds (estimated property taxes, not appropriated)	$560,000,000	$0	$560,000,000
Total Revenues	$2,689,635,700	$10,979,400	$2,700,615,100

Source: Idaho Public School Funding. Idaho State Department of Education, public domain. By permission (2018).

revenues. At the same time, school districts and charter schools received salary and benefit (employer obligations for retirement and FICA) apportionment based on Support Units. As also indicated, the basic support program now includes a career ladder that was introduced for instructional staff in 2015–2016, with pupil service staff added in 2016–2017.[6] State general and dedicated funds are distributed to public schools according to statute.[7]

ADA, as the formula driver, is calculated from public school data submitted to the Idaho State Department of Education on a periodic basis. Two calculations involving ADA are involved: (1) pupil count from the start of the school year through the first Friday in November; and (2) pupil count across the best 28 weeks of the school year. Attendance count is defined by State Board of Education rules as a minimum 2½ hours for kindergarten pupils and a minimum of four hours for grades 1–12. ADA is then converted to Support Units,[8] with divisors taking the size of the school district's or charter school's attendance categories into account. More specifically, the larger the ADA, the larger the divisor and the reverse as ADA goes down. The result is that smaller programs require less ADA to generate a Support Unit, while larger programs require more ADA to generate a Support Unit. This calculation provides more funding per pupil for smaller schools by compensating for smaller class sizes that still require full-time staffing. Divisors also are important to how much funding is provided to grade categories. Table 13.2 provides an example of how a Support Unit ($102,100 FY 2019 estimated statewide average) results in funding distribution. Greater detail is contained in Table 13.3 which breaks down the ADA categories and divisors.

Support Units are used to calculate salary and benefit apportionment (including Career Ladder) and discretionary funds. Support Units based on the attendance period ending on the first Friday in November are used to calculate salary and benefit apportionment. Support Units based on the best 28 weeks are used to calculate discretionary funds.

Staffing is categorized into four areas of Instructional, Pupil Service, Administrative, and Classified. Instructional and Pupil Service staff are placed in a Career Ladder cohort based on FY 2015 and FY 2016 experience and

TABLE 13.2 Idaho ADA Fiscal Model for Pupil Counts FY 2019

Grade Level	Divisor	Funding
Kindergarten	40	$2,600
Elementary Grades 1–6	23 to 12	$4,400 to $8,500
Secondary Grades 7–12	18.5 to 12	$5,500 to $8,500
Exceptional Child	14.5	$7,000
Alternative Grades 6–12	12	$8,500

Source: Idaho Public School Funding. Idaho State Department of Education, public domain. By permission (2018).

TABLE 13.3 Idaho ADA Fiscal Model Pupil Counts Detail FY 2019

Computation of KDG Support Units

Average Daily Attendance	Attendance Divisor	Units Allowed
41 or more	40	1 or more as computed
31–40.99 ADA	—	1.00
26–30.99 ADA	—	0.85
21–25.99 ADA	—	0.75
16–20.99 ADA	—	0.60
8–15.99 ADA	—	0.50
1–7.99 ADA	—	Count as elementary

Computation of Elementary Support Units

Average Daily Attendance	Attendance Divisor	
(300 or more ADA)	23 grades 4, 5, & 6 20 grades 1, 2, & 3	Minimum Units Allowed 15
160–299.99 ADA	40	1 or more as computed
110–159.99 ADA	—	1.00
71.1–109.99 ADA	—	0.85
51.37–71.09 ADA	—	0.75
33.6–51.69 ADA	—	0.60
16.6–33.59 ADA	—	0.50
0.01–16.59 ADA	—	Count as elementary

Computation of Secondary Support Units

Average Daily Attendance	Attendance Divisor	
(750 or more ADA)	23 grades 4, 5, & 6 20 grades 1, 2, & 3	Minimum Units Allowed
750 or more	18.5	47
400–749.99 ADA	16	28
300–399.99 ADA	14.5	22
200–299.99 ADA	13.5	17
100–199.99 ADA	12	9
99.99 or fewer	Units as follows	
Grades 7–12		8
Grades 9–12		6
Grades 7–9		1 per 14 ADA
Grades 7–8		1 per 16 ADA

Computation of Exceptional Support Units

Average Daily Attendance	Attendance Divisor	Minimum Units Allowed
14 or more	14.5	1 or more as computed
12–13.99 ADA	—	1.00
8–11.99 ADA	—	0.75
4–7.99 ADA	—	0.50
0.01–3.99 ADA	—	0.25

Computation of Alternative Secondary Support Units

Average Daily Attendance	Attendance Divisor	Minimum Units Allowed
12 or more	12	1 or more as computed

Source: Idaho Code 330-1002 (4).

education, respectively.[9] For Administrative staff, an average Experience and Education Multiplier index[10] is generated and used to calculate salary and benefit apportionment. These average indexes and Career Ladder average salaries are the primary variables in determining a school district's or charter school's Support Unit value.

Support Units are granted Staff Allowance ratios[11] resulting in a Staff Allowance per school district: Instructional = 1.021; Pupil Service = 0.079; Administrative = 0.075; and Classified = 0.375. Calculation of these variables results in funding distribution as seen in the example in Table 13.4, where it is assumed that the school district has been granted 100 Support Units. However, school districts with less than 40 support units receive an additional 0.5 Instructional FTE and an additional 0.5 Administrative FTE. Districts with less than 20 support units receive an additional 0.5 Instructional FTE in addition to the above provisions for less than 40 support units. Further, no full-time Instructional or Pupil Service staff can be paid less than the minimum dollar amount on the Career Ladder Residency compensation rung[12] for the applicable fiscal year. Administrative and Classified staff base salaries are annually reviewed and determined by the state legislature.

Finally, school districts must hire at least the number of Instructional and Pupil Service staff in order to receive the maximum Instructional and Pupil Service Staff Allowance.[13] This requirement is commonly referred to as the 'use it or lose it' provision. Some exceptions apply. One exception is that charter schools are exempt. Also, in FY 2015 school districts could employ 9.5% less FTE than their staff allowance without penalty. Also, beginning in FY 2016 this requirement was reduced by 1% each year for any school district in which the average class size as determined from prior fiscal year data was at least one student greater than the statewide average class size. Also, virtual instructional expenses up to 15% could be applied to the allowance.

In brief, Idaho's ADA-driven basic support program defines the entitlement per ADA that a school district or charter school receives: *size* (i.e., ADA), *student mix* (i.e., grades served), and *staffing* (i.e., Experience

TABLE 13.4 Idaho Fiscal Model for Staff Ratios FY 2019

Staff Allowance	Multiplier	Count	Positions
Instructional	1.021	100	102.1
Pupil Service	0.079	100	7.9
Administrative	0.075	100	7.5
Classified	0.375	100	37.5

Source: Idaho Public School Funding. Idaho State Department of Education, public domain. By permission (2018).

& Education Multiplier). Other distributions such as pupil transportation, border contracts, exceptional contracts/tuition equivalents, bond levy equalization, and lottery are calculated according to statute and administrative rule. Special distributions such as remediation and the Idaho Reading Initiative are calculated according to appropriation bill intent language.[14]

Table 13.5 provides selected demographic and financial profiles of Idaho schools. The general fiscal model described in the last few paragraphs is evident in table form.

Table 13.6 further develops the financial profile for Idaho's public schools. Table 13.6 identifies totals for all funds on a statewide basis, indicating revenue sources and proportions of totals received and expended for the audited FY 2017 year of record. In table form, it may be seen that Idaho's school supports are derived in amounts approximating 58% from the state, 9% federal, a combined 21% local, and nearly 12% other sources for a $2.8 billion resource base in FY 2017. Expenditures in that timeframe approximated that same income stream and were distributed to an expected range of educational program supports as detailed in Table 13.6.

TABLE 13.5 Idaho Public School Demographic and Fiscal Profile FY 2017

School District Statistics (July 1, 2016–June 30, 2017)			
General Statistics	2016–2017	2015–2016	2014–2015
Local Education Agencies			
School District	115	115	115
Charter Schools (District Sponsored)	10	9	10
LEA Charter Schools	40	39	38
Fiscal Agents	1	1	1
Schools	**724**	**717**	**717**
One Teacher	12	12	12
Elementary	358	351	351
Middle	96	97	97
Secondary	125	123	122
Combined Elementary/Secondary	18	18	19
Charter	50	48	48
Alternative Secondary	53	56	56
Detention Centers	12	12	12

(continued)

TABLE 13.5 Idaho Public School Demographic and Fiscal Profile FY 2017 (continued)

School District Statistics (July 1, 2016–June 30, 2017)

	2016–2017	2015–2016	2014–2015
Employees (Actual)	38,326	37,594	37,244
Administrators (including Principals)	1,400	1,374	1,329
Classroom Teachers	17,701	17,023	17,081
Other Professionals	1,355	1,687	1,324
Non-Certified	17,870	17,510	17,510
Classroom Teacher F.T.E.	15,984	15,306	15,373
Fall Membership	298,787	294,471	291,022
Preschool Special Education	3,049	2,999	2,881
Kindergarten	21,192	21,115	21,553
Elementary	139,278	138,017	136,581
Secondary	135,268	132,340	130,007
Full-Term Average Daily Attendance (A.D.A.)	279,518.77	275,496.09	271,773.80
High School Graduates	18,053	17,432	16,923
Pupil Per Square Mile (Membership divided by 83,577 sq. miles)	3.58	3.52	3.48
Pupil/Teacher Ratio (Membership Divided by Teacher FTE)	18.69	19.24	18.93
Financial Statistics			
Revenue—All Funds Per Full-Term A.D.A.	$10,215	$9,215	$9,330
Local Sources	$2,188	$2,104	$2,045
State Sources	$5,972	$5,635	$5,407
Federal Sources	$875	$903	$882
Other Sources (Sales of Bonds, Fixed Assets)	$1,180	$573	$996
Expenditures—General M & O Fund			
Total Expenditures per Full-Term A.D.A.	$6,809	$6,443	$6,302
Current Expenditures per Full-Term A.D.A.	$6,758	$6,422	$6,251
Expenditures—All Funds			
Total Expenditures per Full-Term A.D.A.	$9,577	$9,203	$8,753
Current Expenditures per Full-Term A.D.A.	$8,279	$7,893	$7,688

Note: Odyssey Charter School closed early in the 2014–2015 school year. Odyssey Charter School did not submit their 2014–2015 financial information as required by Idaho Code 33-01. Therefore, all financial and statistical data relating to Odyssey Charter School has been excluded from their report for 2014–2015.

Source: Idaho State Department of Education, *Financial Summaries, Idaho School Districts and Charter Schools 2016–2017.* www.sde.idaho.gov

TABLE 13.6 Idaho Public School Detailed Fiscal Profile All Funds FY 2017

All Funds—Statewide Total (July 1, 2016–June 30, 2017)

	2016–2017	% of Total	2015–2016	% of Total
Revenue				
Taxes	$517,769,024	18.13%	$493,347,461	19.43%
Other Local	93,811,424	3.29%	86,337,191	3.40%
State Sources	1,669,205,498	58.46%	1,552,318,391	61.15%
Federal Sources	244,672,310	8.57%	248,738,654	9.80%
Other Sources	329,787,841	11.55%	157,996,841	6.22%
Total Revenue	**$2,855,246,097**	**100.00%**	**$2,538,738,538**	**100.00%**
Transfers in	84,501,868		42,395,427	
Total Revenue & Transfers in	**$2,939,747,965**		**$2,581,133,965**	
Expenditures				
Elementary School Program	$553,902,834	20.69%	$524,544,695	20.69%
Secondary School Program	484,571,856	18.10%	456,072,647	17.99%
Alternative School Program	33,947,160	1.27%	33,578,428	1.32%
Vocational-Technical Program	19,736,736	0.74%	17,860,549	0.70%
Special Education Program	175,404,278	6.55%	164,704,059	6.50%
Special Education Preschool Program	9,587,649	0.36%	9,212,016	0.36%
Gifted & Talented Program	9,295,746	0.35%	8,240,979	0.33%
Interscholastic Program	24,453,723	0.91%	23,047,416	0.91%
School Activity Program	5,769,224	0.21%	5,412,300	0.21%
Summer School Program	3,979,279	0.15%	3,939,007	0.16%
Adult School Program	195,357	0.01%	111,053	0.01%
Detention Center Program	1,330,906	0.05%	1,357,634	0.05%
Total Instruction	**$1,322,174,748**	**49.39%**	**$1,248,080,783**	**49.23%**
Attend./Guidance/Health Program	$64,817,601	2.42%	$58,990,208	2.33%
Special Education Support Services Program	56,226,266	2.10%	53,983,838	2.13%
Instructional Improvement Program	69,960,855	2.61%	56,996,643	2.25%
Educational Media Program	21,032,959	0.78%	20,269,671	0.80%
Instruction-Related Technology Program	29,298,076	1.09%	32,601,130	1.29%
Board of Education Program	6,312,394	0.24%	5,426,983	0.21%
District Administration Program	48,715,541	1.82%	44,865,609	1.77%
School Administration Program	127,862,252	4.78%	120,518,681	4.75%
Business Operation Program	29,378,749	1.10%	27,462,726	1.08%
Central Service Program	4,526,771	0.17%	4,946,077	0.19%
Administrative Technology Service	22,171,882	0.83%	18,155,778	0.72%
Buildings–Care Program	119,042,617	4.45%	115,101,756	4.54%
Maintenance–Bldgs. & Equip.	8,769,199	0.33%	6,834,456	0.27%
Maintenance–Student Occupied	78,281,464	2.29%	67,419,959	2.66%

(continued)

TABLE 13.6 Idaho Public School Detailed Fiscal Profile All Funds FY 2017 (continued)

All Funds—Statewide Total (July 1, 2016–June 30, 2017)

	2016–2017	% of Total	2015–2016	% of Total
Maintenance–Grounds	13,844,530	0.52%	9,779,594	0.39%
Security Program	6,693,608	0.25%	6,384,706	0.25%
Transportation–Pupil to School Program	98,516,705	3.68%	93,381,601	3.68%
Transportation–Activity Program	4,970,135	0.19%	4,640,696	0.18%
General Transportation Program	1,660,931	0.06%	1,758,112	0.07%
Other Support Services Programs	6,521,618	0.24%	5,091,272	0.20%
Total Support Services	**$818,604,153**	**30.58%**	**$754,609,496**	**29.76%**
Child Nutrition Program	$110,183,804	4.11%	$109,389,521	4.31%
Community Services Program	4,453,030	0.17%	4,561,622	0.18%
Enterprise Programs	241,903	0.01%	753,041	0.03%
Total Non-Instruction	**$114,878,737**	**4.29%**	**$114,704,184**	**4.52%**
Capital Assets Program-Student Occupied	$35,632,916	1.33%	$38,292,078	1.51%
Capital Assets Program	166,847,570	6.23%	188,100,785	7.42%
Debt Services Program–Principal	119,545,990	4.47%	100,086,173	3.95%
Debt Services Program–Interest	58,499,109	2.19%	57,193,242	2.25%
Debt Services Program–Refunded Debt	40,717,007	1.52%	34,417,424	1.36%
Total Capital Assets & Debt Services	**$421,242,592**	**15.74%**	**$418,089,702**	**16.49%**
Total Expenditures	**$2,676,900,230**	**100.00%**	**$2,535,484,165**	**100.00%**
Transfers Out	84,504,068		42,400,727	
Total Expenditures & Transfers Out	**$2,761,404,298**		**$2,577,884,892**	

MAINTENANCE AND OPERATIONS

Idaho's maintenance and operations fund is detailed in Table 13.7. Consequently, the table provides a breakdown of total historical expenditure supports not evident in the preceding tables.

SUMMARY

Significant changes have occurred in Idaho public school funding. After two decades of relative funding stability, overall spending on Idaho's public schools recently lost considerable ground—a loss that began to reverse with the most recent legislative actions. For a period of several years corresponding with removal of the equalized M&O property tax levying authority in 2006, taxpayers were required to endure unequalized property taxes, with

TABLE 13.7 Idaho Public School Detailed Fiscal Profile All Funds FY 2017

General M & O Fund - Statewide Total (July 1, 2016–June 30, 2017)

	2016–2017	% of Total	2015–2016	% of Total
Revenue				
Taxes	$304,272,560	15.44%	$297,306,495	16.18%
Other Local	41,425,930	2.10%	37,187,618	2.02%
State Sources	1,596,719,017	81.00%	1,485,338,417	80.81%
Federal Sources	9,701,761	0.49%	8,650,583	0.47%
Other Sources	10,311,767	0.52%	2,873,426	0.16%
Total Revenue	**$1,962,431,035**	**99.55%**	**$1,831,356,539**	**99.64%**
Transfers in	8,939,447	0.45%	6,628,731	0.36%
Total Revenue & Transfers in	**$1,971,370,482**	**100.00%**	**$1,837,985,270**	**100.00%**
Expenditures				
Elementary School Program	$494,649,759	25.52%	$468,753,471	25.95%
Secondary School Program	458,343,572	23.65%	433,538,833	24.00%
Alternative School Program	31,868,567	1.64%	28,842,922	1.60%
Vocational-Technical Program	14,518,039	0.75%	12,929,936	0.71%
Special Education Program	123,162,824	6.35%	113,987,887	6.31%
Special Education Preschool Program	7,293,578	0.38%	7,061,347	0.39%
Gifted & Talented Program	9,283,578	0.48%	8,171,335	0.45%
Interscholastic Program	23,419,629	1.21%	22,151,583	1.23%
School Activity Program	5,503,588	0.28%	5,150,246	0.28%
Summer School Program	2,384,748	0.12%	2,492,553	0.14%
Adult School Program	94,913	0.01%	17,299	0.00%
Detention Center Program	929,333	0.05%	1,062,784	0.06%
Total Instruction	**$1,171,452,262**	**60.44%**	**$1,104,160,196**	**61.12%**
Attend./Guidance/Health Program	$60,138,885	3.10%	$55,006,790	3.04%
Special Education Support Services Program	45,685,149	2.36%	42,278,327	2.34%
Instruction Improvement Program	39,988,088	2.06%	30,193,478	1.67%
Educational Media Program	20,704,238	1.07%	19,970,330	1.11%
Instruction-Related Technology Program	19,873,517	1.03%	20,443,951	1.13%
Board of Education Program	6,164,035	0.32%	5,389,393	0.30%
District Administration Program	44,243,305	2.28%	42,040,636	2.33%
School Administration Program	124,909,496	6.45%	117,713,113	6.52%
Business Operation Program	28,661,877	1.48%	26,827,308	1.49%
Central Service Program	3,483,795	0.18%	3,882,290	0.21%
Administrative Technology Service	16,429,707	0.85%	15,054,048	0.83%
Buildings–Care Program	117,513,377	6.06%	113,105,796	6.26%
Maintenance–Bldgs. & Equip.	4,711,457	0.24%	4,160,279	0.23%

(continued)

TABLE 13.7 Idaho Public School Detailed Fiscal Profile All Funds FY 2017 (continued)

General M & O Fund - Statewide Total (July 1, 2016–June 30, 2017)

	2016–2017	% of Total	2015–2016	% of Total
Maintenance–Student Occupied	58,998,639	3.04%	51,742,194	2.86%
Maintenance–Grounds	11,902,981	0.61%	8,600,152	0.48%
Security Program	5,665,102	0.29%	5,295,898	0.29%
Transportation–Pupil to School Program	93,376,595	4.82%	89,355,718	4.95%
Transportation–Activity Program	4,417,894	0.23%	4,082,484	0.23%
General Transportation Program	1,521,271	0.08%	1,684,289	0.09%
Other Support Service Programs	4,505,338	0.23%	3,737,991	0.21%
Total Support Services	**$712,894,746**	**36.78%**	**$660,565,465**	**36.57%**
Child Nutrition Program	$1,690,406	0.09%	$1,515,535	0.09%
Community Services Program	873,448	0.04%	952,021	0.05%
Enterprise Programs	32,460	0.00%	29,454	0.00%
Total Non-Instruction	**$2,596,314**	**0.13%**	**$2,497,010**	**0.14%**
Capital Assets Program–Student Occupied	$3,487,898	0.18%	$986,231	0.05%
Capital Assets Program	7,028,243	0.36%	1,682,109	0.09%
Debt Services Program–Principal	3,665,871	0.19%	3,231,183	0.18%
Debt Services Program–Interest	2,171,466	0.11%	1,894,153	0.11%
Debt Services Program–Refund Debt	0	0.00%	0	0.00%
Total Capital Assets & Debt Services	**$16,353,478**	**0.84%**	**$7,793,676**	**0.43%**
Total Expenditures	**$1,093,296,800**	**98.19%**	**$1,775,016,347**	**98.26%**
Transfers Out	35,009,335	1.81%	31,400,707	1.74%
Total Expenditures & Transfers Out	**$1,938,306,135**	**100.00%**	**$1,806,417,054**	**100.00%**

Source: Idaho State Department of Education, *Financial Summaries, Idaho School Districts and Charter Schools 2016–2017.* www.sde.idaho.gov

evident disparities in funding capacity. Recent changes, however, have reversed those trends, inviting the observation that Idahoans' traditional support for public schools is vibrant.

Idaho's longstanding school finance formula, however, is under constant review and proposals for change. Currently study is underway which may change the fundamental nature of the funding structure. While nothing is yet decided, the following observations are up to date in Idaho's thinking. In September 2018 the legislature's Public School Funding Formula Interim Committee unveiled a draft of a new formula stemming from three years of hearings and testimony. The draft was based on 2018 funding levels, with the most dramatic feature being abandonment of the current ADA-based model in favor of an enrollment-based formula. Highlights of the discussion, led by the Education Commission of the States (ECS), have included additional funding for at-risk students, English language learners, special education and gifted and talented students along with additional funding protection for small schools whereby elementary schools with enrollments of 330 or less and high schools with enrollments of 840 or less would receive increases. Likewise, minimum funding for Idaho's smallest school districts was proposed for districts with 30 or more pupils and including a hold-harmless regardless of whether enrollment actually reaches the minimum. The proposal also folded 17 existing budget line items the new formula, while pulling out 15 others—those 17 line items in the new formula would account for about 90% of all funding. Excluded were funding for transportation, technology, building maintenance, teacher leadership premiums, and literacy funding. Barriers to adoption appear to relate to the specific weights to be applied for funding special education and at-risk pupils, determining how to count at-risk pupils, fractional enrollment for students attending more than one school either through homeschooling or virtual education. If the proposal passes, the committee has recommended holding all school districts harmless until the 2023–24 school year when the new formula would be fully implemented.[15]

NOTES

1. No state-based expert was available to author this chapter at time of publication. Julie Oberle and Tim Hill in the Idaho Department of Education helpfully provided data. The chapter is drawn from multiple sources as footnoted and represents the editorial staff's interpretation of issues, trends and findings regarding the state of Idaho. For additional information and detail, contact the Idaho Department of Education.
2. Idaho Constitution, Article IX § 1.
3. Idaho Center for Fiscal Policy. *Idaho Public School Funding 1980–2013*. Boise, ID (2013). Retrieved from idahocfp.org
4. Ibid.
5. Betsy Russell, "Idaho School Budget Set with 5.9 percent Increase for Next Year; No Rancor or Dissent." *The Spokesman-Review.* (February 19, 2018). Retrieved from http://www.spokesman.com/stories/2018/feb/19/idaho-school-budget-set-with-59-increase-for-next-/
6. Deborah Verstegen, "Idaho." *A Quick Glance at School Finance: A 50 State Survey of School Finance Policies 2018.* Retrieved from; https://schoolfinancesdav.wordpress.com
7. Title 33, Chapter 10, Idaho Code.
8. §33-1002 (4), Idaho Code.
9. §33-1004B, Idaho Code.
10. §33-1004A, Idaho Code.
11. §33-1004, Idaho Code.
12. §33-1004B, Idaho Code.

13. §33-1004 (2), Idaho Code.
14. Idaho Public School Funding. Idaho State Department of Education (2018).
15. Clark Corbin. "School Funding Formula Draft Released. *Idaho Education News*. (2018). Retrieved from https://www.idahoednews.org/news/new-school-funding-formula-draft-released/

CHAPTER 14

Illinois

Michael A. Jacoby
Executive Director/CEO
Illinois Association of School Business Officials

Benjamin Boer
Deputy Director
Advance Illinois

Melissa Figueira
Policy Associate
Advance Illinois

GENERAL BACKGROUND

Article X, Section 1 of The Constitution of the State of Illinois,[1] as amended in 1970, sets forth the primary goals for the funding of public education. It simply states:

> A fundamental goal of the People of the State is the educational development of all persons to the limits of their capacities. The State shall provide for an efficient system of high quality public educational institutions and services. Education in public schools through the secondary level shall be free. There may be such other free education as the General Assembly provides by law. The State has the primary responsibility for financing the system of public education.

Funding Public Schools in the United States and Indian Country, pages 177–192
Copyright © 2019 by Information Age Publishing
All rights of reproduction in any form reserved.

TABLE 14.1 Distribution of Public School Supports Fiscal Year 2017

Year	State $	State %	Local $	State %	Federal $	Federal %	Total $
2017	$11,670.40	35.6	$17,552.80	53.5	$3,602.60	11	$32,825.80

Note: State contribution includes the employer contributions (normal cost and unfunded liability payments) to the state teacher retirement system.

Four key elements to Article X are:

1. The education development of all persons shall allow them to succeed to the "limits of their capacities."
2. The system of public education shall be "efficient."
3. The system of public education shall be "high quality."
4. The "primary responsibility for financing the system" lies with the state, not the local district.

While simple in concept, achieving these key elements has long been elusive for Illinois. Legal attempts to challenge the state's funding system for public education have been unsuccessful due to the opening phrase, "A fundamental goal..." Since a goal is something to be reached in the future, courts have not embraced a suit in equity that would order the legislature to accomplish its goal. Therefore, state spending on education in Illinois provided only 35.6% of all funds for public schools in Fiscal Year 2017, thereby hindering the ability to achieve equitable or adequate educational opportunities for all children (see Table 14.1).[2]

GENERAL FUND APPROPRIATIONS

As detailed in Table 14.2, the Illinois State Board of Education has organized its General Fund appropriations around five principal purposes. Below are the FY 2018 allocations.[3]

BASIC SUPPORT PROGRAM

Decades of advocacy efforts culminated in August 2017 with passage of legislation overhauling Illinois' historically regressive education funding system. Senate Bill 1947 was signed into law on August 31, 2017, becoming *The Illinois Evidence-Based Funding for Student Success Public Act*.[4] The Act put in place a formula that prioritizes equity and allocates state funding to school districts based on pupil needs.

TABLE 14.2 Illinois School Finance Program Elements FY 2018

General Funds	Funding Focus:	FY 2018 Appropriation (in thousands)	% of Total Appropriation
Equity	EBF, Sp Ed, CTPF, Categorical, Early Childhood, Lunch/Breakfast, Truant, Alternative, etc.	$8,053,780.0	98.17%
Quality	Assessments, CTE, Intervention, School Support, etc.	104,568.9	1.27%
Community	After-School, After-School Matters, District Consolidation	22,010.1	0.27%
Educator Recruitment and Recognition	Teach for America, National Board Cert, Mentoring	2,157.4	0.03%
Agency Capacity	Employee Salaries, Benefits, Administration, Operations	21,526.4	0.26%
Total		$8,204,042.8	100.00%

Note: The focus of this chapter is primarily on the Equity line above, which embraces 98.2% of state spending of education.

The new Evidence Based Model (EBM) calculates the cost of a high-quality and highly effective education comprised of interventions having proven impact on student progress. This model has been used as the basis of funding formulae in at least six states. Illinois now uses the EBM as the backbone for its new funding formula by providing a funding target that more accurately captures the necessary funding need from both state and local sources for each individual district.

Following is an overview of the components of the adequacy and distribution methodologies developed for Illinois based on the EBM, now referred to as the Evidence-Based Formula (EBF). There are four major components to the formula:

- A unique *adequacy target* is calculated for each school district in the state, representing the amount of local and state funding students need to receive a high-quality education;
- Each district's *local capacity* is calculated, representing the amount each district can contribute toward its adequacy target from local resources. This is a combination of a calculated contribution target and a proportion of the amount that the district currently raises above its contribution target;
- The formula determines how adequately funded a district currently is via state and local funding or its *percent of adequacy*;
- Finally, the *distribution method* drives equity by pushing new state dollars to those districts calculated to be the least adequately funded.

Calculating the Adequacy Target

The EBF calculates a funding target for each district based on the overall cost of providing a set of research-based interventions, or 'essential elements,' shown by the research literature to positively impact student learning. The cost of staffing and programming for these elements is applied to each district based on demographics to determine a district-specific Adequacy Target that reflects unique student needs.[5] The Adequacy Target provides the foundation for the way state funding is appropriated and distributed.

The list of essential elements is derived from the Evidence-Based Adequacy Model. Responsibility for regularly tailoring these elements to Illinois and determining future costs of delivering programming lies with a professional review panel composed of educators, the Illinois State Board of Education, and members of state educational associations and the General Assembly. The 34 essential elements for the Illinois formula currently include the data shown in Table 14.3.

The process of calculating each district's Adequacy Target causes the model to account for regional variation in cost through application of a Regionalization Factor to each district's calculated raw costs for staffing and programming. This factor is based on the Comparable Wage Index[6] (CWI) which reflects systematic variations in the salaries of college-educated workers who are not educators. Application of such an index reflects the differences in competitive wages across geographical units and time. The CWI for Illinois is normalized each year, using the average weighted index (weighted by average student enrollment or ASE) for the state.

To adjust for dramatic differences in wages between neighboring counties, the formula calculates a Regionalization Factor for each district, using the greater of a county's actual CWI value and the weighted average of the county's CWI and those of its adjacent counties. Additionally, the Regionalization Factor has a floor of 0.9. While regionalizing the Adequacy Target ensures that educators can compete with members of other professions within their county, it was critical to include a lower boundary in order to allow counties to compete with other areas across the state to hire and retain high-quality educators.

Calculating Percent of Adequacy

Once the Adequacy Target has been calculated for each district, the next step to distributing funds is to calculate how well-funded each district currently is, including both the amount of revenue a district can raise in local funds and the amount the district currently receives in state funding.

TABLE 14.3 Evidence-Based Elements in the Illinois Aid Formula

Evidence-Based Elements		PK–5	6–8	9–12
Core FTE		*(per enrolled)*	*(per enrolled)*	*(per enrolled)*
Core Teachers K–3 (Low Income)	Class Size	15		
Core Teachers K–3	Class Size	20		
Core Teachers 4–8 (Low Income)	Class Size	20	20	
Core Teachers 4–8	Class Size	25	25	
Core Teachers 9–12 (Low Income)	Class Size			20
Core Teachers 9–12	Class Size			25
Specialist Teachers	% of Core	20.00%	20.00%	33.33%
		(per enrolled)	*(per enrolled)*	*(per enrolled)*
Instructional Facilitators (Coaches)	1 FTE per	200		
Core Intervention Teachers	1 FTE per	450		
Substitutes		33.33% of average salary		10 for @ FTE
		(per enrolled)	*(per enrolled)*	*(per enrolled)*
Core Guidance	1 FTE per	450	250	250
Nurse	1 FTE per	750	750	750
Supervisory Aides	1 FTE per	225	225	200
Librarian	1 FTE per	450	450	600
Library Aide/Media Tech	1 FTE per	300	300	300
Principal	1 FTE per	450	450	600
Asst. Principal	1 FTE per	450	450	600
School Site Staff	1 FTE per	225	225	200
Per Student				
Gifted	$ per enrolled	$40		
Professional Development	$ per enrolled	$125		
Instructional Materials	$ per enrolled	$190		
Assessment	$ per enrolled	$25		
Computer Technology	$ per enrolled	$285.50	+ $285.50 Tier 1 & 2	
Student Activities	$ per enrolled	$100	$200	$675
Central Services				
Maintenance and Operations	$ per enrolled	$1,038	*Salary Portion = $352.92*	
Central Office	$ per enrolled	$742	*Salary Portion = $368.48*	
Employee Benefits	30% of Salary	30%	+ Norm Cost if applicable	
Diverse Learners		*(per enrolled)*	*(per enrolled)*	*(per enrolled)*
Intervention (Poverty) (DHS count)	1 FTE per	125	125	125
Intervention (EL) (EL count)	1 FTE per	125	125	125
Pupil Support (Poverty)	1 FTE per	125	125	125
Pupil Support (EL)	1 FTE per	125	125	125
Extended Day (Poverty)	1 FTE per	120	120	120
Extended Day (EL)	1 FTE per	120	120	120

(continued)

TABLE 14.3 Evidence-Based Elements in the Illinois Aid Formula

Evidence-Based Elements		PK–5	6–8	9–12
Summer School (Poverty)	1 FTE per	120	120	120
Summer Sch (/EL)	1 FTE per	120	120	120
English Learners (EL)	1 FTE per	100	100	100
Special Ed Teachers	1 FTE per	141	141	141
Psychologist	1 FTE per	1,000	1,000	1,000
Special Ed Instructional Asst	½ FTE per	141	141	141

Determining Local Capacity

Calculation of Local Capacity in the new EBF is intended to accurately account for the amount districts can contribute.

Given budget crises, chronic underfunding, and years of proration, many districts have had to raise property tax rates to offset the lack of reliable and sufficient education funding from the state. Exclusive to state teachers' pension contributions, the state of Illinois contributes 26% of school funding, while local taxes comprise 66% of funding.[7] The national average for state contribution to public schools is closer to 50%. The new formula aims to gradually shift the dynamic in Illinois over time to greater reliance on state funding in order to align more closely with the national average.

The new formula calculates local funding based on both an ideal for each district's local contribution (called the Local Capacity Target [LCT]) and the actual amount each district currently collects in local tax revenues (Real Receipts).[8] The goal of employing a target for calculating local contribution is to work to normalize local contribution across the state. The Local Capacity Target for each district is calculated as follows:

- The formula first creates a Local Capacity Ratio, which is the ratio of a district's Adjusted Equalized Assessed Valuation (AEAV)[9] to the district's Adequacy Target. The Local Capacity Ratio acknowledges both local need and ability to pay, such that the higher a district's EAV, the higher its ratio, and conversely, the larger a district's adequacy target, the smaller its ratio will be.
- In order to standardize the Local Capacity Ratio across school district types,[10] the ratio is adjusted to reflect the number of grades a district serves. Unit districts serve 13 grades, elementary districts serve nine grades, and high school districts serve four grades. To standardize across types, the ratio is therefore multiplied by 9/13 for elementary districts and 4/13 for high school districts.
- To translate the district's Local Capacity Ratio into the percent of adequacy to be funded locally, districts' ratios are then placed on

a normal 'cumulative distribution.' The cumulative distribution is calculated based on the weighted average and weighted standard deviation of the adjusted Local Capacity Ratio for all districts.[11] Placing the Local Capacity Ratio on a cumulative distribution allows for the calculation of the percentile of the ratio for each district.
- The Local Capacity Percentage yielded by placing districts' ratio on the cumulative distribution is then multiplied by the district's Adequacy Target to produce the district's Local Capacity Target.

Using a calculated Local Capacity Target provides a goal for local contribution that works towards normalizing tax rates in the state. However, the primary goal of the formula is to ensure that funding flows to those districts that are currently the least adequately funded. For this reason, the Local Capacity Target is adjusted to consider the amount a district currently receives in local funding, while the Local Capacity Target is treated as a target or goal that districts can work toward over time. For those that collect Real Receipts below their target, the formula uses their LCT. For those districts that collect Real Receipts above their LCT, their real receipts are adjusted downward toward their target to create an Adjusted Local Capacity.

The implication of this adjustment is that high-tax, low-spending districts will have the potential to lower their tax levies to reflect the rates expected by the formula. This potential reduction in tax levy is enhanced by inclusion of a property tax relief fund that provides grants to districts that lower their tax levies. At the same time, districts taxing below their LCT would be able to raise taxes to the calculated amount without impacting their allocation of new state dollars.

The formula makes adjustment to the Local Capacity Target in the following manner and as shown in Figure 14.1.

- Calculates the difference between each district's Real Receipts and their Local Capacity Target;
- Multiplies gap between Real Receipts and Local Capacity Target by district's Local Capacity Percentage;
- Adds that product to district's Local Capacity Target to yield Adjusted Local Capacity.

This dynamic approach to local capacity allows for a more realistic assessment of the ideal funds that could come from local property taxes, but at the same time, it recognizes a portion of receipts already available to fund a district's adequacy target.

Also included in the sum of a district's existing local resources is Corporate Personal Property Replacement Tax (CPPRT). CPPRT is considered local revenue and is based on the corporate personal property tax the district

> **To Recap:**
> Local Capacity = **A. Local Capacity Target (LCT)**, if Real Receipts < LCT
> or
> **B. Adjusted Local Capacity (ALC)**, if Real Receipts > LCT
>
> **Local Capacity Target (LCT)** = Adequacy Target × **Local Capacity Percentage**
> **Local Capacity Percentage** = Conversion of **Local Capacity Ratio** into cumulative distribution
> **Local Capacity Ratio** = (Adjusted EAV / Adequacy Target) × grade level adjustment
> **Real Receipts Adjustment** = (Real Receipts − LCT) × **Local Capacity Percentage**
> **Adjusted Local Capacity (ALC)** = **LCT** + **Real Receipts Adjustment**

Figure 14.1 Evidence-Based Elements in the Illinois Aid Formula.

received prior to the elimination of the personal property tax in 1979. For purposes of the funding formula, the prior year CPPRT distribution from the Illinois Department of Revenue is utilized.

ESTABLISHING BASE FUNDING MINIMUM

The next calculation required by the formula is determining the amount a district currently receives in state funding. Built into the new funding formula is a provision that no district will receive less state funding than was received in the immediately preceding fiscal year. This amount is referred to as a district's Base Funding Minimum (BFM). State revenues per-district from the following sources comprise the Base Funding Minimum: General State Aid (all components); Bilingual or ELL; Special Education Personnel; Funding for Pupils Requiring Special Education Services (Child Funding); and Special Education Summer School. The BFM acts as a guarantee that every district will receive at least the same amount in state funds as it received in the preceding fiscal year. Additional state funding beyond Base Funding Minimum is allocated from the formula in Year 1 based on need. In the next year, the same calculation is repeated, but Base Funding Minimums for Year 2 also include any new funds distributed in Year 1. This means that no district will ever lose money from the state.

It is important to note that the BFM is per-district rather than a per-pupil hold-harmless based on enrollment. Declines in enrollment are still taken into account in calculating a district's Adequacy Target, but a district-level hold- harmless provision protects districts with declining enrollments from seeing dramatic declines in state funding, even if the district is still far from reaching adequacy.

Adequacy Calculation

When calculating adequacy, recognition of additional costs associated with concentrated poverty is included in the essential element of 'class size.' When calculating the cost of this element, the formula accounts for smaller class sizes based on a district's low-income percentage (i.e., for K–3, 1 FTE per 15 low-income students and 1 FTE for every 20 non-low-income students; for 4–12, 1 FTE for every 20 LI students and 1 FTE for every 25 non-LI students).

Base Funding Minimum

Calculation of prior year allocation of state funds used to determine a district's Base Funding Minimum includes funds previously distributed to districts through the poverty supplemental grant. In order to avoid penalizing low-income districts when the system is not adequately funded, the poverty supplemental is discounted when used in the formula by the degree to which the district is adequately funded. This reduces the amount of state funding recognized by the formula and therefore provides more dollars to low-income districts.

Percent of Adequacy

By summing a district's Local Capacity, CPPRT, and its Base Funding Minimum, (i.e., adding together a district's expected local resources and current state funding to find its total amount of 'Preliminary Resources') each district's distance from its Adequacy Target, or its 'Percent of Adequacy' can be calculated. This is done by dividing the district's Preliminary Resources by its Adequacy Target. Districts with a low Percent of Adequacy are the least well-funded or the farthest away from their Adequacy Target. The closer a district's Percent of Adequacy is to 100%, the district is regarded as more adequately funded.

A Dynamic Distribution Methodology

The Percent of Adequacy forms the basis for the distribution methodology, which is designed to reduce the gap between current spending and adequacy for all districts over a period of several years. Those districts that are the least adequately funded (i.e., those having the lowest Percent of Adequacy) receive the majority of new state funds. The amount of time it takes to bring all districts to adequate funding levels is dependent on the amount of new revenue appropriated for education each year.

Based on its Percent of Adequacy, each district is assigned to one of four tiers for funding. A fixed percentage of all new state funds is allocated to each of these four funding tiers. According to the tier into which a district is placed, it then receives funding at a certain percentage of its 'Funding Gap.' A district's funding gap is equal to the district's assigned Tier's Target Ratio times the district's Adequacy Target minus the district's Preliminary Resources. The percent of each tier's funding gap to be filled through the distribution formula is referred to as the Tier's 'allocation rate.' The amount of new funding distributed to each tier is equal to the tier's Funding Gap multiplied by its allocation rate. It is important to note that the Funding Gap is different for each tier. For example, a district in Tier 1 will have a funding gap based on the distance between its funding level and the Tier 1 target ratio and will have another gap between its funding level and 90% of its adequacy target (90% being the Target Ratio of Tier 2). The criteria for placement into each of these tiers as well as the allocation methodology for each is described in Table 14.4.

A Distribution Method that Prioritizes Equity

Under this new formula, education funding could be distributed in one of two ways: either each district could receive funding at a certain percent of their gap to reaching a funding target, or funding could be prioritized to those districts farthest from their target amount by first flowing dollars to those districts farthest from adequacy (basically 'fill from the bottom'). The

TABLE 14.4 Illinois School Funding Tier Structure

	Placement Criteria	Allocation
Tier 1	Includes districts that are the least well-funded. These are all districts below the Tier 1 Target Ratio. This ratio is set dynamically and is based on expending all Tier 1 dollars to close the Funding Gap by each district by 30%. Since determining this value requires calculating the gap closing for each district, it uses an approach called Goal Seek which tries different values for the Target Ratio and then sets the Target Ratio based on that value that uses all the Tier 1 funds.	Tier 1 districts receive 50% of new state dollars. Since these districts are the least well-funded, they receive the greatest amount of new state funding.
Tier 2	Includes all districts with an Adequacy Level below 90% (which means it also includes all Tier 1 districts).	Tier 2 districts receive 49% of new state dollars.
Tier 3	Includes districts with an Adequacy Level between 90% and 100%.	Tier 3 districts receive 0.9% of new state dollars.
Tier 4	Includes districts with an Adequacy level above 100%	Tier 4 districts receive 0.1% of new state dollars.

method in the Illinois Evidence-Based Formula is actually a combination of these two approaches. Since the state bears responsibility for ensuring that all districts are supported in progressing toward adequacy, districts in Tiers 3 and 4 receive funding at a certain percentage of their adequacy target, while districts in Tier 2 receive funding based on their gap to 90% of adequacy. But since Illinois is notorious for having the least equitable education funding system in the nation, the formula uses a 'fill from the bottom' approach for districts in Tier 1, so that districts farthest from their Adequacy Target receive funding to fill a greater proportion of their gap.

Minimum Funding Level and Under-Appropriation

The Minimum Funding Level serves as a mechanism to ensure that the least well-funded districts are receiving the most funding. In a scenario where there is only a small amount of new dollars appropriated, those dollars will be directed to the least well-funded districts. The Minimum Funding Level is set by legislation at $350 million per year. Failure on the part of the state to provide this minimum amount triggers an adaptation to the distribution formula which protects Tier 1 dollars and broadens the set of districts in Tier 1. In this case, the Tier 1 allocation rate is adjusted to 30% multiplied by the ratio calculated by dividing the New State Funds by the Minimum Funding Level.

The formula also adjusts if the state appropriation is less than the amount needed to fund the Base Funding Minimum. In this case, districts in Tier 3 and 4 have their funding reduced to the FY 2017 level (if required). If funding needs to be further reduced, it is done on a dollar-per-pupil basis across all districts. For FY 2018, Total Evidence Based Funding allocation was set at $6.5 billion.

CATEGORICAL FUNDING OUTSIDE THE EVIDENCE-BASED FORMULA

Transportation

School boards of community consolidated districts, community unit districts, consolidated districts, consolidated high school districts, optional elementary unit districts, combined high school unit districts, combined school districts if the combined district includes any district which was previously required to provide transportation, and any newly created elementary or high school districts resulting from a high school unit conversion, a unit to dual conversion, or a multiunit conversion if the newly created district includes any area that was previously required to provide transportation shall provide free transportation for pupils residing at a distance of 1½ miles or more from any school to which they are assigned for attendance maintained within the district, except for those pupils for whom the school board shall certify to the State Board of Education that adequate transportation for the public is available. Further, each school board may provide free transportation for any pupil residing within 1½ miles from the school attended where conditions are such that walking constitutes a serious hazard to the safety of the pupil due to vehicular traffic, effective on the date that the Illinois Department of Transportation grants written approval.[12]

Reimbursement of regular and vocational transportation costs is based on the total cost of operation (adjusted for depreciation) minus local tax revenues (20% minimum threshold) and fees. Reimbursement is prorated if insufficient funds are allocated by the General Assembly. The proration for FY 2018 was approximately 84% compared to 71% in FY 2017. Total FY 2018 allocation was $263 million. Separately, special education transportation costs are reimbursed based on 80% of actual costs and prorated based on appropriation. The proration for FY 2018 was 91% compared to 92% in FY 2017. Total FY 2018 allocation was $387.6 million.

Special Education

Previous special education funding lines for personnel reimbursement ($9,000 per FTE licensed special education teacher and $3,500 per FTE special education paraprofessional and per-pupil funding for students receiving special education services and special education summer school) were absorbed into the Base Funding Minimum calculation under the EBF. Future distributions will be made based on student enrollment through the EBF. Additional special education allocations include:

- *Orphanage Tuition:* Reimburses school districts for per-pupil education cost and approved transportation costs to provide special education service to children residing in orphanages, children's homes, foster families, or other state-owned facilities. Total FY 2018 allocation was $17 million.
- *Private Tuition*: Tuition rates are managed by a Purchased Care Review Board and apply only if the approved cost to educate a student exceeds two times the general per-capita cost for all students (calculated annually in the audited Annual Financial Report). This item was prorated at 90% for FY 2018 compared to 96% in FY 2017. Total FY 2018 allocation was $135.3 million.
- *Special Education Transportation*: (see transportation section above).

English Learners

The program formerly referred to as the Bilingual Grant has been folded into the Base Funding Minimum calculation under the EBF. Future distributions will be made based on the number of students designated as English Learners in each school district through the EBF. Programs are still required to file a grant application in order to retain and receive funding. It is noted that the General Assembly added $29 million to this line prior to folding into the EBF for the purpose of eliminating proration prior to starting the new funding formula.

Early Childhood Education

Early Childhood programs provide resources for early childhood and family education programs. These state and federally funded programs include Preschool for All, Prevention Initiative, and Preschool Development Expansion Programs. Local programs must apply in order to receive funding for Early Childhood programs. The total FY 2018 allocation was $443.7 million.

STATE FUNDING FOR CHARTER SCHOOLS

Charter schools in Illinois are established either by agreement with a local school district or by an Illinois State Charter School Commission. Funding for charters is driven by a Per Capita Tuition Charge (PCTC) which is calculated for each school district in an audited Annual Financial Report. Funding must be within a range of 97%–103% of PCTC. If a charter is established by approval of a local school district board of education, the district submits payment to the charter based on the percent of PCTC required by the agreement. A charter school established by the Illinois State Charter School Commission receives funding directly from the Illinois State Board of Education, with that same amount deducted from state funding allocated to the district in which the charter resides.

TEACHER RETIREMENT

There are three public school retirement systems in Illinois. All three are currently defined benefit programs; however, a new hybrid system (Tier 3) is under development and is likely to be implemented in FY 2020.

- The Teacher Retirement System (TRS) qualifies for Social Security exemption and is for school district employees who are in positions requiring licensure. This includes teachers, local school administrators and central office administrators. There are two active tiers in this system, but for both tiers, the employee contributes 9.0% of salary. Tier 1 includes all applicable employees hired before January 1, 2011, and Tier 2 covers all who were hired on or after that date. Tier 2 is similar to a Social Security benefit, and Tier 1 benefits include an annual compounded cost of living adjustment equal to 3% annually. The State of Illinois is responsible for paying the employer contribution (normal cost), which for FY 2018 was 10.1%. Local school districts contribute 0.58%. In addition, the State of Illinois is responsible for any unfunded liability from prior years. This has grown to a significant amount, and a 50-year ramp was approved in 1994 to address this issue. TRS reports that the unfunded liability at the close of FY 2017 was $73.4 billion, resulting in significant state resources being allocated to address prior decisions to underfund the system. For FY 2017, 76.7% of the state's $ 3.99 billion contribution to TRS was dedicated to paying off a portion of the unfunded liability, and only 23.3% dedicated to the year's pension obligation.[13]
- Chicago Teachers Pension Fund (CTPF) also qualifies for Social Security exemption and operates very similarly to TRS; however, it is applicable only to teachers and administrators in the Chicago Public Schools (CPS). Beginning with FY 2018, the State of Illinois is paying the normal cost for this system, estimated at $221.3 million. This was a part of the final compromise around the Evidence-Based Funding reform. CPS continues to be responsible for the unfunded liability (approximately $11 billion at the close of FY 2017) of this system and receives a deduction to its local capacity target within the EBF to compensate for the annual use of its tax base to pay for the unfunded liability. There is also a statutory ramp for repayment of the CTPF unfunded liability.
- Illinois Municipal Retirement Fund (IMRF) covers all nonlicensed personnel working in public schools and other county and local governmental entities. This applies to all nonlicensed employees who work at least 600 hours annually. IMRF is not qualified for Social Security exemption and therefore is not connected directly to the State of Illinois. School districts pay the employer's normal cost and employees pay a fixed rate of 4.5%. A school district's employer contribution is based on the actuarial analysis of its employees and can vary year to year. Since a school district is, and has always been, required to make its annual payments, IMRF has little to no unfunded liability.

LOCAL SCHOOL REVENUE

There are two primary sources of local revenue for Illinois school districts:

- Property taxes have long been the most substantial source of funding. The property tax is initiated by an annual tax levy set by the local board of education. As noted earlier, 53.5% of all revenue comes from this source. Limits on property taxes come in two forms. (1) Statutory rate limits are set for each fund and can be increased by local referendum; and (2) a Property Tax Extension Limitation Law (PTELL) was initiated in 1991 and applied to the five collar counties around Chicago. In 1994 the new law was extended to Cook County (Chicago). The law limits the increase in property tax extensions to 5% or the Consumer Price Index, whichever is less. Other counties in Illinois may adopt the limitation by referendum. As of FY 2018, 33 counties had adopted the limit and nine counties had rejected it by referendum. Another 54 counties have yet to initiate a PTELL referendum.[14]
- Local fees can also be assessed for textbooks, various elective course related or expendable supplies, student activities, and transportation within 1½ miles of the school. Each district sets its own fees and there is significant variance across the state.

SUMMARY

With 852 school districts, Illinois is a highly diverse state. Approximately 70% of its 1.9 million pupils reside in and around the Chicago metropolitan area. There are many small rural school districts, as well as several other large districts including Peoria, Champaign/Urbana, and the metro area east of St. Louis. This diversity offers many challenges to equity and adequacy of school funding.

The latest reform replacing the general state aid formula with an evidence-based formula holds great promise for closing funding gaps across the state, both related to districts with large low-income populations and districts with little or diminishing local wealth. The goal to achieve fiscal adequacy for all school districts by the year 2027 is now statutory, but its achievement requires approximately $7.2 billion in additional funding.

For a state that has struggled to balance its own budget over the last decade, reaching this ambitious goal will be extremely difficult and will require diligent attention to future appropriations by the General Assembly. The outstanding pension liability will be a further hindrance to achieving fiscal health of the state of Illinois. However, now that the expectation for adequate funding for all students is set, there is hope for a much brighter future for revenue growth in Illinois schools.

NOTES

1. Illinois General Assembly (2018). Retrieved from http://ilga.gov/commission/lrb/con10.htm
2. Illinois State Board of Education 2017 Annual Report, p. 9. Dollars in millions.
3. Illinois State Board of Education (2018): Retrieved from https://www.isbe.net/Documents/FY_2019_Budget_Book.pdf
4. Public Act 100-0465.
5. Michelle Turner Mangan, Ted Purinton, Anabel Aportela, "Illinois School Finance Adequacy Study—Part I: A Comparison of Statewide Simulation of Adequate Funds to Current Revenues," (March, 2010).
6. L. L. Taylor, L.L., and W. J. Fowler W Jr. (2006). A Comparable Wage Approach to Geographic Cost Adjustment (NCES 2006-321). U.S. Department of Education. Washington, DC: National Center for Education Statistics.
7. NCES, Digest of Education Statistics 2016: "Revenues for Public Elementary and Secondary Schools, By Source of Funds and State or Jurisdiction: 2013–14." Retrieved from https://nces.ed.gov/programs/digest/d16/tables/dt16_235.20.asp
8. Real Receipts = Applicable Tax Rate (ATR) * AEAV, ATR = Operating Tax Rate (OTR) where OTR is prior year OTR, less transportation.
9. AEAV = 3-year average EAV, or prior EAV if prior has declined by 10% or more compared to 3-year average.
10. Illinois has three different types of school districts (elementary, high school, and unit) which serve different grade configurations. Elementary district means a school district organized and established for purposes of providing instruction up to and including grade 8; High school district means a school district organized and established for purposes of providing instruction in grades 9 through 12; Unit districts serve grades K–12.
11. Both the weighted average and weighted standard deviation are calculated by weighting the districts' Effort Index by enrollment.
12. Illinois State Board of Education (2018). Retrieved from https://www.isbe.net/Pages/Funding-and-Disbursements-Transportation-Programs.aspx
13. Teachers' Retirement System (2018). Retrieved from https://www.trsil.org/news-and-events/pension-issues/unfunded-liabilities
14. Illinois Department of Revenue (2018). Retrieved from http://www.revenue.state.il.us/localgovernment/propertytax/ptell.htm

CHAPTER 15

Indiana

Marilyn A. Hirth, Ph.D.
Associate Professor
Purdue University

GENERAL BACKGROUND

Before 1930, Indiana schools relied primarily on local revenue from property taxes, supplemented by state distributions from a dedicated common school fund and a state tax levy for special relief to districts with low taxable wealth.[1] In 1933, in order to provide poorer school districts with a proportionately greater share of state funds than wealthier districts, the state began to assume a substantial share of local school costs, distributing funds raised through a new gross income tax as tuition support on a per teaching unit basis.[2] In 1949, the Indiana legislature adopted a traditional minimum foundation type formula to fund public schools. From 1949–1973, districts were given a guaranteed minimum grant (foundation) for imposing a minimum property tax rate (called the qualifying rate) and if they did so, the state guaranteed a specified number of dollars per pupil (called the foundation).[3] Regardless of property tax wealth, each district was guaranteed at least a minimum number of dollars to spend. Consequently, wealthy districts with higher assessed valuations per pupil raised more money than poorer districts.[4]

Major reform occurred in 1973 when legislation was passed to reduce property tax rates and to slow their increase.[5] The tax reform program not only froze the property tax, but also effectively dictated to each school district the number of dollars it could raise and spend each year from its general fund.[6] Districts could request an excess levy only through approval by voter referendum.

Funding Public Schools in the United States and Indian Country, pages 193–209
Copyright © 2019 by Information Age Publishing
All rights of reproduction in any form reserved.

In 1993 the Indiana General Assembly made several changes to the foundation program. Formula revisions were the result of school finance litigation in *Lake Central School District*.[7] Agreement was reached between plaintiffs and the governor who promised to have the state legislature make changes to the funding formula if they dropped the litigation. A reward-for-effort formula was phased in over a six-year period.[8]

In 2006, the legislature adopted a 'money follows the child' formula. This meant the amount of state money available for each regular education pupil would be the same, and the school corporation educating the child would receive the money for that student. Prior to 2006, the formula had contained a minimum guarantee, whereby a school district was assured of receiving at least the same amount of money distributed through the formula in the previous year, plus a fixed percentage increase to that amount. The minimum guarantee was eliminated from the 2006 formula.[9]

Another major change to school funding occurred again in 2008 when the Indiana legislature passed Public Law 146. P.L. 146 eliminated property tax levies as a general fund revenue source for school districts. P.L. 146 also capped Indiana districts' ability to raise revenues from the local property tax without voter approval.[10] To phase in the impact of the new law, the state provided school districts with levy replacement grants in 2009 and 2010 that offset losses greater than 2% of property tax revenues. In 2011 the levy replacement grant program expired, and school districts experienced the full impact of the law. As a result, property taxes for homesteads were capped at 1%, agricultural land at 2%, and nonresidential real property at 3% of total assessed value.[11]

Due to economic recession and lower than projected sales tax revenue, in 2010 the state cut $300 million from public education, and school corporations were forced to make significant reductions in force with cuts to other areas of their budgets.[12] As a consequence of this series of formula revisions, legal challenges to the constitutionality of the state's system for funding schools ensued.[13] In *Bonner v. Daniels*,[14] the Indiana Supreme Court held the constitutional claims in the case to be without merit. In *Hamilton Southeastern et al, v. Daniels*,[15] plaintiffs dropped the case before the judge issued a ruling; plaintiffs' decision was due to changes the state legislature had made to the funding formula, paying school corporations for pupils actually enrolled and phasing out funding to corporations with declining enrollments.

In 2015, the Indiana legislature made two significant changes to the school funding formula. Full-day kindergarten was funded through Basic Tuition Support rather than by categorical grant. Starting in 2016, full-day kindergarten students counted as a full 1.0 ADM and received the full foundation amount in the Basic Tuition Support calculation.[16] Changes to the Complexity Index was a second change, transitioning from free or reduced lunch to textbook assistance, but the programs had the same eligibility criteria.[17] In 2016 and 2017, the Complexity Index was changed to be based on the percent of students in the Supplemental Nutrition Assistance Program (SNAP), the Temporary Assistance for Needy Families (TANF) program, or those receiving foster care assistance.[18]

The 2017 Indiana legislature passed HEA 1009–2017, overhauling school corporation finance reporting and budgeting effective January 1, 2019. It eliminated the General Fund, Transportation Fund, Bus Replacement, Capital Project Funds, Art Association, Historical Society, Public Playground, and Racial Balance funds. The governing body for each school corporation was ordered to establish an 'Education Fund' for payment of expenses allocated to pupil instruction and learning under IC 20-42.5. The governing body of each school corporation was required to create an 'Operations Fund' to be used by the school corporation after December 31, 2018 under IC 20-40-18-1. The operations fund was generally to be used to pay non-academic expenses, consolidating the Transportation, Bus Replacement, Capital Projects, Art Association, Historical Society, Public Playground, and Racial Balance funds and levies. The legislature also passed HEA 1167 Section 29, permitting a school corporation by resolution to transfer to its education fund or operations fund any money that had been deposited to its rainy day fund.[19]

BASIC SUPPORT PROGRAM

Indiana school funding follows a statutory formula, created and revised by the General Assembly as part of the biennium budget process as found in Indiana Code 20-43 . The Indiana General Assembly appropriates funds for state tuition support. This appropriation supports three different programs: (1) state tuition support; (2) Choice Scholarship program; and (3) the Mitch Daniels Early Graduation Scholarship program. The school funding formula only applies to state tuition support, while the other two programs operate under different parameters.[20]

State Tuition Support

The Tuition Support program is the primary source of funding. Referenda levies and other miscellaneous sources provide additional revenue. In the current funding formula, state Tuition Support represents the total of Basic Tuition Support (which provides foundation funds) and four categorical grants.[21] The base amount of funding a school corporation receives reflects the Foundation Funding Amount (adjusted for Transition to Foundation) multiplied by ADM (derived from the number of pupils attending the school corporation).[22] This amount is referred to as 'Basic Tuition Support.' Basic Tuition Support amounts are reported on a per-pupil basis unless otherwise noted.[23] When the amount of Basic Tuition Support is added to the state's current categorical grants, this amount is referred to as 'State Tuition Support.' The state's categorical grants include the Honors Grant, Special Education Grant, Career & Technical Education Grant, and Complexity Grant. This value represents total state funding provided for educational purposes.[24] A simplified version of the funding process is illustrated in Figure 15.1.

State tuition support is the sum of all of grants, i.e., the Basic Grant, the Complexity Grant, the Honors Diploma Grant, the Career and Technical Education Grant, and the Special Education Grant. State tuition support is not a pre-determined amount, but varied by a school corporation's formula results based on actual data counts.[25] Table 15.1 identifies the state appropriation for tuition supports for Fiscal Years 2014–2017. Information

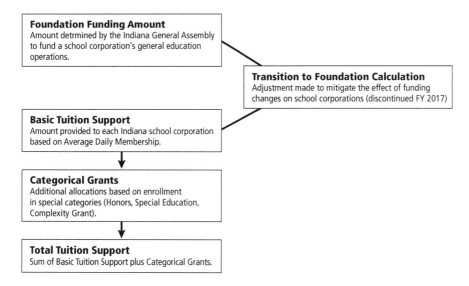

Figure 15.1 Indiana Foundation Funding Program 2015–2017 Biennium. *Source:* Sugimoto, Equity Analysis of the 2015–2017 Indiana School Funding Formula," p. 6.

TABLE 15.1 State Tuition Support Appropriations			
FY 2014	FY 2015	FY 2016	FY 2017
$6,622,800,000	$6,691,600,000	$6,820,300,000	$6,980,500,000

about each of the state tuition support grants follows afterward. The source of information was the *Indiana K–12 State Tuition Support Annual Report* (May 2017) as provided by the Indiana Department of Education Office of School Finance.

Basic Grant[26]

The Basic Grant for Fiscal Years 2014–2016 was comprised of a base amount per pupil, which consisted of the foundation amount plus a transition to foundation amount. The base amount per pupil was multiplied by the number of students to calculate the Basic Grant based on fall and spring ADM counts. Virtual charter schools received 90% of the foundation amount per pupil without a transition to foundation as part of the calculation. Charter schools were funded identically to traditional public schools, with the exception of new charter schools. New charter schools were funded at the foundation amount per pupil beginning FY 2016. The FY 2017 year basic grant was the same for all school corporations and was set at the foundation amount, with the exception of virtual charter schools which received 90% of the foundation amount. Table 15.2 shows the foundation amount for Fiscal Years 2014–2017.

Complexity Grant[27]

The Complexity Grant utilized demographic factors to provide additional funding based on each school corporation's percentage of students who met certain criteria as described for Fiscal Years 2014–2017. In FY 2014, additional funding was based on school corporations' percentages of pupils who qualified for free or reduced lunch in FY 2013, with an additional augmentation for those school corporations having a percentage of at least 33% participation. In FY 2015, complexity funding was based on the percentage of students eligible for free textbooks in 2014, with an additional augmentation for those school corporations with a percentage of at least

TABLE 15.2 Foundation Amounts[a]

FY 2014	FY 2015	FY 2016	FY 2017
$4,569	$4,587	$4,967	$5,088

Source: Indiana Department of Education Office of School Finance (May 2017).
[a] Sugimoto, Equity Analysis of the 2015–2017 Indiana School Funding Formula,"p. 8.

TABLE 15.3 Complexity Grant Totals[a]			
FY 2014	FY 2015	FY 2016	FY 2017
$1,144,499,350	$1,151,408,366	$891,554,291	$887,063,363

Source: Indiana Department of Education Office of School Finance (May 2017).
[a] Sugimoto, Equity Analysis of the 2015–2017 Indiana School Funding Formula," p. 9.

25% participation. The Complexity Index for FY 2016 and FY 2017 used the sum of the following data:

- Percentage of students qualifying for Supplemental Nutrition Assistance Program (SNAP), Temporary Assistance for Needy Families (TANF), or who received foster care services in FY 2015; plus
- A transitional percentage based on the FY 2015 year Complexity Index; plus
- An augmentation for traditional public school corporations whose complexity percentage decreased by more than one-tenth from the previous year and whose FY 2015 percentage of English Language Learners was at least 25%.

The calculation results were multiplied by $3,489 to determine the FY 2016 Complexity Grant, and by $3,539 to determine the FY 2017 Complexity Grant. Table 15.3 shows the amounts distributed for the Complexity Grant for Fiscal Years 2014–2017.

Honors Diploma Grant[28]

The Honors Diploma Grant was based on the number of pupils in the previous school year who received an academic honors diploma or a Core 40 diploma with technical honors. In FY 2014 and FY 2015, the Honors Grant provided $1,000 per honors diploma. For FY 2016 and FY 2017, the grant provided $1,400 for each student who, in the previous school year, received an academic honors diploma or a Core 40 diploma with technical honors and who also qualified for Supplemental Nutrition Assistance Program (SNAP), Temporary Assistance for Needy Families (TANF), or who received foster care services. The 2017 Honors Grant also provided $1,000 for students who received an honors diploma and did not qualify for SNAP, TANF, or receive foster care services. Indiana Code 20-43-10-2 limited use of Honors Diploma Award monies for: (1) staff training, program development, equipment and supply expenditures or other expenses related to the school's honors diploma program; or (2) programs for high

TABLE 15.4 Honors Grant Totals[a]			
FY 2014	FY 2015	FY 2016	FY 2017
$22,033,000	$23,227,000	$24,234,800	$24,711,200

Source: Indiana Department of Education Office of School Finance (May 2017).
[a] Sugimoto, Equity Analysis of the 2015–2017 Indiana School Funding Formula,"p. 10.

ability students. Table 15.4 shows the amounts distributed for the Honors Diploma Grant for Fiscal Years 2014–2017.

Special Education Grant[29]

The Special Education Grant was based on the number of special education students being served on December 1. The special education data collection was used to gather information on students receiving Special Education services on December 1 for the first required collection window and in April for the second required collection window for the school year. Table 15.5 shows the amounts distributed for the Special Education Grant for Fiscal Years 2014–2017.

Career and Technical Education Grant[30]

The Career and Technical Education Grant provided additional funding for career and technical courses. Grant amounts were based on the number of pupils, number of credit hours, and the rating given to courses. The ratings consisted of high/moderate/low need and high/moderate/low wage. For Fiscal Years 2014–2015, the grant amount was also based on number of students in other vocational programs and the number of students participating in a career and technical program in which students from multiple schools were served at a common location. In Fiscal Years 2016–2017, the 'other vocational programs' category of funding was divided into three categories: the number of students enrolled in an introductory career and technical course, the number of students enrolled in a foundational career and technical course, and the number of students enrolled in an apprenticeship, a cooperative education program, or a work-based learning

TABLE 15.5 Special Education Grant Totals[a]			
FY 2014	FY 2015	FY 2016	FY 2017
$516,903,719	$523,795,979	$544,217,100	$550,956,483

Source: Indiana Department of Education Office of School Finance (May 2017).
[a] Sugimoto, Equity Analysis of the 2015–2017 Indiana School Funding Formula,"p. 11.

TABLE 15.6 Career and Technical Education Grant Totals[a]

FY 2014	FY 2015	FY 2016	FY 2017
$98,579,175	$97,091,350	$105,821,750	$109,641,000

Source: Indiana Department of Education Office of School Finance (May 2017).
[a] Sugimoto, Equity Analysis of the 2015–2017 Indiana School Funding Formula," p. 13.

course. Table 15.6 shows the amounts distributed for the Career and Technical Grant for Fiscal Years 2014–2017.

Choice Scholarship Program[31]

The Choice Scholarship Program is Indiana's vehicle for providing state aid to pupils attending private schools. Shortly after the program was started in 2011 a group of teachers, school officials and parents who opposed vouchers sued the state on the grounds the program was unconstitutional. In March 2013 the Indiana Supreme Court ruled that, under the state's voucher program, Indiana tax dollars can be used to finance private school tuition. The vote was unanimous.[32]

Pursuant to Public Law 217-2017, I.C. 20-51, and 512 I.A.C. 4-1, the Choice Scholarship Program was passed as part of House Enrolled Act 1003-2011(Public Law 92-2011) and provides Choice Scholarships to students in households that meet eligibility and income requirements. The program provides funds to assist with payment of tuition and fees at a participating Choice school. For the 2011–2012 school year, Choice Scholarships were limited to 7,500 students. For the 2012–2013 school year, Choice Scholarships were limited to 15,000 students. Beginning with the 2013–2014 school year, the student cap was removed and Choice Scholarships were available to any student who met eligibility and income requirements. During the 2013 Session of the Indiana General Assembly, the program was further expanded to include eligibility components related to special education, siblings, and failing schools. During the 2017 session, the Pre-K Track was added.

Mitch Daniels Early Graduation Scholarship Program[33]

Pursuant to Public Law 217-2017, Indiana Code 21-12-10 allows eligible students to receive a $4,000 Mitch Daniels Early Graduation Scholarship upon meeting all graduation requirements by the end of grade 11. For FY 2017, scholarships totaling $997,380.50 were distributed to 250 students.

ENROLLMENT AND PROGRAM COUNTS

Table 15.7 shows statewide membership (ADM) counts for Fiscal Years 2014–2017 for all programs discussed so far. Figure 15.2 provides a graphic overview of the average fall and spring ADM and scholarship accounts.

TABLE 15.7 Statewide Membership Counts for FY 2014–2017[a]				
	FY 2014	FY 2015	FY 2016	FY 2017
School Corp. Fall ADM	989,696.28	988,647.02	1,024,916.24	1,027,134.65
School Corp. Spring ADM	982,965.11	982,388.84	1,020,006.00	1,022,221.38
Choice Scholarships	19,809.00	29,148.00	32,686.00	34,299.00
Mitch Daniels Early Graduation Scholarship	265.00	288.00	259.00	309.00

Source: Indiana Department of Education Office of School Finance (May 2017).
[a] Indiana Department of Education Office of School Finance, *Indiana K–12 State Tuition Support Annual Report*, 5.

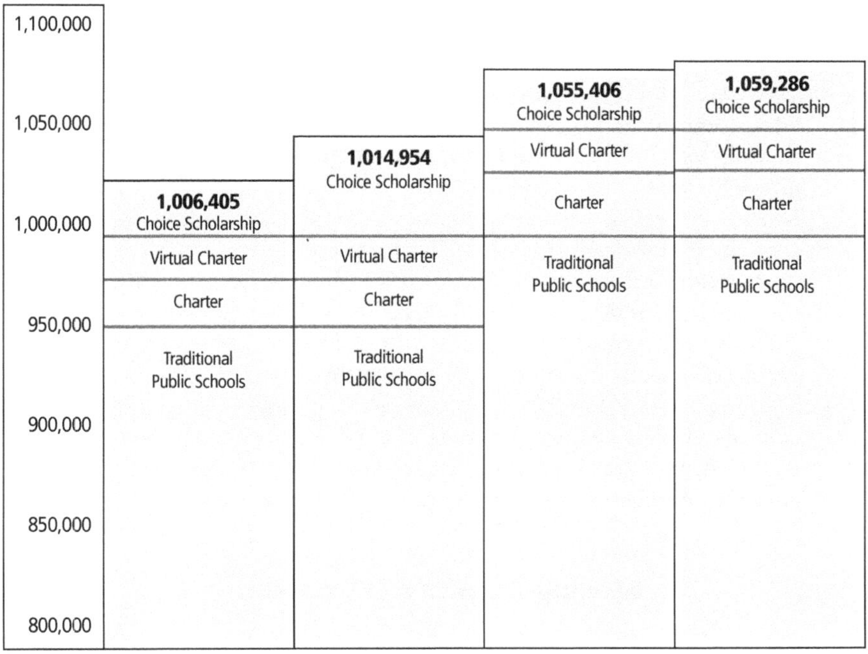

Figure 15.2 Average of Fall and Spring ADM and the Scholarship Accounts (Indiana Department of Education Office of School Finance, *Indiana K–12 State Tuition Support Annual Report*, 6). Source: Indiana Department of Education Office of School Finance (May 2017).

SOURCES OF SCHOOL SUPPORT

Practically all Indiana public school revenues are derived directly or indirectly from some taxing vehicle.[34] Dollars for state support to local public school corporations are appropriated by the Indiana General Assembly from the General Fund or dedicated funds of the state. Dedicated funds include monies from the Hoosier Lottery. Revenues to the state General Fund include monies generated by sales and use taxes, individual income tax, and corporate income taxes.[35]

Locally, various forms of taxation are used to generate monies for schools and for civil units of government. The local taxes are charged, collected, and provided to the governmental units in a more direct way than state revenues. Examples of local taxes charged include the property tax, license excise tax, commercial vehicle excise tax, financial institutions tax, and special county equalizing school taxes in Lake and Dearborn counties. Other sources of income are nontax items including receipts from transfer tuition, property sales, gifts, contributions, and earnings from investments.[36]

House Enrolled Act 1009-2017 created a significant series of changes to the fund structure for school corporations. Beginning January 1, 2019, all school corporations have two primary funds:

- *Education Fund:* The Education Fund is the primary fund through which school corporations pay for classroom expenditures. It is analogous to the general fund. School corporations do not impose a levy for the Education Fund; instead, funding for the education fund is derived from state revenues. Specifically, IC 20-40-2-2 states that the governing body of each school corporation shall establish an education fund for the payment of expenses that are allocated to student instruction and learning. As the statute is currently written, the education fund is the exclusive fund to pay for expenses allocated to student instruction and learning.[37]
- *Operations Fund:* The Operations Fund is broadly used to pay for a school corporation's non-classroom expenditures. It is a combination of the former Transportation, Bus Replacement, Capital Projects, Art Association, Historical Society, and Public Playground funds.[38]

REFERENDUM TAX LEVY FUND

The Referendum Tax Levy Fund[39] was established by the 2002 Indiana General Assembly as a separate fund. Reasons for a referendum tax levy included: (1) the governing body determines that it cannot, in a calendar year, carry out its public educational duty unless it imposes a referendum tax levy; (2) the governing body determines that a referendum tax levy should be imposed to replace property tax revenues that the school corporation will not receive because of the application of the circuit breaker credit under IC 6-1.1-20.6. Approved referendum levies are outside the circuit breaker credit calculations. In other words, schools should receive all taxes generated by the referendum tax levy. Additionally, schools may pursue a Referendum Capital Projects Debt Levy.

RAINY DAY FUND

I.C. 36-1-8-5.1 permits a political subdivision, including public school corporations, to establish a Rainy Day Fund[40] to receive transfers of unused and unencumbered funds. Excluding debt service funds and assuming the transfer is authorized by ordinance or resolution, in any year the school corporation may transfer not more than 10% of the school corporation's total annual budget for that fiscal year to the rainy day fund. The DLGF may not reduce the actual or maximum permissible levy of a school corporation as a result of a balance in the school corporation's rainy day fund.

OTHER FUNDING

In addition to the Basic Tuition Support, additional funding is provided to supplement state support of regular education programs. These include programs for gifted and talented education, non-English speaking, early intervention and reading diagnostic assessment, adult learners, National School Lunch, Teacher Appreciation, and curricular materials.

Gifted and Talented Education

Pursuant to P.L. 217-2017,[41] the purpose of this program is to support school corporation high-ability programs. The High Ability Education program includes funding to assist local schools in the development and implementation of their programs and services for high-ability students K–12. It also includes organizing and developing a state infrastructure of resources and communication for high-ability programs. Table 15.8 details the extent of participation.

TABLE 15.8 Extent of Gifted and Talented Education Participation		
Number of Grants Awarded	Individual Amounts Available	Total
312	$13,000–$147,957	$11,932,563

Note: Extent of Participation: Grants were awarded to 312 local education agencies for the 2016–2017 school year.

Non-English Speaking Program

Pursuant to P.L. 217-2017, the 1999 Indiana General Assembly enacted the Non-English Speaking Program (NESP).[42] This program provides funds to local public school corporations with a concentration of students having a primary language other than English or limited English proficiency, as determined by WIDA W-APT and ACCESS assessments.

The Indiana General Assembly increased funding for the NESP during the 2017 legislative session and added complexity to the NESP funding formula. The new legislation included a $250 base per-pupil allocation, with additional funding for local education agencies with an ELL population comprising 5% or more of total enrollment. A second layer of funding exists for those with an ELL population comprising 18% or more of total enrollment. Initial allocations for the 2017–2018 grant were based on the 2016–2017 ELL student count collected through the Language Minority (LM) report. All program funds are allocated to school corporations, with no funds retained at the state level for administration.

Early Intervention Program and Reading Diagnostic Assessment

Pursuant to P.L. 217-2017, the Early Intervention Program[43] focuses on early grade level intervention (first and second grades) to improve the reading readiness and reading skills of students who are at risk of not learning to read.

Adult Learners Fund

Pursuant to Public Law 217-2017 I.C. 20-24-7-13.5, the Adult Learners fund[44] is for charter schools serving students who are at least 22 years of age and who have dropped out of high school before receiving a diploma. State law provides a listing of charter schools eligible to receive Adult Learner funds. The appropriation funds a full-time equivalency count of students at $6,750 per pupil for the fiscal year. The charter schools specified are removed from the state tuition support formula and funded through this appropriation.

National School Lunch Program

Pursuant to P.L. 217-2017 and I.C. 20-26-9-1 thru I.C. 20-26-9-17, each school district's grant is a pro-rata share of the appropriated amount based on that district's percentage of the total paid meals served in the state during the previous school year. The amount appropriated is the required state match for participation in the National School Lunch Program.[45] Funds are distributed annually, usually in the month of October, for the previous school year. The October 2016 distribution was $4,893,199 for the 2015–2016 school year.

Teacher Appreciation Grant

Pursuant to P.L. 217-2017 and I.C. 20-43-10-3.5, the Teacher Appreciation Grant[46] (formerly known as the Annual Performance Grant) was added by HEA 1001 (the Biennial Budget) during the 2017 legislative session of the General Assembly. It awards stipends to highly effective and effective teachers in their annual evaluations. Both school corporations and charter schools are eligible for the grant, as well as entities participating in interlocal cooperatives. These stipends are based on a formula described in I.C. 20-43-10-3.5.

Curricular Material Reimbursement

Pursuant to P.L. 217-2017 and I.C. 20-33-5, the purpose of Curricular Material Reimbursement funding[47] is to provide reimbursement to school corporations, charter schools, and accredited nonpublic schools for a portion of costs incurred during a school year in providing classroom instruction to children who meet the federal free and reduced lunch standards.

CHARTER SCHOOLS

In Indiana, a charter school is a public school operating under a contract, or charter, entered into between the school's organizer and a charter school authorizer (sometimes referred to as a charter school sponsor). Under I.C. 20-24, charter schools are established to serve the different learning styles and needs of public school students; to offer them appropriate and innovative choices; to afford varied opportunities for professional educators; to allow freedom and flexibility in exchange for exceptional levels of accountability; and to provide parents, students, community members, and local entities with an expanded opportunity for involvement in the public school system.[48] Charter schools in Indiana can be authorized by any one of the following: (1) a governing body; (2) a state educational institution that offers a four-year baccalaureate degree; (3) the executive as defined in I.C. 36-1-2-5 IC of a consolidated city; (4) the Indiana Charter School Board; or

(5) a nonprofit college or university that provides a four-year educational program in which it awards a baccalaureate or more advanced degree. Unlike many states, Indiana's legislation does not place a limit on the number of charter schools that can open in the state.[49]

Charter schools receive basic tuition support from the state but do not have the authority to levy local taxes. In Indiana, funding follows the pupil. This means that, if a student chooses to enroll in a charter school, the charter school will receive state funding on a per-pupil basis in order to provide an education for that student. Similarly, if a student chooses instead to enroll in a traditional district school, the district school will receive state funding associated with that student. In this manner, the school providing education to a student is the school receiving the state funding associated with that student.[50]

TEACHER RETIREMENT

In 1995, the Indiana General Assembly shifted the teacher retirement pension responsibility from the state to local school districts. Prior to 1995, the state paid 8.5% of certified employees' salary and the school district paid 3% of those same salaries. Effective July 1, 1995, two funds were established: pre-1995 and post-1995. The pre-1995 fund included any certified employee currently on payroll; under the change, the school district contributed 3% to the TRF, with the state paying another 8% into the TRF. The post-1995 fund included all new certified employees hired after July 1, 1995, with the school district contributing 11.5% of certified employee salaries to the TRF, while the state made no reimbursement to the school district. In 2001, the General Assembly increased the school district's contribution to the post-1995 fund to 12%.[51]

TAX CREDITS, DEDUCTIONS, AND EXEMPTIONS

Circuit Breaker Credits

The Indiana General Assembly made significant changes to school finance in 2008 that affected property tax collections in 2008 and beyond.[52] I.C. 6-1.1-20.6-7.5 allowed a credit against any person's property tax liability for property taxes first due and payable after 2009. The amount of credit was the amount by which the person's property tax liability attributable to a homestead exceeded 1%; residential, agricultural, and long term care property exceeding 2%; and nonresidential real and personal property exceeding 3% of the gross assessed value of the property that is the basis for taxes for that calendar year. The exception to this limit enters when the limits to property tax liability were expected to reduce in 2010 the aggregate property tax revenue that would otherwise be collected by all units of local government and school corporations in the county by at least 20%, or when property taxes imposed in an eligible county to pay debt service or make lease payments for bonds or leases issued or entered into before July 1, 2008 are not considered for purposes of calculating the credit. If a school corporation were to pursue a referendum for operating and/or debt service, the tax rate would be outside the circuit breaker calculation. Under the act, debt service funds were 'protected funds' for circuit breaker purposes, meaning nondebt funds would receive the impact of circuit breaker credits prior to debt service funds. Units were required to fully fund debt service obligations in an amount sufficient to pay any debt service or lease rentals on outstanding obligations, regardless of any reduction in property taxes due to circuit breaker credits.

NOTES

1. Marilyn R. Holscher, "Funding Indiana's Public Schools: A Question of Equal and Adequate Educational Opportunity," *Val. U. L. Rev.* 25, no. 2 (1991), p. 288.
2. Ibid. p. 288.
3. Robert Lehnen and Carlyn Johnson, "Financing Indiana's Public Schools: Update 1989," Indianapolis, IN: School of Public and Environmental Affairs, (1989), p. 1.
4. Ibid, p. 2.
5. Carlyn Johnson and Robert Lehnen, "Reforming Indiana's School Finance Formula, 1973–1990: A Case of Unanticipated Outcomes," *Journal of Education Finance* 18, no. 3 (1993) p. 266.
6. Ibid, p. 266.
7. *Lake Central School District et al. v. State of Indiana et al.*, Newton County Circuit Court, Indiana Cause No. 56 Col-8703- CP-81
8. Marilyn Hirth and Edward Eiler," Indiana's Formula Revisions and Bonner v. Daniels: An Analysis of Equity and Implications for School Funding," *Educational Considerations* 39, no. 2(2012) p. 38.
9. Ibid, p. 39.
10. Marilyn Hirth and Christopher Lagoni, "A Demographic Analysis of the Impact of Property Tax Caps on Indiana School Districts," *Educational Considerations* 41, no. 2 (2014): 8.
11. Indiana Department of Local Government Finance, *Circuit Breaker Fact Sheet*, 2008.
12. Hirth and Eiler, "Indiana's Formula Revisions and Bonner v. Daniels: An Analysis of Equity and Implications for School Funding" p. 39.

13. See *Bonner ex. Rel. Bonner v. Daniels* 907 N.E. 2d 516 (Ind. 2009), and *Hamilton Southeastern Schools et al. v. Daniels*, Hamilton Superior Court. Cause No. 29 D01 1002 PL 198, filed February 10, 2010.
14. *Bonner ex. Rel. Bonner v. Daniels* 907 N.E. 2d 516 (Ind. 2009).
15. *Hamilton Southeastern Schools et al. v. Daniels*, Hamilton Superior Court. Cause No. 29 D01 1002 PL 198, filed February 10, 2010.
16. Thomas J. Sugimoto, "Equity Analysis of the 2015–2017 Indiana School Funding Formula", Bloomington, IN: *Center for Evaluation and Educational Policy*, (2016) p. 9.
17. Ibid, p. 9
18. Ibid, p. 10.
19. *Digest of Public School Finance in Indiana 2017–2019 Biennium*, Indianapolis, IN: Indiana Department of Education, p. 1.
20. Indiana Department of Education Office of School Finance, *Indiana K–12 State Tuition Support Annual Report*, May 2017.
21. Sugimoto, Equity Analysis of the 2015–2017 Indiana School Funding Formula," p. 1.
22. Ibid., p. 5.
23. Ibid., p. 5.
24. Ibid., p. 6.
25. Ibid., p. 14.
26. Ibid., p. 8.
27. Ibid., p. 9.
28. Ibid., p. 10.
29. Ibid., p. 11.
30. Ibid., p. 12.
31. This section is from *Digest of Public School Finance in Indiana 2017–2019 Biennium*, p. 22.
32. Scott Elliott and Tim Evans, *The Indianapolis Star*, March 26, 2013. Retrieved from: https://www.usatoday.com/story/news/nation/2013/03/26/indiana-school-voucher-ruling/2021021/
33. Ibid., p. 27.
34. This section is from *Digest of Public School Finance in Indiana 2017–2019 Biennium*: 1.
35. Ibid., p. 1.
36. Ibid., p. 1.
37. Ibid., p. 3.
38. Ibid., p. 3.
39. Ibid., pp. 6–7.
40. Ibid., p. 7.
41. Ibid., p. 30.
42. Ibid., p. 32.
43. Ibid., p. 29.
44. Ibid., p. 28.
45. Ibid., p. 31.
46. Ibid., p. 33.
47. Ibid., p. 34.

48. Indiana Charter School Board. Retrieved from: https://secure.in.gov/icsb/2447.htm
49. Ibid.
50. Ibid.
51. Denise Seger (2003). *The Impact of an Unfunded Teacher Retirement Mandate on Two Midwestern Metropolitan School Districts* (Order No. 3113869). Available from Dissertations & Theses @ CIC Institutions; ProQuest Dissertations & Theses Global. (305313941). Retrieved from: https://search.proquest.com/docview/305313941?accountid=13360
52. *Digest of Public School Finance in Indiana 2017–2019 Biennium,* 7.

CHAPTER 16

Indian Country

Alex RedCorn, Ed.D.
Osage
Assistant Professor
Kansas State University

Meredith L. McCoy, Ph.D.
Turtle Mountain Band of Chippewa descent
Royster Fellow
University of North Carolina-Chapel Hill

Hollie J. Mackey, Ph.D.
Northern Cheyenne
Associate Professor
University of Oklahoma

INDIAN COUNTRY: AN INTRODUCTION TO FINANCIAL AND BUREAUCRATIC CONSIDERATIONS[1]

Introduction[2]

Over 600,000 American Indian, Alaska Native, and Native Hawaiian students attend schools every day in every state across the United States. They attend public, private, charter, and federal government schools in rural, urban, and suburban settings, placing the responsibility for educating Indigenous students on all educational institutions. This results in an educational system where complex financial structures reach into all institutions serving Native students. This chapter introduces the financial and bureaucratic landscape, including pertinent history, associated with financing education across Indian Country.

The Indigenous peoples and nations of the United States continuously work in and across educational bureaucracies to advocate for self-determination in education for their people. Each of the more than 570 sovereign Native nations possesses an inherent right to govern its peoples and territories. At the same time, 93% of Native students attend state public schools which also share responsibility for their education.[3] This creates a complex tapestry of overlapping sovereignties, jurisdictional gray areas, and competing curricular interests that complicate contemporary Indian education. Unfortunately, these interlocking legal and curricular structures are often inscrutable to many policymakers and practitioners across federal, state, and local levels of education. The purpose of this chapter is to provide educational leaders, policymakers, and stakeholders a foundational understanding of American Indian education financing landscapes with the hope that a more thorough knowledge of these systems and their histories will facilitate more effective partnerships at all levels between stakeholders and Native nations. Furthermore, the hope is to build collective capacities to acknowledge the trust responsibility held by the federal government with Indigenous peoples and nations, while also navigating overlapping and interwoven jurisdictions and responsibilities.

This chapter presents a broad overview of diverse local contexts across Indigenous communities in the U.S., representing a range of unique perspectives and exceptionalities. For example, Alaska Natives and Native Hawaiians have unique histories and legal standing that are specific to their educational contexts and sometimes differ from Native nations whose territories are located in what is currently termed the contiguous lower 48 states. Anyone working toward developing a deeper understanding of the complex legal, political, and social contours of Indian education should resist the urge to generalize across diverse groups because understanding the local contexts of Indian education is crucial.

The chapter begins by acknowledging the perspectives of Indigenous peoples on topics relative to school finance by drawing connections to major historical moments in American Indian education and showing the relationships between land dispossessions, attempts to erase and assimilate Indigenous peoples, and educational systems. These histories are important because they provide the legal foundation upon which today's complicated financial regulations rest. After acknowledging these important foundational perspectives, the chapter offers an overview of various bureaucracies associated with financing education across Indian Country. It concludes with a list of primary bureaucracies and funding streams associated with P–12 Indian education. By acknowledging the complicated and interwoven past of Indigenous peoples and the U.S., the chapter provides a foundation for practitioners navigating entangled relationships going into the future.

Acknowledgment of Indigenous Peoples' Perspectives on Education Finance

Indian education in the U.S. should be guided by Tribal self-determination and fulfillment of federal trust responsibilities. Conversations about Indian education are often reduced to oversimplified dialogue about language and culture rather than the multifaceted sociopolitical components comprising Indian education systems. It is important to provide context that assists in developing a deeper understanding of American Indian education systems for those unfamiliar with this specific student population, the bureaucratic landscape, and its legal foundations pertinent to education finance.

Native nations of the U.S. occupy a unique position with legal roots unlike any other demographic group, as sovereign nations operating in a government-to-government relationship alongside federal, state, and local governments.[4] The U.S. Supreme Court has affirmed that tribal sovereignty originates from Indigenous peoples' inherent rights to self-governance; therefore, conversations about Indian education in the U.S. must begin by acknowledging that Indigenous peoples' participation in contemporary American education systems is a function of their unique legal status, not a special privilege granted to Native nations. Contemporary Native nations exercise self-determination in education through government-to-government negotiations, pushing back against centuries of colonialism built on conquest and erasure. Lomawaima asserts that educating Native students should be seen as a "500-year-old battle for power: first, the power to define what education is—the power to set its goals, define its policies, and enforce its practices—and second, the power to define who native people are and who they are not."[5] Negotiating and signing treaties were a key component to that battle for power as early colonists sought more land. As McCoy stated:

> When the United States of America was founded as a country, it entered into treaties with Indian tribes. It did so pursuant to the U.S. Constitution. It did so pursuant of the federal policy of recognizing Indian tribes as separate sovereign nations. And, it did so as a means of acquiring Indian land.[6]

In total, the federal government signed 370 treaties with Native nations between 1778 and 1871.[7] Many of these treaties provided educational provisions for Indigenous nations.[8] The U.S. Congress formally ended the practice of signing treaties with Native nations by passing the Indian Appropriations Act of 1871; however, this Act did not invalidate existing federal treaty obligations to Native nations. Treaties are living documents obligating the U.S. to uphold agreed-upon provisions for Indigenous peoples in perpetuity.

While this history has been well documented by historians, anthropologists, and legal scholars, non-Native education practitioners have historically paid less attention to the histories of displacement, dispossession, and deculturalization. With this in mind, it is important that those involved in education policy and practice acknowledge the following: (1) American education finance is rooted in Indigenous land dispossessions and assimilation; (2) all stakeholders are responsible for Indian education; and (3) Indigenous people have always shaped the educational experiences of their children, and schools must partner with Native nations, families, and communities moving forward.

American Education Finance Rooted in Indigenous Land Dispossessions and Assimilation

The founding of all 50 states was possible only through American Indian land dispossession. This occurred through theft, warfare, and subsequent treaties that disproportionately advantaged the U.S.[9] As a result, Henry M. Teller, Secretary of the U.S. Department of the Interior from 1882–1885, noted that education "... is not a gratuity, but a debt due the Indians."[10] Land acquired through these treaties was not only used to access natural resources, but also supported ongoing efforts of conquest through cultural erasure and deculturalization through education.[11] While federal lands held in trust are not taxable, all lands taxed for public education are Indigenous lands acquired through conquest and corresponding negotiations. In this way, school finance formulas among the states and tax bases that are tied to the land, property, and resources are inherently tied to Indigenous land dispossessions.

Corresponding to these land dispossessions and removal of Indigenous peoples, some of the earliest forms of federal education finance used contracts with religious missionary organizations to promote the assimilation of Indigenous people.[12] These contracts expected missionaries to provide agricultural and moral instruction, building on an already centuries-old legacy of forcing Indigenous people to convert to Christianity. In 1819, the U.S. Congress passed the Civilization Fund Act to contract with "... capable persons of good moral character..." to teach English reading and writing, math, and European-style agriculture. The law, which had been passed thanks in part to the lobbying of religious organizations, formally set aside funds for such groups to assimilate Indigenous people.[13] In this way, assimilation to whiteness and to Christianity became the original foundation for Indian education, and much of what occurred in the subsequent hundreds of years was aligned with this original mission. In spite of this, many Native nations today are teaching their own languages, histories, and cultures in the schools that serve their students.

The Civilization Fund Act was passed just prior to the beginning of the federal removal process for the Cherokee, Chickasaw, Creek, Choctaw, and Seminole Nations. These Nations had many of the trappings white society had told them they needed to be 'civilized'—the Choctaw nation ran its own academy, the Cherokee nation had a national newspaper, and several nations operated highly lucrative enterprises on their territories. Children of high ranking bureaucrats and diplomats often learned fluent English in their work as cultural and economic intermediaries.[14] And yet, such initiatives did not prevent dispossession when white settlers wanted their land.

Between 1823 and 1832, the U.S. Supreme Court decided three cases which forever changed the direction of relationships between Native nations and the U.S. In brief, these decisions laid the legal groundwork for American Indians to be uniquely classified as domestic dependent nations, a category first used by the Marshall Court that has since caused extensive debate in Indian law.[15] Two aspects of tribal sovereignty involving Native nations' inherent rights to self-government emerged from these cases: first, that "tribes are under the protection of the federal government" and second, that "tribes hold sufficient powers of sovereignty to shield themselves from any intrusion by the states and it is the federal government's responsibility to ensure that this sovereignty is preserved."[16] These cases have had major repercussions for how education finance works since they cement the federal government's responsibility to provide for Native nations and also clarify that their status is equal to, and not lesser than, that of the states. These developments are foundational to understanding the federal government's unique trust responsibility to the over 570 federally recognized Native nations in the U.S. This trust relationship, which includes a fiduciary responsibility for Indian education, creates an obligation for the federal government to act in ways that protect the interests of Native nations.

As the story of American 'progress' evolved during westward expansion, settlers continued to utilize education as a powerful tool for conquest that worked alongside land dispossession to establish settler control over Indigenous lands. The General Allotment Act of 1887 (also known as the Dawes Act), for instance, forced many Native nations to partition their lands into individual ownership, a practice that ultimately caused extensive Indigenous land loss and enabled settlers to overtake Indigenous lands. Today, the taxing of these same lands fuels education finance for public schools in communities across the U.S.

Temporally, this land dispossession corresponded with an increased focus on Indian education where leaders sought to solve the 'Indian problem' through assimilationist education.[17] After the end of the Indian Wars in the late 1800s, the federal government began to directly operate Indian schools, many of which were off reservation in vacant military facilities. The first of these federal boarding schools was the Carlisle Indian Industrial School, led by General Richard Henry Pratt. Pratt believed that the solution to the 'Indian Problem' was to assimilate Native children through exposure to white social norms in school classrooms, while reducing exposure to Native languages, customs, and worldviews.[18] Throughout the country, hundreds of boarding and day schools operated between the 1870s and 1970s, some of which continue today in modified form under the Bureau of Indian Education (BIE). Throughout the early history of these often militaristic schools, formal policy prohibited Indigenous languages and cultural practices. The schools primarily focused on using technical and vocational training to prepare Indigenous students to participate in the American economy at the lowest levels of the workforce.[19] Resources dedicated to this effort help paint a picture of this era—the $2,936,080 spent on the schools in 1900 when they served 21,568 students would be worth over $88 million today, or only about $4,086 per pupil for the year.[20]

By the 1920s, progressive Americans became more vocal about this approach to educating Indigenous peoples, leading to one of the most famous documents associated with Indian Education: *The Problem of Indian Administration*, often referred to as the Meriam Report. This report was a comprehensive government investigation authored by Lewis Meriam in 1928 at the Institute of Government Research (now the Brookings Institute). The Brookings Institute team (including Henry Roe Cloud, a Ho-Chunk educator) spent time with Native communities across the country gathering information for the report.[21] Researchers found that the boarding school system was extremely harmful, identifying students' lack of access to sanitary living conditions and adequate medical care, as well as school administrators' failure to create safe learning environments and the "dangerously low" amount of available funding.[22] The report constituted an indictment of the government's past methods and a formal charge to change. Indian education systems today are still working to heal the wounds of this era and to implement recommendations outlined in the report.

The Meriam Report did not represent the end of boarding schools, which continue to operate in altered form through the present, but it did represent the transition away from overtly assimilationist schooling. As Deloria and Lytle described, "by the mid-1920s... many boarding schools were being closed and day schools were being consolidated. It was the first indication at the reservation level that the government knew its goal of assimilation had been a miscalculation of major proportions."[23] As federal Indian policy began to shift its rhetoric away from assimilation (as evidenced by policies like the Indian Reorganization Act of 1934 which officially ended allotment), so did its formal policies for education.[24]

These early developments in the 1800s and into the 1900s reflect how the federal government was experimenting with its trust responsibility to Native nations. This trust responsibility continues to structure Indian education today. Its unique fiduciary responsibility is a foundational component of Indian education in the present, even though the federal government has not always adequately funded or managed it. Lack of funding for BIE facilities' construction and upkeep continues to be a frequent talking point among advocates and lawmakers, among other topics.[25] While not all funding in American Indian education stems from this trust responsibility, almost all Indian education financing, bureaucracy, and programming in and across the various systems is connected to it. The importance of respecting this history is paramount, as noted by Patsy Whitefoot, former president of the National Indian Education Association (NIEA), a national advocacy organization that has promoted Indian education since 1970:

> [R]eversing negative trends within Native education...is possible only if the federal government upholds its trust responsibility to tribes. Established through treaties, federal law, and U.S. Supreme Court decisions, this relationship includes a fiduciary obligation to provide parity in access and equal resources to all American Indian and Alaska Native students, regardless of where they attend school. It is important to state that under the federal government's trust corpus in the field of Indian education, the obligation is shared between the Administration and Congress for federally-recognized Indian tribes.[26]

All Stakeholders Are Responsible for Indian Education

While current state and federal leaders are not responsible for the education system's origins in land dispossession and assimilation, many of the system's original aims continue under their direction, often accepted as 'the way things are' or 'the way education works.' Research and scholarship continues to show how achievement gaps exist between American Indians and Alaska Natives (AI/AN) and their non-AI/AN peers (discussed in more detail below), while also outlining how curricula and policy are inherently tied to power, privilege, colonialism, conquest, and cultural erasure.[27] In addition to the federal trust responsibility for education, state governments, state education agencies (SEAs), local education agencies (LEAs), tribal governments, and tribal education departments and/or agencies (TEDs/TEAs) all have roles and responsibilities with Indian Education. While many involved in education policy and practice outside of high Indian enrollment (HIE) schools may believe that Indigenous students are not 'their problem,' in reality, *93% of American Indian children attend public schools across the nation.*[28] With over 600,000 Indigenous students in classrooms across the country, a figure which surpasses total enrollment numbers of many states, the vast majority of those students are attending rural, suburban, and urban public schools. Therefore, many policymakers and practitioners already serve Indigenous students without knowing it. Ignoring Indigenous students during financial decisionmaking, even if they occupy a very small minority of enrollments, implicates leaders in the ongoing cultural erasure occurring through educational systems.

This is not a new problem in Indian education. As early as the 1890s, Native students were beginning to attend public schools.[29] States protested, often on the basis that Native students were not their responsibility. In response, Native people brought multiple court cases against state governments to ensure that states served Native students too. Of these, *Piper v. Big Pine School District of Inyo County*[30] in 1924, *Grant v. Michaels et. al.*[31] in 1933, and *Myers v. Board of Education*[32] in 1994 are the most well-known. In *Myers*, considered by some as the '*Brown v. Board*' of Indian Country, the U.S. Supreme Court held that the federal government never intended to have sole responsibility for Indian education and that no state can deny public education to Native students on the basis of race or political status as citizens of Native nations.[33] States and local school districts are therefore also responsible for providing educational opportunities to Native youth, including identifying the financial resources to provide for that schooling.

Since most states rely primarily on property taxes for school revenues and may serve students living on reservation lands held in trust by the federal government (lands which cannot be taxed by the states in most cases), Congress passed the Johnson O'Malley (JOM) Act of 1934.[34] JOM initially allowed the federal government to contract with states to provide supplemental support for education and other services. According to the 1976 federal Task Force on Indian Education, JOM offered "...federal recognition of a continuing unique responsibility for Indian education in spite of the states' legal obligation to educate Indians just as other citizens." Its major initial impact was "...continuing tuition payments, which had been made to local school districts for decades by the federal government in lieu of property taxes for Indian education in public schools."[35] An amendment in 1936 broadened the parameters to allow the Secretary of the Interior to contract with "any state, school district, tribal organization, or Indian corporation." Still, Native nations were rarely involved in decisions about how to use such funds during the early days of the JOM program.[36]

Initially, states contracting through JOM often moved the money into their general funds since regulations were unclear and there were no requirements to provide additional programming or services for Indian students. When Impact Aid laws were introduced in the 1950s to serve the same purposes of offsetting tax-free federal lands, JOM took on a new focus that asked recipients to offer supplemental programming to meet the unique needs of Indian students. However, the practice of continuing to roll JOM monies into the general fund without supplemental services continued.[37] In other words, states and public schools often used money intended to meet the unique needs of Indian students to simply supplement their general fund while never making an effort to meet the unique needs of Indian students or provide culturally relevant education. This resulted in many social and legal protests in the 1970s to ensure the appropriate usage of JOM funds. For example, a group of parents brought this issue to court in *Natonabah v. Board of Education of the Gallup-McKinley County School District*[38] and won, with the court ruling that JOM funds should be used to "...meet Indian educational problems under extraordinary and exceptional circumstances."[39]

While progress was made, many still critique SEAs and LEAs for collecting money intended for Indian students rather than using it to help generate culturally relevant programming or curricula. Taking money intended for Indian children without consulting tribal governments, families or community members is a form of resource theft. In this form of neo-colonialism, educational leaders see money provided to Indians in a similar manner that settlers saw land a few generations before—free with no obligation. Adding insult to injury, this money represents what was promised to Native nations in exchange for that land.

As many in education finance understand, increasing money and resources can lead to improved student outcomes.[40] Too often, educational leaders have pursued funding opportunities that exist to fulfill the federal trust responsibility for American Indian students without prioritizing the culturally relevant programming particular to American Indian students for which such funding was intended. Alongside these efforts, many also overlook how culturally responsive learning improves student outcomes, and stories of American Indian student performance nationwide have been well documented.[41] As described by Mackey, the National Center for Education Statistics has consistently found math and reading achievement gaps between American Indian and Alaska Native (AI/AN) students compared to their non-AI/AN peers.[42] Furthermore, Faircloth and Tippeconnic studied graduation rates in several states with the largest percentages of American Indian students, finding that on average AI/AN students had the lowest graduation rates (46.6%) compared to their peers in all other racial/ethnic groups (Whites, 69.8%; Blacks 54.7%; Asian, 77.9%; Hispanics, 50.8%).[43] As American Indian education leaders continue to explore ways to overcome the intergenerational trauma associated with America's efforts to assimilate and erase American Indian peoples, there is clearly a need to prioritize culturally responsive programming across systems.

Given the reality that Indigenous peoples are attending schools found across all states and territories, all leaders have a responsibility to dedicate resources toward meeting the unique needs of American Indian students. Stakeholders who are new to Indian education systems should begin to build their understanding of Indian education as a responsibility for all, and those who finance education in all 50 states must pay attention to the needs of Indigenous students in their schools in order to push back against these trends.

Indigenous People Have Always Shaped the Educational Experiences of Their Children, and Schools Must Partner with Native Nations, Families, and Communities Moving Forward

The Indigenous peoples of North America have long maintained systems of education predating contact with Europeans, systems which often used student-driven, locally relevant learning strategies that Western education might describe as place-based learning, experiential learning, character education, simulations, apprenticeships, and storytelling.[44] As with any society anywhere in the world, each Native nation developed pedagogical tools in response to its place-based physical and sociopolitical contexts. Indigenous systems of learning continue today, but are too often viewed through terms such as tradition or heritage rather than education—as if they are a glimpse into the past without acknowledging their role in the present.

While Indigenous education is often labeled under these names, a deeper look would reveal that many Indigenous systems of teaching and learning are still in practice outside of U.S. public school systems, and they still work to prepare children to meaningfully contribute to their communities as adults. These learning systems persist as Native nations work to revive and maintain traditional pedagogies and Native languages in the schools and community events that Native youth attend.[45] It is important to recognize and value Indigenous ways of teaching and learning in schools. In this way, Lomawaima asserts, "Indigenous education should never be trivialized as informal, as if its lessons were accidental or unplanned."[46] In other words, schools offer one version of education within brick and mortar walls, while community events offer another learning environment; these events that occur outside of the school are still education and often carry a distinct degree of formality and structure. That these systems of teaching and learning continue today is evidence of ongoing survival and resistance to colonialism.

As Lomawaima points out, while there is a tragic genocidal component to the historic educational experiences for Native people, there are also elements of survival, persistence, and adaptation. She states:

> Native peoples... have done better than survive; they have created means and ways to thrive. They have learned to make do and get by when times were tough, through personal sacrifice and commitment to guiding principles and practices of life understood as both secular and sacred, both rooted in place and capable of surviving transplantation. They have kept languages, religions, ceremonies, crop plants, springs, and children alive in spite of active persecution, land dispossession, hostile governance and regulation, and outright kidnapping. Adversity is a hard teacher.[47]

Lomawaima's words help deepen thinking about how to perceive institutions of education serving Indigenous peoples in the United States.

Today, Indigenous leaders are advocating for policy that mandates culturally responsive learning environments for Indigenous students using the same school systems that were intended to erase Indigenous ways of life. These are efforts to prioritize educational environments with curriculum and instruction more strongly connected to those Indigenous learning systems which have long survived outside of American schools. While many would argue there is still much work to be done, recent legislation has attached funding mechanisms to meet the unique cultural learning needs of American Indian students, as well as ensuring input and/or administrative oversight from Native nations and peoples. As an example, in order to receive Title VI Indian education formula grant funding under ESSA, there are now policies requiring LEAs to consult with local Native nations in order to receive funding.[48] Also, while states, school districts, tribal organizations, or Indian corporations might apply for JOM monies, if the school board is not composed of a majority of Indians then JOM policy requires the existence of Indian Education Committees formed by parents of Indian children to act as an oversight body for the administration of JOM funds.[49] The degree to which these policies are successful or appropriately followed is an ongoing debate, but the growth of policies such as these signal recognition that the priorities of mainstream education systems in America have not always aligned with Native nations, students, and families. At the same time, they also acknowledge that current school systems can help resolve some of the disparities and dispossessions they helped to create—as long as Native peoples and nations have a voice in the matter.

Given these historic legal foundations, stakeholders must recognize and acknowledge that funding American Indian education is not simply about advocacy in multiculturalism; it is also about countering historical assimilation while honoring the legal roots and fiduciary responsibility into which America entered in exchange for land.

Landmarks in Indian Education Finance and Law for Native Students[50]

Table 16.1 provides an overview of select developments specifically related to law and policy changes that directly influenced tribal, federal, state, and local funding structures for serving Native students, both in terms of appropriations and in terms of admission to state schools. Table 16.1 is not exhaustive, and some politically visible landmarks related to Indian education are not included: e.g., the Indian Reorganization Act of 1934, the Problem of Indian Administration Report of 1928, the Indian Relocation program of the 1950s, and the Indian Education—A National Tragedy, A National Challenge of 1969. Table 16.1 focuses on specific education law, policy, and bureaucratic developments.[51]

MAPPING THE CURRENT FINANCIAL LANDSCAPE ASSOCIATED WITH INDIAN EDUCATION

Having established historical and legal foundations for understanding Indian education, the chapter next outlines the primary funding streams, bureaucracies, and institutional perspectives in Indian Education.

Bureau of Indian Education in the Department of the Interior

From a federal perspective, the Bureau of Indian Education (BIE) is the federal entity charged with managing federal Indian schools, and the mission of the institution has largely shifted away from its assimilationist past. The BIE is one of two federally funded school systems in the U.S., the other being Department of Defense (DOD) schools. BIE serves approximately 46,700 students (8% of the Indian student population) through 183 elementary and secondary schools and/or dormitories across 23 states and 64 reservations. Of these schools, 52 are under the direct administration of the BIE; another 131 are tribally controlled under contracts through the Indian Self-Determination and Educational Assistance Act[52] (sometimes called '638 schools' or '638 contracts') or Tribally Controlled Grant Schools Act[53] (sometimes called '297 schools' or as having '297 grant boards'). The BIE also provides supplemental base operation funding to 33 post-secondary schools consisting of 29 Tribal Colleges and Universities (TCUs), two tribal technical colleges, and directly operates two post-secondary schools—Haskell Indian Nations University (HINU) and Southwestern Indian Polytechnic Institute (SIPI). While the BIE (and BIA) remains a primary

Indian Country ▪ 223

TABLE 16.1 Landmarks in Indian Education Finance and Law for Native Students

1819	PL 15-85 Civilization Fund Act passed. The Act authorized the federal government to contract with "capable persons of good moral character" to teach European-style agriculture to adults and reading, writing, and math to children as part of the federal government's "civilization" program.
1879	The Carlisle Indian Boarding school was founded, marketing federal expansion in the direct administration of Indian schools.
1924	*Piper v. Big Pine School District*. Alice Piper sued the Big Pine School District in California for denying her admission to school on the basis of being Native American. Though Big Pine School attorneys argued that serving Native students would be a financial burden to their district, the California Supreme Court held that the state must admit Native students to state-supported schools. PL 67-85 in the same year, the Snyder Act passed, making all Native people citizens of the United States. This later had implications for court cases about admitting Native students to state-funded public schools.
1933	*Grant v. Michaels et al.* The Montana Supreme Court ruled that states with constitutional mandates for a free public education must serve all students, including Native students, even in the presence of a nearby federal Indian school.
1934	PL 73-167 Johnson-O'Malley Act of 1934 passed. The law initially passed to allow the federal government to contract with states to provide for education, healthcare, and other needs of rural Native communities, conveying federal funds to states to compensate for the non-taxable trust lands on which many Native students live. Today, it provides funding for educational programs that meet the unique needs of Native students, including programs to revitalize Native languages and cultures. JOM funds *cannot* be used for a school's general infrastructural costs.[a]
1950	Impact Aid (PL 815 and PL 874) passed. It provided financial support to schools serving non-taxable federally impacted areas, including Indian trust lands, Alaska Native Settlement Claims Act lands, and lands utilized by branches of the U.S. military, as a way to compensate for the lack of property tax revenues for the schools.[b]
1964	PL 88-452 The Economic Opportunity Act passed. Native students have also benefited from its programs, which include Head Start, Upward Bound, and the Indian Community Act Program.
1965	PL 89-10 Elementary and Secondary Education Act of 1965 passed. Though it did not create any grants specific to Native students, it extended Impact Aid to support local education agencies (LEAs) serving federally affected areas, including tribal lands.

(continued)

TABLE 16.1 Landmarks in Indian Education Finance and Law for Native Students (continued)

1966	PL 89-750 Education Amendments of 1966 passed. The amendments addressed Native students in Bureau-operated schools. In addition, Impact Aid expanded coverage for certain previously uncovered Native students.
	In addition, the Rough Rock Demonstration School was founded on the Navajo Nation. An advancement in educational self-determination, this was the "first school to be overseen by a locally elected, all-India governing board, and the first to incorporate systematic instruction in the native language and culture." Using funds from both the Office of Economic Opportunity (OEO) and the BIE, this school was supervised by the Demonstration in Navajo Education, Inc. board.
1967	PL 90-247 Education Amendments of 1967 passed. Its attention to differently abled students included differently abled Native students. These amendments also expanded operation costs for Bureau-operated schools and provided construction funds for LEAs whose students lived on federal Indian trust lands.
1970	PL 91-230 Education Amendments of 1970 passed. Under the Bilingual Act, it allowed tribal organizations to apply for grants. ESEA also created pathways for hiring teachers through the national Teacher Corps.
1972	PL 92-318 Education Amendments of 1972 passed. It included the Indian Education Act, which significantly expanded ESEA attention and funding for Native students, including through the creation of the Office of Indian Education and the National Advisory Council on Indian Education. It also included Alaska Natives under programs available to "Indians."
1974	PL 93-380 Education Amendments of 1974 passed. It allowed funding for professional development for teachers and project/program administrators working with Native youth. The amendments created fellowships for Native youth to pursue graduate and professional degrees.
	PL 93-644 Separately, the 1974 Native American Programs Act passed as part of a reauthorization of the Economic Opportunities Act, creating the Administration for Native Americans (ANA) within the Department of Health and Human Services (HHS). The ANA was authorized to advocate for Native peoples within federal programs and policies, as well as to provide funds and technical assistance for certain community projects.
1975	PL 93-638 Indian Self-Determination and Education Assistance Act of 1975 passed. Separate from ESEA, this law allowed the Department of the Interior, Department of Education, and Department of Health and Human Services to contract directly with or make grants directly to federally recognized tribes to provide services otherwise provided by these agencies.

(continued)

TABLE 16.1 Landmarks in Indian Education Finance and Law for Native Students (continued)

Year	
1978	PL 95-471 The Tribally Controlled Community College Assistance Act of 1978 passed, securing stable funding for tribally controlled postsecondary educational institutions.
	PL 95-561 In addition, the Education Amendments of 1978 passed, creating funds for regional Indian education support centers. In keeping with the Indian Self-Determination and Education Assistance Act of 1975, the 1978 Amendments required that the Bureau of Indian Education "facilitate Indian control for Indian affairs in all matters relating to education." It ordered a new policy for recruiting Native educators to teach in Bureau schools and expanded ESEA to cover not only the "special educational needs" of Native youth but also their "special educational or culturally related academic needs."
1980	PL 96-374 Education Amendments of 1980 passed. It created the Advisory Council on Native Hawaiian Education and ordered a study of the available federal and state funds for Native Hawaiian education programs.
1984	PL 98-511 Education Amendments of 1984 passed, including the Indian Education Amendments of 1984. These amendments required the Bureau of Indian Affairs schools develop a fiscal accounting system for the Bureau, the Office of Indian Education, each BIA school, and any schools authorized under the Indian Self-Determination and Education Assistance Act.
1988	PL 100-297 The Augustus F. Hawkins-Robert T. Stafford Elementary and Secondary School Improvement Amendments of 1988 passed. It renewed Indian Education and Impact Aid, among other programs, and expanded grants available for serving Native students from the Department of Education. The amendments established a new title for the education of Native Hawaiians. They also created the Office of Indian Education within the Department of Education, which was ordered to establish an auditing system for at least 25% of the LEAs supported under the Indian Education Act of 1988 and to submit an annual report to Congress with its findings. The amendments authorized funds to develop tribal education departments to administer tribes' education programs. Included in the Amendments with the Tribally Controlled Schools Act of 1988, which authorized grants for operations and administrative costs associated with tribally controlled schools. "297 boards" provide oversight for the use of these funds. The amendments also authorized the convening of a White House Conference on Indian Education.
1991	PL 102-524 Native American Languages Act of 1991 passed. Separated from ESEA, it authorized the Department of Health and Human Services to administer grants to tribal governments and Native organizations for Native language revitalization programs.
1994	PL 103-382 Improving America's Schools Act (IASA) of 1994 passed, renewing ESEA. The IASA combined American Indian, Native Hawaiian, and Alaska Native education into Title IX of the ESEA. It also included the Native Hawaiian Education Act and the Alaska Native Education Equity, Support and Assistance Act.
	Meyers v. Board of Education. Sometimes thought of as the *Brown v. Board* for Native students, *Meyers* ruled that all stakeholders—federal, state, and tribal—have a responsibility to Native students and that Native students have a right to an equal educational opportunity.[d]

(continued)

TABLE 16.1 Landmarks in Indian Education Finance and Law for Native Students (continued)

Year	Landmark
1999	PL 106-568 Omnibus Indian Advancement Act passed. Instead of authorizing new grants, it authorized the BIA to create an external non-profit organization called the American Indian Educational Foundation to raise money to support the educational advancement of students affiliated with Bureau schools.
2001	PL 107-110 No Child Left Behind Act of 2001 passed. American Indian, Native Hawaiian, and Alaska Native Education moved to Title VII.
2006	PL 109-394 Esther Martinez Native American Languages Act of 2006 passed, amended the Native American Programs Act of 1974. The Esther Martinez Act provided financial support for Native language revitalization. Esther Martinez grants are currently administered by the ANA.
2007	PL 110-134 The Improving Head Start for School Readiness Act passed, creating the National American Indian/Alaska Native Head Start Collaboration Office (NAIANHSCO). This office focused on building collaborations with stakeholders invested in early childhood programs administered by Native nations.
2014	The Obama Administration created the General Indigenous Initiative which included, among several other elements, a set of new Native Youth Community Project (NYCP) grants.[e]
2015	PL 114-95 Every Student Succeeds Act of 2015 passed. American Indian, Native Hawaiian, and Alaska Native education moved to Title VI, adding mandatory consultations with Native nations for the first time. Grants from 2001 were continued, and new grants provided support for programs related to sustaining language and culture.
2018	*Yazzie v. State of New Mexico* and *Martinez v. State of New Mexico* court rulings held that inadequate funding for education violated the New Mexico's constitutional mandate for a free public education as well as protections for English language learners, low-income students, and Native students. The court ordered the state legislature to create a funding and accountability plan to ensure that districts adequately prepare all students to be college and career ready.[f]

[a] Bureau of Indian Education (BIE). Johnson O'Malley. (Washington D.C., Bureau of Indian Education, 2018). Retrieved from https://www.bie.edu/JOM/
[b] US Department of Education. Office of Impact Aid Programs. (Washington D.C., US Department of Education, 2017) Retrieved from https://www2.ed.gov/about/offices/list/oese/impactaid/index.html
[c] Teresa L. McCarty, "School as Community: The Rough Rock Demonstration," *Harvard Educational Review* 59(1989): 484.
[d] Baca, "Meyers v. Board of Education."
[e] More at https://obamawhitehouse.archives.gov/nativeamericans/generation-indigenous and https://genindigenous.com/
[f] Louise Martinez, et al., v. Secretary-Designate of the New Mexico Public Education Department, No. D-101-CV-2014-00793 (State of New Mexico, County of Santa Fe, First Judicial District 2018); Wilhelmina Yazzie, et al., v. State of New Mexico, Hannah Skandera, et. al., No. No. D-101-CV-2014-02224 (State of New Mexico, County of Santa Fe, First Judicial District 2018).

Source: Meredith L. McCoy. Adapted from "Contextualizing ESSA: A Critical Race Theory Analysis of Settler Colonial Structures and Indigenous Agency in Federal Indian Education Policy, 1819–2018," pp. 207–211. Unpublished doctoral dissertation. University of North Carolina-Chapel Hill (2019). By permission.

institution of education across Indian Country, there persists a constant struggle for adequate funding via the federal government's upholding of its fiduciary responsibilities, particularly regarding resources and upkeep with facilities.[54]

Funding for BIE elementary and secondary schools is determined by formulas, special needs, or specific appropriations. The Indian School Equalization Program[55] (ISEP) provides base funding according to a formula that computes an average daily membership (ADM) and weighted student units (WSUs) for characteristics such as grade level, presence of dormitories, special education needs, small schools with enrollments of less than 100 students, and schools with gifted and talented and language development programs. The U.S. Congress sets the total available amount, and in Fiscal Year 2018, the BIE's distribution per WSU was $5,642.96 based on 70,579 WSUs.

Beyond ISEP, the BIE is responsible for administering other elementary and secondary school appropriated funds for early childhood programs, programs to improve student and school performance, student transportation, and tribal grant support costs ($174,932,000). Furthermore, the BIE also administers funds for the TCUs ($69,793,000), technical colleges ($7,414,000), HINU and SIPI ($22,117,000) and Johnson-O'Malley (JOM) Assistance Grants allocated by the BIA to tribes and the BIE to public schools.[56]

The BIE appropriations also include funds to supplement six TCU budgets, post-secondary scholarships and adult education programs totaling $36,002,000 in FY 2018 for BIA tribal allocation programs and $5,442,000 for BIE-funded graduate scholarships.

BIE appropriations for facilities operations and maintenance was $126,160,000, an amount allocated to elementary and secondary schools, HINU, and SIPI per a facilities formula. In 2016, the BIE funded school facilities containing about 19,410,000 square feet.

In addition to the BIE-appropriated funds, the BIE receives about $215,000,000 from the Department of Education's appropriations for elementary and secondary schools that BIE allocates to schools based on student ADM and special needs. The majority of funds are allocated to schools by formula.[57]

The U.S. Department of Education and Department of Health and Human Services

Indian Education financing can be found across several federal offices. Outside of the BIE, the U.S. Department of Education (ED) and the Department of Health and Human Services (HHS) also provide financing and oversight for Indian education.

Within ED, the Office of Indian Education (found in the Office of Elementary and Secondary Education) administers various grant programs, the most visible being the Title VI formula grants that are often referenced generically as 'Indian Ed.' However, a variety of ED funding mechanisms have unique associations with Indian education, most of which primarily go to public schools. As noted above, some also go to the BIE across a variety of programs. According to a report by the Congressional Research Service, Indian education programming can be linked to the following:

- Titles I-A: Grants to LEAs
- Title I-B: State Assessment Grants
- Title II-A: Supporting Effective Instruction
- Title III-A: English Language Acquisition
- Title IV-B: 21st Century Community Learning Centers
- Title VI-A: Indian Education Programs (*NYCP, STEP, Professional Development*)
- Title VI-C: Alaska Native Education Equity
- Title VII: Impact Aid
- IDEA Part B: Special Education Grants to States
- IDEA Part C: Early Intervention for Infants and Toddlers with Disabilities
- MHVAA: Education for Homeless Children and Youths
- Perkins Native American Career and Technical Education Program (NACTEP).[58]

In FY 2016, ED spent $1.1 billion on Indian Elementary-Secondary Education Programs, including BIE set-asides. Of this amount, Impact Aid accounted for almost 60% ($626 million).

HHS also plays a role in financing Indian Education. The Administration for Native Americans (ANA), which is under the Administration for Children and Families (ACF), manages grants related to Indigenous language education and preservation, such as the Esther Martinez Immersion and Native Language Preservation and Maintenance (P&M) programs, among other programs.[59] HHS also administers Head Start and Early Head Start grants through the Office of Head Start (OHS), also under ACF, which funds programs to Native nations for early childhood education. In OHS, Region XI is specifically associated with Head Start programming for federally recognized Native nations, which serves around 20,000 students across 26 states, with approximately 85% of students being AI/AN.[60] The National American Indian and Alaska Native Head Start Collaboration Office supports these programs through a contract with OHS.[61] Table 16.2 later provides more detail related to these Indian education funding streams for both the ED and HHS.

Tribal Education Departments/Agencies: A Growing Role

Tribal Education Departments (TEDs), also referred to as Tribal Education Agencies (TEAs), are the arms of tribal governments responsible for executing the educational agenda for Native nations. As Bowers outlined in a report for the Tribal Education Department's National Assembly (TEDNA), more than 200 tribes have TEDs, and *32 different states have TEDs operating within their borders.*[62] The size and capacities of these institutions can vary widely, along with roles and responsibilities, with some TEDs taking on administrative oversight of schools (i.e., BIE schools under '638 contracts') and others running a few federally funded programs for their citizens.[63] Furthermore, while some TEDs have sufficient funds acquired through economic enterprises and tribal LLCs which allow them to operate with a large staff of paid employees, others function with a handful of staff members tasked with administering federal programs such as JOM, higher education scholarships, Head Start, and more. Given this diversity, it would be illogical to make generalizations about TEDs across Native nations.

While the U.S. Congress has authorized the direct funding of TEDs as a discretionary program since FY 1989, no appropriations were made until the Obama administration's STEP and TED programs in 2015, despite many requests from prominent organizations representing Indian Country.[64] The STEP program, administered through the U.S. Department of Education's Office of Indian Education, is designed to promote collaboration between TEAs, SEAs, and LEAs, as well as to build capacity for TEAs to conduct certain administrative functions.[65] This was first piloted in 2012–2015, and the first full round of funding ($1,766,232) was granted to five communities across Idaho, Montana and Oklahoma for 2015–2019. The TED program, which is administered out of the BIE, is intended to also build TEAs' capacities to take on a more direct role in the education of their youth, particularly in communities with BIE schools. In 2015, the TED program provided $700,000 to four Native nations with BIE schools.[66]

While often left out of conversations about funding in Indian Education, TEDs are beginning to gain more attention as an active player in the field. New ESSA requirements mandate that certain LEAs and SEAs engage in consultations with Native nations in order to receive funding. TEDs can provide a formal institution to potentially address consultation requirements and assert the nation's views on how federal Indian Education dollars are spent with their students.[67] Since TEDs vary widely in their capacities to take on administrative responsibilities and programming, education practitioners will need to learn about the specific TED programming or other tribal government offices operating near their locales. In this new ESSA landscape, it is imperative that leaders recognize that TEDs are a manifestation of tribal sovereignty and even though current law and policy tends to still prioritize LEAs and SEAs, TEDs have an important role to play.[68] TEDs have an interest in advocating for their tribal citizens in whatever schools they attend, whether they be located in rural (66%) or urban and suburban school settings (33%) and whether they attend federal Bureau of Indian Education schools (7%) or general public schools (93%).[69]

Given the reality that over 90% of American Indian students attend public schools, TED partnerships have become an important part of the education landscape.[70] There are many cases in which TEDs have offered substantial resources to programs and employees that are of direct benefit to LEAs serving their citizens. For example, the Osage Nation of Oklahoma has no existing K–12 BIE school within the local community, and using dollars raised through Osage Nation enterprises they pay for language teachers, tribal education advocates, and tutors, among other initiatives, to work among the rural LEAs operating within reservation boundaries. Furthermore, they spearheaded a partnership with Tulsa Community College that allows Osage and non-Osage high school juniors and seniors across several rural LEAs to take college level coursework in Osage Nation facilities. This illustrates how fostering productive partnerships can help TEDs, LEAs, and SEAs work together to dedicate resources toward shared goals that benefit all students. Therefore, SEAs and LEAs would be wise to make sure they are building strong relationships with TEDs. Such relationships must respect the unique sociocultural needs of American Indian students and the voices of Native nations. For helpful guides on how to build such relationships, see the National Indian Education Association's *Building Relationships with Tribes* series.[71]

State-Tribal Relationships in Gaming and Education

Given the government-to-government relationship between states and Native nations, there are a variety of ways that partnerships are developed and formalized between these two political entities. For example, the STEP program mentioned above is an example of a grant program that enhances collaboration between TED/TEAs, SEAs, and LEAs. Some broader considerations regarding state-tribal partnerships are outlined in the next paragraphs.

Tribes are sovereign nations and have authority that is equal to and not lesser than that of the states. As a result, tribes maintain rights to self-governance and to economic development. One mechanism for tribal economic development is gaming, though gaming is also constrained by laws about what is permissible within a given state. After *California v. Cabazon Band of Mission Indians*[72] affirmed Native nations' rights to engage in many types of gaming (referred to under the law as Class I and Class II gaming), the Indian Gaming Regulatory Act of 1988[73] (IGRA) created a regulatory structure for gaming in Indian Country. This structure established pathways for state-tribal compacts for Class III gaming and statutorily protected Indian gaming as a way for Native nations to promote self-sufficiency through economic development. Native nations use gaming as a means for generating revenue for social services, including education. Since the 1990s, there have been hundreds of state-tribal gaming compacts and agreements signed across 27 states, many of which are tied to education financing for tribal governments and state governments alike.[74] Each of these compacts is generated in a specific sociocultural, economic, and political environment; given the diversity of compacts, this mechanism for generating revenue for states and Native nations does not operate uniformly across the nation.

For example, the state of Oklahoma has 38 federally recognized Native nations within its boundaries (not all of which engage in gaming), and in FY 2017, tribes collected over $2.2 billion in gaming revenue. As per state-tribal gaming compacts, $134 million went to the state of Oklahoma through exclusivity fees associated with Class III electronic games and non-house-banked card games, and of that $117.6 million went to the Education Reform Revolving Fund.[75] While this money is intended to be a supplemental source of education funds, critics of Oklahoma's funding model claim the state uses this money to fill an ongoing shortfall to maintain funding levels without increasing revenues. This is particularly important during a time of financial crisis for education in Oklahoma, highlighted by a highly publicized statewide teacher walkout in 2018 that focused on demands for higher pay, replacing outdated instructional materials, and resolving classroom overcrowding. Also of note, these tribally raised monies are essentially rolled into the general fund with no obligation or accountability for public schools to generate unique programming and/or curricula for American Indian students; however, the State of Oklahoma pays for an Executive Director of Indian Education and has been working on significant curricular reform in recent years for and about American Indians at the state level, all occurring outside of gaming compact contexts. For Oklahoma, the window to renegotiate these compacts opens in 2019, as they expire in 2020, and there is considerable discussion about allowing 'ball and dice' games, such as roulette and craps, in order to raise revenues in the wake of the Oklahoma teacher walkout. Native nations in the state will also have the opportunity to negotiate whether monies might go specifically to unique programming and curricula for American Indian students. As another example, Native nations in Arizona contribute 1% to 8% of their annual gaming revenues to the state, of which 56% goes to public schools through the Arizona Department of Education Instructional Improvement Fund, also with no requirements for set-asides specific to education for Indian students. Since 2004, the cumulative amount that Native nations have provided to support Arizona public education through gaming compacts has exceeded $624.7 million.[76]

Education is one of many social services supported by Native nations, and just as state governments debate education finance and fiscal management, tribal governments also have to make hard decisions about what to do with limited resources. From the perspective of Native nations, gaming and other enterprises are one potential mechanism to help expand funding for education programming. Still, it is important to note that gaming remains controversial in many contexts, and not all tribal nations engage in gaming, nor is its sustainability certain. Of those that do, many do not turn a significant profit. For that reason, it would be inaccurate to think that the existence of a tribal casino equates to lucrative funding for education. It would also be inaccurate to think that just because a Native nation reaches a degree of self-sufficiency in the context of educational programming, that LEAs, SEAs, and the federal government shed their responsibility for providing appropriate educational funding to American Indians.

Among the hundreds of state-tribal gaming compacts that impact education financing, some Native nations and states have recently begun engaging in state-tribal compacts and MOUs specific to education outside the context of gaming. In 2013, the Washington state legislature passed the Engrossed Second Substitute House Bill (E2 SHB) 1154, which paved the way for state-tribal education compact schools (STECs), of which there are now five in the state. The bill authorized state-tribal education compacts between the Superintendent of Public Instruction and Native nations, allowing schools covered by the compacts to work under modified regulations for staffing, standards, funding, admissions, and accountability.[77] As another example, the state of Wisconsin's Executive Order 39, issued in 2004, recognizes the sovereignty of the 11 Native nations within the state and laid a foundation for encouraging consultation and cooperation between tribes and the state.[78] This led to development of the Wisconsin State-Tribal Consultation Initiative, and now almost every department in Wisconsin's executive branch has created state-tribal consultation policies with input from local Native nations. Additionally, Wisconsin's independent agency overseeing education, the Department of Public Instruction (DPI) headed by an independently elected state constitutional officer, has begun the process of building MOUs with local Native nations that are specific to fostering collaboration and resource sharing for the purpose of improving the quality of educational services provided by both entities. According to DPI, the Lac du Flambeau Band of Lake Superior Chippewas was the first to formalize an MOU with the Wisconsin DPI, followed by the Bad River Band of Lake Superior Chippewas, the Oneida Nation, and the Red Cliff Band of Lake Superior Chippewas.[79] The DPI has also created a guide to help local school districts establish their own MOUs with Native nations.

Beyond compacts and MOUs, some states have mandated systemic changes for the improvement of education for and about American Indians.

Wisconsin appropriated funding for the DPI American Indian Studies Program in its 1989–1991 biennial budget bill (referenced as Wisconsin Act 31). This program has also helped develop several state statutes that mandate more appropriate American Indian curricular content in schools and teacher training.[80] The act of developing MOUs between the Wisconsin DPI and Native nations are a way to help all parties work together to meet these state statutes, federal law, and be proactive in addressing the educational needs of school-aged students in Native nations.[81] Furthermore, Washington's *Since Time Immemorial*[82] initiative and Montana's *Indian Education for All*[83] programming are also positive steps toward addressing the ongoing ways in which curricula across the country marginalize and erase American Indian worldviews.[84] It should be acknowledged that while these developments are applauded throughout Indian Country, they address such deep-seated systemic issues that additional resources are needed at all levels of systems to help support the transition in the form of professional development, institutional liaisons, educator training, travel, new positions, development of new coursework, new materials, and so on.

All these developments demonstrate the importance of building strong relationships between states and Native nations.

Taxes and Indian Land Ownership

Understanding that many education finance systems are rooted in property taxes, the laws and policies surrounding Indian land ownership and taxing are relevant to education finance for public schools serving Native children on Indian land. The degree to which education financing is tied to the power of taxation impacts Indian education since laws arising from the Commerce Clause of the U.S. Constitution often "[prohibit] tribal governments from taxing and bonding against Indian lands, with consequences for schools that serve Native students in the form of inadequate buildings and facilities."[85] The federal government's role in education services for Native students helps compensate for this lack of revenue, yet schools relying primarily on federal funds for operation are consistently underfunded.

There are three primary types of ownership associated with Indian land—restricted fee land, trust land, and fee simple.[86] Even on Indian trust land, where the Native nation has jurisdiction, there are still restrictions related to taxation since the title is held by the Secretary of the Interior. Due to these regulations, as the National Congress of the American Indian has observed, "tribal governments lack parity with states, local governments, and the federal government in exercising taxing authority. For example, tribes are unable to levy property taxes because of the trust status of their land, and they generally do not levy income taxes on tribal members."[87] In addition, many reservations face high rates of poverty and lack sufficient opportunities for employment, leaving tribes "unable to establish a strong tax base structured around the property taxes and income taxes typically found at the local state government level."[88] Where tribes are able to generate revenue through taxes, these are often inadequate to support the wide array of government services the tribe must provide.

The political consequences of tax systems vary widely across all Native nations, considering that each locale varies in terms of population size, poverty, wealth, economic development, and geographic footprint. It is therefore not realistic for some nations to aggressively pursue other forms of taxing for the purpose of education even if they have the power to do so.

These land and taxation laws play an important role in the financing of SEAs and LEAs located on or near tribal communities and serving American Indian students. While programs such as Impact Aid help offset the costs associated with educating Indian students attending these public schools (without requirements to spend on Indian education programming), this can generate political tensions, particularly when tribal nations pursue land buyback efforts to reclaim land lost during allotment. In these cases, such actions are seen as a threat to local education financing. Some communities use Payment in Lieu of Taxes (PILT) which can "help local governments carry out such vital services as firefighting and police protection, construction of public schools and roads, and search-and-rescue operations." These are payments made for tax exempt lands as "one of the ways the Federal Government can fulfill its role of being a good neighbor to local communities."[89]

It should also be noted there are 229 nations in Alaska and that the Alaska Native Claims and Settlement Act of 1971[90] (ANCSA) created a different framework than the land into trust process used for nations in the 'lower 48.' As the National Congress of American Indians describes, "Originally, ANCSA allotted 40 million acres of land, divided among 12 [now 13] for-profit regional Native corporations and 220 village corporations, established to manage Alaska Native lands and resources."[91] While Indigenous nations of Alaska operate in these frameworks, Native Hawaiians also operate in unique circumstances compared to Native nations found within the contiguous 48 states. Additionally, there are several Native nations that operate under the status of state recognition, and this status also comes with unique circumstances regarding land ownership, jurisdiction, and taxation.[92]

Primary Funding Streams for Education across Indian Country

Table 16.2 lists funding streams associated with Indian education. The list is not exhaustive, but these represent some of the most common

TABLE 16.2 Primary Funding Streams and Bureaucracies Associated with P–12 Education Across Indian Country

Funding Stream	Details	Eligible Recipients
State Funding Formulas		
Funding formulas found across all 50 states	With 90% of American Indian students attending public schools, state laws and policies associated with school funding are essential bureaucratic components to funding the education of American Indian education. Many of the grants found below are intended to supplement this funding.	LEAs and other institutions eligible for funding according to state laws and policies.
Native Nations and Tribal Education Departments/Agencies (TEDs/TEAs)		
Funding opportunities through and with Tribal Nations	With over 570 federally recognized Native nations, these governments are an essential piece of the bureaucratic landscape in terms of funding for Indian Education. While their make-up and capacities vary widely, many Native nations administer education programs with funds raised through local enterprise, or through federal grants (many listed below). Even when not administering programs directly, partnerships through consortia agreements and/or consultation with Native nations are requirements for various grants.	Most likely recipients are citizens of each Native nation, although non-Natives and/or other enrolled Natives often benefit from programs administered through Native nations.
Bureau of Indian Education (BIE), U.S. Department of the Interior		
Indian School Equalization Program (ISEP)	Formula that distributes funds to BIE schools and dormitories for basic operation costs.	BIE operated schools, and tribally operated schools that are administered by tribes or tribal organizations under a PL 93-638 contract or PL 100-297 grant.
Johnson O'Malley (JOM)	The JOM program provides supplemental education funds in order to meet the unique needs of eligible Indian students; funding is on a formula-basis. Until the passage of the Johnson O'Malley Supplemental Indian Education Program Modernization Act (PL 115-404) on Dec. 31, 2018, the JOM program previously used student counts from 1995. This recent development requires the Department of the Interior to annually update the count of Indian students eligible for JOM. A local Indian Education Committee must be involved in the administration of this program.	Any state, school district, tribal organization, Indian corporation, or previously private BIE funded school with eligible AI/AN children.

(continued)

TABLE 16.2 Primary Funding Streams and Bureaucracies Associated with P–12 Education Across Indian Country

Funding Stream	Details	Eligible Recipients
TED Program	A grant program to promote administrative capacity building for Native nations with BIE schools. Last issued in 2015.[a]	TEAs with BIE funded supply in their community may apply.
Office of Indian Education (OIE), Office of Elementary and Secondary Education in U.S. Department of Education		
Title VI Indian Education Formula Grant Program (as authorized by section 6116 of ESEA as amended by ESSA)	Formerly Title VII under *No Child Left Behind* Formula grant designed to help schools that serve American Indian students to meet their unique cultural, language, and education needs. New under ESSA: Mandatory consultations with Native nations or Indian organizations may apply depending on AI/AN enrollment percentages, size of program, and distance from Native nations.[b] *Professional development grants for specialized American Indian educator training programs are also included under Title VI, but the list of eligible recipients is different. They include Institutions of Higher Education (IHEs) and Tribal Colleges and Universities (TCUs), and encourage consortium agreements with Native nations when appropriate.*	LEAs with a threshold of Indian student enrollment are the primary recipients (with applicable exemptions), eligible BIE funded schools, Indian Tribes, Indian Organizations, or Indian Community Based Organizations (ICBOs).[c]
Native Youth Community Projects (NYCP)	Discretionary demonstration grant program with a focus on improving achievement for AI/AN students. Since 2015, this program has focused on community led programs which emphasize college and career readiness while also meeting the unique cultural needs of American Indian students.	SEAs, LEAs, BIE schools, Indian Tribes, Indian Organizations, institution of higher education, (IHEs), a tribal college or university (TCU), or a consortium of these may apply.[d]
Native American Language Program (NAL@ED)	Discretionary grant program intended to support Indigenous language maintenance and revitalization in schools as envisioned by the Native American Languages Act of 1990.	Indian tribes, TCUs, TEAs, LEAs, BIE-funded schools, Alaska Native Regional Corporation, and non-profits (tribal, Alaska Native, Native Hawaiian, or other); a nontribal for-profit organization may apply.[e]
State-Tribal Education Partnership Program (STEP)	Discretionary/competitive grant program intended to promote collaboration among SEAs, LEAs, and TEAs and build capacity for TEAs to take on some administrative responsibilities.	TEAs, or a consortium of TEAs, in partnership with SEAs and LEAs may apply.[f]

(continued)

Indian Country ▪ 237

TABLE 16.2 Primary Funding Streams and Bureaucracies Associated with P–12 Education Across Indian Country

Funding Stream	Details	Eligible Recipients
Administration for Native Americans (ANA),[g] Office of the Administration for Children and Families in U.S. Department of Health and Human Services		
Native Languages Preservation and Maintenance (P&M)	Competitive grant program intended to support the development and implementation of curriculum and education projects that enhance Native languages preservation and restoration efforts in Native communities.[h]	Federally recognized tribes as recognized by the BIA; incorporated non-federally recognized tribes; incorporated state-recognized tribes; consortia of Indian tribes; incorporated non-profit multi-purpose community-based Indian organizations; Urban Indian centers; Alaska Native villages as defined in the ANCSA and/or non-profit village consortia; incorporated non-profit Alaska Native Associations in Alaska with village-specific projects; non-profit Alaska Native Regional Corporations/Associations in Alaska with village-specific projects; non-profit Alaska Native Regional Corporations/Associations in Alaska with village-specific projects; non-profit Alaska native community entities or tribal governing bodies (Indian Reorganization Act or Traditional Councils) as recognized by the BIA; Public and non-profit private agencies serving Native Hawaiians; national or regional incorporated non-profit Native American organizations with native American community-specific objectives; public and non-profit private agencies serving native peoples from Guam, American Samoa, or the Commonwealth of the Northern Mariana Islands; Tribal colleges and Universities, and colleges and universities located in Hawaii, Guam, American Samoa, and/or the Commonwealth of the Northern Mariana Islands that serve Native American Pacific Islanders.[i]
Esther Martinez Immersion	Competitive grant program focused on supporting community-driven Native American language revitalization projects. Funding supports three-year projects being implemented by Native American Language Nests and Survival Schools.[j]	
Native Youth Initiative for Leadership, Empowerment, and Development (I-LEAD)	Competitive grant program intended to "support local community projects that foster Native youth resiliency, and to empower Native youth across four broad domains of activity: (1) Native youth leading (leadership development), (2) Native youth connecting (building positive identity, community connection, and social-emotional health), (3) Native youth learning (education success), and (4) Native youth working (workforce readiness)."[k] While there are currently grantees operating these programs, there are no I-LEAD competitions for FY 2018.	

(continued)

TABLE 16.2 Primary Funding Streams and Bureaucracies Associated with P–12 Education Across Indian Country

Funding Stream	Details	Eligible Recipients
Office of Head Starts (OHS),[a] Office of the Administration for Children and Families (ACF) in U.S. Department of Health and Human Services (HHS)		
Head Start and Early Head Start Programs	Provides early childhood services to low-income children through grants funded and administered through the Office of Head Start (OHS), which serves 156 federally recognized tribes with AI/AN Head Start and Early Head Start programs in 26 different states.	Federally recognized tribal nations
	Region XI funds Head Start grant programs to federally recognized tribal nations. The National American Indian and Alaska Native Head Start Collaboration Office (NAIANHSCO) supports this work across all 26 states, but it funded through OHS by contract.	

Source: Original table from authors.

[a] Office of the Assistant Secretary–Indian Affairs, "Eight Tribes Receive Nearly $2.5 Million in Grants." (November 5, 2015).
[b] Generally, LEAs with 50% or more Native students in their student population or who have received more than $40,000 in Title VI Indian Education funds must consult with the Native nations of the students they serve. See National Indian Education Association, "Building Relationships with Tribes."
[c] U.S. Department of Education, "Indian Education — Formula Grants to Local Education Agencies," U.S. Department of Education Programs, 2017, https://www2.ed.gov/programs/indianformula/index.html.
[d] U.S. Department of Education, "Indian Education — Demonstration Grants for Indian Children," U.S. Department of Education Programs, 2018, https://www2.ed.gov/programs/indiandemo/applicant.html.
[e] U.S. Department of Education, "Native American Language Program," U.S. Department of Education Programs, 2017, https://www2.ed.gov/programs/nal/eligibility.html.
[f] U.S. Department of Education, "State Tribal Education Partnership Program."
[g] Carmelia Strickland (Director, Division of Program Operations, Administration for Native Americans) contributed to the content of this section (Personal Communication, Dec. 18, 2018)
[h] Administration for Native Americans, "About Native Languages."
[i] 42 USC Sec 2991b and 45 CFR Sec 1336.33
[j] Ibid.
[k] Administration for Native Americans, "SEDS Special Program Areas."
[l] Angie Godfrey (Region XI Program Manager; Office of Head Start) contributed to the content of this section (Personal communication, Dec. 18, 2018)

programs and bureaucracies associated with funding education across Indian Country via SEAs, LEAs, TEDs/TEAs, and the federal government. When viewing the table, it is emphasized that with such a large percentage of American Indian students attending public schools (93%), state funding remains one of the primary funding streams for the education of Native students. With BIE schools then carrying approximately 7% of Native student enrollment, this firmly establishes public schools and federal BIE schools as the primary institutions of education for Indian Country. Furthermore, it is acknowledged that with over 570 federally recognized Native nations and the growth of TEAs/TEDs discussed previously, the Native Nations are beginning to take a more active role and should be regarded as an important part of the bureaucratic and financial landscape of Indian education; they are included here, though not all Native nations currently have TEDs as part of their governance systems. The remainder of Table 16.2 highlights a variety of federal programs associated with Indian education, all of which have different policies and/or eligibilities. Education leaders should *always* be cognizant of their unique local contexts at the intersection of LEAs, SEAs, and Native nations.

Additionally, federal grants increasingly require input from Native nations as a way to support Indigenous rights to self-determination regarding Indian education funds. Depending on local capacities and geographies, there are also many programs that offer opportunities to engage in formal consortia partnerships to attain eligibility. A caution must be given to non-Indian educators exploring funding opportunities with Indian communities: Native communities often receive requests to partner with non-Indian institutions for grants, and this is completely acceptable. However, too often these institutions prioritize their reputation and acquisition of funds over the needs and voices of Indian institutions and stakeholders, which is not an ideal foundation on which to build collaborative and productive partnerships. Often, these kinds of partnerships create an illusion, on paper, that a productive two-way partnership is in place when in reality it is heavily one-sided. Not all partnerships operate this way, but given the long history of exploitative relationships, all stakeholders will need to demonstrate a commitment to long-term, meaningful partnerships. It is therefore recommended that non-Indian institutions explore ways to engage in ongoing and substantive partnership building with Indian institutions and their stakeholders beyond grants.

CONCLUSION

Indian education is a complex bureaucratic network of overlapping sovereignties, jurisdictions, and responsibilities that rests on an important legal foundation—the federal trust responsibility. This network places responsibility on all institutions of education that serve Indian students, even when enrollments are a small percentage of the student body. While current stakeholders are not personally responsible for the traumatic histories inflicted on Indigenous peoples through conquest, land dispossessions, and education, these are inherited legal systems and political histories whose legacies must be addressed. Positive change can be jointly achieved by ensuring that Native nations have a stronger voice in programming, curricula, and spending; by building ongoing collaborations that center on Indigenous perspectives; and by adequately funding educational systems that support Native nations and Native students.

NOTES

1. Following the National Congress of American Indians (NCAI), a national Indian advocacy organization, we use the term "Indian Country" in a broader sense to refer to "tribal governments, Native communities, cultures, and peoples," with an understanding that Indian education involves stakeholders both inside and outside of Native nations and reservations. "Indian Country" (both capitalized) differs from "Indian country," a legal term that describes "the area over which the federal government and tribes exercise primary jurisdiction" and refers narrowly to specific territories, lands, and governments. See National Congress of American Indians, "Tribal Nations and the United States: An Introduction" (Washington, D.C.: National Congress of American Indians, n.d.), http://www.ncai.org/resources/ncai_publications/tribal-nations-and-the-united-states-an-introduction. Throughout this chapter, we use Native and Indigenous interchangeably to refer to students and nations. We use Indian, American Indian, or tribal primarily where such terms are associated with formal laws, policies, and government offices. These general terms facilitate a discussion of policy and finance across multiple settings; where possible, however, it is important to use the specific names each individual or nation prefers.
2. The authors want to thank those who provided insights for this chapter: Jacob Tsotigh, National Indian Education Association; Cornel Pewewardy, Professor Emeritus, Portland State University; Joe Herrin, Bureau of Indian Education; David O'Connor, American Indian Studies Program, Wisconsin Department of Public Instruction; Carmelia Strickland, Administration for Native Americans; Angie Godfrey, Office of Head Start.
3. National Indian Education Association, "Native Nations and American Schools: The History of Natives in the American Education System" (Washington, D.C.: National Indian Education Association, n.d.). In addition to the more than 570 federally-acknowledged Native nations, dozens more state-recognized and unrecognized groups are currently seeking federal recognition—an important status marker with implications for accessing education funding. With many non-recognized nations in the ongoing pursuit of recog-

nition, education leaders should make efforts to stay current on the status of local Native nations.
4. National Congress of American Indians, "Tribal Nations and the United States."
5. K. Tsianina Lomawaima, "Educating Native Americans," in *Handbook of Research on Multicultural Education*, eds. James A. Banks and Cherry A. McGee Banks (New York, NY: Macmillan, 1995): 331.
6. Melody L. McCoy, *The Evolution of Tribal Sovereignty over Education in Federal Law since 1965* (Boulder: Native American Rights Fund, 2005), http://www.narf.org/wordpress/wp-content/uploads/2015/01/gold.pdf.
7. National Congress of American Indians, "Tribal Nations and the United States," 16.
8. Margaret Connell Szasz, *Education and the American Indian: The Road to Self-Determination since 1928*, 3rd ed., rev. and enl. (Albuquerque, N.M.: University of New Mexico Press, 1999), 8–9.
9. For more, see Vine Deloria and Clifford M. Lytle, *American Indians, American Justice* (Austin: University of Texas Press, 1983); Szasz, *Education and the American Indian;* McCoy, *The Evolution of Tribal Sovereignty.*
10. Helen Maynor Scheirbeck et al., "Report on Indian Education; Task Force Five: Indian Education; Final Report to the American Indian Policy Review Commission." (Washington, D.C.: Government Printing Office, 1976): 67.
11. For more, see Jon Reyhner and Jeanne Eder, *American Indian Education: A History* (Norman: University of Oklahoma Press, 2004); David Adams, *Education for Extinction: American Indians and the Boarding School Experience, 1875–1928* (Lawrence, Kan.: University Press of Kansas, 1995); Joel Spring, *Deculturalization and the Struggle for Equality: A Brief History of the Education of Dominated Cultures in the United States*, 8th ed. (New York, NY: McGraw-Hill, 2016).
12. Szasz, *Education and the American Indian.*
13. James E. Seelye, Jr. and Steven A. Littleton, eds., *Voices of the American Indian Experience* (Santa Barbara, California: Greenwood, 2013).
14. For more, see Margaret Connell Szasz, *Indian Education in the American Colonies, 1607–1783*, Bison Books ed. (Lincoln: University of Nebraska Press, 2007) and Margaret Connell Szasz, ed., *Between Indians and White Worlds: The Cultural Broker* (Norman: University of Oklahoma Press, 1994).
15. *Cherokee Nation v. Georgia*, 30 U.S. 1 (1831); *Johnson v. M'Intosh*, 21 U.S 543 (1823); *Worcester v. Georgia*, 31 U.S. 515 (1832).
16. Deloria and Lytle, *American Indians, American Justice*, 32.
17. For more, see Reyhner and Eder, *American Indian Education;* Adams, *Education for Extinction;* Spring, *Deculturalization and the Struggle for Equality.*
18. Adams, *Education for Extinction*, 52.
19. For more, see Brenda Child, *Boarding School Seasons: American Indian Families, 1900–1940* (Lincoln: University of Nebraska Press, 1998); Clyde Ellis, *To Change Them Forever: Indian Education at the Rainy Mountain Boarding School, 1893–1920* (Norman: University of Oklahoma Press, 1996); K. Tsianina Lomawaima, *They Called It Prairie Light: The Story of Chilocco Indian School* (Lincoln: University of Nebraska Press, 1994).
20. Adams, *Education for Extinction*, 26–27.

21. Matt Villeneuve, "The Whole Indian Problem Is Essentially an Educational One: The Problem of Indian Administration and the Mt. Pleasant Indian Industrial Boarding School, 1893–1934" (Session Paper, November 9, 2018).
22. Brookings Institution and Lewis Meriam, "The Problem of Indian Administration; Report of a Survey Made at the Request of Honorable Hubert Work, Secretary of the Interior, and Submitted to Him, February 21, 1928" (Institute for Government Research, 1928): 427.
23. Deloria and Lytle, *American Indians, American Justice*, 12.
24. See Table 16.1 later for a detailed list of key law and policy changes for P–12 Indian Education, with emphasis on 1900-Present.
25. See "Indian Elementary-Secondary Education: Programs, Background, and Issues" (Government Printing Office, 2017), https://www.everycrsreport.com/reports/RL34205.html and Ahniwake Rose, "Testimony of the National Indian Education Association: Before the United States House of Representatives Committee on Appropriations Subcommittee on Interior, Environment, and Related Agencies. National Indian Education Association," 2018, http://www.niea.org/wp-content/uploads/2016/02/NIEAs-Testimony-Before-House-Appropriations-Subcommittee-on-Interior-Environment-for-the-FY-2019-Budget.pdf
26. Patricia L. Whitefoot, "Re: Secretary's Proposed Statewide Assessment System Regulations," September 9, 2016, http://www.niea.org/wp-content/uploads/2016/02/NIEAs-Comments-on-the-Assessment-Regs.pdf
27. For more, see: Vine Deloria and Daniel R. Wildcat, *Power and Place: Indian Education in America* (Golden, Colo.: American Indian Graduate Center, 2001); Gloria Ladson-Billings, *Critical Race Theory Perspectives on the Social Studies: The Profession, Policies, and Curriculum* (Greenwich: Information Age Publishing, 2003); K. Tsianina Lomawaima and Teresa L. McCarty, "When Tribal Sovereignty Challenges Democracy: American Indian Education and the Democratic Ideal," *American Educational Research Journal* 39, no. 2 (2002): 279–305; Hollie J. Mackey, "The ESSA in Indian Country: Problematizing Self-Determination Through the Relationships Between Federal, State, and Tribal Governments," *Educational Administration Quarterly* 53, no. 5 (2017): 782–808; Sarah B. Shear, "Cultural Genocide Masked as Education: U.S. History Textbooks Coverage of Indigenous Education Policies," in *Doing Race in Social Studies: Critical Perspectives* (Charlotte: Information Age Publishing, 2015), 13–40; Sarah B. Shear et al., "Manifesting Destiny: Re/Presentations of Indigenous Peoples in K–12 U.S. History Standards," *Theory and Research in Social Education* 43, no. 1 (2015): 68–101; Wayne Journell, "An Incomplete History: Representation of American Indians in State Social Studies Standards," *Journal of American Indian Education* 48, no. 2 (2009): 18–32; Sarah B. Shear et al., "Toward Responsibility: Social Studies Education That Respects and Affirms Indigenous Peoples and Nations" (National Council for the Social Studies, 2018), https://www.socialstudies.org/positions/indigenous-peoples-and-nations.
28. National Indian Education Association, "Native Nations and American Schools."

29. Irving G. Hendrick, "The Federal Campaign for the Admission of Indian Children into Public Schools, 1890–1934," *American Indian Culture and Research Journal* 5, no. 3 (1981): 13–32.
30. 193 Cal. 664 (1924).
31. 94 Mont. 452 (Mont. 1933).
32. 905 F.Supp. 1544 (D. Utah 1995).
33. Lawrence R. Baca, "Meyers v. Board of Education: The Brown v. Board of Indian Country," *University of Illinois Law Review* 5 (2004): 1155–80.
34. 25 U.S.C. 452 et seq.
35. Helen Maynor Scheirbeck et al., "Report on Indian Education," 73.
36. Timothy LaFrance, *Handbook of Federal Indian Education Laws* (Boulder: Native American Rights Fund, 1982).
37. Ibid.
38. 355 F. Supp. 716 (D.N.M. 1973).
39. In LaFrance, T. 1982; supra at 726.
40. Bruce D. Baker, "Does Money Matter in Education?" (Albert Shanker Institute, 2016), http://www.shankerinstitute.org/sites/shanker/files/moneymatters_edition2.pdf
41. Jacqueline Jordan Irvine and Willis D. Hawley, "Culturally Responsive Pedagogy: An Overview of Research on Student Outcomes," Teaching Tolerance (Southern Poverty Law Center, 2011), https://www.edweek.org/media/crt_research.pdf
42. Mackey, "The ESSA in Indian Country"; "National Indian Education Study 2011:The Educational Experiences of American Indian and Alaska Native Students at Grades 4 and 8" (Washington, D.C.: National Center for Education Statistics, 2011), https://nces.ed.gov/nationsreportcard/pdf/studies/2012466.pdf
43. Susan C. Faircloth and John W. Tippeconnic, "The Dropout/Graduation Rate Crisis Among American Indian and Alaska Native Students: Failure to Respond Places the Future of Native Peoples at Risk" (The Civil Rights Project/Proyecto Derechos Civiles at UCLA and the Pennsylvania State University Center for the Study of Leadership in American Indian Education, 2010), https://www.civilrightsproject.ucla.edu/research/k-12-education/school-dropouts/the-dropout-graduation-crisis-among-american-indian-and-alaska-native-students-failure-to-respond-places-the-future-of-native-peoples-at-risk/faircloth-tippeconnic-native-american-dropouts.pdf
44. David H. DeJong, *Promises of the Past: A History of Indian Education* (Golden, Colo.: Fulcrum, 1993); The Consortium of Johnson O'Malley Committees of Region IV, State of Washington, *The Way It Was (Anaku Iwacha): Yakima Legends*, 1974.
45. For more on this see Tarajean Yazzie-Mintz, "From a Place Deep Inside: Culturally Appropriate Curriculum as the Embodiment of Navajo-Ness in Classroom Pedagogy," *Journal of American Indian Education* 46, no. 3 (December 2007): 72–93; J. Kay Fenimore-Smith, "The Power of Place: Creating an Indigenous Charter School," *Journal of American Indian Education* 48, no. 2 (January 1, 2009): 1–17; Teresa L. McCarty and Tiffany S. Lee, "Critical Culturally Sustaining/Revitalizing Pedagogy and Indigenous Education Sovereignty,"

Harvard Educational Review 84, no. 1 (Spring 2014): 101-124,135-136; Tiffany S. Lee and Teresa L. McCarty, "Upholding Indigenous Education Sovereignty Through Critical Culturally Sustaining/Revitalizing Pedagogy," in *Culturally Sustaining Pedagogies: Teaching and Learning for Justice in a Changing World*, ed. Django Paris and H. Samy Alim (New York, NY: Teachers College Press, 2017); Jerry Lipka, Nancy Sharp, and Betsy Brenner, "The Relevance of Culturally Based Curriculum and Instruction: The Case of Nancy Sharp," *Journal of American Indian Education* 44, no. 3 (September 2005): 31–54.

46. Tsianina Lomawaima, "Education," in *The World of Indigenous North America*, ed. Robert Warrior (New York, 2015): 367.
47. Ibid., 384.
48. National Indian Education Association, "Building Relationships with Tribes: A Native Process for ESSA Consultation" (Washington, DC: National Indian Education Association, 2016), http://www.niea.org/for-advocates/education-priorities/state/essa-implementation/niea-consultation-guides/; National Indian Education Association, "Building Relationships with Tribes: A Native Process for Local Consultation Under ESSA" (Washington, D.C.: National Indian Education Association, 2017), http://www.niea.org/wp-content/uploads/2018/01/NIEA-LEA-Guide-FINAL.pdf
49. 25 CFR 273.15.
50. For additional histories of Indian Education, see Adams, *Education for Extinction*; K. Tsianina Lomawaima and Teresa L. McCarty, *"To Remain an Indian": Lessons in Democracy from a Century of Native American Education* (New York, NY: Teachers College Press, 2006); Reyhner and Eder, *American Indian Education*; Thomas Thompson, ed., *The Schooling of Native America* (Washington, D.C.: Office of Education, 1978); Szasz, *Indian Education in the American Colonies;* Szasz, *Education and the American Indian,* among others.
51. Table 16.1 is a modified version of a table from Meredith L. McCoy's working manuscript on Indian education finance.
52. 25 U.S.C. ch. 14, subch. II § 5301 et seq.
53. Bureau of Indian Education, "Bureau of Indian Education Strategic Direction 2018–2023" (Washington, D.C.: Department of the Interior, 2018), https://www.bie.edu/cs/groups/xbie/documents/site_assets/idc2-086443.pdf
54. See "Indian Elementary-Secondary Education"; Rose, "Testimony of the National Indian Education Association."
55. 25 U.S.C. 13, 2008; Public Law 107-110, 115 Stat. 1425.
56. HINU and SIPI were appropriated $16,885,000 in FY 2018 to cover costs during a change in the fiscal year from an October-to-September cycle to an academic year cycle of July 1 to June 30. Future funding will be on the July 1 to June 30 cycle. The $22,117,000 and the $16,885,000 apply to the period from October 1, 2017 to June 30, 2019.
57. The dollar amounts listed above are from the BIE 2018 appropriations, and the student count numbers are from the BIE's student count system. Appropriations details in this section were provided by BIE Financial Systems Specialist, Joe Herrin, via personal communication, November 30, 2018.
58. "Indian Elementary-Secondary Education"

59. Administration for Native Americans, "About Native Languages," Administration for Native Americans, An Office of the Administration for Children and Families, 2018, https://www.acf.hhs.gov/ana/programs/native-language-preservation-maintenance/about; Administration for Native Americans, "SEDS Special Program Areas," Administration for Native Americans, An Office of the Administration for Children and Families, 2017, https://www.acf.hhs.gov/ana/seds-special-initiatives
60. Sara Bernstein et al., "Descriptive Data on Region XI Head Start Children and Families: AI/AN FACES Fall 2015–Spring 2016 Data Tables and Study Design" (Washington, D.C.: Office of Planning, Research, and Evaluation, 2018), https://www.acf.hhs.gov/sites/default/files/opre/aian_faces_technical_report_final_to_opre_508.pdf
61. National American Indian and Alaska Native Head Start Collaboration Office, "National American Indian/Alaska Native Head Start Collaboration Office: Strategic Plan 2015–2020" (Washington, D.C.: National American Indian and Alaska Native Head Start Collaboration Office, 2016), https://eclkc.ohs.acf.hhs.gov/sites/default/files/pdf/aian-strategic-plan-2015-2020.pdf
62. Amy Bowers, "Tribal Education Departments Report" (Boulder: Tribal Education Departments National Assembly, 2011), https://www.narf.org/nill/resources/education/reports/tednareport2011.pdf
63. Dawn M. Mackety et al., "American Indian Education: The Role of Tribal Education Departments" (Denver: McRel, 2009).
64. Melody L. McCoy, "An Historical Analysis of Requests for Direct Federal Funding for Tribal Education Departments for Fiscal Years 1989–2004," Indian Education Legal Support Project: Tribalizing Indian Education (Boulder: Native American Rights Fund, 2003), http://www.narf.org/wordpress/wp-content/uploads/2015/01/maroon.pdf
65. U.S. Department of Education, "State Tribal Education Partnership Program," U.S. Department of Education Programs, 2015, https://www2.ed.gov/programs/step/index.html
66. Office of the Assistant Secretary–Indian Affairs, "Eight Tribes Receive Nearly $2.5 Million in Grants: Funds Help Tribes Take Control of Own Educational Programs," (November 5, 2015), https://www.bie.edu/cs/groups/xbie/documents/text/idc1-032163.pdf
67. National Indian Education Association, "Building Relationships with Tribes."
68. Mackey, "The ESSA in Indian Country."
69. The Education Trust, "The State of Education for Native Students" (Washington, D.C.: The Education Trust, 2013).
70. Andrea D. Beesley et al., "Profiles of Partnerships Between Tribal Education Departments and Local Education Agencies" (Washington, D.C.: Institute of Education Sciences, National Center for Education Evaluation and Regional Assistance, REL Central, 2012), https://ies.ed.gov/ncee/edlabs/regions/central/pdf/REL_2012137_sum.pdf
71. National Indian Education Association, "Building Relationships with Tribes."
72. 480 U.S. 202 (1987).
73. 25 U.S.C. ch. 29 § 2701 et seq.

74. Office of Indian Gaming, "Indian Gaming Compacts," U.S. Department of the Interior–Indian Affairs, n.d., https://www.bia.gov/as-ia/oig/gaming-compacts
75. Oklahoma Office of Management and Enterprise Services, "Oklahoma Gaming Compliance Unit Annual Report: Fiscal Year 2017" (Oklahoma City: Oklahoma Office of Management and Enterprise Services, 2017), https://ok.gov/OSF/documents/GameCompAnnReport2017-e.pdf
76. Arizona Department of Gaming, "Tribal Contributions," Arizona Department of Gaming, n.d., https://gaming.az.gov/tribal-contributions; Arizona Department of Gaming, "Tribal Contributions from Gaming Revenue to the State, Cities, Towns, & Counties–As of August 1, 2018," Arizona Department of Gaming, 2018, https://gaming.az.gov/sites/default/files/Cumulative%20TC%20amts%20-%20States%20FY2019%20-%20at%20081418_0.pdf
77. State of Washington Office of Superintendent of Public Instruction, "State-Tribal Education Compact Schools (STECs)," Office of Native Education, 2018, http://www.k12.wa.us/IndianEd/STECs.aspx
78. Wisconsin State Tribal Initiative, "Wisconsin State Tribal Relations Initiative," Wisconsin State Tribal Relations Initiative, n.d., http://witribes.wi.gov/
79. An updated list can be found at Wisconsin Department of Public Instruction, "American Indian Studies: Memorandum of Understanding (MOU)" Wisconsin Department of Public Instruction, n.d., https://dpi.wi.gov/amind/mou
80. Wisconsin Department of Public Instruction, "American Indian Studies: State Statutes," Wisconsin Department of Public Instruction, n.d., https://dpi.wi.gov/amind/mou
81. David J, O'Connor, Education Consultant for the Wisconsin American Indian Studies Program, contributed to the content pertinent to the State of Wisconsin (Personal Communication, January 14, 2019).
82. Washington Office of Superintendent of Public Instruction, "Since Time Immemorial: Tribal Sovereignty in Washington State," Since Time Immemorial, 2017, http://www.k12.wa.us/IndianEd/TribalSovereignty/default.aspx
83. Montana Office of Public Instruction, "Indian Education," Indian Education, n.d., https://opi.mt.gov/Educators/Teaching-Learning/Indian-Education.
84. Shear, "Cultural Genocide Masked as Education"; Shear et al., "Manifesting Destiny"; Journell, "An Incomplete History"; Shear et al., "Toward Responsibility."
85. National Indian Education Association's FY2018 Budget Request, "The Federal Trust Responsibility to Native Education." (Washington D.C.: National Indian Education Association, 2017), 2. Found at: http://www.niea.org/wp-content/uploads/2016/03/NIEA-FY-2018-Budget-2-21-17-3.pdf
86. Restricted Fee land is land held by Native individuals who must receive permission from the Department of Interior (DOI) in order to sell or pass land to heirs. This land is often associated with the allotment era (as discussed previously) through families that never relinquished ownership of this land, even under guardianship of non-Native people. Trust land is land that is held in trust under title of the Secretary of the Department of Interior for a Native nation or individual, and this land falls under the jurisdiction of the Native

nation and federal government. Both restricted fee and trust land are exempt from state and local taxes. If a Native nation purchases land as fee simple, a deed purchase just like any other business or individual might do, it is taxable until it undergoes a fee-to-trust review process by the DOI and is taken under title of the Secretary. National Congress of American Indians, "Tribal Nations and the United States."
87. National Congress of American Indians, "Taxation," National Congress of American Indians, n.d., http://www.ncai.org/policy-issues/tribal-governance/taxation
88. Ibid.
89. U.S. Department of the Interior, "Payments in Lieu of Taxes," U.S. Department of the Interior, 2018: para. 3. https://www.doi.gov/pilt
90. Public Law 92-203 (1971).
91. National Congress of American Indians, "Tribal Nations and the United States," 26.
92. For more on Alaska Native education, see Alaska Native Knowledge Network, "History of Alaska Native Education," Alaska Native Knowledge, 2011, http://ankn.uaf.edu/Curriculum/Articles/History/. For more on Native Hawaiian education, see Native Hawaiian Education Council, "History," Native Hawaiian Education Council, n.d., http://www.nhec.org/about-nhec/history/

CHAPTER 17

Iowa

Patti Schroeder
School Finance Director
Iowa Association of School Boards

Shawn Snyder
School Finance Director
Iowa Association of School Boards

GENERAL BACKGROUND

Iowa's schools were originally created by each community's members when enough money had been raised to pay a teacher, provide a school, and purchase essential books and supplies. In 1864, a new state governance system was established by the legislature, creating local school boards and defining local board methods of operation. In 1868, Iowa Judge Dillon determined that school districts have only those powers which are expressly granted or necessarily implied in governing statutes, also known as Dillon's Rule.[1]

At one time there were over 5,000 school districts in Iowa. In the 1950s, the legislature adopted a reorganization law that required all areas of the state to be in a school district offering a kindergarten through grade 12 (K–12) education program, and reorganizing school districts so that no district had fewer than 300 pupils. School districts continued to be governed by local school boards, and operations of school districts were supported by property taxes. The method of fully financing school districts through property taxes remained in place until the mid-1960s. At that time, Iowa taxpayers sought the state's assistance in reducing the local property tax burden.

In 1967, the state adopted a new way to fund Iowa's school districts by equalizing the property tax burden by county on a per-pupil basis. In 1971, the first state foundation program was adopted. This formula, (also known as the school finance formula), substantially increased state aid to school districts. The goals of the state foundation formula were "to equalize educational opportunity, to provide a good education for all the children of Iowa, to provide property tax relief, to decrease the percentage of school costs paid from property taxes, and to provide reasonable control of school costs."[2] Over the years, other components were added to the school finance formula.

Iowa is one of the few states where the school finance formula has not been successfully challenged through the court system. This is primarily because Iowa law establishes a *maximum* cost per pupil that, when multiplied by a district's enrollment, largely represents the maximum amount (ceiling) or spending authority a district can spend to educate students in the district. In this way, the Iowa school foundation formula has generally been considered equitable on a per-pupil basis across the state.

BASIC SUPPORT PROGRAM

General Fund

The Iowa School Foundation Formula calculates the maximum spending authority (ceiling), as well as the mix of property tax and state aid that go into funding spending authority. The state foundation formula is pupil-driven: i.e., most elements of spending authority, as well as funding levels, are based on district enrollment or subsets of enrollment multiplied by a cost per-pupil amount or by enrollment multiplied by a weighting factor applied to either enrollment or cost per-pupil amount.

First, the state foundation formula calculates a maximum school district spending amount (ceiling) which is referred to as maximum spending authority.

Maximum Spending Authority

Maximum Spending Authority is a calculation that is the sum of the Combined District Cost, preschool formula funds, the instructional support levy program (ISL), any modified supplemental amount approved by the school budget review committee (SBRC), miscellaneous income, and unspent balance from the prior fiscal year. Table 17.1 depicts how it works, along with the components making up the overall spending authority and the corresponding revenue sources to fund these components of spending authority.

TABLE 17.1 Basic Support Program Components		
Spending Authority Components		Revenue Sources
Previous Unspent Balance		Cash Reserves
Miscellaneous Income		State/Federal Other
SBRC Modified Supplement Amount		Local Taxes
Preschool Formula		State Aid
ISL and Educational Improvement		Additional Levy
Dropout Prevention		
AEA Flow-Through		
State Categorical Supplements		
Special Education Weighting		
Total Regular Program	Combined District Cost Components	State Aid
		Uniform Levy

Combined District Cost

Combined District Cost (see Table 17.1) is a term at the core of the spending authority calculation, and it equals the summation of the Regular Program District Cost, Supplementary Weighting District Cost, Special Education District Cost, categorical supplements (Teacher Salary Supplement, Professional Development, Early Intervention Supplement, and Teacher Leadership Supplement), funds for supplemental weighting, Area Education Agency Media, Education Services, Special Education Support, and Dropout Prevention funding. Some of these components are defined next:

- *Regular Program District Cost:* equals the district cost per-pupil amount times the district's budget enrollment and represents the majority of spending authority (about 74%), as well as the majority of the funding a district receives. The cost per pupil and any increase in the cost per pupil from year to year is set by the legislature. Budget enrollment is the number of school-aged children residing in a school district on October 1 of the year prior to the year being budgeted;
- *State Foundation Aid:* equals Regular Program State Foundation Cost Per Pupil times Weighted Enrollment (the sum of the Budget Enrollment, Supplementary Weighting, and Special Education Weighting). This determines the level of state aid and property taxes for funding purposes.
- *State Categorical Supplements:* include funding for:
  - Teacher Salary Supplement—additional funding for teachers' salaries;

- Professional Development—additional funding for district level professional development;
- Early Intervention Supplement—additional funding for more teachers at the early elementary level to reduce class size;
- Teacher Leadership Supplement—additional funding to provide teacher leaders and mentors to improve teaching effectiveness.

Each of these categorical funding sources has a district cost per-pupil which, when multiplied by the Budget Enrollment, creates additional spending authority as well as additional funding. Combined District Cost also includes:

- *Special Education District Cost:* equals the Regular Program District Cost Per Pupil times the Special Education Weighting times the number of special education pupils identified with needs at a given level. The higher the needs for a special education child, the higher the weighting as presented in Table 17.2.
- *Supplementary Weightings:* weightings and funding breakdowns for special education and other categories are shown in Table 17.3.

Other Components of Combined District Cost

There are other components of Combined District Cost. The most significant ones from a funding aspect are highlighted below.

- *Area Education Agency (AEA) Flow-through Funding:* AEAs and regional educational resource centers cannot levy property taxes, so for budgetary purposes AEA funding flows through each school district's budget that is within an AEA boundary. AEAs receive regular program, special education, media, educational services and categorical supplements cost per-pupil amounts which, when multiplied by the district's enrollments within an AEA, make up the spending authority and funding for that AEA. In the past few years, the legislature has reduced AEAs funding by $7.5 million (permanent reduction) and up to an additional $15.0 million per year.

TABLE 17.2 Special Education Weighting Factors

Level	Weighting	Regular Program Weighting	Total Weighting (in per-pupil terms)
I	0.72	1.0	1.72
II	1.21	1.0	2.21
III	2.74	1.0	3.74

TABLE 17.3 Special Education and Other Weightings FY 2018 Estimated School Finance Amounts

Weighting Category	Weight	State Aid[a]	Property Tax	Total	# Districts
Special Ed. 1	24,236.64	$143,335,489	$18,788,838	$162,124,327	333
Special Ed. 2	16,842.14	99,604,416	12,996,111	112,600,527	333
Special Ed. 3	23,257.12	137,542,608	18,014,122	155,556,730	330
Total Special Ed.	**64,335.90**	**$380,482,513**	**$49,799,072**	**$430,281,585**	**333**
Shared Students	55.44	327,872	42,644	370,516	49
Shared Teachers	181.47	1,073,214	143,081	1,216,295	66
Community College Courses	3,121.69	18,461,675	2,413,674	20,875,349	333
Whole Grade Sharing	41.90	247,797	32,480	280,276	6
Regional Academy	31.60	186,882	25,849	212,731	1
ICN	1.72	10,172	1,337	11,510	41
Operational Functions	3,232.00	19,114,048	2,543,839	21,657,887	228
Supplementary Shared Weight Total	**6,665.82**	**$39,421,649**	**$5,202,905**	**$44,624,564**	**333**
At-Risk	2,392.18	14,147,353	1,851,876	15,999,228	333
English as a Second Language	4,500.54	26,616,194	3,496,725	30,112,919	239
Reorganization	382.50	2,262,105	301,398	2,564,503	8
Total Supplementary Weight	**13,941.04**	**$82,447,311**	**$10,853,903**	**$93,301,214**	**333**
Re Education Agency Sharing	99.04	22,878	7,121	$29,999	1
Total Weighting	**78,375.98**	**$462,953,702**	**$60,660,096**	**$523,612,797**	**333**

Notes:
Special Ed. 1	Weighting of 0.72.
Special Ed. 2	Weighting of 1.21.

(continued)

TABLE 17.3 Special Education and Other Weightings FY 2018 Estimated School Finance Amounts (continued)

Weighting Category	Weight	State Aid**	Property Tax	Total	# Districts
Special Ed. 3	Weighting of 2.74.				
Shared Students	Weighting of 0.48.				
Shared Teachers	Weighting of 0.48.				
Community College Courses	Weighting of 0.46 for liberal arts and science courses and 0.70 career tech.				
Whole Grade Sharing	Weighting of 0.10 per student for eligible districts.				
Regional Academy	Weighting of 0.10 per student—total weighting for a district cannot be less than 10.0 or more than 15.0.				
ICN	Weighting of 0.05.				
Operational Functions	Weighting based on specific function. Maximum per district cannot exceed 21.0.				
At-Risk	Calculated by formula.				
ESL	Weighting of 0.22.				
Reorganization	Eligible districts that reorganized receive Whole Grade sharing weighting received in year prior to reorganization for three years.				
AEA Sharing	Weighting based on formula for eligible AEAs.				

Additional Notes:

In general, weightings are based on the portion of time the student attends the specific program.

[a] State aid and property tax amounts are based on IASB calculations and include funding for additional property tax relief to cover the increase in the FY 2014–FY 2018 State cost per pupil due to the State percent of growth rate ($83 per pupil).

Funding amounts are based on individual calculations and may not match the Department of Management's Aid and levy worksheet totals.

Totals and subtotals may not sum due to rounding.

AEA = Are Education Agency
ESL = English-as-a-Second-Language
ICN = Iowa Communications Network

Sources: Iowa Department of Management, School Aid File; Iowa Department of Education, Certified Enrollment file; IASB analysis and calculations.

- *Dropout Prevention Funding:* Local Iowa school boards can approve additional funding, financed solely with local property taxes, for services for potential and returning dropouts to aid this group of students in staying, progressing, and graduating from high school. The maximum a local board can approve is subject to legislative limitation and a 25% match of other funds from the district.
- *English as a Second Language (ESL):* Iowa provides additional funding for the specific needs of students who speak English as their second language. The funding level is based on the number of English language learners identified by the district multiplied by a weighting factor of 0.22 times the cost per student amount for that district. This is included as part of supplementary weighting.
- *Gifted and Talented Funding:* Iowa also provides funding to help with the educational needs of gifted and talented students. The funding level is based on the number of identified gifted and talented students multiplied by a dollar per-pupil amount which was set at $38 per identified pupil in FY 2000 but has been allowed to grow and is currently at $62 per identified pupil. A district is required to provide a 25% match to these funds.
- *Home Schooling Assistance Program Funding:* Iowa provides funding to help with instruction and support services for home-schooled students and their parents. The funding is based on a weighting factor of .3 of 1% multiplied by the number of home-schooled children in a district times the cost per-pupil amount for that district.

Other Components of Spending Authority Beyond Combined District Cost

There are other components not included in the Combined District Cost that, when added together, help make up the maximum spending authority for a district:

- *Preschool Funding:* The legislature created a statewide voluntary four-year-old preschool program, offering free preschool to four-year-olds and funding it with state resources. Spending authority and funding is at half the cost per pupil times the number of four-year-olds enrolled in preschool.
- *Instructional Support Levy Program (ISL):* Districts can receive spending authority and funding up to 10% of their regular program funding level for additional instructional support. Since ISL is funded locally through either property taxes or a mix of property and income surtaxes, it requires board approval and must be reapproved every

five years by the board, or every ten years through local election. There is a state aid component to this funding, but it has not been funded in recent years.

- *Modified Supplemental Amount:* School districts may be provided additional spending authority that is beyond the funding generated through the school foundation formula. This is called modified supplemental amount because the school district's spending authority may be modified and approved by the Iowa School Budget Review Committee (SBRC) to reflect factors specific to the individual school district for such things as opening new school buildings, asbestos removal, or negative special education balances, among other reasons. While modified supplemental amount increases spending authority, it does not increase funding. Funding only comes if the district is willing and can, within limitations set by the legislature, increase its property taxes for cash reserves.
- *Negative special education balances:* A unique and desirable aspect of Iowa school finance is that the SBRC must grant a modified supplemental amount to school districts that certify they have negative special education balances. Federal law requires that school districts spend whatever is necessary to provide for the educational needs of special education students. Special education funding calculated in the school foundation formula is generally not sufficient to fully pay for a school district's special education programming, and districts must use other general fund resources to make up the difference. To receive additional spending authority for its negative special education balances, a school district must certify after year-end to the SBRC that the district does have a negative special education balance, and that it will fund the modified supplemental amount with unexpended cash balance or cash reserve levy. Based on this certification, the SBRC grants additional spending authority. Thus, districts may be able to recoup the funds from a negative special education balance in the succeeding year if the district board approves the use of property taxes to do so.[3]
- *Miscellaneous Income:* This is any general fund revenue that is not part of the combined district cost. In other words, if general fund revenue received by a school district is not from the uniform levy, state foundation aid or the additional levy, it is miscellaneous income.[4] These funding sources are also a component of spending authority. Examples include revenue received from other districts for open enrollment into the district, federal, state and local grants received outside the school foundation formula, and investment income.
- *Unspent Balance:* The last element of a school district's total spending authority is the unspent balance. The title 'unspent balance' is

somewhat misleading since it seems to indicate that funds in hand were not spent when, in fact, it may only mean that total spending authority was unspent. Unspent balance is the difference between spending authority and *actual* expenditures. To the extent funds are available, unspent balance can be used for onetime expenditures. It is against the law for a district to have a negative unspent balance; if negative, a district is required to develop, gain SBRC approval, and implement a corrective action plan. While the unspent balance may not be backed by cash on hand, a school district can generate funds for spending its unspent balance by levying for cash reserve. This is called the cash reserve levy.

- *Cash Reserve Levy:* Within legislative limitations, a district can approve a property tax rate to provide working capital or cash for unforeseen events. However, it is important to note that while this levy brings in cash, it does not bring in spending authority.

The Combined District Cost is funded by a Uniform Levy, State Foundation Aid, Property Tax Replacement Payments, and an Additional Levy (see Table 17.1 earlier).

- *Uniform Levy:* The uniform levy is a property tax levied equally against the taxable property valuation in each school district in the state. The uniform levy is $5.40 per $1,000 of taxable valuation. Because taxable valuation per pupil is different from one district to the next, the amount of funding raised in this manner differs significantly between districts.
- *State Aid:* Under the Iowa school finance formula, funding is equalized at 87.5% of the regular program cost per-pupil amount for each district. It is state money, or state foundation aid, that funds the difference between the amount received by the district from the uniform levy up to the foundation percentage of 87.5% of the state cost per pupil.[5] In addition to the regular program foundation, state foundation aid also includes state aid for the state categorical supplements (teacher salary, professional development, early intervention, and teacher leadership), and AEA special education support services. The difference between the equalization at 87.5% and 100% is then funded by an additional property levy, beyond the uniform levy.
- *Property Tax Replacement Payments:* There are several calculations that have been added to the formula over time to provide additional property tax relief: i.e., allowing state aid to fund parts of the formula that before were funded with property taxes. These property tax relief efforts have kept down the use of local property taxes in

funding schools and have significantly increased state aid, but are a wash to school districts, as state aid replaces property taxes.

- *Additional Levy:* To fully fund a district's cost per pupil, the school foundation aid formula charges an additional property tax levy to bring the overall mix of property taxes and state aid to 100% of the value calculated by the cost per pupil times enrollment.[6] Under the formula, variances in property tax rates among school districts are partially due to the additional levy. A larger property tax rate is needed for a lower taxable valuation per-pupil school district to fully fund its district cost per pupil than the property tax rate needed in a higher taxable valuation per-pupil district. Also, the additional levy provides the revenue to fund a portion of the AEAs, dropout prevention, and if a district is eligible, a budget adjustment (also referred to as budget guarantee) provision.
- *State Percent of Growth and Supplemental State Aid:* These are terms used in Iowa to describe the amount the state legislature allows the cost per pupil to grow from one year to the next. Prior to FY 2014 the state percent of growth was funded with a mix of property taxes and state aid. However, since FY 2014 the increase has been entirely funded with state aid as another method to hold down property tax growth in school districts. Each categorical supplement is also allowed to grow by the state percent of growth established each year.
- *Budget Adjustment* (also known as Budget Guarantee): This is a unique feature of the Iowa Foundation Aid formula. If a district has a budgeted regular program cost that is less than 101% of the previous year's regular program cost, the district (with board approval through resolution) may receive a budget adjustment to increase the total regular program funding to an amount that is 101% of the prior year's regular program funding. A district may be in this situation and be eligible if district enrollment decreases are greater than the impact of the state percent of growth or increase from one year to the next. The budget adjustment is funded entirely through local property taxes.[7]

Figure 17.1 illustrates the equalizing aspect of the foundation percentage. In Figure 17.1, both school districts are identical in every respect except taxable valuation per pupil. District A has the 'average' taxable valuation per pupil, while District B has a taxable valuation per pupil 50% higher than District A. District B generates nearly 50% more from the uniform levy per-pupil which means state aid falls by a corresponding amount, so that both districts' mix of property tax and state aid are equalized at the state foundation percentage of 87.5%.

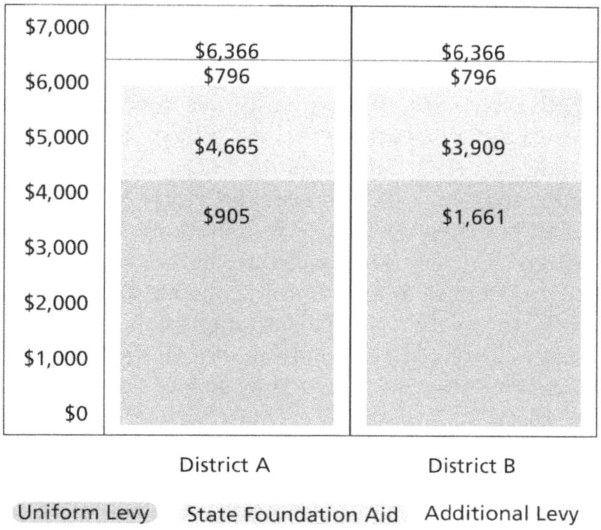

Figure 17.1 School Aid Per Pupil Funding.

OTHER FUNDING SOURCES—NON-GENERAL FUND

In addition to the School Foundation Formula and the General Fund, there are other levies and revenue sources that can be approved by a school district or by the voters of the district:

- *Management Levy:* The management levy is a tax that can be levied annually by a school board. There is no maximum rate limit or dollar limit on the amount levied. However, the management levy may only be used to fund an early retirement program, unemployment compensation, judgements, costs of mediation and arbitration, tort liability, and property insurance.[8]
- *Physical Plant and Equipment Levy (PPEL):* The PPEL is a property tax levy comprised of two levies—the regular physical plant and equipment levy (up to $0.33), and the voter-approved physical plant and equipment levy (up to $1.34). The maximum amount of the joint levies may not exceed $1.67 per $1,000 of taxable valuation. This funding may be used for such stated purposes as purchase of grounds, construction of schoolhouses, technology hardware, non-instructional software, asbestos removal, and bus purchases.[9]
- *Public Education and Recreation Levy (PERL):* The PERL may be levied at $0.135 per $1,000 taxable valuation by a simple majority vote of

the voters residing in the school district to establish and maintain public recreation places and playgrounds in district school buildings or on the grounds, and to support adult and community education. Once PERL is in place, the levy continues until the school board or the voters vote to discontinue the levy by a simple majority.[10]

- *General Obligation (GO) Bond Indebtedness Levy:* A school district may issue bonds, contract indebtedness, and levy property tax to pay the principal and interest on bonded indebtedness for a period not to exceed 20 years. The levy is made against all property in the school district. The proposition to issue bonds, contract indebtedness, and levy property tax to pay the principal and interest on the bonded indebtedness may be submitted to voters on specified school election dates. The proposition must be approved by 60% of those voting. The levy may not exceed $2.70 per $1,000 taxable valuation in any one year unless the voters approve a one-time election to set the maximum at $4.05 per $1,000 taxable valuation in a year. This additional levy must be approved by 60% of the total votes cast in favor of a $4.05 levy. If either election fails, a school board must wait six months from the date of the election before holding another election.[11]
- *Secure an Advanced Vision for Education (SAVE) Funds:* Another unique and desirable feature of Iowa school finance is a dedicated one-cent statewide sales tax for school infrastructure. The state increased sales tax from 5.0% to 6.0%, designating that the increase be used for school infrastructure or district property tax relief. The statewide penny is slated to be repealed at the end of 2029. However, legislation has been introduced to extend this funding through 2049. Most of the revenue from the penny tax is deposited in the Secure an Advanced Vision for Education (SAVE) Fund. All school districts receive the same per-pupil amount multiplied by its district enrollment. By law, these funds can be used for infrastructure needs, such as construction, reconstruction, remodeling, repair or purchasing schoolhouses, land, stadiums, or gyms. Funds can also be used to purchase revenue bonds for infrastructure needs as approved by a district's local school board, to be paid back with sales taxes over a limited period. Each school district's revenue purpose statement is approved by voters and provides further details on how SAVE funds can be used by the district.[12] SAVE funds can also be used for any PPEL or PERL purpose or to reduce the property tax levies of PPEL or PERL. If a district does not have an approved revenue purpose statement, then proceeds from SAVE are required to be used to reduce any debt levy, regular or voter approved PPEL, PERL, payment for principal and interest of revenue bonds, and for the payment or retirement of bonds issued for school infrastructure purposes.[13]

SUMMARY

The Iowa School Foundation Formula (also known as the School Finance Formula) creates a maximum spending authority (ceiling), as well as a method to calculate the mix of property taxes and state aid to fund the authority. Funding is equalized so that districts with lower taxable valuation per pupil and therefore less ability to generate property taxes are made whole to the 87.5% level by state aid, while districts with higher taxable valuation generating more property taxes receive less state aid. The formula is pupil-driven, that is, most components of the formula are based on district enrollment or subsets of district enrollment multiplied by a cost per-pupil amount or by multiplying enrollment by a weighting factor applied to the enrollment or cost per pupil. The formula is designed to provide equitable funding to address each student's needs, no matter where in Iowa that student resides. The state General Fund appropriation for K–12 in Iowa accounts for about half the monies appropriated by the State of Iowa and is augmented by property taxes at the local level. Table 17.4 summarizes the many components of the Iowa School Foundation Formula.

TABLE 17.4 FY 2018 School Foundation Aid Funding by Area (in millions)

Program Funding		FY 2018
	Regular Program District Cost	$3,244.1
	Regular Program Budget Adjustment	$23.6
	District Supplementary Weighting	$93.3
	District Special Education Instruction	$430.3
	District Teacher Salary Supplement	$279.4
	District Professional Development Supplement	$31.7
	District Early Intervention Supplement	$34.5
	Teacher Leadership Supplement	$157.4
	AEA Special Ed Support District Cost	$159.6
	AEA Special Ed Support Adjustment	$1.5
	AEA Media Services	$28.3
	AEA Ed Services	#31.3
	AEA Teacher Salary Supplement	$15.8
	AEA Professional Development Supplement	$1.9
	Dropout and Dropout Prevention	$120.1
	Combined District Cost	**$4,630.9**
	Statewide Voluntary Preschool Program	$78.2

(continued)

TABLE 17.4 FY 2018 School Foundation Aid Funding by Area (in millions) (continued)

		FY 2018
State Aid	Regular Program	$1,940.9
	Supplementary Weighting	$81.3
	Special Education Weighting	$375.1
	Property Tax Adjustment Aid (1992)	$8.5
	Property Tax Replacement Payment (PTRP)	$46.8
	Adjusted Additional Property Tax—General Fund	$24.0
	Statewide Voluntary Preschool Program	$78.2
	Minimum State Aid	$0
	State Aid from General Fund	**$3,179.6**
	Excess from SAVE Fund	$9.7
	Total State Aid (includes Non-General Fund)	**$3,189.3**
Local Property Tax	Uniform Levy Amount	$862.1
	Additional Levy	$612.7
	Total Levy to Fund Combined District Cost	**$1,474.7**
	Commercial/Industrial Uniform Levy Replacement	$26.3
	Commercial/Industrial Additional Levy Replacement	$19.5
Other Levies: Local Property Tax	Cash Reserve	$224.7
	Instructional Support Levy	$138.1
	Management Levy	$137.0
	Education Levy	$0.8
	Physical Plant and Equipment Levy—Board Approved	$55.4
	Physical Plant and Equipment Levy—Voter Approved	$139.8
	Public Education and Recreation Levy	$2.7
	Debt Service	$180.1
	Total Other Levies—Property Tax	**$878.6**
Other Levies: Income Surtax	Education Levy	$0.1
	Instructional Support Levy	$91.2
	PPEL—Voter Approved	$10.1
	Total Other Levies—Income Surtax	**$101.4**

Source: Iowa Legislative Services Agency and IASB.

NOTES

1. An impactful ruling with broad application, originating in *City of Clinton v. Cedar Rapids and Missouri River R.R.*, 24 Iowa 455 (1868).
2. Iowa Code § 257.31(10).

3. Iowa Code § 257.31(14).
4. Iowa Code § 257.2(9).
5. Iowa Code § 257.1(2).
6. Iowa Code § 257.4.
7. Iowa Code §257.14.
8. Iowa Code § 298.4.
9. Iowa Code § 298.2.
10. Iowa Code §300.
11. Iowa Code § 298.18.
12. Iowa Code § 423f.
13. Iowa Code § 423f.3.

CHAPTER 18

Kansas

David C. Thompson, Ed.D.
*Skeen Endowed Professor
Department Head Educational Leadership
Kansas State University*

S. Craig Neuenswander, Ed.D.
*Director of School Finance
Kansas State Department of Education*

John M. Heim, Ph.D.
*Executive Director
Kansas Association of School Boards*

Randy D. Watson, Ph.D.
Kansas Education Commissioner

GENERAL BACKGROUND

The Kansas Legislature began providing funding for public schools in 1937 when it established aid for elementary schools.[1] Secondary schools were aided beginning in 1955.[2] Additional emergency aid was added in 1959.[3] Sweeping school consolidation occurred beginning in 1963, dramatically reducing the state's approximately 2,800 school districts to only 311 by 1969.[4] Legislative enactment of the state's first true school finance formula likewise followed in this same timeframe, known as the School Foundation Act (SFA) of 1965.[5]

This formula broke conceptual ground in Kansas by creating a mindset supporting general state aid. Unique features were an adjustment per school district for teacher training and experience, along with a pupil-teacher ratio multiplier tied to each district's position relative to the state average. These elements combined to establish a state duty to fund schools and acknowledged the need to better equalize educational opportunity among districts.

Major reform occurred again in 1973 as the state enacted the School District Equalization Act.[6] Known as SDEA, it was essentially a reward-for-effort formula. Reform occurred again in 1992 with enactment of the School District Finance and Quality Performance Act[7] (SDFQPA) which established a floor and caps on revenue and expenditure via a strongly structured foundation aid plan. Responding to economic distress tied to steep state tax reductions and political change, in 2015 the state abandoned the SDFQPA, substituting a system of block grants known as Classroom Learning Assuring Student Success Act[8] (CLASS) which froze school aid at prior year levels extending through Fiscal Year 2017 when a new aid formula was expected. In 2017, the state enacted the School Equity and Enhancement Act[9] (SEEA), which again in response to political change restored in most ways the key elements of the former SDFQPA foundation aid plan. Long-term effects of the recent intervening years and restorations are yet to be determined.[10]

All these state aid plans were vigorously litigated. The SFA (1965) fell under state court scrutiny,[11] leading to enactment of SDEA (1973) which in turn was litigated[12] and led to the SDFQPA (1992). The state remained embroiled in court battles over equitable and adequate funding levels and aid distribution methods as plaintiffs repeatedly challenged amendments to the SDFQPA[13] and nearby tax cuts, in part leading to enactment of the SEEA (2017). The state supreme court continues to retain jurisdiction primarily on adequacy grounds, recently adding a requirement for an inflation factor. Elements of the state legislature continue to promote a constitutional amendment to limit or bar judicial interference in school funding matters.[14]

BASIC SUPPORT PROGRAM

General Fund

The School Equity and Enhancement Act of 2017 essentially reinstated and renamed the former SDFQPA general fund foundation aid plan that operated from 1992–2015. Key restorations were elimination of the block grant philosophy, a return to floors and caps on per-pupil revenue and expenditure levels, and restoration of the weighted enrollment concept, with per-pupil weightings added to a uniform base amount per pupil. Weightings are meant to adjust for at-risk, high-density at-risk, bilingual, special education, career technical education, high enrollment, low enrollment, declining enrollment, new school facilities, ancillary school facilities, cost of living, virtual enrollment, and transportation differences among the state's 286 school districts. These weightings are based in the principle of vertical equity meant to adjust for differences in pupils' educational needs. Weightings function as multipliers against base aid for student excellence (a legislatively established uniform budget per pupil amount), with base state aid serving horizontal equity by setting an expenditure floor/cap adjusted by these vertical weights. While essentially restoring the SDFQPA, the new SEEA formula also made several refinements involving certain weights, enrollment count dates, at-risk funding, all-day kindergarten, early childhood education, local option budget, and scholarship tax credits.

Operationally, the general fund state aid formula is expressed as two parts as shown in Figure 18.1.

Base Aid for Student Excellence (BASE) is the foundation uniform per pupil amount. BASE is a legislatively determined amount, derived partly from historical expenditure levels, partly from legislative quantification of educational need as determined by either cost studies or legislative preference, and ultimately is reconciled to match the legislatively appropriated amount assigned to public schools once the entire state's budget for the next fiscal year is passed into law. All districts receive the BASE amount per full-time equivalent (FTE) pupil or a proration thereof for part-time pupils. Once the BASE amount is set, enrollment adjustments are applied via total weighting factors indicated earlier using the process shown in Form 150[15] in the Kansas budget software. The result is Total Financial Aid (TFA). The final step is to calculate the local district's share which is then subtracted from TFA to result in State Financial Aid as shown in Form 148.[16] The outcome is a foundation aid plan built on a statewide uniform base budget per pupil adjusted by pupil weights tied to educational need under a uniform general fund tax rate.[17] The aid formula is reviewed and appropriated in each annual legislative session. However, since Kansas is a cash basis law state, if state revenues falter, aid reductions may occur since the state constitution does not permit deficit-spending.

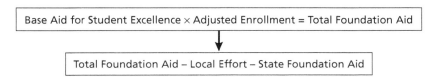

Figure 18.1 Kansas Basic Support Formula. *Source:* Kansas Legislative Research Department, 2014–2015 School Year School District Finance & Quality Performance Act & Bond & Interest State Aid Program—July 1, 2014. Modified by KSDE to reflect SEEA January 2018.

Under the new 2017 general fund state aid formula, the per-pupil BASE amount was set at $4,006 for FY 2018. Pupil weighting adjustments are shown in Table 18.1.

The new 2017 SEEA made changes and improvements to the restored foundation aid plan. New highlights for 2017 were:

- *Base aid* increased to $4,006 in 2017–18 and $4,128 in 2018–19. Out-year increases were estimated at $4,190 in 2019–20; $4,253 in 2020–21, and $4,317 in 2021–22. Beginning in 2019–20, estimates are to be based on the Midwest consumer price index.
- *Ancillary facilities and cost of living* were continued.
- *Declining enrollment* weighting was reduced 50% in the 2017–18 school year and was eliminated beginning 2018–19.

TABLE 18.1 Pupil Weighting Adjustments

Weight	Factor
Low Enrollment	1.014331
High Enrollment	0.035040
Bilingual	0.395 or .185 headcount, whichever is higher
K–12 At-Risk (free lunch)	0.484
High Density At-Risk 50% or more free lunch of 212.1 pupils per square mile plus 35.1% free lunch;	0.105
or 35%–49% free lunch	0.7 multiplier after subtracting 35% from total at-risk count
Four-year-old At Risk	0.5 FTE
Facilities	0.25 multiplier to FTE in new facility*
Ancillary Facilities	Weight calculated after approved tax appeal ÷ BASE = weight*
Special Education	Weight calculated by SPED aid ÷ BASE = weight*
Declining Enrollment	Weight calculated after special tax levy ÷ BASE = weight*
Cost of Living	Weight calculated from density graph ÷ BASE = weight*
Transportation	Weight calculated from density graph ÷ BASE = factor*
Virtual Enrollment	Separate formula: full-time students = $5,000 Part-time students = $1,700/FTE Students over 19 = $709 per credit earned

* Additional conditions and restrictions apply.
Source: Kansas Legislative Research Department. 2014–2015 School Year School District Finance & Quality Performance Act & Bond & Interest State Aid Program—July 1, 2014. Adjusted for 2017 legislative changes.

- *At-risk funding* remained based on free lunch count; the at-risk weighting was increased from .456 to .484.
- *High-density at-risk* computation was changed to permit districts to choose between computing by attendance center or school district for 2017–18 and 2018–19.
- *All-day kindergarten* funding at 1.0 FTE was enacted for all pupils.
- *New facilities* funding was changed to include only bond elections held prior to July 1, 2015 with a .25 weighting.
- *Bilingual education* was changed to use the higher of .395 of contact hours or .185 of bilingual headcount.
- *Low and high enrollment* weighting was reinstated as in law prior to 2014–15.
- *Early childhood* funding was expanded by increasing state aid for four-year-old at-risk programs.
- *Mentoring and professional development* were provided partial funding.
- *Utilities, property and casualty insurance* were added as options for payment from the capital outlay fund.
- *Tax credit scholarship* options were granted for low-income pupils from the 100 lowest performing schools beginning July 1, 2018.
- *Nonresident out-of-state pupil counts* were changed for state aid purposes. Pupils count as 1.0 FTE for 2017–18 and 2018–19, reducing to .75 for 2019–20 and 2020–21, and .5 in 2021–22 and thereafter.

These changes were accompanied by increased appropriations to fund programs and to at least partially address the state supreme court's judicial monitoring where estimates of new required monies have ranged as high as $800 million. Selected amounts are shown in Table 18.2. Total state aid appropriated to all 286 school districts for General Fund purposes was $2,805,882,976 for FY 2018, and total General Fund budgets, excluding special education, in all districts reached $2,814,962,687. State aid was 99.7% of total general fund budgets.

SUPPLEMENTAL GENERAL FUND

The 1992 SDFQPA scheme allowed school districts to engage additional local leeway spending within limits. Earlier reference to revenue and expenditure floors and caps in Kansas originated with SDFQPA, as all previous aid formulas were either unregulated local control or were built on reward-for-effort equalization as in the case of the SDEA of 1973. The initial SDFQPA created a base budget per pupil adjusted by program weights which resulted in the base budget amount serving as a uniform horizontal equity measure

TABLE 18.2 Selected Funding Amounts FY 2018

Program	2017–18	2018–19	2019–20	2020–21	2021–22
Base State Aid for Student Excellence (BASE)	4,006	4,128	CPI Est. 4,190	CPI Est. 4,253	CPI Est. 4,317
General State Aid	161,111,776	85,858,910	42,780,000	43,470,000	44,160,000
Special Education Fund Formula	12,000,000	12,000,000	12,000,000	12,000,000	12,000,000
Increased Funding 4-Year-Old At-Risk	2,000,000	2,000,000	2,000,000	2,000,000	2,000,000
Mentoring	800,000	Same as prior year	Same as prior year	Same as prior year	Same as prior year
Professional Development	1,700,000	Same as prior year	Same as prior year	Same as prior year	Same as prior year
New Facilities	13,000,000	(2,000,000)	(2,000,000)	(2,000,000)	(2,000,000)
Extraordinary Need	2,593,452				
Military-Second Count	1,500,000				
Total	194,705,228	97,858,910	54,780,000	55,470,000	56,160,000

Source: Kansas State Department of Education. Proposed School Finance Plan Senate Bill 19—6-5-17 Major Policy Provisions. Computer Printout SF17-232

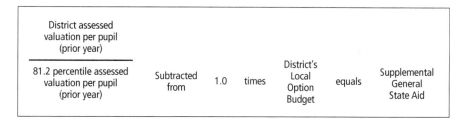

Figure 18.2 Local Option Budget Calculation FY 2018. *Source:* Kansas Legislative Research Department. 22014–2015 School Year School District Finance & Quality Performance Act & Bond & Interest State Aid Program–July 1, 2014.

as well as an expression of vertical equity. However, the SDFQPA also provided school districts with additional local option spending leeway known at the time as Local Enhancement Budget (LEB) which later was restyled as the Local Option Budget (LOB). At inception, the LEB was rightly named since it was meant to provide local choice for program enhancement. Over time, districts came to rely on it for funding basic services in the absence of state aid increases. Districts continue to rely on LOB for basic supports, and its optional nature today is accurate only in that districts are not required to levy the accompanying additional property tax, although LOB adoption is nearly universal statewide for the reasons indicated.

The SEEA of 2017 preserved the LOB (named Supplemental General Fund in statute) and granted new local authority to increase this funding stream. Any district may now choose to levy up to an additional 33% of its State Financial Aid entitlement (see SFA earlier in Table 18.1). To help offset this induced horizontal inequality, the state of Kansas provides equalized aid to the LOB, although at a different ratio than for TFA. Historically, the state has equalized the LOB in each district to the 81.2 percentile of assessed valuation per pupil, meaning that any district below that percentile is aided as if it were at that benchmark, while any district having an assessed valuation above the 81.2 percentile receives no LOB aid.

The LOB follows the formula shown in Figure 18.2. Calculation of each district's LOB authority follows Form 155[18] in the Kansas budget software. Total state aid appropriated to all 286 school districts for LOB purposes was $454,500,000 for FY 2018, and total LOB budgets in all districts reached $1,106,491,631. State aid was 41.1% of total LOB budgets.

COMPENSATORY EDUCATION

Compensatory education programs are integrated via pupil weightings built into each school district's general fund budget, along with operation of categorical funds. Kansas provides general fund weightings as shown earlier in Table 18.1. Specific compensatory programs include K–12 at-risk, four-year-old at-risk, and bilingual education.

Funding for K–12 at-risk programs is determined by the number of pupils qualifying for free meals. Districts receive an additional 0.484 weighting for each qualifying pupil. If more than 35% of district pupils qualify for free meals, an additional high-density weighting is added. Total state aid to all 286 school districts for K–12 at-risk education was $413,095,114 for FY 2018, representing 14.7% of total general fund budgets, excluding special education.

The state also provides funding for four-year-old at-risk programs. Pupils must meet specific at-risk criteria to qualify and are funded as one-half FTE pupils.[19] Total state aid to all 286 school districts for four-year-old at-risk education was $14,866,266 for FY 2018, representing 0.5% of total general fund budgets, excluding special education.

Local districts also receive an additional weighting for bilingual education programs. Districts are funded on the higher of 0.395 times the bilingual pupil contact hours, or 0.185 times the number of identified bilingual pupils. Total state aid to all 286 school districts for bilingual education was $42,661,095 for FY 2018, representing 1.5% of total general fund budgets, excluding special education.

SPECIAL EDUCATION

Although special education was included in the earlier description of general fund pupil weightings in Kansas, the actual program operates as a separate fund. Inclusion in the general fund in Kansas is an artifice designed to temporarily inflate a school district's general fund for purposes of levying for local option budget authority. The effect is to increase the tax yield for LOB purposes since LOB is calculated based on the size of the general fund. Special education services state aid is therefore first deposited to the district's general fund and then transferred to its own special education fund.

Kansas school finance is characterized as intensely enrollment-driven, as the foundation aid formula relies on pupil counts expressed as FTE for all calculations and distribution of revenues. Special education is the exception to this principle by being tied to the classroom unit. Consequently, the funded unit is the classroom teacher.

Organization and operation of special education services in Kansas conform to any of three models: district-provided, interlocal agreements, and cooperatives. District-provided services are self-descriptive as a single district budgets, directs, and controls services. Interlocals are multi-district entities organized as quasi-districts with separate budget authority. Cooperatives are also multi-district entities hosted by a member district, but with different legal structure wherein the host district carries the cooperative's special education budget on its books. In both cases, member districts share costs through member assessments. The choice of organization is often dictated by district size and cost-efficiency considerations perceived by the membership.

Calculation of special education services aid follows Form 118 of the Kansas budget software.[20] Key elements are number of certified special education teachers, number of paraprofessionals, and teacher and pupil costs related to travel. The model recognizes that itinerant services are inherent to special education. Special education in Kansas is a reimbursement model, wherein costs are incurred locally and reimbursed by the state. However, state aid is not intended to fully cover the cost of special education, leaving school districts to fund the shortfall by budgeting general fund monies for transfer to the special education fund. The state is statutorily required to provide 92% of the excess cost of special education.[21] For FY 2018 state aid was approximately 78.5% of excess cost.

Special education aid in Kansas is based on a projected cost per teacher, set annually by the state. Special education teachers are employees of the district or interlocal. The district bears any cost difference if it provides a higher salary for its local teachers; if in an interlocal agreement, member assessments are adjusted to cover any of these unfunded salary costs as the interlocal has its own salary schedule. The state further provides .4 funding for paraprofessionals hired by the district/interlocal/cooperative. State aid is therefore the product of 1.0 FTE teachers plus .4 FTE paraprofessionals multiplied by the allowable state per-teacher amount. For FY 2018, the state amount was $28,250. The resultant calculation yields the following procedure: [Estimated State Aid = xFTE teachers + xFTE paras * $28,250]. Special education service units can affect these costs via salary schedules and by balancing licensed teacher and paraprofessional positions.

Transportation services form the other major cost calculation in Kansas special education. Costs are reimbursed by the state in a cost-share ratio. Form 118 permits transportation salaries and benefits, insurance, equipment and maintenance, along with mileage costs for service delivery. Transportation costs are reimbursed at an 80% cost share with the district. A provision is made for maintenance in lieu of services for certain educational needs. Provision is also available for catastrophic services. The state and special education service providers also have access to all federal special education monies according to the state plan.

Total state aid to all 286 school districts for special education was $445,981,646 for FY 2018, and total special education budgets in all districts reached $906,491,448.

GENERAL TRANSPORTATION

Pupil transportation is a huge expense in Kansas given a largely rural and vast geography, and state aid to transportation is a weighting in every district's general fund calculation. Pupils residing at least 2.5 miles from school are aided via a cost reimbursement formula, although others may ride at district expense. The state calculates a per-pupil cost using a complex density-cost graph that takes into account pupil sparsity. Operationally, the formula plots a curve of best fit for each district to yield a cost per pupil which is then multiplied against the number of transported pupils. This cost is tied to base state aid, thereby including it as a weighting to the general fund. Calculation of transportation weighting is seen in Form 150 (Table III).[22]

Total state aid to all 286 school districts for general transportation was $102,575,232 for FY 2018, and total student transportation budgets in all districts reached $157,394,355. State aid was 65.1% of total student transportation budgets.

SCHOOL FACILITIES

The state of Kansas provides a general fund weighting for school districts that commence operation of new classroom facilities. The enrollment of the new school is multiplied by a factor of .25 provided other conditions are met. The weighting is calculated in Form 150[23] and is available only to districts exercising a minimum 25% LOB authority and which held a bond election prior to July 1, 2015 using bond money for new schools or classroom additions. The weighting is available upon commencing operation of the new facilities and is limited to two years thereafter.

Total state aid to all 286 school districts for school facilities was $16,570,017 for FY 2018. State aid was 0.6% of total general fund budgets, excluding special education.

CAREER AND TECHNICAL EDUCATION

Kansas provides an additional 0.5 weighting for each FTE pupil enrolled in approved vocational courses. This weighting is added to the district enrollment and multiplied by the BASE.[24] Total state aid to all 286 school districts for career and technical education was $37,783,390 for FY 2018. Career and technical state aid was 1.3% of total general fund budgets, excluding special education.

VIRTUAL EDUCATION

Local Kansas school districts may offer virtual courses, with funding for virtual pupils included in the general fund, but under a different formula than traditional pupils. Full-time virtual pupils are funded at $5,000 per FTE and part-time pupils are funded at $1,700 per FTE. Virtual pupils over the age of 19 are funded at $709 per credit earned up to a maximum of six credits.[25]

Total state aid to all 286 school districts for virtual education was $31,343,680 for FY 2018. Virtual education state aid was 1.1% of total general fund budgets, excluding special education.

SPECIAL LEVIES

School districts may levy additional local property tax to provide funding for three specific areas of additional costs in some districts. Ancillary school facilities weighting allows districts with extraordinary enrollment growth to petition the State Board of Tax Appeals for authority to levy an additional property tax for up to two years to defray new facility start-up costs that were beyond the costs financed in a bond election. A second option exists for districts experiencing enrollment decline. Such districts may appeal to the State Board of Tax Appeals for authority to levy an additional property tax for up to two years in an amount not greater than the revenue lost due to declining enrollment. After the initial two years, the district's levy authority continues, but phases out over a six-year period. The third levy is available to districts with average appraised home values greater than 125% of the state average. This cost-of-living weighting may not exceed 5% of a district's general fund budget and is subject to protest petition by local district voters.

Financing for these three funds is converted to a pupil weighting and becomes part of the state finance formula.[26] Revenue is generated entirely by local property tax in the districts utilizing these funds, with no state aid provision. Total funding for 2018 was $54,800,000.

CAPITAL OUTLAY

The state of Kansas provides considerable latitude to school districts in the use of their separate capital outlay funds. This fund is generally used for maintenance and upkeep and cash projects involving school facilities and equipment. Many school districts use this fund to accumulate cash reserves, either through scheduled transfers from the general fund or by an authorized special tax levy. The 2017 SEEA expanded uses of the capital outlay fund to include utilities and property and casualty insurance.

School districts may locally levy up to 8 mills of property tax to fund the capital outlay. State aid for capital outlay was not provided from 2009 through 2014. The Kansas Legislature began funding state aid again in 2015, and implemented the current state aid formula in 2017, in response to a state supreme court ruling. The formula is equalized with the median assessed valuation per pupil (AVPP) receiving 25% state aid. Each $1,000 in AVPP above the median receives 1% less state aid. Each $1,000 below the median receives 1% additional state aid.

Total state aid to all 286 school districts for capital outlay was $60,530,000 for FY 2018, and total capital outlay revenue in all districts reached $362,518,579. State aid was 16.7% of total revenue.

FOOD SERVICES

All Kansas school districts are expected to operate a food service program in full compliance with federal and state regulations. Districts are free to structure food services in-house or to contract with outside vendors. Virtually all districts engage in a four-way cost sharing in accord with local funding preferences. Reimbursement rates by federal and state government carry the first part of costs, with the remainder shared by local districts and pupils. Each district is free to determine food service costs and to set the local prices and cost-shares. Each school board determines its participation, generally by scheduled transfer from the general fund to the food service fund. Any unfunded difference represents the cost to pupil. The process is seen in Form 162[27] of the state budget software.

Total state aid appropriated to all 286 school districts for food service was $2,510,486 for FY 2018, and total food service budgets in all districts reached $294,635,231. State aid was 0.9% of total budgets.

STATE FUNDING FOR NON-PUBLIC SCHOOLS

Kansas has only minimally engaged in public funding for non-public schools, and typically has done so through mandated provision of certain shared services or by in-kind contributions. As a broad characterization, the state does not make provision for direct payment of state resources to private or parochial schools. The state does provide transportation for both public and nonpublic schoolchildren. Other sharing of services as mandated in federal law is observed.

The state currently has ten charter schools under the direct supervision of their local school districts. Charter schools in Kansas are independent public schools operating within a school district and are free of charge to parents and open to all pupils. These charter schools are subject to all rules and regulations pertaining to accreditation and other accountability within the state's charter guidelines.[28]

The most direct involvement of Kansas public monies in non-public schools is by a tax credit provision initially adopted by the state legislature in 2014 and amended in the new SEEA of 2017. Under the SEEA, low-income pupils from the 100 lowest performing schools were granted tax credit scholarship options. Low income is defined as qualifying for free lunch programs. Qualified donors may make contributions and receive a 70% tax credit. A $500,000 per year contribution cap applies to donors. Qualified donors include corporations, insurance companies, or individuals. In 2017, $687,254 in scholarships were awarded to 204 students. A total of $5,200,421 has been contributed to the program since 2015, resulting in tax credits of $3,640,295.

OTHER STATE AIDS

The state provides various other aid to public schools including driver education, motorcycle safety, professional development, and mentor teacher programs. See Form 195 in the Kansas budget software.[29]

Capital Improvement

The state provides capital improvement aid for school districts' facilities following after successful local bond elections. State aid rates are based on assessed valuation per pupil (AVPP), with two separate formulas. Bond elections passed prior to July 1, 2015 generate state aid based on the median AVPP district receiving 25% state aid. Each $1,000 in AVPP above the median receives 1% less state aid. Inversely, each $1,000 below the median receives 1% additional state aid. For elections held after July 1, 2015, the district with the lowest AVPP receives 75% state aid. Every $1,000 increase in AVPP decreases state aid by 1%. This formula change reduces state aid to districts by 23%–25%.

Total capital improvement expenditures for 2018 were $556,628,656. Capital improvement state aid was $188,593,226 of that amount, or 33.9%.

Retirement

The Kansas Public Employees Retirement System (KPERS) applies to all public schools in Kansas. KPERS administers three defined benefit retirement systems: the Kansas Public Employees Retirement System, the Kansas Police and Firemen's Retirement System, and the Kansas Retirement System for Judges. Schools are included under the public employee system.

School employees contribute to KPERS through payroll deduction. There is no school district contribution, as the state considers itself to be the payor for the employer share. The state's contribution for public school districts in 2018 was $390,319,670.

REVENUE

State revenue for aid payments to local school districts is primarily derived from income, sales, and property taxes as well as a variety of small fee funds and assessments. State revenue receipts have been volatile in recent years as the state legislature significantly reduced income taxes in 2012, forcing reliance on other revenue sources and cash balances. The 2017 legislature restored many of the income tax reductions. For 2018 total state aid to school districts was approximately $4,450,385,000.

Federal revenue primarily funds Title programs, including special education, and food service. Smaller amounts of federal revenue help fund career and technical education, capital improvement, and grants. Approximate 2018 total federal revenue to school districts was about $500,000,000.

Local revenue is calculated after state and federal revenues are known. School districts apply the state aid formula for each specific fund, subtract that amount and any federal funds from the budget, and levy the difference locally. Local school board revenue authority is limited to the property tax and a few miscellaneous fees. For 2018 local revenue was approximately $1,650,000,000.

The exception to this practice is the school district general fund budget. Every school district is statutorily required to levy 20 mills property tax for the general fund. Prior to 2015 the 20-mill levy was collected by counties, distributed directly to school districts and treated as local revenue. In 2014 the state legislature determined that counties should send that tax to the state, with the state distributing it back to local districts as state aid. For 2018 total state aid included approximately $643,101,000 from the 20-mill general fund levy.

SUMMARY

Table 18.3[30] summarizes several views of Kansas public education funding for Fiscal Years 2016–2019. On a grand scale, P–12 education budgeted at $3.39 billion represents 21% of the state's total $15.9 billion budget for

TABLE 18.3 Four-Year General Fund Expenditure Analysis

Agency	Actual FY 2016	Education State General Fund Expenditures FY 2016–FY 2019		
		Approved FY 2017	Approved FY 2018	Approved FY 2019
Department of Education	$3,009,361,008	$3,098,992,761	$3,394,152,246	$3,326,877,540
Kansas State Library	4,042,473	3,864,035	3,872,811	3,881,357
School for the Blind	5,303,584	5,403,988	5,386,299	5,435,726
School for the Death	8,682,249	8,813,828	8,830,008	8,899,869
State Historical Society	3,463,309	4,248,847	4,264,833	4,281,056
For Hays State University	32,086,541	32,822,540	32,776,775	32,921,990
Kansas State University	99,136,520	97,401,226	97,138,169	98,482,390
KSU-Ext. Systems and Ag. Research	44,927,198	46,074,407	45,798,391	45,902,644
KSU-Veterinary Medical Center	14,247,551	14,587,491	14,438,520	14,528,680
Emporia State University	29,810,819	30,770,432	30,967,221	30,566,179
Pittsburg State University	34,196,948	35,386,387	34,698,414	34,793,676
University of Kansas	131,946,948	131,848,578	132,101,617	133,733,053
University of Kansas Medical Center	104,300,352	108,473,031	105,805,795	106,310,695
Wichita State University	72,046,788	71,717,393	71,090,543	71,875,016
Board of Regents	197,415,113	191,138,334	190,828,800	190,888,582
Total	$3,790,967,111	$3,881,543,278	$4,172,118,442	$4,109,378,453

FY 2018. Differently viewed, public elementary and secondary schools represent approximately 81% of P–20+ education budgets. Finally and overall, P–12 education represents 51% of the state's $6.6 billion[31] general fund where most of education's costs reside. In perspective, these costs provided services to nearly a half-million school-aged children in 2018.

NOTES

1. K.S.A. 72-5009.
2. K.S.A. 72-5702.
3. K.S.A. 72-6403.
4. See broad history at http://www.kslegresearch.org/KLRD-web/Publications/Education/2016-School-Finance-Overview.pdf
5. K.S.A. 72-7001.
6. K.S.A. 72-7030 et seq.
7. K.S.A. 72-6410. See formula operation at http://www.ksde.org/Portals/0/School%20Finance/budget/Legal_Max/sdfandqpa_2014-15.pdf?ver=2014-09-26-161228-583
8. K.S.A. 72-6463 et seq. See more broadly http://www.kslegresearch.org/KLRD-web/Publications/Education/2016_school_finance_history.pdf
9. K.S.A. 72-5131 et seq.
10. Early analysis has begun. See, for example, Shiloh J. Vincent, *A Longitudinal Study of Selected State School Aid Formula Changes in Kansas 1992–2017, with Emphasis on the Classroom Learning Assuring Student Success (CLASS) Act of 2015*. Unpublished doctoral dissertation, Kansas State University (2018); see also Kellen J. Adams, *An Overview of Selected Impacts and Reconceptualization of State Aid to Public School Infrastructure in Three Representative Kansas School Districts*. Unpublished doctoral dissertation, Kansas State University (2018).
11. *Caldwell v. State* No. 50616 (Kan. Dist. Ct. Aug. 30, 1972).
12. *Knowles v. State Bd. of Educ.*, 547 P.2d 699 (Kan. 1976).
13. Among others see *Mock v. State* (1991); numerous iterations of *Montoy v. State* (1999–2006); likewise *Gannon v. State* (2010–2017, citations omitted).
14. http://www.kslegresearch.org/KLRD-web/Publications/Education/2017-Article6-ProposedConstitutnlAmndmnts.pdf
15. Tab F150. Retrieved from http://www.ksde.org/Agency/Fiscal-and-Administrative-Services/School-Finance/Budget-Information/USD-Budget-Software
16. Tab F148. Retrieved from http://www.ksde.org/Agency/Fiscal-and-Administrative-Services/School-Finance/Budget-Information/USD-Budget-Software
17. Not discussed here is the concept of taxpayer equity, wherein the state partly derives revenue to fund the school aid formula from a statewide uniform property tax rate for schools. This element completes the underlying philosophy of pupil/taxpayer equity via a uniform base per pupil budget (horizontal pupil equity), weightings (vertical pupil equity), uniform tax levy (horizontal taxpayer equity), and state aid making up the difference between tax yield

and budget authority (vertical taxpayer equity). The concept of adequacy is not addressed here.
18. Tab F155. Retrieved from http://www.ksde.org/Agency/Fiscal-and-Administrative-Services/School-Finance/Budget-Information/USD-Budget-Software
19. Tab F150. Retrieved from http://www.ksde.org/Agency/Fiscal-and-Administrative-Services/School-Finance/Budget-Information/USD-Budget-Software
20. Tab F118. Retrieved from http://www.ksde.org/Agency/Fiscal-and-Administrative-Services/School-Finance/Budget-Information/USD-Budget-Software
21. K.S.A. 72-3422
22. Tab F150. Retrieved from http://www.ksde.org/Agency/Fiscal-and-Administrative-Services/School-Finance/Budget-Information/USD-Budget-Software
23. Tab F150. Retrieved from http://www.ksde.org/Agency/Fiscal-and-Administrative-Services/School-Finance/Budget-Information/USD-Budget-Software
24. Tab F150. Retrieved from http://www.ksde.org/Agency/Fiscal-and-Administrative-Services/School-Finance/Budget-Information/USD-Budget-Software
25. Tab F150. Retrieved from http://www.ksde.org/Agency/Fiscal-and-Administrative-Services/School-Finance/Budget-Information/USD-Budget-Software
26. Tab F242. Retrieved from http://www.ksde.org/Agency/Fiscal-and-Administrative-Services/School-Finance/Budget-Information/USD-Budget-Software
27. Tab F162. Retrieved from http://www.ksde.org/Agency/Fiscal-and-Administrative-Services/School-Finance/Budget-Information/USD-Budget-Software
28. http://www.ksde.org/Agency/Division-of-Learning-Services/Career-Standards-and-Assessment-Services/CSAS-Home/Graduation-and-Schools-of-Choice/Charter-Schools
29. Tab F162. Retrieved from http://www.ksde.org/Agency/Fiscal-and-Administrative-Services/School-Finance/Budget-Information/USD-Budget-Software
30. Kansas Legislative Research Department, *FY 2018 Appropriations Report*, p2-141.
31. Kansas Legislative Research Department, *FY 2018 Appropriations Report*, p1-1.

CHAPTER 19

Kentucky

William E. Thro, JD
General Counsel
University of Kentucky

GENERAL BACKGROUND

Any discussion of school finance in the Commonwealth of Kentucky must deal with two realities. First, there are great disparities between Appalachia and the rest of the state. Henry Caudill's 1963 classic, *Night Comes to the Cumberlands*,[1] inspired President Johnson's War on Poverty,[2] but that war was lost in Eastern Kentucky.[3] By any objective measure, the 54 Kentucky counties[4] served by the Appalachian Regional Commission lag behind the rest of the Commonwealth and the nation.[5] In terms of per capita income, poverty rate, percentage of adults with a high school diploma, percentage of adults with a college degree, and homes with broadband access, the non-Appalachian counties of Kentucky (population 3.2 million) closely track the national average,[6] but the Appalachian counties (population 1.1 million) represent the worst of American poverty.[7]

Second, Kentucky believes in local government and local control. Despite a population of only 4.3 million and a relatively small geographic area, Kentucky has 120 counties, more than any state except Texas, Georgia, and Virginia.[8] Each of those 120 counties has a school district, and there are an additional 53 independent school districts or a total of 173 districts.[9] Consequently, Kentucky does not and cannot take advantage of efficiencies associated with economies of scale.

This chapter on school finance in Kentucky has three distinct sections. Section I discusses the school finance litigation that is the foundation of

Kentucky school finance in the twenty-first century. Section II discusses the current school finance system. Section III examines future challenges to financing education in Kentucky.

THE FOUNDATION OF KENTUCKY SCHOOL FINANCE
ROSE V. COUNCIL FOR BETTER EDUCATION

The foundation of Kentucky's school finance system is *Rose v. Council for Better Education*,[10] a 1989 decision where the Kentucky Supreme Court invalidated *every* statute dealing with K–12 education.[11] In doing so, *Rose* recognized that educational equality depends not on money or racial desegregation, but involves the complex interaction of multiple factors.[12] Twenty years later in *Horne v. Flores*,[13] the U.S. Supreme Court reached a similar conclusion.[14] Both the courts in other states and the academy generally ignore this aspect of *Rose*, but it represents a profound truth.[15]

Three aspects of *Rose* are particularly important. First, it is faithful to the constitutional text. Second, it acknowledged local control as an implicit constitutional value. Third, it recognized the need for the legislature, not the judiciary, to solve the constitutional problem.

Faithful to the Constitutional Text

Rose was faithful to the constitutional text. Kentucky's education clause provides, "[t]he General Assembly shall, by appropriate legislation, provide for an efficient system of common schools throughout the state."[16] In describing how these "few simple, but direct words" establish "the will of the people with regard to the importance of providing public education in the Commonwealth,"[17] the court explained:

> Several conclusions readily appear from a reading of this section. First, it is the obligation, the sole obligation, of the General Assembly to provide for a system of common schools in Kentucky. The obligation to so provide is clear and unequivocal and is, in effect, a constitutional mandate. Next, the school system must be provided throughout the entire state, with no area (or its children) being omitted. The creation, implementation and maintenance of the school system must be achieved by appropriate legislation. Finally, the system must be an efficient one.[18]

In resolving the critical issue—the meaning of "efficient"—*Rose* considered "foreign cases, along with our constitutional debates, Kentucky precedents and the opinion of experts in formulating the definition of 'efficient' as it appears in our Constitution."[19]

However, instead of adopting a quality standard adopted by another branch of government, *Rose* developed its own standard. Not surprisingly, it failed. The court declared that:

> [A]n efficient system of education must have as its goal to provide each and every child with at least the seven following capacities: (i) sufficient oral and written communication skills to enable students to function in a complex and rapidly changing civilization; (ii) sufficient knowledge of economic, social, and political systems to enable the student to make informed choices; (iii) sufficient understanding of governmental processes to enable the student to understand the issues that affect his or her community, state, and nation; (iv) sufficient self-knowledge and knowledge of his or her mental and physical wellness; (v) sufficient grounding in the arts to enable each student to appreciate his or her cultural and historical heritage; (vi) sufficient training or preparation for advanced training in either academic or vocational fields so as to enable each child to choose and pursue life work intelligently; and (vii) sufficient levels of academic or vocational skills to enable public school students to compete favorably with their counterparts in surrounding states, in academics or in the job market.[20]

As noted in 1998, "[i]f this standard is taken literally, there is not a public school system in America that meets it."[21] A standard that is extraordinarily difficult to meet and is substantively vague is inappropriate. While that criticism is still valid, the Kentucky courts' refusal to enforce the standard tempers the criticism. After almost three decades, the *Rose* standard is not substantive, but merely aspirational.

Acknowledged Local Control As a Constitutional Value

While Kentucky does not have an explicit constitutional provision concerning local control, *Rose* implicitly recognized local control as a structural constitutional value. The court seemed aware that the General Assembly would never contemplate abandoning local school districts when it observed:

> In no way does this constitutional requirement act as a limitation on the General Assembly's power to create local school entities and to grant to those entities the authority to supplement the state system. Therefore, if the General Assembly decides to establish local school entities, it may also empower them to enact local revenue initiatives to supplement the uniform, equal educational effort that the General Assembly must provide. This includes not only revenue measures similar to the special taxes previously discussed, but also the power to assess local ad valorem taxes on real property and personal property at a rate over and above that set by the General Assembly to fund the statewide

system of common schools. Such local efforts may not be used by the General Assembly as a substitute for providing an adequate, equal, and substantially uniform educational system throughout this state."[22]

In effect, the court seemed to be harmonizing the structural constitutional value of local control with the textual constitutional value of federalism.

The Legislature Must Solve the Constitutional Problem

Third, *Rose* recognized the need for the legislative branch, not the judiciary, to solve the constitutional problem. *Rose* invalidated the entire educational *system*,[23] but it emphasized that "the *sole responsibility*...lies with the General Assembly."[24] The court was careful "not to instruct the General Assembly to enact any specific legislation" or "direct the members of the General Assembly to raise taxes."[25] The court's role was to "only decide the nature of the constitutional mandate."[26] Instead of creating a judicial solution,[27] the court "directed the General Assembly to recreate and redesign a new system" that would guarantee all children the opportunity for an adequate education through a *state* system."[28]

THE CURRENT KENTUCKY SCHOOL FINANCE SYSTEM

Overview

In 1990, immediately after *Rose*, The General Assembly—implicitly acknowledging both political reality and the constitutional limitation of local control—chose to enact reform rather than a revolution. Instead of dividing and consolidating school districts, moving to a system of centralized financing or radically altering teacher compensation, the legislature chose a path that retained the present school districts, continued a significant degree of local financing, and devoted additional resources to the current teacher compensation scheme.[29]

Specifically, the legislature passed the Support Educational Excellence in Kentucky (SEEK) program which provides the foundation for school finance.[30] Administered by the Kentucky Department of Education, SEEK attempts to ensure that each school district has sufficient funds to provide a constitutionally sufficient education to every child. Essentially, the state guarantees to each district a certain amount of funding per pupil (Guaranteed Base Funding) and enhances this amount for certain children with unique circumstances (adjustments or add-ons).[31] The sum of the

Guaranteed Base Funding and the adjustments is the Adjusted SEEK Base Funding.[32]

Local school districts are required to make a Local Effort by imposing real and personal property taxes.[33] To the extent the Local Effort fails to generate the amount of the Adjusted Seek Base Funding, the state makes up the difference (Calculated State SEEK Funding).[34] Additionally, local school districts have the option of raising additional revenue, some of which the state will match. Finally, the state provides a set amount of capital funding ($100) for each pupil.

Guaranteed Base Funding

During each two-year budget cycle, the Kentucky General Assembly establishes a per-pupil amount of funding.[35] Each school district receives a Guaranteed Base Funding amount, which is calculated by multiplying the per-pupil funding amount by the prior year's average daily attendance[36] with adjustment for enrollment growth.[37] If a district experiences dramatic decline in enrollment, there are statutory provisions to minimize the impact.[38]

Adjustments to the SEEK Guaranteed Base

Because it costs more to educate certain children, there are add-on adjustments for: (1) at-risk children; (2) children who receive instruction in a home or hospital setting; (3) exceptional children with disabilities); and (4) limited English proficiency children.[39] In addition, because transportation costs vary widely, school districts with greater transportation costs receive an adjustment.[40]

At-Risk Funding. Local school districts receive an additional 15% of Guaranteed Base Per Pupil Funding Amount for every child who receives free lunch under the federal government's school lunch program.[41]

Home and Hospital Funding. If a child is receiving instruction in a home or hospital setting under the provisions of state law, then the school district receives an additional sum of money equal to the Guaranteed Base Funding amount per pupil less $100.[42]

Exceptional Child Funding (Individuals with Disabilities). Local school districts receive additional funds for any pupil who receives service under the Individuals with Disabilities Education Act. State law divides these students into three categories: (1) low incidence disabilities; (2) moderate incident disabilities; and (3) high incidence disabilities.[43] School districts receive an additional 24% of base funding for each child with low incidence disabilities; an additional 117% of base funding for each child with moderate incidence disabilities; and an additional 235% of base funding for each child with high incidence disabilities.[44]

Limited English Proficiency Funding. School districts receive an additional 9.6% of the Guaranteed Base Per Pupil Funding for each Limited English Proficiency student.[45] Federal law determines whether a child qualifies as Limited English Proficiency.

Transportation Funding. Kentucky law establishes a complex formula for calculating transportation costs.[46] The state's school districts are divided into density groups based on based frequency, length, and type of transportation provided by the district.[47] Each density group then receives a set amount of money per pupil being transported by the district.[48] To the extent the school district transports students to local vocational schools or to the Kentucky School for the Deaf or to the Kentucky School for the Blind, it receives additional transportation money.[49]

Required Local Effort. As a condition of receiving any SEEK funding, Kentucky law requires each local school district to levy a minimum equivalent tax rate of 30 cents per $100 in assessed value of property and motor vehicles.[50] As noted earlier, to the extent the required local effort fails to generate the amount required for the school district's Adjusted SEEK Base Funding, the state makes up the difference through Calculated State SEEK Funding.[51]

Optional Local Effort. In addition to the required local effort, school districts have two options to raise additional revenues. First, under Tier One Funding, school districts are permitted to raise up to 15% of the district's Adjusted SEEK Base Funding (Guaranteed Base Funding + Adjustments).[52] If a district pursues this option, then the state will equalize the additional revenue. The level of equalization is set during each two-year budget cycle and generally helps property poor districts more than property rich districts.[53] Second, under Tier Two Funding, school districts—with the approval of the voters—may impose additional taxes and raise up to 30% of the district's Adjusted SEEK Base Funding plus the revenue raised in Tier One. The state does not match Tier Two Funds.[54]

Capital Outlay Funds. With respect to capital funding, the state guarantees that each school district will receive $100 per pupil per year.[55] Local districts are required to generate a portion of this $100 through a local property tax.[56]

THE FUTURE OF KENTUCKY SCHOOL FINANCE

A generation after it was first established, the SEEK plan remains in place.[57] Although the state has managed to maintain and even slightly increase the amount of per-pupil funding in the SEEK program, the state has steadily decreased the amount by which it subsidizes transportation.[58] This decrease reflects the ever-increasing financial pressures on Kentucky's school finance system. Two factors are particularly relevant—the costs of funding of the Kentucky Teacher Retirement and the dramatic increase in costs of other governmental programs. The remainder of this section discusses both factors.

Funding Kentucky's Public Employment Retirement System

Kentucky's defined benefit pension system for teachers and other public employees is both generous and ultimately unsustainable. To calculate the pension benefit, the state multiplies a teacher's years of service by the average of the three highest years' salary and then multiplies that total by a benefit factor (2.5%).[59] Teachers are generally able to retire with unreduced benefits after 27 years of service, or the age of 60, whichever comes first.[60] Conceivably, teachers can retire before age 50 and receive two-thirds pay for the rest of their lives. Those who work until age 65 generally will receive up to 100% of their active pay.

For a variety of reasons, Kentucky's public pension systems are unable to meet future obligations.[61] Estimates of unfunded liability range from $33 to $84 billion. Moreover, the substantial amount of unfunded liability has led national bond rating agencies to downgrade Kentucky's credit rating, thereby increasing the cost of debt funding for roads and other infrastructure projects. In order to solve the pension crisis, the legislature must either substantially reduce benefits or increase expenditures on pensions, or some combination. Given state constitutional constraints on reducing benefits, solving the pension crisis likely will involve increased expenditure on pensions. If expenditures on pensions are increased, it is virtually inevitable that the state will reduce expenditures for K–12 education. Ironically, the educational quality for Kentucky's children will suffer because the state will need to pay retirement benefits for the teachers who taught Kentucky's parents.

Costs of Other Governmental Functions

Finally in addition to the public pension crisis, governmental expenditures—particularly those associated with a former governor's 2013 Executive Order expanding Medicaid—are rising far faster than tax revenues. Because the Kentucky constitution requires a balanced budget, the legislature will either have to increase revenue, cut spending including spending on K–12 education, or some combination of the two measures. Although modest tax reform was enacted in 2018 (over the governor's veto) which should result in additional revenue, the state continues to face a dire budget situation.

CONCLUSION

Thirty years after *Rose* prompted significant reform of all aspects of education, Kentucky's SEEK system of school financing remains in place. However, financial pressures, particularly those related to the public pension crisis, continue to undermine SEEK. As the legislature contemplates hard choices, it seems likely that there will be at least some reduction to per-pupil expenditures. Such an action will make a second school finance case almost inevitable.

NOTES

1. See Henry M. Caudill, *Night Comes to the Cumberlands* (1963).
2. See John Cheves, Bill Estep, and Linda Blackford, *Fifty Years of Night* 74 (2014) (Kindle Edition) (chronicling the current conditions of Appalachian Kentucky on the fiftieth anniversary of Caudill's work).
3. See Kevin D. Williamson, *Left Behind:* "An Elegy for Appalachia," *National Review* December 16, 2013 p. 28.
4. Those counties are Adair, Bath, Bell, Boyd, Breathitt, Carter, Casey, Clark, Clay, Clinton, Cumberland, Edmonson, Elliott, Estill, Fleming, Floyd, Garrard, Green, Greenup, Harlan, Hart, Jackson, Johnson, Knott, Knox, Laurel, Lawrence, Lee, Leslie, Letcher, Lewis, Lincoln, McCreary, Madison, Magoffin, Martin, Menifee, Metcalfe, Monroe, Montgomery, Morgan, Nicholas, Owsley, Perry, Pike, Powell, Pulaski, Robertson, Rockcastle, Rowan, Russell, Wayne, Whitley, and Wolfe.
5. See Chives, Estep, and Blackford, p. 3320 (chart comparing Appalachian Counties, non-Appalachian Counties, and nation as a whole).
6. For example, non-Appalachia Kentucky has a per capita income of $25,130 and the nation has a per capita income of $28,501. The poverty rate is 16% for non-Appalachia Kentucky and 14% for the nation. The percentage of adults without a high school diploma is identical (14%). Non-Appalachia Kentucky is slightly below the United States in terms of adult college graduates (28%–24%) and has an identical broadband rate (98%).
7. To illustrate, Appalachia Kentucky has a per capita income of $ 18,158 and the nation has a per capita income of $28,501. The poverty rate is 25% for Appalachia Kentucky and 14% for the nation. The percentage of adults without a high school diploma is 26%; almost double the national norm of 14%.

Appalachia Kentucky is far below the United States in terms of adult college graduates (28%–12%) and substantially trails broadband rate (98%–87%).
8. See United States Census Bureau, *Geographic Areas Reference Manual* (2018). Retrieved from https://www.census.gov/geo/reference/garm.html)
9. See Kentucky Department of Education, *Kentucky Education Facts* (2018). Retrieved from https://education.ky.gov/comm/edfacts/Pages/default.aspx)
10. 790 S.W.2d 186 (Ky. 1989).
11. For a discussion of the long-term significance of *Rose*, *see* Scott R. Bauries, *Forward: Rights, Remedies, and Rose*, 98 Ky. L.J. 703 (2010); William E. Thro, *Judicial Humility: The Enduring Legacy of Rose v. Council for Better Education*, 98 Ky. L.J. 717 (2010); R. Craig Wood, *Justiciability, Adequacy, Advocacy, and the "American Dream,"* 92 Ky. L.J. 739 (2010).
12. Some scholars call for a renewed emphasis on financial resources. *See* William S. Koski & Rob Reich, *When "Adequate" Isn't: The Retreat from Equity in Educational Law and Policy and Why It Matters*, 56 Emory L.J. 545, 547 (2006).
13. *Horne v. Flores*, 557 U.S. 443 (2009). For some early observations about the impact of *Horne*, *see* William E. Thro, *The Many Faces of Compliance: The Supreme Court's Decision in Horne v. Flores*, 75 School Business Affairs 14 (October 2009).
14. *Horne*, 557 U.S. at 459-71.
15. But see D. Frank Vinik, *The Contrasting Politics of Remedy: The Alabama and Kentucky School Equity Funding Suits*, 22 J. Educ. Fin. 60 (1996).
16. Ky. Const. § 183.
17. *Rose*, 790 S.W.2d at 205.
18. Ibid.
19. Ibid. at 210.
20. *Rose*, 790 S.W.2d at 212.
21. William E. Thro, *A New Approach to State Constitutional Analysis in School Finance Litigation*, 14 J. L. & Pol. 525, 548 (1998).
22. *Rose*, 790 S.W.2d at 211-12 (footnotes omitted).
23. The court declared that:

> Lest there be any doubt, the result of our decision is that Kentucky's *entire system* of common schools is unconstitutional. There is no allegation that only part of the common school system is invalid, and we find no such circumstance. This decision applies to the entire sweep of the system-all its parts and parcels. This decision applies to the statutes creating, implementing and financing the *system* and to all regulations, etc., pertaining thereto. This decision covers the creation of local school districts, school boards, and the Kentucky Department of Education to the Minimum Foundation Program and Power Equalization Program. It covers school construction and maintenance, teacher certification-the whole gamut of the common school system in Kentucky.
>
> While individual statutes are not herein addressed specifically or considered and declared to be facially unconstitutional, the statutory system as a whole and the interrelationship of the parts therein are hereby declared to be in violation of Section 183 of the Kentucky Constitution. Just as the bricks and mortar used in the construction of a schoolhouse, while contributing to the building's facade, do not ensure the overall structural ad-

equacy of the schoolhouse, particular statutes drafted by the legislature in crafting and designing the current school system are not unconstitutional in and of themselves. Like the crumbling schoolhouse which must be redesigned and revitalized for more efficient use, with some component parts found to be adequate, some found to be less than adequate, statutes relating to education may be reenacted as components of a constitutional system if they combine with other component statutes to form an efficient and thereby constitutional system. *Rose*, 790 S.W.2d at 215.

24. *Rose*, 790 S.W.2d at 216.
25. *Ibid.* at 212.
26. *Ibid.*
27. For example, the court could have ordered specific reforms such as a finance system that did not utilize local property taxes, a system of public school vouchers, a transformation of the teacher certification process, the consolidation or division of school districts, or the centralized administration of education.
28. *Rose*, 790 S.W.2d at 212.
29. This is not a criticism of the profound and significant reforms undertaken by the Kentucky Education Reform Act. Rather, it is an acknowledgement that the pre-*Rose* and post-*Rose* educational systems are structurally the same.
30. Kentucky Department of Education, SUPPORT EDUCATION EXCELLENCE IN KENTUCKY (SEEK) EXECUTIVE SUMMARY FOR THE 2014-15 ACADEMIC YEAR (2015). Retrieved from https://education.ky.gov/districts/SEEK/Pages/default.aspx).
31. If enrollment rises dramatically during the academic year, the state may provide additional funds. *See* Ky. Rev. Stat. § 158.060(1).
32. *SEEK Executive Summary*, p. 3.
33. See Ky. Rev. Stat. § 160.470(9)(a). Currently, the tax rate is 30 cents per $100 in assessed value.
34. *SEEK Executive Summary*, p. 3.
35. Ibid. p. 1.
36. The statute provides that average daily attendance is the aggregate days attended by pupils in a public school, adjusted for weather-related low attendance days if applicable, divided by the actual number of days school is in session, after the five (5) days with the lowest attendance have been deducted. Ky Rev. Stat § 157.320(1). In addition, there are adjustments "for virtual and performance based attendance, students under or over the funding age, and students residing in one district who attend in another district without a properly executed transfer agreement." *SEEK Executive Summary, supra* note 30, at 1.
37. Ibid.
38. Ky Rev. Stat. § 157.360(9) and (10).
39. *SEEK Executive Summary, supra* note 30, at 1.
40. Ibid. p. 2.
41. *SEEK Executive Summary*, p. 1.
42. *See* Ky. Rev. Stat. 157.270. The $100 reduction is intended to prevent capital outlay funding from being used for students who do not actually attend public schools. *SEEK Executive Summary, supra* note 30, at 2.
43. See Ky. Rev. Stat. § 157.200.

44. *SEEK Executive Summary*, p. 2.
45. *SEEK Executive Summary*, p. 3.
46. See Ky. Rev. Stat. § 157.370.
47. Specifically, the statute:
    requires a graph to be constructed utilizing the district's gross transported pupil density. At least nine different density groups must be identified by analyzing the results of the gross transported pupil density calculations. A smoothed graph of cost is then developed for each density group to determine the average cost per pupil per day.
    Costs shall be determined separately for county school districts and independent school districts. The cost of transportation includes all costs recorded for the transportation to and from schools in the general current expense fund and function 2700 (student transportation). Each district in an identified density group receives funding based on the average cost per pupil per day for that group as determined by the smoothed graph which provides an incentive for districts to supply transportation services efficiently. In addition, independent districts are limited to the lowest average cost per pupil per day for their district or the lowest average cost per pupil per day for a county school district. *SEEK Executive Summary*, p. 2.
48. As the Kentucky Department of Education explained:
    The cost of transportation includes amounts representing depreciation of district-owned buses. A district will theoretically receive 100% of the state bid price or actual purchase price of a bus after year 10 and 124% of the state bid price or actual purchase price of a bus at the end of the funding cycle after year 14. *SEEK Executive Summary*, p. 2.
49. Ibid. p. 3.
50. See Ky. Rev. Stat. § 160.470(9)(a).
51. *SEEK Executive Summary*, p. 3. Additionally, "[i]f local share using the prior year assessment increased by four percent (4%) plus the value of current year new property is less than local share using the current year assessment, that difference is the amount of additional funding to be provided." *Id.*
52. Ibid.
53. Ibid.
54. Ibid.
55. Ibid.
56. Ibid.
57. Various studies during the early 2000's concluded that the SEEK system was both equitable and adequate. However, recent events and the slow growth in total funding cast doubt on those conclusions.
58. See Kentucky Center for Economic Policy, *Governor's Budget Cuts Education, Eliminates Some Programs* at 1 (January 17, 2018) (observing that the State's share of transportation costs had declined from sixty-four percent to fifty-one percent from 2008 to 2018).
59. Ky. Rev. Stat. §§ 161.220(9); 161.620.
60. See Ky Rev. Stat. § 161.600.

61. By one measure, Kentucky's public pension systems are the worst funded among the fifty States. *See* Standard & Poor's, *U.S. State Pensions Weak Market Returns Will Contribute to Rise in Expense* (2016).

CHAPTER 20

Louisiana

Janet M. Pope Ed.D.
Executive Director
Louisiana School Boards Association

Dannie P. Garrett, III
Attorney at Law, LLC

Markey W. Pierré, MBA, Ph.D.
President and Managing Partner
Southern Strategy Group of North LA

GENERAL BACKGROUND

The Louisiana constitution tasks the state legislature with establishing and providing for a public education system in Section I of Article VIII. In Section 13(B) of Article VIII, the Louisiana constitution gives the State Board of Elementary and Secondary Education (BESE) responsibility for annually developing and adopting "...a formula which shall be used to determine the cost of a minimum foundation program of education in all public elementary and secondary schools as well as to equitably allocate the funds to parish and city school systems." The constitution tasks the Louisiana legislature with annually setting aside funds "...sufficient to fully fund the current cost to the state of such a program as determined by applying the approved formula in order to ensure a minimum foundation of education in all public elementary and secondary schools." These sections of the state constitution establish the legislative basis for the Minimum Foundation Program (MFP).[1]

The MFP is the process used by Louisiana to determine how local and state dollars are distributed across local school districts. The MFP is approved annually by the BESE and the legislature. The MFP determines the minimum district funding requirements, or the cost of education, for all public schools. This cost is calculated by adding together the base per-pupil amount, determined in legislation, and special allocations for at-risk and special education pupils and others.

The MFP helps to equitably distribute funds to all school systems, including local school districts and the Recovery School District. The state contributes the difference between the local contribution to the MFP and the minimum district funding requirement. The MFP provides incentives for local support. The state provides extra funds to local districts that exceed the required contribution of approximately 35%. Thus, districts with a greater local contribution can receive extra money from the state. This is in addition to the minimum district funding requirement. The state provides more money to districts that provide a greater percentage of their minimum district funding requirement. Thus, the amount of local funding is important because it directly contributes to the district's funding and also indirectly contributes by encouraging additional state-level funding.

BASIC SUPPORT PROGRAM

Overview of Louisiana's Minimum Foundation Program

The Louisiana constitution, Article VIII §13 establishes an obligation for the state to fund K–12 public education. Subsection A says "The legislature shall appropriate funds to supply free school books and other materials of instruction prescribed by the State Board of Elementary and Secondary Education to the children of this state at the elementary and secondary levels." Subsection B goes beyond books and materials to institute a minimum foundation program for public education funding—the MFP. It further mandates that there is also a local contribution. The MFP is designed to be based on the cost of providing public education and to equitably allocate the funds to parish and city school systems and other local school systems such as the Recovery School District schools (RSD), Louisiana State University (LSU), and Southern Laboratory schools, Office of Juvenile Justice schools, New Orleans Center for Creative Arts, Louisiana School for Math, Science and the Arts, Thrive and Legacy Type Charter schools."[2]

Prior to the 1987 Amendment to Article VIII §13, the legislature determined how much the state would fund the MFP. Since the 1987 amendment, the legislature is now obligated to fully fund the MFP, showing prioritization by the voters of Louisiana for K–12 public education.

Prior to 1997, the MFP was crafted under BESE by determining the cost of K–12 public education by line item, such as teacher salaries and state contributions to state retirement systems, in which school board employees are required to participate. Since 1997, the MFP is constructed as a block grant to local school systems and charter schools without line items to establish what costs are being funded and at what levels.

Important Factors in the Louisiana MFP Formula[3]

Adoption and Implementation Process:
- The formula for the upcoming fiscal year must be submitted by the BESE to the state legislature by March 15.
- The legislature considers the formula submitted by the BESE during the legislative session. If the legislature agrees with the formula filed in resolution, the resolution is adopted. If the resolution does not meet legislative approval, then the resolution is rejected and returned to the BESE.
- The BESE has the option to revise the formula contained in resolution; resubmit the same formula; or take no action. Louisiana law provides that if no resolution is adopted, the existing formula will remain in effect.

Basic Components of the Louisiana School Finance System:
- Determine the cost of a minimum program of education;
- Equitably distribute funds across all school systems;
- Provide incentives for local support.

Structure of the MFP Formula:
- The allocation for Fiscal Year 2019 totaled over $3.7 billion in support of 69 school districts, 140+ charter schools, and designated special schools;
- The formula is designed with separate calculations to provide funding for varying educational needs and costs;
- The current formula has four components or 'levels.'

Level 1 Funding
- Level 1 calculations utilize pupil counts and special student characteristics as the basis for determining the basic cost of education in each community across the state;
- Upcoming fiscal year projections are funded based on pupil count taken in the previous year on February 1;

- Students must qualify to be counted, both for base and weighted counts as applicable, according to the Student Membership Definition set forth in BESE policy;
- Level 1 allocated approximately $2.4 billion (67%) of the most recent total MFP allocation.

Student Count

The first step in the calculation is to determine the Weighted Student Membership Count as seen in Figures 20.1–20.2.

Figure 20.1 Calculating Louisiana Weighted Student Membership Count.

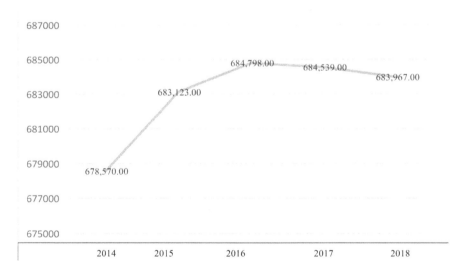

Figure 20.2 Calculating Louisiana Weighted Student Membership Count. *Source:* February 1 student count throughout the years found in the Louisiana Minimum Foundation Program (MFP) Reference Library under "MFP Budget Letter." https://www.louisianabelieves.com/resources/library/minimum-foundation-program *Note:* Student enrollment increased in Louisiana Public Schools 2010–2017. There was a slight decrease in enrollment on February 1, 2018

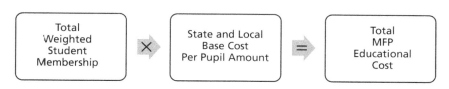

Figure 20.3 Calculating Louisiana Total MFP Educational Cost.

The second step in the calculation is to determine the Total MFP Educational Cost as seen in Figure 20.3:

Base Cost Per Pupil Amount
- The state and Local Base Cost Per-Pupil Amount is the amount utilized as the starting point for calculation of the cost of education in school districts and schools across Louisiana. This amount is used exclusively in the Level 1 cost calculation and is **not** the final pupil allocation that each district receives;
- From 2000–01 to 2008–09, the MFP formula included a 2.75% increase to the Base Cost Per-Pupil Amount. The initial intent of the 2.75% was to address rising costs in delivering a quality education;
- From 2008–09 to 2013–14, the Base Cost Per Pupil remained the same;
- From 2014–15 to 2018–19, the Base Cost Per-Pupil amount remained at $3,961. During this time, the legislature appropriated additional funding for K–12 education outside the formula to address specific needs and priorities.

Sharing of Level 1 Total MFP Educational Cost
- The next step in the calculation is to determine the proportion of the total MFP educational cost to be shared between the state and the city and parish school systems.
- The proportion is based on the ability of the school systems to support education in their communities through local sales and property tax revenues. This calculation is often referred to as the "wealth measurement." This calculation utilizes data on local ad valorem, sales, and other revenue amounts.

Figure 20.4 shows total Level 1 State and Local Allocations through the years FY 2013 (formula year 2015), FY 2014 (formula year 2016), FY 2015 (formula year 2017), FY 2016 (formula year 2018) FY 2017 (formula year 2019).

The second step continues as follows:

- To determine the Local Cost Allocation in the MFP, the formula measures the potential of each city and parish school system to generate local revenue, rather than the actual amount collected. This

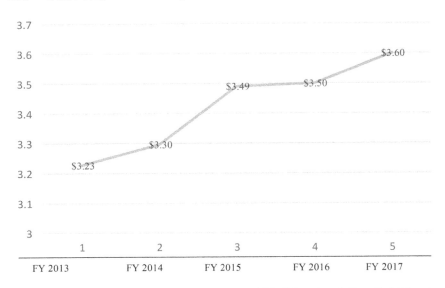

Figure 20.4 Sharing of Level 1 Total Louisiana MFP Educational Cost (in billions). *Source:* Total Level 1 State and Local Cost Allocations throughout the years found in the Louisiana Minimum Foundation Program (MFP) Reference Library under "Table 1: State Level Summary." https://www.louisianabelieves.com/resources/library/minimum-foundation-program

method accounts for differences in the ability of city and parish school systems to raise local revenue;
- Ad valorem millages and sales tax rates are utilized in the calculation at a level appropriate to yield the 65/35 percent split;
- To determine districts' potential to generate revenue, the calculation multiplies statewide computed tax millages and rates against actual ad valorem tax assessments and sales tax bases;
- Each district will have a different allocation based on its unique situation. The percentage of cost funded by the state may range from a high of 89% to a low of 25%. Each year, as school systems are more or less able to support education costs through increases or decreases in local revenues, the formula adjusts the state and local allocations upward or downward as applicable;
- Overall, the formula attempts to ensure an average state contribution of 65% and an average local contribution of 35%, creating statewide equity in the formula.

State and Local Contributions

Once the Local Cost Allocation is determined, the next step is to calculate the State Cost Allocation as seen in Figure 20.5.

Figure 20.5 Calculating Louisiana State Cost Allocation.

Level 2 Funding

- In the early years of the formula, some city and parish school systems did not have local revenue sufficient to meet the minimum local allocation required;
- Local school systems identified two obstacles to increasing local revenues at the time: (1) Taxpayers were not regularly willing to tax themselves more heavily; and (2) under the new formula, if a city or parish school system became more able to support education costs by becoming "wealthier," then the Level 1 allocations were decreased;
- As a result, a provision was added to the formula providing an incentive or reward to school systems taxing themselves above the minimum required level of financial support;
- To be eligible for the Level 2 Reward, a city or parish school system must generate local revenue above the local allocation required in Level 1. Any amount above the established minimum would be eligible for the reward calculation;
- The reward amount was about one-third of local revenues above the contribution required in Level 1;
- For some years, all city and parish school systems have met the required minimum local revenue level;
- The majority of city and parish school systems currently receive the reward, except for a few school systems which are not eligible because local revenues are above the cutoff point;
- In FY 2017, Level 2 allocated approximately $489 million, or 13% of the total allocation.[4]

Level 3 Funding

- Level 3 contains allocations added to the formula over years due to requests from the Louisiana legislature to fund specific items;
- These allocations are determined on a per-pupil basis;
- This funding is in addition to the funding provided in Level 1 and Level 2;
- In FY 2017, Level 3 allocations totaled over $628 million (17%) of the total allocation;[5]
- Categories of funding include a continuation of teacher pay raises provided by the legislature in 2001–02, 2006–07, 2007–08,

and 2008–09 and support worker pay raises in 2002–03, 2006–07, 2007–08;[6]
- Support for increasing mandated costs of health insurance, retirement, and fuel allocation provides $100 per pupil to help defray the costs of these expenses.

Level 4 Funding
- Level 4 provides funding for specific programs and schools, each with a unique allocation method. In FY 2017, Level 4 allocated over $107 million (3%) of total allocation, with $45 million for programs and $62 million for other public schools;
  - *Foreign Language Associates Allocation*—provides additional salary allocations of $21,000 per teacher to a school system or school employing foreign language teachers—statewide maximum of 300 teachers. The stipend allocation provides a $6,000 installation stipend for first-year foreign language associate teachers and a $4,000 retention stipend for second and third year teachers;
  - *Career Development Fund (CDF) Allocation*—provides approximately 6% MFP funding for specific courses providing career training for students;
  - *Supplemental Course (SCA) Allocation*—provides $59 per pupil for each student enrolled in grades 7 to 12 to support the cost of secondary course choices above and beyond the traditional classroom. Beginning in 2017–18, SCA allocation increased to $59 per pupil.[7]
  - *High-Cost Services (HCS) Allocation*—provides funding for pupils ages 3–21 with a current IEP who are currently receiving services with costs greater than three times the average per-pupil expenditure;
  - *Other Public Schools Allocation*—LSU and Southern Lab schools, Legacy Type 2 Charter schools, Office of Juvenile Justice (OJJ) schools, New Orleans Center for Creative Arts (NOCCA), Louisiana School for Math, Science, and the Arts (LSMA) and Thrive Academy of Baton Rouge (THRIVE).

Further, the definition of city, parish, or local public school systems and schools includes city or parish school systems, Recovery School District including operated and Type 5 charter schools, Louisiana School for Math, Science, and the Arts (LSMSA), New Orleans Center for Creative Arts (NOCCA), THRIVE, New Type 2 Charter schools, Legacy Type 2 Charter schools, Type 3B Charter schools, Office of Juvenile Justice (OJJ) schools, and Louisiana State University and Southern University Lab schools.[8]

Mid-year Student Count Adjustments

The formula provides funding for midyear adjustments for student gains and losses during the year. Two midyear adjustments are provided using the following:

- October 1 Count: February 1 count compared to October 1 count; The State Cost Allocation per pupil multiplies increase/decrease in students.
- February 1 Count: October 1 count compared to February 1 count; Increase/decrease in students multiplied by one-half of the State Cost Allocation per-pupil.

Use of Funds

The MFP Resolution requires that state MFP funds shall only be expended for educational purposes:

- Expenditures are related to the operational and instructional activities of city, parish, or other public school systems or schools including:
  – Instruction, pupil support, instructional staff programs, school administration, general administration, business services, operations/maintenance of plant services, student transportation, food services, enterprise operations, community services, facility acquisition and construction services, and debt services;[9]
  – A significant portion of expenditures paid using MFP funds includes teacher salaries and benefits, including retirement since these expenses make up approximately 85% of all educational costs.

Expenditure Requirement

Expenditure requirements for the MFP are extensive and include the following principles and operations:

- The MFP is a block grant from the state to local school systems and schools;
- The block grant philosophy provides flexibility to school systems and schools in budgeting funds to spend as they see fit as long as program requirements outlined in BESE are met;
- The MFP funds should be blended with other funds to support the total cost of education;

- To provide appropriate accountability for funds spent on K–12 education, the MFP Resolution requires an annual measurement and report on the manner in which general fund dollars, state and local funds combined, are spent;
- A 70% expenditure requirement requires public school systems and schools receiving MFP funds to spend 70% of general fund (state and local) dollars on the areas of instruction and school administration at the school building level;
- In the most recent measurement, 130 of a total 177 school districts and schools met the 70% requirement;
- The 47 entities not meeting the 70% requirement were required to submit a plan to the LDOE detailing efforts over the next year to make budget and spending adjustments;
- In many cases, the reason entities did not meet this requirement was due to special circumstances, e.g., high transportation costs with rural schools.

MFP Appropriation History

The MFP's recent appropriation history is illustrated in Figure 20.6 across Fiscal Years 2014 through 2018. Figure 20.7 details an historical

	2013–2014	2014–2015	2015–2016	2016–2017	2017–2018
Total	$3,565,826,163	$3,565,826,163	$3,684,986,335	$3,678,498,272	$3,707,203,252
Change		1.79% increase	1.52% increase	0.18% decrease	0.078% increase
State General Fund	$3,302,972,099	$3,333,357,104	$3,400,239,001	$3,396,745,776	$3,436,831,987
Statutory Dedication	$262,854,064	$296,467,826	$3,400,239,001	$281,752,496	$270,373,265

Figure 20.6 MFP Recent Appropriation History FY 2014–2018.

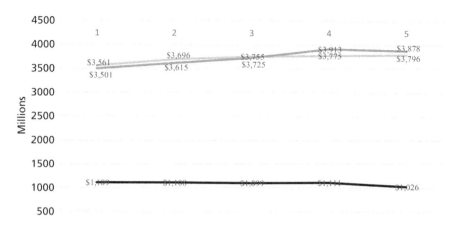

Figure 20.7 Louisiana K–12 Federal, State, and Local Education Revenues FY 2013–2017

summary of all K–12 education revenues in Louisiana across Fiscal Years 2013 through 2017.

MFP Taskforce

In August 2013, the State Board of Elementary and Secondary Education convened the MFP Task Force to provide an advisory recommendation for the MFP. The Task Force represented a cross-section of education stakeholders. The Task Force met from September through December to discuss various issues relative to the formula including costs, local revenue availability, and funds distribution. The MFP Task Force adopted a final recommendation in December, to be considered in March of the following year. The resolution annually recreated the MFP taskforce with the same goals and purpose.

MFP Formula Budgeting Cycle

The MFP follows a budget cycle calendarized as follows:

- August to December—Research and presentations;
- January to February—BESE considers possible revisions to the MFP formula for the upcoming fiscal year;
- March—BESE makes the final decision on the structure of the MFP formula and submits the proposed formula along with an estimated cost to the legislature via resolution for consideration;
- April to June—state legislature considers the MFP formula.

MFP Detail Parts—Effect for FY 2018–2019[10]

For Fiscal Year 2019, the following bulleted points indicate changes affecting the MFP:

- Base Per Amount (Level 1)= $3,961;
- $3,855 per HCR 130 of 2011—set annually by the BESE with the approval of the Joint Legislative Committee on the Budget, or an increase of 2.75% over the prior year per-pupil amount if the MFP continues to operate under the previous resolution because the legislature did not adopt a new resolution;[11]
- Add-on weights—based on pupil characteristics, recognizing the extra cost of instruction for specific categories of students or classes;
- Low Income and/or English Language Learner Weight (22%);
- Career and Technical Education Units (6%);
- Special education pupils;
- Other Exceptionalities (150%);
- Gifted and Talented (60%);
- Economy of scale up to 20% (for school systems with less than 7,500 students).[12]

LOUISIANA RETIREMENT SYSTEM

Title 11, the general retirement law, mandates that the legislature will appropriate the nonemployee portion of the actuarial cost of the state retirement system in which school employees have mandated membership. This obligation has been recognized by the courts,[13] as the state argued that it is meeting its obligation by embedding state retirement funding into the block grant, even though the discrete amount of that funding is indeterminable. The court accepted that argument that the MFP block grant includes funds dedicated to the state retirement systems, even though this ruling raises a charter school issue.

The system requires that the local school board then passes through retirement funds embedded in the MFP to the retirement system. For public school employees who are in the retirement system (including traditional public schools where employees are mandatory members and charter schools opting into the retirement system), the school governing body forwards between 19 and 22% of total payroll to the retirement system, ostensibly from those dollars embedded in the MFP. A recent review shows that approximately $1 billion of the $3.4 billion MFP is passed through to local school boards to the retirement systems[14] For charter schools opting out of the retirement system, state dollars embedded in the MFP and dedicated to meeting the retirement obligation of the state are never provided to the retirement system; yet the charter school retains those dollars to use toward operating costs, including the hiring of for-profit charter operators in a number of schools.

LOCALLY GENERATED EDUCATION FUNDING

Local funds for public education come from two sources: a five mill tax levied without election, and an ad valorem or sales taxes levied only after election by local voters.

Ad valorem taxes levied by a school board are subject to the Homestead Exemption. The Homestead Exemption provides that the first $75,000 in value of a home is not subject to ad valorem tax. There are rural parishes where upward of 80% of homes are valued at less than $75,000, meaning there are some rural properties entirely exempt from school board ad valorem taxes. Louisiana also has several special ad valorem provisions that freeze a home owner's property value, so that the Assessor cannot recognize appreciation of that home's value; thus the homeowner does not owe property taxes on the appreciated value of the home, even if that home value is frozen below $75,000.

Additionally, imposition of a sales tax by the school board, in addition to an election, also requires permission of the Louisiana legislature.[15] The legislature has authority (and has exercised it in the past) to exempt specific sales transactions from the local sales taxes approved by local voters.

CHARTER SCHOOL FUNDING

Charter schools law[16] in Louisiana provides that such organizations be granted per-pupil funding in the same amount as both the state MFP and the de facto per-pupil local tax revenue levied by the local school board. Additionally, charter schools receive the second element of funding from the state that equals the amount of local tax levied by the local school board and the vote of the people – even taxes levied before the charter school was established and thus not considered at the time the voters approved the taxes. The state then withholds this additional charter school payment from the local school board's state MFP allocation, which has the effect of local school board taxes aiding the funding of charter schools over which the local school board has no authority, nor which were approved by local voters.

In several parishes, local school boards have been left in a circumstance of being obligated to fund a specific purpose, based on tax dedication approved by voters, yet those funds have been diverted to one or more local charter schools, resulting in the school board having to pay dedicated expenses without accompanying dedicated revenue. Additionally, charter schools are not obligated to use dedicated revenues per the dedication imposed by voters. Recent data indicate that such redirection of local tax revenues is almost $250 million annually.[17]

VOUCHER PROGRAM

Louisiana's voucher program is funded through a discrete line item, identified as student scholarships, for educational excellence in the subgrantee assistance category found in HB1 State General Fund.[18] The voucher program allows for payment of tuition at nonpublic schools, up to the value of the state MFP plus the local de facto per-pupil funding from local tax revenues.

SUMMARY

In October 2018, the Louisiana Department of Education and the State Board of Elementary and Secondary Education convened the first MFP Task Force meeting for the purpose of providing an up-to-date presentation regarding the history of the MFP. The Louisiana School Boards Association Executive Director reported to the Task Force that there continues to be various issues relative to the MFP, including costs, local revenue availability, and funds distribution. Other topics included an increase to the MFP of 2.75%, raises for certified teachers and uncertificated personnel, and rising costs of health insurance for school systems.

NOTES

1. Louisiana Constitution Article VIII, §13. Retrieved from http://senate.la.gov/Documents/Constitution/Article8.htm
2. 2018–2019 MFP Formula SCR 48, Senator Morrish. Retrieved from http://www.legis.la.gov/legis/ViewDocument.aspx?d=1098695
3. Louisiana MFP Overview 2016–2017. Retrieved from https://www.louisianabelieves.com/docs/default-source/minimum-foundation-program/2016-2017-overview-of-mfp-formula.pdf?sfvrsn=3
4. MFP FY 2016–17 Level 2 allocations. Retrieved from https://www.louisianabelieves.com/docs/default-source/minimum-foundation-program/2016-2017-circular-no-1160—mfp-budget-letter—tables-1-4.pdf?sfvrsn=6
5. MFP FY 2016–17 Table 3A. Retrieved from https://www.louisianabelieves.com/docs/default-source/minimum-foundation-program/2016-2017-circular-no-1160—mfp-budget-letter—tables-1-4.pdf?sfvrsn=6

6. MFP Library Each Year Table 3A for yearly comparisons. Retrieved from https://www.louisianabelieves.com/resources/library/minimum-foundation-program
7. HCR 7 of 2017. Retrieved from http://www.legis.la.gov/legis/BillInfo.aspx?s=17RS&b=HCR7&sbi=y
8. 2018–2019 MFP Formula SCR 48, Senator Morrish. Retrieved from http://www.legis.la.gov/legis/ViewDocument.aspx?d=1098695
9. The MFP has never included any funding for the costs of building public schools, making Louisiana only one of a few states that provide no such funding *Which States Fund Costs for Public School Buildings*. Retrieved from https://www.infrastructurereportcard.org/how-your-state-funds-school-construction/
10. Louisiana 2018 Regular Legislative Session Senate Concurrent Resolution (SCR) 48. Retrieved from http://www.legis.la.gov/legis/ViewDocument.aspx?d=1098695
11. Louisiana 2011 Regular Legislative Session House Concurrent Resolution (HCR) 130. Retrieved from https://www.louisianabelieves.com/docs/minimum-foundation-program/2011-2012-house-concurrent-resolution-130-mfp-resolution.pdf?sfvrsn=4
12. 2018–2019 MFP Budget Letter. Retrieved from https://www.louisianabelieves.com/docs/default-source/minimum-foundation-program/bese-approved-fy18-19-mfp-resolution.pdf?sfvrsn=3
13. EBRPSS vs. LSERS (no citation, 2012)).
14. 2016–2017 Projected UAL Costs. Retrieved from http://www.lsba.com/Images/Interior/trsl_insurance_costs.pdf
15. Article VI §29.
16. LRS 17:3991.
17. 2016–2017 MFP Budget Letter-Excel. Retrieved from https://www.louisianabelieves.com/resources/library/minimum-foundation-program
18. 2016–2017 MFP Budget Letter-HB1 p. 133. Retrieved from http://www.legis.la.gov/Legis/ViewDocument.aspx?d=1013096

CHAPTER 21

Maine

Staff Writer[1]

GENERAL BACKGROUND[2]

Maine became a state in 1820, with its constitution established in the same year. Article VIII, governing educational provisions, declared:

> A general diffusion of the advantages of education being essential to the preservation of the rights and liberties of the people; to promote this important object, the Legislature are authorized, and it shall be their duty to require, the several towns to make suitable provision, at their own expense, for the support and maintenance of public schools; and it shall further be their duty to encourage and suitably endow, from time to time, as the circumstances of the people may authorize, all academies, colleges and seminaries of learning within the State . . .[3]

The state of Maine first began providing revenue for public schools in 1828. The earliest revenue came from public land sales and was granted to towns through a per-pupil formula. A banking tax was created in 1872, collecting a 1 mill property tax that was also distributed on a per-pupil basis, making it the first instance of the state engaging a statewide tax for school redistribution purposes. In 1974, Maine adopted a true statewide uniform property tax featuring a required tax rate, with matching state monies. Due to unpopularity given the tax's impact on wealthier towns, the provision was repealed and replaced in 1977. The revision refocused the tax away from the state as collector, but still provided aid based on local ability to pay as measured by tax capacity. State aid under the new plan was sourced from

Funding Public Schools in the United States and Indian Country, pages 311–324
Copyright © 2019 by Information Age Publishing
All rights of reproduction in any form reserved.

state income and sales taxes. In 2004, a statewide referendum set state aid at 55% of local costs.

The state aid plan was revised in 2005, with a new school funding formula known as the Essential Programs and Services (EPS) model. The EPS was designed to rely on research in best practices on student success. The EPS tied funding to state standards (i.e., the Maine Learning Results[4]) rather than being linked to either prior-year expenditures as the base for budgeting or to local school board budget preferences, although local boards had discretion to spend local dollars above the EPS. In 2016, voters approved a 3% income tax surcharge for high income earners; however, the state legislature subsequently repealed the surcharge while simultaneously increasing state school aid by $162 million.

BASIC FUNDING PROGRAM

Essential Programs and Services Plan

The Essential Programs and Services (EPS) plan serves as Maine's basic funding scheme. Using a complex set of cost factors, the state determines the amount, level, and cost of education components needed by school districts tied to the Maine Learning Results standards. The EPS allocation depends on student, staff, and school variables, resulting in individualized operating cost rates for each local school district.

As indicated, the state provides a 55% cost-share ratio for total EPS operating costs. The local share is based on property valuation. The state covers 100% of approved EPS special education costs for most school districts, and up to 33% for minimum subsidy receiving districts. The state provides added support for geographically isolated schools, and island schools are automatically included. Qualified school districts are adjusted for sparsity using grade-level enrollments, where qualification depends on threshold factors including K–8 <15 enrollment and minimum distance from the nearest school that could accept the headcount; and 9–12 <200 enrollment. The state also accounts for grade-level differences in the EPS through staffing ratios resulting in different supports based on grade span and district size.[5]

Key EPS Elements[6]

The EPS is defined as those programs and resources deemed essential for students to meet the Learning Results standards. The EPS formula determines the state and local shares for each School Administrative Unit (SAU). As indicated, the formula is based on years of research on high performing cost-effective schools as judged by the state of Maine. Expressed as a formula, the EPS reads as:

EPS for the SAU − Required Local Share = State Share

Key State Share Components

The EPS takes into account a set of cost components in determining the aid formula's outcome. The EPS accounts for:

- *Student Demographics:* includes SAU pupil counts for PreK–K, grades 1–5, 6–8, 9–12, and specialized student populations;
- *EPS per-Pupil Rate for the SAU:* includes per-pupil amounts tailored to each SAU to reflect costs for personnel, administration, and instructional support;
- *Weighted Amounts:* includes additional per-pupil amounts for Limited English Proficiency (LEP) and economically disadvantaged pupils;
- *Target Amounts:* includes additional per-pupil amounts for four-year-old PreK pupils, K–2 pupils, student assessment, and technology resources;
- *Other Adjustments:* includes isolated small schools, adult education, and equivalent instruction variables.

Key Required Local Share Components

The EPS takes into account three variables in setting the local contribution to the EPS formula. The local share is defined as:

- *Valuation by town* as provided by the Maine Revenue Service. This variable annually defines local ability to pay;
- *Percent of students by town* within a combined school district. This variable is used to determine the distribution of the total allocation by town;
- *Mill expectation.* This variable is set by calculating the required funding level for each year.

Brief Results of EPS Rates

EPS dollars per pupil across Fiscal Years 2010–2019 are shown in Table 21.1. Table 21.2 next examines K–12 statewide total averages and growth in per-pupil operating costs as defined in the EPS across a longer time FY 1992–2017. Total state funds for the period FY 2012–2019 are then visually illustrated in Figure 21.1.

TABLE 21.1 State Average EPS Rates FY 2010–2019

School Year	Elementary	Secondary
FY 2018–19	$6,720	$7,211
FY 2017–18	$6,634	$7,117
FY 2016–17	$6,584	$7,078
FY 2015–16	$6,596	$7,064
FY 2014–15	$6,505	$6,963
FY 2013–14	$6,415	$6,859
FY 2012–13	$6,342	$6,784
FY 2011–12	$6,254	$6,705
FY 2010–11	$6,138	$6,566
FY 2009–10	$5,976	$6,405

Source: Maine Department of Education. (2018). https://www.maine.gov/doe/funding/gpa/eps

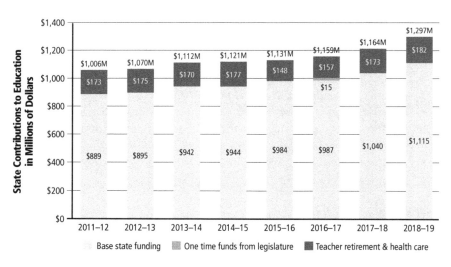

Figure 21.1 Total State EPS Dollars FY 2012–2019. *Source:* Maine Department of Education. (2018). https://www.maine.gov/doe/funding/gpa/eps

TABLE 21.2 Statewide EPS Operating Costs Per-Pupil FY 1991–2017

Fiscal Year	Per Pupil Operating Cost	Annual Percentage Change
2016–17	$11,859.95	4.3%
2015–16	$11,348.78	3.2%
2014–15	$10,990.51	4.0%
2013–14	$10,545.58	5.0%
2012–13	$10,021.47	2.9%
2011–12	$9,726.80	1.0%
2010–11	$9,629.62	–0.3%
2009–10	$9,662.93	0.4%
2008–09	$9,624.71	2.6%
2007–08	$9,370.00	6.1%
2006–07	$8,801.79	6.5%
2005–06	$8,229.51	5.7%
2004–05	$7,761.24	5.5%
2003–04	$7,330.59	4.3%
2002–03	$7,018.79	5.4%
2001–02	$6,640.44	6.1%
2000–01	$6,233.15	6.6%
1999–00	$5,819.69	5.9%
1998–99	$5,474.60	6.0%
1997–98	$5,146.99	4.1%
1996–97	$4,938.29	4.0%
1995–96	$4,738.41	2.9%
1994–95	$4,600.02	4.1%
1993–94	$4,411.02	2.5%
1992–93	$4,299.19	1.7%
1991–92	$4,226.97	1.3%

Source: https://www.maine.gov/doe/funding/reports/perpupil. December 2018. Operating costs refer to general fund and exclude major capital outlay, debt service, transportation, and tuition receipts.

Condensed Overview of EPS Calculation[7]

Calculation of the EPS is a complicated and lengthy process. Figure 21.2 provides an abbreviated version of the steps leading to determination of state and local shares.

Maine's Funding Formula for Sharing the Costs of PreK–12 Education Between State and Local:
- Determine the EPS Defined Cost for each Unit (Total Allocation)
- Determine the Required Local Share of those Costs (Local Contribution)
- The Difference Between the Two is the State Share (State Contribution)

Section 1 Attending Pupil Counts
- Uses average of October attending pupil counts for the school unit from the previous two years as reported in Synergy.
- Attending student counts are based on where students are educated. Public school district attending student counts include: (1) students from the local district attending schools in the district; plus (2) students from outside the district who are tuitioned in.
- Separated by PreK–K, 1–5, 6–8, and 9–12 for calculation of EPS determined ratios for each grade level.

Section 1 B1-8: Staff Positions Part 1—Full Time Equivalent (FTE) Staff
- EPS has determined ratios of FTE Staff to Students necessary for each grade level and position.
- Current Staff to Student Ratios are shown in table; adjustment is made if the total number of PreK-12 students from Section 1 Line A3 is less than 1200:
    - EPS FTE Total is determined by dividing the Average Attending Pupils from Section 1 Line A3 for each Grade Level by the EPS Ratio; then adding the results for the four grade levels.
    - Actual FTE Totals are obtained from the NEO Staff module as entered by the SAU and downloaded each December 1.
    - Percentage of EPS is determined by dividing the EPS FTE Total by the Actual FTE Total.

Position	PreK–K	Under 1,200	1–5	Under 1,200	6–8	Under 1,200	9–12	Under 1,200
A. Teachers	15:1	15:1	17:1	17:1	17:1	17:1	16:1	16:1
B. Guidance	350:1	315:1	350:1	315:1	350:1	315:1	250:1	225:1
C. Librarians	800:1	720:1	800:1	720:1	800:1	720:1	800:1	720:1
D. Health	800:1	720:1	800:1	720:1	800:1	720:1	800:1	720:1
E. Ed. Techs	114:1	103:1	114:1	103:1	312:1	281:1	316:1	285:1
F. Library Techs	500:1	450:1	500:1	450:1	500:1	450:1	500:1	450:1
G. Clerical	200:1	180:1	200:1	180:1	200:1	180:1	200:1	180:1
H. School Admin.	305:1	275:1	305:1	275:1	305:1	275:1	315:1	284:1

Figure 21.2 Essential Programs and Services State Calculation for Funding Public Education (ED279). *(continued)*

Section 1 B1-8: Staff Positions Part 2—Adjusted EPS Salary
- The EPS Staff Salary is determined using a Salary Matrix. Years of Experience and Education Level Attained are important factors in determining the Minimum Teacher Salary for the EPS funding formula. The data entered by the SAU into the NEO Staff Module is used along with the Salary Matrix to determine the minimum teacher salary for each EPS Staff Position—the total of those positions is then used in this calculation.
- Actual salaries are ultimately determined by local contract agreements.
- Adjusted EPS Salary is calculated by multiplying the SAU data in EPS matrix salary amount by the % of EPS. That amount is then distributed to the Elementary and Secondary columns based on the percentage of attending pupils determined in Section 1A.

Section 1 Lines C1-4: Computation of Benefits
- Benefits are calculated using the EPS determined percentage for each category.
- The current EPS salary benefits percentage amounts for each of the following categories are (A) Teachers, Guidance, Librarians and Health (19%); Education and Library Technicians (36); Clerical (29%); School Administrators (14%).

Section 1 Lines D1-7: Other Support Per-Pupil Costs
- Other Support Per-Pupil Costs are calculated based on the EPS determined Per Pupil Amount.
- The most recent (FY 18) EPS Per Pupil amounts for each of the following support costs are shown in the table:

Other Support Costs	PreK–K	9–12
1) Sustitute Teachers (½ day)	42	42
2) Supplies and Equipment	373	514
3) Professional Development	64	64
4) Instructional Leadership Support	28	28
5) Co- and Extra-Curricular Support	39	123
6) System Administration/Support	92	92
7) Targeted System Administration/Support	46	46
8) Operations and Maintenance	1,089	1,294

B7: 9-12 Equivalent Instruction Pupils Basic Count Operating Cost Allocation is determined by using the average of the two most recent "October Equivalent Instruction Pupils" count (as reported in the State Student Information System) times the Secondary SAU EPS Rate as determined in Section 1 of the ED279 report.

Figure 21.2 (continued) Essential Programs and Services State Calculation for Funding Public Education (ED279). *(continued)*

Section 2: (Operating Cost Allocations)—Lines C1-6: Weighted Counts

4YO/PreK, K–8 and 9–12 Disadvantaged Percentage is calculated by dividing the PreK-8 Elementary Free & Reduced Lunch (FRL) Eligible most recent October 1 count by the Total PreK–8 Subsidy in the most recent October 1 count as reported in the State Student Information System. (Example: FRL PreK–8 Count 697 ÷ Total PreK–8 Subsidy Count 1,435 = 0.4857 disadvantaged percentage).

4YO/PreK, K–8 and 9–12 Disadvantaged Weighted Count Operating Cost Allocation is determined by multiplying the percentage of pupils eligible for free & reduced lunch by the most recent October 1 4YO/PreK Pupils (Line B1) and by the average K–8 (Line B2) or 9–12 (Line B3) pupils; then multiplying that number of disadvantaged pupils by the EPS determined weight (.15 at this time) and finally multiplying by the Elementary or Secondary SAU EPS Rate as determined on page 1 of the ED279 report. (Example: 0.4857 × 103.0 = 50.0 × 0.15 = 7.5 × 6,577 = $49,327.50).

4YO/PreK, K–8 and 9–12 Limited English Proficiency Weighted Count Operating Cost Allocation is determined by multiplying the number of limited English proficiency students that are provided services through programs approved by the Department of Education most recent October 1 count by the weight as determined depending on the total number of LEP students in the SAU and then multiplying that by the Elementary or Secondary SAU Rate as determined on page 1 of the ED279 report.

Section 2: (Operating Cost Allocations)—Lines D1-8: Targeted Funds

4YO/PreK, K–8 and 9–12 Student Assessment Targeted Funds Operating Cost Allocation is determined by multiplying the most recent 4YO/PreK October 1 pupils from line B1 basic counts; and the average K–8 or 9–12 pupils from line B2 & B3 basic counts respectively, by the EPS determined rate (currently 48.00).

4YO/PreK, K–8 and 9–12 Technology Resources Targeted Funds Operating Cost Allocation is determined by multiplying the 4YO/PreK October 1 pupils from line B1 basic counts; and the average calendar year K–8 or 9–12 pupils from line B2 & B3 basic counts respectively, by the EPS determined rate; currently 102.00 for Elementary and 308.00 for Secondary.

4YO/PreK and K–2 Pupils Targeted Funds Operating Cost Allocation is determined by multiplying the count of 4YO/PreK October 1 students and Kindergarten to grade 2 calendar year average students by the EPS determined weight, currently .10 and then by the EPS determined rate; currently set at the Elementary SAU Rate as determined on page 1 of the ED279 report.

Figure 21.2 (continued) Essential Programs and Services State Calculation for Funding Public Education (ED279). *(continued)*

4YO/PreK, K–8 and 9–12 Disadvantaged Students Targeted Funds Operating Cost Allocation is determined by multiplying the disadvantaged counts from lines C1, C2, & C3 by the EPS determined weight, currently .05 and then by the EPS Elementary and Secondary EPS rates as determined on page 1 of the ED 279 report.

Section 2: (Operating Cost Allocations)—Lines E1-2: Isolated Small School Adjustment

Isolated Small School Adjustment: A school administrative unit is eligible for an isolated small school adjustment when the unit meets the size and distance criteria established by the commissioner and outlined below. The isolated small school adjustment must be applied to discrete school buildings that meet the criteria for adjustment. The adjustment is not applicable to sections, wings or other parts of a building that are dedicated to certain grade spans.

Section 2: (Operating Cost Allocations)—Operating Allocation Totals

Operating Allocation Totals equals the sum of the Total Allocations from Section 2 lines B) Basic Counts, C) Weighted Counts, D) Targeted Funds and E) Isolated Small School Adjustments.

Percentage of EPS Transition Amount = 100.00%.

Adjusted Total Operating Allocation Amount = Operating Allocation Totals times EPS Transition Percentage.

Section 3: Other Allocations—A) Other Subsidizable Costs

Line A1: Gifted & Talented Expenditures from 2016–2017—an allocation for Gifted & Talented Programs is determined using the most recent audited reported financial data of approved actual expenses or the approved budget, whichever is less, increased by an inflation adjustment, currently 1.5%.

Line A3: Special Education–EPS Allocation—weighted per pupil amounts for each special education student plus adjustments.

Base Component—Each identified special education student is weighted at 1.5 for up to 15% of the resident enrollment.

Prevalence Adjustment—Special education identified students above the 15% receive an additional .38 weight.

Special Education—EPS Allocation:
- Base Component Identified up to 15% (1.5 × EPS Rate × 295 Pupils) = $2,819,020.00

Figure 21.2 (continued) Essential Programs and Services State Calculation for Funding Public Education (ED279). *(continued)*

- Prevalence Adjustment Identified above 15% (.38 × EPS Rate × 0 Pupils) = $0.00
- Size Adjustment for <20 Pupils (.29 × EPS Rate × 0 Pupils) =
- High Cost In-District Adjustment =
- High Cost Out-of-District Adjustment =
- Federal Revenues Adjustment (to exclude Federal Revenues) =
- Maintenance of Effort Adjustment (to adjust 2013–14 actual expenses) =
- Special Education—EPS Allocation Amount =
- Example: $0.00 $115,956.00 $319,043.00 $–470,810.00 $585,476.64 $3,368,685.64

Small Districts—Districts with fewer than 20 students with disabilities receive an adjustment to reflect lower student-staff ratios.

High Cost In-District—Students educated within the district estimated to cost more than three times the special education per-pupil base amount are identified as high cost in-district and an adjustment is made.

Maintenance of Effort—Districts are given a hold-harmless adjustment that is equal to at least the previous year's per-pupil expenditure minus adjustments for the loss of high cost students and shift in staff.

Line A4: Special Education—High-Cost Out-of-District Allocation

High Cost Out-of-District—Students educated outside the district estimated to cost four times the special education per-pupil base amount are identified as high cost out-of-district and an adjustment is made.

Special Education Model—FY2019
Special Education Allocation Calculation
- Step 1: Base Component
- Step 2: Prevalence Adjustment
- Step 3: Size Adjustment
- Step 4: High Cost In-District Adjustment
- Step 6: EPS Special Education Allocation
- EPS Maintenance of Effort Adjustment Calculation

High-cost Out-of-District Adjustment—Taken outside of the formula
- Separate allocation

Federal Revenues
- Removed from the formula completely
- No longer impacting the special education allocation

Section 3: Other Allocations—A) Other Subsidizable Costs

Line A5: Transportation Operating–EPS Allocation—an allocation for Transportation based on Pupil Density or Miles Driven; whichever is greater.

Figure 21.2 (continued) Essential Programs and Services State Calculation for Funding Public Education (ED279). *(continued)*

Line A6: Approved Bus Allocation—an allocation for bus purchases based on the amount approved for bus purchases made in the previous year.

Section 3: Other Allocations—B) Teacher Retirement Amount (Normalized Cost)

Line B: Teacher Retirement Amount (Normalized Cost)—an allocation for Teacher Retirement 'Normalized Costs' (Employer's Share) to be paid by the SAU to the Maine State Retirement System. The amount is an estimate provided for each SAU by MePERS.

Section 3: Other Allocations—Lines C1-5) Debt Service Allocations

Debt Service—Includes principal and interest costs for approved major capital projects in the allocation year. Major capital means school construction projects including onsite additions to existing schools; new schools; the cost of land acquired in conjunction with projects otherwise defined; the building of or acquisition of other facilities related to the operation of SAUs. Note: this is for approved State subsidizable debt service only—this does not include Local Only Debt Service.

Approved Leases & Lease Purchases—Lease costs for school buildings when the leases, including leases under which the school administrative unit may apply the lease payments to the purchase of portable, temporary classroom space, have been approved by the commissioner for the year prior to the allocation year.

Section 3: Other Allocations—Total Combined Allocation

Includes Section 2 Adjusted Total Operating Allocation, Other Subsidizable Costs, and Total Debt Service Allocation.

Section 4: Calculation of Required Local Contribution—Mill Expectation

Line A) Subsidizable Pupils by Member Municipality:

> Distribution by Town of the Total EPS Allocation (Example):
> The EPS Total Allocation is distributed to each member town based on their respective percent of the Average Calendar Year Subsidizable (Resident) Pupils.
>
> Town A Operating Allocation Distribution = 974.5 ÷ 2,276.5 = 42.81% × 23,617,444.04
> = $10,110,627.79
> Town A Debt Allocation Distribution = 42.81% × 1,258,003.24 = $538,551.19
> Total Municipal Allocation Distribution for Town A = $10,649,178.98

Figure 21.2 (continued) Essential Programs and Services State Calculation for Funding Public Education (ED279). *(continued)*

> **Line B) State Valuation by Member Municipality:**
>
> > Required Local Contribution to the Town EPS Allocation:
> > The required local contribution (Ability to Pay) to the Town Allocation of EPS is equal to the two-year average of the Town's State Certified Valuation times the established mill expectation, but not to exceed the Total Town Allocation as determined in Section 4 Line A.
> > $$\text{Town A} = 827{,}766{,}667 \times (8.48 \div 1{,}000 = .00848) = \$7{,}019{,}461.34$$
>
> **Line C) Required Local Contribution = the lesser of the previous two calculations:**
> The required local contribution is either the Distribution of the Total Allocation by Town amount as calculated in Section 4 Line A or the State Valuation two-year average of the Town times the mill expectation as calculated in Section 4 Line B—whichever is less. The State Contribution by Municipality (prior to adjustments) is the difference between the Total Allocation by Municipality and the Required Local Contribution by Municipality.
>
> Section 5A provides the Total Allocation, Local Contribution and State Contribution amounts prior to any adjustments. Section 5B lists adjustments that may occur throughout the fiscal year to the State Contribution for those items listed above. Adjustments may add to the State Contribution or reduce the State Contribution depending on the type of adjustment.
>
> | Section 5: Totals and Adjustments | | Contribution | |
> |---|---|---|---|
> | | Total Allocation | Local | State |
> | **Total Allocation, Local Contribution, State Contributions** | $20,433,467.21 | $7,064,898.75 | $13,368,568.46 |
> | Totals after adjustment to Local and State Contributions | $20,433,467.21 | $7,064,898.75 | $13,368,568.46 |
> | **Other Adjustments to State Contribution** | | | |
> | 1) Plus Audit Adjustment | | | $0.00 |
> | 2) Less Audit Adjustments | | | $0.00 |
> | 3) Less Adjustment for Unappropriated Local Contribution | | | $0.00 |
> | 4) Less Adjustment for Unallocated Balance Excess of 3% | | | $0.00 |
> | 5) Special Education Budgetary Hardship Adjustment | | | $0.00 |
> | 6) Career & Technical Education Center Adjustment | | | $0.00 |
> | 7) Plus Long-Term Drug Treatment Centers Adjustment | | | $0.00 |
> | 8) Regionalization and efficiency assistance | | | $0.00 |
> | 9) Bus Refurbishing Adjustment | | | $0.00 |
> | 10) Less Maine Care Seed–Private | | | ($13,388.68) |
> | **Adjusted State Contribution** | $20,433,467.21 | $7,064,898.75 | $13,355,179.78 |
> | Local and State Percentages Prior to Adjustments | Local Share = 34.58% | State Share = 65.42% | |
> | Local and State Percentages After Adjustments | Local Share = 34.64% | State Share = 65.36% | |
> | FYI: 100% EPS Allocation | | | |
>
> **Section 5F: Adjusted Local Contribution by Town for Warrant Article**
> Section 5F provides the Adjusted Local Contribution Amount by Town for use in the budget warrant articles.

Figure 21.2 (continued) Essential Programs and Services State Calculation for Funding Public Education (ED279).

SUMMARY

Maine's school finance system is extensive and marked by recent change. It is also exhaustively analyzed at legislative and other levels.[8] The state chamber of commerce in 2018 provided a synopsis of recent changes to Maine school funding, saying in relative part:

Budget negotiations in 2017 resulted in a number of changes to education funding. The final budget repealed a 3% income tax surcharge in exchange for an additional $162 million for elementary and secondary education ($48 million for 2018 and $114 million for 2019). The budget also made some substantive changes to the EPS funding formula:

1. Projected Pre-K (four-year-old program) enrollment was added to the funding formula. Districts can now get state funding for Pre-K students up front, rather than having to pay for new and expanded programs with 100% local funds for the first year;
2. The definition of kindergarten was expanded to include four-year-old programs, ensuring that districts will receive the state funding share for these students;
3. Title I money will no longer supplant state funding but will supplement those funds, providing greater support for schools with higher shares of economically disadvantaged students;
4. More funding was added for economically disadvantaged students: an additional funding weight of 0.15 for each economically disadvantaged student, and extended learning programs for economically disadvantaged students receive an extra additional weight of 0.05;
5. The funding weight for special education students was increased;
6. The 2018–2019 state budget also includes $5 million per year for one-time funding for consolidation of school administrative districts, to encourage efficient delivery of educational services.[9]

NOTES

1. No state-based expert was available to author this chapter at time of publication. Valuable conversations occurred with Joanne Allen and Tyler Backus in the Maine Department of Education that provided helpful insight. The chapter is drawn from multiple sources as footnoted and represents the editorial staff's interpretation of issues, trends and findings regarding the state of Maine. For additional information and detail, contact the Maine Department of Education.
2. This section closely follows Maine State Chamber of Commerce, "How Is Public Education Funded in Maine?" (2018). Retrieved from http://www.educatemaine.org/docs/17-029_EDME-FundingPrimer-FNL-web.pdf

3. Constitution of the State of Maine. Retrieved from https://www.maine.gov/legis/const/
4. Maine Department of Education. "Maine Learning Results." Retrieved from https://www.maine.gov/doe/learning/content/mathematics/learning results
5. Description of the EPS in the preceding two paragraphs partly relies on Deborah A. Verstegen, "A Quick Glance at School Finance: A 50 State Survey of School Finance Policies." *Maine.* (2018). Retrieved from https://schoolfinancesdav.wordpress.com
6. This section closely follows Maine Department of Education, "School Funding—General Purpose Aid (GPA). Retrieved from https://www.maine.gov/doe/sites/maine.gov.doe/files/inline-files/EPS%20Cost%20Component%20Calculations%20ED279%20Line%20by%20Line_updatedSeptember2017.pdf. Retrieved December 18, 2018.
7. An excellent and exhaustive tutorial updated for FY 2019 is found at https://www.maine.gov/doe/sites/maine.gov.doe/files/inline-files/EPS%20Cost%20Component%20Calculations%20ED279%20Line%20by%20Line_updatedSeptember2017.pdf
8. This section is taken from Maine State Chamber of Commerce, "How Is Public Education Funded in Maine?" (2018). Retrieved from http://www.educatemaine.org/docs/17-029_EDME-FundingPrimer-FNL-web.pdf
9. Ibid.

CHAPTER 22

Maryland

Laura Checovich, Ph.D.
University of Maryland

Jennifer King Rice, Ph.D.
Dean of Education University of Maryland

GENERAL BACKGROUND[1]

The modern school finance system in Maryland has its roots in the Education Article of the Maryland Code passed in 1978. The now-defunct 1978 formula distributed state and local taxes in a way meant to equalize funding across school districts and to account for differences in local wealth. The Lee-Maurer formula established a per-pupil statutory foundation level which is the minimal per-pupil base amount that each school district must spend annually.[2] The state and school districts shared the cost of funding the formula up to the foundation level according to a percentage based on district wealth. The formula also established a uniform local tax rate designed to ensure that each district would contribute its share of the foundation funding based on local wealth.[3]

In addition to the foundation amount, the state provided supplemental funding, regardless of district wealth, based on the enrollment of children with special needs and the population density of a district. Despite the state's intention to equalize funding across districts, the foundation level was set too low to offset differences in wealth between districts and disparities in spending remained.[4]

A lawsuit *Hornbeck v Somerset County Board of Education*[5] challenged the equity of the funding system. Boards of education of three counties, the school commissioners of Baltimore City, numerous school superintendents, and a number of taxpayers, students, parents, and public officials challenged the existing funding formula. The group argued that the Lee-Mauer formula was insufficient to equalize funding across districts and violated the Equal Protection Clause of the 14th Amendment. In 1983, the *Hornbeck* court set a new funding standard in Maryland, ruling that all students were guaranteed, "an adequate education measured by contemporary educational standards."[6]

In the decade that followed, the ACLU and the City of Baltimore initiated numerous lawsuits arguing that the state's education finance system was not providing an 'adequate' education to all students. The state responded to the pressures by creating the Commission on Education Finance, Equity, and Excellence (often referred to as the Thornton Commission). The Thornton Commission met for three years between 1999 and 2002 and was charged with studying and making recommendations on how the state could:

- ensure adequate school funding;
- reduce funding inequities among school districts; and
- ensure excellence in school systems and student performance.

The Thornton Commission identified four major goals: adequacy, equity, simplicity, and flexibility. To ensure adequate funding, the Commission recommended that school funding be based on the "costs associated with meeting state performance standards, including the ... costs associated with providing services to students with special needs."[7] Based on recommendations of the Thornton Commission, the Maryland General Assembly passed the *Bridge to Excellence in Public Schools Act of 2002*.[8] The Act restructured Maryland's public school finance system and increased state aid through a new school finance formula that accounted for differences in local wealth and linked resources with students' needs (see Table 22.1). The goal was to ensure that all schools were adequately funded to meet state education standards.

Under the new formula, the state allocated per-pupil foundation funding to school systems in inverse proportion to district wealth. In addition, the program included a guaranteed tax base, a geographic cost adjustment, and weights to compensate districts for the additional cost of educating students from special needs groups.[9,10]

Chapter 288 of the *Bridge to Excellence* Act required the state to conduct a follow-up study of the adequacy of education funding approximately ten years after enactment.[11] In 2016, the General Assembly created the Commission on Innovation and Excellence, made up of legislators and other stakeholders, to review recent adequacy studies and make recommendations for revising the state's education finance formula, accountability measures, and requirements for district master plans.[12] Using a gap analysis that compares Maryland to international and domestic "top performers,"

TABLE 22.1 Total State Aid for Education[a] (in Millions)

	Fiscal Year	State Education Aid	$ Change from Prior Year	% Change from Prior Year
	2002	$2874		
Bridge to Excellence Phase-in Years	2003	$3103	$229	8.0
	2004	$3292	$189	6.1
	2005	$3606	$314	9.6
	2006	$2990	$384	10.6
	2007	$4456	$466	11.7
	2008	$5147	$691	15.5
	2009	$5355	$208	4.0
	2010	$5484	$128	2.4
	2011	$5692	$209	3.8
	2012	$5751	$59	1.0
	2013	$5814	$62	1.1
	2014	$5903	$90	1.5
	2015	$6035	$132	2.2
	2016	$6127[b]	$92	1.0
	2017	$6302[c]	$175	1.0
	2018	$6352[d]	$50	1.0

[a] State of Maryland, *Legislative Handbook Series–Volume IX–Education in Maryland* (Annapolis: Department of Legislative Services, 2014), p. 66.
[b] State of Maryland, Overview of State Aid to Local Governments–Fiscal 2016 Allowance. Retrieved from http://mgaleg.maryland.gov/Pubs/BudgetFiscal/2016fy-state-aid-local-governments.pdf, 38.
[c] State of Maryland, Overview of State Aid to Local Governments–Fiscal 2017 Allowance. Retrieved from http://dls.maryland.gov/pubs/prod/InterGovMatters/SteAidLocGov/Overview-of-State-Aid-to-Local-Governments-Fiscal-2017-Allowance.pdf, 35.
[d] Ibid. p. 38.

preliminary recommendations released in January 2018 focused on early childhood education, highly qualified and diverse teachers and leaders, college and career readiness pathways, resources for at-risk students, and governance and accountability. The Commission will develop recommendations, and the General Assembly is expected to consider changes to the finance formula during the 2019 legislative session.

GENERAL AND SUPPLEMENTAL FUNDS

A majority of the state funds allocated for public education in Maryland are collected annually through state taxes and amassed into the state's general fund. General fund revenues are collected through state income taxes, retail sales taxes, and the state lottery. Other sources of general fund revenue include the corporate income tax, alcohol and tobacco sales taxes, and others.[13] Together these tax collections contributed to the $6.3 billion in state aid to education in Fiscal Year 2013. Some additional funds for education are collected through the state's various special funds which are made up of revenues that are statutorily mandated for specific purposes, including financing education.

The adequacy model has three components:

1. Providing districts, through a combination of state and local funding, with a uniform per-pupil base amount of funding that the state estimates to be the minimum amount required to provide general educational services;
2. Adjusting funding provided to districts to account for the costs associated with providing educational services to special education students, English language learners and students eligible for free and reduced-price meals;
3. Adjusting funding provided to districts to account for the local or regional differences that impact the costs of providing educational services.

Under the adequacy model, state aid is distributed chiefly based on total enrollments, enrollment of students with special needs, and local wealth (measured through property value).[14] However, there is considerable variability across Maryland's 24 LEAs (23 counties and Baltimore City) on the number of at-risk students they serve, the relative costs of providing educational services, and their local wealth. Maryland uses a wealth equalization formula, and consequently, individual LEAs vary in the shares of state, local, and federal funds that make up final budgets.[15]

Figure 22.1 is a visual representation of how the Maryland funding model works. The state funds the foundation level in inverse proportion to local wealth. Building on the foundation, the state adds targeted funds for special student populations. The state provides additional funds through small grants and monies for transportation and facilities costs. Finally, the county adds supplemental funds based on its local wealth and willingness (effort) to provide additional funding.

State funds are allocated to LEAs through three mechanisms: 1) general education aid, 2) targeted education aid, and 3) other funds.

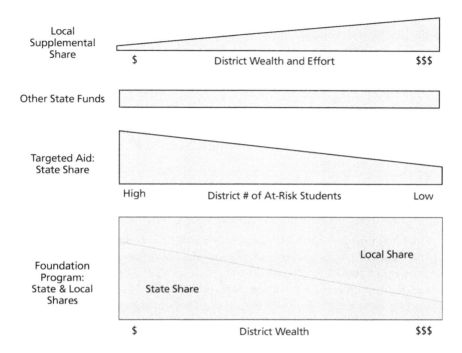

Figure 22.1   Maryland Funding Model.

GENERAL EDUCATION AID

General Education Aid funded programs provide LEAs with the minimum level of funding determined by the state to be essential for providing general educational services. The General Education Funds are made up of the foundation program and the geographic cost of education index.

The Foundation Program

Accounting for nearly half of the aid provided to education by the state, the foundation program uses a formula to determine a minimum per-pupil funding level and the share of the per-pupil funding carried by the SEA and by the LEA.[16] The formula includes a wealth equalization adjustment that measures a district's wealth by determining the eligible level of assessable property and net taxable income.[17] Due to the adjustment, districts with higher wealth contribute more of the cost while the state picks up the larger share for poorer districts.

The *state's share* of the foundation program for a specific district is calculated with the following formula:

$$\text{(Per-pupil foundation} \times \text{Local enrollment)} - \text{(Local contribution rate} \times \text{Local wealth)}$$

The local contribution rate is determined by multiplying the state's overall local contribution (50%) by the total cost of the foundation program and then dividing by the total local wealth. The FY 2018 state foundation aid totaled more than $3.2 billion.[18]

Geographic Cost of Education Index (GCEI)

The Geographic Cost of Education Index (GCEI) is designed to account for regional differences in costs of educational resources that are outside of the control of the LEA.[19] The GCEI has two components: (1) a personnel cost index that accounts for wage differentials, and (2) a nonwage index that accounts for differences in the costs of procuring non-personnel supplies, other than capital expenditures.[20] Of Maryland's 24 local school districts, 13 are designated 'high cost' and receive GCEI funds. Those thirteen districts serve around 80% of Maryland's public school students.[21]

The index's influence on the state funding sent to LEAs is calculated with the following formula:

$$\text{FTE enrollment} \times \text{Per-pupil foundation amount} \times \text{(GCEI value} - 1)$$

Originally, the GCEI model was included in the state general aid program as an add-on to the foundation program and the state was not required to fully fund it, or even to fund it at all.[22] In 2015, after a brief period when the Index was not funded, the state legislature passed legislation mandating that the GCEI be fully funded and included in state spending on education.[23] The FY 2018 foundation program includes $139 million in GCEI grants to districts.[24]

Guaranteed Tax Base

The GTB provides additional funds to jurisdictions with less than 80% of the statewide wealth per pupil, up to 20% of the per-pupil foundation.[25] In FY 2018 the state allocated $50.3 million to nine school systems under the GTB program.[26]

TARGETED EDUCATION AID

Targeted aid programs provide LEAs with additional funds based on enrollments of students with special educational needs, adjusted for local wealth. The funds are allocated to school systems based on the estimated cost, above and beyond the foundation cost, of educating special education students, students eligible for free and reduced-price lunch, and students with limited English proficiency. Each type of targeted aid is distributed through the following formula:

(State aid amount per at-risk pupil × Enrollment of at-risk students) / (Local wealth per pupil / Statewide wealth per pupil)

Compensatory Education

Maryland allocates compensatory education funds to LEAs to support students at risk of not meeting state academic achievement standards. LEAs are required to develop plans that promote the improved academic performance of all students, not just those identified as at-risk. This model is similar to that of the federal Title I grants—schools with the most at-risk students are identified for funding, but the spending should comprehensively support the entire school. Students are identified as at risk of not meeting state standards based on their eligibility for free and reduced-price meals as well as by local wealth, an accepted indicator of poverty and a predictor of low test scores.[27]

Under the *Bridge to Excellence* Act, the weight applied to free and reduced-price lunch students is 0.97, or an additional 97% of the base (see Table 22.2). Combining these funds with funds allocated for poor students by the federal government under programs like Title I brings the aid per student to approximately 1.1 times the aid provided at the base per-pupil funding level.[28] The FY 2018 state budget included $1.3 billion for compensatory education.[29]

TABLE 22.2 Targeted Aid Category Weights

Targeted Aid Category	Weight
Compensatory (poverty indicator)	0.97
Special Education	0.74
Limited English Proficiency	1.00

Special Education

In Maryland, funds are allocated to LEAs for the "free appropriate education for students with disabilities up until age 21." Appropriate special education services are available to most students within their local public school or specialized programs within the public schools. However, when appropriate educational services are not available in the public schools, the funds can be used to provide aid for nonpublic school placements.

Under the *Bridge to Excellence* Act, the weight applied to special education students is 0.74, or an additional 74% of the base. Combining these funds with funds allocated for special education by the federal government brings the aid for each special education student to nearly 1.2 times the aid provided at the base per-pupil funding level.[30] The FY 2018 state budget included almost $424 million for special education funding.[31]

Limited English Proficiency

Maryland allocates funds to LEAs with the goal of supporting and promoting improved English language instruction for students with limited English proficiency (LEP). Students are identified for services based on the English Language Proficiency test given at the time of enrollment. The test is designed to identify the English language proficiency of students whose primary language is not English.[32]

Under the *Bridge to Excellence* Act, the weight applied to LEP students is 1.00, or an additional 100% of the base. Combining these funds and funds allocated for limited English proficiency students by the federal government under programs like Title III brings the aid per student to approximately 1.1 times the aid provided at the base per-pupil funding level.[33] In FY 2018 the state allocated just under $249 million for LEP.[34]

OTHER FUNDS

Other funds are distributed to LEAs by the state for a variety of purposes.[35,36] Funds for each of these programs are distributed either by formulas based on enrollments or by individual measures of eligibility. Numerous programs exist, including teacher development, science and mathematics initiatives, career and technology education, and gifted and talented. Several of the key programs are described below.

Nonpublic Placements

The state and local education agencies share the cost of special education students who require nonpublic school placements in order to meet their needs. The county contributes two times the basic cost of educating a student in the county plus the amount of the local share of basic costs of educating a child in the county. The state then covers 70% of costs above the base amount.[37]

Food Service

Maryland requires that all public schools provide subsidized or free nutrition programs to all eligible students. The state provides the LEA with funds to match the federal funds provided for the National School Lunch Program and allocates those funds as a percentage of the total federal funds allocated during the second prior fiscal year. Maryland has participated in the Community Eligibility Option of the *Healthy, Hunger-Free Kids Act*[38] since it was invited to pilot the program in 2014.[39] At this time three districts (including all 177 schools in Baltimore City) in the state are participating in the program.[40] Total funding for food service in the state in FY 2018 was just under $440 million, including $11.2 million in state aid.[41]

Public School Construction Program

Maryland allocates funds to public school instruction based on a state and local cost-sharing formula that takes into account factors including local wealth, at-risk student populations, enrollment growth, economic condition of the county, and local effort for school construction. The cost-sharing formula is updated every three years, and the minimum state share is 50% of total costs. The Interagency Committee on School Construction, under the authority of the State Board of Public Works, recommends capital improvement projects to the Governor for inclusion in the proposed capital budget. Total state funding appropriated for K–12 school construction in FY 2018 was $343 million, or one-third of FY 2018 capital spending. This included $280 million for the traditional school construction program, $40 million to districts with high enrollment growth, and $6 million for aging schools to upgrade fire protection, plumbing, roofing, HVAC, high-tech wiring, and asbestos and lead paint abatement.[42,43]

Adult Education

The Department of Labor, Licensing and Regulation is responsible for the funding and oversight of adult education and workforce development services in the state. In most places, adult education is provided at the local community college; however, in certain circumstances the local boards of education are involved in providing adult education services.[44]

Student Transportation

Maryland requires all school systems to provide transportation for all public school students to and from school. State aid is distributed to districts based on a two-part formula with a base grant and per-pupil grants for students with special transportation needs and increases in enrollment. In recent years, due to fiscal constraints, the base grant has been limited to 1% growth per year. In FY 2018, the state allocated $276 million to student transportation.[45]

Funding for Charter Schools

Under Maryland law, charter schools are entitled to commensurate funding with traditional public schools in their local jurisdiction. Charter schools receive the same per-pupil amount as other schools in their district and they may not charge tuition or raise funds in any way that does not comply with the laws, regulations, and policies of their school district.[46] Unlike in other states, Maryland's charter schools do not receive any state aid to support their facilities.[47]

LOCAL SHARE

Maryland's LEAs do not have independent authority to collect taxes and, therefore, require their corresponding county governments to raise funds to cover the LEA budgets. Thus, state law mandates that Maryland's counties provide a share of the costs through state formulas. County funds account for nearly half of the total funding for Maryland's school systems. In addition to county funding provided through the state funding formula, all 24 counties in Maryland provide supplemental funds to their LEA. These funds are not mandated by the state and are based on local taxing capacity and the local willingness to support education and are subject to the state's maintenance of effort requirement.

Counties are required to maintain a minimum annual appropriation to the LEA budget that is the greater of either (1) the local share of foundation program, or (2) the per-pupil amount provided in the previous year. This rule is in place to ensure a more equal partnership between the counties and the state in funding education. Because most counties have historically contributed funds in excess of their required foundation amount, county contributions are generally maintained from year to year.[48]

Counties can apply for waivers from the maintenance of effort requirement if its "fiscal condition significantly imped[es] the county's ability to fund the maintenance of effort requirement."[49] When six of the state's 24 counties applied for waivers in 2012, the state was unable to meet their requests for increased state funds and the counties were allowed to reduce their funding without penalty. This led the Maryland General Assembly to renew its interest in the funding formula and to provide funding for an adequacy study as mandated under the 2002 *Bridge to Excellence* legislation.

SUMMARY

State education aid for K–12 schools increased from $4 billion in FY 2006 to $6.3 billion in FY 2018. State funding accounted for 47.8% of 2018 revenue raised for public elementary and secondary schools, with 47.9% coming from local sources and 4.3% coming from federal sources. The average per-pupil allocation in the state was $15,467, one of the highest in the nation. The recommendations of the Commission on Innovation and Excellence in Education, to be considered during the 2019 legislative session, are likely to have a significant effect on the level and structure of school funding in the state.

NOTES

1. Much of this chapter is based on briefs prepared for the Maryland Equity Project. *Funding Formulas and Revenue Streams: A Primer on Public School Finance in Maryland* and *Financing Public Education in Maryland: A Brief History*. Retrieved from https://education.umd.edu/research/centers/mep/research/k-12-education
2. Molly Hunter, Maryland Enacts Modern, Standards-based Education Finance System: Reforms Based on Adequacy Cost Studies, *National Access Network, Teachers College, Columbia University* (2002). Retrieved from http://www.schoolfunding.info/resource_center/research/MDbrief.pdf
3. 1978 Maryland code- Section 5-202 (b).
4. Hunter (2002).
5. 295 Md. 597 (1983); 458 A.2d 758.
6. Hunter (2002).

7. State of Maryland and Alvin Thornton, *Commission on Education Finance, Equity, and Excellence: Final Report* (2002), 52. Retrieved from https://msa.maryland.gov/megafile/msa/speccol/sc5300/sc5339/000113/000000/000013/unrestricted/20030011e.pdf
8. Senate Bill 856 (2002).
9. Senate Bill 856—*Bridge to Excellence in Public Schools Act*. Retrieved from http://mgaleg.maryland.gov/2002rs/bills/sb/sb0856e.pdf
10. Ibid.
11. Senate Bill 856.
12. Senate Bill 905—*Commission on Innovation and Excellence in Education*. Retrieved from http://mgaleg.maryland.gov/2016RS/chapters_noln/Ch_701_sb0905E.pdf
13. State of Maryland—Department of Budget and Management, *Frequently Asked Questions about Maryland's Budget*. Retrieved from http://dbm.maryland.gov/budget/Pages/FAQs.aspx
14. William J. Glenn, Mike Griffith, Lawrence O. Picus, and Allan Odden, *Analysis of School Finance Equity and Local Wealth Measures in Maryland* (Denver: Augenblick, Palaich & Associates, 2015), p. 25.
15. State of Maryland, *Legislative Handbook Series—Volume IX—Education in Maryland* (Annapolis: Department of Legislative Services, 2014), 63.
16. Ibid. p. 70.
17. Wealth Equalization = (local contribution rate X local wealth) where the local contribution rate is measured by (per-pupil foundation X 50% X FTE enrollment)/the wealth base.
18. State of Maryland, *Maryland State Budget Book, Volume II* (Department of Budget and Management, 2017). Retrieved from http://dbm.maryland.gov/budget/Documents/operbudget/2019/Proposed/Volume2.pdf
19. William Duncombe and Dan Goldhaber, *Adjusting for Geographic Differences in the Cost of Educational Provision in Maryland* (2003). Retrieved from http://dlslibrary.state.md.us/publications/exec/msde/agdcepm_2003.pdf
20. Ibid.
21. Genevieve Demos Kelley, *A GCEI Primer: Everything You Need to Know about Maryland's Geographic Cost of Education Index* (*Prince George's County Advocates for Better Schools website, May 27, 2015*). Retrieved from https://pgcabs.org/2015/05/27/a-gcei-primer-everything-you-need-to-know-about-marylands-geographic-cost-of-education-index/
22. Jennifer Imazeki, *A Geographic Cost of Education Adjustment for Maryland* (Denver: Augenblick, Palaich & Associates, September 2015).
23. Associated Press, *Md. Lawmakers Approve Mandated Full Funding for GCEI* (CBS Baltimore, April 14, 2015). Retrieved from http://baltimore.cbslocal.com/2015/04/14/md-lawmakers-approve-mandated-full-funding-for-gcei/
24. Ibid. *Maryland State Budget Book, Volume II* (2017).
25. State of Maryland, Department of Legislative Services, *Overview of Education Funding in Maryland* (2018). Retrieved from http://dls.maryland.gov/pubs/prod/Educ/OverviewOfEducationFundingInMaryland.pdf , p. 7.
26. Ibid. *Maryland State Budget Book, Volume II* (2017).

27. State of Maryland, *Legislative Handbook Series–Volume IX–Education in Maryland* (Department of Legislative Services, 2014), p. 97.
28. Ibid.
29. Ibid. *Maryland State Budget Book, Volume II* (2017).
30. State of Maryland, *Legislative Handbook Series–Volume IX–Education in Maryland*, p. 92.
31. Ibid. *Maryland State Budget Book, Volume II* (2017).
32. State of Maryland–Maryland State Department of Education. (n.d). *Identification of ELLs and Home Language Survey*. Retrieved from http://marylandpublicschools.org/MSDE/programs/title_III/i_ell_hls.html
33. Ibid. *Legislative Handbook Series–Volume IX–Education in Maryland* p. 100.
34. Ibid. *Maryland State Budget Book, Volume II* (2017).
35. Other funding provided by the state to LEAs include supplemental grants to LEAs whose local shares of the foundation level grow at a lower than expected rate, payments for teacher pensions, the provision of net taxable income grants, a guaranteed tax base for spending over the foundation level, declining enrollment grants, and many other small programs.
36. Ibid. *Legislative Handbook Series–Volume IX–Education in Maryland*), pp. 103–114.
37. Ibid. p. 95.
38. P.L. 111-296 (2010).
39. Ibid. *Legislative Handbook Series–Volume IX–Education in Maryland* p. 108.
40. http://www.mdhungersolutions.org/community-eligibility/
41. Ibid. *Maryland State Budget Book, Volume II* (2017).
42. Ibid. *Legislative Handbook Series–Volume IX–Education in Maryland* p. 130.
43. Ibid. *Maryland State Budget Book, Volume II* (2017).
44. Ibid. *Legislative Handbook Series–Volume IX–Education in Maryland* p. 110.
45. Ibid. *Maryland State Budget Book, Volume II* (2017).
46. State of Maryland–Maryland Department of Education, *Charter School Program Overview*. Retrieved from http://www.marylandpublicschools.org/msde/programs/charter_schools/
47. Education Commission of the States, *Does the State Provide Direct Facilities Funding or Other Facilities Assistance to Charter Schools?* (2016). Retrieved from http://ecs.force.com/mbdata/mbquest2rte?rep=CS152324
48. Ibid. *Legislative Handbook Series–Volume IX–Education in Maryland* p 115.
49. Ibid.

CHAPTER 23

Massachusetts

Glenn Koocher, MPA
Executive Director
Massachusetts Association of School Boards

GENERAL BACKGROUND

The current school funding system in Massachusetts has evolved into a multifaceted program of state appropriations, local property tax revenues, and a small element of private and fee-based revenue. The majority of local funding is based on local property taxes, while state reimbursements and general grants are linked to need but justified by a complex set of assessment and accountability measures.

Unlike public school finance in most of the nation where school districts are county-based or where revenues rely on the independent school district as the appropriating and taxing authority, Massachusetts school districts largely operate as the department of education for the city or town government. In those municipalities, school committees operate as the municipal legislature for schools with authority to initiate the local education budget, set policy, retain the school superintendent, and negotiate collective bargaining agreements. In cities, the municipal chief executive officer is usually an ex officio member of the school committee and often, but not always, the chair, creating an element of check and balance between the local branches of government. School budgets require, at some point prior to finality, the approval of the local appropriating authorities (city councils, town councils, town meeting, and select boards), depending upon the historical structure of municipal government.

Funding Public Schools in the United States and Indian Country, pages 339–350
Copyright © 2019 by Information Age Publishing
All rights of reproduction in any form reserved.

Public regional and vocational technical school districts exist as independent municipalities, again overseen by elected school boards whose budgets must be approved by a minimum of two-thirds of member municipalities. A network of over 65 Commonwealth charter schools operate as independent state agencies but are funded by the direct diversion of state financial aid away from districts from which students enroll in charter schools. The expropriation of state funds to be diverted to charter schools is set at the average per-pupil expenditure for the 'sending' districts for the students' cohorts.

In Massachusetts, school districts are usually the educational department of municipal government. They are overseen by the school committees which have autonomous policy-making authority and fiduciary responsibilities shared with the municipal executive (mayor, city or town manager) and a municipal legislature that may be a city or town council or town meeting, which are the formal appropriating authorities.

Prior to 1993, school district revenues were largely derived from property tax revenues with additional state financial aid provided through general appropriation and several other budgetary line items to support special education, vocational schools, and a range of other designated areas. Because of the economic disparities among cities and towns, economically advantaged school districts enjoyed significantly higher budgets per capita than their disadvantaged counterparts. Also, a public referendum enacted in 1980[1] restricted the ability of cities and towns to raise revenues from property taxes, thus increasing reliance on state appropriations to fund schools.

In 1993, acting in concert, several parties at interest including teachers' unions, school committees, representatives of the business community, and others began to conceive a means of correcting the inequities in funding. Conceptualizers took advantage of the opportunity to devise a more broad response that included an alignment within a master plan to raise standards, create more consistent curricula, and create a better balance between rich and poor districts.

Concurrently, led by teachers' unions, other public education stakeholders and legal and advocacy organizations, an equity lawsuit was filed in 1991 seeking to invoke provisions of the state constitution[2] as the basis for requiring the legislature to end the broad disparity between wealthy and economically disadvantaged school districts. In June 1993, the state legislature, having anticipated the verdict in the *McDuffy*[3] case, enacted comprehensive education reform within days of issuance by the Massachusetts Supreme Judicial Court of a landmark decision invoking the provisions of the state constitution that prescribed a special obligation of the state and its local magistrates to cherish[4] public education in the broadest sense. The court called upon the legislature to ensure that school funding would be not only adequate, but also equitably distributed among the school districts. Legislators, anticipating the court decision, had taken the mission a step further by approving the framework for comprehensive school and district assessment systems, a set of standards for proficiency, and stronger requirements for educator proficiency as a means of promoting and measuring the effectiveness of the new investments.

The state legislature, known since the 1630s as the General Court, enacted the Massachusetts *Education Reform Act*[5] (MERA). The statute reorganized school district governance, accountability, assessment, and finance all at once. It created a coordinated system consisting of a state-developed curriculum framework with a new system of accountability and assessment measures to gauge progress. The law clarified and expanded the role and authority of the school superintendent as chief executive with authority over personnel and daily operations and school principals as local educational leaders. The role of locally elected school committees was clarified to hiring superintendents, setting policy, preparing and implementing budgets, overseeing fiduciary responsibilities, and negotiating collective bargaining with unions.

MERA also instituted a system of competition via school choice for interdistrict transfers that would allow students to leave their home district for another in exchange for a $5,000 diversion of local funds. A system of charter schools, the largest group of which are called Commonwealth Charter Schools, is operated as independent state agencies in exchange for a significantly larger diversion, specifically, the full average per pupil expenditure for each student in each sending district.

Critical elements of MERA were major revisions to the state school funding system as found in several sections of Chapter 70 of the Massachusetts General Laws.[6] Hence, the proposals are known as The Chapter 70 funding system. Simply put, the system organized the largest source of state aid to education based on:

- Calculation of a 'Foundation Budget' based on criteria necessary to determine an adequate education for students in each school district. This calculation was designed to set a reasonable and defensible standard for the court's interpretation of the state constitutional mandate;
- Prescribed measurement of 'wealth' to determine the share of the Foundation Budget that each district would be able to bear, also known as the local contribution; and
- Implied obligation of the state to provide, over time, sufficient state financial aid to fill the gap between the Foundation Budget for each district and the ability of those districts to pay their share, or local contribution.

Although arguments persist as to whether the original calibrations and subsequent efforts to keep pace with inflation have sustained a truly adequate budget, the basic structure remains in effect today. By 2000, every school district had achieved a full foundation budget through a combination of a $2 billion infusion of state funds and local appropriations, largely from property taxes.

It is important to note that between 1993–2000, Massachusetts and the nation experienced a period of unprecedented economic expansion, generating the state revenue growth necessary to reach this full funding goal. In the intervening years, a succession of governors and legislatures recommended and appropriated sufficient funds to ensure that every district can be operated at Foundation Budget levels, a fact noted by the Supreme Judicial Court when it when it rejected an attempt to revive a new equity lawsuit in 2005.[7]

In the 25 years following adoption of MERA, state financial aid under the Chapter 70 program has grown to represent 41% of the total consolidated Foundation Budgets across the state.

CALCULATING THE FOUNDATION BUDGET AND CHAPTER 70 FINANCIAL AID[8]

School districts are required to budget at the level of Required Net School Spending (RNNS). This is a function of spending in previous years as adjusted for an inflation factor. Districts are free to fund above RNNS if local revenue will sustain that budget.

Expenditures above the required level are not calculated in the Foundation Budget. In other words, a wealthy community having the property tax revenue to sustain a school district budget of 20% higher than the Foundation Budget may do so at its own expense, and without additional Chapter 70 aid. In Fiscal Year 2017, the total consolidated RNNS spending across Massachusetts was $10.241 billion, while total net school spending reached $12.679 billion.

As an example of the disparity, contrast the examples of Chelsea, a gateway city with high numbers of transient, migrant, and economically disadvantaged people with the affluent suburb of Lexington, ten miles away. Both districts have virtually identical enrollments of 7,100 pupils. However, Chelsea serves 4,200 low-income children while Lexington hosts only 450. In FY 2017, RNNS the spending requirement for Chelsea was $87.449 million, a function of high need for a high-risk population. Lexington, on the other hand, had a RNNS of $69.116 million on the theory that a wealthy district needs fewer programs and services to provide an adequate education. However, actual spending in Chelsea was $89.210 million and state financial assistance totaled $71.7 million; Lexington, on the other hand, spent $117,314 million for its public schools and received only $11.631 million in Chapter 70 funds, a reflection of the willingness and ability of a wealthy town to use its own wealth to pay most of its school budget on its own. In other words, while the Foundation Budget system helped level the playing field economically and relieved a distressed city of most of its burden—a significant improvement over an earlier era—wealthier communities continue to be able to provide more resources and services to their children.

Step 1 Calculating What is Adequate

Simply stated, calculation of the Foundation Budget is derived by multiplying the average per-pupil allocation for 11 separate expense categories by the number of students in each of 11 census cohorts based on data provided by the home district. Additional funds are built into the calculation for students enrolled in special education based on a statewide estimate that 3.75% of in-district enrollment and 1% of out-of-district students utilize these services in aggregate for the state. Finally, a further calculation is added for 'economically advantaged' students at elementary and secondary levels.

Step 2 Calculating Ability of a District to Pay its Share

Originally, the wealth of a community was calculated on the basis of taxable property values. Subsequently, in response to objections that real property values were inaccurate in describing overall wealth, a second factor (earned taxable income) was added. A formula blending the two then set a determination of wealth and the portion of the foundation budget that a community or regional district should bear. This 'target share,' in addition to the state appropriation would, in theory, provide a full Foundation Budget to the school district.

Step 3: Ensuring a Fully Funded Foundation Budget

Since 2000, the legislature has appropriated and specified that sufficient funds be provided to ensure that every school district collects locally and receives from the state sufficient revenue to fund the Foundation Budget. In recent years, efforts to make major changes to the Foundation Budget have stalled, but rather than recalibrate the elements of the formula, per-pupil adjustments have been made (i.e., $30 per pupil across the board to all districts for FY 2018) which have provided a temporary political solution.

OTHER SOURCES OF STATE AND LOCAL REVENUE

There are several additional sources of state financial aid to school districts. They include:

- *The Special Education Circuit Breaker* provides reimbursement to districts for those cases in which the cost of individual student services exceeds four times the average per-pupil expenditure for the Commonwealth. The FY 2018 threshold was $43,094. For these cases, districts receive in the subsequent year reimbursement of 75% of total case costs, minus the amount of threshold. In FY 2019, the estimated cost of this account was $318 million. This budget item is popular because, unlike Chapter 70 which is partly economic need-based, the cases involving the Circuit Breaker are driven by clinical requirements of services provided to students and are more evenly shared among all districts;
- *Regional Transportation Aid* is provided to regional school districts to defray costs of transporting students in regional school districts. The original intent of the legislation for this appropriation was for 100% reimbursement. More recent economic challenges reduced funding to 73% in FY 2018;
- *Charter School Mitigation Funding* is provided to districts whose children enroll in Commonwealth Charter Schools. As noted earlier, when a student enrolls in a Commonwealth Charter School, the state diverts the full average per-pupil cost for the sending district from the Chapter 70 allotment to the charter school. The mitigation program was legislated to be 100% of the full expropriation in the first year of student enrollment, followed by 25% of the diversion in each of the following four years. This account is subject to annual legislative appropriation and has been significantly underfunded, although diversions to fund charter schools have remained at the average total district spending per student;
- *School Building Authority grants* are provided by the Massachusetts School Building Authority to underwrite the capital costs of new and renovated facilities. This program is funded by a 1% allocation from the total revenue gathered from the 6.25% sales tax;
- *Grants to districts hosting inner-city students* in suburban schools under a METCO program, an initiative of early desegregation programs in Boston and Springfield;
- *Grants to support students who are homeless* as provided in the McKinney/Vento Homeless Assistance Act;[9]
- *Grants to support the cost of school breakfast and lunches* as a local match to federal programs[10]
- *Funds for temporary immigrant, migrant, and transient* students;
- *Additional funds* for underperforming districts;

- *Several earmarked funds* for special products in cities, towns, and regions.

Additionally local funds are available. Local revenue sources include some of the following:

- *Personal Property Tax* revenue is assessed locally by cities and towns. Municipalities that are members of regional school districts and regional vocational technical school districts contribute a share of local property taxes based on student enrollment and any special provisions of the regional district agreements in effect. On average, 59% of all Foundation Budgets are supported by the property tax;
- *Districts may retain certain revolving funds* into which are deposited such revenues as school lunch payments, athletic fees and gate receipts, and a reserve for special education costs. There are more than a dozen permitted revolving funds that can be deployed strategically for authorized purposes;
- *School Committees are authorized to accept* gifts, bequeaths, sponsorships, and other donations;
- *About 40 communities have established School Foundations* to supplement tax revenues.

For FY 2018, the Foundation Budget by category among Massachusetts school districts resembles the data shown in Table 23.1 which provides cost centers, dollars attributed, and percentages of total budget.[11] Table 23.2

TABLE 23.1 Fiscal Year 2018 Massachusetts Foundation Budget by Category

Cost Center	Budget Dollars	Percent of Total
Administration	$269,429,414	5%
Pupil Services	$247,795,730	2%
Maintenance	$1,170,510,982	11%
Benefits	$1,046,746,500	10%
Special Education Tuition	$212,281,179	2%
Instructional Leadership	$640,552,127	6%
Teachers	$4,732,621,675	46%
Other Teaching Services	$887,194,829	9%
Professional Development	$165,409,638	2%
Instructional Materials	$528,421,238	5%
Guidance/Psych Services	$278,210,530	3%
Total	$10,379,173,843	100%

TABLE 23.2 Sample Massachusetts School District Foundation Calculation

	(1)	(2)	(3)	(4)	(5)	(6)	(7)	(8)	(9)	(10)	(11)	(12)	(13)	Total[a]
		Kindergarten									**Base Foundation Components**			
	Pre-School	Half-Day	Full-Day	Elementary	Jr High/Middle	High School	ELL PK	ELL K Half	ELL KF–12	Voca-tional	Special Ed. in District	Special Ed. Out of District	Economically Disadvantaged	
Foundation Enrollment	130	272	6	1,436	1,022	1,356	0	1	39	67	153	40	573	4,128
1. Administration	24,642	51,558	2,274	544,361	387,421	514,034	0	190	14,784	25,398	400,302	104,654	0	2,069,618
2. Instructional Leadership	44,504	93,117	4,108	983,174	699,724	928,401	0	342	26,702	45,872	0	0	0	2,825,945
3. Classroom and Specialist Teachers	204,062	426,961	18,836	4,508,132	2,823,445	5,509,051	0	2,364	184,394	462,747	1,320,896	0	1,800,080	17,260,967
4. Other Teaching Services	52,336	109,503	4,831	1,156,256	592,363	654,317	0	322	25,109	32,330	1,233,302	1,599	0	3,862,269
5. Professional Development	8,070	16,885	745	178,407	137,646	177,071	0	84	6,558	14,465	63,720	0	39,619	643,271
6. Instructional Equipment & Tech	28,675	59,998	2,647	633,491	450,855	957,133	0	221	17,205	82,760	53,997	0	0	2,286,981
7. Guidance and Psychological	14,847	31,064	1,371	328,045	310,777	516,883	0	152	11,859	25,539	0	0	0	1,240,538
8. Pupil Services	5,905	12,355	545	195,756	227,564	696,245	0	68	5,316	34,401	0	0	0	1,178,157
9. Operations and Maintenance	56,666	118,564	5,231	1,251,864	965,910	1,242,626	0	590	46,027	114,909	447,157	0	278,009	4,527,553
10. Employee Benefits/Fixed Charges	56,191	117,569	5,187	1,241,417	873,488	1,079,272	0	520	40,006	82,516	503,207	0	177,401	4,176,773
11. Special Ed Tuition	0	0	0	0	0	0	0	0	0	0	0	964,695	0	964,695
12. Total	495,899	1,037,574	45,776	11,020,903	7,469,193	12,275,032	0	4,853	377,961	920,937	4,022,581	1,070,948	2,295,109	41,036,767
13. Wage Adjustment Factor	103.0%											Foundation Budget per Pupil		9,941
14. Economically Disadvantaged Decile	3													

[a] Total foundation enrollment does not include columns 11 through 13, because those columns represent increments above the base. The pupils are already counted in columns 1 to 10.
Total foundation enrollment assigns pupils in pre-kindergarten and half-time kindergarten an enrollment count of .5.
Special education in-district headcount is an assumed percentage, representing 3.75 percent of K to 12 non-vocational enrollment and 4.75 percent of vocational enrollment.
Special education out-of-district headcount is also an assumed percentage, representing 1 percent of non-vocational K-12 enrollment.
Economically disadvantaged headcounts are the number of pupils in columns 1 through 10 who are directly certified as eligible for the Supplemental Nutrition.
Each component of the foundation budget represents the enrollment on line 1 multiplied by the appropriate state-wide foundation allotment.
The wage adjustment factor is applied to underlying rates in all functions except instructional equipment, benefits and special education tuition.
The foundation budget shown on this page may differ from the final number used in the formula, due to rounding error.

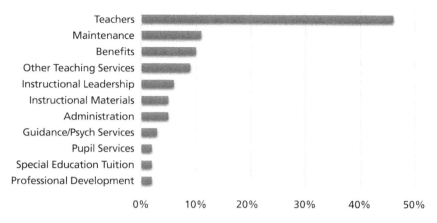

Figure 23.1 Percent of Statewide Foundation Budget.

shows a sample Massachusetts school district's Foundation Budget calculation, while Figure 23.1 graphically illustrates the same distribution.

SUMMARY

Conclusions about public school finance in Massachusetts include earlier discussion in this chapter, which can be distilled to several succinct points. First, evaluation of the state's funding formula rests in defining a legislatively mandated adequate level of funding, which in Massachusetts' case is called the school district's 'foundation budget.' The goal of the Chapter 70 formula is to ensure that every district has resources to meet its foundation budget through an equitable mix of local property taxes and state aid. The foundation budget is likely the most important factor used in calculating a district's state aid. Second, the foundation budget has its origins in three key events: (1) the Massachusetts Business Alliance for Education's release of *Every Child a Winner*,[12] an influential report establishing the groundwork for the 1993 *Education Reform Act*; and (3) the *McDuffy* case leading to the Act itself, which for the first time set a required foundation level of spending, with the requirement that it be met through a required local contribution and a supplemental amount of state aid."[13] The succinct observations about the formula are:

- *Foundation enrollment is a key factor in determining a school district's foundation budget and Chapter 70 state education aid.* Enrollment plays a central role not only because of the total number of pupils, but also because there are differences in costs associated with educational programs, grade levels, and student needs.

- *When districts' foundation budgets are presented in per-pupil terms, variation is evident.* The FY 2018 statewide average is $11,026 per pupil. After separating vocational districts to a separate category, urban centers are higher than other types of districts by more than $1,400 per pupil.
- *Foundation enrollment is comprised mostly of local resident students attending their own community local or regional school district.*[14] The most common structure is for a community to operate its own K–12 system and to belong to a vocational regional school district. About 94% of publicly-funded schoolchildren enroll in the school district associated with their cities and towns of residence. Only about 6% of public schoolchildren attend in settings other than their home districts, including charter schools, inter-district school choice, private special education schools or other appropriate programs, and vocational students attending out of district for valid reasons.
- *A district's foundation budget is derived by multiplying the number of pupils in 13 enrollment categories by cost rates in 11 functional areas.* A district's total foundation enrollment equals the sum of full day headcounts plus the students in prekindergarten and half-day kindergarten counted as half-time.
- *Special education and low-income costs are treated as costs above the base.* Three cost categories reflect the additional resources needed to educate these populations. Those categories are in-district special education, out-of-district special education, and economically disadvantaged status.
- *Once a district's foundation enrollment is calculated, it is applied to specific cost rates in 11 functional areas to arrive at the upcoming year's foundation budget.* These rates are based on a model school budget that reflects the major cost centers of school spending. Briefly said, the rates are tied to different types of students, so that costs are higher in upper grades, for ELL students, for vocational students, and for special education and low income pupils.
- *Foundation budget rates are adjusted each year by a statutorily defined inflationary factor.* Chapter 70 stipulates usage of the ratio of the current year's third-quarter inflation index to the prior year's third-quarter index.
- *The wage adjustment factor gives districts greater aid for higher school costs due to geographic realities.* The rationale is that it is teacher costs will be higher if the district is to be competitive in a market basket model. Massachusetts uses 23 labor market areas related to this adjustment.

Massachusetts school funding today is illustrated in Figure 23.2.

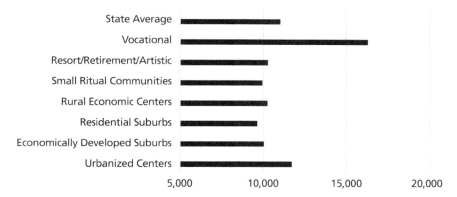

Figure 23.2 FY 18 Foundation Budget per Pupil by District Type. *Source:* Massachusetts Department of Elementary and Secondary Education (2018). http://www.doe.mass.edu/FinanceFunding.html. See also *Demystifying the Chapter 70 Formula: How the Massachusetts Education Funding System Works* (2010). http://www.massbudget.org/report_window.php?loc=Facts_10_22_10.html

NOTES

1. Proposition 2½, Chapter 580 of the Acts of 1980.
2. Constitution of the Commonwealth of Massachusetts (1780).
3. *McDuffy v. Secretary of the Executive Office of Education*, 415 Mass. 545 (1993).
4. Mass. Constitution, Chp 5 § 7.
5. Massachusetts Educational Reform Act, St. 1993, c. 71.
6. General Laws, Commonwealth of Massachusetts, Chapter 70: School Funds and State Aid for Public Schools.
7. *Hancock v. Driscoll*, 822 N.E.2d 1134 (2005).
8. A highly detailed history and outline of the Foundation Budget can be found at the website for the Massachusetts Department of Elementary and Secondary Education and school funding in Massachusetts can be found at http://www.doe.mass.edu/finance/chapter70/ and at Massachusetts Budget and Policy Center at http://www.massbudget.org/report_window.php?loc=Facts_10_22_10.html
9. PL 100-77 (1987).
10. National School Lunch Act, 42 USC 1751.
11. Any district's FY 2018 calculations can be seen on the foundation budget report available in the FY 2018 Chapter 70 formula spreadsheet http://www.doe.mass.edu/finance/chapter70/chapter-18p.html. The columns going across the page are the fourteen enrollment categories used in the foundation budget calculation.
12. *Every Child a Winner*, Massachusetts Business Alliance for Education (MBAE), 1991. Retrieved from http://www.mbae.org/every-child-a-winner/

13. *Building on 20 Years of Massachusetts Education Reform.* Retrieved from http://www.doe.mass.edu/commissioner/BuildingOnReform.pdf
14. For foundation enrollment, resident students also include Horace Mann charter students, and foreign exchange students (who do not pay tuition).

CHAPTER 24

Michigan

Brett Geier, Ed.D.
Associate Professor
Western Michigan University

GENERAL BACKGROUND

In 1993, the state of Michigan experienced an unprecedented conundrum related to financing its public schools. Kalkaska Public Schools, a district in northern Michigan, closed approximately two-thirds of the way through the school year due to insufficient funds. This travesty made headlines in many of the nation's most prominent media outlets–an entire school district had to close early because it lacked the financial resources to operate.[1] In 1994, Michigan took drastic action to change the method of funding public schools. Commonly known as Proposal A, this formula purported to provide stability, adequacy, and equity to the revenue allocated to schools. Debate remains strong after 24 years of Proposal A as to whether Michigan has provided adequate revenue streams for public education.

The crisis that enveloped Michigan was twofold. First, the pre-Proposal A funding system used a power equalization formula based primarily on ad valorem taxable value for a local school district, which resulted in substantial horizontal inequity among local school districts.[2] Secondly, because the amount of revenue available to schools was dependent on the local school district's home property values, ad valorem taxes among the various localities were unequal, and in some cases demonstrated significant discrepancies among these entities. During this time, approximately 80% of all school funding came from local sources, most notably ad valorem taxes.[3] Michigan's property owners paid well over the average amount of their national counterparts. During 1993, Michigan residents' ad valorem tax was 35% higher than the national average. Any decrease in property tax would inevitably reduce the amount of revenue allocated for local public schools' operating budgets. The majority of citizens recognized the need for quality schools and the reliance on the property owners to operate them. However, ad valorem taxes became incommensurate with other states, and the school funding system did not represent equity among all property owners.

BASIC SUPPORT PROGRAM

The amended section of the Michigan constitution in 1994 directed the state legislature to establish the initial per-pupil foundation floor for each district. A majority of schools that could be characterized as 'poor,' or more specifically below the $4,200 threshold, saw a substantial increase in per-pupil funding as a result of Proposal A. The per-pupil funding for schools in Fiscal Year 1994 provided an enhanced representation of the wealth disparities seen in Michigan prior to Proposal A's passage.

The state's first objective was to establish a minimum level of per-pupil funding. Multiple ideas were investigated, yet rejected for various reasons. For example, some individuals suggested an averaging of allocations to bring immediate equity among all school districts. The averaging concept was unacceptable to parents in high-revenue districts, as this would require a leveling down of the foundation grant, which would be politically unacceptable. A more enticing approach was to raise up the lowest funded schools, thereby 'raising the floor.' Out of this philosophy, the state decided to establish the foundation grant based on three levels: the minimum grant, the basic grant, and the maximum grant.

The minimum grant established a floor so that all school districts would receive at least this minimum. For FY 1995 the amount was set at $4,200. The basic grant was the minimum amount the state mandated all schools to receive. In concert with this objective, the state decided to increase payments in various phases until all districts arrived at the basic grant. A sliding scale was employed, which allowed districts that were farther away from the basic grant to receive larger allocations, ensuring they would reduce the gap more expeditiously. In FY 1995, the minimum grant was set at $4,200 and the basic was set at $5,000. A final objective regarding the foundation grant was to set a maximum amount the state would guarantee, which was $6,500. In contrast to the name, the maximum grant did not represent the highest per-pupil amount in the foundation program. The amount only dictated the level at which the state would provide funding as part of the foundational grant; local voter approval was required for districts that were raising more than that amount prior to Proposal A.

In FY 1995, 51 school districts exceeded the $6,500 maximum grant allocation. Districts exceeding the maximum foundation grant were afforded the opportunity to retain the revenue above the maximum grant. Those districts were provided a safeguard against having to reduce their per-pupil allocation. The hold-harmless provision was enacted by voters in each respective district, which allowed a corresponding operating millage to be levied in order to secure the per-pupil allocation prior to Proposal A. The millage levied for the hold-harmless revenue was assessed separately from any other category.

Proposal A adjusted the authority for raising operating revenue away from local school districts to the state. In FY 1994, local taxpayers were responsible for 63% of general operating revenue, while the state share was 37%. Simply by enactment of Proposal A, the percentages almost uniformly inverted, with the state responsible for 80% and the local district responsible for 20%.[4] The new law required that all homestead property[5] earmarked for school operation be taxed at a rate of six mills. This was defined as the State Education Tax (SET). Local school district constituents were required to approve the mills assessed on non-homestead[6] property.[7] The local non-homestead millage was set at a maximum 18 mills. Therefore, a total of 24 mills could be levied on homestead and qualifying non-homestead properties for general operating revenue, unless a school district was considered a hold-harmless district, whereby the local voters must approve a separate millage rate separate from the non-homestead millage to meet the hold-harmless provision.

Various methods have been employed during the life of Proposal A to adjust the foundation grant on an annual basis. In concert with the executive branch, the state legislature now annually establishes the foundation grant based on a number of variables and priorities, most notably the revenue forecast for the following year. Mechanisms utilized by Michigan to determine foundation allowances are:

- The automatic foundation index to adjust the basic grant;
- The 2× formula sliding scale used for districts below the basic grant;
- Equal per-pupil adjustments for all districts; and
- Separate equity payments.

The per pupil foundation grant for FY 2018 was $7,361. Figure 24.1 below is an illustration of the per-pupil foundation amount in 1993–94 (the school year before Proposal A) to 2017–18.

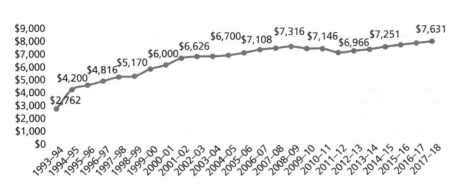

Figure 24.1 Per-Pupil Foundation Grant 1993–94 through 2017–18. *Source:* Kathryn Summers, *Overview of K–12/School Aid* (Michigan: Senate Fiscal Agency, 2017), 20.

Proposal A Funding Formula

Ironically, with the various components that were integrated into the foundation grant, the formula for determining actual allocation for each local district was abecedarian. The formula incorporated the foundation allowance with the pupil enrollment for the local district. In addition, various categorical grants were added to the total revenue to provide remediation for vertical inequity. The current formula for determining a local school district's revenue based on the per-pupil foundation is as follows:

Total Revenue = Foundation Grant × Full Time Equivalency Student Enrollment (FTE) + Categoricals − Homestead Taxable Value

Student Enrollment—The Blended Count

The enrollment algorithm, which now provides the total count for pupil enrollment, has been fairly consistent since the inception of Proposal A. The state has occasionally modified the finer details of the formula for various reasons, which has caused some school districts a loss of revenue, or more recently a slight increase. Figure 24.2 shows the general overall decline of student enrollment in Michigan, with charter schools slightly increasing.

Determining student enrollment is completed with two count days during the calendar year. The spring count (February) is 10% of the FTE, with the fall count (October) worth 90%. Percentages have been adjusted several times since Proposal A's inception. The formula below shows how enrollment was calculated for the 2017–2018 school year. For example, if XYZ school district had a student count of 1,000 for the winter count and 1,200

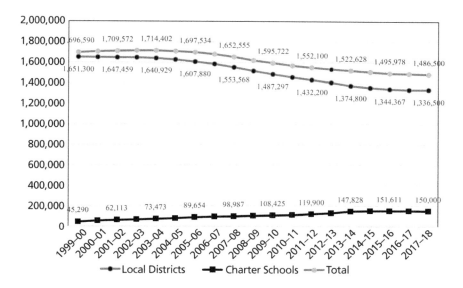

Figure 24.2 Pupil Enrollment Count. *Source:* Kathryn Summers, *Overview of K–12/School Aid* (Michigan: Senate Fiscal Agency, 2017), 35.

students in the fall count, the total FTE for this school is $(1{,}000 \times .10) + (1{,}200 \times .90) = 1{,}180$. The local school district reports 1,180 students as its total FTE and uses this number in the foundation grant formula.

[February 2017 FTE Count × (10%)] + [October 2017 FTE Count × (90%)]
= Total FTE for 2017–18 School Year

TRANSPORTATION

Michigan does not provide fiscal resources for general school transportation, although the state is legally responsible for approved costs associated with transporting special education students (see footnote 19 later) at a rate slightly over 70%. The state did allocate $3,730,300 in FY 2018 for bus driver safety instruction or evaluation, and to reimburse for costs associated with the inspection of school buses.[8]

SPECIAL EDUCATION

Accounting for revenue allocated to students identified for special education services is difficult in Michigan.[9] In 2016, the state reported that local districts spent approximately $2.7 billion for special education services.[10] School districts receive a foundation allowance on behalf of each special needs student, just as they do for general education students.[11] This foundation allowance provides a minimum per-pupil funding amount. Michigan has approximately 200,000 students who require these services, and providing adequate funding is arduous.[12] Most of the funding for special education comes from local property taxes levied by one of Michigan's 56 intermediate school districts (ISDs).[13] Each ISD levies a special education millage on local property owners to pay for services they provide directly or that they pay other school districts to provide.[14] Intermediate school districts may not levy more than 1.75 times their 1993 special education millage rate approved by local residents.[15] Because these millages are a function of the total property value in a district, large disparities in special education per-pupil funding can occur from ISD to ISD.[16] The state assists in alleviating some of these disparities by providing a categorical grant that gives additional monies to lower-funded ISDs.[17] Larger payments are provided to ISDs that have lower property values.[18]

Additional payments are made to fund special education due to the 1997 ruling in *Durant v. State of Michigan*.[19] The Michigan Supreme Court ordered the state to reimburse local school districts and ISDs for 28.6% of total approved special education costs and 70.4% of total approved transportation costs. For a small percentage of special education students who are placed in institutions by a court or state agency, the state reimburses those districts 100% of approved expenses. For a small group of school districts, another layer of funding is provided to ensure they are held harmless by a payment guarantee that does not fall below 1997 levels. While state and local funds combine to provide the largest share of revenue for local school districts and ISDs, federal funds from the Individuals with Disabilities Education Act (IDEA) are provided. For many school districts, these revenues do not cover the entire expense for special education programs, thus, the district's general fund must pay for this gap.

GIFTED AND TALENTED EDUCATION

Michigan funds gifted and talented programs by creating line items in the budget for various initiatives established by the education community and enacted by the legislature. For example, in FY 2018 $1,750,000 was allocated for dual enrollment incentive payments, $750,000 for an advanced placement incentive program to increase the number of pupils who participate and succeed in advanced placement and International Baccalaureate programs, and $2,800,000 to provide competitive grants that provide pupils with expanded opportunities to improve math, science and technology skills by participating in FIRST robotics.[20]

BILINGUAL EDUCATION

For FY 2018, the state of Michigan allocated $6,000,000 to provide grants to districts offering programs of instruction for pupils of limited English-speaking ability. Districts must administer the Wida assessment, and reimbursement is either $410 or $620 per full-time English language learner based on Wida scores. To be eligible for funding, districts must allow the Michigan Department of Education to audit records and must provide a report on usage of funds.

CAPITAL OUTLAY AND DEBT SERVICE

Primary financial responsibility for maintaining and constructing public school buildings in Michigan resides with the local school district. Michigan law allows public schools to use up to 20% of general operating revenues to finance capital projects; however, it is rare for public schools to use their main operating funds for this purpose. Local school districts are legally authorized to borrow money by taking out debt through resolution bonds. Local districts sell bonds, which raises a certain amount of revenue, and a tax is levied on local property to pay off the principal and interest over time. These bonds must be approved by a majority of local voters. More than 85% of Michigan's school districts currently charge taxpayers to pay down various outstanding debt. Most states offer local school districts some type of direct aid for facility expenses through reimbursements, matching grants, or other appropriations, but Michigan does not afford school districts this service. Michigan does allow school districts to have their debt 'qualified' by the state. A qualified loan is one that can use the state's credit rating, which is almost always more favorable than the rating individual school districts could get and usually translates to lower interest rates and borrowing costs. The state essentially guarantees its faith and credit that if the district fails to make payments, the state will assume the debt. Districts that do not want to abide by the state's terms for qualified borrowing can gain voter approval to issue nonqualified bonds for capital projects. However, the total debt for those voter-approved bonds is limited to 15% of SEV, or three times more than can be issued by a simple school board vote. Total debt limits do not apply to state-qualified bonds.

    A second funding method available to Michigan school districts for capital projects is the sinking fund. Sinking funds are established as separate savings accounts for certain projected facility costs. Sinking fund levies cannot exceed three mills, nor last more than ten years (prior to 2016, these limits were five mills and 20 years). These funds can be used to buy land, build or repair facilities, install infrastructure for technology and security, as well as purchase computer equipment and software. About 30% of Michigan school districts use voter-approved sinking funds, most of them at a lower rate.

EDUCATOR RETIREMENT

In 1945 the Michigan legislature enacted the Michigan Public School Employees Retirement Act (MPSERS). This Act was originally designed to provide pension benefits, excluding health care, for retired school employees.[21] Article 9, Section 24 of the Michigan constitution codified MPSERS in 1963. Health care benefits were not constitutionally embedded, but rather legislatively enacted in 1975. At that time, the state required all local school districts to bear partial costs of the program at the rate of 5% of salary for all public school employees. Substantial change occurred in 1994 with Proposal A which placed most of the responsibility for the retirement program on the local school district. The per-pupil foundation allowance increased for most districts in 1995; however, local districts became responsible for the amount defined by MPSERS, which was established at 14.56% the first year. This change transferred future obligations and assigned a significant portion of solvency of the retirement system to the local school districts.[22] The rate districts must pay has notably increased, intensifying the financial burden for all districts. Legislation enacted by the state in 2012 created multiple categories for employees to enter for retirement and provided a cap for local school districts. In addition, the state enacted legislation that established a payment to member schools, which is earmarked to be remitted to the state to pay for the unfunded actuarial accrued liability rate. In FY 2018, based on the teacher retirement program selected, districts paid from a low 32.28% to a high 38.48% of the teacher's salary. In this same cycle, the state paid 11.32% of those yearly totals to reduce a district's obligation. Infusing additional state dollars, modifying pension programs from defined benefit to defined contribution, and estimating lower return rates for state investments were enacted to mitigate the increasing financial burden on school districts, which will lower state funding obligations in the future.

The legislation enacted in 2012 was an effort to eliminate a growing unfunded accrued liability in MPSERS. In FY 2013, the accrued unfunded liability rose to $62.7 billion with actuarial value of assets of $38.4 billion for a fund ratio of 61.3%.[23] The fund ratio amplified a downward trend in the financial health of the MSPERS program, as Michigan maintained a public educator retirement system that was 72% funded in FY 2010.[24]

The state allocated three line items in its FY 2018 budget to specifically address MPSERS costs. First, $148,969,000 was allocated to make payments to districts to offset a portion of retirement contributions owed by districts. Second, $1,160,784,000 was allocated to pay the difference between the uncapped MPSERS contribution rate and the capped rate that school employers paid. Third, $23,100,000 was provided to cover additional costs to MPSERS for a defined contribution cost for new hires.[25] At the same time, enrollment in Michigan public school districts was declining; from 2004–2012, 425 of the 549 districts witnessed loss of enrollment, while statewide enrollment declined by 13.2%. A reason for enrollment losses (apart from flight due to the economy) was the increased presence of charter schools; since 2004, the number of charter schools increased from 199 to 298. These schools enrolled approximately 120,000 students, equating to 9% of all public and charter school students in the state.[26] Very few charter schools participate in MPSERS. This drain of student enrollment decreases the number of teachers needed in traditional public schools, which reduces the number of workers per retiree.

OTHER CATEGORICAL FUNDS

While a majority of public school funding in Michigan comes from the per-pupil foundation grant (approximately 70%), categorical aid provides a secondary method for funding schools.[27] Categorical aid allocated in Michigan frequently addresses vertical equity issues for students who require added costs above the per-pupil foundation.[28] Two of the largest categorical allocations are for at-risk and special education students. For FY 2018, the state allocated over $510 million for at-risk students known as Section 31a.[29] Students qualiFY for 31a monies by being documented as having two of six at-risk factors. For special education, the state allocated over $1.3 billion in this same period to provide payment for special education membership, special education transportation, and other special education categorical programs.[30] These categorical allocations allow the state to identify any special interests and to provide funding: for instance, over $37 million was allocated for career and technical education programs, over $3 million for bus driver instruction and bus inspections, and over $8.5 million to assist schools in Flint as a result of the declaration of emergency due to the water crisis.[31]

FUNDING OF CHARTER SCHOOLS

Charter schools receive district foundation allowances just like traditional local public school districts. However, a charter school's foundation allowance is equal to the lesser of the foundation allowance of the surrounding conventional school district and the basic foundation allowance. The basic foundation allowance for FY 2018 was $7,631. Interestingly, in the spring of 2018, the Michigan legislature began reviewing proposed legislation that has the goal of allowing charter schools to receive a portion of Intermediate School District (ISD) enhancement millages levied against ISD property owners[32]—currently charter schools are not entitled to a portion of these funds.

EARLY CHILDHOOD EDUCATION

Over several past budget cycles, the state of Michigan made improving funding for early childhood programs a priority. In several categorical funds, the state allocated monies to various uses by early childhood programs. In FY 2018, almost $244 million was provided in formulas to eligible ISDs for comprehensive compensatory education programs to improve the school readiness of at-risk four-year-olds.[33] An approved school readiness program must include an age-appropriate educational curriculum, nutritional services, health screening, plan for parent involvement, and referrals for community social services.[34] At least 90% of the children participating in the program must be from families with income levels no more than 250% of the federal poverty level, with children from poorer families awarded slots before children from families with higher incomes.[35] Of the total appropriation, $10 million was earmarked for reimbursement of transportation costs at no more than the actual cost of transporting to the program.[36] An Early Childhood Block Grant Program ($13,400,000) was established to provide an application detailing proposed uses of early childhood funding.[37] Of this total appropriation, $2.5 million was earmarked for home visits to at-risk children and their families, to improve school readiness, to reduce the number of pupils retained in grade level, and to reduce the number of pupils needing special education.[38]

LOCAL SCHOOL REVENUE

Local obligation of tax revenue is required as part of the state per-pupil aid formula. Just as a six-mill levy is placed on homestead property in a local school district, an 18-mill tax is levied on all non-homestead property such as businesses, second homes, and qualifying farmland. The revenue raised from this levy can be calculated by multiplying the 18 mills by the total non-homestead taxable value of the school district.[39] Local revenue sources are a primary component for financing school building maintenance and construction (see capital outlay and debt service section earlier).

FOOD SERVICES

The school lunch program in Michigan is made up of both a federal and state component, but the state distributes both payments. The federal program is calculated under the Richard B. Russell *National School Lunch Act*.[40] Michigan's federal allocation in FY 2018 was $545,695,100. The state payment, equaling 6.0127% of a district's program costs, was $22,495,100 in FY 2018. The state reimbursement is a directive by the court in the *Durant* decision (see footnote 19). The state also allocated $4,500,000 to reimburse districts for the cost of providing breakfast, which is statutorily required under certain circumstances.[41]

STATE AID FOR PRIVATE SCHOOLS

Article VIII, Section 2 of the Michigan constitution delineates that no public monies shall be allocated to pay for any private, nonpublic pre-elementary, elementary, or secondary school. The Michigan legislature allocated $2.5 million in the past two budget cycles ($5 million total) to private schools to help them cover the cost of complying with state mandates. However, a Michigan Court of Claims held that the disbursement of public money for private schools violated the Michigan constitution.[42]

EARMARKED STATE REVENUES

Michigan is somewhat unique from other states in that a majority of its public schools are funded through a special fund established by the state known as the State School Aid Fund (SSAF). The SSAF has earmarked funds that may be used only to support public education in Michigan.[43] In FY 2018, the gross amount appropriated to the SSAF was approximately $12,642,370,400, which was 87% of the $14.6 billion public school budget.[44] The following are sources of revenue statutorily or constitutionally allocated to the SSAF (percentage of obligation varies):

- State Sales Tax
- State Use Tax
- State Income Tax
- State Education Tax

- Real Estate Transfer Tax
- Casino Gaming Tax
- State Lottery
- Cigarette Tax
- Liquor Tax[45]

SUMMARY

For FY 2018, Michigan allocated a total of $14,578,863,900 for education funding, which represented 26% of the state's total $56.5 billion budget. This budget served 1,520,065 students.

NOTES

1. Isabel Wilkerson, "Tiring of Cuts, District Plans to Close Schools," *New York Times*, March 21, 1993.
2. Citizens Research Council of Michigan, *Distribution of State Aid to Michigan Schools*, Report 317, August 2011. Per-pupil revenue in Michigan had a range of $2,700 to $10,000.
3. Joe Carrasco and Kathryn Summers-Coty, "K–12: A Moving Target" (Michigan Senate Fiscal Agency, 2002). Retrieved from: http://www.senate.michigan.gov/sfa/publications/notes/2002notes/notesjulaug02carrascosummers.pdf
4. House and Senate Fiscal Agencies, "School Finance in Michigan Before and After the Implementation of Proposal A: A Comparison of FY 1993–94 and FY 1994–95 Approaches to K–12 School Funding in Michigan," *The Michigan School Aid Act Compiled and Appendices* (Lansing, MI: Senate Fiscal Agency, July/August 1994), 5.
5. Homestead property is defined as a taxpayer's primary residence, including noncommercial agricultural property.
6. Non-homestead property is defined as all other property such as business, rental property, vacation homes, and commercial agriculture.
7. Kathryn Summers, *The Basics of School Funding* (Lansing, MI: Senate Fiscal Agency, 2012), p. 10.
8. Kathryn Summers, *Appropriation Line Item*, 20.
9. Ben DeGrow, *How School Funding Works in Michigan* (Michigan: Mackinac Center for Public Policy, 2017), p. 8
10. Ibid.
11. Ibid.
12. Ibid., p. 9.
13. Ibid.
14. Ibid.
15. Ibid.
16. Ibid.
17. Ibid.

18. Ibid.
19. *Durant v. State of Michigan*, 563 N.W.2d 646 (1997) (The Michigan Supreme Court held that special education, special education transportation, and the school lunch program are required by state law. It found that the state had been funding these programs at levels proportionally below those appropriated in 1978, when the Headlee Amendment was adopted and enacted. Through a different Special Master appointed by the Court of Appeals in 1995, state funding percentages from 1978 were determined for these services. The supreme court issued a monetary remedy for the amount of underfunding and a percentage the state must pay local school districts and ISDs for these services).
20. Kathryn Summers, *Appropriation Line Item*, pp. 19–23.
21. Tom Gantert, "Public School Pension System Totally Broken: Taxpayers on the hook," *CAPCON: Michigan Capitol Confidential* (June 24, 2013). Retrieved from: http://www.michigancapitolconfidential.com/18797
22. Mich. Pub. Act 300 (2012).
23. Financial Services for Office of Retirement Services, *Michigan Public School Employees Retirement Services: Comprehensive Annual Financial Report for the Fiscal Year Ended September 30, 2013* (Michigan: MPSERS, 2013).
24. Ibid.
25. Kathryn Summers, *Appropriation Line Item*, 27–28.
26. Cate Long, "Michigan's Pension Problem," *Reuters* (November 20, 2013). Retrieved from: http://blogs.reuters.com/muniland/2013/11/20/michigans-pension-problem/
27. William J. Price, *Michigan School Finance: A Handbook for Understanding State Funding Policy for Michigan Public Schools Districts* (Houston, TX: National Council of Professors of Educational Administration, 2012), 37.
28. Ibid.
29. Kathryn Summers, *Appropriation Line Item*, p. 9.
30. Ibid., p. 14.
31. Ibid., pp. 2–28.
32. Regional Enhancement Millage Allowed for Charter Schools, Cyber Schools and ISDs of 2017, S.B. 574, Mich. Leg. (2017).
33. Kathryn Summers, *Appropriation Line Item*, p. 11.
34. Ibid.
35. Ibid.
36. Ibid.
37. Ibid., p. 12.
38. Ibid.
39. Mich. Rev. Sch. Code § 380.1211 (2018).
40. Chapter 281 of the 79th Congress, Approved June 4, 1946, 60 Stat. 230 As Amended Through P.L. 115–141, Enacted March 23, 2018.
41. Kathryn Summers, *Appropriation Line Item*, pp. 10–11.
42. Lori Higgins, "Judge: Public Money for Private Schools Violates Michigan constitution," *Detroit Free Press*, April 26, 2018, Retrieved from https://www.freep.com/story/news/education/2018/04/26/public-money-private-schools-michigan-constitution/555598002/

43. Price, *Michigan School Finance*, p. 9.
44. Bethany Wicksall, "Budget Briefing School Aid" (lecture, House Fiscal Agency, Lansing, MI, January 17, 2018).
45. Price, *Michigan School Finance*, pp. 10–14.

CHAPTER 25

Minnesota

Nicola Alexander, Ph.D.
University of Minnesota

GENERAL BACKGROUND

The Minnesota constitution[1] requires the state legislature to provide for operation of its public elementary and secondary schools.[2] The Minnesota school finance system is the method by which the legislature fulfills that responsibility. Minnesota has a biennial budget, where the governor makes proposals to the legislature regarding the state's operating budget in odd years, with proposed capital expenditures made in even years. Until the early 1900s, local school boards contributed almost all of the funds used for operating public elementary and secondary schools through property taxes levied locally. In the early part of the 20th century, the state supplemented local contributions with limited amounts of state appropriations to school districts.

Minnesota eventually developed a state aid program that provided all districts with a flat grant per pupil weighted for grade level, and provided some districts with additional equalized amounts based on district property valuation as a measure of district wealth. These efforts on the part of the state, however, were not sufficient to stem the rapid and uneven rise in local property taxes that marked the late 1960s. In response, the 1971 legislature substantially increased the amount of equalized state foundation aid per weighted pupil and imposed a uniform statewide limit on the property tax rates that districts could establish. Just two years later, the 1973 legislature eliminated flat grants and substantially increased the established foundation aid so that low spending districts had per-pupil revenues that approximated the state average. For the next ten years, from 1973 to 1983, the legislature refined the foundation aid formula by modifying the foundation aid and required local tax effort without changing the basic structure of the program.

The 1983 legislature enacted a new foundation aid program that became effective in the 1984–85 school year. The new program replaced the existing system with a five-tier foundation aid formula. The main characteristics of the new program were equal access to revenue, recognition of specific cost differences, and more discretion on the part of school boards in choosing the necessary level of revenue.

By 1987, the legislature had replaced the foundation aid program with a modified funding formula called the general education revenue program, effective for the 1988–89 school year. In 1988, 52 outer-ring suburban and rural school districts representing 25% of the state's K–12 enrollment filed a lawsuit against the Minnesota school finance system. The suit in *Skeen v. State*[3] claimed that Minnesota's school finance system was unconstitutional because the system was not uniform and school districts received disparate amounts of government aid. In 1989, a Minnesota trial court ruled that three parts of the finance mechanism were unconstitutional: (1) debt levy; (2) referendum levy; and (3) 302 revenue;[4] the state appealed the ruling. In 1993, the Minnesota Supreme Court reversed the trial court and held the state's school finance system constitutionally permissible.

The components of Minnesota's school finance formula have remained relatively stable since 1989. In general, each component reflects legislative perspective on school district funding needs. Components cover differential costs tied to economies of scale (e.g., small school revenue, operating sparsity revenue, transportation sparsity revenue); differences in the needs of students served (e.g., English learner revenue, compensatory revenue, extended time revenue); programmatic costs (e.g., gifted and talented revenue); and the status of enrollment (e.g., declining pupil revenue).

In Fiscal Year 2003, Minnesota changed the way it calculated property taxes and brought some of these revenue streams under the auspices of the state. At that time, even though the bulk of the funding system was still structured as if it was foundational, it largely operated as a flat grant. From 2003–2015, the general education formula revenue was funded solely with state aid. The state established a Student Achievement Levy in FY 2013 to generate an additional $20 million annually statewide in general education revenue, which was first effective in school year 2014–2015. It was a limited version of the local tax rate in place under the previous foundational formula, but this newest incarnation of the local levy was slated to be short-lived as the 2015 legislature passed legislation phasing out the levy over two years beginning in FY 2018.

The latest embodiment of the school finance system's general education revenue is the primary source of general operating funds for Minnesota's 331 public school districts and 165 charter schools, in place for FY 2018. Enrollment is the primary driver of Minnesota's school finance system, and the state distributes aid to each adjusted pupil unit. Adjusted pupil units reflect average daily membership weighted by the grade level of the student, where one voluntary prekindergarten student is weighted 0.6 pupil unit; a student in required kindergarten through grade 6 is weighted 1.0 pupil unit; a student in grades 7 through 12 is counted as 1.2 pupil units. Prior to FY 2015, the state adjusted the pupil count to reflect the organizational level in which the student was served as well as whether the student was in a district with stable, declining, or rising enrollments. In FY 2015, the enrollment status of the district was subsumed as one of the components in the general education aid formula, and districts with declining enrollment from year to year are now eligible for declining enrollment revenue. Thus, adjusted pupil units currently reflect average daily membership, weighted only by organizational level of the student served.

Most general education revenue is for the general operation of the school district and is not restricted by the state for a specific purpose. In addition to general education revenue, school districts also receive state appropriations through categorical aids, which are funds designated for specific purposes such as special education and school integration/desegregation. General education revenue pays for operating expenses of the district including employee salaries, fringe benefits, and supply costs.

GENERAL EDUCATION PROGRAM

Minnesota finances elementary and secondary schools through a combination of state-collected taxes and locally collected property taxes.[5] There are three categories of funding under this finance system: (1) State education finance appropriations; (2) state paid property tax credits; and (3) property tax levies. State education finance appropriations are funded with state-collected taxes and comprise general education aid and categorical aids. State paid property tax credits reflect the amounts paid by the state to compensate for reductions in local property tax revenues tied to state property tax credits. Property tax levies are largely made with voter approval, but in some instances are at the discretion of individual school boards. Voter-approved levies usually authorize excess operating referenda and debt service levies.

The general education aid program has 13 subcomponents; revenue from this aid accounts for almost four-fifths of annual education finance appropriations, reflecting a majority of all financial support for Minnesota's school districts. This funding reflects flat grants, foundational aid, and equalized support and is grounded in principles of adequacy, horizontal equity, and vertical equity. These funding components reflect not only a minimum level of funding, but also adjustments for a variety of district, pupil, and programmatic needs.

Basic General Education Formula Revenue

The biggest subcategory of general aid is the basic general education formula revenue, which establishes the minimum (or foundational) level of per-pupil unit funding for school districts. This aid is set each year in legislation, and all school districts are eligible for this basic amount. This funding accounted for 70.8% of all general education revenue in FY 2017. Each district's share is determined by multiplying the formula allowance by the district's adjusted pupil units.[6] For FY 2017, the formula allowance was $6,067 per pupil unit. This portion of Minnesota's school finance system superficially resembles a standard foundation program comprised of a formula allowance and an established local tax rate. However, from FY 2003 through FY 2014 the established local tax rate was set at 0%, essentially causing this portion of the funding mechanism to operate as a flat grant.

As noted earlier, the state legislature established a Student Achievement Levy to act as a limited version of the old general education levy that was in place prior to FY 2003. This levy, based on adjusted net tax capacity calculated for the prior year, was set at a rate of 0.30% for FY 2017. Districts are not required to tax to the maximum level allowed. However, if a district chooses to tax itself less than the established levy rate, the district's share of total general education revenue state aid not subject to an aid/levy split is reduced proportionately. Other levies for the general education program include the local portions of equity, transition, operating capital, referendum, and local optional revenue. The local portions of general education revenue (excluding basic general education formula) are equalized.

Supplemental Components in the General Education Program

There are 12 additional components to the general education program aid besides the basic general education revenue. These adjustments include aid to address differences among districts in four major areas:

1. *programmatic needs*: extended time revenue, gifted and talented revenue, learning and development revenue, revenue for staff development;
2. *economies of scale and district structure*: declining enrollment revenue, secondary sparsity revenue, elementary sparsity revenue, transportation sparsity revenue, small school revenues, and operating capital revenue;
3. *needs of students served*: basic skills revenue (compensatory revenue and English learners);
4. *district wealth*: referendum revenue, equity revenue, local optional aid.

> General Education Revenue = (Basic revenue + extended time revenue + gifted and talented revenue + declining enrollment revenue + small schools revenue + basic skills revenue + secondary sparsity revenue + elementary sparsity revenue + operating capital revenue + transportation sparsity revenue + equity revenue + transition revenue + referendum revenue (board approved) + referendum revenue (voter approved) + local optional revenue) x Pupil units.

Figure 25.1 Components of Minnesota's General Education Program Revenue. *Source:* Fiscal Analysis Department of the Minnesota House of Representatives. (2016). Financing Education in Minnesota 2016–2017

Operationally, the total general education program is expressed in Figure 25.1.

Table 25.1 provides data on each component of the general education program formula for FY 2017. It includes information on the number of districts that received aid from the specified programs; total aid appropriated for that formula component; the established formula amount for each revenue component; and whether or not that revenue stream is equalized.

The general education program had key changes in the formula for FY 2017 as highlighted in bullet form.

- Basic formula allowance increased from $5,948 per pupil unit in FY 2016 to $6,067 per pupil unit in FY 2017. The associated tax rate fell from .35% to .33% in the same period;
- Beginning in FY 2017, English Learner (EL) students became eligible for EL revenue for up to seven years (increased from six years);
- For Fiscal Years 2017, 2018, and 2019, equalized revenue is multiplied by a factor of 1.25 for metro districts and 1.16 for nonmetro districts. In FY 2017 only, the state fully funded the 1.16 adjustment for nonmetro districts. Beginning in FY 2020, all districts are eligible for the 1.25 adjustment.

The governor's priorities for FY 2017 included the following.[7]

- $25 million to expand availability of and participation in prekindergarten programs;
- $12.4 million to help train and attract up to 1,200 teacher candidates by 2021;
- $10 million to help districts not participating in alternative teacher pay systems to develop teacher development and evaluation programs;

TABLE 25.1 Detailed Description of Minnesota's General Education Program for FY 2017[a]

State aid component	Number of receiving districts	Total state aid	Formula amount per eligible adjusted pupil unit	Equalized aid[b]
Basic revenue	331	$5.6B	$6,067	No
Extended time revenue	135	$65.4M	$5,117	No
Gifted & talented revenue	331	$12.05M	$13	No
Declining enrollment	178	$9.05M	$1,699[c]	No
Small schools revenue[d]	162	$16.4M	Up to $544	No
Basic skills revenue	331	$559.59M	Based on number and concentrations of eligible students	No
Sparsity (elementary and secondary sparsity revenue)	102	$27.4M	Based on enrollment and geographic attendance area	No
Operating capital revenue	331	$209.6M	$188–$243	Yes
Transportation sparsity revenue	302	$66.6M	Up to $1,026	No
Equity revenue[e]	331	$110.56M	$50–$177	Yes
Transition revenue	200	$29.89M	Varies	Yes
Referendum revenue (board and voter approved)	331	$154.5M	1st tier: Up to $300 2nd tier: $300–$760 3rd tier: $760–$1,517	Yes
Local optional revenue	314	$60.51M	Up to $424	Yes

Source: Adapted from Fiscal Analysis Department of the Minnesota House of Representatives. (2016). Financing Education in Minnesota 2016–2017.

[a] While charter schools are considered school districts and are also funded through the education finance mechanism used for traditional public school districts, the table refers only to traditional public school districts.
[b] Equalized aid refers to aid distributed using guaranteed tax base (also known as power equalization, guaranteed revenue, and guaranteed tax yield).
[c] This amount is times the difference between the current year and previous year weighted pupil count.
[d] Charter schools are ineligible for small schools revenue.
[e] Excludes all districts in cities of the first class; i.e., Minneapolis, St. Paul, and Duluth for the equalized portion; however, all districts receive a flat rate of an additional $50 per pupil unit.

- $2.75 million to increase the number of sites implementing Positive Behavioral Intervention and Supports (PBIS) systems in schools and districts throughout the state;
- $2 million to increase the number of community schools receiving state grants in 2017. These grants allow schools to partner with community agencies to provide on-site health and dental clinics, mental

health services, family resource centers, college access information, out-of-school program information, and other family support services;
- $2 million in FY 2017 and $540,000 a year thereafter to build and maintain an online system for Individual Education Plans (IEPs);
- $1 million to implement a comprehensive early childhood system to better connect children and families to resources that support healthy child development. Targeted to Minnesota families with children prenatal through age 8.

Total state aid appropriated in FY 2017 to all 331 school districts and 165 charter schools for the general education program amounted to $6.86 billion. An additional $2 billion was spent on categorical programs in that same period. State education finance appropriations totaled $8.9 billion in FY 2017, which accounted for 41.7% of the Minnesota's general fund dollars.

State appropriations for programs differ from revenues calculated based on the formula for those programs because of statutory requirement that the state pays most education aids over a two-year period. Under this law, a majority percentage of a current year's entitlement must be paid in the current year, plus the adjusted balance of the previous year's entitlement. For FY 2017, state appropriations equaled 90% of the current year's entitlement plus the final 10% payment from the prior fiscal year.[8]

COMPENSATORY EDUCATION

Compensatory education programs are integrated into Minnesota's general education program as illustrated earlier in Figure 25.1 and Table 25.1. Along with funding for English Learners, compensatory revenue is a part of the basic skills revenue stream of that program. School sites generate funding levels based on numbers and concentrations of students eligible for free and reduced priced lunch (FRL) served at the site; the higher the concentration of eligible students, the higher the level of compensatory revenue that is generated. The level of concentration that influences the level of funding is capped. Even though compensatory education is included as part of the general education program, there are restrictions on how this money can be spent. Thus, compensatory revenue must be reserved in a separate account, and each district must produce an annual report describing how compensatory revenue was spent at each site within the district.

The formula for this revenue stream is calculated for each site using the following steps which results in the number of compensatory pupil units:

- *Multiply* 100 by the ratio of the number of pupils eligible for free lunch plus half of the number of pupils eligible for reduced price meals to the school site's total enrollment. That is:
- [100 × [(number of free lunch students + .5 number of reduced lunch students)] / School ADM]
- *Calculate* a building weighting factor equal to the lesser of 1, or the building's concentration factor divided by .80.
- *Multiply* the compensation pupils calculated in step 1 by the weighting factor calculated in step (2) by .60[9]

The total amount of compensatory revenue generated is as follows.

(Basic Formula Allowance − $415) × .6 × Compensatory Pupil Units

For FY 2017, the formula would read: ($6,067 − $415) × .6 × Compensatory pupil units.

Beginning FY 2016, school boards could allocate up to 50% of compensatory revenue on a district-wide basis. Prior to 2016, the district had to distribute those funds to the schools that generated them. All districts received some portion of the $544.85 million in compensatory revenue, which accounted for 6.9% of FY 2017 general education aid.

SPECIAL EDUCATION

Special education funding is a major portion of all categorical aid that the state appropriates to school districts. State aid for this category amounted to $1.25 billion (61.9%) of all state categorical aid for FY 2017. There are four categories of special programs: (1) special education aid; (2) special education excess cost aid; (3) home-based travel aid; and (4) special pupil aid.

All operating districts receive special education aid, but the amounts vary among districts. Prior to FY 2015, Minnesota used a partial cost reimbursement basis for funding special education, where districts received special education aid for the current year based on covering 69% of certified special related expenditures in the previous fiscal year. The state has since adopted a census-based model which takes into consideration overall district enrollment, poverty concentration, district size, and the average costs of educating students with different primary disabilities.[10]

There are three average cost categories for determining the special education aid needed:[11]

- *Category 1* includes those with the primary disability areas of autism spectrum disorder, developmental delay, and severely multiply impaired, i.e., $10,400 times the December 1 child count;

- *Category 2* includes those with the primary disability areas of deaf and hard-of-hearing and emotional behavioral disorders, i.e., $18,000 times the December 1 child count;
- *Category 3* includes those with the primary disability areas of developmentally cognitive severe-profound, physically impaired, visually impaired, and deafblind.

Because the census-based approach is new in Minnesota, the state has included provisions to essentially hold school districts harmless. Thus, initial aid for the current year was calculated based on prior year fiscal calculations to include the least of:

- 62% of the district's old formula special education expenditures, excluding expenditures spent on transportation;
- 50% of the district's nonfederal special education expenditures, excluding expenditures spent on transportation; or
- 56% of the product of the sum of the census-based amounts.

Special education excess cost aid is intended to address vertical equity by compensating districts that have large unreimbursed special education costs relative to the district's general education revenue.[12] Excess cost aid is calculated based on the greatest of: (a) 56% of the difference between the district's unreimbursed nonfederal special education costs and 7% of the district's general education revenue; (b) 62% of the difference between the district's unreimbursed 'old formula' special education costs and 2.5% of the district's general education revenue; or (c) zero.

Home-based travel aid reimburses 50% of the travel costs of personnel providing home-based travel services to children under age five with a disability.[13]

Special pupil aid is a catch-all category, where districts are reimbursed for special education costs not covered by other special education funding; it also covers unreimbursed spending for students with disabilities who reside in public or private residential facilities in the district and for whom there is no specified school district of residence.[14]

GENERAL TRANSPORTATION

Pupil transportation is a huge expense, and the state of Minnesota largely addresses that cost as part of its general education revenue program. No categorical aid exists for transportation, a function accounting for 5.7% of a district's budget on average.[15] While additional transportation needs are considered for rural districts via sparsity aid (including transportation sparsity revenue), there is no comparable funding for districts located in more densely populated areas. The formula to calculate transportation sparsity revenue employs a complex density and sparsity index; the actual formula uses logarithms to calculate a revenue amount.[16]

CAPITAL IMPROVEMENTS

The state provides capital improvement aid for school districts' facilities in its general education program in the support provided for operating capital revenue and long-term facilities maintenance revenue.

School Facilities

School facilities are covered by operating capital revenue under the general education program and by categorical aid for long-term facilities maintenance revenue (LTFMR). Operating capital revenue is used for repair and betterment of facilities, acquisition of land, purchase or lease of equipment, and purchase of books. Even though operating capital revenue is part of the general education program, this revenue must be used for specified capital projects and may not be used for general operating purposes.[17] It is an equalized formula, with an equalizing factor of $15,740 of a district's adjusted net tax capacity. The equalized amount was set to increase to $19,972 in FY 2018 and to $22,912 in FY 2019.[18]

Capital Outlay

School districts are responsible for funding their ongoing capital needs as well as major building construction projects. The preceding discussion on school facilities covered financing for ongoing capital needs; this section focuses on major building projects.

To finance major building projects, districts often borrow money through the sale of bonds and levy an annual tax to repay the money over a period of years. This pay-as-you-use strategy contrasts with the alternative of pay-as-you-go, where districts build up money in reserves to finance major capital projects. The amount of debt service revenue needed each year is equalized at varying rates depending on the ratio of the amount of debt service revenue to the district's total adjusted net tax capacity. Debt service for traditional general obligation bonds is calculated differently from use for long-term maintenance programs. For FY 2017, debt service levels were equalized at $4,430 for the amount of debt service totaling between

15.74% and 26.24% of the district's adjusted net tax capacity and at $8,000 for the amount of debt service exceeding 26.24% of the district's adjusted net tax capacity.[19] Debt service amounts qualifying for debt equalization are general debt service amounts for land acquisition, construction costs, and capital energy loans.

Because of the importance and cost of major construction projects, the Minnesota Department of Education is required to provide review and comment on each major project for which the district plans to issue a sale of bonds. Any project that requires an expenditure of more than $2,000,000 except for certain deferred maintenance projects must be submitted by the district to the commissioner for review and comment unless the school district has an outstanding capital loan, in which case the project must be submitted for review and comment for any expenditure in excess of $500,000. There are three ratings that the commissioner can apply to the proposed project: (1) positive; (2) unfavorable; and (3) negative. With a positive rating, the district can hold a referendum to authorize the sale of bonds and can proceed with the project on a simple majority of the voters. If the project receives an unfavorable rating, the district can hold a referendum to authorize the sale of bonds but can only proceed if it receives 60% approval of the voters. If the project receives a negative rating, the district cannot proceed with the project. Prior to referendum, the findings of the commissioner must be published in the legal newspaper of the district.[20]

The LTMFR aid replaced the previous Health and Safety, Alternative facilities, and Deferred maintenance revenue programs. Beginning in FY 2017, all districts and charter schools became eligible for this funding, with detailed restriction on its use. Further, districts may issue general obligation bonds for this funding. This revenue must not be used for "construction of new facilities, remodeling of existing facilities, purchase of portable classrooms, to finance a lease purchase agreement, energy efficiency projects, facilities used for postsecondary instruction, violence prevention, security, ergonomics or emergency communication devices."[21] This revenue is an equalized levy, designed so that districts with large portions of agricultural land, of which a smaller portion contributes to the net tax capacity of the district, is eligible for increased LTMFR. The program was scheduled to be phased in over three years. For FY 2017, the amount allowed was $193 times adjusted pupil units; the amount granted to charter schools was $34 times adjusted pupil units for the same period.

CAREER AND TECHNICAL EDUCATION

Only districts offering career and technical programming are eligible for revenue under this program. These education services comprise courses that were formerly called vocational programs including agricultural, business, technology, and health occupations courses. This revenue is comprised of equalized state aid and local levies. Revenue from this program equals 35% of the district's approved expenditures for career and technical programming, but not less than the revenue authority for the previous year provided that the revenue does not exceed 100% of the district's career and technical expenditures for that year. Unlike most other programs in Minnesota's school finance plan, the revenue for the career and technical levy is recognized in the same year for which taxes are payable. Thus, the levy for taxes payable in 2017 was recognized as revenue in FY 2017. On average, expenditures for these programs account for 1.25% of districts' general fund expenditures.

VIRTUAL EDUCATION

Minnesota offers categorical aid for telecommunications access revenue. This is a reimbursement program for eligible tele-communications and internet access costs from the previous fiscal year. To access these funds, school districts must apply for federal internet funding, called e-rate funding. Revenue is calculated based on a district's eligible costs for the prior year minus any e-rate funding received that exceeds $16 per pupil.

SPECIAL LEVIES

School districts may levy additional local property tax to provide funding for operating and capital expenditures. These levies are equalized and are part of the general education funding program. There are three primary categories of special levies: (1) referendum revenue; (2) local optional revenue; and (3) equity revenue.[22]

Referendum revenue allows districts to increase the revenue available in the district's general fund and is generated with both voter approval and, in more limited cases, approval of the school board. Unlike other revenue streams that are based on adjusted net capacity of a school district (a small portion of the total market value), referendum revenue is based on market value. Minnesota provides three equalization tiers for referendum revenue, which is subject to an annual cap. For FY 2017, the standard cap was estimated to be $1,891.49 per adjusted pupil unit. The cap is adjusted annually for inflation based on the urban consumer price index. Only districts eligible for sparsity revenue can have district referendum revenue that exceeds this cap. Districts are also eligible for up to $424 per pupil unit in local optional revenue.

Minnesota's funding system also allows for equity revenue, which is aimed at reducing the disparity in revenue per pupil unit on a regional basis. There are two primary regions, the seven-county metropolitan area and the rest of the state. Minnesota uses a set of three formulas to calculate equity revenue: (1) regular equity; (2) low-referendum equity; and (3) supplemental equity. Regular equity revenue is calculated by ranking all districts in each region based on their total and basic referendum revenue. Any district below the 95th percentile is eligible for regular and low-referendum equity revenue unless it is a district in a city of the first class (i.e., Minneapolis, St. Paul, and Duluth). Low referendum equity was created to provide additional aid for districts with referendum amounts per pupil unit below 10% of the state average referendum amount. For FY 2017, the state average referendum amount was $770 per pupil unit. Prior to FY 2005, a district's equity revenue was provided entirely in state aid. For FY 2017, about $26 million in equity revenue was provided in state aid; the remaining $84 million was raised through the levy.[23]

Finally, under the safe school's levy program a district may also levy up to $36 per pupil unit for the costs of peace officers used for school liaison services, drug prevention programs, gang resistance education programs, and other programs that are aimed to enhance the physical, mental, and emotional health of students. Districts that are members of an intermediate school district may levy an additional $15 for these same purposes.[24]

FOOD SERVICES

All Minnesota school districts are expected to operate a food service program in full compliance with federal and state regulations. Food service funds are part of the operating funds of districts but are separate from their general funds. Categorical aid for districts includes school breakfast and school lunch aid. Under the school breakfast aid, schools are eligible to receive 55¢ for each fully paid breakfast and 30¢ for each reduced-price breakfast served to students in grades 1 through 12.[25] Schools are eligible to receive up to 12.5¢ of state funding for each lunch served. Districts receive 40¢ per reduced price lunch meal served.[26]

STATE FUNDING FOR NONPUBLIC SCHOOLS

Minnesota has two categories for funding nonpublic pupils: (1) nonpublic pupil aid[27] and (2) nonpublic pupil transportation.[28] Public school districts receive this aid for the benefit of their nonpublic school students.

Nonpublic pupil aid may be used for supplying secular textbooks and other instructional materials; it also includes provision of health services and secondary guidance and counseling services. The textbook funding level is based on the average amounts expended per pupil in public schools for similar materials two years prior; this amount is multiplied by a factor equal to the growth in the basic formula amount between the second prior year and the current year. Health service reimbursements are based on actual costs per pupil or on the average cost of providing those services to public school students two years prior, whichever is less. Guidance and counseling services are reimbursed based on actual costs per secondary pupil or the average cost of providing those services to public secondary school students two years prior, whichever is less. State aid for nonpublic pupil transportation reimburses public school districts for the cost per pupil of providing transportation services. It is based on the cost of transportation two years prior and adjusted for the change in general education formula allowance between the current year and two years prior.

OTHER STATE AIDS

Minnesota provides various other categorical aid to public K–12 schools including American Indian Education Aid, Alternative Teacher Compensation Revenue (QComp), Achievement and Integration Revenue (AIM), Literacy Incentive Aid, Library Programs, Abatement Revenue, Advanced Placement and International Baccalaureate Programs, and Consolidation Transition Revenue. The AIM is relatively unique to Minnesota and is intended to pursue racial and economic integration, increase student achievement, and reduce economic disparities in Minnesota's public schools.[29]

RETIREMENT AND OTHER POST-EMPLOYMENT BENEFITS

The Minnesota system provides retirement benefits for teachers, administrators, nurses, librarians, social workers, counselors, and other professional personnel employed in Minnesota's public schools, including charter schools. There are two teacher retirement fund associations: the Teachers Retirement Association (TRA) which is statewide; and a separate retirement fund association for teachers employed by the St. Paul district.

Since FY 1989, school districts have been required to make all employer contributions for teacher retirement and Social Security directly from their undesignated general fund revenue. No separate categorical aid for teacher retirement exists. However, special state aid is paid by the state to the statewide retirement fund for teachers employed by Minneapolis and

Duluth and the St. Paul retirement fund to reduce the unfunded liability in those funds.[30]

Many Minnesota school districts have offered post-employment benefits to their employees. These benefits are in addition to the employee pension benefits provided by teacher retirement systems and the Public Employee Retirement Association (PERA). The largest share of these benefits consists of promises to pay certain health costs of retired employees. These benefits give rise to a liability under Statement No. 45 of the Governmental Accounting Standards Board (GASB), and in Minnesota, generally refers to retiree health benefits.[31]

REVENUE

State revenue for aid payments to local school districts is primarily derived from income, sales, and property taxes as well as a variety of small fee funds and assessments. In FY 2017, school districts had $11.6 billion available from state and local sources (excluding local fees). Of that amount, $8,855,886,000 was in state appropriation, $s24,096,000 was in the form of state tax credits, and $2,626,021,200 came from net levies. Net levies are certified levies minus tax relief aids.

In the FY 2016–2017 biennium budget, Minnesota raised $44.5 billion in general fund revenue, of which 51.7% came from individual income tax, 24.9% came from sales tax revenue, 6.2% came from corporate taxes, and 4% came from revenue generated from the statewide property tax. General fund revenues are expected to increase to $47.7 billion in the next biennium, FY 2018–2019.

SUMMARY

Table 25.2 provides data on Minnesota's E–12 and higher education general fund dollars for FY 2016–FY 2019. Overall funding for E–12 education rose by 4.6% from FY 2016 to FY 2017, but that increase is expected to slow somewhat over the next biennium, with general fund expenditures expected to increase by 4.3% from FY 2017 to FY 2018, and to rise by 3.2% from FY 2018 to FY 2019. If inflation is considered, the annual increase from FY 2016 to FY 2017 was 2.5%.[32]

State aid to E–12 schools has consistently accounted for about 85% of the over $10 billion spent on E–20+ education budgets. Overall, in the 2016–2017 biennium, P–12 education represented 25% of the state's $74.6 billion all funds and 41.7% of general funds, where most of the state's education

TABLE 25.2 Minnesota State General Fund Expenditures on Education, E–12 and Higher FY 2016–FY 2019 (in thousands)

	Actual FY 2016	Actual FY 2017	Estimated FY 2018	Estimated FY 2019
E–12 Education aids	$8,465,943	$8,851,626	$9,235,745	$9,540,492
Department of Education	$22,605	$28,130	$27,199	$24,874
Board of Teaching	$0	$931	$3,481	$3,493
Minnesota State Academies	$12,307	$13,378	$14,026	$14,352
Perpich Center for Arts Education	$6,530	$7,268	$8,335	$6,973
Total E–12 Education	**$8,507,385**	**$8,901,333**	**$9,288,786**	**$9,590,184**
Office of Higher Education	$229,343	$251,804	$262,861	$256,495
University of Minnesota	$625,549	$629,049	$658,686	$648,636
Minnesota State	$672,925	$673,516	$731,019	$721,919
Mayo Foundation	$1,351	$1,351	$1,351	$1,351
Total Higher Education	**$1,529,168**	**$1,555,720**	**$1,653,917**	**$1,628,401**
Total Education	*$10,036,553*	*$10,457,053*	*$10,942,703*	*$11,218,585*

Source: Adapted from data obtained from Minnesota Department of Management and Budget, https://mn.gov/mmb/assets/fba-nov17fcst-summary_tcm1059-319763.pdf

costs reside. These dollars funded programs for the state's 856,687 public school students.

The percentage of total general fund expenditures devoted to elementary and secondary education is expected to decrease slightly over the next three biennia. That is, in the 2016–2017 biennium, 41.7% of general funds went to E–12 education; in 2018–2019 biennium, 41.2% of the general fund dollars is expected to go to E–12 education. If present trends continue, by the 2020–2021 biennium, only 40.6% of the state's general fund dollars will go to funding K–12 education.[33] While the proportion of the general fund budget devoted to public elementary and secondary education is expected to decrease, the dollars devoted to this category are expected to increase. In the omnibus bills for 2016–2017 biennium, Minnesota devoted $17.4 billion of its general fund dollars to E–12 education; this amount is expected to increase to $18.8 billion in the 2018–19 biennium, and $19.5 billion in the 2020–21 biennium.

NOTES

1. Minnesota Constitution, Article XIII, Section I states "The stability of a republican form of government depending mainly upon the intelligence of the people, it is the duty of the legislature to establish a general and uniform system of public school. The legislature shall make such provisions by taxation

or otherwise as will secure a thorough and efficient system of public schools throughout the state."
2. The discussion of the general background is largely taken from the Minnesota House of Representatives, Research Department, Minnesota School Finance: A Guide for Legislators (December 2017).
3. *Skeen v. State of Minnesota*, 505 N.W.2d 299 (Minn. 1993).
4. https://law.justia.com/cases/minnesota/supreme-court/1993/c5-92-677-2.html
5. The discussion of the elements of the Minnesota school finance program comes primarily from the annual publications of the Minnesota House of Representatives Fiscal Analysis Department; i.e., Financing Education in Minnesota (year).
6. Pupil unit reflects the average daily membership count weighted by grade level where one voluntary prekindergarten student is weighted 0.6 pupil unit; a student in required Kindergarten through grade 6 is weighted 1.0 pupil unit; students in grades 7 through 12 are counted as 1.2 pupil units.
7. Nicola A. Alexander, "Minnesota State of the States," *Journal of Education Finance* 42, no. 3(2017): 287–288.
8. Minnesota Statute 127A.45. See also, Fiscal Analysis Department. (2016). Financing Education in Minnesota 2016–2017.
9. Minn. Stat. §§ 126C.05, subd. 3; 126C.10, subd. 3; 126C.15. See also Fiscal Analysis Department. (2016). Financing Education in Minnesota 2016–2017 and Minnesota House Research Department. (2016). Minnesota School Finance: A Guide for Legislators.
10. See also, Fiscal Analysis Department. (2016). Financing Education in Minnesota 2016–2017, p. 36.
11. Ibid. See also Minn. Stat. §§ 126A.76.
12. Minn. Stat. §§ 125A.79.
13. Minn. Stat. §§ 125A.75, 1.
14. Minn. Stat. §§ 125A.75,3.
15. See Minnesota Department of Education for statewide expenditure averages for major expenditure categories for FY 2016 available at http://w20.education.state.mn.us/MDEAnalytics/DataTopic.jsp?TOPICID=79.
16. Fiscal Analysis Department. (2016). Financing Education in Minnesota 2016–2017, p. 22.
17. Minnesota House Research Department, *Minnesota School Finance: A Guide for Legislators* (2016), 40.
18. Minn. Stat. §§ 126C.10, 13.
19. Minn. Stat. §§ 123B.53. See also Fiscal Analysis Department, *Financing Education in Minnesota 2016–2017* (2016), 48.
20. Minnesota House Research Department, *Minnesota School Finance: A Guide for Legislators* (2016), 40. Also, see Minn. Stat. §§ 123B.70; 123B.71.
21. Fiscal Analysis Department. (2016). Financing Education in Minnesota 2016–2017, p. 44.
22. For the statute related to referendum revenue, see Minn. Stat. §§ 126C.17; for statute related to local optional revenue, see Minn. Stat. §§ 126C.10, 2e; for the statute related to equity revenue, see, Minn. Stat. §§ 126C.10, 24-28 1. See

also Fiscal Analysis Department, *Financing Education in Minnesota 2016–2017* (2016), 23–26; 31–34.
23. Minnesota House Research Department, *Minnesota School Finance: A Guide for Legislators,* (2016), 31.
24. Minn. Stat. §§ 126C.44. See also Fiscal Analysis Department, *Financing Education in Minnesota 2016–2017 (2016) 54.*
25. Minn. Stat. §§ 124D.1158.
26. Minn. Stat. §§ 124D.111.
27. Minn. Stat. §§ 123b.40-123b.48.
28. Minn. Stat. §§ 123b.92
29. Minn. Stat. §§ 124D.862
30. Minn. Stat. §§ 354.42; 354.43; 354,435; 354.436; 355.01-355.08 (Statewide TRA); 354A.12 (St. Paul; Cities of the First Class). See also, Minnesota House Research Department, *Minnesota School Finance: A Guide for Legislators* (2016), 114.
31. Minnesota House Research Department, *Minnesota School Finance: A Guide for Legislators* (2016), 118.
32. Inflation was calculated using the CPI index provided by the US Bureau of Labor Statistics. See historical table of indices at http://www.usinflationcalculator.com/inflation/consumer-price-index-and-annual-percent-changes-from-1913-to-2008/
33. Minnesota Management and Budget. (July 2017). See especially, https://mn.gov/mmb/assets/fba-nov17fcst-pie-charts_tcm1059-319765.pdf

CHAPTER 26

Mississippi

Judy Rhodes
*Director (Retired)
Office of Educational Accountability
Mississippi Department of Education*

GENERAL BACKGROUND

Mississippi became a state in 1817, and the first of four state constitutions was adopted in that same year. A fourth constitution was adopted in 1890; that adoption stands today, although it has been frequently amended and updated across the decades since its origin. The latest amendment came in 2013. The Mississippi constitution's education article places it among the barest of all 50 states, reading only:

> The Legislature shall, by general law, provide for the establishment, maintenance and support of free public schools upon such conditions and limitations as the Legislature may prescribe.[1]

Current Context

Education funding in Mississippi has been fraught with argument and revision.[2] Recent history is generally regarded as beginning in 1997 when the state legislature passed the Mississippi Adequate Education Program (MAEP) in an effort to address two primary problems: low student achievement, and fiscal inequity among school districts. Background for the initiative was that Mississippi schoolchildren were being outperformed by other

Funding Public Schools in the United States and Indian Country, pages 383–390
Copyright © 2019 by Information Age Publishing
All rights of reproduction in any form reserved.

states. In contrast, almost every other state was spending more per pupil despite fewer challenges. Additionally, Mississippi districts with low tax bases were worse off than those in more prosperous communities because more affluent Mississippi communities were able to supplement state funding, making education's quality as defined by available resources a consequence of residence.

The Mississippi legislature subsequently engaged consultants, legislators, and other experts to study the situation. The outcome was two acts in legislation: the Mississippi Accountability System, and the Mississippi Adequate Education Program (MAEP). The Mississippi Accountability System significantly raised standards for teachers and students. The Mississippi Curriculum Test (MCT[1]), MCT[2], and the current MCT[3] were developed to measure student achievement, and schools were thereafter to be rated on test scores. The Children First Act of 2009 raised stakes, calling for removal of superintendents and school boards in chronically low performing schools.

The MAEP was a legislative commitment to provide resources to teachers and schools, tied to the new accountability system. The system meant to hold districts and individual schools accountable for academic performance, with the MAEP providing a formula determining the necessary funding for each district to provide an adequate education. Importantly, the MAEP capped the portion of funding a local school district is required to provide.

The MAEP was intended to erase inequities by ensuring that children across Mississippi would be granted access to an adequate education without relationship to local wealth. In brief, the MAEP was meant to determine the per-pupil cost of a good education after accounting for the local district's responsibility. The MAEP's difference was meant to be the level of funding required from the state legislature.

MISSISSIPPI ADEQUATE EDUCATION PROGRAM OPERATION[3]

The Mississippi Adequate Education Program (MAEP) in place today, covering 142 independent school districts, is a formula that functions as a minimum foundation by producing a base student cost, i.e., an amount thought to be required in order to provide each student an adequate education. Each school district provides up to 27% of base student cost through a local contribution derived from local ad valorem taxes. The legislature is required to fund the difference between what local communities can provide and total base student cost. That amount is then multiplied by the district's average daily attendance (ADA) to determine the MAEP allocation.

The MAEP is scheduled for recalculation every four years, adjusted for inflation by multiplying 40% of base student cost by the current rate of inflation as computed by the state. The MAEP is meant to account for differences, including salaries and benefits, textbooks and materials, operational costs, transportation, special education, vocational education, gifted education, and alternative education. The MAEP is not meant to pay for administrative costs, leaving that expense to local shares. Other MAEP funding outside the formula relates to teacher supplies, National Board Certification, early childhood education initiatives, and costs for operating the Mississippi Department of Education.

Table 26.1 is taken from the Mississippi Department of Education's explanation for operation of the MAEP.

TABLE 26.1 Mississippi Adequate Education Program Detail 2018

What is the MAEP

MAEP is the state aid formula used to establish adequate current operation funding levels necessary for the programs of each school district to meet a successful level of student performance as established by the Mississippi State Board of Education using current statistically relevant state assessment data.

Purpose

To ensure that every Mississippi child, regardless of where he/she lives, is afforded an adequate educational opportunity as defined by the State Accountability System.

MAEP FUNDING FORMULA

$$\text{ADA} \times \text{Base Student Cost} + \text{At-Risk Component} - \text{Local Contribution} + 8\% \text{ Guarantee} = \text{MAEP Formula Allocation}$$

$$\text{MAEP Formula Allocation} + \text{Add-on Programs} = \text{Total MAEP District Funding}$$

Base Student Cost Calculation

District Selection Process

Districts determined to be successful *and* efficient in four areas of school operations are selected for determining base student cost;

Successful district: defined by the State Board of Education using current statistically relevant assessment data;

Efficient school district: in each of the following Efficiency Components, a mean score for all districts is determined (only districts meeting successful status and above are selected for cost component calculations).

- Instruction teachers per 1,000 students;
- Administrator/staff ratio;
- Maintenance and operations (M&O spending per 100,000 square feet); and (maintenance staff per 100,000 square feet);
- Ancillary librarians and counselors per 1,000 students.

Districts scoring one standard deviation above or two standard deviations below the mean for each component are ruled efficient;

Districts meeting the successful and efficient standard are used to calculate the average cost for each component.

(continued)

TABLE 26.1 Mississippi Adequate Education Program Detail 2018

By law, average cost for each component is calculated using expenditure data from the second preceding year.

Average Costs of the Four Components are Added Together
to Obtain the Base Student Cost.

To provide stability for appropriation and budgeting, base student cost is calculated every four years rather than annually. An inflation adjustment is computed in the years between recalculation by multiplying 40% of base student cost times the current inflation rate as computed by the state's economist.

Example: FY 08 BSC × 40% × CPI = FY 09 Inflation Component $4,574 × .40
× .03 (3% inflation rate) = $54

In this example, for FY 2009 $54 would be added to the FY 2008 BSC to arrive at FY 2009 BSC of $4,519.

Once Base Student Cost is determined, district allocations are calculated using the following formula:

ADA × Base Student Cost + At-Risk Component–Local Contribution
+ 8 % Guarantee = MAEP District Allocation

Definitions of Program Elements

Average Daily Attendance (ADA):
- Grades K–12 months 2–3 of preceding year;
- Excludes self-contained special education ADA;
- High growth component: for any district having consistent growth in ADA in the three-year period prior to the appropriation, the average percent growth in ADA over those three years is added to the ADA for the district.

At-Risk Component:
- 5% of base student cost, multiplied by numbers of free lunch participants on October 31 of the preceding year;
- As base student costs increase, the amount for At-Risk increases;
- Added into total before calculation of the local contribution.

Local Contribution:
- uses 2nd preceding year's data;
- Reduced by ad valorem tax reduction grants;
- Yield from 28 mills + ad valorem in lieu payments;
- Capped at 27% of program costs, including the At-Risk component.

8% Guarantee:
- Incorporated to ensure that a district receives a formula allocation of at least what was received in 2002 plus 8%.

Add-On Programs:
- Transportation;
- Special Education;
- Gifted Education;
- Vocational Education;
- Alternative Education.

(continued)

TABLE 26.1 Mississippi Adequate Education Program Detail 2018

Transportation:
- Determined by the ADA of transported students in a school district;
- The allowable cost per student is calculated using a rate table approved by the State Board of Education which associates the rate allowed to the transported density of the district;
- Density is determined by dividing transported ADA by total square miles in the district. The lower the density, the higher the rate. The higher the density, the lower the rate. The total amount of transportation funding allowed is dictated by the state legislature. The total of all district transportation funding cannot exceed amounts appropriated for such purposes;
- Additional special education and vocational transportation allotment is administered by the Deputy Superintendent and the Office of School Building and Transportation and is interfaced with the Office of Educational Accountability and the Office of School Financial Services.

Special Education:
- A teacher unit is added for each approved program for exceptional students, with funding based on certification and experience. Program approval criteria and special education teacher units are administered through the Office of Instructional Programs and Services, Office of Special Services and is interfaced with the calculation.

Gifted Education:
- A teacher unit is added for each approved program for gifted (artistic, intellectual, academic) students, with funding based on certification and experience of the approved teacher. Program approval criteria and gifted teacher units are administered through the Office of Instructional Programs and Services, Office of Academic Education and are interfaced with the Office of Educational Accountability, Office of School Financial Services.
- The 1993 legislature mandated that, beginning in 1993–94, each school district must have an intellectual gifted program. The mandate begins with grade 2 and increases by one grade each year until grade 6 is mandated in 1997–98. No other programs or grades are mandated, and the mandate applies to intellectual programs in grades 2–6 only.

Vocational Education:
- One-half (½) teacher unit is added for each approved vocational program, with funding based on certification and experience of the approved teacher. Program approval criteria and vocational education teacher units are administered through the Office of Vocational-Technical Education and interfaced with the Office of Educational Accountability.

Alternative School Programs:
- Three quarters of one percent (0.75%) of the district's ADA (grades 1–12, elementary and secondary special education self-contained and ungraded) or 12 students, whichever is greater, is multiplied by the statewide average per-pupil expenditure in public funds for the immediately preceding school year.

MAEP Formula Allocation + Add-on Programs = Total MAEP District Funding

Source: Mississippi Adequate Education Program (MAEP). (2018). http://tpcref.org/wp-content/uploads/ MAEP_Explanation.pdf

OTHER PROGRAMS[4]

District-Based Components

As observable in Table 26.1, the state of Mississippi provides almost none of the typical categorical supports common to many states. Namely:

Density or Sparsity for Small Schools Adjustment
None.

Grade Level Differences
None.

Declining Enrollment or Growth
If a school district has a consistent pattern of growth over the three-year period prior to the annual appropriation, the average percent of growth is added to the district's ADA.

Capital Outlay and Bond Debt Service
Bonded indebtedness for Mississippi school districts is limited to 15% of assessed property valuation. Additional authority for notes and certificates of indebtedness is limited to the amount a three mill tax levy can raise for ten years. No state support is evident.

Transportation
State aid to transportation in Mississippi is based on the ADA for transported pupils and a density formula and rate table. The result is the lower the density, the higher the rate. The rate table provides greater amounts per pupil to districts with fewer pupils per square mile. This is an add-on program amount.

Student-Based Components

As observable in Table 26.1, the state of Mississippi provides fiscal supports for the areas of special education, low income, compensatory and at-risk education, gifted and talented education, career and technical education, and alternative education programs. Namely:

Special Education
Teacher units are added for each approved program for exceptional students. Funding is based on the certification and experience of the approved teacher. This is an add-on program amount.

Low Income, Compensatory, and At-Risk Education
MAEP has an at-risk component based on 5% of Base Student Cost times the number of free lunch participants as of October 31 of the previous year.

English Language Learner and Bilingual Education
None.

Gifted and Talented Education
Teacher units are added for each approved program for gifted and talented students. Funding amounts are based on the certification and experience of each teacher. This is an add-on program amount.

Career and Technical Education
One-half of a teacher unit is added for each approved program. Funding amounts are based on certification and experience of each teacher. This is an add-on program amount.

Alternative Program Education
Based on three quarters of one percent (0.75%) of the school district's ADA for grades 1–12 or 12 students, whichever is greater, is multiplied by the state average per-pupil expenditure in the previous year. This is an add-on program amount.

Preschool Education
None.

STEM Education
None.

State Support for Nonpublic Schools

Mississippi provides aid to distribute and loan books to nonpublic schools that maintain the same academic standards as public schools. The state regards such contribution as demonstrating nondiscriminatory practices.

Charter Schools

Charter schools in Mississippi must be approved by the Charter School Authorizer Board as defined in state statute. Four such charter schools were in place for 2018–2019. Charter schools are funded in the same manner as other public school districts. Projected charter enrollment is used for the initial funding calculation and is later reconciled with actual ADA.

SUMMARY

In 2018, the Mississippi legislature passed House Bill 1592, increasing overall K–12 appropriation by $12.8 million which included a $3.1 million increase for the MAEP and $2.5 million for Pre-K programs. Critics alleged that HB 1592 underfunded the MAEP for Fiscal Year 2019 by approximately $240 million, arguing simultaneously that the law reduced funding by $37 million compared to two years prior. Critics also argued that the Public School Building Fund, which by statute is entitled to $20 million annually, received no appropriation. Overall, critics claimed Mississippi schools were underfunded at a rate of $1,300 per pupil compared to the neighboring states of Alabama, Arkansas, Louisiana, and Tennessee.[5] The same critics alleged that Mississippi's educational scene was riddled with challenges, including efforts to inject public funds into private schools while exempting those schools from standards, oversight, and accountability: initiatives accompanied by efforts to change funding laws in ways that would result in complete and total legislative deference.

NOTES

1. Mississippi Constitution, Article 8. Retrieved from https://www.sos.ms.gov/Education-Publications/Documents/Downloads/Mississippi_Constitution.pdf
2. This section borrows heavily from Parents Campaign for Better Schools, "Mississippi Adequate Education Program" (2018). Retrieved from http://www.msparentscampaign.org/education-funding.html?id=34
3. Ibid. This section continues to rely on http://www.msparentscampaign.org/education-funding.html?id=34
4. This section partly relies on Deborah Verstegen, "A Quick Glance at School Finance: A 50 State Survey of School Finance Policies: Mississippi." (2018). Retrieved from https://schoolfinancesdav.files.wordpress.com/2018/09/24-mississippi.pdf
5. Parents Campaign. "It's a Wrap! Here's our Take." (March 28, 2018). Retrieved from http://www.msparentscampaign.org/component/content/article?id=1550

CHAPTER 27

Missouri

Staff Writer

GENERAL BACKGROUND

Missouri funds public elementary and secondary schools through a combination of local, state, and federal revenue sources directed to its 518 school districts. Of these, 70 are elementary districts. Additionally, there are 36 charter schools and three state board of education-operated schools. Missouri has only one virtual school. In total, for the 2017–18 school year approximately 884,000 students attended these school configurations. State funds in 2018 reached approximately $6 billion, representing over 20% of the total state budget. State revenues are from earmarked funds and general revenue funds. In recent years, total shares of Missouri's public school funding have shifted more toward local school districts given severe statutory and legislative budget restraints.

The education clause of the Missouri constitution states in two relevant parts:

Article IX, §1,3 provides: A general diffusion of knowledge and intelligence being essential to the preservation of the rights and liberties of the people, the general assembly shall establish and maintain free public schools...

Article IX, §3(b) provides: [I]n no case shall there be set apart less than twenty-five percent of the state revenue... to be applied annually to the support of the free public schools.[2]

Constitutional litigation has marked Missouri's recent history.[3] Briefly, in 1990 suit was filed in *Committee for Educational Equality v. State*[4] on equity and adequacy claims. A trial court held in 1993 that the system was in violation of the state constitution, ordering the state to provide equal educational opportunities to all children. The legislature responded with the Outstanding Schools Act[5] of 1993, increasing taxes to pay for a revised school funding formula that accompanied significant program reforms. In 2005, the legislature again engaged in school funding changes by enacting Senate Bill 287[6] providing a new school aid scheme. By 2009, the law had again been exhaustively litigated, with the state supreme court ruling against plaintiff claims of unconstitutionally disparate and inadequate provisions.[7] The court reasoned that the 25% minimum level of funding required in Article IX §3(b) of the state constitution defined adequacy and that plaintiffs were attempting to read additional adequacy mandates into the minimum provision required of the state. Other school funding-related litigation not developed here has also marked the state.[8]

BASIC SUPPORT PROGRAM

Missouri's school finance formula today is the 2005 law setting out a foundation aid plan based on student needs. The formula consists of four main components:

$$\text{State Adequacy Target} \times \text{Weighted Average Daily Attendance} \times \text{Dollar Value Modifier} - \text{Local Effort} = \text{State Funding}$$

State Adequacy Target

Calculating the formula first requires knowing a baseline cost for pupils with no special needs or services. Once the baseline is known, multipliers comprising the Weighted Average Daily Attendance (WADA) are used to grant more money to school districts to compensate for the additional cost of certain students's program needs.

The baseline is called the State Adequacy Target (SAT). It is defined as a measure of the average spending per pupil in schools meeting state standards (i.e., Performance Districts). The SAT is intended to recalculate every year, but state deficits have led to several years without adjustment.

Weighted Average Daily Attendance

The WADA factor measures attendance in each school district and adjusts state aid so as to create pupil weights for poverty, special education, and limited English proficiency. This measure is utilized to determine additional funding for Free or Reduced Lunch (FRL), special education (IEP), or Limited English Proficient (LEP) students. The adjusted number of students in FRL, IEP, or LEP programs in each district is calculated by multiplying the average percentage of students in a particular program in 'Performance Districts' by the district's ADA. If this figure is higher than the actual number in the district, every student above the adjusted number becomes a weighted student for per-pupil funding purposes. The total number of weighted students a district serves is the WADA.[9]

Since the SAT represents the 'cost' of an education in Missouri, the state school finance formula only distributes WADA funds to school districts that reflect high concentrations of students in particular groups. To receive these monies the school district must exceed a threshold, i.e., if the district is average or below in the number of students in a particular category, the state assumes no extra money is warranted. For Fiscal Years 2017–18, threshold percentages were as follows:

FRL threshold = 36.12%
IEP threshold = 12.16%
LEP threshold = 1.94%[10]

The current school finance formula utilizes the following weights:

FRL weight = .2
IEP weight = .7
LEP weight = .60[11]

Dollar Value Modifier

The result of the WADA multiplied by the SAT is next adjusted by the Dollar Value Modifier (DVM). This factor is a cost of providing educational services in areas of the state having high cost of living. The DVM adjusts for higher expenses such as prevailing wages or costs of construction. For example, the DVM formula compares the regional wage ratio for a school district (i.e., the average salary in the area) with the state median wage per job. The formula assumes that higher income areas will have proportionally higher costs of living. Importantly, all school districts are held constant in that low cost of living areas are not penalized as the school aid formula does not take money away from districts.

Local Effort

The local effort is next deducted from the product of these successive calculations. That is, the formula causes school districts with relatively low assessed valuations and resultantly low district tax levy yields to receive more state dollars relative to other districts: i.e., the lower the assessed value, state aid increases after all other factors are equal on a per pupil weighted basis. For purposes of determining the state's contribution to a local school district, the measure primarily reflects how much revenue a school district sets as its tax levy. Local tax revenue is calculated by multiplying the school district's assessed property values by the local property tax levy. The state utilizes a performance tax levy of $3.43 per $100 assessed valuation for calculations of uniform local effort.

Other variables factor into determining local effort. For example, collector and assessor fees are subtracted from the levy. Other revenue sources also contribute to total local effort: e.g., Proposition C, a statewide 1% sales tax, is collected and redistributed to school districts based on the WADA so that 50% of Proposition C revenue goes to school districts and is counted as local effort. Additional local revenue comes from the state-assessed railroad utility tax.

Broadly viewed, the bulk of the state's share of funding Missouri's public schools comes from general state revenues collected through state income and sales taxes. Oher state revenue is provided by gaming taxes, lottery proceeds, and other miscellaneous taxes. In contrast, the local share comes primarily from a local tax levy against the assessed valuation of each school district.

State Funding

The sum of successive calculations results in state aid eligibility in the consequent dollar value. Totals are shown in Table 27.1 later in the chapter.

Hold-Harmless School Districts

Each year, about 33% of Missouri school districts are categorized as eligible for 'hold-harmless' funding—a provision that the state legislature utilizes to help protect against local revenue losses that might befall districts as a result of the current school aid formula.[12] For example, districts can use the highest WADA calculation from either the current or previous two years' experience. The net effect is to allow for quick increases in state aid, while alternatively allowing districts with declining enrollments to preserve funding at a higher level from the previous year. Additionally, the SAT cannot decline absent legislative action so that even if recalculation of the SAT in any year yields a lower number, the SAT remains constant at the local level. Even in the calculation of local effort, the system is designed to give school districts more state money: e.g., by pegging local tax calculations to

2004 assessment levels and by allowing assessed value to decrease (but not increase), the state shelters some districts from funding losses.

SPECIAL LEVIES

While Missouri's school aid formula is designed to intervene in fiscal equity distribution as described in previous sections, school districts can have tax levies higher than the performance tax levy of $3.43 per $100. In effect, this provision makes Missouri's school finance scheme a minimum foundation plan by allowing local taxation above the established funding floor.

Each school district therefore has statutory authority to establish its own tax rate subject to local election. "If a district's tax levy is lower than the state's performance tax levy, it will actually have less money locally than the estimated figure of the state...if a district has a tax levy higher than the state's target, it will be able to raise additional funds with no penalty."[13]

SPECIAL EDUCATION

Special education grant funds are distributed to Missouri school districts in order to help alleviate the added costs of educating students with disabilities. In FY 2017, these funds were projected to serve approximately 128,000 students.

Special Education High Needs Fund

The Special Education High Needs Fund provides additional monies to school districts serving high need students whose educational costs exceed three times the district's current expenditure per ADA. In FY 2017, it was estimated by the state that approximately 3,300 high needs students were served by this fund.

Students with Severe Disabilities

Missouri's State Board Operated Programs comprise a set of schools designed to serve students with severe disabilities who cannot be educated within the local school district. Three such programs operate in the state:

- Missouri School for the Blind;
- Missouri School for the Deaf;
- Missouri Schools for the Severely Disabled.[14]

TRANSPORTATION

Missouri provides transportation for public school children. Historically, the aid plan operated as a reimbursement of allowable costs limited by district-specific efficiency factors. Current key components of the transportation calculation are based in ridership-tracking which occurs as the state audits eligible and ineligible rider data. These include (1) ridership; (2) mileage; (3) allowable costs; (4) eligible costs; (5) cost factor; (6) entitlement; and (7) appropriation adjustment. Definitionally, these are regulated as follows.

Ridership

- Students living more than 3.5 miles from school must be provided transportation services;
- All students can be transported by local board decision;[15]
- Funding is available for students who live one mile or more from school;
- No funding is available for students living less than one mile from school (except when required by IEP);
- Ineligible riders are students who live less than one mile from school or are non-resident students.

Allowable Costs

- Allowable costs are costs for transporting students,[16] administrative services, and costs paid to other school districts.[17]

Eligible Costs

- Eligible costs are those costs remaining after allowable costs have been reduced by the cost associated with ineligible miles. The cost factor is the efficiency rating in the school district's Calculation for State Transportation Aid used to measure the efficiency of the district's transportation program. The cost factor is calculated by comparing the district's actual cost per-pupil mile to a predicted cost per- pupil mile as obtained through a curvilinear regression analysis.

Cost Factor

Also known as an efficiency rating, if the cost factor is 100% it means that the school district's cost per pupil mile equals the predicted cost per pupil mile and is efficient under the transportation formula. A 4% variance is built into the formula, thereby allowing a district's cost factor to be 104% or below without violating efficiency.

Entitlement

Entitlement is the state aid eligibility resulting from the transportation formula calculations. Entitlement is 75% of the school district's eligible costs after being reduced for any inefficiency.

Appropriation Adjustment

The appropriation adjustment is a percent legislatively applied to school districts' entitlement. The percent is calculated by adding all districts' entitlements together and comparing the total to the available legislative appropriation. The appropriation adjustment changes each month a live payment is made as districts make changes to the transportation data.

Order of Calculation

Calculating transportation eligibility and entitlement follows an order of calculation. Missouri's school districts know their current individual transportation subsidy amounts by following the prescribed calculation order, that is:

- Allowable Cost;
- Cost for Eligible Miles;
- Cost Adjusted for Ineligible Students Affecting the Calculation;
- Cost Adjusted for Inefficiency;
- Reimbursable Cost Reduced to 75%;
- Entitlement Reduced by Appropriation.[18]

CAREER AND TECHNICAL EDUCATION

Missouri provides aid to local school districts operating approved Career and Technical Education (CTE) programs. CTE contains a range of programs and services that provide training to assist students in gaining employment, continuing their education, or retraining to gain new industry skills. In FY 2016, the state of Missouri reported that approximately 96% of students who completed secondary career education programs were placed in employment, continuing education, or military service. These programs served approximately 179,000 secondary students in FY 2016.[19]

CAPITAL OUTLAY

The state of Missouri does not have a capital outlay distribution formula. All expenditures and debt service are the responsibility of local school districts. Per state accounting rules and regulations, school district bond escrow accounts must be shown separately on the district's general ledger. Debt Service Funds must be held in separate bank accounts. A school district's Capital Project Fund must be used to account for all facility acquisition, construction, equipment, lease purchase principal and interest payments, and other capital outlay expenditures. The Debt Service Fund is used to account for monies used to retire bond debt.

FOOD SERVICE

In Missouri, the largest proportion of revenue for school food service is provided by the federal government under school nutrition services. Several federal programs provide funding to Missouri schools for school breakfast, lunch, milk, and after-school snacks. Students from low income families are provided meals and after-school snacks free or at a reduced rate. During FY 2016, an average 570,000 Missouri schoolchildren per day received school lunch at an average cost of $3.14 per meal. Approximately 276,000 children received school breakfast at an average cost of $2.36 per meal in that same year.[20]

STATE FUNDING FOR OTHER PUBLIC SCHOOLS

At the time of this writing, the state of Missouri had 36 charter schools. Charter schools are free, public schools and typically are funded in exactly the same manner as all public school districts in Missouri – however, certain notable exceptions apply. The hold-harmless provision under the Missouri school finance formula does not apply to charter schools because they fall only under the current formula because they were not in existence under the previous formula (a condition of eligibility for hold-harmless aid). Additionally, Missouri's charter schools have no taxing authority and must cover their facility costs from state and local general aid.

Charter schools in Missouri may be organized as part of a local school district or as a separate local education agency. Consequently, Missouri charters may be viewed as a charter school within a school district or viewed independently like a traditional school district.[21,22] In this situation, a school district pays the charter school a portion of funds that exceeded the tax performance levy. A school district which exercises a tax rate above $3.45 must share those funds generated beyond this rate.[23] If a charter school is granted LEA status, the Missouri Department of Elementary and Secondary Education (DESE) funds the charter school within the foundation formula. "Additionally, DESE distributes the revenue to the charter school that the incidental and teacher funds raised in excess of the performance tax levy."[24]

OTHER STATE AIDS[25]

The state of Missouri has a number of other state aids for specific needs and purposes, including the following programs:

School Age Afterschool Program

The School Age Afterschool Program provides funding to school districts and community-based organizations to improve academic achievement and individual development.

Child Care Development Fund Program

The Child Care Development Fund Program (CCDF) provides funding to start new or expand existing afterschool programs. In FY 2016, approximately 3,500 students were enrolled in CCDF programs.

21st Century Community Learning Center Program

The 21st Century Community Learning Center Program (CCLC) provides funding for centers offering academic, artistic and cultural enrichment opportunities during non-school hours for students in high poverty areas and low performing schools. In FY 2016 approximately, 29,000 students were enrolled in CCLC programs.

Virtual Schools Program

The Virtual Schools Program provides funds for a virtual public school. State-funded slots are available for medically fragile students. This program was projected by the state of Missouri to serve approximately 1,700 students in FY 2017.

Small Schools Program

The Small Schools Program provides extra funding in the foundation formula for Missouri school districts having average daily attendance of 350 or fewer students.

Title I

Title I provides federal funding to schools to implement strategies for raising student achievement in schools with high numbers of children living in poverty who are costlier to educate.

RETIREMENT

The state of Missouri contributes 1.75% of teacher salaries to retirement. The state has a five-year vesting period. All certificated employees are required to be a member of the Public School Retirement System (PSRS) of Missouri; however, the St. Louis and Kansas City public school districts are under separate systems. The state allows individual school districts to decide whether they will offer Social Security coverage to teachers. The Public Education Employee Retirement System (PEERS) of Missouri is primarily for non-teacher school employees. PEERS members participate in the federal Social Security program, but most PSRS members do not. PSRS members contribute at a higher rate to their retirement system than do PEERS members, and the benefit factors used in retirement benefit calculations are different. PSRS members who participate in Social Security pay into PSRS at 66% of the normal PSRS contribution rate.[26]

SUMMARY

Table 27.1 presents a current snapshot of P–12 education funding in Missouri. The table presents a detailed list of specific elementary and secondary education programs, relevant section numbers, and FY 2017 funding levels and sources. In effect, Table 27.1 profiles a state serving two large urban areas and numerous small rural communities with hundreds of school districts varying in size. Within that profile are small, relatively wealthy

TABLE 27.1 Missouri Elementary and Secondary Education Programs Fiscal Year 2019

Program	Budget Section	FY17 GR	FY17 Federal	FY17 Other	FY17 Total
Financial and Administrative Operations	2.005	$1,978,513	$2,639,052	$0	$4,617,565
Foundation-Equity Formula	2.015	$1,911,051,403	$0	$1,433,639,865	$3,344,691,268
Foundation-Small Schools Programs	2.015	$15,000,000	$0	$0	$15,000,000
Foundation-Transportation	2.015	$36,024,611	$0	$69,273,102	$105,297,713
Foundation-Career Education	2.015	$50,069,028	$0	$0	$50,069,028
Foundation-State Board Operated Programs	2.015	$42,604,843	$5,724,357	$1,876,355	$50,205,555
Foundation-Virtual Schools Program	2.015	$200,000	$0	$389,778	$589,778
Dropout Reduction (Community Partnerships)	2.017	$150,000	$0	$0	$150,000
Tutoring program (KCPS)	2.018	$0	$0	$100,000	$100,000
Math and science tutoring (St. Louis)	2.019	$150,000	$0	$0	$150,000
Urban Teaching	2.020	$3,000,000	$0	$0	$3,000,000
School Safety	2.025	$700,000	$0	$0	$700,000
STEM careers	2.027	$50,000	$0	$0	$50,000
School Nutrition Services	2.030	$3,412,151	$318,031,026	$0	$321,443,177
Missouri Scholars & Fine Arts Academies	2.031	$750,000	$0	$0	$750,000
Early Grade Literacy	2.041	$103,000	$0	$0	$103,000
Division of Learning Services	2.050	$3,983,579	$10,366,532	$3,009,997	$17,360,108
Adult Learning and Rehabilitation Services	2.050	$0	$0	$33,648,236	$33,648,236
School Age After-School Program	2.065	$0	$21,908,383	$0	$21,908,383

(continued)

TABLE 27.1 Missouri Elementary and Secondary Education Programs Fiscal Year 2019 (continued)

Program	Budget Section	FY17 GR	FY17 Federal	FY17 Other	FY17 Total
MAP (Missouri Assessment Program) Performance Based Assessment Program	2.070	$13,472,213	$7,800,000	$4,311,255	$25,583,468
Career Education Distribution	2.075	$0	$21,000,000	$0	$21,000,000
Dyslexia Training Program	2.077	$100,000	$0	$0	$100,000
Title I	2.080	$0	$250,000,000	$0	$250,000,000
Innovative Educational program strategies	2.085	$0	$1,500,000	$0	$1,500,000
Programs for the gifted	2.090	$0	$0	$9,027	$9,027
Advanced Placement	2.095	$100,000	$315,875	$0	$415,875
Title II (Improve Teacher Quality)	2.100	$0	$44,000,000	$0	$2,432,000
Public Charter School Program	2.105	$0	$2,432,000	$0	$2,432,000
Title VI, Part B (Federal Rural and Low-Income Schools)	2.110	$0	$3,500,000	$0	$3,500,000
Title III, Part A (Language Acquisition)	2.115	$0	$5,400,000	$0	$5,400,000
Federal Refugee Program	2.120	$0	$300,000	$0	$300,000
Trauma Informed	2.126, 2.078	$200,000	$0	$0	$200,000
Teacher of the Year program	2.130	$0	$40,000	$0	$40,000
Charter Education Initiatives	2.137	$10,000	$0	$0	$10,000
Disability Determination Program	2.140	$0	$0	$21,000,000	$21,000,000
Adult Education & Literacy	2.150	$5324,868	$9,999,155	$0	$15,324,023
Special Education Grant	2.160	$0	$244,873,391	$0	$244,873,391

(continued)

TABLE 27.1 Missouri Elementary and Secondary Education Programs Fiscal Year 2019 (continued)

Program	Budget Section	FY17 GR	FY17 Federal	FY17 Other	FY17 Total
Special Education High Need Fund	2.165	$26,965,141	$0	$19,590,000	$46,555,141
Readers for the Blind	2.185	$25,000	$0	$0	$25,000
Blind student literacy	2.190	$231,953	$0	$0	$231,953
Missouri Special Olympics Program	2.205	$100,000	$0	$0	$100,000
Missouri Charter Public School Commission	2.215	$2,203,000	$500,000	$2,750,000	$5,453,000
Missouri Commission for the Deaf and Hard of Hearing	2.220	$445,547	$0	$303,437	$748,984
Missouri Assistive Technology Council	2.225	$0	$808,482	$3,577,427	$4,385,909
Children's Services Commission	2.230	$0	$0	$8,000	$8,000

Source: Missouri Budget Project. "Budget Basics: K–12 Education, FY 2019 An Introduction to Missouri's K–12 Education Services and Funding." (2019). http://www.mobudget.org/wp-content/uploads/2019/01/K-12-2019-Budget-Primer.pdf

suburban school districts that surround the large urban areas. The Missouri school finance formula has both proponents and critics—advocates for the status quo point to funding based on weighted students, cost of living adjustments, and performance targeting, while critics point to school districts essentially determining their own tax rates in ways that are to their advantage along with allowing very small school districts to exist which critics say creates severe diseconomies of scale that the state ultimately funds at the larger state's expense. Upcoming legislative sessions will no doubt be difficult, as the state's economic and legal troubles have made it harder to equitably and adequately fund the Missouri aid plan.

NOTES

1. No state-based expert was available to author this chapter at time of publication. The chapter is drawn from sources as footnoted and represents the editorial staff's best interpretation of issues, trends and findings regarding the state of Missouri. For additional information and updates and detail, contact the Missouri Department of Elementary and Secondary Education.
2. Mo. Const. art. IX, sec. (a).
3. This section partially follows and expands on SchoolFunding.Info, "Missouri." (2019). Retrieved from http://webcache.googleusercontent.com/search?q=cache:7CylKOh393UJ:schoolfunding.info/+&cd=1&hl=en&ct=clnk&gl=us&client=safari
4. No. CV190-1371CC, slip op. (Cir. Ct. Cole County January 1993).
5. Senate Bill 380 Outstanding Schools Act. (1993). Retrieved from https://dese.mo.gov/governmental-affairs/legislation/previous-legislation/SB380.
6. Missouri Joint Committee on Legislative Research. "Session Laws of Missouri." (2005). Retrieved from http://www.moga.mo.gov/SessionLaws/2005/Part01_PREFACE.pdf
7. *Committee for Educational Equality v. State of Missouri*, 294 S.W.3d 477, 482 (Mo. 2009) (en banc).
8. See, e.g., cases surrounding Missouri troubles involving accreditation loss by certain school districts and a state law allowing voluntary transfer of students between districts, with resulting argument about funding insufficiency brought on by such transfer. These cases went to the point of a practical conflict between the transfer law and a constitutional provision (the Hancock Amendment prohibiting the state from imposing unfunded mandates on schools). As cases in point, *Breitenfeld v. Clayton School District*, 399 SW 3d 816 (2013) and relatedly *Blue Springs R-IV School District v. School District of Kansas City* 415 S.W.3d 110 (2013).
9. Children's Education Alliance of Missouri. *Missouri Education Funding Formula and Interactive Maps, School Funding General Overview*, (2019). Retrieved from https://www.ceamteam.org/missouri-education-funding-formula-interactive-maps/
10. RSMo §163.011.

11. RSMo §163.011.
12. James. V. Shuls, *A Primer on Missouri's Foundation Formula for K–12 Public Education, 2017 Update*. Show Me Institute Policy Study, No. 10, March 2017.
13. Ibid, p. 14.
14. Missouri Budget Project. *Budget Basics: K–12 Education, 2017: An Introduction to Missouri's K–12 Education and Funding* (2017).
15. RSMo §167.231.
16. RSMo §304.060.
17. 5 CSR- 261.040.
18. Debra Clink, Manager Student Transportation, Missouri Department of Elementary and Secondary Education, *How Does the Transportation Calculation Work?* October, 2018.
19. Missouri Budget Project. Budget Basics: K-12 Education, 2017.
20. Ibid.
21. RSMo §160.41.
22. James. V. Shuls, *A Primer on Missouri's Foundation Formula*. Show Me Institute Policy Study (2017). If a charter school were part of a local district without separate LEA status, the funds to the charter school are essentially flow through funds based on the same formula described previously. The charter school attendance and resultant weights are reported within the school district data. Within "... the district formula, local effort [is] subtracted. By not subtracting the local effort here, the district is paying the charter school the entirety of the funds calculated for the charter school by the WADA, adequacy target, and DVM.
23. Ibid, p. 18.
24. Ibid.
25. Missouri Budget Project. *Budget Basics: K–12 Education* (2017).
26. PSRS/PEERS Public School & Education Employee Retirement Systems of Missouri (2019). Retrieved from psrs-peers.org

CHAPTER 28

Montana

Christiana Stoddard, Ph.D.[1]
Montana State University

GENERAL BACKGROUND

The Montana state constitution, Article X, Section 1 sets out the main role of the state in providing public elementary and secondary education:

> It is the goal of the people to establish a system of education which will develop the full educational potential of each person. Equality of educational opportunity is guaranteed to each person of the state. The state recognizes the distinct and unique cultural heritage of the American Indians and is committed in its educational goals to the preservation of their cultural integrity. The legislature shall provide a basic system of free quality elementary and secondary schools... (and) shall fund and distribute in an equitable manner to the school districts that state share of cost of the basic elementary and secondary school system.[2]

The current system of school finance stems from a series of legal challenges beginning in 1985, when 64 school districts filed suit against the state claiming violations of these rights as laid out in the state constitution. The state supreme court in *Helena*[3] found for plaintiffs in 1989, stating that the state of Montana "...failed to provide a system of quality public education granting to each student the equality of educational opportunity guaranteed under Article X, Section I of Montana's constitution." After other suits were filed in the 1990s,[4] House Bill 667 was enacted in 1993. HB 667 established the current method of school funding for all public school districts in the state, using a formula that created maximum and minimum general fund budget levels for all districts. Each school district was required to be within that range on or before 1998. Senate Bill 460 (1999 session) and Senate Bill 390 (2001 session) expanded the capacity of districts to adopt budgets that exceed the maximum level. This basic model is in use today.

During the 2000s, legal challenges[5] to the state's funding system focused on the issue of whether the state adequately funded education. In the *Columbia Falls* case, the court found that the state's share of school district spending was inadequate. The Montana Supreme Court subsequently upheld this decision. Consequently, the 2007 legislative session provided additional funding which further expanded districts' general fund, as well as one-time only payments to the miscellaneous programs fund.

In addition to general state support, a 2005 special legislative session added four explicit components to districts' general fund that reflected specific state priorities. These included funding for components known as Quality Educator, At-Risk Student, Indian Education for All, and American Indian Achievement Gap. The 2013 legislative session added an additional component, the Data for Achievement component.

BASIC SUPPORT PROGRAM

The largest component in Montana school district budgets comes from the general fund. As noted, Montana's general fund has both a set minimum Base Amount of School Equity (BASE) and a set maximum level. Montana also has other special purpose funds discussed in the following sections of this chapter. These include (among others) funds for transportation, building reserves, tuition, retirement, and debt service.

The BASE fund has three main components.

- *The first component* is a basic entitlement portion, driven by student enrollment. The minimum BASE amount is 80% of the enrollment-based entitlement, while the maximum is 100% of entitlement. Districts can adopt either the higher of the maximum or the adjusted prior year's budget, but they cannot adopt a budget below the minimum;
- *The second component* is for special education. It is funded based on special education's allowable costs. More discussion occurs later regarding special education operation;
- *The third component* is for the five state-funded priorities. These include funding for Quality Educator, Indian Education for All, American Indian Achievement Gap, At-Risk Student, and Data for Achievement. These are all funded at 100% for every school district.

State Entitlement

The largest component of BASE funding is determined by the state entitlement. This is based on student enrollment. The term for enrollment used in Montana is ANB, or 'average number belonging.' The relationship between the basic entitlement and enrollment is nonlinear to ensure adequate resources for smaller schools. The state entitlement is specified for elementary school districts without 7–8 grades, districts with 7–8 grades, and high school districts. For Fiscal Year 2018, entitlements were as follows.

Elementary Districts Without 7–8 grades:
- Basic entitlement of $51,149 for the first 250 pupils, plus an additional $2,558 for every 25 ANB over 250;
- A per-ANB entitlement of $5,471. This rate decreased by $.20 per ANB for each additional elementary ANB up to 1,000 ANB. The per-ANB entitlement was $5,271.20 for each ANB over 1,000.

7–8 grades:
- Basic entitlement of $102,299 for the 7–8 grade programs, plus $5,115 for every 45 ANB over 450;
- The per-ANB entitlement per elementary rate for K–6, high school rate for 7–12.

High School Districts:
- Basic entitlement of $306,879 plus $15,345 for every additional 80 ANB over 800;
- A per-ANB entitlement of $7,005. This rate decreased by $.50 per ANB for each additional high school ANB up to 800 ANB. The per-ANB entitlement was $6,605.50 for each ANB over 800.

SPECIAL EDUCATION

Montana provides state funds for school districts' special education services and is comprised of several categories:

Instructional Block Grant (IBG) and *Related Services Block Grant* (RSGB). The IBG comprises 52.5% of special education monies. The RSBG provides an additional 17.5%. These block grants are based on the ANB of a school district. Monies are spent on allowable special education costs as defined in statute.[6] Allowable costs include instructional services, equipment and supplies, adaptive equipment or technology, and facility modification costs, but not administrative services or other overhead costs. Districts provide a 25% local contribution match to state funds. Consequently, districts provide $1 in local funds for every $3 received from the total block grant. If a school district is a member of a special education cooperative, the state pays the district's RSBG directly to the cooperative;

Reimbursement for Disproportionate Costs. This category provides 25% of available funds. Districts with unusually high special education costs may be eligible for additional special education reimbursements;

Additional administrative/travel funding for special education cooperatives. This category provides 5% of special education monies. Special education's costs involve the services of specialists such as speech or physical therapists and psychologists. Large school districts are often able to pay for these special services through their own programs, but smaller districts may not have adequate resources to run a freestanding special education program. The result is that small and midsize school districts may pool resources by forming a cooperative to maximize their special education services.

Table 28.1 provides information on total appropriations in Montana for these special education categories over the last several years.

OTHER STATE-FUNDED PRIORITIES

During the 2005 special legislative session, four new components were added to school districts' general fund: namely, Quality Educator, At-Risk Student, Indian Education for All, and American Indian Achievement Gap. Subsequently, the 2013 legislative session added an element called the Data for Achievement component. These components introduced the following enhancements.

Quality Educator. Each district and special education cooperative received a $3,185 payment in FY 2018 for each full-time equivalent

TABLE 28.1 Montana Special Education Funding Categories and Amounts FY 2015–2018

Category	FY 2015	FY 2016	FY 2017	FY 2018
Instructional Block Grant	$22,518,282	$22,518,282	$22,518,282	$22,728,260
Related Services Block Grant	$7,506,094	$7,506,094	$7,506,094	$7,576,087
Disproportionate Costs	$10,722,992	$10,722,992	$10,722,992	$10,82,981
Cooperativs	$2,144,598	$2,144,598	$2,144,598	$2,164,596
Total	**$42,891,966**	**$42,891,966**	**$42,891,966**	**$43,391,924**

licensed educator and for other licensed professionals employed by the school district including registered nurses, licensed practical nurses, physical therapists, speech language professionals, psychologists, licensed social workers, counselors, occupational therapists, and nutritionists;

At-Risk Student. Likewise, the At-Risk Student payment addressed the needs of at-risk students, with money distributed in the same manner that Title I monies are distributed to schools. For FY 2018, the legislature appropriated $5.36 million across all schools;

Indian Education for All. Similarly, each district received an Indian Education for All payment to implement the provisions of the Montana constitution Article X, Section 1(2) and the statutory requirements in recognition of American Indian cultural heritage (20-1-501, MCA). In FY 2018, the Indian Education for All payment equaled the greater of $100 for each district or $21.36 per ANB;

American Indian Achievement Gap, For FY 2018, every school district received payment of $210 for each American Indian student enrolled in the district;

Data for Achievement. For FY 2018, the payment was equal to $20.46 per budgeted ANB.

STATE AND LOCAL REVENUES

In the latest year available (FY 2017), Montana public school districts received approximately 44% of all funding from the state, 27% from local property taxes, 9% from county sources, 8% from non-tax local sources, and 12% from federal sources. These proportions have remained roughly the same since FY 2013.

Statewide total and per-pupil general fund budgets appear in Table 28.2. Greater detail regarding major sources of state and local revenue follows after Table 28.2.

TABLE 28.2 Montana Statewide Total and Per Pupil General Fund Budgets FY 2015–2018

	FY 2015	FY 2016	FY 2017	FY 2018
Total General Fund	$1.04B	$1.07B	$1.10B	$1.11B
State Revenue	$664M	$685M	$703M	$740M
Local Revenue	$296M	$308M	$314M	$356M
Other Revenue	$82M	$79M	$80M	$18M
Total Per-Pupil Budget	$7,257	$7,433	$7,537	$7,626
Total State Support Per Pupil	$4,631	$4,750	$4,832	$5,067

BASE Mill Levy

The BASE mill levy is the state-determined minimum local property tax revenue that districts are required to raise. Consequently, this levy is not determined by a vote.

The core of the current Montana school finance system is built around the principle of a Guaranteed Tax Base (GTB), which is designed to mitigate equity issues stemming from differences in property tax revenue. A district's revenue-generating capacity is calculated based on the district's taxable value (or mill value) divided by student enrollment (ANB). State aid is given to districts with ratios below the state guarantee. The guaranteed ratio is 193% of the statewide average ratio. However, this 193% multiplier is scheduled to increase over the next several years, as funding that previously went to districts under block grants is being redistributed through the GTB. The GTB multiplier is set to be 216% for 2019, 224% in 2020, and 232% in 2021.

The BASE mill levy is the local property tax revenue from non-voted local levies, as well as state subsidies based on the GTB. The total BASE mill levy covers 35.3% of the basic and per-ANB entitlement, and 40% of the special education allowable cost payment.

As of 2017, local property tax revenue was $134 million, increasing to $166 million in 2018. GTB aid for 2017 was $163 million, increasing to $195 million in 2018.

State Aid

Direct state aid typically makes up about 45% of school funding and comprises about 64% of school districts' general fund budgets. State aid contributes to districts' budgets in the following ways:

- 44.7% of each school district's basic and per-ANB entitlement comes from direct state aid;
- Special Education Allowable Cost payments come in the form of the Instructional Services Grant, Related Services Block Grant, and Reimbursement for disproportionate costs;
- 100% of the five state priority payments comes in the form of Quality Educator, At Risk Student, Indian Education for All, American Indian Achievement Gap, Data for Achievement components;
- Aid for the Guaranteed Tax Base as described above.
- Non-levy revenue and fund balance reappropriation as defined. Non-levy revenues include oil and gas production revenue, interest earnings, rental of buildings or equipment, summer school revenues,

tuition payments from other districts for transfer students, and school block grants. The Natural Resource Development Funding (NRD) payment was established in 2015 to provide payment to each school district in proportion to the district's direct state aid and to reduce local property taxes in support of the general fund. This was restricted in 2017, as discussed later in the school facilities section;
- Schools also typically have year-end as well as fund balances that can be reappropriated to the following year, but the amount that can be carried over is limited by law;
- Voted and non-voted local levies for the Over-BASE (above minimum up to maximum) general fund. These have no state equalizing GTB aid attached.

Property taxes therefore have several components: i.e., the local school district property tax (varies by district and includes BASE and Over-BASE funds); a statewide equalization mill levy of 40 mills and a countywide equalization mill levy of 55 mills that fund direct state aid; transfer payments for the GTB aid; state transportation aid; and state special education funding. There is also a six-mill levy for the university system.

SCHOOL FACILITIES

School facilities in Montana are funded by several sources. Under the federal *Enabling Act*[7] of 1889, 5.2 million acres of federal land were ceded to the state for school support. Income from school trust lands are currently reserved to funding BASE aid. If interest and earnings from the school trust lands exceed $56 million in a single year, the excess amount goes to the school major maintenance account.

The Building Reserve Fund is used for future construction and renovation. It is comprised of four funds.[8]

- *District Safety Subfund* which transfers funds for facilities to school safety and security;
- *District Voted Levy Subfund* which is levied for building reserves approved by voters for future construction, renovation, and land purchase;
- *District Transition Subfund* or voted transition levies;
- *District Permissive Levy Subfund* for facility maintenance and repair (the maximum permissive levy is ten mills per fiscal year (20 mills for a K–12 district).

Senate Bill 307 was passed in FY 2017 to create a District Permissive Levy Subfund for major maintenance and building improvement expenditures for public schools. This law determines the annual amount that can be budgeted by a school district for major maintenance. The total was set at $15,000 + $100 × ANB, where ANB is from the prior fiscal year. This maximum amount may be funded through local levies, with some state support for low property wealth districts. As noted, the maximum local levy is ten mills.

Senate Bill 260 established a school facilities fund using the coal severance tax trust fund.[9] Starting July 2017, 75% of the amount in the coal severance tax bond fund in excess of the amount required to meet all principal and interest payments over the coming year on bonds payable from the coal severance tax bond fund was set to be transferred to the school facilities fund.

CHARTER SCHOOLS

Montana is often listed as a state having no charter school laws. However, limited forms of charter schools are permitted.[10] This provision allows charter schools that are approved and managed by local school boards, using the same teacher licensing union eligibility and collective bargaining agreements. In 2016, Bozeman High School's Bridger Alternative Program became the state's first charter school. A second charter school features a partnership between Libby and Troy.

STATE AID FOR PRIVATE K–12 SCHOOLS

The Tax Credit Scholarship Program was passed by the Montana state legislature in 2015. Individuals and corporations can receive a 100% state tax credit for contributions to a Student Scholarship Organization (SSO), which provides scholarships for students to attend private schools or to receive tutoring. The maximum tax credit for individuals is $150, and the total budget cap for the state is $3 million. The maximum scholarship is 50% of the statewide average per-pupil expenditure; there are no eligibility requirements.

EARLY CHILDHOOD EDUCATION

Montana provides limited funding for preschool education. Federal funds provide the majority of subsidized preschool seats. In 2017, the Montana legislature also imposed a fee on large hospitals funding pilot programs. To date, this fee is the only source of state funds for preschool.

TRANSPORTATION

The Transportation Fund is used to pay basic costs of transportation (bus purchase, driver salaries, bus maintenance, and the cost of building bus barns). Bus transportation is reimbursed for 180 days. The state generally reimburses 50% of each district's transportation budget. Parental consent is required for rides of more than one hour.

BILINGUAL EDUCATION

House Bill 113 allows state funds to be used as matching funds for federal or private grants for Indian language immersion programs.

TEACHER QUALITY

As noted earlier when describing general aid components, one of the areas of state aid to the general fund is for quality educators. Districts and special education cooperatives are eligible to receive payment for each fulltime equivalent licensed educator and for other licensed professionals employed by the school district, including registered nurses, licensed practical nurses, physical therapists, speech language professionals, psychologists, licensed social workers, counselors, occupational therapists, and nutritionists.[11] The FY 2019 rate per Quality Educator is set at $3,245. Additionally, the Board of Public Education publishes a list of critical educator shortage areas. Teachers in those areas may be eligible for up to three years of student loan repayment under HB 119.

TEACHER RETIREMENT

All teachers in Montana participate in the state's Teacher Retirement System (TRS). This is a defined benefit system. Contributions are based on year of hire. Teachers hired after 2013 contribute 8.15% and districts contribute 8.47%, with increases for newer start dates. Retirement eligibility is age 60 with five years of service, or at any age after 25 years service. Benefits are approximately 1.67 multiplied by years of service, multiplied by average final compensation. The Retirement Fund is funded by a countywide levy to pay the district's share of the employer contributions, TRS contributions, and Social Security and Medicare taxes.

NOTES

1. The author thanks the Montana Office of Public Instruction, School Finance Division, for its collaboration during the chapter's writing.
2. https://leg.mt.gov/bills/mca_toc/CONSTITUTION.htm (1972).
3. *Helena Elementary School District No. 1 v. State*, 769 P.2D 684 (1989);
4. See, e.g., *Helena Elementary School District No. 1 v. State*, 236 Mont. 44, 55, 769 P.2d 684, 690 (1989), *amended by* 236 Mont. 61, 769 P.2d 684 (1990). *Montana Rural Education Association v. State*, No. BDV-91-2065 (Mont. 1st Jud. Dist. Ct. July 22, 1993) (Combined Order Concerning Mootness Issue).
5. See, e.g., *Columbia Falls Elementary School District No. 6 v. State*, 109 P.3d 275 (2005); *Columbia Falls Elementary School District No. 6 v. State*, 2008 Mont. Dist. LEXIS 483; *Montana Quality Education Coalition v. State*, Cause No. ADV-2011-1076 Consent Decree (2012).
6. Montana Code Annotated. 20-7-431. Retrieved from https://leg.mt.gov/bills/mca/20/7/20-7-431.htm
7. 25 Stat. 676, chps. 180, 276–284, enacted February 22, 1889.
8. Montana Code Annotated 20-9-502. Retrieved from https://leg.mt.gov/bills/mca/20/9/20-9-502.htm
9. Senate Bill 260, Montana Legislature 2017. Retrieved from https://leg.mt.gov/bills/2017/billhtml/SB0260.htm
10. Standards of Accreditation (Administrative Rules of Montana – Title 10, Chapter 55, ARM accreditation standards 10.55.604 Chapter 55). Retrieved from http://www.mtrules.org/gateway/ChapterHome.asp?Chapter=10%2E55
11. See Montana Code Annotated 20-9-306 (16) and 20-9-326, 20-9-327.

CHAPTER 29

Nebraska

Joel Applegate, Ed.D.
Superintendent Cozad Public Schools

Bryce Wilson, MPA, CPA
*Administrator of Financial and Administrative Services
Nebraska Department of Education*

Jeffrey Zacharakis, Ed.D.
Professor Kansas State University

GENERAL BACKGROUND

Historically, funding for Nebraska's public schools was based on the local property tax. Property taxes were solely established to fund public education under the Common Schools Act, which was passed by the Nebraska Territorial Legislature in 1855.[1] Until the mid-1960s, the general property tax was laid at both local and state levels. Indeed, the entirety of state government was financed primarily through property taxes until 1954 when voters approved a constitutional amendment adopting an income and/or sales tax meant to automatically eliminate the general property tax, although no enabling statutory action was taken.[2] In 1965, the legislature developed the first income tax, triggering the 1954 amendment for the first time. As a result, until 1965 the property tax functioned as the principal funding source for all state governmental revenue in Nebraska.

As part of the 1966 statewide general election, opponents of the new income tax law launched a repeal referendum. At the same time, the Nebraska Farm Bureau developed a petition to completely erase property taxes

---

Funding Public Schools in the United States and Indian Country, pages 417–429
Copyright © 2019 by Information Age Publishing
All rights of reproduction in any form reserved.

from the state constitution. Voters, leaving the state with no real source of statewide revenue, approved both questions.[3]

The 1967 Nebraska legislature consequently faced real issues. In response, the legislature approved the Nebraska Revenue Act[4] of 1967, which included both sales tax and income tax provisions. The 1967 legislature also established the state's first comprehensive school funding reform law known as the School Foundation and Equalization Act.[5] Three components key to school funding under the new law were:

- *Foundation aid*—Funding based on the number of students in attendance in a school district;
- *Equalization aid*—Funding based on property valuation in such a way as meant to equalize funding between school districts with differing levels of property wealth; and
- *Incentive aid*—Funding provided to school districts that chose to offer summer school programs, employed teachers with advanced degrees, or both.[6]

Unfortunately, the state legislature did not fully fund the new school finance plan. The main reluctance was a concern that property tax relief was less than expected. As a result, state aid under the School Foundation and Equalization Act only reached a maximum 13%, with much of the remaining share dependent upon local property taxes.[7]

Not until the 1980s did the Nebraska legislature begin to intensively focus on public education and its fiscal support issues. In 1985, the legislature passed Legislative Bill (LB) 662,[8] which required elementary school districts to consolidate with K–12 districts because property owners in elementary districts were paying lower property taxes than K–12 districts, i.e., tax havens. LB 662 also increased sales taxes to generate more funding for schools. However, voters mounted a referendum to reject the new law because it forced school district consolidation. Voters repealed LB 662 during the 1986 referendum, once again leaving school tax issues unresolved until the 1990 legislative session.

In 1990, the Nebraska legislature passed LB 1059.[9] LB 1059 was supported by the Nebraska School Financing Review Commission, which had been created in 1988 to review the state's school finance system.[10] Recommendation from the Commission was that the tax burden on property owners was excessive, with inequities and an unsteady tax base for school districts. The Commission also stated that because of these inequities, there was no assurance that all students had equitable access to needed educational services.

Also in 1990 at the same time the Commission was making its recommendations, a group of landowners filed suit in *Gould v. Orr*.[11] Plaintiffs argued that the funding system for Nebraska schools was inadequate and failed to provide equal educational opportunities because the state lacked a uniform tax system.

The combination of recommendations from the Commission and the lawsuit gave legislative impetus to LB 1059, which eventually replaced the School Foundation and Equalization Act of 1967. LB 1059 also survived a gubernatorial veto and ballot repeal initiative. As such, LB 1059 created inclusive funding reform for Nebraska schools and became known as the Tax Equity and Educational Opportunities Support Act (TEEOSA). TEEOSA had two main purposes: (1) to provide fiscal equity for both taxpayers and schools, and (2) to provide educational opportunities for all students. In the end analysis, LB 1059 sought to move away from reliance on property taxes toward reliance on sales and income taxes to fund K–12 schools. LB 1059 also amended school spending growth rates to a range of about 6.5%.

Another legislative bill introduced in 1990 sought to consolidate school districts. LB 259[12] addressed the need for school districts to offer all grades. There were three types of school districts in Nebraska at the time: (1) elementary only, (2) high school only, and (3) K–12 districts. LB 259 required elementary-only districts to merge with high school-only or K–12 districts. LB 259 was introduced due to concern that school districts with high schools were paying more property tax than elementary-only districts. From 1990 to 2007, reorganization and consolidation of schools reduced the number of districts from 845 to 271; today, the state of Nebraska has only 244 operating school districts.

Although first introduced in 1990, TEEOSA is still the same formula in use today, though it has been tweaked several times. Many changes made were due to budget constraints, including the stresses brought on by the recession in 2008. The recession reduced state funding by an estimated $189 million (2011–2012) and $222 million (2012–2013). Perennial issues continue to persist, as property tax relief—a concern in the 1960s—is still a top stressor for schools today. Nebraska's school funding profile in 2019 still finds the property tax and other local taxes providing a majority of monies for local school districts. The state's other major revenue sources (income and sales taxes) increasingly continue to be a point of contention, just as it was in the past despite evidence that a broader tax base better equalizes and relieves property tax burdens.

BASIC SUPPORT PROGRAM

Approximately three decades later, TEEOSA still serves as the funding formula for Nebraska's public schools. The main concept underlying TEEOSA is:

$$\text{Needs} - \text{Resources} = \text{Equalization Aid}$$

TEEOSA is structured to provide state aid to school districts in order to help supply the dollar difference between local districts' resource inadequacy and state-approved educational needs. The difference is called 'equalization aid.' Definitionally:

- *Needs* = what it costs a school district to educate students;
- *Resources* = local property taxes and other revenue sources;
- *Equalization Aid* = allocation from the state to offset the difference between needs and resources of a school district.

Local Sources

Nebraska's public school districts derive revenue from local, state and federal sources. Although local property taxes continue to be the largest proportion, many state attempts have been made to reduce reliance on the property tax for schools. In Fiscal Year 2017, approximately $2.1 billion (56%) in school funding came from local sources. Local funding includes residential and business taxes, with total property tax equating to $1.87 billion (89%) of total local funding (FY 2017). Other local revenue includes sales tax, motor vehicle tax, tuition/fees, and transportation. Figure 29.1 illustrates the role of local sources in fiscal resource proportions.

State Sources

The state share of Nebraska's P–12 school fiscal support in FY 2017 was roughly $1.41 billion (37%).[13] State support is seen synonymously with TEEOSA, which is the largest state funding source. Almost $1 billion in state funding was distributed through TEEOSA in FY 2017.[14]

TEEOSA offsets school districts' fiscal resource differences that stem from wealth variations that limit districts' ability to raise sufficient revenue through local taxation. Starting in FY 2018, every school district was entitled to receive some state aid through the formula due to 2016 legislative changes. However, even after recent changes, not all schools receive equalization aid, as only about 25% ultimately are equalization aid-eligible. Figure 29.1 illustrates the role of state sources in fiscal resource proportions.

Federal Sources

Nebraska's school districts participate in federal revenue eligibility through various school district entitlements and other programs. Almost

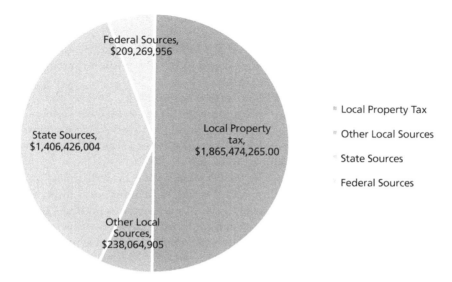

Figure 29.1 Federal, State, Local and Other Resource Shares for Nebraska Public Schools FY 2017. *Source:* Nebraska Department of Education. School Finance and Organizational Services, 2016/17. Statewide Annual Financial Report. (NDE, 2017).

$209 million in federal funds was received in FY 2017.[15] Figure 29.1 illustrates the role of federal sources in fiscal resource proportions.

TEEOSA Structure and Operation

Nebraska's state school aid formula known as TEEOSA is a complicated plan. Most revenue flows through TEEOSA in the form of equalization aid. The formula uses a four step process to determine needs of school districts on dimensions of determining needs, calculating available resources, determining equalization aid, and adjusting for additional items to finally determine total state aid.

Step 1: Determining Needs

The first step in TEEOSA is to determine the needs of each school district. Needs are defined as the approved costs to educate students in a district. Calculation of needs includes 17 components.[16] The largest component is basic funding (83% of total need). Basic funding is determined by creating a comparison group of school districts. Comparison groups are comprised of 10 schools larger and 10 schools smaller as measured by student count.[17] These groups are used to help equalize spending among differently sized districts.

Components making up the needs calculations are[18] as follows:

- *Basic Funding*—the major piece of TEEOSA's formula needs definition. Equalized spending is averaged using 10 schools larger and 10 schools smaller by student count;
- *Poverty Allowance*—for school districts completing a poverty plan which includes activities, curriculum and goals to meet the educational needs of students in poverty. Money received is calculated so that a district having a greater concentration of students in poverty will receive more funding up to a limit;
- *Limited English Proficiency (LEP) Allowance*—for school districts completing an LEP plan of activities which includes curriculum and goals to meet the educational needs of students with limited English proficiency. The district is funded based on a per-student factor;
- *Focus School & Program Allowance*—for school districts having a focus school, defined as a school that has been labeled for a specific curriculum purpose—i.e., low performing. The program allowance is for those schools designated in a Learning Community for the purpose of a diversity plan;
- *Summer School Allowance*—for school districts that hold summer school for at least three hours per day for 12 summer weeks. Funding is calculated using a per-student factor;
- *Special Receipt Allowances*—the second largest component of the needs calculation. It includes special education, state wards, and accelerated or differentiated curriculum programs;
- *Transportation Allowance*—a district's amount is determined by the lesser dollar of two calculations on actual prior year transportation expenditures or route miles traveled. It is calculated as four times the state mileage rate;
- *Elementary Site Allowance*—for school districts having more than one elementary attendance center more than seven miles apart. It can also be a city or village having only one elementary school;
- *Distance Education & Telecommunications Allowance*—based on actual expenditures, the allowance is determined by transmission costs to provide distance learning classes;
- *System Averaging Adjustment*—for school districts with enrollments greater than 900 formula students that levy more than $1.00 per $100 of property tax valuation and whose basic funding per formula student is less than the average of all districts having enrollments greater than 900 formula students;
- *New School Adjustment*—for districts having constructed a new school building because of increasing enrollment. The amount of need

calculated for this funding is based on the district's basic funding per formula student;
- *Student Growth Adjustment*—school districts with increased enrollment can apply and receive an amount based on the K–12 estimated year-end student count and the district's basic funding per formula student;
- *Community Achievement Plan Adjustment*—this adjustment applies to schools in the Learning Community that achieve standards based on written improvement plans;
- *Limited English Proficiency Allowance Correction*—a school district may receive a reduction to its needs based on actual expenditures and based on not meeting the requirements of its written plan;
- *Poverty Allowance Correction*—a school district may receive a reduction to its needs based on actual expenditures and having not met the requirements of its written plan;
- *Student Growth Adjustment Correction*—a school district will receive an increase in need if student growth is higher than the estimated student growth. Inversely, a decrease in need will follow if actual growth is lower than estimated student growth.

Step 2: Calculating Resources

The second step in TEEOSA is calculating resources by determining how much funding a school district has to fund its needs. There are four components to calculating resources:

- *Local effort rate*—the largest component. It is a hypothetical property tax rate that estimates how much funding a school district could raise locally. The local effort rate for 2016/17 was $1.00 per $100;
- *Allocated Income Tax*—a share of income taxes paid by taxpayers in the school district which is given back to districts;
- *Other Revenues*—includes interest earned on investments and tuition collected from other districts;
- *Net Option Funding*—applies when a school district receives funding for students who transfer to a school district from a home school district, meaning the net of more students optioning into the district than optioning out.[19]

Step 3: Determining Equalization Aid

The third step in TEEOSA is determining state aid for equalization purposes. Equalization provides funding necessary to educate a student when a school district cannot generate enough local funding. "In 1990/91, nearly 90% of the state's K–12 schools (250 of 278) received equalization aid. About 31% of the state's school districts (75 of 245) received equalization aid in 2016/2017."[20] The formula expressed earlier in text is operational in Step 3.

Step 4: Additional Items in Determining Total State Aid

The last step in TEEOSA finds some components of resources (net option funding [10%], allocated income tax [4%], and other state aid [1%]) added back into the funding of equalization aid to determine total state aid to school districts. Table 29.1 illustrates the basic formula for calculating state aid, where:

Equalization Aid (85%) + Additional Components = Total State Aid

Table 29.2 provides a summary of system-calculated outcomes of TEEOSA, so that total contributions are revealed and detailed.

Other Provisions Affecting TEEOSA

In 1990, the Finance Review Commission believed that limits to school district budget growth were important to the new funding system. A major concern for the Commission was to ensure that a part of new state aid monies would be used to keep local property taxes low, rather than simply being added to the budget.[21] In 1996, a property tax levy limit was added by the state legislature. This levy limitation placed a ceiling on the property tax rate that may be assessed against the taxable valuation of school districts (i.e., the same levy limit identified earlier as $1.05 for each $100 of property value). An example of the impact is provided in text box.

> (Assessed Valuation) × (Property Tax Levy) (divided by $100) = Property Tax Request
> $8000,000,000 $1.05 $840,000,000 $8,400,000
>
> *Source:* Nebraska Department of Education School Finance and Organization. *2018/19 Budget Text for Nebraska Public School Districts.* p. 17.

The net result was that school districts must keep within the taxing levy limit and spending limit (budget authority) when developing a budget.

Described next are three methods by which the state of Nebraska calculates school district budget authority: (1) the budget-based method; (2) the formula needs method; and (3) the student growth method. All three methods are calculated, with districts granted the greatest of the three results. Budget authority only applies to the General Fund.

Budget Based Calculation Method

The Budget Based Calculation uses information from the 2017/18 LC-2 (Lid Computation Form). The steps in the 2018/19 Budget Based Calculation are detailed below:

TABLE 29.1 TEEOSA Structure and Operation

Step 1 Needs	Step 2 − Resources	Step 3 = Equalization Aid	Step 4 + Additional Items	Final Determination = Total State Aid
Basic Funding (83%)	Local Effort Rate (79%)		Net Option Funding	
Special Receipts Allowance (6%)	Other Actual Receipts (16%)		Learning Community Transition Aid	
Poverty Allowance (4%)	Net Option Funding (3%)		Allocated Income Tax	
LEP Allowance (2%)	Allocated Income Tax		Community Achievement Plan Aid	
Transportation Allowance (2%)	Learning Community Transition Aid		Prior Year State Aid Correction	
Focus School & Program Allowance	Community Achievement Plan Aid			
Summer School Allowance				
Elementary Site Allowance				
Distance Education				
Adjustment				
Averaging Adjustment				
New School Adjustment				
Student Growth Adjustment				
Correction				
Community Achievement				
Plan Adjustment				
Poverty Allowance				
Adjustment				
LEP Allowance Adjustment				
Non-Qualified LEP				
Adjustment				

Source: Nebraska Department of Education (NDE), "Tax Equity and Education Opportunities Support Act (TEEOSA) Certification of 2017/18 State" (Lincoln: NDE, 2017).

TABLE 29.2 Nebraska 2018/19 State Aid Calculated by System	
Formula Needs	$3,535,590,990
Yield from Local Effort Rate	$2,517,496,035
Net Option Funding	$102,541,643
Income Tax Rebate	$42,333,888
Other Receipts	$504,003,571
Community Achievement Plan	$6,197,049
Total Resources	$3,172,538,781
Equalization Aid	$848,435,395
Transition Aid	$906,222
Total State Aid Calculated	$1,000,414,197

Condensed from 2018/19 State Aid Certification (March 1, 2018). https://cdn.education.ne.gov/wp-content/uploads/2018/02/1819SA_SACalc-TEEOSA_A1.pdf

$$(GFBE - SGF - SPED - GFLE) \times 1.015$$

Step 1: The 2017/18 Total General Fund Budget of Disbursements and Transfers (GFBE) is reduced by 2017/18 Special Grant Funds (SGF), 2017/18 Special Education Budget of Disbursements and Transfers (SPED), and 2017/18 General Fund Lid Exclusions (GFLE). This calculation represents the adjusted general fund budget of expenditures on Line B-140 of the LC-2.

Step 2: The adjusted general fund expenditures from Step 1 are grown by the Basic Allowable Growth Rate of 1.5%.

Student Growth Adjustment Method

The Student Growth Adjustment calculation uses information from the 2017/18 Lid Computation Form (LC-2), the 2018/19 Student Growth Adjustment, and the 2018/19 Student Growth Correction from the 2017/18 State Aid Certification. The steps in the 2018/19 Student Growth Adjustment Calculation are as follows:

$$((GFBE - SGF - SPED - GFLE) + (SGA +/- SGACORR))$$

Step 1: The 2017/18 Total General Fund Budget of Disbursements and Transfers (GFBE) is reduced by 2017/18 Special Grant Funds (SGF), the 2017/18 Special Education Budget of Disbursements and Transfers (SPED), and the 2017/18 General Fund Lid Exclusions (GFLE). This calculation represents the adjusted general fund budget of expenditures on Line B-140 of the LC-2.

Step 2: The 2018/19 Student Growth Adjustment (SGA) is adjusted by the 2017/18 Student Growth Correction from the 2018/19 State Aid Certification is added/subtracted to the Adjusted General Fund Expenditures calculated in Step 1.

Formula Needs Based Calculation Method

The Formula Needs Based Calculation uses information from the 2018/19 State Aid Certification (TEEOSA Need) and the 2017/18 LC2. The steps in the 2018/19 Formula Needs Based Calculation are as follows:

$$((FN \times 1.10) - (SPED \times 1.015))$$

Step 1: The 2018/19 Formula Needs (FN) of the school district are increased by 110%.
Step 2: The increased 2018/19 Formula Needs are then reduced by the 2017/18 Special Education Budget of Disbursements and Transfers (SPED) that has been grown by the Basic Allowable Growth Rate (BAGR) of 1.5%.

OTHER STATE AID PROGRAMS

TEEOSA was designed to be comprehensive and consequently includes programs otherwise regarded as categorical in many states. Selected state aid programs are highlighted in the following headings—refer to Table 29.1 earlier for scope and detail of general financing involving typical categorical supports.

Special Education

Special education funding in Nebraska receives its largest dollar proportion from the federal government. In 2016–2017, the state received $67 million in federal revenue through the Individuals with Disabilities Education Act (IDEA) grants. IDEA directs how states provide services to children with disabilities.[22] Currently, the state of Nebraska provides $212 million in special education revenue. Federal funds for special education are passed through at the 100% level of allowed cost, while state funds for special education are reimbursed at the 50% level of allowed cost.[23]

Other Funds

The state of Nebraska maintains many funds that exceed the scope of this chapter. Consequently, selected funds are identified and briefly discussed here.

Depreciation Fund

A major fund used by Nebraska school districts is known as the Depreciation Fund. The Depreciation Fund was established to reserve monies for eventual capital outlay uses. Such monies are reserved and typically come from each school district's General Fund. Under these circumstances, a school district will show monies as an expense to the district's General Fund via transfer to the district's Depreciation Fund. The purpose is to spread costs for potential capital outlay projects over many years in order to avoid a disproportionate tax effort in a single year to pay for these projects.[24]

Activities Fund

The Activities Fund is widely used by Nebraska school districts for operations of quasi-independent student organizations, inter-school athletics, and other self-supporting or partially self-supporting school activities. Failing to have this account within the district's General Fund would misrepresent the financial position of school operations and would complicate adding of net expenses received or incurred by conducting school services. Under Nebraska law, the impact is important—if negative balances are incurred in the Activities Fund, the school district's General Fund must cover the deficit by transferring district funds to the Activities Fund.

Special Building Fund

A Special Building Fund is available for establishment in every Nebraska school district for the purpose of making improvements to capital assets. Examples of uses for the Special Building Fund include acquiring or improving sites and/or erecting, altering or improving school facilities. The tax levy for this fund is set at a maximum .014¢ per $100 assessed valuation.[25] Monies collected for construction and/or related costs and all other income associated with this fund must be accounted for through this fund structure. Importantly, general fund monies cannot be used for the purposes of this fund.

SUMMARY

In the long view, Nebraska has been struggling with reliance on property taxes to fund public schools since 1855—i.e., it is an issue as old as Nebraska's territorial legislation.[26] Throughout the 1960s, 1980s, 1990s and extending to today, heavy reliance on local property taxes to fund the state's public schools is still an unresolved issue. Significantly, Nebraska's school funding formula continues to rely heavily on local sources of revenue. Also significantly, Nebraska ranks 48th nationally in fiscal support for public schools.[27]

NOTES

1. Michael S. Dulaney, *The History of the Nebraska Tax Equity and Educational Opportunities Support Act* (Unpublished doctoral dissertation, University of Nebraska (2007).
2. Ibid.
3. Kay Stilwell Bergquist, Renee Fry, Kevin O'Hanlon, Dylan Grundman, Tiffany Seibert Joekel, Micaela LaRose, and Tiffany Friesen. *Investing in Our Future: An Overview of Nebraska's Education Funding System.* OpenSky Policy Institute (2018), p5.
4. Neb. Rev. Stat. 77-1784 (1967).
5. Neb. Rev. Stat. §79-1340 (Cum. Supp. 1967).
6. Ibid., Bergquist, p. 5.
7. Ibid., Dulaney, p. 4.
8. Neb. Rev. Stat. 77-662 (1985).
9. LB 1059 (1990). Session Laws §32.
10. Ultimately decided in 506 N.W.2d 349 (1993).
11. 506 N.W.2d 349 (1993).
12. See Neb. Rev. Stat. 79-413 (1990).
13. Nebraska Department of Education. School Finance and Organizational Services, 2016/17 Statewide Annual Financial Report. Retrieved from http//www.education.ne.gov/fos (accessed January 20, 2019).
14. Ibid.
15. Ibid.
16. Nebraska Department of Education. Finance and Organizational Services, "Tax Equity and Educational Opportunities Support Act Certification of 2016/17 State Aid." http//www.education.ne.gov/fos/state-aid (accessed January 20, 2019).
17. Victoria Rosenboom, Kristin Blagg, Cary Lou, Victoria Lee, and Stipca Mudrazija. *School District Funding in Nebraska: Computing the Effects of Changes to the TEEOSA Formula.* Urban Institute (October 2018), p. 6.
18. Ibid. Bergquist, p. 27.
19. Ibid. p. 11.
20. Ibid.
21. Ibid. p. 15.
22. Nebraska Department of Education. *Rule 51: Regulations and Standards for Special Education programs.* January 1, 2017 (Revised).
23. Nebraska Department of Education. School Finance and Organizational Services. Retrieved from www.education.ne.gov/fos/special-education-reporting-information (accessed January 26, 2018).
24. Nebraska Department of Education. *Program Budgeting, Accounting, and Reporting System for Nebraska School Districts: 2016 User's Manual* (2016).
25. Ibid.
26. Ibid, Bergquist, p. 18.
27. U.S. Census Bureau, Public Elementary–Secondary Education Finance Data (2016).

CHAPTER 30

Nevada

Staff Writer[1]

GENERAL BACKGROUND

Revenues in support of Nevada's public K–12 schools for Fiscal Year 2014 were approximately $4.3 billion. This represented a decrease of 2.4% from FY 2009 when revenues totaled $4.5 billion, which was the highest amount over the last ten years. However, compared to FY 2005 revenues of $3.39 billion, school funding increased 28% from FY 2005–2014.

Financial support for Nevada's public schools is a shared responsibility. The local share in FY 2014 totaled 54.8% ($2.4 billion), while state revenue reached 35.9% ($1.6 billion). Federal revenue totaled 9.3% ($0.4 billion) in that same year, an amount slightly above the national average of 8.7%.

A large portion of local funding in Nevada derives from the state-mandated Local School Support Tax (LSST) and the Ad Valorem Property/Mining Tax. Consequently, the local share has been one of the highest in the nation. However, the recent Great Recession affected the amount of local school revenue, forcing a higher percentage of state funding for education.

At the same time, there are notable differences between Nevada's averages and the experience in each Nevada school district. For example, high mineral wealth in Eureka County caused about only 2.2% of total local school revenue in the Eureka County School District to come from state aid in FY 2016. In contrast, the Lincoln County School District received about 70.4% of total revenue from state aid.

Funding percentage distributions vary among Nevada school districts as the result of a formula equity process factoring in wealth and operating and transportation costs when determining state support for each

Funding Public Schools in the United States and Indian Country, pages 431–442
Copyright © 2019 by Information Age Publishing
All rights of reproduction in any form reserved.

TABLE 30.1 Nevada Local, State, and Federal Shares in K–12 Costs FY 2016

District	Dollars				Percentage		
	Local	State	Federal	Total	Local	State	Federal
Carson City	$42.4	$38.5	$8.9	$89.8	47.3%	42.8%	9.9%
Churchill	$16.9	$19.6	$5.1	$41.7	40.6%	47.1%	12.3%
Clark	$1,962.7	$958.7	$283.1	$3,204.7	61.2%	29.9%	8.8%
Douglas	$42.2	$20.9	$4.7	$67.8	62.2%	30.8%	7.0%
Elko	$74.1	$43.7	$6.7	$124.5	59.5%	35.1%	5.4%
Esmeralda	$0.9	$1.7	$0.2	$2.8	32.7%	60.6%	6.7%
Eureka	$10.1	$0.2	$0.3	$10.6	94.6%	2.2%	3.2%
Humboldt	$25.0	$10.8	$3.7	$39.5	63.3%	27.3%	9.4%
Lander	$12.1	$0.9	$0.7	$13.7	88.3%	6.4%	5.3%
Lincoln	$3.6	$10.9	$1.0	$15.5	23.3%	70.4%	6.3%
Lyon	$29.3	$52.6	$9.7	$91.7	32.0%	57.4%	10.6%
Mineral	$2.8	$4.0	$1.1	$7.9	35.6%	50.8%	13.6%
Nye	$20.9	$31.2	$7.9	$60.1	34.8%	52.0%	13.2%
Pershing	$3.7	$7.3	$1.0	$12.0	30.5%	61.1%	8.4%
Storey	$5.8	$1.5	$0.3	$7.7	76.4%	19.1%	4.6%
Washoe	$359.5	$209.1	$72.4	$640.0	56.1%	32.6%	11.3%
White Pine	$7.5	$8.7	$1.4	$17.6	42.5%	49.4%	8.1%
State Sponsored Charter Schools	$13.7	$5.6	$5.6	$263.0	5.2%	92.7%	2.1%
Statewide	$2,633.4	$1,664.1	$414.16	$4,711.6	55.9%	35.5%	8.8%

Source: Legislative Counsel Bureau Fiscal Analysis Division. "Nevada Plan for School Finance." (2017). https://www.leg.state.nv.us/Division/Fiscal/NevadaPlan/Nevada_Plan.pdf

school district. Differences can be seen in federal, state, and local shares in Table 30.1.

BASIC SUPPORT PROGRAM

The 1967 Nevada legislature approved Senate Bill 15,[2] revising the state's plan for financing elementary and secondary schools, thereby creating the 'Nevada Plan.' In so doing the legislature declared "the proper objective of state financial aid to public education is to ensure each Nevada child a reasonably equal educational opportunity."[3]

The Nevada Plan is a statewide, formula-based funding scheme for public K–12 schools. The plan provides state aid to school districts equaling the difference between the school district's basic support guarantee and local available funds raised by mandatory taxes minus local funds attributed to pupils residing in a county but attending a charter school or a university school for gifted pupils.[4] The plan does not include targeted formula funding for individual student differences; however, the state provides categorical funding for programs including Class-Size Reduction, Career and Technical Education, Adult High School Diploma, Special Education, English Learner, Victory and Turnaround Schools (low-income students), and Gifted and Talented Education (GATE).[5]

Nevada Plan

Under the Nevada Plan, the state provides an amount of funding for each local school district and charter school. Such revenue, which includes guaranteed funding, is derived from both state and local sources. As currently constituted, guaranteed funding provides roughly 80% of general fund monies. The plan includes state support received through the Distributive School Account (DSA) plus locally collected revenues from the LSST, and one-third of proceeds from the 75¢ property tax as required in law.[6]

To determine the level of guaranteed funding, a basic per-pupil support amount is established for each school district during each legislative session. The amount is formula-based, taking into consideration the demographic characteristics of each school district. Average operating and transportation costs and a wealth adjustment are factored in to determine the basic per-pupil support amount. The wealth adjustment factor is based on district ability to generate revenue above the guaranteed funding. For charter schools, the basic per-pupil support amount varies and is tied to the school district of origin for each pupil, e.g., virtual charter schools enrolling students from multiple in-state school districts receive differing basic per-pupil support amounts related to the home school districts of the attending pupils.[7]

The corresponding basic per-pupil support amount is next multiplied by the school district's or charter school's weighted apportionment enrollment. Effective in FY 2016, the official enrollment for apportionment purposes (Average Daily Enrollment, or ADE) is reported quarterly in October, January, April, and July. Disabled 3–4-year-olds and kindergarteners are multiplied by 60% and added to the total to derive total weighted enrollment. Beginning FY 2018, kindergarteners are counted as a 1.0 FTE.

The Nevada Plan is visually represented in Figure 30.1.

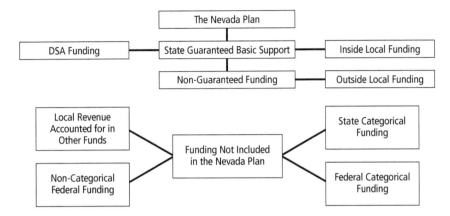

Figure 30.1 The Nevada Plan. *Source:* Legislative Counsel Bureau Fiscal Analysis Division. The Nevada Plan for School Finance: an Overview (2017), p. 10.

Formula Components[8]

The formula elements identified in Figure 30.1 are developed next in bullet form to explain their purpose and assignment.

- *DSA Funding* includes:
  - State General Fund appropriations
  - A share of the annual slot tax
  - Investment income from the Permanent School Fund
  - Federal mineral land lease receipts
  - Out-of-state LSST revenue that cannot be attributed to a particular county
  - Transfers of IP 1 (2009) room tax revenues
  - Medical marijuana excise tax (75 percent)
  - Beginning in FY 2018, recreational marijuana excise tax and license fees (less the cost of administration)
- *Inside Local Funding* includes:
  - LSST
  - One-third of the proceeds from the 75-cent property tax
- *Outside Local Funding* includes:
  - Two-thirds of the proceeds from the 75-cent property tax
  - Share of basic governmental services tax distributed to school districts
  - Franchise taxes
  - Interest income
  - Tuition
  - Rent
  - Opening General Fund balance

- *Non-Categorical Federal Funding* includes;
  - Impact received in lieu of taxes for federally impacted areas
  - Forest reserves
- *Federal Categorical Funding* includes:
  - Nutrition Education (e.g., National School Lunch Program)
  - Title I Program
  - Special Education Programs
  - Vocational Education Programs
  - Other School Improvement Programs, including programs under the federal Every Student Succeeds Act
- *Other Funding* includes:
  - Capital Projects—General Obligation Bonds
  - 'Pay as You Go' Debt Service

District-Based Components

The Nevada Plan also includes formula adjustments that refine local contributions and needs. District-based components are developed in bullet form next to explain their purpose and assignment.

- *Density/Sparsity of Small Schools* includes:
  - Guarantee is based on number of school district attendance areas in which educational services must be provided due to distances involved. This constitutes adjustment for rural and urban area characteristics.
- *Grade Level Differences* includes:
  - Eligible (IEP-only) prekindergarten pupils are weighted 0.6; all others weighted 1.0. Funding is provided for grades 1–3, and up to grade 6 when applicable through a class-size reduction program. Funds for FY 2018 totaled $147,445,963, and $152,142,582 for FY 2019. These funds were to hire 1,944 teachers to reduce class sizes in these grades to a ratio.
- *Pupil Weights for District/School Size* includes:
  - The DSA groups school districts into five groups (large, centralized, rural, small, and very small) according to common attributes (i.e., size, cost structure, degree of urbanization).
- *Declining Enrollment or Growth* includes:
  - For any district or charter school experiencing a drop in quarterly enrollment of 5% or more vs. the comparable quarter of the prior year, DSA guarantees hold-harmless payment using the ADE of the comparable quarter of the prior year.
- *Capital Outlay and/or Debt Service* includes:
  - Total bonded indebtedness of a county school district may not exceed 15% of the total of the last assessed valuation of taxable property, excluding motor vehicles, in the county school district.[9,10]

Student-Based Components

The Nevada Plan includes program cost adjustment factors, including funds for special education, low income/compensatory education, English Language Learner/bilingual education, gifted/talented education, career and technical education, preschool education, and STEM programs. These are developed later under individual major chapter headings.

Formula Structure and Operation

Public school funding in Nevada occurs through the Distributive School Account (DSA). The Nevada Plan guarantees every school district and charter school base-level funding on a per-pupil basis. Locally collected taxes (i.e., inside revenue) contribute to the guaranteed funding pool by offsetting the basic support guarantee to each county school district. Local taxes are added as nonguaranteed outside revenue by county. Figure 30.2 graphically illustrates the formula's structure and operation.

Total Operating Expenditures, including Salaries and Benefits
Minus
Projected Outside Local Revenue
Equals
Guaranteed Regular Basic Support
Plus
Cost of Additional Programs (e.g., Special Education, Class Size Reduction)
Equals
Total Required Support
Minus
Projected Inside Local Revenue
Equals
Total State Share
Minus
Miscellaneous State Revenues (e.g., Slot Tax)
Equals
State's General Fund Obligation

Figure 30.2 Nevada Formula Structure and Operation. *Source:* Legislative Counsel Bureau Fiscal Analysis Division. "The Nevada Plan for School Finance: An Overview (2017), p. 13.

Formula Impact and Amounts 2018[11]

Translation of the formula into impacts amounted to a statewide average basic support per pupil for FY 2018 of $5,897. The guaranteed per-pupil amount varied, ranging from $5,700 to $21,469. Revenue sources adding to the DSA funding guarantee pool included the state general fund, room tax, slot tax, medical and recreational marijuana taxes and fees, federal mineral lease revenue, out-of-state sales tax (LSST), and the permanent school fund. Expenses included salary and benefits of licensed and administrative staff, and transportation and equipment costs. Applicable locally collected taxes included the Public School Operating Property Tax (PSOPT) at $0.75 per $100 assessed value and Net Proceeds of Mining (NPM) (one-third guaranteed inside revenue, two-thirds nonguaranteed outside revenue), and the instate Local School Support Tax (LSST) sales tax of 2.60% (100% guaranteed inside revenue), as well as governmental services tax, franchise fees, and unrestricted federal revenues (each 100% nonguaranteed outside revenue).[12]

In FY 2018, Nevada implemented the New Nevada Education Funding Plan, augmenting the DSA. The new plan provides $1,200 per-pupil additional funding for restricted groups of pupils related to ELL and for low achievers who are not on an IEP.[13]

Table 30.2 illustrates the impact of the DSA for the 2015–2017 biennium.

SPECIAL EDUCATION

Historically, Nevada funding for special education was provided on a classroom unit basis, with the amount per unit legislatively established on an annual basis. Unit funding is typically designed to fund licensed personnel, rather than funding the individual pupil. In 2015, the Nevada legislature enacted Senate Bill 508[14] dictating that state funding for students with disabilities would move from a per-unit basis to a new system of distributing funding proportionally to each school district and charter school largely tied to numbers of students with disabilities not to exceed 13% of the total pupil enrollment for the district or charter school. The 2015 legislature further approved a general fund appropriation of $5 million for FY 2017 for the purpose of establishing a Special Education Contingency program for extraordinary expenses and related services for pupils with significant disabilities.[15]

For FY 2018, special education funding of $185,170,566 was allocated to eligible school districts and charter schools using the following factors: federal maintenance of effort minimums, inflation, enrollment growth to a maximum enrollment cap of 13% of total enrollment at each district/charter, and a multiplier equity adjustment. FY 2018 special education funding

TABLE 30.2 The Nevada Plan

	Governor Recommended (Millions)			Legislatively Approved (Millions)			Percent Change
	FY 16	FY17	2015–2017 Biennium	FY 16	FY 17	2015–2017 Biennium	
Total Operating Expenditures	$3,332	$3,437	$6,769	$3,353	$3,458	$6,811	0.6%
Less: Projected Local Revenues Outside the DSA	$(647)	$(670)	$(1,317)	$(647)	$(661)	$(1,308)	-0.7%
Less: Non-Basic Support Programs	$(139)	$(169)	$(308)	$(139)	$(19)	$(3,080)	0.1%
Total Regular Basic Support[a]	$2,545	$2,598	$5,143	$2,567	$2,628	$5,195	1.0%
Plus: Programs Other Than Basic Support	$313	$349	$662	$295	$331	$626	-5.4%
State Guarantee							
Total State Required Support[a]	$2,858	$2,947	$5,805	$2,862	$2,959	$5,821	0.3%
Less: Local Inside Revenues	$(1,441)	$(1,525)	$(2,966)	$(1,445)	$(1,520)	$(2,965)	0.0%
Distributive School Account							
Total State Share[a]	$1,417	$1,422	$2,839	$1,417	$1,439	$2,856	0.6%
Less: Miscellaneous DSA Revenues	$(316)	$(328)	$(644)	$(318)	$(330)	$(648)	0.6%
Less: Transfers of Categorical Funding[b]	$(2)	$(2)	$(4)	$(5)	$(7)	$(12)	
General Fund Support	$1,100	$1,092	$2,191	$1,094	$1,103	$2,196	0.2%

[a] Totals may not balance due to rounding
[b] Categorical funding to be transferred to Other State Education Programs Account (BA 2699) and Remediation Trust Fund (BA 2615)

Source: Legislative Counsel Bureau Fiscal Analysis Division. "The Nevada Plan for School Finance: An Overview (2017), p. 14.

was expressed as a multiplier of the statewide average basic support of $5,897 with multipliers ranging from 1.54 to 2.53. Supplemental funding up to $1.5 million was allocated to pay for students in excess of the 13% cap at $3,305.79 per pupil (50% of the statewide average special education per-pupil rate).[16]

LOW INCOME/COMPENSATORY/AT-RISK EDUCATION

During the 2015–2017 legislative biennium, the Nevada legislature enacted Senate Bill 447 which was targeted to underperforming schools in the 20 poorest zip codes in the state. Specific services were required in the bill, especially wrap-around and family engagement initiatives. Known as Victory Schools,[17] the biennium budget maintained the current $50 million in support of existing Victory schools through 2019.

ENGLISH LANGUAGE LEARNER/BILINGUAL EDUCATION

Under Senate Bill 504[18] the Nevada legislature and its Department of Education administer the Zoom Schools initiative. Aimed at English Language Learners, these intensive services have resulted in increased academic achievement and improvements in English language proficiency. The Zoom Schools program granted $46,048,905 for FY 2018 to K–12 schools having the highest percentage of pupils who are limited English proficient or otherwise eligible for designation as limited English proficient and who are academically lowest performing. Nearly 20,000 students have received services since enactment of SB504, with about 17,000 recipients in a single school district and more than 1,500 others in rural areas.

GIFTED AND TALENTED EDUCATION

As indicated earlier, the Nevada Plan includes components relating to profoundly gifted and talented pupils. Nevada has provided $6,374,243 for Gifted and Talented Education (GATE) under Senate Bill 544.[19] These funds are restricted to GATE pupils and are administered through a process that includes state-approved assessments and procedures relating to instructional time and other provisions.

CAREER AND TECHNICAL EDUCATION

Nevada engages Career and Technical Education (CTE) through program clusters.[20] Federal funding supplemented state funds in the amount of $ 12,543,822 for FY 2018. Approximately 30% of funds were distributed through competitive review, with restrictions regarding eligible areas for participation.

PRESCHOOL EDUCATION

The Office of Early Learning and Development (ELD) in the Nevada Department of Education administers early childhood state and federal funding, including programs and grants covered under Nevada State Pre-K; Pre-K Development Grant; Head Start State Collaboration Office Grant; Early Childhood Comprehensive Systems Grant; and Child Care and Development Fund (CCDF) Quality Dollars. Programs funded through the CCDF Quality Dollars include Silver State Stars QRIS; Nevada Registry; Pre-K Standards and Early Learning Guidelines; Early Childhood Substitute Network; and T.E.A.C.H. Early Childhood Scholarship program.[21] Early Childhood Education funding for FY 2018 was $3,338,875.

STEM (SCIENCE, TECHNOLOGY, ENGINEERING, MATH)

The 2016–2017 school year was designated in the state of Nevada as the Year of STEM. Accompanying funding included the Nevada Ready 21 program which provided $10 million to implement one-to-one student computing tied to 24/7 mobile device access for each student. Expansion plans are in development.[22]

TRANSPORTATION

The funding formula also recognizes each school district's transportation costs by including 85% of actual historical costs adjusted for inflation. The formula adjusts transportation aid through the basic support guarantee by including transportation as a factor. After subtraction, districts with positive numbers receive added per-student revenue, while districts with negative numbers receive a per-pupil deduction to the final basic support.

CHARTER SCHOOLS

Nevada law makes provision for state-administered and district-administered charter schools. For FY 2019, approximately 49 charter schools were serving over 35,000 students across the state. As indicated earlier, charter schools receive funding through the Nevada Plan, but because charter schools have no access to local tax bases, the entire basic support guarantee is state-funded.

As identified earlier, the charter school funding allocation is based on the per-pupil rate inside the Nevada Plan, taxes in the county where each pupil resides, minus a charter school sponsorship fee. As indicated earlier, for some charter schools all pupils reside in one county and therefore a single funding rate per pupil applies. For other charter schools, students reside in multiple counties and therefore generate multiple funding rates. Table 30.1 earlier showed that during FY 2016 charter schools received approximately $263 million in support of programs and pupils.

SUMMARY

School finance continues to be a concern in Nevada, as is the common case in other states. A study[23] in 2018 suggested revisions to the Nevada Plan that would include at least:

- *A formula that is cost-based* with a base amount and adjustments for student and district characteristics tied to state standards;
- *A formula that is responsive to student needs through program weights* reflecting needs to include at-risk, English learner, special education and more—a weighting formula instead of categorical funding streams to better serve the proposed educational deficiency;
- *A formula that is responsive to district characteristics* through adjustments sensitive to district size, wage index, and a necessarily small schools adjustment.
- *A formula that is transparent and flexible* by providing resources through straightforward base and weights so that the plan is easily understood.
- *A formula that is equi*table, with consideration for the interplay between all levels of support and which recognizes equity criteria.

NOTES

1. No state-based expert was available to author this chapter at time of publication. Early correspondence with Nate Hanson in the Nevada Department of Education provided helpful insight. The chapter is drawn from multiple sources as footnoted and represents the editorial staff's interpretation of issues, trends and findings regarding the state of Nevada. For additional information and detail, contact the Nevada Department of Education. This chapter borrows heavily from the public domain, i.e., Legislative Counsel Bureau Fiscal Analysis Division. "The Nevada Plan for School Finance: An Overview

(2017). Retrieved from https://www.leg.state.nv.us/Division/Fiscal/Nevada-Plan/Nevada_Plan.pdf
2. Statutes of Nevada, 889 (1967).
3. Citing Legislative Counsel Bureau Fiscal Analysis Division. "The Nevada Plan for School Finance: An Overview (2017), p. 6.
4. Nevada Revised Statutes [NRS] 387.121.
5. Legislative Counsel Bureau Fiscal Analysis Division. "The Nevada Plan for School Finance: An Overview (2017), p. 7.
6. NRS 387.195.
7. Legislative Counsel Bureau Fiscal Analysis Division. "The Nevada Plan for School Finance: An Overview (2017), p. 7.
8. Ibid p. 11.
9. Ibid.
10. (NRS 387.400).
11. Portions of the remainder of the chapter draw from Deborah Verstegen, "A Quick Glance at School Finance: A 50 State Survey of School Finance Policies." *Nevada*. (2018). Retrieved from https://schoolfinancesdav.wordpress.com and from Legislative Counsel Bureau Fiscal Analysis Division. "The Nevada Plan for School Finance: An Overview (2017).
12. Verstegen (2018).
13. Ibid.
14. Senate Bill 508, Chapter 536 (2015).
15. Legislative Research Council Bureau, "Summary of Legislation." (2015). Retrieved from http://epubs.nsla.nv.gov/statepubs/epubs/292049-2015.pdf
16. Verstegen (2018).
17. Nevada Department of Education. Victory Schools. Retrieved from http://www.doe.nv.gov/VictorySchools/
18. Senate Bill 504 (2017).
19. Senate Bill 544 (2017).
20. Nevada Department of Education. "Career and Technical Education (2018). Retrieved from http://www.doe.nv.gov/CTE/
21. Nevada Department of Education. Office of Early Learning and Development (2018). Retrieved from http://www.doe.nv.gov/Early_Learning_Development/
22. Verstegen (2018).
23. Education Commission of the States. "Nevada School Finance Study." Denver, CO (2018). Retrieved from https://www.leg.state.nv.us/App/InterimCommittee/REL/Document/12828

CHAPTER 31

New Hampshire

Staff Writer[1]

GENERAL BACKGROUND

New Hampshire became a state in 1776, and its original constitution was replaced in 1783. The state constitution's education article today provides that:

> Knowledge and learning, generally diffused through a community, being essential to the preservation of a free government; and spreading the opportunities and advantages of education through the various parts of the country, being highly conducive to promote this end; it shall be the duty of the legislators and magistrates, in all future periods of this government, to cherish the interest of literature and the sciences, and all seminaries and public schools...[2]

Interpreting New Hampshire's education clause has not been without controversy. State constitutional litigation and legislation have been important parts of the New Hampshire school finance landscape. Legislation has been regularly revised, and litigation has led to state landmark cases affecting school funding in conceptual and practical ways.

New Hampshire's school finance struggles are generally marked from 1999, as the state changed its school funding scheme to include a statewide property tax in response to a state supreme court ruling in *Claremont v. Governor*.[3] In what would become a series of rulings known as *Claremont I, II, and III*,[4] the court held that the state constitution "imposes a duty on the State to provide a constitutionally adequate education to every educable child and to guarantee adequate funding" and the legislature and governor have a responsibility to define "the specifics of" an adequate education.[5] In *Claremont II*, the court followed up, declaring the then-current school finance system unconstitutional because it failed the constitutional test that it be proportional and reasonable. Proportional and reasonable referred to how taxpayers in some lower wealth school districts paid more than 400% of the local property tax rate of those in higher wealth districts. The New Hampshire high court ordered the state to provide a four-part remedy: define a constitutionally adequate education; determine the cost; fund an adequate education statewide; and ensure its delivery through an accountability system.[6]

Compliance litigation followed. In 2002, the state supreme court ordered the legislature to hold school districts accountable for educational productivity,[7] whereon the legislature enacted an accountability statute. A few years later, school districts that had lost revenue after legislative changes in 2005 filed suit, and in 2006 a trial court in *Londonderry* held for plaintiffs. On appeal,[8] the state supreme court upheld, saying that the state had failed to define an adequate education and required legislative redress by June 30, 2007. The legislature met the deadline, enacting an adequacy definition that set content standards among other enumerations. In 2008, the state supreme court dismissed[9] on the grounds that the case was moot since the offending statute had been replaced.

In the ensuing years, the state legislature entertained over 80 proposed constitutional amendments addressing judicial review of educational funding, although all failed during contentious debate. In 2015, the Dover school district sued the state for failing to adequately fund education. The suit challenged a statutory funding cap, claiming that it violated the court's requirement to adequately fund schools. The office of the Attorney General subsequently announced it would not defend the state cap. In 2016, a superior court upheld the district's claims in *Dover*.[10] Talk of new lawsuits persisted in 2018, with the media reporting on consultations with plaintiff attorneys.

BASIC SUPPORT PROGRAM[11]

Following after the litigation history in New Hampshire, state education fiscal support is first conceptualized as Adequate Education Aid. Aid is further conceived as the 'Cost of an Opportunity for an Adequate Education' as determined in statute.[12] These statutes specify how aid is calculated and distributed.

Adequacy Aid is calculated using the Average Daily Membership (ADM) of students residing within a municipality. A full-time student enrolled in school for the entire year would have an ADM of 1.00. If a student moves midyear, s/he is counted as a fractional ADM in each municipality. For Fiscal Year 2020 Adequacy Aid, the ADM from the 2018–19 school year applies. Total ADM for a municipality consists of:

- Students attending a school operated by their resident district;
- Students tuitioned by the resident district to a district-operated school in New Hampshire or another state;
- Students tuitioned by the resident district to a nonpublic school, such as a special education program;
- Kindergarten students counted as no more than .50 ADM (half-day programs);
- Home school students enrolled in high school academic courses at the rate of 0.15 ADM per course and counted only if the appropriation has excess funds available;
- Preschool students excluded;
- Charter schools students excluded, except as provided in RSA 194-B:11.

Cost of Adequacy

In New Hampshire, the base per-pupil cost and additional costs for certain students are adjusted every two years for inflation and used for both years of the state's biennium. Statute specifies that the U.S. Bureau of Labor Statistics' Consumer Price Index for All Urban Consumers, Northeast Region, special aggregate index of services less medical care services, must be used to make adjustments.[13] For the biennium starting July 1, 2019, this inflation adjustment is set to increase by 2%.

For FY 2020 and FY 2021, the base per-pupil rate is set at $3,708.78 per ADM. Adequacy includes an additional rate for certain students as follows:

- $1,854.38 for a free or reduced price meal-eligible student. This eligibility determination is based on household income rather than participation in a lunch program. Students from households receiving TANF or SNAP are automatically eligible. Others are certified if parents/guardians provide income information;
- $1,995.21 for a special education student who has an individualized educational plan (IEP);
- $725.63 for an English Language Learner receiving English Language instruction. Students who have advanced to the monitoring stage are not included;
- $725.63 for each 3rd grade pupil whose achievement score on the state assessment for reading is below the proficient level, provided the student is not already counted in any of the above three categories. Students not taking the test are excluded.

For each municipality, the cost of an opportunity for an adequate education is calculated by applying the base rate and applicable additional rates to the ADM of each student.

Determining Adequacy Grants

Statewide Education Property Tax Assessment

Each December, the New Hampshire Department of Revenue Administration determines the minimum tax rate needed to raise at least $363 million from the Statewide Education Property Tax (SWEPT) for the subsequent school year. The tax rate, rounded to the nearest ½¢, is applied to equalized valuations without utilities.[14] Municipalities collect the SWEPT and send the total assessment amount directly to school district(s). Within cooperative districts, the assessment amount is credited to individual towns. While municipalities are responsible for collecting and distributing this tax revenue, SWEPT is a state tax, not a local tax. For FY 2020, a tax rate of $2.06 per thousand is applied to April 2017 equalized values.

Preliminary Grant

When the SWEPT assessment is subtracted from the cost of adequacy, the balance is the preliminary grant. If SWEPT is more than the cost of adequacy, then the preliminary grant is zero.

Stabilization Grant

A new funding formula was enacted for FY 2012 and was intended to ease the impact on municipalities facing a decrease in aid. The New Hampshire legislature utilized a stabilization grant to cover decreases. Not all municipalities received a stabilization grant in 2012. For FY 2020, the stabilization grant is set at 84% of the FY 2012 amount. This grant is being phased out over 25 years by reducing the rate by 4% each year.

Inclusion of Home-School Course Credit

Prior to the final payment of adequacy grants in April of each year, the New Hampshire Department of Education determines if appropriations allocated in the state budget for adequacy aid are sufficient for inclusion of an ADM credit of 0.15 for each home-schooled enrollment.

Total Grant

A municipality's total grant is the sum of its preliminary and stabilization grants. For final calculation in Spring 2020, the total grant cannot be less than 95% of the November 15, 2018 estimate and must include home-schooled course credit funding if applicable.

Program Allocation Amounts in New Hampshire[15]

Tables 31.1 and 31.2 illustrate supports for New Hampshire school districts for FY 2017. Table 31.1 provides a state summary of revenues and expenditures for the academic year 2016–17. Table 31.2 shows estimated expenditures for all school districts during the same time period and includes amounts by grade level and cost per pupil.

TABLE 31.1 Revenue and Expenditure Profile for New Hampshire School Districts FY 2017

Revenue Sources	Amount	Percent
Local Taxation	$1,859,885,529	60.1%
Tuition, Food & Other Local Revenue[a]	555,285,537	1.8%
Equitable Education Aid	926,491,022	29.9%
Other State Sources	80,818,756	2.6%
Federal Sources	173,816,060	5.6%
Other (Includes insurance settlements)	77,644	0.0%
Total Net Revenues	**$3,096,374,548**	**100.0%**
Sale of Bonds & Notes[b]	65,316,584	
Distribution of Expenditures		
Regular Instruction[a]	$1,199,964,323	40.8%
Special Programs[a]	566,549,771	19.2%
Vocational Programs[a]	39,306,678	1.3%
Other Instructional Programs	48,653,918	1.7%
Student Support Services	222,533,410	7.6%
Instructional Staff Support	105,349,693	3.6%
General Administration and Business	126,818,929	4.3%
School Administration	161,566,524	5.5%
Business Services	18,601,970	0.6%
Plant Operations	237,987,563	8.1%
Pupil Transportation	128,816,686	4.4%
Non-Public Programs	454,419	0.0%
Community Programs	6,222,108	0.2%
Bond & Note Interest	45,629,499	1.6%
Charter Schools/Other Agencies	2,636,468	0.1%
Food Service	33,860,801	1.2%
Total Recurring Expenditures	**$2,944,952,760**	**100.0%**

(continued)

TABLE 31.1 Revenue and Expenditure Profile for New Hampshire School Districts FY 2017 (continued)

Revenue Sources	Amount	Percent
Facility Construction	104,341,482	
Total Expenditures	**$3,049,294,242**	
Bond & Note Principal Payment	87,756,967	

[a] The following adjustments have been made to State Total DOE-25 data.
Deducted from Revenues:
Tuition from other NH school districts — 98,511,241
Transportation from other NH school districts — 381,688
Food service revenues except interest — 36,229,683
Services provided other NH school districts other than food — 1,620,639
Total Revenue Adjustments: — $136,743,251
Deducted from Expenditures:
Regular, Special and Vocational Tuition from other
NH school districts — $104,166,493
Food service revenues except interest — 36,229,683
Total Expenditure Adjustments: — $140,396,176

[b] Bonds & Notes must be repaid with revenues from other sources. To avoid double-counting revenues, these amounts are shown below the total revenue line.

Source: New Hampshire Department of Education "Financial Reports." https://www.education.nh.gov/data/financial.htm

SELECTED PROGRAM SUPPORTS

New Hampshire provides aid to targeted priorities within and beyond the general aid scheme. Sections below outline the selected areas of special education, catastrophic aid, tuition, pupil transportation, school building aid, charter schools, and kindergarten.

Special Education

New Hampshire provides an allocation for special education on an ADM basis.[16] This aid is intended to assist districts in complying with accounting for revenues that offset expenditures for special education programs and services. For FY 2018, state aid amounted to $54,353,188.20 which was distributed by formula to 40 school districts.

The state also provided catastrophic aid to qualifying school districts. Catastrophic aid is based on the number of students. Districts are cost-eligible for 80% funding; provision is also made for 100% cost-eligible funding.[17]

TABLE 31.2 Estimated Expenditures for New Hampshire School Districts FY 2017

Part A–Estimated Expenditures	Elementary	Middle	High	Total
Operating Expenses for Public Schools	$1,325,415,626	$495,128,095	$797,859,404	$2,618,403,125
Tuition[a]	24,674,041	16,056,203	121,532,901	162,263,145
Transportation	68,288,720	25,545,743	44,821,310	138,655,773
Elem and Sec Current Expenditures[a]	$1,418,378,387	$536,730,041	$964,213,615	$2,919,322,043
Capital Items (other than facilities reported below)				22,371,256
Interest on debt				43,963,778
Total Recurring Elementary and Secondary Expenditures				$2,985,657,077
Facility Construction & Acquisition				143,593,907
Total Expenditures for Elementary and Secondary Education				$3,129,250,984
Current Expenditures Not Part of Public Elementary and Secondary Education				
Summer School				$3,275,962
Non-Public Programs				112,733
Adult Education & Community Programs				2,054,723
Allocation to Charter Schools/Other Agencies				682,528
Total Expenditures[b]				$3,135,376,930
Part B–Estimated Pupil Memberships	Elementary	Middle	High	Total
Average daily membership	83,793	32,244	49,644	165,681
Part C–Estimated Cost Per Pupil	Elementary	Middle	High	Total
Operating Expenses for Public Schools[c]	$15,817.74	$15,355.67	$16,071.62	$15,803.88
Tuition	294.46	497.96	2,448.09	979.37
Transportation	814.97	792.26	902.85	836.88
Elem and Sec Current Expenditures[a]	$16,927.17	$16,645.89	$19,422.56	$17,620.13

(*continued*)

TABLE 31.2 Estimated Expenditures for New Hampshire School Districts FY 2017 (continued)

Capital Items (other than facilities)	135.03
Interest on debt	265.35
Total Recurring Elementary and Secondary Expenditures	$18,020.51
Facility Construction & Acquisition	866.69
Total Expenditures for Elementary and Secondary Education	18,887.20
Current Expenditures Not Part of Public Elementary and Secondary Education	
Summer School	19.77
Non-Public Programs	0.68
Adult Education & Community Programs	12.40
Allocation to Charter Schools/Other Agencies	4.12
Total Expenditures	$18,924.17

[a] Does not include inter-district tuition transfers.
[b] Does not include Bond Principal repayment of $88,656,701.
[c] For districts using the state average cost for tuition.

Source: New Hampshire Department of Education "Financial Reports." https://www.education.nh.gov/data/financial.htm

Kindergarten Aid

Aid is available to school districts operating full-day public kindergarten programs.[18] For FY 2018, state kindergarten aid was $10,728,603.71.

Tuition and Transportation Aid

New Hampshire provides school district reimbursement for Career and Technical Education tuition costs, along with aid for transportation.[19] Additionally, tuition and transportation for alternative education is available. For FY 2019, CTE tuition and transportation aid to school districts totaled $6,724,228.01 for tuition and $675,771.99 for transportation—a total of $7.4 million.

Building Aid

New Hampshire provides support to school districts for infrastructure.[20] District aid entitlement along with October and April payments are reported. For 2018, $ 33,700,315 aid was available to 82 school districts.

Charter Schools

In the 2018–19 school year, New Hampshire had 28 public charter schools in operation.[21] Charter schools are eligible for state aid paid by ADM. For FY 2018, a total 4,804 ADM charter school students were recorded, with $31,065,068.50 in state aid paid. Another $1,233,807.44 was made available in the form of differentiated aid. Total special education differentiated aid to charter schools was paid in the amount of $716,836.76.

State Support for Nonpublic Schools

In 2012, New Hampshire began providing education tax credits.[22] Enabling statutes made available an 85% business tax credit for contributions to a nonprofit scholarship organization which awards scholarships for private school tuition and home school expenses. Qualifying students must have been enrolled in a public school in the previous year; must have received a scholarship in the previous year; or must have a family income less than 300% of the federal poverty level.

SUMMARY

New Hampshire school funding faces uncertainty, as facts are in dispute. For 2017–18, the basic allocation was $3,636.06 per pupil, an amount that could be adjusted to a maximum $8,121.57 for certain student categories. Cumulatively, the average amount of state funding was approximately $4,476 per pupil, but the New Hampshire Department of Education reported about $15,310 as the average actual annual per pupil cost. Critics are restless, arguing that the percentage of K–12 education costs paid by the state of New Hampshire is among the five lowest states in the nation.[23]

Table 31.3 provides a summary of estimated expenditures by major category relating to the state aid formula.

TABLE 31.3 Estimated Expenditures for New Hampshire School Districts FY 2017	
2016–17 ADM	166,101.48
Base Adequacy Aid $3,636.06	$603,954,940.50
F&R ADM	45,473.07
F&R Differentiated Aid $1,818.02	$82,670,954.35
SPED ADM	28,484.70
ELL ADM $1,956.09	$55,718,633.17
SPED Differentiated Aid	4,732.22
ELL Differentiated Aid $711.40	$3,366,504.06
Grade 3 Reading Below Proficient ADM	2,151.74
Grade 3 Reading Differentiated AID $711/4-	$1,530,745.15
Total Calculated Cost of an Adequate Education	$747,241,777.23
SWEPT @ $2.170	$363,099,673
Preliminary Grants = Cost of Adequacy Less SWEPT	$413,677,464.72
FY 2012 Stabilization Grant	$158,480,276.00
In Preliminary Grant > 0 and ADM > 0 then FY12 Stabilization @88%	$138,234,410.16
FY 2018 Grants	**$552,207,689.68**

Source: New Hampshire Department of Education. Adequacy Aid Memo 2019 Updated. https://www.education.nh.gov/data/state_aid.htm

NOTES

1. No state-based expert was available to author this chapter at time of publication. Early correspondence with Caitlin Davis in the New Hampshire Department of Education provided helpful insight. The chapter is drawn from multiple sources as footnoted and represents the editorial staff's interpretation of issues, trends and findings regarding the state of New Hampshire. For additional information and detail, contact the New Hampshire Department of Education.
2. N.H. Const. Pt. 2, art. 83.
3. *Claremont School District v. Governor*, 635 A.2d 1375 (1993).
4. *Claremont I*, 635 A.2d. 1375 (1993); *Claremont II* 703 A.2d 1353 (1997); and *Claremont III*, 744 A.2d 1107 (1999).
5. 635 A.2d 1375 (1993).
6. SchoolFunding.Info. "New Hampshire." Retrieved from http://schoolfunding.info/litigation-map/new-hampshire/#1485150611794-bca14785-8203
7. *Claremont v. Governor*, 794 A.2d 744 (2002).
8. *Londonderry School District Sau #12 & a. v. State of New Hampshire*, Opinion Issued September 8, 2006.
9. *Londonderry Sch. Dist. v. State*, 958 A. 2d 930 (N.H. 2008).
10. *City of Dover v. State*. No. 219-2015-CV-312 (2016).
11. This section follows closely from New Hampshire Department of Education, "FY202 Adequate Education Aid: How the Cost of an Opportunity for an Adequate Education is Determined." Retrieved from https://www.education.nh.gov/data/ documents/fy2020_explained.pdf
12. RSA 198:38 through 198:42.
13. RSA 198:40-d.
14. (RSA 76:3 and RSA 76:8.).
15. This section relies in significant part on the New Hampshire Department of Education website's data tables. https://www.education.nh. gov/data/financial.htm
16. RSA 32:11-a.
17. See RSA 186-C:18 for legislation which describes the calculation and distribution of aid.
18. See RSA 198:48-c for legislation describing the calculation and distribution of aid.
19. See RSA 188-E:7 through 9 for legislation which describes the calculation and distribution of aid.
20. See RSA 198:15 for legislation which describes the calculation and distribution of aid.
21. See RSA 194-B:11 for legislation that describes the calculation and distribution of aid.
22. https://www.revenue.nh.gov/quick-links/education-tax-credit.htm
23. John Tobin, "Worsening Inequities in School Funding." The New Hampshire Center for Public Interest Journalism (May 18, 2018) Retrieved from http://indepthnh.org/2018/05/18/the-worsening-inequities-in-nh-school-funding/

CHAPTER 32

New Jersey

Luke J. Stedrak, Ed.D.
Assistant Professor
Seton Hall University

GENERAL BACKGROUND AND AID FORMULA BASIC DESIGN

Since 1973, the New Jersey state supreme court has handed down a series of decisions in an effort to uphold the state's constitutional requirement of a 'thorough and efficient' system of public education for all students. In *Robinson v. Cahill*[1] the court determined that the system of financing public education in New Jersey was unconstitutional. Since that groundbreaking case, the state's high court has repeatedly imparted numerous rulings, variously known as the *Abbott*[2] decisions, to provide all students in New Jersey with equal access to quality public education. During that time, the court better defined what a thorough and efficient education really means. Goertz et. al. make the point that through these court decisions:

> [T]he New Jersey Supreme Court has defined an adequate education as one that prepares a student to be a citizen, to be competitive in the labor market, to participate fully in society, and to appreciate music, art and literature, all as measured by students' mastery of the state's core curriculum standards.[3]

These court decisions have also resulted in increased state aid for education and, importantly, more funds directed to poorer urban districts, also known as the *Abbott* districts.

Robinson v. Cahill

The New Jersey state constitution was amended in 1875 to require the institution of a thorough and efficient system of education. In 1970, a lawsuit was brought against the state of New Jersey and the cities of Jersey City, Paterson, Plainfield and East Orange, asserting that the state's funding formula for public schools discriminated against students from economically disadvantaged school districts. In 1973, the New Jersey supreme court deemed unconstitutional the state's system of primarily using property taxes to fund public schools and called for a new funding system. As a result of the court's decision in *Robinson*, the state legislature established the Public School Education Act of 1975 (also known as Chapter 212).[4] The act had three major goals.

- *Guarantee* that school districts of unequal property wealth would receive equal resources for equal tax rates;
- *Compensate* districts for the extra costs of educating students with extraordinary educational needs; and
- *Narrow* per-pupil expenditure disparities through a system of expenditure caps.

With the Act of 1975, New Jersey's legislators aimed to level the playing field to ensure that all students were able to receive a thorough and efficient education as written in the state constitution. Under the Act, school districts were able to raise funds as though their tax bases were equal to a guaranteed tax base (GTB). If school districts could not generate all necessary funds under their actual tax bases, the state would provide equalization aid to make up the difference.

Abbott I

Despite changes to the state's funding formula, a lawsuit was filed against the state of New Jersey on behalf of 20 children attending schools in Camden, East Orange, Irvington, and Jersey City. Plaintiffs asserted that the Public School Education Act of 1975 failed to provide a thorough and efficient education for all students.

Plaintiffs argued that under the then-current funding formula, the state provided roughly 40% of funds for all school operating costs, with the remainder of funds generated by the property tax. According to plaintiffs, due to vast property wealth differences among school districts, there were equally vast discrepancies in per-pupil expenditure. As a result of these disparities, plaintiffs argued that students in poorer school districts did not receive the same high-quality education as students in both average and economically advantaged school districts. In 1985, the New Jersey supreme court transferred the case to an administrative law judge for initial hearing. This decision, known as *Abbott I*,[5] was the first in a myriad of *Abbott* decisions that would be reached over the course of the next three decades. The series of *Abbott* decisions would profoundly shape education for students in New Jersey, helping to level the playing field for economically disadvantaged students in the state.

Abbott II

The New Jersey Supreme Court minced no words in *Abbott*, saying:

> [T]he children of poorer urban districts are as capable as all others; [...] their deficiencies stem from their socioeconomic status; and that through effective education and changes in that socioeconomic status, they can perform as well as others. [The state's] constitutional mandate does not allow [the state] to consign poorer children permanently to an inferior education on the theory that they cannot afford a better one or that they would not benefit from it.

In 1990, the New Jersey supreme court handed down the second *Abbott*[6] decision, ruling that the Public School Education Act of 1975 was unconstitutional as applied to 28 'poorer urban' school districts (this number would later be increased to 31 districts, which would be known as the Abbott districts). The court found that schools in those poorer urban districts were unable to meet the needs of students under the state's funding formula. Furthermore, the court found that the then-current system of funding public schools was neither thorough nor efficient as applied to poorer urban districts. According to the court, "... the poorer the district and the greater its need, the less the money available and the worse the education." The court determined that the Public Education Act of 1975:

> [Must] be amended to assure funding of education in poorer urban districts at the level of property-rich districts; that such funding cannot be allowed to depend of the ability of local school districts to tax; that such funding must be guaranteed and mandated by the State; and that the level of funding must also be adequate to provide for the special educational needs of these poorer urban districts in order to redress their extreme disadvantages.

Although the court acknowledged that simply fixing the funding disparity would not solve all of the educational inequalities that existed at that time between schools in low-income areas and schools in affluent areas, it also asserted that (if used wisely) it could help schools in low-income districts provide students with higher quality education. The current system under the Act enabled school districts to raise as much money as needed to provide a thorough and efficient education. If those school districts were unable to raise all necessary funds, the state would provide the difference. Despite this policy, the court found that schools in poorer urban areas were still failing, and under the current system had no "likelihood of achieving a decent education tomorrow, in the reasonable future, or ever."

Consequently, the court found the Act's funding scheme to be flawed. Under the scheme, local tax revenues were supplemented by state aid, known as equalization aid, to ensure that districts in poorer areas were able to reach the guaranteed tax base (GTB). The court found that the Act was only fully funded twice, once for the 1977–78 school year, and again for the 1978–79 school year. While the Act promised that all school districts would be funded at a 134% guaranteed base level, funding over the years had varied from 129% to 134%.

The court also noted several limitations with equalization aid, one of which greatly affected low-income school districts in New Jersey. The equalization aid that a district received under the Act was based on the budget for the previous year, not for the current school year. The court illustrated how a district with an equalization aid level of 80% of the district's budget could be impacted by the practice of using the previous year's budget:

> Assume that district has a $4.2 million dollar budget for this year, representing a spending increase of $200,000 (last year's budget was $4 million). For $4 million of that $4.2 million budget, 80% aid will be forthcoming—the district will have to raise only $800,000 locally to have a total of $4 million. But to get the extra $200,000, the school district will have to raise that entire amount on its own tax base, and the impact on its tax rate will be five times as much as it would have been (because, on the assumption given, the state would have paid 80% of that $200,000 but for this "prior year" equalization tax rule.

The example showed that, under the Act, there was tremendous potential that poorer urban school districts would be financially unable to meet the needs of their students and ultimately unable to provide them with the thorough and efficient education that they had a constitutional right to receive.

Quality Education Act

In response to the *Abbott II* decision, New Jersey's governor and state legislature signed the *Quality Education Act*[7] (QEA) into law in July 1990. The QEA specifically was designed to comply with the New Jersey supreme court's ruling, which mandated that all students in the state of New Jersey would be supported by similar educational resources. The intent of the QEA was to "enhance educational opportunities for New Jersey's children by guaranteeing all school districts an adequate level of state aid."[8] The QEA identified 30 urban school districts as having special needs and aimed to provide those districts with increased financial support. Under the QEA, the Commissioner of Education was directed to determine an equity spending cap, permitting special needs districts to increase their spending budgets. In 1991, the QEA was amended to alleviate school districts' tax burdens, provide property tax relief, and also impose spending limitations. Ultimately, the QEA aimed to level the playing field for New Jersey's children by ensuring educational equity, improving the quality of education, and imposing greater accountability for school spending.

Under the QEA's funding system, known as the 'foundation funding program', the state department of education would determine a basic amount of money that would be spent for every child's education, regardless of socioeconomic status of the district. The QEA, which was funded primarily through taxes and the state education aid, determined how the various types of state aid would be distributed. Those types of state aid included: (1) state foundation aid; (2) categorical aid (including aid for special education, bilingual education, at-risk students, and county vocational schools); (3) other state aid for transportation, pension and social security costs, debt service; and (4) transition aid.

State foundation aid was a key piece of the QEA. It was distributed to schools to help finance operating costs such as teacher salaries, textbooks and supplies, administrative costs, maintenance, utilities, and out of district tuition. In order to calculate the amount of state foundation aid that a school district would receive, the state first determined the district's maximum foundation budget, or 'appropriate overall spending level'. The maximum foundation budget was based on the district's enrollment and the foundation amount, or the amount of money, determined by the state, to provide each student with a quality education. For the 1991–92 school year, the foundation amount was $6,640 per student. For the 30 high needs urban districts, the amount of foundation aid would increase by 5%; for the 1991–92 school year, this amounted to $332, resulting in a foundation amount of $6,972 per pupil. According to the rationale used in creating the formula, the additional state aid for those schools would help to address their special needs.

As various programs required different levels of funding, weights were assigned to grade and program categories to determine the amount of foundational funding required for each program. The foundation was multiplied by the foundation weight to determine the weighted foundational amount. For example, a student attending full-day kindergarten or preschool was assigned a foundation weight of 1.00, and thus was entitled to a weighted foundation amount of $6,640 in 1991–92. A student attending a half-day kindergarten or pre-school program was assigned a weight of .5 and thus entitled to a foundation amount of $3,320. Grades 1–5 were assigned a foundation weight of 1.00; grades 6–8 were assigned a foundation weight of 1.10; and grades 9–12 were assigned a weight of 1.33, thus a weighted foundation amount of $8,831 per pupil in 1991–92.

Once a foundation amount was established, the state then determined the school district's 'fair share,' or how much of that money the district should be able to generate through local taxes. In addition to the foundation amount, a facilities component was also used to determine the districts' maximum foundation budget. This amount was set at $107 for the 1991–92 school year.

Categorical aid was also provided to districts to cover the costs of additional programs such as special needs programs, bilingual programs, at-risk student programs and vocational programs. Other state aid was also provided under the QEA for districts to cover the costs of pension and social security, as well as transportation aid. Finally, transition aid was also provided for school districts that would be receiving less state aid under the QEA. Transition aid aimed to help districts ease into the transition of a four-year period; after 1995–96 transition aid would be completely eliminated.

Although state legislators aimed to comply with the *Abbott II* ruling by implementing the QEA, the Education Law Center reactivated the *Abbott* case in 1992, asserting that the QEA violated the court's ruling.[9]

Abbott III

In 1994, the New Jersey supreme court upheld a superior court's decision that the QEA was unconstitutional based on its failure to assure parity of regular education expenditures between special needs districts and the more affluent districts.[10] Although under the QEA there was a significant increase in state aid (approximately $700 million) to the 30 special needs districts and no increase in aid to wealthier districts, the court ultimately determined that the QEA failed to achieve parity among poorer and wealthier school districts in the state. According to the court, while the QEA authorized the special needs districts to *spend* enough each year to achieve parity by the 1995–1996 school year, the Act did not guarantee funding sufficient to *pay* for the authorized level of spending. Under the QEA, the Commissioner of Education was directed to determine an equity-spending cap for the 30 special needs districts; this increase in spending would enable special needs districts to spend as much per pupil as wealthier school districts, also known as I and J districts.[11]

According to the court, while it was theoretically possible to use the equity-spending cap to achieve parity in terms of per-pupil spending among special needs districts and wealthier districts, the equity-spending cap was never exercised and there was no link between the equity-spending cap and the maximum foundation budget. In fact, at the time of the court's ruling, the equity-spending cap had not been calculated for the 1993–94 school year. The court ruled that because the QEA's design for achieving parity depended on the *discretionary* action of the executive and legislative branches, the state failed to *guarantee* funding for each district. The court also specified concerns regarding how special needs districts were using the additional state aid received under the QEA. According to the court, the state needed to monitor use of the increased state aid to ensure that the additional funding was being used for supplemental programs to meet the needs of students. Although each special needs district was required to develop an educational improvement plan under the QEA, the court found no evidence to suggest a correlation between the increased state aid and the educational improvement plan. Furthermore, the court asserted that the state failed to study which supplemental programs would best support students in the special needs schools, such as full-day kindergarten programs or health services. According to the court, simply providing increased funding to special needs schools would not improve the quality of education or ensure educational equity.

New Jersey Core Curriculum Content Standards

Following after the *Abbott III* decision, state legislators worked to reform education funding to ensure that all students in the state of New Jersey would receive a thorough and efficient education as mandated by the state constitution. The reformation was implemented in 1995, when the governor executed the New Jersey Core Curriculum Content Standards[12] (NJCCCS). The standards provided an extensive outline of what all students should know and be able to do at each stage of their elementary, middle, and high school career. The standards were an effort to define the meaning of 'thorough' in the context of the 1875 state constitutional guarantee that students would be educated within a thorough and efficient system of free public schools.

The standards were designed to ensure that public education in New Jersey would prepare all students to compete in a competitive global workforce. Comprehensive standards were created for the following categories: Cross-Content Workplace Readiness, Visual and Performing Arts, Comprehensive Health and Physical Education, Language Arts and Literacy, Mathematics, Science, Social Studies, and World Language. The standards provided educators with a list of 'cumulative progress indicators' that indicated what all students should know and be able to do by the end of grades 4, 8, and 12.

School districts had the autonomy to develop their own curriculums that would enable students to achieve the goals laid out in the NJCCCS.

Implementing the NJCCCS was the first step in complying with *Abbott III* and ensuring that New Jersey students would receive a thorough and efficient education. The second step was reforming how state aid was distributed to school districts across the state. In December 1996, the governor signed the Comprehensive Education Improvement and Financing Act[13] (CEIFA) into law, linking state standards to state aid.

Comprehensive Education Improvement and Financing Act

The CEIFA was designed to ensure that all students in the state of New Jersey, whether in regular or special needs school districts, would receive a thorough and efficient education. CEIFA was very different from the earlier Quality Education Act because it truly focused on providing students with both a *thorough* and *efficient* education by linking state standards to state aid. While the QEA used a complex formula to determine which schools required the most funding based on socioeconomic status and enrollment, CEIFA linked state aid to the amount of funding schools would need in order to meet the specific goals of the new NJCCCS.[14]

Under CEIFA, a thorough education was defined as an education that met the NJCCCS. Efficient education was defined as a set of standards that were considered essential to meeting the NJCCCS such as class size, administrators/teachers per student, schools per district, and types and amounts of classroom supplies, services and materials, that are considered to be sufficient to achieve the state content standards. Local revenue would be used to fund all other school expenses, which were considered non-essential.

The CEIFA preserved the foundational funding structure established in the 1990 QEA. Under CEIFA, this foundation funding was referred to as the 'T & E' amount, defined as the amount of per-pupil funding needed to implement the NJCCCS.[15] In 1996, the T & E amount was set at $6,720. This number was based on a model education delivery system designed by the state as well as average salaries of school staff. The T & E level for the 30 special needs districts was set as 1.05 times that amount, thus $7,056 in 1996. Under CEIFA, school districts could generate additional revenue through local taxes, thus resulting in disparate per-pupil expenditures; however, the additional revenue was considered unnecessary in terms of providing students with a thorough and efficient education.

The CEIFA also addressed the court's concern in *Abbott III* that special needs school districts needed supplemental educational programs and support services. The act established Early Childhood Program Aid (ECPA) and Demonstrably Effective Programs Aid (DEPA). Through ECPA, special needs districts would receive additional funding for early childhood programs such as full day kindergarten, preschool programs, and other services. DEPA provided funding for special services such as health programs and social service programs for students in special needs districts.

Another important component of CEIFA was measuring performance indicators. Prior to the implementation of CEIFA, student performance was not evaluated until eighth grade. Under CEIFA, New Jersey students would be evaluated in fourth grade with the Elementary School Proficiency Assessment (ESPA), eighth grade through the Early Warning Test (EWT), and in high school through the High School Proficiency Assessment (HSPA). The purpose of the new evaluation system was to give educators and administrators an indication of whether students were meeting the performance goals of the NJCCCS, and what areas required improvement.

Through CEIFA, New Jersey state legislators once again aimed to provide a thorough and efficient education for all students via school funding. In January 1997, The Education Law Center returned to the New Jersey state supreme court to assert that the new funding act violated the *Abbott* rulings.

Abbott IV

In 1997, the New Jersey supreme court in *Abbott IV*[16] declared the CEIFA unconstitutional as applied to special needs districts. The court found that, like QEA, the CEIFA did not insure adequate funding for special needs districts. While CEIFA attempted to link standards to state aid, the court found that there was no concrete system in place ensure that special needs districts had the resources to implement the NJCCCS, rendering it unconstitutional. The court also found that CEIFA failed to address school facilities in the special needs districts, which were in dire condition.

The court asserted that the 'model school district' used to determine the T & E or foundation amount was not representative of a successful school district in the state of New Jersey. The state argued that the additional funds that school districts were able to generate by local revenue under CEIFA were unnecessary to student achievement, and therefore wealthier school districts, although successful, were not used to develop the model school district used in the funding formula. The state claimed that wealthier districts frivolously spend excess capital and therefore should not be used in developing a model school district; however, the court disagreed, asserting that the level of spending for education in the wealthier districts is not attributable solely to inefficiency or directed to educational luxuries. Furthermore, the court found no evidence to support the assertion that all amounts spent by Livingston, Princeton, Millburn, and the other successful districts in excess of the T & E amount constituted educational inefficiency. According to the xourt, those additional funds that successful, wealthier districts were able to generate would only further the disparity between special needs districts and regular districts.

Ultimately, the court determined that one of the key problems with CEIFA was that it treated all school districts equally, rather than taking into account the additional needs of the special needs districts. According to the court:

> [CEIFA] is incapable of assuring that opportunity for children in the special needs districts for any time in the foreseeable future. Although the educational content standards prescribed by the new act are an essential component of a thorough and efficient education, the primary infirmity of the new act inheres in its funding provisions that fail to assure expenditures sufficient to enable students in the special needs districts to meet those standards. Furthermore, the supplemental aid provided by the new act bears no demonstrable relationship to the real needs of the disadvantaged children attending school in the special needs districts.

Although deemed unconstitutional, the court declared that CEIFA may someday result in the improvement of the educational opportunity available to all New Jersey public school students.

In response to *Abbott IV*, the state provided $246 million to the Abbott districts or 30 special needs districts for the 1997–98 school year in order to equalize spending.

Abbott V

In May 1998, the New Jersey supreme court handed down another decision in *Abbott V*,[17] requiring the Commissioner of Education to implement whole-school reform for the 30 special needs districts through Success for All,[18] a comprehensive initiative designed to increase student achievement. The Success for All program focused on reading, writing, and language arts and was designed to help at-risk students succeed in reading. In addition, the court directed the Commissioner to implement full-day kindergarten in the special needs districts. The court also ruled that the special needs districts could request additional funding to implement supplemental programs if the district was able to demonstrate need. The court held:

> If a school demonstrates the need for programs beyond those recommended by the Commissioner, including programs in, or facilities for art, music, and special education, then the Commissioner shall approve such requests and,

when necessary, shall seek appropriations to ensure the funding and resources necessary for their implementation.

The decision in *Abbott V* required implementation of a comprehensive set of reforms for special needs districts, as well as a means for the districts to appeal for additional funding as needed.

The groundbreaking *Abbott* decisions enabled the state of New Jersey to assure funding parity; as a result, students in special needs districts would receive the same per-pupil funding as students in wealthier school districts. The state was—and continues to be—a pioneer in needs-based school reform, helping students in low-income areas achieve academic success.[19]

BASIC SUPPORT PROGRAM

New Jersey's basic support program for funding public schools was set in legislation in 2008 via the School Funding Reform Act[20] (SFRA). The formula incorporated both wealth equalization and categorical aid. Wealth-equalized aid sought fiscal equality by assuring that each school district would receive adequate funds based on local ability to generate tax revenue. The formula called for categorical aid to be disbursed based on a combination of student data and costs associated with pupil-driven performance categories. The SFRA was expressed formulaically as:

Adequacy Budget = (Base Cost + At-Risk Cost
[Based on eligibility for free and reduced lunches]

+

Limited English Proficient Cost

+

Combination [of Limited English Proficient and At-Risk] Cost

+

Special Education Census)

×

Geographic Cost Adjustment

Although the SFRA has been modified over time,[21] categorical aid is still provided based on the following categories: (1) special education, (2) security, (3) transportation, (4) pre-school, (5) debt service aid/benefit payments, and (6) school choice aid.[22]

DEMOGRAPHIC, REVENUE AND EXPENDITURE PROFILES

New Jersey ranks 47th in total land area compared to the 50 states; however, it is ranked second among densely populated states with approximately 1,195.5 people per square mile.[23] Although New Jersey is geographically small compared to the rest of the nation, this densely populated and diverse state is ranked among those states generating and spending the most money on public elementary and secondary education.[24] For Fiscal Year 2012, New Jersey generated $27,091,705,000 in public school system revenue. It ranked fifth among states generating the most public school system revenue, behind only California ($66,581,317,000), Illinois ($29,153,117,000), New York ($58,803,445,000), and Texas ($51,294,202,000).[25] New Jersey generated a median per pupil revenue amount of $19,012 in FY 2012, approximately 62% greater than the national median per-pupil revenue of $11,770. While national median per-pupil revenue decreased for FY 2012 by approximately 2.9%,[26] New Jersey's increased 6.6%.

Demographic Profile

Although New Jersey ranks fifth among the states that generate the most revenue for public education, it is not ranked among the top five states that have the largest populations or largest enrollments. For FY 2012, California had the highest state population with approximately 38,041,000 residents.[27] New Jersey ranked eleventh in states with the highest population, with a total of 8,865,000 inhabitants.

California also had the highest number of pupils enrolled in public schools in 2012, with a total of 6,203,034 students, followed by Texas with 4,844,744 students, and Florida with 2,658,559 students. New Jersey had the 11th highest enrollment with a total of 1,330,330 students.[28]

While New Jersey ranked 11th both in terms of state population as well as enrollments, it ranked 7th among states with the highest personal income for FY 2011. California had the highest personal income with a total approximately $1,683,204,000,000, followed by Texas with $1,053,552,000,000 and New York with $1,012,406,000,000. New Jersey reported total personal income of approximately $471,188,000,000 in 2011.[29]

Revenue Profile

For FY 2012, New Jersey reported $27,091,705,000 in public school revenue.[30] About 5.2% of total revenue ($1,407,750,000) was received from the federal government, 39.31% ($10,650,713,000) from state government, and 55.5% ($15,033,242,000) from local government.

Federal Revenue

In FY 2012 the 50 states and the District of Columbia reported $603.5 billion in total revenue, with 10.1% coming from the federal government ($60.7 billion), 45.1% from state government ($272.4 billion), and 44.8% from local government. In comparison, New Jersey generated only 5.2% of total public school revenue from federal sources. Compared to the top ten states generating the most revenue for public education in 2012, New Jersey generated the least amount of federal revenue[31] (U.S. Census Bureau, 2014).

Sources of federal revenue included funding for Title I, IDEA, child nutrition, and vocational programs, as well as non-specified sources of funding and direct federal aid. Approximately 27% of federal funding to New Jersey ($364,859,000) was for special education. Title I funding accounted for 21% ($293,448,000). Federal child nutrition programs accounted for 20% ($271,261,000). Another 30% ($413,291,000) was received for other and non-specified programs distributed by the state for a variety of federal grant programs such as the Workforce Investment Act, Title V, the Safe and Drug-Free Schools and Community Act, and Mathematics, Science and Teacher Quality grants.[32] Finally, federal funding for vocational programs accounted less than 1% ($8,264,000) of New Jersey's total federal revenue in FY 2012.

State Revenue

For FY 2012, 57% ($5,993,469,000) of all state revenue that New Jersey generated for public school education was through General Formula Assistance. General Formula Assistance includes revenue from income tax and sales tax, as well as non-categorical state assistance programs. Non-categorical programs include foundation funding, flat grants, and state public school fund distributions.

State payments on behalf of local educational agencies (LEAs) accounted for $1,661,998,000 (16%) of state revenue that New Jersey generated in 2012. This revenue was not bestowed directly on school districts; instead, the funds were used for benefits such as employee funds and health benefits. Additionally, revenues may be used to repay school districts for textbooks, telecommunications and school buses provided by the state.

Funding for compensatory programs amounted to $841,039,000 (8%) of public school revenue in 2012. Special education funding accounted for $873,704,000 (8%), an amount approximately 2% higher than the national average. Approximately 1% of state revenue in New Jersey was for transportation programs, with no state revenue generated for vocational programs.[33] Other and non-specified state aid amounted to $903,554,000 (9%); this revenue was used to support the central or school business office in data processing, staff services, and payments for fiscal services. Some revenue is included in this category because it was used for more than one of the programs mentioned in this section and therefore could not be placed in a distinct category.[34]

Local Revenue

Nationally, local sources of revenue accounted for approximately 44% of total public elementary-secondary school system monies in the 50 states and the District of Columbia in FY 2012.[35] In New Jersey, local revenue accounted for a larger percentage of total revenue, as in FY 2012 fully 57% came from local governments.[36]

Since New Jersey relies heavily on property taxes to fund its schools, it is no surprise that it is a state well known for high real estate taxes. New Jersey ranked as the state with the highest median real estate taxes paid in 2009. Further, New Jersey had the highest median real estate taxes as a percentage of median home value in 2009 at 1.89%. In comparison, the state with the lowest median real estate taxes as a percentage of median home value was Louisiana at only .18%.[37] New Jersey's high taxation was born out as 84% ($12,565,156,000) of local revenue came from property taxes in 2012.[38] About 6% ($892,459,000) of local revenue came from parent government contributions which are tax receipts and other amounts appropriated by a parent government and transferred to its independent school system. Revenue from non-school local government amounted to 2% ($250,477,000) of total local revenue. School lunch charges amounted to another 2% ($259,352,000), while less than 1% came from tuition and transportation charges. Another 2% ($292,389,000) of New Jersey's total local revenue came from other charges. Finally, 4%, ($522,573,000) came from other local revenue.[39]

New Jersey is ranked among the states that generate the most revenue for public education. But the majority of New Jersey's public elementary and secondary education resources comes from local sources, with the bulk derived from property tax.

Expenditure Profile

The United States spent $593.8 billion in FY 2012 on public elementary and secondary education. Current spending accounted for $524 billion (88%) of the total expenditure; capital outlay accounted for $50.2 billion (8%); and other expenditures accounted for $19.7 billion (3%) of total spending. In perspective, New Jersey is regarded as high-spending; in that year, New Jersey's total spending amounted to $25,663,828,000 on public schools, earning it fifth place position among states spending the most on schools. About $24,356,836,000 (95%) of funds in New Jersey was used for current spending; another $940,557,000 (3.6%) was allocated to capital outlay; and $366,415,000 (1.4%) was assigned to other expenses.

Of the $524 billion current spending on public schools in the U.S. in FY 2012, approximately $316.6 billion (60%) was spent on instruction; $179.8 billion (34%) went to support services; and $27.5 billion (5%) went to other expenditures. Approximately $14,491,817,000 (59%) was spent on instruction; $8,921,990,000 (37%) was spent on support services to include salaries, wages, and employee benefits; and $943,929,000 (4%) was allocated for other expenses. By comparison in the five states spending the most on public education, New York allocated the highest percentage (70%) to instruction, while California, Illinois, New Jersey, and Texas spent 59% of total expenditures on instruction. Further comparing, New York spent 27% on support services, while Illinois and New Jersey each allocated 37% to support services, while California and Texas expended about 35%. Of the $8,921,990,000 that New Jersey spent on support services, $2,370,498,000 (27%) went to pupil support services for recordkeeping, social work, student accounting, counseling, student appraisal, record maintenance, and placement services. It also included payments made for medical, dental, psychological, nursing and speech services. About $708,738,000 (8%) went to instructional staff support services which including expenditure for supervision of instruction service improvements, curriculum development, instructional staff training, and media, library audiovisual, television, and computer assisted services. About $471,495,000 (5%) was allocated to general administration to include spending for the board of education and office of the superintendent. Payments for school-level administration amounted to $1,141,896,000 (13%). Operation and maintenance of plant was $2,446,947,000 (27%) of total capital disbursement for support services. These funds were expended for building services such as electricity, heating, and air conditioning, as well as maintenance of grounds, property insurance, and security.[40]

New Jersey pupil transportation amounted to $1,215,611,000 (14%) of total expenditures for FY 2012. Other non-specified support services amounted to $566,605,000 (6%), a category that included payments for business support such as in the areas of budgeting, payroll, auditing, and accounting as well as payments for central support such as in the areas planning, research and development.

Finally, school systems in the U.S. in 2012 spent $50,153,239,000 on capital outlay. Approximately 78% of those funds was allocated to construction, 6% to maintaining building and grounds, 4% to instructional equipment, and 12% to other equipment. Additionally, U.S. schools spent $17,951,538,000 in interest on debt and $1,750,817,000 to payments to other governments, which includes payments made to states, counties, cities, and special district school housing authorities including repayment of loans and debt service payments to entities that incur debt instead of the school system as well as payments made to other school systems. In comparison, New Jersey's school systems allocated $940,577,000 to capital outlay; these funds were distributed very similarly to national averages, with approximately 77% of total capital outlay allocated to construction, 6% to maintaining land and existing structures, 4% to instructional equipment, and 13% to other equipment. New Jersey's public school systems also spent $326,161,000 in interest payments on debt and $40,254,000 was allocated to other governments.[41]

Per-Pupil Expenditure Profile

As indicated, New Jersey ranked fourth among states with the highest per-pupil expenditure for Fiscal Year 2012. By comparison, California had the highest revenue per pupil but expended only $9,183 per pupil, while New Jersey spent on average $17,266 per pupil. The state with the lowest mean per-pupil expenditure was Utah, spending on average $6,206. The state with the highest per-pupil expenditure was New York, spending an average $19,552. These data stood across from the average per-pupil expenditure in the U.S. coming in at $10,608.[42] Although national per-pupil spending did not change from FY 2011 to FY 2012, per-pupil spending increased in New Jersey by 8.1%, while New York's per-pupil spending increased 2.5% and the District of Columbia's effort decreased by –5.4%. Other examples included Alaska's increase of 4.3% and Vermont's increase of .4%.

According to the National Education Association, New Jersey had the second highest starting teacher salary in the 2012–2013 school year, with an average of $48,631.[43] New Jersey ranked fifth among states with the highest overall teacher salaries, averaging $68,797, behind New York ($75,279), Massachusetts ($73,129), the District of Columbia ($70,906) and California ($69,324). With high educator salaries, it is understandable that New Jersey ranks among the states spending the most per-pupil. Examples of instructional expenditure amounts during that year included a national average per-pupil expenditure for instruction of $6,430, while New Jersey spent $9,964 and New York spent $13,582 per pupil.

Instructional costs in New Jersey are expected to increase over the next few years, especially given implementation of the Partnership for Assessment of Readiness for College and Careers (PARCC) examinations.[44] New Jersey spent about $25.50 per pupil for testing during the 2014–2015 school year, amounting to approximately $22 million. As a result of PARCC, within four years that cost could increase to $108 million. This controversial exam first made its debut in 2009 and is a computer-administered test covering all students in grades 3–11 in Arkansas, Colorado, District of Columbia, Illinois, Louisiana, Maryland, Massachusetts, Mississippi, New Jersey, New Mexico, Ohio, and Rhode Island.

Finally and although New Jersey is ranked fourth among states spending the most on public schools, the Census Bureau only takes into account the cost of instruction (salaries and wages, employee benefits) and support services (pupil support, instructional staff support, general administration, and school administration). Excluded in this calculation are capital outlay, debt service and interfund transfers per-pupil. For FY 2011, the New Jersey Department of Education revised its reporting calculation to include following indicators: pensions and social security payments, transportation costs for all students (including those bussed to schools outside the district), food service expenditures, payments made by the district to other public and private school districts, debt service, legal services, and estimates of school districts' share of debt service paid by the state for construction grants and School Development Authority Projects.[45] This calculation paints a more detailed picture of how funds are allocated to school districts and enables a more accurate comparison among districts. Concomitantly, a recent development instituted by a former governor maintains that, prior to any new money being allocated to a school district, comprehensive reports must be submitted to the state illustrating how money was spent in prior academic years—the concept of balancing the budget and increased district accountability are the end goal to show how funding was spent on student development.

Table 32.1 shows recent yearly amounts for New Jersey per-pupil expenditures for all operating types by major categories.

TABLE 32.1 State Average All Operating Types of Expenditures in New Jersey School Districts Fiscal Years 2015–2018

Total Spending Per Pupil 2015–16 Costs Amount per Pupil: $20,316 2016–17 Costs Amount per Pupil: $20,849	**Total Legal Services Costs Per Pupil** Per Pupil Amount (15–16 actual costs):$47 Per Pupil Amount (2016–17 actual costs): $47 Per Pupil Amount (2017–18 budget): $43
Budgetary Per Pupil Cost 2015–16 Actual Costs Amount per Pupil: $14,940 2016–17 Actual Costs Amount per Pupil: $15,258 2017–18 Budgeted Costs Amount per Pupil: $15,955	**Administration Salaries and Benefits** Per Pupil Amount (15–16 actual costs): $1,309 Per Pupil Amount (2016–17 actual costs): $1,344 Per Pupil Amount (2017–18 budget): $1,895
Total Classroom Instruction Per Pupil Amount (15–16 actual costs): $8,828 Per Pupil Amount (2016–17 actual costs): $8,999 Per Pupil Amount (2017–18 budget): $9,447	**Total Operations of Maintenance of Plant** Per Pupil Amount (15–16 actual costs): $1,779 Per Pupil Amount (2016–17 actual costs): $1,812 Per Pupil Amount (2017–18 budget): $1,895
Classroom Salaries and Benefits Per Pupil Amount (15–16 actual costs): $8,301 Per Pupil Amount (2016–17 actual costs): $8,464 Per Pupil Amount (2017–18 budget): $321	**Salaries/Benefits - Operations of Maintenance of Plant** Per Pupil Amount (15–16 actual costs): $898 Per Pupil Amount (2016–17 actual costs): $906 Per Pupil Amount (2017–18 budget): $954

(continued)

TABLE 32.1 State Average All Operating Types of Expenditures in New Jersey School Districts Fiscal Years 2015–2018 (continued)

Classroom General Supplies and Textbooks Per Pupil Amount (15–16 actual costs): $296 Per Pupil Amount (2016–17 actual costs): $288 Per Pupil Amount (2017–18 budget): $321	**Board Contributions to the Food Service Program** Per Pupil Amount (15–16 actual costs): $47 Per Pupil Amount (2016–17 actual costs): $74 Per Pupil Amount (2017–18 budget): $48
Classroom Purchased Services and Other Per Pupil Amount (15–16 actual cost): $232 Per Pupil Amount (2016–17 actual costs): $246 Per Pupil Amount (2017–18 budget): $286	**Extracurricular Costs** Per Pupil Amount (15–16 actual costs): $289 Per Pupil Amount (2016–17 actual costs): $299 Per Pupil Amount (2017–18 budget): $319
Total Support Services Per Pupil Amount (15–16 actual costs): $2,377 Per Pupil Amount (2016–17 actual costs): $2,437 Per Pupil Amount (2017–18 budget): $2,577	**Personal Services - Employee Benefits** % of Total Salaries (15–16): 29.7% %of Total Salaries (2016–17): 30.1% % of Total Salaries (2017–18): 32.7%
Support Services Salaries and Benefits Per Pupil Amount (15–16 actual costs): $2,058 Per Pupil Amount (2016–17 actual costs): $2,098 Per Pupil Amount (2017–18 budget): $2,196	**Total Equipment Cost** Per Pupil Costs (15–16): $85 Per Pupil Costs (2016–17): $88 Per Pupil Costs (2017–18): $73
Total Administrative Costs Per Pupil Per Pupil Amount (15–16 actual costs): $1,635 Per Pupil Amount (20166–17 actual costs): $1,679 Per Pupil Amount (2017–18 budget): $1,726	

Source: State of New Jersey Department of Education (2018). https://www.nj.gov/cgi-bin/education/csg/18/csggrsum.pl?string=L.%20ALL&maxhits=10000

SUMMARY

Although geographically small, New Jersey is a densely populated and diverse state ranking among the top spenders in the nation on public education. For FY 2012, New Jersey ranked fifth among states that generated and spent the most for public elementary and secondary education. The majority of school funding in New Jersey comes from local sources. In 2012, about 56% came from local revenue, 39% from state revenue, and 5% from federal revenue. Consequently, New Jersey is a state with high property taxes.

While New Jersey is ranked among the top state spenders, it is also one of the most diverse states. "New Jersey has among the most intensely economically and racially segregated public school districts in the nation."[46] Some New Jersey districts report student poverty rates of 80%, while wealthier districts report 4%.[47] In light of need-based differences, it is important to keep in mind that some students need more financial support than others. The per-pupil expenditure is calculated by a simple mathematic equation—total spending divided by total students. This equation does not take into account the needs of students.

Per-pupil revenue and per-pupil spending are used to compare education funding within a state or among states. Assessing spending by pupil may not be the best indicator of funding and spending because all students across the state are treated equally regardless of need. The amount of funding per-pupil comparison is highly inappropriate and misleading, according to the former head of the Division of Finance for the New Jersey Department of Education, because it fails to take into account the differences in revenues and expenditures generated by the stark variations in concentrations of student poverty and other student needs.[48]

The Ed Law Center recommends using a Funding Per Weighted Pupil calculation to assess per-pupil spending within a state. This calculation takes into account the needs of at risk students, limited English proficiency (LEP) students, and students who are both LEP and at-risk. If the Census Bureau used a weighted formula such as what the Ed Law Center proposes, it would paint a much clearer picture of how education funding is being distributed.[49]

While New Jersey has remained in the spotlight for high property taxes and high teacher salaries, it is clear that education's expenses are paying off. According to the *Quality Counts 2015 State Report Card*,[50] a comprehensive analysis of state performance in public education, New Jersey ranked second. The report grades states based on three categories: Chance for Success, K–12 Achievement, and School Finance. New Jersey earned a B for Overall State Grade (the highest letter grade awarded in category), a B+ in Chance for Success, a B+ in School Finance, and a B- in Student Achievement. By comparison, the nation earned a C for Overall Performance, C+ in Chance for Success, C in School Finance, and C- in Student Achievement.

A pioneer in needs-based school reform, New Jersey continues to improve its school finance system to ensure parity funding and thereby help impoverished students achieve academic success. Decades of groundbreaking *Abbott* decisions have shaped New Jersey's school finance in an effort to ensure a 'thorough and efficient' education for all as outlined in the state constitution. Each *Abbott* decision has allowed the New Jersey supreme court to better define what constitutes a thorough and efficient education and how to provide children in the state of New Jersey with equal access to high quality education. According to the Ed Law Center:

> New Jersey has a high degree of "equity" in its school finance system, with small gaps between the poor and wealthiest districts. Many states do not spend enough on public education and have large funding gaps among districts, with low poverty districts far outspending higher poverty districts.[51]

New Jersey continues to make changes to its funding model to ensure equity for students within the state.

NOTES

1. 62 N.J. 473 (1973).
2. See, e.g., *Abbott v. Burke* (1985), 495 A. 2d 376 - NJ: Supreme Court; *Abbott v. Burke* (1990), 575 A. 2d 359 - NJ: Supreme Court; *Abbott v. Burke* (1994), 643 A. 2d 575 - NJ: Supreme Court; Abbott v. Burke (1997), 693 A. 2d 417 - NJ: Supreme Court; *Abbott v. Burke* (1998), 710 A. 2d 450 - NJ: Supreme Court.
3. M.E. Goertz and M. Weiss (2009). "Assessing Success in School Finance Litigation: The Case of New Jersey." *Education, Equity and the Law.* No. 1. New York: The Campaign for Educational Equity.
4. Public School Education Act of 1975, N.J. STAT. ANN. 18A:4A,7A,1-33 (West 1989); Quality Education Act of 1990, ch. 52, §§ 1-33, 1990 N.J. Laws 587-613 (codified at N.J. STAT. ANN. §§ 18A:7D-1 (West Supp. 1994)).
5. *Abbott v. Burke*, 100 N.J. 269, 495 A.2d 376, N.J.,1985.
6. *Abbott v. Burke*, 119 N.J. 287 (June 1990).
7. 1990 N.J. Laws 587 (codified as amended at N.J. STAT. ANN. §§ 18A:7D (West 1999)), *repealed by* 1991 N.J. Laws 200 & Comprehensive Educational Improvement and Financing Act of 1996, 1996 N.J. Laws 954.
8. J. Ellis and R.J. Swissler, Funding Education under the Quality Education Act of 1990. New Jersey Department of Education (1991). Retrieved from http://www.njleg.state.nj.us/PropertyTaxSession/OPI/FundingEducation.pdf
9. New Jersey Department of Education. (n.d.). Abbotts—History of Funding Equity. Retrieved from http://www.state.nj.us/education/archive/abbotts/chrono/
10. *Abbott III* 643 A. 2d 575 (1994).
11. New Jersey school districts are grouped into District Factor Groups which are a measure of the school districts' socioeconomic status. The categories are: A, B, CD, DE, FG, GH, I, and J. The lowest SES school districts are labeled as A or B, while the highest SES districts are labeled as I or J.
12. https://www.nj.gov/education/cccs/
13. ftp://www.njleg.state.nj.us/19961997/PL96/138_.htm
14. M.E. Goertz and M. Edwards. "In Search of Excellence for All: The Courts and New Jersey School Finance Reform." *Journal of Education Finance*, (1999) 25(1), 5–31.
15. State of New Jersey (1996). Comprehensive Educational Improvement and Financing Act. http://www.njleg.state.nj.us/PropertyTaxSession/OPI/BriefExplanationCEIFA.pdf
16. 693 A. 2d 417 (1997).
17. 710 A. 2d 450 (1998).
18. https://www.state.nj.us/education/archive/abbotts/wsr/shu/chap2.htm
19. Ed. Law Center. "The History of Abbott v. Burke." (n.d.). Retrieved from http://www.edlawcenter.org/cases/abbott-v-burke/abbott-history.html
20. "School Funding Reform Act of 2008" (SFRA), P.L.2007, c.260.
21. As amended, NJ S2 (2018). Retrieved from https://www.billtrack50.com/BillDetail/985333

22. New Jersey Department of Education. "A Formula for Success: All Children, All Communities." Retrieved from http://nj.gov/education/sff/reports/AllChildrenAllCommunities.pdf.
23. States Ranked by Size and Population (2012). Retrieved from http://www.ipl.org/div/stateknow/popchart.html
24. S.Q. Cornman. "Revenues and Expenditures for Public Elementary and Secondary School Districts: School Year 2011–2012 (Fiscal Year 2012)." National Center for Education Statistics (2015). Retrieved from http://nces.ed.gov/pubs2014/2014303.pdf
25. Ibid.
26. The National Center for Education Statistics adjusted the 2011 median per-pupil total revenues to account for inflation from 2011–2012.
27. U.S. Census Bureau. (2014). *Public Education Finances: 2012.* Retrieved from http://www2.census.gov/govs/school/12f33pub.pdf
28. Ibid.
29. Ibid.
30. See S. Q. Cornman. "Revenues and Expenditures for Public Elementary and Secondary School Districts: School Year 2011–2012 (Fiscal Year 2012)." National Center for Education Statistics (2015). Retrieved from http://nces.ed.gov/pubs2014/2014303.pdf Further, the Census Bureau reports that New Jersey generated a total of $26,616,365 in elementary and secondary revenues. The National Center for Data Statistics includes financial information from independent charter school districts, while the Census bureau only collects information for school districts that are considered a government entity as defined by the Census Bureau. Charter schools with boards that are not elected or appointed by elected officials are not included in the data provided by the Census Bureau (NCES, 2015).
31. U.S. Census Bureau. (2014). *Public Education Finances: 2012.* Retrieved from http://www2.census.gov/govs/school/12f33pub.pdf
32. Ibid.
33. Ibid.
34. Ibid.
35. According to the Census Bureau, total public elementary-secondary school revenue in 2012 was $594,531,633,000. Total local revenue from local sources in 2012 was $264,567,460,000.
36. According to the Census Bureau, New Jersey's public schools generated a total of $26,616,365,000 in federal, state and local aid in 2012. $14,843,386,000 came from local sources in 2012.
37. Tax Foundation's Data Analysis Division. (2010). New census data on property taxes on homeowners. Retrieved from http://taxfoundation.org/article/new-census-data-property-taxes-homeowners-2
38. The Census Bureau reported a total of $14,843,386,000 in local revenue for the 2012 fiscal year.
39. U.S. Census Bureau. (2014). *Public Education Finances: 2012.* Retrieved from http://www2.census.gov/govs/school/12f33pub.pdf
40. Ibid.
41. Ibid.

42. Ibid.
43. National Education Association. "2012–2013 Average Starting Teacher Salaries by State." (n.d.). Retrieved from http://www.nea.org/home/2012-2013-average-starting-teacher-salary.html
44. Kelly Heyboer, NJ Advance Media. "PARCC Exams: How Pearson Landed the Deal to Produce N.J.'s Biggest Test." (2015). Retrieved from https://www.nj.com/education/2015/03/parcc_exams_how_pearson_landed_the_deal_to_produce.html
45. New Jersey Department of Education. (2013). "Taxpayers' Guide to Education Spending 2013." Retrieved from http://www.state.nj.us/education/guide/2013.
46. Ed. Law Center. The Right to Special Education in New Jersey. (2008). Retrieved from http://www.edlawcenter.org/assets/files/pdfs/publications/Rights_ SpecialEducation_Guide.pdf
47. Ed. Law Center. The Right Way to Compare NJ Education Funding. (2010). Retrieved from http://www.edlawcenter.org/news/archives/school-funding/the-right-way-to-compare-nj-education-funding.html
48. Ibid.
49. Ibid.
50. Education Week. (2015). *Quality Counts Introduces New State Report Card; U.S. Earns C, and Massachusetts Ranks First in the Nation.* [Press Release]. Retrieved from http://www.edweek.org/media/qualitycounts2015_release.pdf
51. Law Center. The Right Way to Compare NJ Education Funding. (2010). Retrieved from http://www.edlawcenter.org/news/archives/school-funding/the-right-way-to-compare-nj-education-funding.html

CHAPTER 33

New Mexico

Staff Writer[1]

GENERAL BACKGROUND[2]

New Mexico became a state in 1912, and its constitution today devotes three clauses in particular support of public schools. Article XII[3] defines state responsibility for public education:

> §1 provides "A uniform system of free public schools sufficient for the education of, and open to, all the children of school age in the state shall be established and maintained;"
>
> §8 provides "The legislature shall provide for the training of teachers in the normal schools or otherwise so that they may become proficient in both the English and Spanish languages, to qualify them to teach Spanish-speaking pupils and students in the public schools and educational institutions of the state, and shall provide proper means and methods to facilitate the teaching of the English language and other branches of learning to such pupils and students;"
>
> §10 provides "Children of Spanish descent in the State of New Mexico shall never be denied the right and privilege of admission and attendance in or other public educational institutions of the state, and they shall never be classed in separate schools, but shall forever enjoy perfect equality with other children in all public schools and educational institutions of the state...."

Notwithstanding, debate about public school funding and attendant litigation have marked New Mexico's history. In the early 1970s, plaintiffs began a challenge to the constitutionality of the state's education finance system alleging that expenditures impermissibly varied depending on local school district wealth. Settlement was reached before trial when the New Mexico legislature shifted funding for schools to the state level in search of providing more equal resources to each district. The 1974 Public School Finance Act[4] resulted in state funding exceeding 80% of education's costs.

Despite changes to the school aid formula, school facilities in many low wealth school districts deteriorated. In 1998, districts again sued in *Zuni School District v. State*,[5] claiming that the funding system for capital projects was unconstitutional because local districts still bore primary responsibility for funding bricks and mortar. A trial court ordered the state to implement a uniform funding system for capital improvements.

By 2001, a proposal to fund a $1.2 billion capital program was legislatively defeated. Instead, the state offered a $400 million capital program and created a school funding scheme aimed at establishing a standards-based adequacy level for all school districts. However, the new system faltered, and in 2006 an additional $90 million was directed to capital projects in high growth areas. Although plaintiffs argued that the added funding was unfair to smaller districts, the cause was vacated in 2008.

In 2007, a New Mexico school funding lawsuit made its way to the U.S. Supreme Court, holding in *Zuni Public School District No. 89 v. Department of Education*[6] that federal impact aid deducted from state aid eligibility through the state school finance plan was constitutional. Plaintiff school districts were located on federal and tribal lands with poor property tax bases, qualifying them for federal impact aid. The argument was based in federal impact aid provisions prohibiting a state from offsetting federal aid by reducing state aid to local districts, together with an exception in the statute permitting a state to reduce its own local funding on account of the federal aid if the Secretary of Education found that the state program 'equalizes expenditures' among local school districts.[7] Federal wealth neutrality tests had shown compliance so that no fault was found in New Mexico's aid offset.

Particularly impactful recent litigation occurred in the consolidated actions of *Martinez v. State* and *Yazzie v. State*. Two separate groups of parents of educationally disadvantaged Latino and Native American students had filed adequacy lawsuits charging that the state had denied children a 'uniform' and 'sufficient' education as guaranteed by Article XII §1 of the state constitution, along with claims of violating the state's equal protection clause. The lawsuits had attacked the state's funding level, a claim supported by an external evaluation[8] concluding the state was underfunding schools by approximately $350 million. Other claims were imbedded, including arguments involving special education and teacher evaluation. State efforts to dismiss[9] were denied in 2014, and the cases were consolidated for trial.

In July 2018, a New Mexico district court held the state's school finance system to be in violation of the state's education clause, its equal protection clause, and its due process clause.[10] The court gave the state until April 2019 to take "...immediate steps to ensure that New Mexico schools have the resources necessary to give at-risk students the opportunity to obtain a uniform and sufficient education that prepares them for college and career."[11]

BASIC SUPPORT PROGRAM[12]

New Mexico's school funding formula roots originated in the Public School Finance Act of 1974[13] which attempted to guarantee a fairer statewide distribution of legislative dollars. The formula was seen as innovative at the time because it dramatically reduced reliance on local property taxes.

The current state aid formula uses factors to differentiate the cost of serving students with different needs and other school district variables. The state aid formula is membership-based, wherein enrollment uses multipliers by grade level, pupil counts in special education, bilingual education, and at-risk programs, along with teacher training and experience, district and school size, and other factors. The resulting number of 'units' is multiplied by a dollar value set by the New Mexico Public Education Department for total program cost. That amount is then adjusted for local and federal revenue, resulting in a state equalization guarantee tied to appropriation levels. In the end, each school district or charter school receives a lump sum based on the funding formula. Formula dollars are not earmarked — a local district or charter school can allocate monies according to local priorities as long as various statutory and regulatory guidelines are met.

Most state school funding in New Mexico is sourced from the state's general fund. Sources of funding include the public schools' share of interest earned on the land grant permanent fund, the depository for certain income earned through activity on state trust land, and other income from state trust lands designated to benefit public schools. Federal Mineral Leasing Act revenues are also appropriated to schools for purchasing instructional materials and are distributed outside of the formula, as are state and federal funds for transportation and other categorial expenses and specific special programs managed by the New Mexico Public Education Department.

Formula Structure and Operation[14]

New Mexico's school finance formula is illustrated in Figure 33.1 and Figure 33.2. Figure 33.1 identifies the revenue sources comprising school

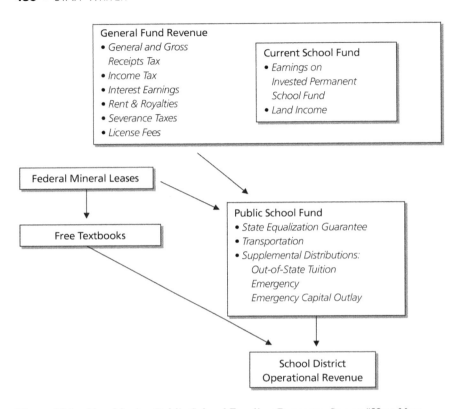

Figure 33.1 New Mexico Public School Funding Revenue. *Source:* "How New Mexico Public Schools are Funded." New Mexico Public Education Department, School Budget and Finance Analysis Bureau (April 2016), p.1. https://webnew.ped.state.nm.us/wp-content/uploads/2017/12/SBFAB_home_How-New-Mexico-Schools-Are-Funded-4-7-16.pdf

funding, while Figure 33.2 parses the interplay among major equalization formula elements. In sum, an array of resources is fed to a state aid formula that is a product of adjusted pupil membership multiplied by teacher experience and education indices plus adjustments for special features related to local school district variables.

Almost all revenue shown in Figure 33.1 is distributed to schools through the Public School Fund. An exception is the Free Textbook appropriation which is made from federal mineral leasing revenue.

The Public School Fund is comprised of three distinct distributions. The State Equalization Guarantee (SEG) makes up more than 90% of school districts' operations revenue. The Transportation distribution relies on a regression analysis of prior year transportation expenditures to determine

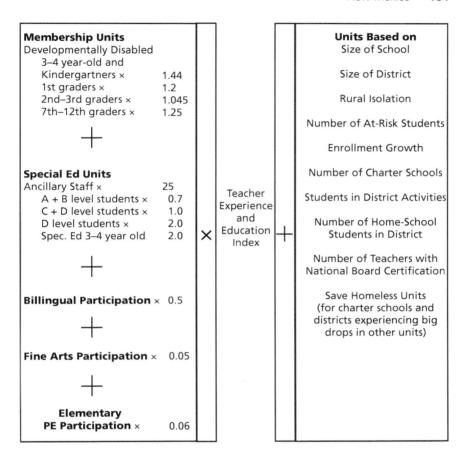

Figure 33.2 New Mexico Public School Funding Formula Elements 2018. *Source:* New Mexico Legislative Finance Committee. "Finance Facts: Public School Funding Formula." (April 2018). https://www.nmlegis.gov/Entity/LFC/Documents/Finance_Facts/finance%20facts%20public%20school%20funding%20formula.pdf

base funding. Supplemental distributions make up the remainder, with elements relating to out-of-state tuition, emergency funds, and emergency capital outlay. As indicated, formula dollars received by local school districts are not earmarked so that districts have significant spending latitude within statutory and regulatory guidelines.

As indicated, Figure 33.2 identifies the major program costs contained in the state equalization formula. The primary driver is program cost differentials based in pupil needs assessment. A program cost for each school district is determined by multiplying the pupil full-time equivalency (FTE) by grade level by the respective cost differentials, with the result called 'units.'

> Sum of Units × T&E Multiplier Index = Adjusted Program Units + Unit Adjustments = Grand Total Units
>   ↓
> Grand Total Units × Unit Value* = Program Cost − 75% Non-Categorical Revenue − Conservation Deducts
>   = **STATE GUARANTEE**
>
> * The initial program unit value was $4,053.55 for 2017–18.

Figure 33.3 New Mexico Public School Funding Formula Calculating 2018. *Source:* Staff Writer (2019).

Units are next summed and multiplied by the district's Training and Experience Index (T&E) to produce the adjusted program unit. There is an accompanying list of add-ons to the adjusted program unit as shown in the right side column of Figure 33.2.

The SEG derives from these program cost calculations. A school district's SEG is the amount of money the state guarantees to defray most of the school district's program cost. The exact amount is determined by adding together revenue coming into the district as the result of a required half-mill property tax levy plus Impact Aid revenue after excluding special education revenue plus any revenue generated through Forest Reserve funds. The result is multiplied by 75% to determine the revenue for which the state takes credit. The product is then subtracted from program cost as seen in Figure 33.3.[15]

Revenues flowing to New Mexico's public schools are therefore driven by needs-based FTE variables adjusted for local differences in a state/local funding partnership. The state equalization guarantee can be expressed as in Figure 33.3.

CHARTER SCHOOLS

Since 1993, the state of New Mexico has actively participated in the charter school movement. Charter schools may be authorized either by local school districts or by the State Public Education Commission.[16] In 2018–2019, 56 charter schools were authorized in the state of New Mexico. Growth is limited to 15 new charters opening each year. Similarly, charter school are limited to enrolling no more than 10% of students in the district where the charter is located. In the 2013–2014 school year, approximately 84 charter schools enrolled slightly more than 21,000 students. By comparison, 26,340 students were attending 97 charter schools in 2018, accounting for approximately 7.5% of statewide total school enrollment.[17]

Funding for New Mexico's charter schools closely adheres to how the state's regular public schools are financed. Per-pupil funding is nearly identical, with state-authorized charter schools also eligible for all relevant federal funds. Consequently, New Mexican charter schools may not receive less than 98% of school-generated program costs, and authorizers may deduct 2% of program costs for administrative fees.[18] The school choice option extends beyond charter schools, as school districts are allowed to operate magnet schools and open enrollment policies generally permit transfer from any low performing public school to any eligible school of choice.[19]

Charter schools are also eligible for facility assistance in New Mexico. Per-pupil state funds are available to assist with lease payments, and charters can apply for tax-exempt bonds from the state facilities authority. Charters also can access tax-exempt county debt, and school districts must share local facilities funds and must make available unused district facilities.[20] Virtual schools are not explicitly allowed; however, regulations for distance learning, including online schools, encompass charter schools that offer distance learning programs, all of which must be located in the state.[21]

SUMMARY

Although New Mexico's 1974 school finance formula was long regarded as highly equalized due to its centralized nature and independence from heavy reliance on local property tax bases, it is not without critics today. The *2018 Kids Count Data Book*[22] ranked New Mexico last among the 50 states in 2018. The charter school footprint is growing, and at the same time per-pupil spending has declined in New Mexico, down from $10,477 per pupil in Fiscal Year 2010 to $9,535 in FY 2014.[23] Although New Mexico spent more on schools than several surrounding states in the comparison timeframe, pupil performance lagged in the same era. And particularly the recent litigation in *Martinez* in late 2018 created uncertainty about the future as the court retained jurisdiction, warning that injunctive relief would be granted if the legislature failed to provide solutions by the prescribed date. Importantly, the court also defined at-risk to include students along economic dimensions, finding that the vast majority are at risk given that 71.6% of students in New Mexico fit the profile of low income and more.[24]

The goals of plaintiffs and reformers say that solutions are only available through a school funding system that:

- *Embraces, reflects, and incorporates the cultural and linguistic heritage* of diverse communities as a foundation for all learning;
- *Provides extended learning opportunities* like summer school and more time in the classroom;

- *Values teachers and educators* and puts them in a position to succeed;
- *Allows all children to access early learning* and pre-kindergarten programs;
- *Offers services such as counseling and health clinics* that promote learning;
- *Ensures [that] schools receive financial resources* required to meet the needs of all children.[25]

NOTES

1. No state-based expert was available to author this chapter at time of publication. The chapter is drawn from multiple sources as footnoted and represents the editorial staff's interpretation of issues, trends and findings regarding the state of New Mexico. For additional information and detail, contact the New Mexico Public Education Department.
2. This section borrows from and adds extended documentation and interpretation to the discussion found at SchoolFundingInfo.com, "New Mexico." (2019). Retrieved from http://schoolfunding.info/litigation-map/new-mexico/
3. N.M. Constitution, As adopted January 21, 1911, and as Subsequently Amended by the People in General and Special Elections 1911 through 2017. New Mexico Compilation Commission (2017). Retrieved from http://www.sos.state.nm.us/nmconst2017.pdf
4. Ch. 8, §16 (1974).
5. CV-98-14-II (Dist. Ct., McKinley County Oct. 14, 1999).
6. 550 U.S. 81 (2007).
7. 20 U. S. C. §7709(b)(1).
8. American Institutes for Research. "An Independent Comprehensive Study of the New Mexico Public School Funding Formula: Final Report." (2008). Retrieved from https://www.air.org/sites/default/files/downloads/report/An-Independent-Comprehensive-Study-New-Mexico-Public-School-Funding-Formula-2008.pdf
9. Motion to dismiss in *Martinez* (November 14, 2014). Retrieved from http://schoolfunding.info/wp-content/uploads/2017/01/Denied-NM-motion-to-dimiss.pdf
10. *Martinez et. al. v. State of New Mexico* No. D-101-CV-2014-00793 consolidated with *Yazzie et. al. v. State of New Mexico* No. D-101-CV-2014-02224. Decision & Order. 1st Judicial District Court. Filed July 20, /2018. Retrieved from http://schoolfunding.info/wp-content/uploads/2018/08/Martinez-NM-decision-2018-1.pdf. See also Court's Findings of Fact and Conclusions of Law and Order re Final Judgment. 1st Judicial District Court. Filed December 20, 2018. Retrieved from http://nmpovertylaw.org/wp-content/uploads/2019/01/Courts-Findings-of-Fact-and-Conclusions-of-Law-2018-12-20.pdf.
11. Ibid. *Martinez*, p. 74.
12. Formula descriptions and interpretations hereafter rely in significant part on data found at the New Mexico Legislature's site https://www.nmlegis.gov; also, related links including https://www.nmlegis.gov/Entity/LFC/Finance_Facts (2018), as well as the New Mexico Public Education Department's

School Budget and Finance Analysis site https://webnew.ped.state.nm.us/bureaus/school-budget-finance-analysis/.
13. As amended, Chapter 22, Article 8 NMSA (1978).
14. This section closely follows Hanna Skandera and Paul Aguilar, "How New Mexico Public Schools are Funded." New Mexico Public Education Department, School Budget and Finance Analysis Bureau (April 2016). Retrieved from https://webnew.ped.state.nm.us/wp-content/uploads/2017/12/SBFAB_home_How-New-Mexico-Schools-Are-Funded-4-7-16.pdf.
15. Description condensed from Skandera and Aguilar, "How New Mexico Public Schools are Funded." New Mexico Public Education Department, School Budget and Finance Analysis Bureau (April 2016). Retrieved from https://webnew.ped.state.nm.us/wp-content/uploads/2017/12/SBFAB_home_How-New-Mexico-Schools-Are-Funded-4-7-16.pdf. *Additional note:* Districts participating in the Utility Conservation program have an additional subtraction from the program cost to be held in a separate fund for that program. Similarly, 90% of amounts under the Energy Efficiency and Renewable Energy Bonding Act are deducted for transfer to the New Mexico Finance Authority.
16. New Mexico Public Education Department, Public Education Commission. (2019). Retrieved from https://webnew.ped.state.nm.us/bureaus/public-education-commission/.
17. NewMexicoKidsCan. "What Are Charter Schools? A Look at New Mexico's School Landscape." (2019). Retrieved from https://nmkidscan.org/wp-content/uploads/sites/15/2018/06/NM-CharterSchools.pdf.
18. N.M. Stat. Ann. § 22-8B-13.
19. National Conference of State Legislatures, Interactive Guide to Public School Choice. "New Mexico. (2019). Retrieved from http://www.ncsl.org/research/education/interactive-guide-to-school-choice.aspx#/
20. Education Commission of the States: Individual State Profile. "New Mexico." (January 2018). Retrieved from http://ecs.force.com/mbdata/mbstprofile?Rep= CSP17&st=New%20Mexico
21. N.M. Admin. Code 6.30.8, N.M. Admin. Code 6.80.4.18. For more detail, see Education Commission of the States, fn. 19 above.
22. Annie E. Casey Foundation. "2018 Kids Count Data Book: State Trends in Child Well-Being." (2018). Retrieved from https://www.nmvoices.org/archives/12369
23. NewMexicoKidsCan.org. "State of Education in New Mexico 2018." (2019). Retrieved from https://nmkidscan.org/wp-content/uploads/sites/15/2017/09/SoE-NM-WEB.pdf
24. SchoolFundingInfo.com, "New Mexico." (2019). Retrieved from http://schoolfunding.info/litigation-map/new-mexico/
25. New Mexico Center on Law and Poverty. "Education: The Opportunity." (2019). Retrieved from http://www.nmpovertylaw.org.

CHAPTER 34

New York

Brian O. Brent, Ph.D.
Professor
Associate Dean for Graduate Studies
University of Rochester

Karen J. DeAngelis, Ph.D.
Associate Professor
Chair Educational Leadership
Associate Dean for Academic Programs
University of Rochester

GENERAL BACKGROUND

The state of New York employs a system of fiscal federalism, with funding for public schools deriving from three sources: approximately 4% from federal sources, 42% from state formulae aids and grants, and 55% from local sources.[1,2]

The state's general fund provides approximately 78% of the funds supporting state aid for public schools, wherein the major sources of revenue are state income and sales taxes. About 10% of state support for public schools comes from the School Tax Relief program (STAR), and the balance of support (approximately 12%) from a Special Revenue Fund that accrues state lottery, video lottery terminal, and commercial gaming receipts.[3] The state earmarks all lottery and gaming proceeds for public P–12 education. The state has also established that the general fund will guarantee any shortfalls in lottery revenues for schools.[4]

Funding Public Schools in the United States and Indian Country, pages 487–504
Copyright © 2019 by Information Age Publishing
All rights of reproduction in any form reserved.

In 2007, the state enacted Foundation Aid to replace approximately 30 funding streams. The state now distributes revenue to school districts using about 40 aid programs. Foundation Aid, the state's largest aid program, accounts for approximately 68% of total state aid.[5] The state also allocates aid to districts based on wealth-equalized percentages of actual expenditures (e.g., building aid, and flat grants per pupil e.g., textbook aid).

Over the decades, state aid as a percentage of total expenditures has varied considerably. State aid as a percent of local expenditures was 31.5% in 1944–45. By 1968–69, this figure had increased to 48.1%. In the 1970s, state aid levels gradually declined to 37.6%. Throughout the 1980s, state aid levels increased steadily and again exceeded 40%, followed by decline during the fiscal crisis of the early 1990s. In 2001–2002, state aid as a percent of total expenditures reached an all-time high of 48.2%. State aid declined markedly again in 2011–2012 following the downturn in the economy. In 2016–2017, the state's share of total expenditures was approximately 42%.[6]

The state has 674 school districts employing eight or more teachers and are eligible for 'regular' state aid.[7] The state's five largest urban districts, commonly referred to as the Big Five, are fiscally dependent on city governments for local funding (i.e., Buffalo, New York City, Rochester, Syracuse, and Yonkers). All other districts are fiscally independent (i.e., having independent taxing and borrowing authority). The state also has 37 Boards of Cooperative Educational Services (BOCES) that provide shared educational services and programs to component districts. Currently, BOCES services are not available for the Big Five city school districts.

The state provides a need/resource capacity indicator for each school district as a measure of the district's ability to meet student needs with local resources. This index is a ratio of a district's estimated poverty percentage (i.e., census poverty and free- and reduced-price lunch percentages) and its combined wealth ratio (see Table 34.1).

TABLE 34.1 New York School District Need/Resource Capacity

Need/Resource Capacity	Number of Districts
Big Five City Districts–High Need	5
Urban/Suburban–High Need	45
Rural–High Need	153
Average Need	336
Low Need	135

Source: The University of the State of New York, The State Education Department, *Need/Resource Capacity Categories* (2018). http://www.p12.nysed.gov/irs/accountability/2011–12/NeedResourceCapacityIndex.pdg

BASIC SUPPORT PROGRAM

Foundation Aid

Introduced in Fiscal Year 2008, New York relies on a foundation aid formula to allocate general (unrestricted) aid to public school districts.[8] In FY 2018, the state distributed an estimated $17,174.2 million in foundation aid, representing 68% of the total state aid distributed statewide.[9] The state bases the formulae on four components:[10]

- Adjusted Foundation Amount (AFA);
- Expected minimum local contribution per pupil;
- Number of total aidable foundation pupil units (TAFPU) in the district;
- Foundation Aid payable.

Adjusted Foundation Amount

The state holds that AFA "reflects the average per-pupil cost of general education instruction in successful school districts... it is adjusted annually to reflect change in the consumer price index."[11] Expressed as a formula:

$$\text{AFA} = \text{Foundation Amount} \times \text{CPI Change} \times \text{Phase in Foundation \%} \times \text{Regional Cost Index (RCI)} \times \text{Pupil Need Index (PNI)}$$

For FY 2018, AFA = $6,340 × 1.013 (CPI) × 1.0 (Phase in %) = $6,422, before RCI and PNI were factored in.[12]

Regional Cost Index. The state adjusts a district's AFA amount using a Regional Cost Index (RCI) based on an analysis of labor market costs in non-education fields. Enacted in 2006, the RCIs for New York's nine labor regions are shown in Table 34.2.[13]

TABLE 34.2 New York Regional Cost Index

Region	RCI
Long Island/NYC	1.425
Hudson Valley	1.314
Finger Lakes	1.141
Capital District	1.124
Central New York	1.103
Western New York	1.091
Southern Tier	1.045
Mohawk Valley	1.000
North Country	1.000

Pupil Need Index. The state further adjusts a district's AFA amount by a Pupil Need Index (PNI) to recognize the additional costs of educating students in need.[14] Expressed as a formula, the following occurs.

$$PNI = 1 + \text{Extraordinary Needs (EN\%)} \text{ (Min = 1, Max = 2)}$$

where

$$EN\% = (\text{Extraordinary Needs (EN) Count}/\text{Base Year Public School Enrollment}) \times 100$$

where

$$EN = (\text{Free and Reduced-Price Lunch Count} \times .65)$$
$$+ (5\text{--}17 \text{ Census Poverty Count} \times .65)$$
$$+ (\text{English Language Learner Count} \times .5)$$
$$+ \text{Sparsity Count (for districts with fewer than 25 pupils per square mile)}$$

where

$$\text{Sparsity Count} = (25.0 - \text{Base Year Enrollment per square mile})/50.9$$

Expected Minimum Local Contribution per Pupil

The Expected Minimum Local Contribution is the amount the state expects districts to contribute to the adjusted foundation amount and represents their "fair share of the total costs of general education."[15] The contribution amount is the lesser of two figures.

$$(\text{Selected Actual Value}/\text{Total Wealth Foundation Pupil Units})$$
$$\times \text{Local Tax Factor (LTF)} \times \text{Income Wealth Index (IWI)}$$

or

$$\text{Adjusted Foundation Amount}$$
$$\times (1 - \text{Foundation Aid State Sharing Ratio})$$

Local Tax Factor. For the FY 2018 school year, the Local Tax Factor (LTF) was 0.0162[16]

Income Wealth Index. The Income Wealth Index (IWI) is set as minimum = 0.65, max = 2. The IWI is calculated as IWI = 2014 District Adjusted Gross Income (AGI) Per Pupil/2015–16 Statewide Average AGI.

Foundation Aid State Sharing Ratio. The wealthier a district is when compared to the state average, the lower the sharing ratio. The Foundation Aid State Sharing Ratio (FASSR) equals the largest of the following ratios (max = 0.900):

1.37 − (1.23 × Foundation Aid Combined Wealth Ratio)
1.00 − (0.64 × Foundation Aid Combined Wealth Ratio)
0.80 − (0.39 × Foundation Aid Combined Wealth Ratio)
0.51 − (.0173 × Foundation Aid Combined Wealth Ratio)

For high need/resource capacity districts, the FASSR is multiplied by 1.05.[17]

Foundation Aid Combined Wealth Ratio. The Foundation Aid Combined Wealth Ratio (FACWR) is expressed in the following calculation:

$$0.5 \times \frac{\text{District Selected Actual Value}/2016\text{–}16 \text{ TWPU}}{\$558,500}$$

$$+$$

$$0.5 \times \frac{\text{District Selected AGI}/2016\text{–}16 \text{ TWPU}}{\$193,000}$$

The FACWR balances equally a district's income per pupil and property wealth per pupil relative to statewide averages. A district with a FACWR of 1.0 indicates that the district is of average wealth. A district with a FACWR below 1.0 is a district of below-average wealth. A district with a FACWR above 1.0 is a district of above-average wealth.

Total Wealth Pupil Units

The Total Wealth Per Pupil Units (TWPU) equals the sum of: (1) average daily membership [i.e., enrollment]; plus (2) full-time equivalent enrollment of resident pupils attending public school elsewhere, less the full-time equivalent enrollment of nonresident pupils; plus (3) the full-time equivalent enrollment of resident pupils with disabilities attending a BOCES full-time.[18]

Selected Total Aidable Foundation Pupil Units

The foundation aid formula, identified as Selected Total Aidable Foundation Pupil Units (TAPFU), weights students according to a set of rules depending on the following:

TAPFU = Average Daily Membership (ADM)
+ (Summer Average Daily Membership × .12)
+ weighted foundation pupils with disabilities (WFPWD)

where

ADM equals the total number of students enrolled during a session divided by the number of days in the session (e.g., 180).

Weighted Foundation Pupils with Disabilities. Determining the Weighted Foundation Pupils with Disabilities (WFPWD) follows the definition provided, where WFPWD = 1.41 multiplied by the full-time equivalent enrollment of pupils with disabilities (as determined by a district's committee on special education) who receive the following services:[19]

- *Placement* for 60% or more of the school day in a special class, or
- *Home or hospital instruction* for a period of more than 60 days, or
- *Special services or programs* for more than 60% of the school day, or
- *Placement* for 20% or more time of the school week in a resource room.

WFPWD also includes 0.5 multiplied by the full-time equivalent of declassified pupils who are in their first year of regular instruction.

Foundation Aid Payable

The Fiscal Year 2018 budget provided for a number of Foundation Aid set-asides, including $170.3 million for Magnet Schools, $67.48 million for Teacher Support, and $2,723.1 million to support students with disabilities. New York City was required to set aside $50.48 million for attendance improvement/dropout prevention programs. There was also a $150 million Community School set-aside to support school-based "academic, health, mental health, nutrition, counseling, legal and other services to students and their families in failing schools and other higher need districts."[20] Expressed as a formula, it reads:

Foundation Aid Payable = Foundation Aid Base
+ phase-in foundation aid increase + additional increase.

TRANSPORTATION

Transportation aid[21] supports district cost of transporting pupils to and from school daily, BOCES, shared programs at other schools, and occupational programs within the district.[22] In FY 2018, the state distributed an estimated $1,716.6 million in transportation aid. Approved expenditures included operational costs associated with a school district's transportation supervisor's office and for the operation of district-owned buses, contracted buses, and public service vehicles (subway included).[23] Nonallowable transportation expenditures included the cost of transporting nondisabled pupils living 1.5 miles or less from school and field trips. An important realization is that transportation aid is property wealth equalized (i.e., selected sharing ratio) and adjusted for district pupil sparsity (i.e., enrollment per square mile). Expressed as a formula, the sum of the selected sharing ratio cannot exceed 90% or be less than 6.5%.[24]

$$\text{Transportation Aid} = \text{Approved Transportation Expenditures} \times (\text{Selected Sharing Ratio} + \text{Sparsity Factor})$$

FACILITIES

Building Aid

School districts can receive Building Aid[25] for expenditures and financing incurred to construct, renovate, purchase, or lease school buildings. Building Aid is also available to remediate lead-contaminated drinking water[26] and improve school safety systems.[27] The Facilities Planning Unit of the State Education Department must approve all building plans. In FY 2018, the state allocated $3,054.6 million in Building Aid.[28] The local share for an average wealth district was .49. The maximum BAR was 0.95 for most districts, and 0.98 for high need/resource capacity districts.[29] Formula expression is as follows.

$$\text{Building Aid} = \text{Aidable Building Expenditures} \times \text{Building Aid Ratio}$$

where

$$\text{Building Aid Ratio (BAR)} = 1.000 - 0.51 \times \frac{(2014 \text{ Actual Valuation}/2015\text{--}16 \text{ RWADA})}{\$702,400}$$

RWADA = Resident Weighted Average Daily Attendance

Expanding Our Children's Education and Learning (EXCEL)

Expanding Our Children's Education and Learning (EXCEL)[30] provides supplemental funding for selected types of construction projects, including education technology, health and safety, accessibility, physical capacity expansion, and energy. The state is authorized to issue a maximum of $2.6 billion in bonds and notes (a maximum of $1.8 billion for New York City [NYC]). NYC has received its full allocation, and other districts have received $737 million in funding, supporting approximately 3,000 projects.[31]

TEACHER RETIREMENT

The New York State Teachers' Retirement System (NYSTRS) was established in 1921 by the New York legislature to administer retirement, disability and death benefits for eligible public school teachers, teaching assistants, counselors, and administrators in the state, excluding those in New York City which has its own retirement system. As of June 30, 2017, NYSTRS served 822 employers, including public school districts, BOCES, higher education institutions, and charter schools, and 428,579 members.[32]

The NYSTRS is funded through employer and member contributions and investment income. The employer contribution rate (ECR) is a uniform percentage of member payroll that is set annually at a level needed to cover benefits. The ECR for the 2017–18 academic year was 9.80%.[33] Benefits and eligibility rules for members are based on a tier structure according to date of initial membership, with the most recent tier 6 applying to those who entered the system on or after April 1, 2012. Member contributions vary by tier, ranging from no annual contribution for Tiers 1 and 2 members to a variable rate contribution based on annual gross salary for Tier 6 members.[34]

SPECIAL EDUCATION

New York's Foundation Aid formula provides additional weighting for students with disabilities. To ensure that school districts meet federal maintenance of effort provisions for students with disabilities, each district must set aside a portion of its current year Foundation Aid.[35] The Public Excess Cost Set-Aside[36] provided an estimated $2,723.1 million in FY 2018. The state provides additional aid to students with disabilities through a number of programs. Highlighted next are those most noteworthy.

Private Excess Cost Aid for Pupils in Approved Private School Placements or in State Operated Schools

The state provides wealth-equalized aid for students with disabilities who attend approved private schools, Special Act School Districts, the New York State School for the Blind, or the New York State School for the Deaf.[37] The Department of Education and the Division of Budget must annually approve tuition charges to each private school.[38] In 2017–18, the state allocated an estimated $392.4 million to Private Excess Cost Aid. Formulaically expressed as:

Aidable Excess Cost = Approved Tuition Paid − Basic Contribution

where

Private Excess Cost aid per pupil = Aidable Excess Cost × Private Excess Cost Ratio × FTE of each pupil in base year

where

Private Excess Cost Ratio = 1.0 − (Combined Wealth Ratio × 0.15) (minimum ration = 0.50)

where

Total Aid = the sum of aid for all pupils

Public High Cost Excess Cost Aid

A school district can receive Public High Cost Excess Cost Aid[39] for pupils with disabilities enrolled in resource-intensive programs operated by public schools or BOCES. In FY 2018, the state allocated an estimated $607.1 million to Public High Cost Excess Cost Aid. The wealth-equalized formula for calculating Public High Cost Excess Cost Aid for each student is as follows: [40]

Annualized Education Cost − (3 × Approved Operating Expense per pupil) × Excess Cost Aid Ratio × 2016–2017 FTE Enrollment)

where

Excess Cost Aid Ratio = 1.000 − (Combined Wealth Ratio × 0.51) (Minimum ratio = 0.25)

COMPENSATORY EDUCATION

New York supports the provision of compensatory education needs and services by including a Pupil Needs Index (PNI) in the calculation of Foundation Aid. The PNI drives more resources to those districts with higher percentages of students eligible for free- and reduced-price lunch (FRPL), in poverty, and English Language Learners. In addition, Foundation Aid is dependent on pupil count weightings (e.g., students with disabilities).

GIFTED AND TALENTED EDUCATION

The state of New York does not provide direct state aid to school districts for gifted and talented education. However, it funds other programs to advance high school students' academic achievement. For example, following the expiration of the federal AP Test Fee Program, in 2017 the state began using state funds to cover the remaining AP exam fees for low-income public school students who qualify for the College Board's fee reduction. The FY 2018 budget allocation of $2.0 million funded exam costs for 68,000 low-income students.[41]

In addition, the state provides funding for 55 early college high school programs which support public school students to earn college credits while still in high school. The FY 208 budget expanded funding from $5.3 million to $6.76 million.[42]

BILINGUAL EDUCATION

The Commissioner's Regulations[43] established the standards for English Language Learners (ELLs)/Multilingual Learners (MLLs) that New York public school districts are required to meet. To assist districts in meeting these standards, New York's Education Department (NYSED) operates seven Regional Bilingual Education Resource Network (RBERN) centers at regional BOCES as well as one statewide RBERN. These centers provide training, professional development, and technical assistance to improve districts' programs and practices for ELLs/MLLs.[44] In the FY 2018 budget cycle, $15.5 million was allocated to support regional bilingual education programs at RBERN centers and innovative programming, such as two-way bilingual education.[45]

FUNDING FOR CHARTER SCHOOLS

Charter schools are authorized by the New York State Charter Schools Act of 1998.[46] Amendments to the law in 2007 and 2010 increased caps on the number of charter schools in the state from an initial cap of 100 to 200 in 2007, and then to 460 in 2010. Districts in the state pay a per-pupil tuition rate to charter schools for each district resident student enrolled in a charter school. The annual per-pupil rate has been the base amount provided by the district plus supplemental increases provided by the state. Starting in FY 2019, the base amount increases each year by a district-specific inflator equivalent to the average change over three years in the district's expenditures.[47] The rate includes any state and federal funds collected for students with disabilities.

To lessen the impact of significant increases in charter school transfers on school districts, the state provides transitional aid to 23 districts (excluding New York City). Impact is determined by the effect on districts' enrollments or budgets.[48] The FY 2018 state allocation for this program was $39.3 million.[49]

STATE AID FOR PRIVATE K–12 SCHOOLS

Pursuant to Chapters 507 and 508 of the Laws of 1974, New York provides aid to private schools for costs associated with state-mandated efforts, including data collection and reporting, taking attendance, and testing. The FY 2018 state appropriation for these activities totaled $180.99 million. Additional private school aid was provided in the budget for academic intervention services ($0.92 million), safety equipment ($15.0 million), STEM and immunization recordkeeping ($12.0 million), classroom technology and connectivity projects ($25.0 million), and support for public school students placed in special education programs in other settings; these settings included private schools, Special Act school districts, and state-operated schools in Rome and Batavia ($392.43 million). The latter excluded an additional $103.10 million in state funds for students attending eight private schools for the deaf, two private schools for the blind, and one private school for students with multiple disabilities. In addition, a portion of the state's allocated $34.4 million in subsidies for school lunch and breakfast programs in FY 2018 was provided to nonpublic schools.[50]

EARLY CHILDHOOD EDUCATION

In FY 2015, the state of New York committed $1.50 billion over five years to phase-in full-day prekindergarten programs for four-year old children.[51] Through a competitive grant program, $340 million of this amount was allocated in FY 2018 with $300 million designated for programs in New York City. An additional $5 million was provided to expand half-day and full-day programs for three- and four-year old children in high-need districts. In 2018, the state also passed legislation to consolidate over a three-year period multiple existing prekindergarten programs into its Universal Prekindergarten Program. Total allocations for Universal Prekindergarten reached $415.56 million in FY 2018.[52]

Pursuant to Section 4410 of the Education Law, the state also allocated $1,035.0 million in FY 2018 to support preschool special education programs and related services for three- and four-year-olds with disabilities.

The state's allocation covered approximately 59.5% of the costs of services for these children.[53]

Pursuant to Section 3602(9) of the Education Law, the state also provides conversion funds to incentive districts to establish and expand full-day kindergarten programs. In the 2018 budget, $1.7 million was set aside for conversion aid. The amount of aid received by districts is calculated as the product of the current year Selected Foundation Aid and the growth in enrollment in full-day kindergarten between the current year and the base year. Districts receiving this aid in a prior year are not eligible to receive it again, although the state considers one-time exceptions.[54]

OTHER CATEGORICAL PROGRAMS

The state allocates additional aid to districts for a variety of educational purposes. Highlighted briefly are several of the more noteworthy categorical aids.[55]

BOCES Aid

Districts other than the Big Five city districts are eligible to receive Board of Cooperative Educational Services (BOCES) aid.[56] The state's 37 BOCES provide services to two or more component school districts upon request, including career and technical education, special education, summer school general instruction, itinerant teacher services, technology services, and staff development.[57] In FY 2018, the state allocated an estimated $893.8 million in BOCES aid. Approved service costs are distributed among component districts in proportion to their level of participation.[58] BOCES aid is equalized by either a district's property tax rate or its relative property value per pupil.

Special Services Aid for Five Large City School Districts and Noncomponents of BOCES

The state provides Special Services[59] aid to the Big Five city school districts and any district that is not part of a BOCES in lieu of BOCES aid for career education, computer administration, and academic improvement. In FY 2018, the state allocated an estimated $262.3 million in Special Services aid.

Textbook Aid

Districts receive Textbook Aid[60] equal to the district's actual expenditures for eligible materials up to a maximum of $58.25 multiplied by the number of students enrolled in the district or nonpublic schools (i.e., flat grant per pupil). Districts are to loan textbooks aided under this program to nonpublic school students on an equitable basis. In FY 2018, the state allocated an estimated $178.1 million in Textbook Aid.[61]

Educational Technology Aids

School districts are eligible for aid to purchase or lease educational technology hardware and software.[62] For FY 2018, the state reimbursed districts for computer software expenses up to $14.98 per pupil based on public and nonpublic school enrollment for an estimated total of $46.0 million in Computer Software Aid. Instructional Computer Hardware and Technology Equipment Aid reimburses districts for hardware expenses up to a wealth-adjusted $24.20 per pupil. For FY 2018, the state allocated and estimated $37.97 million in Hardware and Technology Equipment Aid.[63]

Library Materials Aid

Districts are eligible to receive $6.25 in library aid per pupil based on the number of students enrolled in public and nonpublic school within the district's boundaries (i.e., flat grant per pupil).[64] Districts are required to loan library materials equitably among public and nonpublic school students. In FY 2018, the state allocated an estimated $19.2 million in Library Materials Aid.[65]

LOCAL SCHOOL REVENUE

Property Taxes

Real property taxes constitute the primary source of local revenue for New York's schools (approximately 91%).[66] Personal property, such as automobiles, is not subject to school taxes.

Nonproperty Taxes

New York state sales tax laws reserve 4% for the state and permit counties the option of supplementing this amount to support county services. Five counties (out of 57 statewide) share a portion of local sales taxes with approximately 163 school districts.[67] In these counties, the county portion of the sales tax is prorated among districts based on enrollment. In addition, state law requires that school districts receive a portion of payments in lieu of taxes (PILOTS) in areas where Industrial Development Agencies have granted tax exemptions.[68] Small city school districts can also levy a utility tax.

TAX CREDITS AND EXEMPTIONS

The School Tax Relief Program (commonly referred to as STAR) provides state-funded partial exemptions to homeowners for owner-occupied primary residences.[69] Enacted in 1997, STAR took effect in the 1998–99 school year. STAR provides two classes of exemptions. The Basic STAR exemption exempts the first $30,000 of property value for homeowners who earn less than $500,000 per year. The Enhanced STAR exemption provides an increased benefit for senior citizens (age 65 and older) who earn less than $86,000 per year by exempting the first $66,800 of the full value of their primary residences. In 2016, the law changed so that instead of applying to a local assessor for exemption, new homeowners now register with New York state and receive a STAR credit in the form of a check. The dollar value of the credit is generally equal to the amount of the exemption.

STAR does not provide additional educational revenues. The state makes payments to school districts to compensate for amounts equal to lost property tax revenue. Although STAR revenue goes to districts to support schooling, its purpose is different than state aid. State aid strives to equalize revenue (i.e., foundation aid) or foster the purchase of educational resources and services (e.g., textbook aid and transportation aid). STAR provides property tax relief.

In 2016, New York instituted a property tax credit program. Eligibility requires living in a school district that is complying with the New York state property tax cap (see below), receive either the Basic or Enhanced STAR exemption of credit, and have an annual income less than $275,000.[70] In 2019 when fully phased in, those making less than $75,000 will receive a rebate equal to 80% of their Basic STAR savings. The percentage decreases for higher income levels, falling to 7.5% for those with incomes between $200,000 and $275,000. Enhanced STAR recipients will receive credits equal to 34% of their STAR savings.

New York state provides an additional exemption for income-poor senior citizens.[71] School districts can opt to reduce the taxable assessment of seniors' homes by as much as 50%. For the 50% exemption, the law allows school districts to set the maximum annual income limit between $3,000 and $29,000. Districts may provide exemptions of less than 50%, the so-called sliding scale option, to senior homeowners whose annual income is high as $37,399.99. School districts can opt to reduce property tax liabilities similarly for qualifying disabled persons.[72] In addition to these exemptions, New York allows a ten-year property tax exemption for newly constructed or reconstructed agricultural structures.[73]

TAX AND SPENDING LIMITS

Chapter 97 of the Laws of 2011 established a tax levy limit (commonly referred to as the property tax cap) on all local governments (i.e., counties, cities, towns, villages, and fire districts) and independent school districts.[74] The property tax cap does not apply to New York City. The other Big Five dependent school districts (i.e., Buffalo, Rochester, Syracuse, and Yonkers) are subject to the legislation as components of their city governments. The property tax cap first applied to FY 2012.

The law established a limit on the annual growth of property taxes levied to 2% or the rate of inflation as specified by the Consumer Price Index for all urban consumers, whichever is lower. The property tax cap cannot be less than zero. There are a few narrowly defined exclusions to the cap "including certain costs of significant judgments arising out of tort actions" (i.e., any amount that exceeds 5% of the prior year tax levy) and "unusually large year-to-year increases in pension contribution rates" (i.e., greater than two percentage points).[75] The cap also excluded the tax levy needed to support the local share of capital expenditures. The property tax cap calculation is subject to noteworthy modifications. Beginning in FY 2013, districts could carryover over up to 1.5% of unused tax levy growth to the following year. For example, if a district increased its tax levy 1% in a year when its cap was 2%, the district could add 1% to the subsequent year's levy cap. The tax cap formula also included a 'quantity change factor' that provided an upward adjustment for certain types of tax base growth, such as new residential and nonresidential construction. Finally, a proposed levy not exceeding the property tax cap would require the approval of a simple majority of voters. A proposed levy exceeding the property tax cap required approval of 60% of voters. If the district failed to obtain a supermajority, the levy would remain the same as the previous year's levy.

NOTES

1. This chapter highlights the New York state system of school finance pursuant to the Laws 2017. To report accurately on these laws we rely extensively on the following source: The University of the State of New York, The State Education Department, Office of State Aid (2017) *2017–2018 State Aid Handbook: State Formula Aids and Entitlements for Schools In New York State As Amended by Chapters of the Laws of 2017*. Retrieved from https://stateaid.nysed.gov/publications/

handbooks/handbook_2017.pdf Readers of this chapter should refer to this and other referenced sources to verify the accuracy of interpretation and reporting of each respective section and provision.
2. Handbook, p. 5.
3. Ibid.
4. The University of the State of New York, The State Education Department, Fiscal Analysis and Research Unit (July 2017). *State Aid to Schools: A Primer: Pursuant to Laws of 2017*.Retrieved from http://www.oms.nysed.gov/faru/PDFDocuments/Primer17-18A.pdf
5. 2017–18 State Aid Handbook, p. 7.
6. The University of the State of New York, The State Education Department, Fiscal Analysis and Research Unit (January 2018). *Analysis of School Finances in New York State School Districts 2015–16.* Retrieved from http://www.oms.nysed.gov/faru/PDFDocuments/2017_Analysis_a.pdf
7. State Aid to Schools: A Primer, p. 14.
8. [Section 3602 (2 and 4) and 211-d of the Education Law].
9. 2017–18 State Aid Handbook, p. 7.
10. 2017–18 State Aid Handbook, p. 7.
11. 2017–18 State Aid Handbook, p. 7.
12. 2017–18 State Aid Handbook, p. 7.
13. 2017–18 State Aid Handbook, p. 8.
14. 2017–18 State Aid Handbook, p. 9.
15. State Aid to Schools: A Primer, p. 23.
16. 2017–18 State Aid Handbook, p. 10.
17. State Aid to Schools: A Primer, p. 27.
18. 2017–18 State Aid Handbook, p. 10.
19. Ibid. p. 12.
20. New York State Division of the Budget, Education Unit (October 31, 2017). *Description of 2017–18 New York State School Aid Programs,* p. 6. Retrieved from https://www.budget.ny.gov/pubs/archive/fy18archive/enactedfy18/2017-18EnactedSchoolAid.pdf.
21. Section 3602(7) of the Education Law.
22. 2017–18 State Aid Handbook, p. 28.
23. Ibid. p. 28.
24. Ibid. p. 30.
25. Section 3602(6) of the Education Law.
26. Chapter 296 of the Laws of 2016.
27. NY Safe Act, Chapter 1 of the Laws of 2013.
28. *Description of 2017–18 New York State School Aid Programs,* p. 11. Retrieved from https://www.budget.ny.gov/pubs/archive/fy18archive/enactedfy18/2017-18EnactedSchoolAid.pdf.
29. 2017–18 State Aid Handbook, p. 24 .
30. Section 3641(14) of the Education Law.
31. 2017–18 State Aid Handbook, p. 26
32. New York State Teachers' Retirement System (2017). *Comprehensive Annual Financial Report Fiscal Years Ended June 30, 2017 and 2016,* p. 10. Retrieved from https://www.nystrs.org/Library/Publications/Annual-Reports

33. 2017 Annual Financial Report, p. 12.
34. 2017 Annual Financial Report, p. 18.
35. 2017–18 State Aid Handbook, p. 43.
36. Section 3602(4.c).
37. Section 4405(3) of the Education Law.
38. 2017–18 State Aid Handbook, p. 41.
39. Section 3602(5) of the Education Law.
40. 2017–18 State Aid Handbook, p. 42.
41. Description of 2017–18 New York State School Aid Programs, p. 21. Also see http://www.p12.nysed.gov/ciai/gt/ap/
42. Ibid.
43. CR Part 154-2.
44. See http://www.nysed.gov/bilingual-ed/regional-supportrberns
45. Description of 2017–18 New York State School Aid Programs, p. 13.
46. Education Law §2851[3].
47. See http://www.nyccharterschools.org/funding
48. Section 3602(41) of the Education Law.
49. 2017–18 State Aid Handbook, pp. 38–39.
50. Description of 2017–18 New York State School Aid Programs, p. 16.
51. Section 3602-ee of the Education Law.
52. Description of 2017–18 New York State School Aid Programs, p. 19, 25.
53. Ibid. p. 16
54. 2017–18 State Aid Handbook, p. 48.
55. Those interested in the full set of available aids can turn to the 2017–18 State Aid Handbook.
56. Section 1950(5) of the Education Law.
57. 2017–18 State Aid Handbook, p. 45.
58. Ibid, p. 45.
59. Section 3602(10) of the Education Law.
60. Ibid, Section 701.
61. Description of 2017–18 New York State Aid Programs, p. 9.
62. Sections 751-754 of the Education Law.
63. Description of 2017–18 New York State Aid Programs, p. 9.
64. Section 711 of the Education Law.
65. 2017–18 State Aid Handbook, p. 48
66. Ibid, p. 5
67. State Aid to Schools: A Primer, p. 27.
68. Ibid, p. 27.
69. Section 425 of the Real Property Tax Law.
70. New York State Department of Taxation and Finance (2018). Property tax relief credit. Retrieved from https://www.tax.ny.gov/pit/property/property-tax-relief.htm.
71. Section 467 of the Real Property Tax Law.
72. Ibid, Section 459..
73. Ibid, Section 483.
74. Office of the New York State Comptroller, Division of Local Government and School Accountability (2018). *Property Tax Cap: Summary of Legislation.*

Retrieved from https://www.osc.state.ny.us/localgov/realprop/pdf/legislationsummary.pdf
75. New York State Department of Taxation and Finance and the New York State Department of State (nd). *The Property Tax Cap: Guidelines for Implementation.* Retrieved from https://www.tax.ny.gov/pdf/publications/orpts/capguidelines.pdf

CHAPTER 35

North Carolina

Eric A. Houck, Ph.D.
University of North Carolina-Chapel Hill

Kyle Abbott
University of North Carolina-Chapel Hill

GENERAL BACKGROUND

The state of North Carolina passed its first public school law in 1839, which established a funding system combining state and local funds. The state provided two dollars for every dollar local governments collected from taxes, an early form of matching fund with required local effort. The law further divided the state into districts with five schools per district and established a board of 'superintendents' to oversee each county's schools. In 1852, the General Assembly established the Office of General Superintendent of Common Schools, the precursor to the Department of Public Instruction. After the Civil War, the 1868 state constitution provided for free education for all children. It established the State Board of Education, which had the authority to set state standards and regulated teacher licensure, among other duties.[1]

In the 20th century, North Carolina's system of school funding evolved into something more recognizable to modern scholars. The General Assembly passed the Compulsory Attendance Act in 1913, established city school districts in 1921, and set a minimum funding level in 1931 through the School Machinery Act. The School Machinery Act was a mechanism to provide resources to meet the constitutional mandate of a free and uniform education for all students in the state. The School Machinery Act also repealed earlier provisions that required local effort in order to receive a state match and provided for local bonding authority for construction of schools; thereby establishing a tradition of local responsibility for capital costs and state responsibility for current costs.[2] With some modification, the logic of the School Machinery Act motivates North Carolina's current funding mechanism.

The U.S. Supreme Court's *Brown v. Topeka Board of Education*[3] in 1954 brought the challenge of integration to North Carolina schools. Throughout the late 1950s and into the 1960s and 1970s, the state slowly integrated its all-Black and all-White systems. Thomas J. Pearsall, then chairman of the state's Special Advisory Committee on Education, proposed an early version of a voucher, whereby students could use state dollars to go to a private school if their parents did not want them to attend an integrated school. However, the 1964 U.S. Civil Rights Act ended the effort by disallowing federal funds to go to any segregated school district.[4]

Post-integration, the legislature accelerated the rate of modernization. The General Assembly passed all-day kindergarten for all students in 1977, followed by the Basic Education Program (BEP) in 1985. The BEP is the cornerstone of North Carolina's policy and finance régime built on a systemic reform framework of defining standards, assessing performance, and holding schools and leaders accountable.[5] The BEP established statewide standards across all subject areas and gave the state board the authority to "describe the education program to be offered to every child in the public schools."[6] This authority also included "funds appropriated for that purpose."[7] In 1990, the state began issuing report cards for each school, reporting student outcomes.

Legal History

The North Carolina funding mechanism has been challenged on the basis of both equity and adequacy concerns. In 1987, the North Carolina Court of Appeals dismissed a case arguing for increased vertical equity in the state funding mechanism in *Britt v. North Carolina*.[8] The North Carolina supreme court refused to hear the case.

The 1997 *Leandro v. North Carolina*[9] was a landmark case in school finance, establishing adequacy as a principle of a constitutional funding formula. Low-wealth rural districts, as well as high-poverty urban districts, cited the inability to raise sufficient local revenue as a disequalizing force in school funding. The court upheld the funding structure as constitutional, but also ruled unanimously that all students have a right to 'a sound, basic education' as evidenced by performance on state standardized tests. Just as importantly, the court placed the burden of education provision on the state instead of on local districts. Efforts to hold the state accountable to this decision from the bench have continued to the present day, although the legislature has taken little heed of the court's pronouncements.

STATE AID FORMULA

The Basic Education Program (BEP) rests on a system of allotments based on pupil counts, making North Carolina's system a distinct minority among state finance mechanisms. Only seven states still use a resource-allocation system instead of a weighted-student model.[10] The state currently uses 37 different allotments, or a specific amount of resources determined by the funding formula. Allotments are largely dependent on each district's average daily membership (ADM). The 37 allotments are divided into two major categories: position-based allotments allocate personnel positions and categorical allotments allocate dollar grants. They can be further divided by function. Base Allotments are used to provide materials, staffing, and services necessary for district activities. Grant/Application Allotments are used for acquiring improvement funds through a competitive grant process. Local Education Agencies (LEAs) are allotted dollar amounts based on student counts. LEAs with low wealth or enrollment are given allotments to account for economic capacity and effort. Table 35.1 lists allotments by category and includes each allotment name and Program Report Code (PRC). Employee allotments take a majority of resources. Across all allotments, the state was projected to spend $8.93 billion in the 2017–18 school year on 1,552,638 allotted students, resulting in $5,407 in spending per pupil.[11] The sections that follow outline these components of the funding mechanism.

Position-Based Funding

Table 35.2 presents ratios and bases for position-based funding allocations for the 2017–2018 academic year. North Carolina uses the number of students in ADM to allocate teaching, support, and administrative positions. While LEAs were able to present estimated counts projections for funding, the ADM amount is now based on real counts from the previous year to estimate initial allocations in the current year. The differentiated student counts for ranges of grade levels represents an implicit weighting in the allocation of teacher positions. Also, the basis for salary allocation is the average school district salary of a given LEA in the previous academic year. That is, the state provides different salary amounts for each district based

TABLE 35.1 Allotments by Category and Program Report Code (PRC)

Based Allotments (position based)	Grant/Application (dollar based)	Student Characteristics (dollar based)	LEA Characteristics (dollar based)
PRC 001: Classroom Teachers	PRC 029: Behavioral Support	PRC 032: Children With Special Needs	PRC 019: Small County Supplemental Funding
PRC 002: Central Administration	PRC 030: Digital Learning	PRC 054: Limited English Proficiency	PRC 031: Low Wealth
PRC 005: School Building Administration	PRC 039: School Resource Officer	PRC 063: Children With Special Needs: Special Funds	PRC 024: Disadvantages Student Supplemental Funding
PRC 007: Instructional Support	PRC 040: After School Quality Improvement Grant	PRC 069: At Risk Student Services/Alternative Schools	
PRC 012: Driver Training	PRC 041: Panic Alarms Improvement Grant		
PRC 013: Career & Technical Education (Employment)	PRC 042: Child and Family Support Teams: Nurses		
PRC 014: Career & Technical Education (Program Support)	PRC 043: Child and Family Support Teams: Social Workers		
PRC 015: School Technology Fund	PRC 055: Learn and Earn		
PRC 016: Summer Reading Camps	PRC 066: Assistant Principal Interns: Principal Fellows		
PRC 025: Indian Gaming Fund	PRC 067: Assistant Principal Interns: MSA Students		
PRC 027: Teacher Assistants	PRC 042: Child and Family Support Teams: Nurses		
PRC 034: Academically and Intellectually Gifted			
PRC 036: Charter Schools			
PRC 056: Transportation			
PRC 061: Classroom Materials and Instructional Supplies			
PRC 073: School Connectivity			
PRC 085: Class Reading 3D			
PRC 120: LEA Financed Purchase of School Busses			
PRC 130: Textbooks			

Source: http://www.ncpublicschools.org/docs/fbs/finance/reporting/coa/2012/programreportcodes.pdf
Categorized by Authors (2019).

TABLE 35.2 Funding Ratios for Positions 2017–2018

Category	Formula	Salary Basis
Classroom Teachers		
Kindergarten	1 per 18 in ADM.	LEA Average
Grade 1	1 per 16 in ADM.	
Grades 2–3	1 per 17 in ADM.	
Grades 4–6	1 per 24 in ADM.	
Grades 7–8	1 per 23 in ADM.	
Grade 9	1 per 26.5 in ADM	
Grades 10–12	1 per 29 in ADM.	
Math/Science/Computer Teachers	1 per county or based on sub agreements	
Teacher Assistants	The number of classes is determined by a ratio of 1:21. • K: 2 TAs per every 3 classes • Grades 1–2: 1 TA for every 2 classes • Grade 3: 1 TA for every 3 classes	$35,171
Instructional Support	1 per 218.55 in ADM	LEA Average
Administration		
Principals	1 per school with at least 100 ADM or at least seven state-paid teachers or instructional support personnel. Schools opening after 7/1/2011 are eligible based on at least 100 ADM only.	LEA Average
Assistant Principals	1 month per 98.53 in ADM.	LEA Average
Career Technical Ed. (CTE)	Base of 50 Months of Employment per LEA with remainder distributed based on ADM in grades 8–12.	LEA Average

Source: Initial Allotments Formula Worksheet, http://www.ncpublicschools.org/fbs/allotments/state/

on the salary pool of its individual teaching corps. There is an exception for teacher assistants, who are allocated with a straight standard salary.

Student Categorical Funding

Table 35.3 presents dollar allocations based on student characteristics, along with additional regulatory guidance in the funding mechanism. For example, academically gifted and special education funding is capped at a percentage of students in ADM. Of particular interest is the dollar allocation for gifted and for special education which are capped at 4% and 12.75% of the district ADM, respectively. Additional gifted or special education identified students are funded from local revenue sources. In addition,

TABLE 35.3 Dollar-Based Allocation Based on Student Characteristics

Category	Basis of Allotments
Supplies	$42.46 per ADM in grades K–12.
Noninstructional Support Personnel	$258.05 per ADM.
Academically Gifted Students	$1,322.28 per child for 4% of ADM.
At-Risk Student Services	• Each LEA receives the dollar equivalent of one resource officer ($37,838) per high school. • Of the remaining funds, 50% is distributed based on ADM ($89.10 per ADM) and 50% is distributed based on number of poor children, per the federal Title 1 Low-Income poverty data ($358.14 per poor child). • Each LEA receives a minimum of the dollar equivalent of two teachers and two instructional support personnel ($272,812).
Children with Disabilities	
School Aged	• $4,253.55 per funded child count. • Child count is comprised of the lesser of the April 1 handicapped child count or 12.75% of the allotted ADM.
Preschool	• Base of $64,558 per LEA. • Remainder distributed based on December 1 child count of ages 3, 4, and Pre K–5, ($3,413.70) per child.
Limited English Proficiency	Base of a teacher assistant ($34,673); remainder based 50% on number of funded LEP students ($406.62) and 50% on a LEA's concentration of LEP students ($4,551.36

Source: Initial Allotments Formula Worksheet, http://www.ncpublicschools.org/fbs/allotments/state/

funding for students with disabilities is undifferentiated—every identified student in the state receives the same dollar allocation regardless of the severity or nature of the identified disability. This category was identified for further study in the 2018–2019 legislative session.[12]

District Categorical Funding

Table 35.4 presents funding categories that are dollar allocations based on district characteristics. There is a dollar allocation to LEAs based on size through the small county supplemental funding stream in graduated amounts for districts with ADMs less than 3,200 students. Support for career and technical education is a dollar-based grant that is then graduated based on student counts. Transportation funding is a dollar grant based on formula inputs which include total miles traveled.

TABLE 35.4 Dollar-based Allocation Based on District (LEA) Characteristics

Category	Basis of Allotment	
Small County Supplemental Funding	ADM <	Allotment
	600	$1,710,000
	1,300	$1,820,000
	1,700	$1,548,700
	2,000	$1,600,000
	2,300	$1,560,000
	2,600	$1,470,000
	2,800	$1,498,000
	3,200	$1,548,000
CTE Program Support	$10,000 per LEA with remainder distributed based on ADM in grades 8–12 ($33.54).	
Disadvantaged Student Supplemental Funding	Formula based.	
Low Wealth Supplemental Funding	Formula based.	
Transportation	Formula based.	

Source: Initial Allotments Formula Worksheet, http://www.ncpublicschools.org/fbs/allotments/state/

Perhaps the most important and controversial dollar-based grants based on district characteristics are two funding streams to support disadvantaged students within districts and districts with low fiscal capacity. These allocations are discussed separately, below.

Low Wealth Supplemental Funding

Counties having below-average wealth, as measured by a formula, are eligible for supplemental funding. The formula includes three factors: anticipated total county revenue, tax base per square mile, and per capita income. Anticipated revenue is calculated by estimating the property value in the county plus the revenue the county receives from sales taxes, fines, and forfeitures. The tax base per square mile compares each county's property value per square mile to the state average. Many low-wealth counties have significant areas of swampland, which has zero value. This is meant to equalize counties with different topographies. Per capita income is a three-year average of income in the county compared to the state.[13]

Each factor is weighted to determine eligibility: 40% is anticipated revenue, 10% is density, and 50% is per capita income. These percentages are multiplied by each county's value (e.g., 50% multiplied by 90% of the state average in per capita income). If the total of these percentages is less than 100, the county is considered low wealth. Counties must maintain effort to receive this funding. Each must either have effective tax rates at or above the state average or contribute more dollars to the LEA's per pupil amount than the state average when accounting for wealth. If the county meets neither of these criteria, it receives funding equal to the percentage actually contributed relative to what it is able to contribute.[14]

Low-wealth supplemental funding is more restricted than other allotments. These funds are expendable only for instructional staffing and materials. They are meant to supplement, not supplant, local dollars. The state can sanction the county if it is found to be spending less than 95% of the average local effort per student for the past three fiscal years. LEAs can apply for waivers from this requirement in the event of school closures, loss of federal funds, or some other emergency such as a natural disaster.[15] Most LEAs are eligible for this supplemental funding. In Fiscal Year 2017, 79 LEAs received these funds[16] and they received an average of $315 per pupil.[17]

Disadvantaged Students Supplemental Funding

North Carolina has adapted its allotment system to account for disadvantaged pupils in both high-wealth and low-wealth districts by providing dollar funding equivalents of additional teacher positions based on the count of disadvantaged students pegged to the formula ratios in the broader funding mechanism. North Carolina accounts for disadvantaged pupils in LEAs using a three-step process. First, the fundable disadvantaged population is used to generate additional positions based on a standard teacher-to-student ratio of 1:21. Second, this ratio is adjusted to account for district wealth. If the district is over 90% of the state wealth average (calculated using the Low Wealth Supplemental Funding formula), the teacher-to-student ratio falls to 1:19.9. If the district is between 80% and 90% of the state wealth average, the teacher-to-student ratio falls to 1:19.4. If the district is under 80% of the state wealth average, the teacher-to-student ratio becomes 1:19.1. However, 16 LEAs receiving funds during the FY 2006 program pilot year are still funded at a teacher-to-student ratio of 1:16 due to a hold-harmless provision passed by the General Assembly. Third and finally, these additional teaching positions are converted to dollars using the state average teacher salary and provided as a categorical dollar-based grant.[18]

The state imposes restrictions on this funding. LEAs must use these funds for classroom instruction, intensive in-school and/or after school remediation, purchase of diagnostic software and progress monitoring tools, and providing teacher bonuses and salary supplements. Only 35% of funds may be used for salary enhancements. These funds also have a nonsupplant clause similar to Low Wealth Supplemental Funding.[19] In FY 2014, all 115 LEAs received this supplement averaging $53 per pupil.

Inferred Funding Weights

North Carolina allocates positions and dollars, but it does so differentially based on student, school, and district characteristics. In this sense, the funding mechanism can be considered a weighted model, and state-level administrators have made this argument in regard to recent efforts to alter the basics of the funding mechanism.

One of the challenges of the resource-based funding model North Carolina uses lies in determining structural components that support and provide equitable resource provisions, especially in comparison to other states. Many states use some form of pupil weighting as a driver for their state funding mechanisms; to compare states with these types of mechanisms consists of the relatively simple step of comparing the funding weights for students identified in similar categories. This type of comparison is difficult when seeking to understand the structural equity of the North Carolina mechanism.

To facilitate these comparisons, Table 35.5 takes funding levels reported by the North Carolina School Business Office in testimony before the Joint Legislative Task Force on Education Finance Reform and converts them into pupil weights to demonstrate the relative value the state places on different student, school, and district characteristics. As in other states with student weighting components in their mechanisms, these weights can be 'stacked' for students who exist and are counted within multiple categories.

TABLE 35.5 Inferred Weights of Critical Funding Categories

Illustration of how funding is weighted for students in Kindergarten through Grade 3 (2018)

Funding for Different Students	State Dollars	Weight
Every Student	$5,410.53	1.00
Student from a Low-Income Family	$347.68	0.06
Special Learning Issues (IEPs)	$4,093.14	0.76
Small County	$754.40	0.14
Students Below Grade Level	$105.51	0.02
Disadvantaged Student Supplemental Fund	$263.13	0.05
Low Wealth County	$301.42	0.06
Limited English Proficiency	$839.54	0.16
Intellectually and Academically Gifted	$425.24	0.08
Career and Technical Ed	$0.00	0.00
Cooperative Innovative HS	$0.00	0.00

Source: Levinson, (2018) https://goo.gl/cu2dnT Weights calculated by authors.

PROGRAM EVALUATION

In 2016 the General Assembly's research arm, the Program Evaluation Division (PED), issued a report critical of the allotment system. In the report, PED found that the school funding mechanism results in a resource distribution that favors wealthy counties, limits the ability of districts with high concentrations of students with disabilities to serve that population, and leaves low-wealth and small-county districts behind. Based on these findings, PED recommended the General Assembly either adopt a weighted student funding model or address deficiencies in the existing allotments to improve transparency and accountability. PED argued that a weighted student funding model would be simpler for both LEAs and the public to understand, allowing for better input and buy-in.[20]

In response to the PED report, the General Assembly in 2017 formed a task force of 18 geographically diverse legislators (nine from each chamber) to study weighted student funding models, the required levels of funding necessary to achieve desired outcomes, and how funding should be distributed among the 115 LEAs. The task force's report and recommendations were due October 1, 2018.[21] The state's executive branch had a more muted response to the PED report, advancing arguments that North Carolina promotes equity by assuming the burden for a large percentage of total overall per-pupil funding, thereby reducing the inherent inequities present in allowing local funding based on property tax wealth and also that the sum total of position allocations and categorical allotments provides equitable funding across North Carolina districts in terms that address teacher quality and student needs. Additionally, testimony by school finance officers across the state noted relatively broad support for the status quo and the advantages of position-based allotments.

NEW DIRECTIONS

Finance-related activity with the potential to impact the operation and implementation of funding reform in North Carolina into the next five years includes:

- Efforts to change the state's class size mandates to align with the ratios in the funding model, with implications for both capital construction and teacher hiring, as many LEAs use the difference between the mechanism ratios and the class size legislation to staff positions in the arts and other ancillary subjects;
- Action on the forthcoming report of the Joint Legislative Task Force on Education Finance Reform which has been considering options

to keep and adjust the current mechanism or push toward a more explicit pupil weighting model;
- Starting in 2018, teachers entering the profession in North Carolina were no longer eligible for retirement healthcare benefits. The impact on early-career teachers is unknown;
- Principal pay has been revamped, resulting in some principals potentially earning tens of thousands of dollars less in salary. While the General Assembly employed a one-year hold-harmless, the impact on the principal corps may be dramatic, as principals may wish to retire to lock in higher salaries in their final years of employment rather than work with reduced salaries and their potential impact on retirement benefit calculations;
- The governor's Leandro Commission, tasked with determining solutions to adequately fund the *Leandro* case's 'sound, basic education' mandate, will release findings with implications for levels and mechanisms of funding.

NOTES

1. NC State Board of Education, "Chapter One," History of SBE. https://stateboard.ncpublicschools.gov/about-sbe/history/chapter-one
2. Ibid.
3. 347 U.S. 483 (1954).
4. Benjamin R. Justesen and Scott Matthews, "Part 5: Desegregation and Equality in Public Education," *Public Education* (NCpedia. January 1, 2006). Retrieved from https://www.ncpedia.org/public-education-part-5
5. Anthony R. Rolle, Eric A. Houck, and Ann McColl, "And Poor Children Continue to Wait: An Analysis of Horizontal and Vertical Equity among North Carolina School Districts in the Face of Judicially Mandated Policy Restraints 1996–2006," *Journal of Education Finance 34* no. 1 (2008): 75–102; Marshall S. Smith and Jennifer O'Day, "Systemic School Reform," *Journal of Education Policy* 5 no. 5 (1990): 233–267, DOI: 10.1080/02680939008549074
6. N.C. Gen. Stat. § 115C-81.5 (2017).
7. Ibid.
8. *Britt v. State of North Carolina* 357 S.E.2d 432 (1987).
9. *Leandro v. State,* 488 SE.2d 249 (1997). Retrieved from https://law.duke.edu/childedlaw/schooldiscipline/attorneys/casesummaries/leandrov state/
10. *Allotment-Specific and System-Level Issues Adversely Affect North Carolina's Distribution of K–12 Resources.* Report no. 2016–11. June 4, 2017. Retrieved from https://www.ncleg.net/PED/Reports/documents/K12/K12_Report.pdf
11. Ibid.
12. See finding 7 here: https://www.ncleg.net/documentsites/committees/bcci6701/Final%20Report%20of%20the%20Jt%20Leg%20Study%20Committee%20on%20Division%20of%20Local%20School%20Admin%20Units.pdf

13. North Carolina Department of Public Instruction. *North Carolina Public Schools Allotment Policy Manual.* Retrieved from http://www.ncpublicschools.org/docs/fbs/allotments/general/newpolicies17-18.pdf
14. Ibid.
15. Ibid.
16. North Carolina Department of Public Instruction. *Low Wealth Supplemental Funding.* Retrieved from https://www.ncleg.net/DocumentSites/Committees/JLEDGEOC/2015-2016/Meeting%20Documents/3%20-%20March%2017,%202016/5%20%20DPI_Philip%20Price%20Low%20Wealth%20EDGE%20Presentation.pdf
17. Authors' calculations.
18. North Carolina Department of Public Instruction. *North Carolina Public Schools Allotment Policy Manual.* Retrieved from http://www.ncpublicschools.org/docs/fbs/allotments/general/newpolicies17-18.pdf
19. Ibid.
20. *Allotment-Specific and System-Level Issues Adversely Affect North Carolina's Distribution of K–12 Resources.* Report no. 2016-11. June 4, 2017. Retrieved from https://www.ncleg.net/PED/Reports/documents/K12/K12_Report.pdf
21. North Carolina General Assembly. *Committee Charge.* Retrieved from https://www.ncleg.net/documentsites/committees/BCCI-6685/CommitteeMeetings/Committee Charge.pdf

CHAPTER 36

North Dakota

Jerry Coleman
Director (2009–2017)
School Finance and Organization
North Dakota Department of Public Instruction

GENERAL BACKGROUND

A foundation aid program designed to provide financial assistance to local school districts has been in effect in North Dakota since 1959. This initial program was adopted in part because the legislature recognized that property valuations, demographics and educational needs varied from school district to school district. The following is a condensed version of the evolution of the program.[1]

- Major changes began in the 1970s, introducing equity adjustments and recognizing economies of scale;
- In the early 1980s the state tapped into mineral taxes to supplement the common schools trust fund with the goal of providing 60% of the cost of education from state sources;
- A subsequent bust economy eroded state aid and pushed the funding burden onto local property taxes throughout the 1980s;.
- During this time, legal action on the national level informed many changes the state began to undertake;
- Two equity and adequacy lawsuits[2] provided impetus for structural changes to the major funding formulas. As a condition to staying the second lawsuit, the governor created a commission made up of school leaders, legislators and agency heads with heavy involvement

of stakeholder groups. Largely due to the chemistry of its members, this commission performed much of the heavy lifting in creating and selling an acceptable solution;
- A new formula adopted by the 2007 legislature combined several funding line items with different allocation bases into one comprehensive formula. This was enabled in large part by an improving economy;
- The economy continued to boom due to advancement in hydraulic fracturing for oil recovery and improving commodity prices. Higher tax revenue aided efforts to further reform the K–12 funding formula and provide tax relief;
- The state took the next major step in 2013, as significant property tax relief was integrated into the formula.[3] School district levy authority was dramatically reduced and a per-student payment rate based on the cost of providing an adequate education was adopted. The changes shifted state/local support percentages from roughly 50/50 to 75/25.

BASIC SUPPORT PROGRAM

The main school aid funding formula in North Dakota distributes well over 90% of total state K–12 funding. Transportation and special education excess cost funding have separate appropriations. The formula is driven by average daily membership (ADM) and uses various weights to account for the increased costs associated with school district size and serving students with special needs. In addition, there are adjustments to minimize budget impacts as districts transition to the new formula.

The base per-student rate was set by the legislature at $9,646 for each year of the 2017–19 biennium. The base level funding addresses education and operational costs for school districts. This includes core staffing, administration, operation, professional development, technology and instruction materials.[4]

Table 36.1 describes the basic components of the formula.[5] Part One calculates the base funding level by multiplying weighted student units by the base per-student rate set by the legislature and applies transition adjustments. Part Two determines the funding sources. The local share is 60 mills from local property taxes, plus a designated percentage of other local in-lieu-of property tax sources. The state aid payment provides the amount not funded by local sources.

Student Membership (ADM)

The main driver for the formula is student enrollment, as determined by the ADM of the most recently completed school year. A student's ADM

TABLE 36.1 North Dakota K–12 School Funding Formula		
Part One: Calculate Base Funding Amount		Example District
	A. Student Membership (ADM)	300
+	B. Other Program Weighted ADM	30
=	C. Weighted ADM	30
×	D. C. School District Size Factor	1.13
=	E. Weighted Student Units	363
×	F. Per Student Rate	$9,646
=	G. Total Formula Amount	$3,600,000
Part Two: Determine State Aid Payment		
Local Share	60 mills times taxable valuation	$600,000
	70%–100% of local in lieu revenue	$6,000
State Share	Difference is State Aid Payment	$2,940,000

is calculated by dividing the number of days a student was enrolled in the school district by the number of days in the regular school calendar (the minimum required in North Dakota is 182 days). Membership in less than a full day program is prorated based on hours.

Other Program Weighted ADM

Table 36.2 identifies the weighting factors used to reflect the differential costs of educating students based on factors such school size, special education and limited English proficiency (ELL). The state provides funding for regional education associations (REAs) through a factor in the main funding formula. REAs provide educational support services to member school districts. The funding generated by the factor is forwarded directly to the REA to which the district belongs. The state also provides each REA a $31,250 annual base operating grant.

School District Size Factor

Weighting factors are established for three broad size categories based on school district ADM. Districts with ADM less than 110 receive a factor of 1.36. Districts with ADM between 110 and 900 are assigned a factor ranging from 1.35 down to 1.00. Districts at or over 900 ADM are not adjusted; e.g., their factor is 1.00.[6]

TABLE 36.2 North Dakota Weighting Factory Estimates 2017–18 School Year

Student Based	Weight	ADM Added	Amount Generated
Alt High School	0.250	201	$1,941,740
Alt Middle School	0.150	2	$21,740
Special Ed ADM (based on district ADM)	0.083	8,858	$85,446,294
PK Special Ed ADM	0.170	194	$1,875,858
ELL Level 1	0.400	143	$1,875,858
ELL Level 2	0.280	188	$1,814,413
At Risk	0.025	1,009	$9,734,357
Home-Education (district supervised)	0.200	11	$106,974
Summer Program			
Summer School	0.600	1,261	$12,164,378
Special Ed ESY	1.000	49	$472,847
Isolated School District			
> 275 sq miles and < 100 ADM	0.100	116	$1,114,499
> 600 sq miles and < 50 ADM	1.100	—	—
Other			
Regional Education Association	0.002	209	$2,016,207

Transition Adjustments

When the new funding formula was enacted, consideration was given to minimizing disruption in local budgets due to the changes. This was addressed through transition adjustments based on funding levels in the 2012–13 payment year (the year preceding the formula change). An effective funding rate was established for each school district based on the revenue sources considered in the formula (state aid, property taxes and identified in-lieu of property tax revenue).

- Districts were guaranteed at least the effective rate per weighted student unit received in 2012–13. This rate has been increased periodically by the legislature;
- Districts were limited to a maximum effective rate per weighted student unit received in 2012–13. This limit was put in place to avoid windfalls certain districts would receive due to other unrestricted income not addressed in the formula. This rate has been increased periodically by the legislature;

- In addition, districts were guaranteed the same base level amount in dollars they received in 2012–13. This provided a floor in dollars not tied to enrollment changes.

SUPPLEMENTAL GENERAL FUND

North Dakota provides no supplemental state funds to school districts to reward or equalize for higher local levy effort.

COMPENSATORY EDUCATION

State/local funding generated for compensatory programs is done through weighting factors in the general state aid formula. The following weighting factors were effective for 2017–2018:

- *Alternative education*: A weighting factor of .25 times alternative education ADM generated $2 million for districts operating approved alternative education programs;
- *English language learners:* A weighting factor times English language learner ADM generated $4 million for districts providing programs to students assessed eligible in one of the three highest need categories. The level I factor is .40, the level II factor is .28 and the level III factor is .07;
- *At-risk:* A weighting factor of .025 times the district's free and reduced price lunch percentage times the district's ADM generated $10 million. The free and reduced price lunch percentage is based on a rolling three-year average of eligible students in grades 3–8;
- *Summer programs:* A weighting factor of .60 times extended school year ADM generated $12 million for districts providing approved high school, migrant and remedial elementary summer programs.

Federal title programs provide significant funding to improve education for disadvantaged students. These programs are operated under the rules and regulations of the agency granting the funding. Expenditures for Title I and bilingual programs were $40 million in 2016–17.

SPECIAL EDUCATION

Additional formula funding identified for special education programs is generated through a weighting factor in the state aid formula, applied to the total ADM of the school district. Weights are added for preschool and extended year summer programs required by a student's individual education plan.

Separate funding is set aside at the state level to cover excessive costs of special education and agency placed students. School districts can claim reimbursement for costs over established liability limits depending upon the reason for the student's placement. Generally speaking, students placed by a school district for educational purposes are reimbursed for educational costs exceeding 4.0 times the state average cost of education. Student placements by external agencies for purposes other than education are reimbursed for educational costs exceeding 1.0 times the state average cost of education.

Special education services are provided through 32 special education units. Ten larger school districts operate as single district units, with the remainder organized into multi-district cooperatives. The units are approved by the state and share costs as governed by their by-laws.

Total special education expenditures were $206 million in Fiscal Year 2017. The special education weighting factor added approximately $88 million to state aid payments, and the state separately reimbursed school districts $14 million in excess costs for high cost special education and agency placed students. Federal special education funds provided $33 million.

CAREER AND TECHNICAL EDUCATION

Approved career and technical education programs are funded in part through the State Board for Career and Technical Education,[7] an agency that is also involved in funding programs at designated post-secondary institutions. Local school districts are expected to provide a major portion of funding, and career and technical education programs are augmented by federal aid. School districts and area centers reported spending $57 million on career and technical education programs in FY 2017. Federal sources provided $3 million, and state sources provided $8 million.

VIRTUAL EDUCATION

The North Dakota Center for Distance Education[8] (NDCDE) provides online courses that students can use for credit recovery, advanced placement, or courses not otherwise available in their school districts. The Center operates primarily on a fee basis. It is hosted within the state's Information Technology Division.

GENERAL TRANSPORTATION

State funding for transportation is provided to a maximum of 90% of actual expenditures under a rate schedule that uses the number of miles transported, the number of rides provided, and the type of vehicle used for transporting students to and from school. The following rates were effective for the 2017–19 biennium.

- School buses having a rated capacity of ten or more students are reimbursed at $1.11 per mile plus 30¢ per student ride provided;
- Vehicles with rated capacities of less than ten students are reimbursed at 52¢ per mile;
- Students transported by parents are reimbursed 25¢ per mile where school bus transportation is unavailable.

Total transportation expenditures were at $62 million in FY 2017, with $29 million coming from state sources.

SPECIAL LEVIES

School districts may levy local property tax in several ways. Some levies are under the general authority of the school board, while others require voter approval. School district levy authority was rewritten in 2013 with the implementation of the new integrated funding formula. Numerous special purpose levies were eliminated or combined. The following describes the school district levy authority as it exists today.

Fund Group 1—General Fund

- *General.* The general fund levy may not increase more than 12% in dollars over the previous year, up to a levy of 70 mills on the taxable valuation of property in the school district.[9] Local share in the state aid formula considers 60 of the 70 mills.[10] Voters can override levy restrictions by approving a specified mill levy rate. The approval can be for a period no longer than ten years at a time;
- *Miscellaneous.* Each district can levy up to 12 mills for any school district purpose without restriction;
- *Tuition.* A school district may levy the amount necessary to pay tuition for its students required to be educated in another school.

Fund Group 2—Special Reserve

- *Special Reserve.* Districts may levy up to three mills annually to build a special reserve fund to cover budget shortfalls. The fund cannot exceed an amount raised by a levy of 15 mills. Any excess funds are transferred to the general fund at the end of the year.

Fund Group 3—Capital Projects

- *Building*. Voters can approve up to 20 mills for a building fund dedicated to building maintenance and capital projects;
- *Special Assessment*. The school board has authority to levy the amount necessary to pay special assessments.

Fund Group 4—Debt Service

- *Sinking and Interest*. Voters can approve a levy to service bonded debt. A 60% majority vote is required;
- *Bond Judgment*. The school board may levy to pay any final judgment obtained against the school district.

SCHOOL FACILITIES

Plant operation and maintenance costs are included in the base per-student funding rate used for the state aid formula.

CAPITAL IMPROVEMENT

The state does not provide direct funding for capital improvements. School districts may pay for infrastructure purchases through existing levy authority, building fund levies and bond levies. All construction projects over $150,000 must have approval from the North Dakota Department of Public Instruction.

The state has set up a school construction assistance revolving loan fund to provide low interest loans to school districts. The fund is capitalized at $225 million and is authorized to make 2% loans to school districts that have approval for a bond issue.[11] Low interest loans for emergency purposes are also made available through the North Dakota Department of Trust Lands.

CAPITAL OUTLAY

Projects for North Dakota school districts are funded by local property taxes. For major projects, the local school board may request authority from the voters to issue bonds. A supermajority (60%) of qualified voters voting on the proposed project is necessary for approval.

Total outstanding bonds cannot exceed 10% of the total assessed valuation in the district. The voters confer authority to incur indebtedness at a specified amount, to then sell bonds to raise funding for the proposed project, and finally to establish a sinking and interest fund and associated levy to raise revenue to pay interest and amortize the outstanding principal.[12] School boards may also secure authority from voters to establish and maintain a building fund.[13] This authority may be approved for a maximum of 20 mills per year. Since 1985, school boards have had authority on their own initiative to sell bonds and then pay interest and amortize the principal from the proceeds of the building fund levy. A number of restrictions and requirements apply to such action. Capital project expenditures for 2016–2017 were $225 million.

FOOD SERVICES

The Child Nutrition and Food Distribution[14] office within the North Dakota Department of Public Instruction administers USDA child nutrition programs, nutrition education and training programs, and commodity assistance for schools, institutions and low-income individuals. The state participates through a required match. School districts are expected to operate food services in full compliance with federal and state regulations. Total spending for school food service was reported at $68 million in FY 2017. State receipts were $1.6 million and federal receipts totaled $24 million.

STATE FUNDING FOR NON-PUBLIC SCHOOLS

There are no provisions for direct aid to private schools in North Dakota. Sharing of services mandated by federal law is provided through school districts or special education units. The state has no provisions authorizing charter schools.

OTHER STATE AIDS

The state hosts PowerSchool, a student management information system, and requires school districts to use it. This system provides substantial amounts of data for state reporting and longitudinal data systems. It is funded by a direct state appropriation to the Information Technology Division at a cost of roughly $25 per student annually. K–12 schools connect to the state's communication backbone for broadband, Internet and networking services.

From time to time the legislature provides supplemental grants to school districts to address specific initiatives. These grants do not make up a significant part of school funding. Programs are almost always considered one-time funding but can and have been continued over several biennia. Grants have addressed teacher compensation, declining enrollment, rapid enrollment, supplemental English language learner programs, deferred maintenance, and school safety grants.

Special grant programs authorized for 2017–2019 were supplemental English language learner programs ($500,000) and rapid enrollment grants ($6 million). Supplemental flat grants ($500,000) were awarded to Regional Education Associations in addition to the funding generated through the funding formula. The 2017–2019 state aid appropriation included $800,000 for gifted and talented grants to school districts.

RETIREMENT

The Teachers' Fund for Retirement[15] (TFFR) is a qualified defined benefit public pension plan that is administered through the state's Retirement and Investment Office. The state does not provide direct contributions to the teacher retirement fund. The Legislative Assembly specifies the level of contribution required of both school districts and individual teachers. Employer contribution was 12.75% and member contribution was 11.75% as of July 1, 2014.

REVENUE

State general fund revenue for aid payments to local school districts is primarily derived from income, sales and mineral taxes as well as earnings from trust funds, the state owned bank, and the state owned mill and elevator. An increasingly significant source of K–12 formula funding comes from the common schools trust fund[16] and the foundation aid stabilization fund.[17] These two special funding sources were expected to provide $300 million of the $1 billion state aid distribution for K–12 in the first year of the 2017–2019 biennium.

The federal government provided $127 million in restricted funding in FY 2017, primarily for title, special education and food service programs. Districts received another $41 million in unrestricted federal revenue to compensate for the impact of reservations, military bases and national grasslands.

Local revenue is determined after state, federal and other revenue sources are identified. School districts prepare annual budget certifications, subtract projected state, federal and other sources, and levy the remainder in property taxes within statutory limits. Districts levied taxes of $320 million for general fund purposes in FY 2017. Another $108 million was levied for building funds and debt service.

SUMMARY

Table 36.3 summarizes the state agency appropriations supporting North Dakota public education for the 2017–2019 biennium.[18] Appropriations to

TABLE 36.3 North Dakota Legislative Appropriations–Education 2017–2019

	General Fund	Other Funds	Total
Elementary, Secondary and Other Education			
201 Department of Public Instruction			
226 Department of Trust Lands	$1,435,600,000	$897,500,000	$2,333,100,000
250 State Library	—	$238,500,000	$238,500,000
252 School for the Deaf	$5,600,000	$2,200,000	$7,800,000
253 North Dakota Vision Services/School for the Blind	$4,400,000	$1,200,000	$5,600,000
270 Department of Career and Technical Education	$29,600,000	$12,100,000	$41,700,000
Higher Education			
215 North Dakota University System	$103,900,000	$26,400,000	$130,300,000
227 Bismarck State College	$30,700,000	$73,000,000	$103,700,000
228 Lake Region State College	$12,800,000	$24,100,000	$36,900,000
229 Williston State College	$8,400,000	$19,900,000	$28,300,000
230 University of North Dakota	$134,900,000	$819,900,000	$954,800,000
232 University of North Dakota School of Medicine and Health Sciences	$57,800,000	$154,100,000	$211,900,000
235 North Dakota State University	$129,100,000	$689,400,000	$818,500,000
238 North Dakota State College of Science	$35,200,000	$57,600,000	$92,800,000
239 Dickinson State University	$26,100,000	$29,700,000	$55,800,000
240 Mayville State University	$14,300,000	$30,300,000	$44,600,000
241 Minot State University	$39,900,000	$64,300,000	$104,200,000
242 Valley City State University	$20,500,000	$51,000,000	$71,500,000
243 Dakota College at Bottineau	$7,700,000	$9,600,000	$17,300,000
244 North Dakota Forest Service	$4,400,000	$10,700,000	$15,100,000
Total	$2,108,400,000	$3,214,700,000	$5,323,100,000
Total State Appropriation	$4,310,300,000		$13,553,400,000
K–12 Education	33.3%		17.2%
Other Education	1.1%		2.2%
Higher Education	14.5%		19.8%

support K–12 schools represented 33.3% of total state general fund appropriations. Higher education was 14.5% of total state general fund appropriations. Fall 2016 enrollment in North Dakota public higher education institutions was 37,872. Fall 2016 enrollment in North Dakota public elementary and secondary schools was 106,863.

NOTES

1. A more complete narrative on the legislative history relative to state school funding can be found in the background memorandums prepared by Legislative Council staff for interim education committees. See "Elementary and Secondary Education State Aid and Funding Formula Study—Background Memorandum," Legislative Council. Retrieved from: http://www.legis.nd.gov/files/resource/committee-memorandum/19.9030.01000.pdf
2. *Bismarck Public School District No. 1 v. North Dakota*, 511 N.W.2d 247 (N.D. 1994); *Williston Public School District No. 1 et al. v. State of North Dakota, et al.*, Civil No. 03-C-507 (Dist. Ct. Northwestern Judicial Circuit, N.D. (2003); Agreement to Stay Litigation, *Willison Public School District No. 1 v. State*, No. 03-C-507 (N.D. Dist. Ct. 2006).
3. The term "state school aid integrated formula" is often used for the foundation aid formula because of the significant amount of property tax relief provided through the formula.
4. The legislature, through the interim education funding committee, contracted with Picus, Odden and Associates to study the adequacy of the base level of support. The report can be found in the meeting minutes. See "Minutes of the EDUCATION FUNDING COMMITTEE Monday, June 2, 2014," North Dakota Legislative Branch. Retrieved from: http://www.legis.nd.gov/assembly/63-2013/interim/15-5088-03000-meeting-minutes.pdf?20141016152129.
5. The School Finance and Organization Office of the North Dakota Department of Public Instruction publishes an Excel worksheet on its web page that fully implements the actual formula computation. See "Worksheet for Estimating School District Revenue," School Finance and Organization, North Dakota Department of Public Instruction. Retrieved from: https:/www.nd.gov/dpi/SchoolStaff/SchoolFinance/SchoolDistrictFinance/SchoolDistrictBudgeting/
6. "North Dakota Century Code, Title 15.1-27-03.2—School District Weighting Size Factor," North Dakota Legislative Branch. Retrieved from: http://www.legis.nd.gov/cencode/t15-1c27.html, accessed April 4, 2018.
7. https://www.nd.gov/cte/
8. https://www.ndcde.org
9. Districts may levy an amount in dollars using the alternative levy authority under North Dakota Century Code 57-15-01.1. The conditions necessary to use this authority are rarely met. See "North Dakota Century Code, Title 57-15-01.1—Protection of Taxpayers and Taxing Districts," North Dakota Legislative Branch. Retrieved from: http://www.legis.nd.gov/cencode/t57c15.html

10. The amount considered in the state aid formula cannot increase 12% over the prior year to protect school districts that are unable to levy 60 mills because of the 12% limit on general fund levy increases.
11. "North Dakota Century Code, Title 15.1-36 – School Construction," North Dakota Legislative Branch. Retrieved from: http://www.legis.nd.gov/cencode/t15-1c36.html.
12. "North Dakota Century Code, Title 21-03–Bonds," North Dakota Legislative Branch. Retrieved from: http://www.legis.nd.gov/cencode/t21c03.html.
13. "North Dakota Century Code, Title 57-15-16 – Tax levy for building fund in school districts," North Dakota Legislative Branch. Retrieved from: http://www.legis.nd.gov/cencode/t57c15.html
14. https://www.nd.gov/dpi/SchoolStaff/ChildNutritionFoodDistribution/
15. https://www.nd.gov/rio/tffr/default.htm
16. The common schools trust fund is provided for in Article IX of the Constitution of North Dakota, which provides that the fund is to be used to support the common schools of the state. The fund consists of income from state lands dedicated for the support of schools as well as 10% of oil extraction tax revenue and 45% of tobacco settlement money received by the state. The fund balance is approaching $4 billion dollars and income provided $300 million toward the $2 billion 2017–2019 state aid appropriation.
17. The foundation aid stabilization fund, provided for in Article X of the Constitution of North Dakota, was created by the voters to protect school districts from reductions due to state revenue shortfalls. This fund receives 10% of the oil extraction tax revenue. Once the fund reaches 15% of the general fund appropriation for K–12, the excess may be used for educational purposes. The legislature used $300 million from this fund to support the 2017–2019 appropriation, with $185 million considered one-time funding.
18. Source: "Agency Budget Information—200 Education," North Dakota Legislative Branch. Retrieved rom: http://www.legis.nd.gov/fiscal/agency#agency-200, accessed April 4, 2018.

CHAPTER 37

Ohio

Barbara M. De Luca, Ph.D.
Associate Professor
University of Dayton

GENERAL BACKGROUND

Although becoming a state in 1803, it was not until 1825 that the Ohio legislature established common schools financed with a one-half mill real property tax.[1] This tax increased to one mill in 1873, then 1.8 mills in 1920, and 2.65 mills shortly thereafter in 1921. In 1933, a constitutional change by voters limited the state's ability to impose property taxes and placed it in the hands of local voters, but still limited district-voted authority to 15 mills. Because of this, some districts received less money than when the tax was state-imposed and distributed. By this time, taxes on cigarettes and gasoline also provided revenue for schools.

The Ohio legislature approved a state lottery in 1975, with the promise that lottery money would help schools. However, much (if not most) of the lottery money distributed to schools supplanted money previously allocated through the state budget; it did not add to the amount provided prior to existence of the lottery. The following year, the legislature enacted House Bill 920 limiting property tax revenue to the dollar value of property at the point in time when new mills were initially approved. This meant that when property values increased due to simple growth in market value (not because of improvements to the property), the value of the increase did not generate additional tax until additional mills were approved by voters. It also meant that additional dollars generated were limited to those raised by the additional mills, not those already in place. The average percent of

Funding Public Schools in the United States and Indian Country, pages 531–542
Copyright © 2019 by Information Age Publishing
All rights of reproduction in any form reserved.

property increase was the percent by which existing mills decreased to account for each household's tax liability as a result of HB 920. The percent of the reduction was known as the reduction factor. This legislation remains in place the time of this writing.[2]

A 1981 law permitted local school district patrons to vote on a school district income tax in 0.25% increments. This law was repealed in 1983, but reenacted in 1989. A tax credit for residential and agricultural property of 12.5% is currently in effect for owner-occupied properties; the credit is 10% for properties owned, but not occupied. This credit is in effect for all levies prior to November 2013. Finally, there is a credit for senior homeowners dubbed the Homesite Exemption.

BASIC SUPPORT PROGRAM

Ohio uses a foundation program to support public schools. Each of the 610 school districts must levy a minimum 20 mills to participate in the state aid program. The guaranteed foundation formula amount, known as the 'Opportunity Grant,' was $6,000 per pupil in Fiscal Year 2017. Several factors affected how much of the $6,000 the state grants to each district.

Primary determinants of the basic support program are local district capacity and local district millage rate. Local capacity is the real property value per pupil (PVPP). In FY 2018, the lowest PVPP was $49,606 and the highest was $870,968.[3] Local millage for residential properties in FY 2018 ranged from 20 to 124.63 mills.

The dollar value of the Opportunity Grant is determined as shown in formula below. The 'State Share Index' is a calculation that includes property value adjusted for 30% or more tax-exempt property; income designed to equalize state funding; and district average daily membership (ADM).

$$\text{Opportunity Grant} = \text{Formula Amount} \times (\text{Formula Aid} + \text{Preschool Autism Scholarship ADM}) \times \text{State Share Index}$$

Table 37.1 shows adjustments that add value to the Opportunity Grant, while Table 37.2 shows items that deduct value due to transferring funds to other districts or schools.[4]

OPERATING REVENUE

Public P–12 school districts in Ohio have three revenue sources. Percentage of revenue from the federal government has fluctuated from a low 5.2% in 1997 and 1998 to a high 8.82% in 2010. In 2016, 5.6% of revenues came

TABLE 37.1 Adjustment Adding Value to Ohio Opportunity Grant

Adjustments	Purpose
Targeted Assistance	District with lower capacity
Capacity Aid	Small districts with low capacity
Special Education	6 categories of funding for students with special needs
K–3 Literacy	Promote grade-level reading
Economic Disadvantaged	Address poverty and its effect on educational outcomes
LEP Funding	Additional services for LEP students
Gifted Education	Identify students; provide intervention specialist and coordinator
Transportation	Regular transportation funding students outside two miles of school
Career Technical Education	Additional money for career technical programs
Capacity Aid	Equity money to support districts with weaker tax base
Graduation Bonus	Extra money for each high school graduate
Third Grade Reading Proficiency Bonus	Based on third grade reading proficiency
Transitional Aid Guarantee	Assurance that districts cannot receive less than Guarantee Base
Preschool Special Education	Extra funding to meet special needs of students
Special Education Transportation	Special transportation for students with special needs

TABLE 37.2 Adjustments Deducting from the Ohio Opportunity Grant

Adjustments (transfer)	Purpose
Education Service Center	Student services provided
Open Enrollment	Students entering minus student leaving
Community (charter) School	Money transferred for district students
STEM School	Money transferred for district students
Scholarship (Voucher) Transfer	Voucher student funds for district students

from the federal government. Similarly, state revenue fluctuated from a low 41.85% in 2005 and 2006 to a high 48.9% in 2016. Local districts contributed a high of 50.52% in 1999 and 2000 to a low of 45.6% in 2016.[5]

Federal Revenue

Some federal grant programs are formula-driven, and some are competitive. Table 37.3 identifies some federal formula aid programs and the dollar value of the Ohio award in FY 2017. In addition, in FY 2017 Ohio had

TABLE 37.3 Federal Formula Grant Funds K–12 in Ohio FY 2017

Formula Grant Funds	Ohio Award
Title I Part A	$554,604,331
Title IC-Migrant Education	$2,359,021
Title ID-Neglected and Delinquent State Agencies	$1,067,103
Title II-Supporting Effective Instruction	$76,021,227
Title III-English Language Acquisition	$10,629,695
Title IVB-21st Century Community Learning Centers	$44,356,299
Title IV-Student Support and Academic Enrichment (new 2015)	$15,074,220
Title 6B-Rural and Low Income	$3,950,872
Title VIIB-McKinney-Vento Homeless Children & Youth	$2,663,310
Small, Rural School Achievement Program	$2,303,891
Career and Technical Education	$42,750,001
Funding for Assessing State Achievement	$10,389,196
Impact Aid	$1,488,586
IDEA Part B[a]	$388,312,973

Note: Department of Education, Funds for State Formula-Allocated and Selected Student Aid Programs, Index to State Tables https://findit.ed.gov/search?utf8=%E2%9C%93&affiliate=ed.gov&query=ohio++2016+1%2C275%2C472%2C852

[a] Ohio Department of Education, http://education.ohio.gov/Topics/Special-Education-Data-and-Funding/Special-Education-Part-B-Allocations/Fiscal-Year-FY-15-IDEA-Part-B-Allocation

371,785 free-and-reduced-price-breakfast students and 663,311 free-and reduced-price-lunch students, generating additional federal money.[6] Additionally, other discretionary federal grant funds were received by the state of Ohio; for example the Striving Readers Comprehensive Literacy Program awarded $35 million to the state in FY 2017, along with another $1,833 million in FY 2015 from Math and Science Partnerships.

State Revenue

Every two years, the Ohio state legislature approves a biennial budget. With each new budget, the legislature guarantees that no district will receive less money than it did in the previous year. Similarly, it places a 'Gain Cap' to limit any increases due to changes in the funding formula. The FY 2018 gain cap was 3%.[7]

Of the total general revenue fund, approximately 24.6% of the FY 2019 operating budget was appropriated for public primary and secondary schools. If only state revenue is considered (i.e., federal reimbursements are removed from the total), 35.5% of the operating budget was allocated to K–12.[8] State revenue per pupil was $6,025.85 in FY 2017, accounting for 43.57% of total revenue.[9]

Local Revenue

Local revenue for Ohio's schools is generated from real local property tax and school district income tax. The average number of operating mills per school district was 49.9 for FY 2018. In this same year, residential and agricultural real property valuation accounted for 73.37% of total property value, while all other real property accounted for 20.44%. The average district income tax per pupil for FY 2017 was $1,377.14. Average local revenue per pupil in FY 2017 was $5,779.10, 41.79% of total revenue.[10,11]

Local levy options are extensive in Ohio. Table 37.4 identifies and briefly describes the eight most common levies available to local districts. Aside from the levies voted on by the public in Table 37.4, each political district may impose ten mills without a vote (called 'inside mills'). On average, school districts access about half of these ten mills. Anything above the ten mills must be voted on by the public via one of the levies in Table 37.4.

The basic formula for generating local revenue is: Assessed Property Valuation × Number of Mills = Gross Tax. Assessed property value is 35%

TABLE 37.4 Ohio Local Voter-Approved Levies for K–12 Schools

Levy	Features	Term
Regular Operating Levy	Vote on mills, not dollars	1–5 years or continuous
Emergency Levy	Vote on dollars, not mills; mills adjusted each year to maintain levy dollar value	1–10 years
Incremental Tax Levy	Millage phased in on a regular schedule; maximum of 5 increments	1–10 years
Replacement Levy	For expiring operating levy; original number of mills on new (current) property value	1–5 years
Renewal Levy	For expiring operating levy; original number of mills on old (original) property value	1–5 years
Permanent Improvement Levy	Vote on dollars, not mills. For improvement of school property or purchase of assets lasting at least 5 years	1–5 years or continuous
School Safety and Security Levy	Vote on mills, not dollars	1–10 years or continuous
Combination Levy	Combination of any two of the above, plus bond issue	Term varies on request
Substitute Levy	Votes to substitute an emergency levy; allows for growth based on new construction	1–10 years

Source: Ohio School Finance Blue Book, Robert G. Stabile, 2018–2019 Edition.

TABLE 37.5 Sample Tax Calculation for Ohio School Property Tax

Assessed value of property	$100,000 × .35 = $35,000
Determine millage before RF	5 inside mills = 30 voted outside mills
Apply RF	25%
Determine millage after RF	30 voted outside mills—(30 × .25) = 22.5 + 5 = 27.5
Determine tax liability before credits	$35,000 × 27.5 mil = $962.50 = Gross Tax

of appraised property value, with appraisal updates completed every three years. Because of the reduction factor (RF) contained in HB 920 explained above, the number of mills is the total number of outside mills minus these same mills, multiplied by the reduction factor plus the inside mills. An example is shown in Table 37.5.

Finally, tax credits are subtracted from the gross tax to arrive at net taxes owed. The tax credits include a 12.5% owner-occupied credit (10% for owner, not occupied) and a Homesite Exemption credit for senior homeowners as described earlier.

SPECIAL EDUCATION

Special education funding in Ohio is determined by severity of pupil disability. Table 37.6 identifies the six levels of disability and the per-pupil funding amount for each level for FY 2018. Each dollar value is multiplied by the 'State Share Percent' as described earlier. The resultant dollar value follows the student to the school of attendance.

TABLE 37.6 Ohio Special Education Funding Levels 2018

Category	Disability	Per Pupil Funding
1	Speech and Language Impairments	$1,578
2	Learning, Intellectual, Other Minor Health, Developmentally Delayed Preschool	4,005
3	Deafness, Severe Behavior Disability (SBH)	9,622
4	Visual Impairment, Other Major Health Impairment	12,841
5	Orthopedic Impairment, Multiple Disabilities (other than Deaf-Blind)	17,390
6	Autism, Deaf-Blind, Traumatic Brain Injury	25,637

Source: Ohio Department of Education, FY2018 School Finance Payment Report Line-by-Line Explanation, October 2017. https://education.ohio.gov/getattachment/Topics/Finance-and-Funding/School-Payment-Reports/State-Funding-For-Schools/Traditional-Public-School-Funding/FY2018-SFPR-Funding-Form-Line-by-Line-Explanation.pdf.aspx

COMMUNITY (CHARTER) SCHOOLS

Charter schools, called 'Community Schools' in Ohio, are funded on a per-pupil basis. Community School money is equal to the amount per resident pupil the traditional school district would have received for each individual student for programs known as Opportunity Grant, Targeted Assistance, categorical Special Education, other Special Education Services, K–3 Literacy Funding, Economic Disadvantage Funding, LEP Funding, and Career Tech Funding. Transportation for charter school students is also funded in individual situations. The money is transferred to the charter school of attendance from the student's school district of residence. Nearly 340 Community Schools were available to students in FY 2018.[12]

In FY 2018, the Ohio Department of Education (ODE) provided about $32 million for a competitive grant opportunity for new 'high quality' charter schools to serve educationally and socioeconomically disadvantaged children. The goal of the grant was to improve the quality of charter school education in Ohio for more students. ODE is charged with monitoring the implementation of the plan and evaluating continued progress of the students in the new schools.[13]

SCHOLARSHIPS (VOUCHERS)

Ohio has an extensive voucher program. In Ohio, vouchers are known as 'scholarships.' Table 37.7 identifies each program, eligibility criteria, and the dollar value of the scholarship for FY 2018. In brief, the state provides 60,000 EdChoice scholarships per year for students in failing public schools or for children in low-income households to attend private schools. Students from

TABLE 37.7 Ohio Scholarship Programs 2018

Scholarship	Criteria	Dollar Value
Education Choice (EdChoice)	Student attends failing public school two-of-three years	K–8 = $4,650 9–12 = $6,000
EdChoice Expansion	Household at or within 200% of federal poverty guidelines	K–5 = $4,650
Jon Petershon Scholarship	K–12 student on an IEP in home district	Based on disability = $7,588–$27,000 max
Autism Scholarship	Child identified with autism and has an IEP from home district (Eligibility at age 3)	Lesser of fee for special education program or $27,000
Cleveland Scholarship	Cleveland Municipal School District student may attend private school in Cleveland	K–8 = $4,650 9–12 = $6,000

Source: http://education.ohio.gov/Topics/Other-Resources/Scholarships

about 125 schools were eligible for the EdChoice scholarship in 2018. About 428 schools are providers for EdChoice scholarship students, and 483 are providers for the EdChoice Expansion program. Parents can choose from 376 schools for the Jon Peterson Scholarship and another 289 for the Autism program. Forty-two schools are providers for Cleveland, Ohio students.[14]

FACILITIES

In 1997 as a result of *DeRolph v. State of Ohio*,[15] the state created the Ohio School Facilities Committee (OSFC) to institute and monitor a program to address the K–12 facility issues addressed in the lawsuit. In 2012, the OSFC and the Office of State Architect were combined to create the Ohio Facilities Construction Commission (OFCC), responsible for renovation and construction of state public K–12 buildings and state-supported universities, as well as cultural facilities, state agencies, and charter schools. All OSFC responsibilities were merged into those of the OFCC in 2017.[16]

The OFCC directs several programs for the construction and renovation of K–12 school buildings. One of the major K–12 programs for traditional public schools is the Classroom Facilities Assistance Program (CFAP), in place since 1997.[17] This is a shared program between each school district and the state. Each year the Ohio Department of Education ranks each public school district on a three-year average income-adjusted property valuation per pupil. The rank determines the order in which each district's facility needs are addressed by the OFCC. The ranks are converted to percentiles. Each district's percentile rank identifies the portion of the construction cost that will be paid by the state. The remaining cost is the responsibility of the district.[18]

The Expedited Local Partnership Program (ELPP) allows a district to move ahead of its ranked position in the CFAP to implement a portion of its construction project. There are several other facilities construction programs including one for exceptional needs, two for vocational facilities, one for Regional STEM schools, and one for College Prep Boarding Schools.[19]

Although it is not required, most districts raise their share of the facility money by asking the voting public to pass a bond issue. If the bond issue passes, the board receives all the money from the bond and invests it, pulling out the necessary funds to finance the construction project as it proceeds. At the end of each year (20 or more), the bonds are bought back by the board until no more are outstanding.[20]

Finally, in June 2015 the state approved $25 million for a Community Schools Classroom Facilities Grant Program. In 2016, $17 million was awarded. Eight high-performing schools received this money. Of the remaining $8 million four schools were awarded a total of $4 million in Round 2 in 2018.[21]

TRANSPORTATION

Ohio students are counted as a district transportation student the first time they are transported each day during the first full week in October, known as 'Count Week.' They are not counted a second time from school to home. The state reimburses districts for transporting preschool handicapped students on the regular transportation route, as well as K–12 students living more than one mile from their home school.[22]

In FY 2016, the total cost of transporting all students was $731,994,094 or $876.69 per student. Slightly more than 753,000 public school students, nearly 25,500 charter school students, and 55,876 nonpublic school students were transported in that same year. These numbers included students transported by district/board owned busses and other vehicles, leased and contracted services and buses, and by parents who were reimbursed at some level by the state.[23]

Charter schools may elect to provide their own transportation rather than use the student school-of-residence services.[24]

EXPENDITURES

Table 37.8 shows expenditures during FY 2017 as a percent of total expenditures for traditional public schools and charter schools.

TABLE 37.8 Ohio K–12 School Expenditures FY 2017

Expenditure (Mean)	TPS (*n* = 609)	Charter (*n* = 361)
Classroom Instruction per Pupil	$7,466.42	$7,265.97
Range	$0–$24,247	$452–$7,266
Operating Expenditures	$29,711,187	$3,147,384
Range	$533,176–$741,732,367.90	$140,594–$124,703,328
General Administration per Pupil	$385.93	$1,129.16
Range	$0–$3,029.02	$0–$1,129.16
School Administration per Pupil	$661.79	$1,328.10
Range	$0–$1,670	$0–$9,919.00
Operation and Maintenance per Pupil	$1,141.14	$944.02
Range	$0–$4,405.39	$0–$5,061.00
Classroom Instruction Percent	66.79%	60.53%
Nonclassroom Instruction Percent	33.21%	39.47%

Source: http://reportcard.education.ohio.gov/downloaddata/2016-2017/financial expenditures/fy17_expanded_list.xls

Zeroes do not necessarily mean no expenditure occurred in a given category. Although the Uniform School Accounting System (USAS) User Manual[25] is designed to guide supervisors to file expenditures under specific categories, it is likely that the same expenditure is filed under one of several different categories by different school/district finance managers.

SUMMARY

Ohio's public schools receive federal, state, and local money for traditional public schools and charter schools. Federal government money makes up less than 10% of the total, while state and local monies make up the remainder, with each contributing close to half. Federal money comes primarily in the form of categorical grants promoting equity. Likewise, the goal of some state money is to promote equity, while some promotes adequacy and some is directed to stimulate high quality education. Local money is based completely on wealth or income and the local voter willingness to pay.

Charter schools and voucher programs are major controversial issues in Ohio. Another issue often raised is the effect of HB 920 and the Reduction Factor. This causes Ohio voters to return to the ballot box on a relatively frequent basis. The *DeRolph* case,[26] filed on the basis of inequity and inadequacy, claimed that the state did not provide a 'thorough and efficient' system of common schools, as mandated by the Ohio constitution due to the inequities from district to district and school to school. The biennial budget passed by the state legislature attempts to address those inequities in a variety of ways, but many such as those mentioned above have become very controversial.

NOTES

1. Ohio History Central. Retrieved from http://www.ohiohistorycentral.org/w/Public_Education
2. Richard E. Maxwell and Scott R. Sweetland, *Ohio School Finance: A Practitioner's Guide*, Newark, NJ: Matthew Bender & Company, Inc., a member of LexisNexis, 2008.
3. OhioDepartmentofEducation,FY2017LocalDistrictProfileReport.Retrievedfrom http://education.ohio.gov/Topics/Finance-and-Funding/School-Payment-Reports/District-Profile-Reports/FY2017-District-Profile-ReportLocaldistrict
4. Ohio Department of Education, FY2017 District Profile Report. Retrieved from http://education.ohio.gov/Topics/Finance-and-Funding/School-Payment-Reports/District-Profile-Reports/FY2017-District-Profile-Report
5. Robert G. Stabile, Ohio Finance Blue Book 1998–99 edition, 2002–2003 edition, 2004–2005 edition, 2006–2007 edition, 2008–2009 edition, 2010–2011

edition, 2012–2013 edition, 2014–2015 edition, 2016–2017 edition, 2018–2019 edition.
6. Food Research and Action Center. Retrieved from http://www.frac.org/maps/sbp-state/tables/tab1-sbp-partic.html
7. Robert G. Stabile, Ohio School Finance Blue Book, 2018–2019 edition.
8. Building for Ohio's Next Generation: Budget of the State of Ohio, Fiscal Years 2018–2019. Retrieved from http://obm.ohio.gov/Budget/operating/fy18-19.aspx).
9. FY2017 District Profile Report. Retrieved from http://education.ohio.gov/Topics/Finance-and-Funding/School-Payment-Reports/District-Profile-Reports/FY2017-District-Profile-Report
10. FY2017 District Profile Report. Retrieved from http://education.ohio.gov/Topics/Finance-and-Funding/School-Payment-Reports/District-Profile-Reports/FY2017-District-Profile-Report)
11. Ohio School Boards Association, Understanding School Levies. Retrieved from https://www.ohioschoolboards.org/sites/default/files/OSBAUnderstandingLeviesFactSheet.pdf
12. http://education.ohio.gov/getattachment/Topics/Finance-and-Funding/School-Payment-Reports/State-Funding-For-Schools/Community-School-Funding/Community-School-Funding-Information/FY18-CS-FTE-manual-total-1.pdf.aspx
13. http://education.ohio.gov/getattachment/Topics/Community-Schools/Charter-School-Program-Grant-CSP/CSP_NoticeofGrantOpportunity.pdf.aspx
14. https://scholarship.ode.state.oh.us/
15. 699 N.E.2d 516) 1998); see also Ohio History Central, *DeRolph vs. State of Ohio*. Retrieved from http://www.ohiohistorycentral.org/w/DeRolph_v._State_of_Ohio
16. OFCC, Overview/History http://ofcc.ohio.gov/About/OverviewHistory.aspx
17. OFCC, K–12 Programs http://ofcc.ohio.gov/ServicePrograms/K–12Schools.aspx
18. Ohio Department of Education, FY2017 District Profile Report. Retrieved from http://education.ohio.gov/Topics/Finance-and-Funding/School-Payment-Reports/District-Profile-Reports/FY2017-District-Profile-Report
19. OFCC, K–12 Programs. Retrieved from http://ofcc.ohio.gov/ServicePrograms/K–12Schools.aspx
20. Robert G. Stabile, Ohio School Finance Blue Book, 2018–2019 edition).
21. OFCC, Community School Classroom Facilities Grants. Retrieved from http://ofcc.ohio.gov/ServicesPrograms/CommunitySchoolClassroomFacilitiesGrantsRound2.aspx
22. Ohio Department of Education, T-1 Report Instructions. Retrieved from http://education.ohio.gov/getattachment/Topics/Finance-and-Funding/School-Transportation/School-Transportation-Finance/T-Report-Instructions-Worksheets/T-1-Report-2016-Final-Instructions.pdf.aspx
23. Ohio Department of Education, Pupil Transportation Cost Analysis. Retrieved from http://webapp2.ode.state.oh.us/school_finance/transportation/cost_analysis/f2016_cost_analysis.asp

24. For more information, see Ohio Department of Education, Community School Transportation, https://education.ohio.gov/getattachment/Topics/Finance-and-Funding/School-Transportation/School-Transportation-Finance/T-Report-Instructions-Worksheets/Community-School-Transportation-Manual-v-2-0-3.pdf.aspx
25. David Yost, Auditor of State, Uniform School Accounting System User Manual. Retrieved from https://ohioauditor.gov/ publications/uniform_ school_accounting_system_user_manual.pdf Spring 2013
26. Ohio History Central, DeRolph vs. State of Ohio. Retrieved from http://www.ohiohistorycentral.org/w/DeRolph_v._State_ of_Ohio

CHAPTER 38

Oklahoma

Jeffrey Maiden, Ph.D.
*Professor
Senior Research Director
Institute for the Study of Education Finance
University of Oklahoma*

Shawn Hime, Ph.D.
*Executive Director
Oklahoma State School Boards Association
Advisory Council Chair
Institute for the Study of Education Finance*

GENERAL BACKGROUND

Although equalization of funding among school districts is not required by the Oklahoma constitution, the state legislature has established as a goal the maintenance of a degree of interdistrict funding equity as specified in state statute.[1] Accordingly, Oklahoma has utilized a two-tiered equalization education funding formula since 1981. The legislature annually appropriates state aid to flow through both 'halves' of the formula in a single line item.[2] The state annually provides the largest share of funding for common schools, and education represents the largest single item in the state's annual budget. The local portion of the school funding formula includes yields based on a total of 39 local district mills plus other chargeable local district income.

State funding for Oklahoma schools increased dramatically during the 1990s (mostly during the first half of the decade), due largely to implementation of the Oklahoma Reform and Funding Act of 1990,[3] more commonly known as House Bill 1017. However, the Oklahoma economy severely suffered from the recession of the early 2000s and the Great Recession of the late 2000s and into the year 2010. These downturns affected state funding for education.

Oklahoma is currently divided into 512 local non-charter school districts, down from 547 in 2000. These include independent K–12 districts, as well as dependent districts serving students in grades PK–8. Most local revenues are derived through ad valorem taxation (the 39 mill local levy through a variety of sources). School districts also may levy a maximum five mill building levy and a sinking fund levy for debt service. The state does not provide capital outlay support to local districts. Local districts additionally derive miscellaneous revenues from interest income, gifts, student fees, property sales, transfer fees, tuition, rental and refunds.

BASIC SUPPORT PROGRAM

The state of Oklahoma appropriated nearly $2.5 billion for general funding support to local school districts during Fiscal Year 2018. The basic state support mechanism for Oklahoma school district general funding includes a two-tiered equalization formula. The 'top half' includes a foundation formula coupled with a transportation supplement. The 'bottom half,' the salary incentive aid, is a modified guaranteed yield formula.[4] Currently, an Oklahoma State Aid Task Force has proposed legislation that would converge the two tiers plus the transportation supplement into a single foundation formula.[5]

State formula aid is enrollment-driven, with weighted average daily membership (ADM) used as the formula unit of funding through the foundation and salary incentive formulas (the transportation supplement uses average daily haul, or ADH). Currently, ADM is weighted across three categories. The first is grade level weight[6] and the second weighting category is special education classification.[7] For qualifying districts, ADM may also be adjusted per a small school weight. Districts that do not qualify for the small school weight may qualify for additional isolation funding, which is a grant-in-aid rather than an ADM weight.[8] The teacher index weight, which is applied only to the salary incentive aid, is provided to give districts the fiscal incentive to hire more experienced teachers with graduate degrees.[9]

The foundation program (known locally as the top half of the formula) for a given local school district includes a base support factor ($1,583 for FY 2018) multiplied by the district's weighted ADM. The local foundation program income for the district is subtracted from this product. This income includes the district 15 mill tax levy, 75% of the four mill countywide levy, and collections from state-dedicated revenue sources (i.e., motor vehicle tax collections, gross production tax revenues, rural electrification tax revenues, and school land earnings). State foundation aid for a given district is the difference between the total foundation program and local foundation program income. State-appropriated aid to school districts is thereby disbursed in inverse proportion to local ability to raise revenue.

The salary incentive aid formula (known locally as the bottom half of the formula) is fundamentally a guaranteed yield formula, constituting a second-tier resource equalization program. The local portion of the program is derived from an annual maximum 20 mill levy for each local school district across three separate levies (the local support, emergency, and county levies). For FY 2018, the state guaranteed $72.97 per weighted ADM for every mill levied up to 20 mills.

District aid is calculated semiannually in July and January. Aid is distributed through 11 monthly electronic transfers to local school districts. August through December disbursements are based on the July calculation, while January through June disbursements are based on a January calculation.

The number of 'out of formula' districts (i.e., those ineligible for foundation and/or salary incentive aid because of substantial amounts of local revenue), increased to 71 by FY 2018 (14% of all districts). This increase was likely due in large part to the general increase in local wealth statewide, coupled with decreases in state support dollars since the Great Recession.

Formula adjustments for vertical equity purposes also occur in Oklahoma's funding formula. Particularly, the weighted average daily membership is comprised of the average daily enrollment plus the sum of nine additional possible weights delineated in Title 70 Section 18 of Oklahoma State Statutes. The funding formula uses student- and district-level weights to satisfy vertical equity. Oklahoma funding formula weights are allocated based on identified differences in students, teachers, and district factors that affect the cost to educate students. Similarly, student economic disadvantage is addressed through a per-pupil add-on weight of .25 that is provided in both halves of the formula. This weight is meant to assist local school districts in defraying education costs for students from poverty as defined by qualification for free or reduced lunch services. Additional costs must be paid by districts, supplemented by federal funds. Total state aid formula revenue dedicated to students identified as economically disadvantaged in FY 2018 was $344.5 million, representing 9.9% of state aid formula revenue.

Table 38.1 details FY 2018 common schools state legislative appropriations.

TABLE 38.1 Fiscal Year 2018 Oklahoma Common Schools Appropriations

Purpose	FY 18 Appropriation
Financial Support of Public Schools	$1,870,977,666
General Revenue (GR)	$1,036,429,437
Education Reform Revolving Fund (1017 funds)	$695,407,138
Common Education Technology Fund	$47,372,299
Oklahoma Lottery Trust Fund	$31,369,754
Mineral Leasing Fund	$6,899,038
School Consolidation Assistance Fund	$2,500,000
Amount appropriated from Constitutional Reserve Fund (Rainy Day)	$51,000,000
Flexible Benefit Allowance (appropriated from GR)	**$462,695,967**
Certified Personnel	$299,320,340
Support Personnel	$163,375,627
Support of Public School Activities (appropriated from GR)	**$92,074,033**
Administrative and Support Functions (appropriated from GR)	**$15,681,105**
Lottery Trust Fund Transfers	**$6,971,058**
Total Appropriation	**$2,448,399,829**

Source: Oklahoma State Department of Education, *Oklahoma School Finance Technical Assistance Document,* October 2017.

REVENUE

State Revenue

The Oklahoma legislature annually appropriates monies to support public education, with revenues primarily flowing through the state aid formula. State general fund revenues derive mostly through the state income tax and state sales tax. Oklahoma also includes a state lottery, with 45% of lottery proceeds dedicated to common school funding. The legislature is constitutionally prohibited from using lottery trust fund proceeds to supplant other state funds in support of public education.[10]

Certain revenue sources are earmarked for support of public schools. Proceeds from these sources constitute part of the state's foundation aid to school districts. School land revenues derived from the Permanent School Fund are earmarked for local districts. This fund is administered by the Commissioner of the Land Office.

Rural Electrification Association (R.E.A.) tax revenues are in lieu of property tax collections and are distributed in proportion to the number of miles of transmission lines within each school district. Also, motor vehicle tax collections earmark 35% of fees to local school districts from a separate motor vehicle fund. Proceeds are distributed through each county to school districts based on ADA.

Finally, extractive industries provide a major source of revenue for Oklahoma schools. Gross production tax revenues in the amount of 10% are earmarked for school districts based on an ADA allocation.

Local Revenue

The largest source of local revenue for Oklahoma school districts is ad valorem tax collections. Assessment ratios are constitutionally capped at 35%. Local boards of education are authorized by the state constitution to annually levy 15 mills for general fund education support.[11] The revenue resulting from the 15 mill levy constitutes part of the local district's contribution to the state foundation formula.

Oklahoma school districts are constitutionally guaranteed proceeds from a four mill county wide levy.[12] These revenues are distributed to local districts based on ADA. Part of these revenues constitutes a portion of the local contribution to the state foundation program. In 2018, the State Aid Commission recommended that ADA be eliminated as an enrollment factor in any state aid calculation, to be replaced by ADM.[13]

District voters decide an additional 20 mills for general fund support. These are derived from three separate levies: A ten mill local support levy, a five mill emergency levy, and a five mill county levy.[14] The county levy must be approved by a majority countywide vote and distributed to local districts based on ADA. Proceeds from these 20 mills are equalized by the state through the salary incentive aid formula.

Districts may, with approval of a majority of voters, pass a five mill building fund levy to support capital costs. Proceeds are not equalized by the state. Further, depending on a 60% supermajority voter approval, districts may pass a sinking fund levy to service debt.

Oklahoma school districts do not generate revenue through either income or sales tax. In fact, local income taxation is prohibited by the Oklahoma constitution.[15] Additionally, districts are limited in the amount of ad valorem taxes annually levied for support of local school districts. Districts are only authorized to levy a maximum 39 mills for the support of the general educational program, along with the aforementioned additional five mill building fund. Districts may pass millage to service debt not to exceed 10% of total aggregate district net assessed valuation. By law, fair cash value of real property for tax purposes may be increased no more than 5% per taxable year, thereby limiting revenue growth. Finally, the state legislature, based on State Question 340 passed in 1992, may not increase state taxation rates without approval of a majority of voters participating in a statewide election.

TAX AND SPENDING LIMITS

Districts' administrative costs are statutorily limited according to ADA.[16] Districts exceeding these limits are subject to a state aid penalty, as well as a performance review of budgeting effectiveness and efficiency.[17]

- ADA > 1,500   5% penalty
- 500 > ADA < 1,500 7% penalty
- ADA < 500   8% penalty

FORMULA REWARDS AND SANCTIONS

Financial penalties are possible for Oklahoma school districts under certain conditions. Primarily, penalties are incurred as a result of noncompliance with certain elements of school reform. For example, districts that fail to comply with state-mandated class size restrictions may be penalized accordingly by having commensurate state aid withheld. Districts that employ too many noncertified teachers or which fail to maintain state minimum salary requirements likewise will face a measure of state aid reduction.

SPECIAL EDUCATION

Oklahoma school finance includes special education weights that are used in calculating weighted ADM in both halves of the state aid formula. The additional weights for special education students are shown in Table 38.2[18] These weights have undergone minor modifications, but there has been no substantive revision since implementation of the current formula in 1981. The State Aid Task Force recommended that the categories be revised and modernized and that cost analyses be used to revise the categorical weights.[19] Revenues are not tracked to expenditures. Any additional costs are borne by the local school districts, supplemented by federal funding. Special education funding from the state aid formula was $356.7 million in FY 2018, representing 10.2% of state aid revenue.

TRANSPORTATION

State aid to public school transportation is provided as a supplement to the foundation formula. The supplement is calculated by multiplying average

TABLE 38.2 Oklahoma Special Education Weights 2018	
Specific Learning Disability LD	0.40
Hearing Impaired	2.90
Visually Impaired	3.80
Multiple Disability	2.40
Speech or Language Impairment	0.05
Intellectual Disability	1.30
Traumatic Brain Injury	2.40
Autism	2.40
Emotionally Disturbed	2.50
Orthopedically Impaired	1.20
Other Health Impairment	1.20
Deaf - Blind	3.80
Spec Ed Summer Program	1.20

daily haul (ADH) by a per-capita transportation allowance and then multiplying this product by a transportation factor (1.39 for FY 2018).[20] The ADH for a district represents the number of students legally transported who live at least 1½ miles from school. Transportation supplement proceeds are fully fungible and are not tracked to specific transportation costs. Additional transportation costs are borne by local school districts. The State Aid Task Force proposed legislation to eliminate the transportation supplement.[21] Transportation aid in FY 2018 was $26.3 million, representing less than 1% of total state aid revenue.

FACILITIES AND CAPITAL OUTLAY

The Oklahoma constitution provides a State Public Common School Building Fund to assist school districts with capital outlay costs.[22] However, the Oklahoma legislature has never appropriated monies to the fund, and there is no state funding mechanism to support district capital outlay needs.

Local school districts may annually levy a maximum five mills to support a building fund. Building fund proceeds, with few exceptions as noted below, may not be mixed with the district's general fund. Most funding for capital outlay is derived through the sale of general obligation bonds. School districts may use bond authority only after the approval of at least 60% of the voters voting in an election[23] (bonded indebtedness is the only vote requiring a supermajority in Oklahoma). With passage of a bond issue, a debt service levy is concomitantly approved to service the debt. Although there is no limit on the number of debt service mills a school district may incur, no district may carry debt above a 10% ceiling of net assessed valuation.

Although the Oklahoma general school aid formula has demonstrated a degree of fiscal equity, capital outlay revenues among Oklahoma school districts are largely inequitable. Building fund proceeds cannot support general operations and vice versa. However, there are a few crossover areas that may be supported by either the general fund, building fund, or bond funds.[24] Crossover expenditures from the building fund include a school's utility bills, custodial, maintenance and security salaries, furniture, and insurance premiums. Bond fund expenditures that are also allowable from the general fund include equipment, textbooks, and library books. Therefore, inherent inequity in capital outlays appear to mitigate equities in general funding across Oklahoma districts, as wealthier districts are able to meet crossover funding costs more readily with building or bond fund proceeds, whereas less wealthy districts are more prone to rely more heavily on general fund proceeds to fund these crossover areas.[25]

STATE FUNDING FOR NON-PUBLIC SCHOOLS

The state of Oklahoma does not provide financial support for private schools, though local districts are subject to support provisions encapsulated in federal law.[26]

CHARTER SCHOOLS

Notwithstanding laws regarding public monies and private schools in Oklahoma, charter schools are authorized by the Oklahoma Charter School Act of 2010.[27] According to statute, certain organizations may sponsor charter schools if conditions outlined in statute are met. The Oklahoma State Department of Education lists 30 current charter schools operating in the state.[28] Charter schools receive state aid through the funding formula, based on district location. Statutes provide that a maximum 5% of the state allocation to a charter school may be retained by its sponsor for administrative costs.[29] Oklahoma grants charter authorization to the following organizations.

- School districts;
- Oklahoma State System of Higher Education member institutions;
- Federally recognized Indian Tribes;
- The State Board of Education.

Additionally, four virtual charter schools operate in Oklahoma. Virtual charter schools are governed by the Statewide Virtual Charter School Board[30] which has authority to oversee all virtual charter schools in the state. The board's authority includes regulating virtual charter school applications and sponsoring virtual charter schools.[31]

CAREER AND TECHNICAL EDUCATION

Career and technical education is governed by the Oklahoma Department of Career and Technology Education, with both governance and funding independent from Oklahoma common schools. The system includes 29 technology centers across 58 campuses statewide.[32]

GIFTED AND TALENTED EDUCATION

A student add-on weight of .34 is provided in both halves of the state school funding aid formula to assist local school districts in maintaining programs for gifted students. Additional costs must be borne by districts. State aid generated by the gifted weight was $87.8 million in FY 2018, representing 2.5% of state aid formula revenue.

BILINGUAL EDUCATION

A student add-on weight of .25 is provided for both funding formulas to assist Oklahoma school districts in defraying bilingual education costs. Additional cost must be borne by local districts, supplemented by federal funds. State aid derived from the bilingual weight was $64.9 million in FY 2018, representing 1.9 % of state aid formula revenue.

EARLY CHILDHOOD EDUCATION

Oklahoma students participating in early childhood programs are weighted at 0.7 (half-day students) or 1.3 (full day students) as part of the pupil grade level weight in both halves of the formula. Additional costs are borne by local school districts, supplemented by federal funds.

CATEGORICAL PROGRAMS

Numerous categorical programs were historically included as supplementary state supports outside the formula in Oklahoma. Examples include driver's education, funding for textbooks, and compensatory education among other areas. However, most of these categorical programs have been eliminated and proceeds have instead been appropriated through the state aid formula.

TEACHER RETIREMENT AND BENEFITS

Public school teachers, administrators and staff are members of the Oklahoma Teachers Retirement System (OTRS), a separate entity from the Oklahoma Public Employees Retirement System.[33] The OTRS is based on member contributions through payroll deductions, and districts are not required to fund employee contributions. The employer contribution is 9.5% of the employee's salary. The employee must pay 7% of salary toward the statutorily defined benefit plan.

TECHNOLOGY

The Common Education Technology Revolving Fund was established by statute in 2014.[34] Funds are derived through tax revenue from the gross production of oil and are used as part of the state aid formula.

RECENT/PENDING LITIGATION

No case has been decided since the Oklahoma supreme court upheld the state funding system in *Fair School Finance Council of Oklahoma, Inc. v. Oklahoma* in 1987.[35] *Fair II* in 1990[36] was filed but was never adjudicated.

SUMMARY

Oklahoma led the nation in state funding cuts per pupil as a percentage over the past decade (nearly 25%).[37] This fact exacerbates relatively poor funding levels in the state, given that Oklahoma is regularly among the lowest in per-pupil support for education among the 50 states.[38] Additionally, average Oklahoma teacher salaries are among the lowest in the nation,[39] and Oklahoma school districts are prone to losing teachers to other states, particularly border states—each of which includes higher average teacher salaries.

NOTES

1. 70 O.S. Section 18-101.
2. 70 O.S. Section 18-117.
3. Ok. Laws 1989, 1st Ex. Sess., c. 2. The official title was the Oklahoma Educational Reform Act, though it is more commonly known as HB 1017. Most of

the provisions, with some slight modifications, have been incorporated into Oklahoma statutes. The exceptions included some of the provisions for increased funding for education, primarily through state dedicated sources. These increases failed a statewide vote for constitutional amendment on June 26, 1990 (H.J.R. No. 1005, State Questions 634, 635, and 636).
4. 70 O.S. 18-200.1.
5. Oklahoma State Aid Task Force Regular Meetings February 6 and February 20, 2018.
6. 70 O.S. sec. 18-201.1(B)(1).
7. 70 O.S. sec. 18-201.1(B)(2).
8. 70 O.S. sec. 18-201.1(B)(3).
9. 70 O.S. sec. 18-201.1(B)(4).
10. Ok Const Art X Sec. 41.
11. Ok Const Art X Sec. 9(c).
12. Ok Const Art X Sec. 9(b).
13. Oklahoma State Aid Task Force Regular Meetings February 6 and February 20, 2018.
14. Ok Const Art X Sec. 9(a,d).
15. Ok Const Art X Sec. 5.
16. 70 O.S. Sec. 18-124.
17. 70 O.S. Sec. 3-118.1.
18. 70 O.S. sec. 18-201.1(B)(2).
19. Oklahoma State Aid Task Force Regular Meeting February 20, 2018.
20. 70 O.S. sec. 18-200.1(D)(2).
21. Senate Bill 1015 by Stanislawski, Second Session of the 56th Oklahoma Legislature (2018).
22. Ok. Const. Art. X Sec. 32.
23. 70 O.S. sec. 18-201.1(B)(4).
24. Examples of crossover areas include building utilities, salaries of maintenance staff, and certain technology purposes.
25. Shawn Hime and Jeffrey Maiden, *An Examination of the Fiscal Equity of Current, Capital, and Crossover Educational Expenditures in Oklahoma School Districts*, Institute for the Study of Education Finance (ISEF-01FR, July 2017).
26. *Every Student Succeeds Act*, 20 U.S.C. ch. 28 § 1001 et seq.
27. Ok Stat 70-3-130.
28. See http://www.sde.ok.gov/sde/current-charter
29. 70 O.S. sec. 3-130.
30. 70 O.S. sec. 3-145.
31. See Statewide Virtual Charter School Board, 'Virtual Charter School Authorization and Oversight Process,' November 2017. Retrieved from http://svcsb.ok.gov/Websites/svcsb/images/Virtual%20Charter%20School%20Authorization%20and%20Oversight%20Process%20Manual.pdf
32. Oklahoma Department of Career and Technical education. Retrieved from https://www.okcareertech.org/
33. See https://www.ok.gov/TRS/
34. 62 O.S. Sec. 62-34.90.
35. *Fair School Finance Council of Oklahoma, Inc. v. Oklahoma*, 746 P. 2d 1135 (1987).

36. *Fair School Finance II,* CJ90 7165 (Okl. 1990).
37. Data from the Center on Budget and Funding Priorities, *State General Funding Per Student Still Lower than 2008 in 25 States*. Retrieved from https://www.cbpp.org/state-general-funding-per-student-still-lower-than-2008-in-25-states
38. National Center for Education Statistics, Table 236.70 Current Expenditure per Pupil in Average Daily Attendance in Public Elementary and Secondary Schools, by State or Jurisdiction: Selected Years, 1969–70 through 2014–15. Retrieved from https://nces.ed.gov/programs/digest/d17/tables/dt17_236.70.asp?current=yes
39. National Center for Education Statistics, Table 211.60 Estimated Average Annual Salary of Teachers in Public Elementary and Secondary Schools, by State: Selected Years, 1969–70 through 2016–17. Retrieved from https://nces.ed.gov/programs/digest/d17/tables/dt17_211.60.asp?current=yes

CHAPTER 39

Oregon

Angie Peterman
Executive Director
Oregon Association of School Business Officials

GENERAL BACKGROUND

Oregon's commitment to public education began in the 1830s when New England pioneer John Ball opened the first 'public' school for children of fur trappers who frequented Fort Vancouver. By 1849 the Reverend George Atkinson had authored Oregon Territory's first body of school law, which included the following principles: (1) education should be free; (2) control should be decentralized and local; (3) a permanent school fund should be established; (4) professional standards should be established to provide for the certification of teachers; (5) schools should be tax supported; and (6) educational institutions should practice religious freedom.[1] In February 1859 Oregon became a state, and its constitution included provisions for the establishment of:

A uniform and general system of Common schools (Article VIII, §3);

A Common (Irreducible) School Fund (Article VIII, §2) which provided for the distribution of income to school districts from the sale of land given to the state by the federal government;

A distribution formula for school fund income (Article VIII, §4) by counties in proportion to the number of children between the ages of 4 and 20 years;

A position of a statewide Superintendent of Public Instruction (Article VIII, §1).[2]

Funding Public Schools in the United States and Indian Country, pages 555–573
Copyright © 2019 by Information Age Publishing
All rights of reproduction in any form reserved.

Between 1859 and 1946, voters in Oregon approved a variety of different methods for funding schools, including the county school fund and the elementary school fund. In November 1946 voters approved the Basic School Support Fund (BSSF) initiative which replaced the county school fund and the elementary school fund. Sponsors of the BSSF initiative expected the new law to provide 50% of school operating costs from state resources. The remaining 50% would continue to be provided at the local level. However, the actual percentage of school district funding provided by the BSSF between 1946 and 1990 ranged from a high of 47% in the early years to a low of 22% in the late 1980s. During this time, districts across the state faced the very real possibility of closing their doors early or for some portion of the school year due to lack of funding. Voters were required to approve local levy amounts which school districts could then levy against properties within their boundaries. Between 1972 and 1987 there were 13 districts that closed for a total of 187 days due to lack of funding, impacting 97,611 students.[3]

Pressure to fund public education in Oregon was falling more and more on local taxpayers through the payment of escalating property taxes. Legal struggles began in the early 1970s regarding school fiscal resources, sparking lawsuits based on widely varying local school district property wealth. During that time period, per-pupil spending varied from $675 to $1,795—a difference causally linked to property values and tax rates.[4] Litigation ensued, reaching the state supreme court in 1976 in *Olsen v. State*,[5] with the court recognizing serious equity concerns but nonetheless finding for the defendant state because it saw only a minimum constitutional duty in tandem with a strong tradition of local control of all aspects of schooling. In the words of the state's highest court, "We are of the opinion that Art. VIII, §3, is complied with if the state requires and provides for a minimum of educational opportunities in the district and permits the districts to exercise local control over what they desire, and can furnish, over the minimum."[6]

In May 1987, voters approved a constitutional amendment referred to as 'Safety Net' which allowed school districts to levy the amount last approved by voters. This process continued for a period of five years, during which 98 Oregon school districts fell into the safety net for one or more years.

In 1990, a referendum initiative known as Measure 5[7] was passed by voters to become effective in 1991 that restricted local property taxes and simultaneously required the state to replace lost school revenues from its own coffers. As a constitutional amendment, Measure 5 caused the state legislature to inject new monies, significantly shifting proportions of state/local funding. Simultaneously in an effort to address funding equity issues, the legislature created a new funding formula directed at equalizing revenue among all districts to eliminate the 'have' and 'have not' funding scenario that existed throughout the state.

Despite change stemming from Measure 5, issues of equity spending per pupil were ongoing and returned to Oregon's highest court in 1991 in *Coalition for Equitable School Funding v. State*.[8] Plaintiffs again were denied equity claims. In 1995 *Withers v. State*[9] saw an appeals court holding for defendants when challenged on differential funding effects based in geography, a ruling subsequently confirmed in *Withers II*,[10] with the state supreme court in 2000 again denying review.

Following this continual litigation, voters approved a constitutional amendment in 2000 setting in place the wording of Article VIII §8 'Adequate and Equitable Funding' which read:

> The Legislative Assembly shall appropriate in each biennium a sum of money sufficient to ensure that the state's system of public education meets quality goals established by law, and publish a report that either demonstrates the appropriation is sufficient or identifies the reasons for the insufficiency, its extent, and its impact on the ability of the state's system of public education to meet those goals.

As part of the shift in funding from local taxpayers to the state, the Oregon legislature developed a school funding formula designed to equalize support across all school districts. But despite the equity formula, litigation continued in 2006 with *Pendleton School District v. State*[11] filed on the basis of a uniform and general system of common schools tied to sufficient funding to meet the state's own Quality Education Model (QEM).[12] In 2001, the state legislature had enacted the QEM statute to tie school funding to educational performance indicators instead of basing funding on historic levels and guesswork.[13] *Pendleton* alleged that the state's funding effort fell far short of QEM's adequacy requirement. The state supreme court agreed that the state was deficient in supporting the QEM's quality standards, but it refused to intervene given the language of Article VIII §8 in that the court saw each constitutional provision standing alone and severally enforceable. The court read into the theory of separation of clauses as giving the state an option of either meeting the standard or admitting underfunding, accompanied by reporting why it failed and to simply estimate the impact of underfunding on the educational system.[14]

The QEM was based on prototypical (model) schools designed and funded to meet high standards. The 2018 Final Report[15] from Oregon's Quality Education Commission (QEC) stated, "The State School Fund requirement to fund K–12 schools at a level recommended by the QEC is estimated at $10.734 billion in the 2019–21 biennium, $1.963 billion more than the funding required to maintain the Current Service Level—that is, to simply keep up with inflation and enrollment growth. This funding gap rose from the prior biennium (2017–19), when it was $1.771 billion."[16]

BASIC SUPPORT PROGRAM[17]

K–12 Equalization Formula

The profile of Oregon's public schools contains 197 school districts serving approximately 581,000 pupils in grades K–12. Money for public schools is sourced from state income taxes, lottery funds, local revenue consisting mostly of the property tax, and federal funds. As indicated earlier, the historic dependence on property tax changed in 1990 when voters passed Measure 5, lowering the amount of property taxes dedicated to schools and limiting property taxes for education to $5 per each $1,000 assessed real market value. Soon after, voters passed Measure 50,[18] further limiting local property taxes for schools by placing restrictions on assessed valuation of property and property tax rates. The effect was to shift the vast majority of public school funding from local property taxes to the state's General Fund, which is funded from the state income tax.

The basic school finance plan for Oregon relies on a state aid formula meant to provide fiscal equity among school districts. This complex formula combines the legislatively approved General Fund appropriation with statewide estimates of local revenue deemed part of the formula and then distributes these funds on a per-pupil basis to school districts. Each district calculates its total combined state and local funds, resulting in an allocation per pupil. Each district also receives an additional sum for each child enrolled in more costly programs such as Special Education or English Language Learners. This funding plan resulted in $10.996 billion for the 2017–19 biennium, an increase of $1.23 billion (12.6%) over the 2015–17 budget.

State Revenue

Oregon's school equalization formula was first adopted in 1991, accompanied by phased implementation. Equity as measured by the formula applied to all school districts beginning in 1992–93. By 2007, the legislature had added student weights and some funding to the formula for small high schools, remote small schools, high cost disability students, and other programs previously outside the formula. However, the added weights exceeded available funding, thus depleting the allocation per pupil. Currently, the aid formula is allocated on the basis of 95.5% of the total to K–12 school districts and 4.5% of the total available to Education Service Districts (ESDs).

State School Fund

The State School Fund (SSF) serves as the central pivot point for the Oregon school funding equalization formula. The SSF is divided into multiple program areas in addition to the direct formula funding to K–12 school districts. Each of the following programs is a subtraction from the amount of state-level funding available for distribution to school districts and/or ESDs: (1) state schools such as the Oregon Virtual School; (2) Long Term Care and Treatment education programs for K–12 students; (3) English Language Learner Improvement Fund; (4) Network for Quality Teaching and Learning; (5) School Facilities Grants; and (6) High Cost Disabilities. These programs represent the largest transfers or set-asides. In the 2017–19 biennium these transfers and set-asides totaled approximately $210 million. Transfers and set-asides are then distributed through various programs, but not as part of the per-student funding formula.

The actual SSF equalization formula allocates an amount to each school district that is driven by student enrollment. In 1991 the legislature established a per-student funding amount of $4,500. Since that time, the base allocation per pupil has remained unchanged. To address inflation and the increase in funding available through the formula on a statewide basis, a funding ratio was developed. The ratio is calculated by taking total available formula resources minus the above noted transfers and set-asides minus the estimate of reimbursable transportation costs for home to school transportation. The net funding amount after deductions is then divided by the estimated total weighted student count on an Average Daily Membership (ADM) basis, resulting in the General Purpose Grant per weighted student (ADMw). The General Purpose Grant per ADMw is then divided by the original $4,500 per ADMw, resulting in the estimated funding formula output.

Table 39.1 presents calculation of the Funding Ratio for Fiscal Year 2018–19.

TABLE 39.1 Fiscal Year 2018–19 Estimated Funding Ratio (in millions)

State Appropriation	$4,100.00
Less direct transfers and set-asides	($51.76)
	$4,048.24
Add estimated local revenue	$2,034.15
	$6,082.38
K–12 district allocation @95.5%	$5,808.68
Less additional K–12 direct transfers and set-asides	($48.13)
	$5,760.54
Less estimated transportation grant	($215.78)
Net funding available for distribution to districts	$5,544.76
Estimated Extended ADMw	$708,000
General Purpose Grant per ADMw	$7,832
1991 General Purpose Grant per ADMw	$4,500
Funding Ratio	1.740352801

Education Service Districts

In addition to the 197 public school districts in Oregon, state monies also support 19 ESDs which are set up to provide regional educational support services. The ESD share of statewide K–12 school and ESD general operating revenue amounts to 4.5%, derived from state aid through the SSF and ESD property tax revenue. Before Measure 5, ESDs received no state aid. In 2001 the legislature began a five year phase-in plan to equalize ESD revenue so that, beginning in 2011–12, ESD revenue comprised 4.712% of the sum of component district formula revenue. It should be noted that starting in 2011–12, some school districts were allowed to opt out of ESDs, making those districts eligible for reimbursement of their shares of prorated formula revenues.

School Improvement Fund

The 2007 Oregon legislature appropriated $260 million to the School Improvement Fund from the state General Fund. School districts and ESDs received $126.6 million in Fiscal Year 2008 and $133 million in FY 2009. Funds were targeted for specified uses to improve student achievement. Although the mechanism remains, there have been no appropriations to the School Improvement Fund since the 2007–09 biennium.

Education Stability Fund

In 2002, Oregon voters approved a constitutional amendment[19] converting the Education Endowment Fund to the Education Stability Fund and allowing the principal to be used to fund education. This fund receives 18% of lottery net proceeds, with its size limited to 5% of General Fund revenue. Restrictions applied, however, as use of the principal requires meeting criteria reflective of an economic recession and approval by a 60% majority vote in each legislative chamber; the principal can also be used if the governor declares an emergency and both chambers approve by 60% majority vote. Further restrictions on approved use were that the principal can only be used to fund prekindergarten through higher education, continuing education, and workforce training. Fund earnings currently are used to pay education lottery bond debt (75%) and to provide scholarships (25%).

Local Revenue

For state aid formula purposes, determining the state's share of public school costs requires knowing local revenue requirements. Oregon school districts receive general operating revenue from various sources, with the property tax comprising the primary source. Other local revenue sources include federal forest payments, county school funds, the state Common

School Fund, and state timber sales. These local revenues are included in the school distribution formula and comprise about 33% of state and local formula operating revenue. All of these revenue sources are considered part of the SSF and are utilized to equalize the entire pool of revenue across the state.

In addition, school districts are authorized to ask voters to approve temporary local option levies. Local option revenue is limited to the lesser of: (1) the district's Measures 5 and 50 tax gap; (2) 20% of formula revenue; or (3) $1,000 per weighted pupil (2007–08). The $1,000 was indexed to increase 3% per year beginning in 2008–09. Local levies may be approved for up to five years for operations and up to ten years for capital projects. Local option revenue is in addition to equalization formula revenue.

School districts were granted new tax authority beginning in 2007. Districts were allowed to impose an excise tax on new construction in the district. The Construction Excise Tax rate was capped at $1 per square foot for residential use and $0.50 for nonresidential use, with maximum rates indexed beginning in 2009. The tax on nonresidential use was also restricted to $25,000 per structure or building permit, whichever was less. The legislation exempted certain properties. In the 2015–16 school year, 61 school districts used this option, raising a total of $24.2 million. It is important to note that construction excise tax revenue is in addition to equalization formula revenue.

School districts also receive other revenues which are considered outside the SSF formula. These are generally small amounts derived from investment earnings, student activity funds, donations from foundations and local grants, as well as districts' beginning fund balances.

Federal Revenue

Federal revenue to Oregon schools is characterized by the state as 'federal forest fees' and 'other federal revenue.' Data indicate the state's school districts share approximately $545.8 million in federal resources. In 2018, these resources provided 7.7% of total revenue to Oregon K–12 education.

Table 39.2 presents the state's view of federal, state, and local cost shares for Oregon's public schools.

State Aid Formula Detail[20]

As indicated earlier, Oregon's K–12 school equalization formula provides money from a combination of the SSF and local revenue. It is the sum of a *general purpose* grant, a *transportation* grant, a *high cost disability* grant,

TABLE 39.2 Biennial Formula Federal, State, and Local Shares for Oregon Schools 2010–2017

(Dollars in Millions, unadjusted for inflation)

	Local		Intermediate[a]		State		Federal		Total	
	Amount	%	Amount	%	Amount	%	Amount	%	Amount	%
2009–10	$1,928.0	33.5%	$70.9	1.2%	$2,934.2	51.0%	$820.1	14.3%	$5,753.1	100%
2010–11	$1,949.9	34.4%	$75.1	1.3%	$2,782.4	49.1%	$856.5	15.1%	$5,662.9	100%
2011–12	$1,987.2	34.8%	$74.6	1.3%	$3,028.9	53.1%	$612.3	10.7%	$5,703.0	100%
2012–13	$2,009.7	35.3%	$88.9	1.6%	$3,030.4	53.2%	$565.3	9.9%	$5,694.2	100%
2013–14	$2,073.8	34.0%	$100.2	1.6%	$3,381.9	55.5%	$538.9	8.8%	$6,094.8	100%
2014–15	$2,187.2	33.5%	$126.9	1.9%	$3,662.9	56.0%	$561.2	8.6%	$6,538.1	100%
2015–16	$2,273.7*	33.4%	$127.8*	1.9%	$3,846.7*	56.5%	$559.7	8.2%	$6,807.9	100%
2016–17	$2,399.9	34.0%	$135.7	1.9%	$3,985.6	56.4%	$545.8	7.7%	$7,067.0	100%

Source: Oregon Department of Education. "Statewide Report Card 2017–2018." An Annual Report to the Legislature on Oregon Public Schools. (2018), p. 18. https://www.oregon.gov/ode/schools-and-districts/reportcards/Documents/rptcard2018.pdf Actuals from audited financial reports of School Districts and Education Service Districts Columns may not sum to total due to rounding.

[a] Intermediate refers to revenue from other levels of government, such as county or city.

* Revised

and a *facilities* grant. Distribution is based on need within available funding at the legislative level. Formula expression is straightforward:

District Formula Revenue = State School Fund Grant + Local Revenue + Transportation Grant

State School Fund

The Oregon legislature allocates monies to the SSF derived primarily from the state General Fund and from lottery revenue for formula redistribution to school districts.

Local Revenue

The Oregon school finance formula only includes district local revenue from select sources: (1) operating property taxes collected, including prior years; (2) Common School Fund; (3) County School Fund; (4) federal forest related revenue; (5) state managed county trust forests [Chapter 530]; (6) ESD funds required to be shared with school districts; (7) revenue in lieu of property taxes; and (8) supplantable federal funds.

General Purpose Revenue

Formula expression of the general purpose grant identified earlier is expressed formulaically. Its elements are defined as follows.

$$\text{General Purpose Grant} = \text{Extended Weighted Students (ADMw)} \times \text{\$4,500 Adjusted by Teacher Experience} \times \text{Funding Ratio}$$

Weighted Students

Weighted student count is calculated using ADM. ADM becomes ADMw when extra counts or weights are added based on special categories of pupils' educational needs. Oregon's funding formula allows for the higher of the current year ADMw or the prior year ADMw to be used when determining annual funding. This provides districts with the ability to plan and refine the budget process on a prospective basis. Whichever of the counts is highest is utilized in the funding formula and called extended ADMw.

For 2018, this system resulted in the student weight categories shown in Table 39.3.

Limitations are placed on individual education program weights, so that the count cannot exceed 11% without state department of education approval.

TABLE 39.3 Student Weights 2018

Category	Additional Weight	Count (ADMw)
Special Education and At Risk		
Individual Education Program	1.00	2.00
English Language Learner	0.50	1.50
Pregnant and Parenting	1.00	2.00
Students in Poverty Adjusted	0.25	1.25
Neglected and Delinquent	0.25	1.25
Students in Foster Care	0.25	1.25
Grade and School		
Kindergarten (half-day)	–0.50	0.50
Elementary District	0.90	0.90
Union High School	0.20	1.20
Remote Small School	Varies	

Source: Legislative Revenue Office, "2018 Oregon Public Finance Basic Facts: Research Report #1–18. (2018), p. G5.

Limitations also apply to the category of remote small schools. A school site qualifies for additional ADMw using the following formula:

	Elementary School	High School
ADM less than x (varies by grade level) Distance to nearest same district school more than 8 miles	252 (9 grades)	350 (4 grades)

The formula is refined so that the smaller the school the greater the weight per pupil. The formula is scheduled to change when full-day kindergarten ADM weight becomes the same as other grades.

Teacher Experience

The final part of general purpose revenue is the variable involving teacher experience. The target $4,500 base amount is subject to legislative determination; however, the teacher experience adjustment increases or decreases the target by $25 for each year a district's average teacher experience is greater or less than the statewide average teacher experience level.

Transportation Revenue

Formula expression of the separate transportation grant identified earlier is expressed formulaically. Its elements are defined as follows.

$$\text{Transportation Grant} = 70\% \text{ to } 90\% \text{ of Transportation Costs}$$

School districts are ranked by approved transportation costs per pupil from highest to lowest, with percentage support based on rankings within ranges, so that the top 10% of districts receives 90% of costs; the next 10% receives 80% of costs; and the bottom 80% receives 70% of costs, thereby awarding aid based on efficiency. Eligible transportation costs include: (1) preschool handicapped; (2) elementary pupils more than one mile from school; (3) secondary pupils more than 1.5 miles distant; (4) pupils traveling between facilities; (5) field trips; (6) health and safety needs; and (7) room and board in lieu of transportation.

High Cost Disability Revenue

Formula expression of the high cost disability grant identified earlier is expressed formulaically. Its elements are defined as follows.

$$\text{High Cost Disability Grant} = \text{Up to Sum of Costs above \$30,000 per Disability Student}$$

For students with approved disability costs above $30,000 the state grant pays costs above the $30,000 shouldered by the school district. If applicable, ESD costs can be included in the total. If total costs exceed $35 million statewide, grants are reduced proportionally.

Facility Revenue

Formula expression of the facility grant identified earlier is expressed formulaically. Its elements are defined as follows.

$$\text{Facility Grant} = \text{Up to 8\% of Construction Costs}$$

School districts adding new classroom space are eligible to receive up to 8% of construction costs, excluding land. Portable unit costs, including furnishings and equipment, are grant-eligible. Total grants are capped at $9 million per biennium. Proportional share reduction is engaged if grants exceed the 8% cap.

Other State School Fund Revenue

In 2013, the Oregon legislature created the Network of Quality Teaching and Learning (NQTL) and appropriated $33 million to the network for 2013–15 biennium from the SSF. Later in the same year, the legislature approved another $12 million to NQTL, using an additional distribution from the Common School Fund. For the 2017–19 school years, school districts and ESDs were scheduled to respectively contribute $17.3 million from their shares of formula revenue, so that the total NQTL budget stands at $39.5 million.

The total school district side of Oregon's K–12 equalization formula is shown in Table 39.4. Grants-in-aid are heavily directed toward general purpose. Table 39.5 shows percentages by categories, adjusted for size by ADM before calculation of monies directed toward ESDs. As described earlier, state aid and local revenue for school districts equals 95.5% of the statewide K–12 school and education service district formula revenue for general operating purposes. The remaining 4.5% is earmarked for ESDs as discussed in the next section.

ESD EQUALIZATION FORMULA

Earlier discussion in this chapter indicated that state monies also support 19 ESDs which provide regional educational support services. It was noted that the ESD share of statewide K–12 general operating revenue amounts to 4.5%, derived from state aid through the SSF and ESD property tax revenue. Finally, it was noted that starting in 2011–12, some school districts were allowed to opt out of ESDs, making those districts eligible for reimbursement of their share of prorated formula revenues.

TABLE 39.4 Formula Grant Percentage By District Size 2016–17 Before ESD Share

District Size by ADM	# of Districts	General Purpose	Transportation	High Cost Disability	Facility
0–500	77	94.02%	5.91%	0.07%	0.00%
500–1,000	33	95.10%	4.62%	0.25%	0.03%
1,000–3,000	39	95.81%	3.95%	0.21%	0.03%
3,000–5,000	17	94.83%	3.87%	1.14%	0.16%
5,000–10,000	18	95.87%	3.56%	0.52%	0.05%
10,000 and Greater	13	95.30%	3.66%	0.82%	0.22%

Source: Legislative Revenue Office, "2018 Oregon Public Finance Basic Facts: Research Report #1–8. (2018), p. G6.

ESD Equalization

ESDs in Oregon are funded via a separate equalization formula expressed as follows. The ESD formula assumes that ESD revenue should be proportional to the equalization formula revenue of component school districts. Component school districts are defined as those districts within the boundaries of an ESD.

$$\text{General Services Revenue} = \text{Higher of Balance:} \quad \text{Base Revenue} \times \text{Percent to} \text{ or } \$1.165 \text{ million}$$

General Services Revenue

For ESDs, general services revenue is the same as district base revenue, sourced from the SSF and the local revenue assigned to the ESD. Local revenue is defined in the same manner as for school districts and primarily consists of operating tax collections plus state-managed county trust timber.

Base Revenue and Minimum Base for ESDs

The ESD equalization formula illustrated earlier calls for determination of base revenue by solving for 4.712% multiplied against the sum of school formula revenue of an ESD's component districts. The calculation results in 4.5% of total funding to support ESDs, leaving 95.5% from the state equalization side as discussed earlier. Additional calculations to adjust for staying within percentages and appropriations are required and not discussed here.[21]

District and ESD Summary

A multi-year snapshot of Oregon's combined public school revenue plan is shown in Table 39.5. Growth in revenue per pupil across the years 1992–2019 shows the presumed effect of Oregon school finance reform, although accounting for inflation is not indicated. Over the 14-year period, a 73% growth was recorded, for an annual average increase of 5.2%.

OTHER SELECTED STATE FUNDING PROVISIONS

Charter Schools

Students enrolled in Oregon's charter schools are included in the state's primary funding formula. The formula takes students and weights at the charter school and combines them with students and weights at the

TABLE 39.5 K–12 and ESD Revenue History

Revenue Source	2003–2004	2004–2005	2005–2006	2006–2007	2007–2008	2008–2009	2009–2010	2010–2011	2011–2012	2012–2013	2013–2014	2014–2015	2015–2016	2016–2017	2017–2018	2018–2019
State																
State School Fund	$2,589.8	$2,326.3	$2,566.6	$2,737.7	$2,917.6	$2,911.2	$2,940.1	$2,797.7	$2,754.3	$2,858.8	$3,209.7	$3,440.7	$3,627.5	$3,745.5	$4,101.9	$4,101.9
Local K–12																
Property & Timber Taxes	1,003.4	1,049.4	1,093.6	1,167.2	1,223.7	1,278.0	1,331.3	1,368.4	1,400.1	1,421.3	1,466.5	1,541.6	1,616.5	1,685.8	1,753.3	1,819.0
Other Local	77.5	98.9	112.2	120.0	127.5	102.1	97.9	97.6	86.6	95.8	86.8	92.6	99.2	90.5	94.9	96.5
Excluded from Formula	−19.5	−21.7	0.0	−15.5	−16.5	−17.3	−17.9	−18.1	−18.7	−19.3	−19.9	−20.5	−22.6	−23.6	−24.5	−25.4
Subtotal	1,061.3	1,126.6	1,205.8	1,271.9	1,334.7	1,362.9	1,411.3	1,447.9	1,467.9	1,497.8	1,533.5	1,613.7	1,693.2	1,752.8	1,823.6	1,890.1
Local ESD																
Property Tax & Other Local	72.2	75.1	79.4	83.3	87.1	90.5	94.9	98.0	100.9	102.3	102.2	108.6	113.8	118.6	121.3	125.9
Shared with K–12	0.0	0.0	0.0	0.0	0.0	0.0	0.0	0.0	0.0	0.0	0.0	0.0	0.0	0.0		
Subtotal	72.2	75.1	79.4	83.3	87.1	90.5	94.9	98.0	100.9	102.3	103.3	108.6	113.8	118.6	113.8	118.6
Total Sources	3,723.3	3,527.9	3,851.7	4,092.8	4,339.3	4,364.6	4,446.3	4,343.6	4,323.2	4,456.9	4,846.5	5,163.0	5,434.5	5,616.9	6,039.3	6,110.6
Revenue Allocation																
ESD																
Districts	176.1	170.6	192.0	191.8	204.9	205.8	210.0	205.1	193.2	199.2	209.9	224.1	235.6	244.1	261.5	264.7
Testing/Regional Education		0.0	0.0	0.0	0.6	0.6	0.6	0.6	0.7	0.7	0.5	0.5	0.5	0.5	0.5	0.5
Quality Teaching Network		0.0									7.0	7.0	7.8	7.8	8.6	8.6

(continued)

TABLE 39.5 K-12 and ESD Revenue History

	2003-2004	2004-2005	2005-2006	2006-2007	2007-2008	2008-2009	2009-2010	2010-2011	2011-2012	2012-2013	2013-2014	2014-2015	2015-2016	2016-2017	2017-2018	2018-2019
K-12 School																
Categorical Grants		0.0	1.0	1.0	1.4	8.2	1.2	1.2	1.2	1.2	1.1	1.1	1.1	1.1	3.5	3.5
		0.0														
Small HS Grants		2.5	2.5	2.5	2.5	2.5	2.5	2.5	2.5	2.5	2.5	2.5	2.5	2.5	2.5	2.5
		2.5														
Long Term Care & Pediatric		7.3	7.2	9.8	10.1	9.8	9.8	9.8	9.8	9.8	10.5	10.5	16.5	16.5	18.4	18.4
Nursing		7.1														
Youth Corrections & Detention		11.0	11.0	11.9	12.0	12.5	12.0	12.5	12.0	12.5	10.5	10.5	10.5	10.5	7.5	7.6
Quality Teaching Network		10.3									7.0	7.0	7.8	7.8	8.6	8.6
English Language Learners													6.3	6.3	6.3	6.3
District Equalization Formula	3,520.3	3,331.9	3,630.3	3,869.0	4,099.7	4,119.1	4,205.3	4,106.5	4,098.8	4,225.5	4,593.3	4,895.6	5,139.1	5,321.0	5,723.7	5,791.7
Misc.		6.0	7.6	6.9	8.2	6.2	5.0	5.5	5.0	5.5	4.3	4.2	6.9	6.9	7.4	7.4
		5.4														
Total Allocations	3,723.3	3,527.9	3,851.7	4,092.8	4,339.3	4,364.6	4,446.3	4,343.6	4,323.2	4,560.9	4,846.5	5,163.0	5,434.4	5,624.8	6,039.3	6,110.6

Notes: Dollars in millions.
*Including Quality Teaching and Learning Network and local option equalization grants, starting from 2013–14. Also includes Office of School Facilities carve-out
Source: Legislative Revenue Office, "2018 Oregon Public Finance Basic Facts: Research Report #1–8, (2018), p. G5.

remainder of non-charter schools located in each school district. This total number is the basis for the district's total funding.

The school district then distributes a portion of funding to the charter school based on the number of pupils and weights at the charter school. Distribution is calculated by dividing the district's general purpose grant by the current ADMw for the district. The actual percentage of distribution is based on the charter agreement entered into between the charter school and district. Additional funding issues such as timing and reconciliation increase the complexity of the fiscal and organizational relationship.

Virtual Schools

Each biennium, approximately $1.6 million is transferred from the SSF to the Oregon Department of Education to develop and maintain a statewide program that offers virtual resources to school districts and their personnel.

SUMMARY

Despite increases shown in Table 39.5, education advocates in Oregon hold that schools are underfunded. That position is supported when held up against the state's own QEM Final Report.[22] Data from the Report are detailed in Table 39.6, recounting the shortfall of approximately $1.963 billion in the current biennium discussed at the outset of this chapter. These data were additionally broken down by the QEC as seen in Table 39.7, comparing shortfalls to specific QEM recommended resource levels. All these variables have been a topic of significant discussion over the years, as numerous factors play into the challenges facing Oregon in adequately funding public schools. Evident among those have been the dependence on income taxes, limitations on property tax levies, and a multitude of competing programs that place significant pressure on the legislature when allocating state resources.

In the end, arguments by school advocates consistently point to the escape clause in the Oregon supreme court's ruling in *Pendleton*.[23] In short, advocates for school funding continue to hold that despite a ballot measure passed by voters in 2001 requiring the legislature to appropriate in each biennium enough money to meet the QEM, the legislature is unaccountable because it can alternatively publish a report saying why the state could not fund the model.

TABLE 39.6 Quality Education Model Estimates–2019–21 Biennium

Current Service Level Compared to Fully Implemented QEM Model	Current Service Level	Fully-Implemented QEM	Difference	Percent Difference
Estimated Prototype School Operating Expenditures for 2019–20	$7,404,402,656	$8,322,414,948	$918,012,292	12.4%
Estimated Prototype School Operating Expenditures for 2020–21	$7,621,003,478	$8,565,014,191	$944,101,712	12.4%
2019–21 Biennium Total for Prototype Schools	$15,025,406,134	$16,887,429,139	$1,862,023,004	12.4%
Plus: ESD Expenditures	$722,506,102	$783,057,452	$60,551,350	8.4%
Plus: High-Cost Disabilities Fund for Special Education Students	$70,000,000	$110,000,000	$40,000,000	57.1%
Equals: Total 2017–19 School Funding Requirement	$15,817,912,236	$17,780,486,591	$1,962,574,354	12.4%
Less: Local Revenue not in Formula (local option taxes, grants, etc.)	$1,319,829,897	$1,319,829,897	$0	0.0%
Less: Federal Revenue to School Districts and ESDs	$1,167,003,885	$1,167,003,885	$0	0.0%
Less: Food Service Enterprise Revenue	$83,535,194	$83,535,194	$0	0.0%
Less: PERS Side Account Earnings Net of Debt Service Costs	$176,699,523	$176,699,523	$0	0.0%
Equals: Total Equalization Formula Funding Requirement	$13,070,843,737	$15,033,418,091	$1,962,574,354	15.0%
Less: Property Taxes and other Local Revenues in Formula	$4,299,477,685	$4,299,477,685	$0	0.0%
Equals: 2019–21 State School Fund Requirement	$8,771,366,052	$10,733,940,406	$1,962,574,354	22.4%

Source: Quality Education Commission Report 2018. "Exhibit 27." (August 2018), p. 49. https://www.oregon.gov/ode/reports-and-data/taskcomm/Documents/QEMReports/2018QuemReport.pdf

TABLE 39.7 Cost Impacts of Specific QEM Recommended Resource Levels

The funding gap of $1.963 billion reflects recommended resources that Oregon's current system does not provide. Recommendations contributing most of the funding gap in the 2019–21 biennium are:

Lower class sizes in elementary schools	$454 million
Instructional improvement in all schools (e.g. mentoring, peer review)	$304 million
More teachers (smaller classes) in middle and high schools	$273 million
Additional resources for special education and alternative education	$242 million
More time for teacher collaboration	$107 million
Increased maintenance to better maintain buildings	$69 million
Additional counselors in all schools	$72 million
Added professional development for teachers and building leaders	$51 million
Additional summer school for struggling students	$33 million

Source: Quality Education Commission Report 2018. "Exhibit 27." (August 2018), p. 49. https://www.oregon.gov/ode/reports-and-data/taskcomm/Documents/QEMReports/2018QEMReport.pdf

NOTES

1. Oregon Blue Book 2000–2001, OSBA's Covering Education and Legislative Reports, Tom Rigby, former OSBA Executive Director, William G. Robbins, retired OSU History Professor.
2. Oregon State Legislature. "Constitution of Oregon (2018 Edition)." Retrieved from https://www.oregonlegislature.gov/bills_laws/Pages/OrConst.aspx
3. Oregon Blue Book 2000–2001.
4. SchoolFunding.Info, "Oregon." (2019). Retrieved from http://schoolfunding.info/litigation-map/oregon/#1485195566508-3e4815ca-fcce
5. 554 P.2d 139 (1976).
6. Ibid, p. 27.
7. Oregon Department of Revenue, "A Brief History of Oregon Property Taxation." (2009). Retrieved from https://www.oregon.gov/DOR/programs/gov-research/Documents/303-405-1.pdf
8. 891 P.2d 675 (1995).
9. 891 P.2d 675 (1995).
10. 987 P.2d 1247 (1999) (*Withers II*).
11. 200 P3d 133 (2009).
12. House Bill 2295 (ORS 327.497- 327.506) (2001).
13. Oregon Legislative Committee Services. "Background Brief on Quality Education Model." (May 2004). Retrieved from https://www.oregonlegislature.gov/lpro/Publications/2004DI_Quality_Education_Model.pdf
14. The latest such report was issued by the Joint interim Special Committee on Public Education Appropriation, entitled "Report on Adequacy of Public Education Funding as Required by Article VIII, Section 8, of the Oregon

Constitution: 2017–2019 Education Budget." (January 2018). Retrieved from https://www.oregonlegislature.gov/citizen_engagement/Reports/JISPEA_2018EducationBudget_EdFunding.pdf
15. Oregon Department of Education, Quality Education Commission. "Quality Education Model Final Report." (August 2018). Retrieved from https://www.oregon.gov/ode/reports-and-data/taskcomm/Documents/QEMReports/2018QEMReport.pdf
16. Ibid, pp. 7–8.
17. This section closely follows and relies on Legislative Revenue Office, "2018 Oregon Public Finance Basic Facts: Research Report #1–18. (2018), pp. G1–G11. Retrieved from https://www.oregonlegislature.gov/lro/Documents/2018%20FINAL%20-1.pdf. *Also* integral to the description is Oregon Blue Book, "Public Education." Oregon Secretary of State, (2019). https://sos.oregon.gov/blue-book/Pages/education-public.aspx
18. Oregon Department of Revenue, "A Brief History of Oregon Property Taxation." (2009), p. 3. Retrieved from https://www.oregon.gov/DOR/programs/gov-research/Documents/303-405-1.pdf
19. Oregon Education Stability Fund Amendment, also known as Measure 19 (2002).
20. The following formula description sections are condensed and interpreted from Legislative Revenue Office, "2018 Oregon Public Finance Basic Facts: Research Report #1-18. (2018), pp. G5–G11.
21. See p.G7, Legislative Revenue Office, "2018 Oregon Public Finance Basic Facts: Research Report #1-18. (2018).
22. Joint interim Special Committee on Public Education Appropriation, entitled "Report on Adequacy of Public Education Funding as Required by Article VIII, Section 8, of the Oregon Constitution: 2017–2019 Education Budget." (January 2018). Retrieved from https://www.oregonlegislature.gov/citizen_engagement/Reports/JISPEA_2018EducationBudget_EdFunding.pdf
23. 200 P3d 133 (2009). See earlier discussion around the state high court's either/or legislative option to fully fund the system or explain the failure to do so.

CHAPTER 40

Pennsylvania

Andrew L. Armagost, Ph.D.
*Research and Advocacy Manager
Pennsylvania Association of School Business Officials
Former Assistant Executive Director, Education Committee
Pennsylvania Senate*

Timothy J. Shrom, Ph.D.
*Director of Research
Pennsylvania Association of School Business Officials
Former Business Manager, Solanco School District*

GENERAL BACKGROUND

The education clause of the Pennsylvania constitution declares "the General Assembly shall provide for the maintenance and support of a thorough and efficient system of public education to serve the needs of the Commonwealth."[1] This system of public education in Pennsylvania was formally established in the 1830s through passage of the Common School Fund Act of 1831 and the Free Schools Act of 1834. The Act of 1831 established the first common school fund, with a revenue source directed from the sale of unpatented lands and fees collected from the land office. However, the Act of 1834 formally established a system of public schools throughout the Commonwealth by requiring counties to form school divisions which were made up of the school districts from every ward, township and borough in the several counties. The Act also provided for distribution of state support to fund common schools, providing funds to any county that voted affirmatively to impose a county school tax of not less than twice the amount received from the state. Funding distribution under the Act was calculated using the number of taxable inhabitants in the county. Disbursements went to the counties, which then distributed funds to the school districts. According to Walsh, while the law fixed the appropriation to one dollar for each taxable inhabitant, the General Assembly did not meet this requirement and from 1845 to 1872 the actual amount distributed varied between 38¢ in 1865 and 62¢ in 1872.[2]

In the following years, the state formula for distributing general basic education funding remained mostly unchanged with some few minor attempts at change in 1863, 1897, 1911 and 1919.[3] In 1863, the state attempted to adopt a new distribution of funds based on the number of children attending a school. This calculation, formally enacted through the Appropriations Act of 1863, was found too difficult and was repealed the following year.[4] In 1876, the Commonwealth continued to appropriate funds based on the number of taxable inhabitants in each county and school district.[5] In 1897 the General Assembly attempted to improve distribution of funding on the basis of the number of children, number of teachers, and the number of taxable residents, providing for "one-third of the money annually appropriated for common schools in this Commonwealth to be distributed to each of these categories and for each category to be based upon the counts within the category.[6]

In 1911,[7] the General Assembly consolidated existing laws pertaining to public education into a single omnibus statute and provided the following distribution of state subsidies:

> *Section 2504.* One-half on the basis of the number of paid teachers regularly employed for the full annual term of the school district, not including substitute teachers or teachers employed to fill vacancies which may occur during the school year; such number of teachers to be certified as herein provided;

> *Section 2305.* One-half on the basis of the number of children between the ages of six and sixteen residing in the respective school districts of the several counties of this Commonwealth, as reported to the Superintendent of Public Instruction under the provisions of this act.[8]

By Fiscal Year 1921, total state appropriation for the basic subsidy to school districts reached $8.85 million.[9] The Act of 1921, known as the Edmunds Act, made significant structural changes to the system of public education.[10] In 1927, a major report from a commission established by the state studied school funding throughout Pennsylvania and recommended that the state adopt a form of power equalization to equalize wealth among all school districts, as the report found that assessed value per teacher unit was not equitable across counties as a result of non-uniform assessments. Twenty years later, Act 447 of 1947 established the State Tax Equalization Board (STEB) with a purpose to provide for equalization throughout the state.

Act 14 of 1949, also known as the Public School Code, distributed basic education funding based on school district teaching units multiplied by a base factor enacted into law and the district's standard reimbursement fraction. During FY 1950, the base factor was $2,400 and state appropriation for basic education was $173 million. It is important to note that while Act 14 was never codified into Pennsylvania's consolidated statutes, the Act served as the single authoritative law on the system of public education and has been amended several times, with updates to the formula distributing basic education funding. From 1949 to 2008, dozens of enacted statutes amended Act 14 to change the funding distribution for numerous types of grants and subsidies for public schools.[11]

During FY 2008, Act 61 enacted recommendations of a study commissioned by the governor in 2006. The Act added Section 2502.48 providing for a student-based adequacy target for school districts and distributing funds for FY 2008. Funding for adequacy targets in the subsequent two fiscal years primarily came from federal recovery funding provided to states in response to the 2008 economic recession. Distribution of funds through the student-based adequacy targets for FY 2010 and FY 2011 came through omnibus amendments to the Fiscal Code enacted in those years. Act 24 of 2011 ceased using the student-based adequacy target formula and prescribed for FY 2012 a formula based on factors used prior to Act 61. In the following years, Act 82 of 2012, Act 59 of 2013, Act 126 of 2014 (Fiscal Code) provided for the funding distribution formula.

Act 35 of 2016 was the most recent update to the basic education funding formula. As illustrated later in this chapter, the Act 35 weighted student formula distributes additional funding appropriated beyond the FY 2015 funding level to school districts based on recommendations of the legislative Basic Education Funding Commission established under Section 123 by Act 51 of 2014.

Pennsylvania's long history regarding public education dates back to the earliest days of the nation.[12] Since passage of the 1831 and 1834 acts establishing the system of public education, Pennsylvania's support and funding for schools has developed into a broader funding system covering basic and special education, career and technical education, school construction, employee retirement, pupil transportation and numerous other categories. However, studies show that Pennsylvania school districts are enduring substantial fiscal stress,[13] and growing financial pressures continue to place funding of the system of public education at the forefront of state policy decisions. Summary Tables 40.4 through 40.7 at the end of this chapter illustrate overall state appropriation of grants and subsidies supporting school district revenues by source and expenditures.

Currently, Pennsylvania's courts have moved forward by hearing a lawsuit[14] challenging the constitutionality of the funding scheme in regard to the General Assembly's duty to provide for the maintenance and support of a thorough and efficient system of public education to serve the needs of the Commonwealth. In 2017, the Pennsylvania supreme court overturned precedent and struck down the longstanding political question doctrine[15] in the state and remanded the case to the lower courts. At the time of this writing, the Commonwealth court had issued a memorandum opinion overruling several preliminary objections in the case and was moving forward with a trial scheduled for the summer of 2020.[16]

Statutory language can be found for almost all major aspects of education funding in Pennsylvania's Act 14 of 1949, also known as the Public School Code.[17] Regulations established by the Pennsylvania State Board of Education are located in Title 22 of the Pennsylvania Code,[18] and source data on school finance can be found on the Department of Education website.[19]

BASIC EDUCATION

Pennsylvania Act 35 of 2016 added Section 2502.53 of the Public School Code[20] to provide for a student-weighted formula that distributes any additional state dollars to support basic education funding beyond the amount allocated during FY 2015. The new basic education funding formula distributes support to school districts based on the following methodology. First, the district receives a base amount equal to its 2014–2015 Basic Education Funding allocation. The total base of all Pennsylvania school districts is approximately $5.56 billion. The district then receives a pro-rata share of the total allocation (approximately $538 million in FY 2019) based on the district's weighted student count (WSC) multiplied by its median household income index (MHI) and its local effort capacity index (LECI).

The weighted student count equals the sum of the following: (1) the three-year average daily membership; (2) three poverty weights based on the number of students living in poverty, acute poverty, and concentrated acute poverty; (3) an English language learner weight based on the number of students designated as English language learners; (4) a charter school weight based on the number of students who withdrew from the traditional public school and enrolled in a public charter school; and (5) the sparsity-size adjustment for qualifying school districts.

The three-year ADM is calculated by averaging the school district's three most recent years' ADM. The poverty factor is the sum of the three poverty weights. The three poverty weights are calculated as:

- *the acute poverty* ADM calculated by multiplying the district's ADM by its acute poverty percentage and 0.6;
- *the poverty* ADM calculated by multiplying the district's ADM by its poverty percentage and 0.3;
- *the concentrated poverty* ADM for qualifying districts with an acute poverty percentage equal to or greater than 30% calculated by multiplying the district's ADM by its acute poverty percentage by 0.3.

The English language learner (ELL) weight is calculated by multiplying the number of the school district's limited English-proficient students by 0.6. The charter school (CS) weight is calculated by multiplying 0.2 by the ADM for the district's students enrolled in charter schools and cyber charter schools.

A sparsity/size adjustment (SSA) is calculated for qualifying school districts with a sparsity size ratio greater than the 70th percentile of all districts. The SSA is calculated by dividing the district's sparsity/size ratio by the ratio at the 70th percentile; subtracting 1; multiplying by the sum of (a) through (f); multiplying by 0.7. The sparsity-size ratio is calculated as follows:

- Calculate the sparsity ratio: divide the school district's ADM per square mile by the state total ADM per square mile; multiply by 0.5; subtract from 1;
- Calculate the size ratio: divide the district's ADM by the average of the ADM for all districts; multiply by 0.5; subtract from 1;
- Calculate the combined sparsity-size ratio by weighting the sparsity ratio at 40% and the size ratio at 60%.

The sum of these weights and the three-year ADM provides the weighted student count. Next, calculate the adjusted weighted student count (AWSC) by multiplying the weighted student count by the district's median household income index and the district's local effort capacity index. The median household income index (MHI) is calculated for each district by dividing 1 by the quotient of the district's median household income divided by the state median household income. The local effort capacity index (LECI) equals the sum of the local effort index and the local capacity index.

The local effort index equals the local effort factor multiplied by the lesser of 1 or the excess spending factor.

- The local effort factor is calculated for each school district as: divide its local tax-related revenue by its median household income multiplied by its number of households; multiply by 1,000; divide by the statewide median;

- The excess spending factor is calculated for each district as: divide 1 by its net current expenditures per student-weighted average daily membership divided by the statewide median.

The local capacity index is calculated as: if the school district's local capacity per student-weighted ADM is less than the statewide median, divide its local capacity per student-weighted ADM by the statewide median; if the district's local capacity per student-weighted ADM is equal to or greater than the statewide median, the local capacity index is zero.

- The local capacity per student-weighted ADM for each school district is calculated as: multiply the sum of its market value and personal income by the statewide median local effort rate; divide by its student-weighted ADM;
- The local effort rate for each district is calculated as: divide its local tax-related income by the sum of its market value and personal income.

The result of multiplying weighted student count, median household income index, and local effort capacity index is the school district's AWSC. The amount a district receives through this formula is determined by calculating the district's share of the state total AWSC. That share is then distributed through the total state allocation. In Summary Table 40.4, the state appropriation for basic education funding is line 1.

The Pennsylvania basic education funding formula is expressed as:

$$ADM + PVW + ELL + CS + SSA = \text{Weighted Student Count (WSC)}$$

$$WSC \times MHII \times LECI = \text{Adjusted Weighted Student Count (AWSC)}$$

$$AWSC \times \text{Total Student-Weighted Distribution/State Total AWSC}$$
$$= \text{Prorata Share to District}$$

In addition to basic education funding, Pennsylvania provides two other general education funding appropriations to school districts. First, the state distributes $250 million annually through the Ready to Learn Block Grant, with the prescribed mission to enhance learning opportunities for students and provide resources to innovate at the local level. Section 2599.6 of the Public School Code[21] provides funding for these grants. In Table 40.4 later, state appropriation for this program is line 2. Second, the state distributes funding through the Educational Access Program as single-year or multi-year appropriation to specific districts to support education programs. In prior fiscal years, this appropriation was distributed to certain school districts designated as financially distressed by the Department of Education.

In Table 40.4, state appropriation for this program is part of line 18 representing $23.1 million in FY 2019.

SPECIAL EDUCATION

The state special education funding formula was last amended by Act 86 of 2016 and is distributed pursuant to Section 2509.5 of the Public School Code.[22] The new special education funding formula established three categories of student costs. The three cost categories and corresponding weights are: Category 1 includes students with costs ranging from $1 to $24,999 with a formula weight of 1.51; Category 2 includes students with costs ranging from $25,000 to $49,999 with a formula weight of 3.77; and Category 3 includes students with costs equal to $50,000 or more with a formula weight of 7.46.

School districts receive allocations through two parts. First, the district receives an amount equal to its 2013–2014 Special Education Funding allocation. The total of all Pennsylvania districts is approximately $1.05 billion. Second, the district receives a pro-rata share of the allocated amount (approximately $102.8 million in FY 2019) based on the district's weighted student count (WSC) multiplied by its market value/personal income aid ratio (MVPI) and its equalized mills multiplier (EQM).

In calculating a school district's share of allocated funding, the WSC equals the sum of the special education student count and the sparsity-size adjustment for qualifying districts. The special education student count is calculated by multiplying the number of students in each student category by its weighting. A sparsity-size adjustment is calculated by first calculating the sparsity-size ratio as:

- *Calculate the sparsity ratio*: divide the school district's ADM per square mile by the state total ADM per square mile; multiply by 0.5; subtract from 1;
- *Calculate the size ratio*: divide the district's ADM by the average of the ADM for all districts; multiply by 0.5; subtract from 1;
- *Calculate the combined sparsity-size ratio* by weighting the sparsity ratio at 40% and the size ratio at 60%.

If the school district's sparsity-size ratio is greater than the 70th percentile sparsity-size ratio, divide the district ratio by the 70th percentile ratio; subtract 1; multiply by 0.5; multiply by the weighted-student count. If the district's sparsity-size ratio is less than or equal to the 70th percentile sparsity-size ratio, the sparsity-size adjustment is 0.

After calculating the weighted student count, calculate the adjusted weighted student count by multiplying the weighted student count by the school district's market value/personal income aid ratio and the district's equalized mills multiplier. The equalized mills multiplier is calculated as:

- Calculate the average of the most recent three years of equalized mills;
- If the district's three-year average equalized mills is greater than the 70th percentile equalized mills, its equalized mills multiplier equals 1;
- If the district's three-year average equalized mills is less than or equal to the 70th percentile equalized mills, divide the district's equalized mills by the 70th percentile equalized mills.

The product of these factors is the school district's adjusted weighted student count. The amount a district receives through the formula is determined by calculating the district share of state total adjusted weighted student count. That share is distributed through the total state allocation. In Table 40.4, the state appropriation for special education funding is line 5. Operation of the formula appears next.

$$[C1_n \times 1.51] + [C2_n \times 3.77] + [C3_n \times 7.46] + SSA$$
$$= \text{Weighted Student Count (WSC)}$$

$$WSC \times EQM \times MVPI = \text{Adjusted Weighted Student Count (AWSC)}$$

$$AWSC \times \text{Total State Allocation}] / [\text{State Total AWCS}]$$
$$= \text{Prorata Share of New Special Education Funding}$$

EARLY CHILDHOOD EDUCATION AND EARLY INTERVENTION

During FY 2017, Pennsylvania distributed approximately $192.3 million for high-quality early childhood education and $59.2 million to supplement funds for federal Head Start programs. The state program supporting early childhood education, known as Pre-K Counts, provided grant funding to providers, including school districts, serving high-need populations in underserved communities. The competitive grant program currently provides approximately 25,540 children access to early learning programs. Act 45 of 2007 established the Pre-K Counts program, and grant distributions are prescribed under Section 1514-D of the Public School Code.[23] In Table 40.4, state appropriation for the Pre-K Counts program is line 6. Additionally, the state Head Start supplemental program distributes grant funding pursuant to Sections 1502-D and 1503-D of the Public School Code[24] to supplement federal Head Start programs. The program provides a high-quality, standards-based educational program in addition to health, nutritional and social services. In Table 40.4, the state appropriation for the Head Start Supplement is line 7.

Pennsylvania's Early Intervention program aims to identify and support students displaying needs for special services before entering the elementary grades. Working with early child care providers such as Head Start, the program provides special instruction, family training, psychological services, physical therapy, speech therapy, family counseling and support services. In Table 40.4, the state appropriation for this program is line 4.

CAREER AND TECHNICAL EDUCATION

State reimbursement is provided to school districts for vocational programs focusing on agriculture education, distributive education, health occupations education, home economics education (gainful), business education, technical education, trade and industrial education, or any other occupational-oriented program approved by the Secretary of Education. Pennsylvania's statute regarding reimbursement to districts for career and technical education is distributed pursuant to Section 2502.8 of the Public School Code[25] and was last amended by Act 97 of 1979.

The career and technical education funding formula distributes support to school districts based on the following. The formula calculates the vocational average daily membership (VADM). The VADM is the ADM of students in vocational programs in a district or charter school multiplied by 0.17. For career and technical centers, the VADM is the ADM of students in vocational programs in a career and technology center multiplied by 0.21.

The formula then calculates the base earned for reimbursement. The formula calculates a school district's equalized mills ratio by first computing the difference between the highest equalized mill rate in the state and the district's equalized mill rate. This difference is divided by the difference between the highest equalized millage rate in the state and the lowest equalized millage rate in the state, resulting in an equalized mills ratio. The base earned for reimbursement is calculated by multiplying the equalized mills ratio by $200 and subtracting that product from the state median actual instruction expense per weighted ADM. Under these conditions:

- The fully funded amount equals the lesser of the AIE/WADM or the BER multiplied by the greater of the market value/personal income aid ratio or 0.3750 multiplied by the VADM;

- For the 2000–2001 school year and each school year thereafter, any additional funding provided by the Commonwealth over the amount provided for the 1998–1999 school year would be distributed to area vocational-technical schools, school districts and charter schools with eight or more vocational programs, and to school districts and charter schools offering a vocational agriculture education program;
- Based on Section 2502.6 of the School Code, the actual allocation is proportionately reduced so that the total does not exceed the amount appropriated.

In Table 40.4, the state appropriation for career and technical education funding is line 8. Additionally, Pennsylvania provides grants for career and technical education equipment and job training programs. Equipment grants are awarded to school districts and area vocational and technical schools; in Table 40.4, the state appropriation for the equipment grant program is line 9. The Job Training Program appropriation provides support to educational programs providing job training for economically disadvantaged youth and adults. The appropriation supports programs promoting economic development in regions having higher than average unemployment; assisting youth and adults in increasing technical work skills in order to become economically self-sufficient; and supporting collaboration among coordinating agencies. In Table 40.4, the state appropriation for the job training program is a part of line 18, representing $31.76 million.

PUPIL TRANSPORTATION

Pennsylvania's statute regarding reimbursement to school districts for pupil transportation was last amended by Act 97 in 1979 and is distributed pursuant to Section 2541 of the Public School Code.[26] Each district is required to submit data to the Pennsylvania Department of Education on each vehicle used to provide pupil transportation. A total cost allowance is calculated for each vehicle eligible for subsidy reimbursement by calculating the following: vehicle allowance, mileage allowance, utilized passenger capacity miles allowance, and layover or congested hours allowance. The allowance for each vehicle is a calculation of the age of the vehicle, size of the vehicle, number of students assigned to the vehicle and number of miles the vehicle travels with students. The resulting calculation is multiplied by the annual cost index, resulting in the maximum approved cost for the vehicle. The sum of each vehicle's maximum approved vehicle cost is then multiplied by the school district's market value aid ratio to determine the amount of state subsidy.

The vehicle allowance (Vehicle) is calculated by multiplying the final fraction by the sum of the basic and additional allowances. The basic allowance is calculated using the pupil seating capacity. If pupil seating capacity is 10 or less, the basic allowance is $360. If the pupil seating capacity is greater than 10, the basic allowance is $540. The additional allowance (ADD) is calculated using the age of the bus and pupil seating capacity. If the bus is ten years or less, the pupil seating capacity is multiplied by $15; if the vehicle's age is 11 years or more, the pupil seating capacity is multiplied by $12. The resulting additional allowance is added to the basic allowance and then multiplied by the final fraction. The product is the vehicle allowance.

The mileage allowance (Mileage) is calculated by multiplying the approved annual miles by $0.23. The approved annual miles are calculated by multiplying the approved daily miles by the number of days the vehicle is in use. The utilized passenger capacity miles allowance (UPCM) is determined by calculating the approved annual miles and multiplying that figure by the greatest number of assigned pupils at any one time. The result is the utilized passenger capacity miles and that result is then multiplied by $0.003. The result is the utilized passenger capacity miles allowance. The layover or congested hours allowance (LCH) is calculated by multiplying the approved annual excess hours by $3. The total vehicle allowance is determined by calculating the sum of the four allowances multiplied by a cost index. In Table 40.4, the state appropriation for pupil transportation funding is line 10. An illustration of the pupil transportation formula appears next.

[Vehicle + Mileage + UPCM + LCH] × Cost Index = Total Allowance

The state also provides reimbursement to school districts for a share of pupil transportation costs for non-public and charter school students. The reimbursement rate, last amended by Act 88 of 2002, is prescribed under Section 2509.3 of the Public School Code.[27] Requirements for charter schools are prescribed in Section 1726-A as amended by Act 61 of 2008. Each school district is reimbursed $385 for each nonpublic and charter school pupil transported by the district. In Table 40.4, state appropriation for nonpublic and charter school pupil transportation funding is line 11.

SCHOOL EMPLOYEE BENEFITS

School district spending on employee benefits includes retirement contributions to the pension system, healthcare and social security payments. For FY 2017, total district spending on employee benefits ($7.07 billion) represented 61.9% of total employee salaries ($11.41 billion) and 23.2% of total spending ($30.45 billion).[28]

Most school employees in Pennsylvania are members of the Public School Employees' Retirement System (PSERS). Pursuant to statute,[29] both the employer district and the Commonwealth are responsible for paying a portion of employer contribution rates. Employers are divided into two groups: school entities and non-school entities. School entities are responsible for paying 100% of the employer share. The Commonwealth reimburses school entities for approximately 50% of payments for employees hired on or before June 30, 1994; employees hired after June 30, 1994 face a statutory formula, although not less than one-half of the payment. Non-school entities and the Commonwealth each contribute 50% of the total employer rate.

Total employer contributions for FY 2019 were estimated at $4.6 billion.[30] The employer contribution rate-setting methodology is set in statute.[31] Table 40.1 shows the employer contribution rate history beginning with FY 2012 and the certified projected rates for FY 2019–2023. The table also shows projected rates for employers presuming a 7.25% annual return on pension fund investments. While employee contributions vary, most school employees contribute 7.5% of earnings along with social security/Medicare employee contributions.

In Pennsylvania, pension legacy cost issues remain[32] and pension reform legislation has been a focus of lawmakers.[33] The General Assembly enacted two distinct forms of remedy through Act 120 of 2010 and Act 5 of 2017. Act 120 was the first successful effort at curbing rising pension costs to school districts and the Commonwealth. A key milestone in reform, Act 120 began slowing cost growth and instituted important changes to reduce the cost of Pennsylvania's public pension systems. Reforms implemented by Act 120 included:

- *Creating short-term funding relief* through a series of annual rate collars that artificially limit the amount the employer contribution rate

TABLE 40.1 Pennsylvania School Employer Retirement Contribution 2018 ($ in thousands)

Financial Year	Employer Contribution Rate	Actual District $ Contributions
FY 2011	5.64%	$418,448
FY 2012	8.65%	$939,909
FY 2013	12.36%	$1,333,490
FY 2014	16.93%	$1,819,028
FY 2015	21.40%	$2,326,279
FY 2016	25.84%	$2,847,895
FY 2017	30.03%	$3,376,828

could increase over the prior year's rate to not more than 3% for FY 2012; not more than 3.5% for FY 2013; and not more than 4.5% for FY 2014;
- *Reducing pension benefits for new employees* by lowering the multiplier used to calculate retirement benefits from 2.5% to 2%, returning it to pre-2001 levels;
- *Increasing the retirement age to 65 for new employees*; extending the period for employees to vest from 5 to 10 years; and eliminating the lump sum withdrawal of contributions at retirement; and
- *Implementing a shared risk provision for new employees*, allowing for increased employee contributions if actual investment returns fall below assumed returns.

In 2017 the governor signed into law Act 5 of 2017, fundamentally changing retirement options for newhires beginning January 1, 2019. In addition, the legislation allows current members to opt in to one of three new options. The choice is irrevocable. This legislation introduced two new hybrid defined benefit (DB)/defined contribution (DC) options and a straight DC option for members in the larger State Employee Retirement System (SERS) as well as PSERS. The new classes of service apply to all employees with the exemption of most hazardous duty employees who first become members in the new fiscal year beginning July 1 2019. In Table 40.4, the state appropriation for state's share of pension contributions is line 13.

In addition to pension eligibility, Pennsylvania school employees also participate in the Social Security and Medicare systems. Various public school entities within the Commonwealth (including school districts, intermediate units, and career and technology centers) are eligible for the School Employees' Social Security (state) subsidy. Reimbursement is available to these local education agencies for Social Security and Medicare tax contributions paid on behalf of their employees. This amount is equal to the sum of 0.5 multiplied by the contributions for existing employees and the greater value between 0.5 and the market value/personal income aid ratio for new employees. The appropriation is paid to school districts quarterly following receipt of data from each district. In Table 40.4, the state appropriation for social security funding is line 12.

SCHOOL CONSTRUCTION

Currently, reimbursement to Pennsylvania school districts for the state share of school construction is prescribed by Sections 2571–2580 of the Public School Code.[34] The funding formula has been under review by the

Public School Building Construction and Reconstruction Advisory Committee pursuant to Act 25 of 2016.

In 2012, Act 82 directed the Pennsylvania Department of Education (PDE) to conduct a review of the process by which public school building projects are reviewed and approved for reimbursement. The report found considerable concerns regarding the outdated program and recommended initiating a thorough analysis of the program with the General Assembly. As a result, a committee was formed following passage of Act 25. Among the recommendations for substantial redesign of construction reimbursement, the committee released a new recommended reimbursement formula in the spring of 2018.

The total reimbursable subsidy is found by multiplying the base per full-time equivalent (BASE) by an adjustment factor, a full-time equivalent factor, and a wealth factor. The product is divided by the number of years to calculate the annual subsidy the state will provide. The BASE is the five-year statewide median structural cost per student determined from past completed projects. At the time the report was released, the amount was $18,251 and it was recommended the amount be updated every five years. An adjustment factor (ADJ) would be determined by the governor and General Assembly representing the state share of the BASE from 0 to 1. The full-time equivalent factor (FTE) is the lesser of the school building enrollment or the full-time equivalent building capacity. FTE building capacity is calculated using weighted FTE capacity room schedule based on the proposed room types, capacities and weights shown in Table 40.2.

The wealth factor (WEALTH) proposed in the report was based on similar factors used in the basic education funding formula. To calculate the wealth factor, first multiply the school district's median household income index (MHI) by the district's local effort capacity index (LECI). Next,

TABLE 40.2 Proposed PlanCON Room Schedule for Weighted FTE Capacity

Room Type	Unit FTE Capacity	Weight	Weighted FTE Capacity
Pre–K/Kindergarten Classroom	25	1.0	25
Special Education Classroom	15	1.0	12
Special Education Resource Room	10	1.0	10
Alternative Education Classroom	20	1.0	20
Regular Classroom	25	1.0	25
Art/Music Classroom	25	1.1	28
Career/Tech-Ed/TV Studio	20	1.6	32
Laboratory	25	1.3	33
Library/Gym	50	1.4	70

calculate the statewide median product of this calculation (SDMed). A ratio (RATIO) is determined by dividing the statewide median product by the school district's product. The ratio is multiplied by 0.5 and then that product is subtracted from 1 to calculate the initial wealth factor (FACTOR). If the result is less than 0.1500, the district's initial wealth factor is set at 0.1500. The initial wealth factor is then adjusted by adding the district's sparsity size adjustment and concentrated poverty weight. The result is the district's calculated wealth factor.

The state distributes a reimbursement to school districts by an annual subsidy made over a set number of years (YEARS). Equal payments across years with a maximum ratio to structural cost is set at 65%. The school construction formula is illustrated as:

$$[(SDMed)/(MHI \times LECI)] = RATIO$$
$$[1 - (0.5 \times RATIO)] = FACTOR$$
$$(FACTOR + SSA + POV) = WEALTH$$
$$(BASE \times ADJ \times FTE \times WEALTH)/YEARS = \text{Annual Subsidy}$$

During the advisory commission's study recommending updates, Pennsylvania placed a moratorium on building projects eligible for reimbursement. The state typically appropriates funding for construction reimbursement through the Authority Rentals and Sinking Fund Requirements budget line item. In Table 40.4, the state appropriation for school construction reimbursement is line 14.

CHARTER SCHOOLS

Pennsylvania's charter schools are independently run public schools paid by public tax dollars, authorized and primarily funded by the school districts from which their students come. According to the state courts, "the relationship between a school district and a charter school is not contractual, but regulatory."[35]

Prior to FY 2012, Pennsylvania allocated state funding to school districts as reimbursement for a share of charter school tuition. However, on elimination of several state appropriations after the financial recession, Pennsylvania ceased providing state reimbursement to school districts. Table 40.3 illustrates growth in total tuition paid by school districts to charter schools and the approximate reimbursement from the state to school districts.

Currently, school districts send charter schools a per-pupil payment based on a state-established formula prescribed under Section 1725-A of the Public School Code.[36] Section 1725-A provides that for non-special

TABLE 40.3 Tuition Paid to Charters and State Charter School Reimbursement ($ in millions)

	Financial Year								
	2008	2009	2010	2011	2012	2013	2014	2015	2016
Total Tuition	$621	$717	$806	$960	$1,145	$1,268	$1,436	$1,486	$1,549
State Funds	$161	$228	$228	$219	$0	$0	$0	$0	$0

education students, the charter school shall receive for each student enrolled no less than the budgeted total expenditure per average daily membership of the prior school year, as defined in Section 2501(20), minus the budgeted expenditures of the district of residence for nonpublic school programs; adult education programs; community/junior college programs; student transportation services; for special education programs; facilities acquisition, construction and improvement services; and other financing uses, including debt service and fund transfers as provided in the Manual of Accounting and Related Financial Procedures for Pennsylvania School Systems established by the department. This amount shall be paid by the district of residence of each student.[37]

Additionally, Section 1725-A provides that:

> For special education students, the charter school shall receive for each student enrolled the same funding as for each non-special education student as provided in clause (2), plus an additional amount determined by dividing the district of residence's total special education expenditure by the product of multiplying the combined percentage of Section 2509.5(k) times the district of residence's total average daily membership for the prior school year. This amount shall be paid by the district of residence of each student.[38]

Pennsylvania's charter school law was enacted by Act 22 of 1997. Since then, Pennsylvania's funding formula has caused significant debate and concern. Legislation was introduced in 2017[39] to provide for a charter school funding commission to study the current funding system, much like prior funding commissions established for basic education funding, special education, and school construction.

NONPUBLIC (PRIVATE) K–12 SCHOOLS

In addition to funding for nonpublic school transportation detailed earlier, Pennsylvania also provides funding and services to nonpublic (private) schools across several other support categories such as special education, instructional materials, and support services. For example, Pennsylvania annually appropriates funding to acquire and provide nonsectarian textbooks, instructional materials and equipment that are loaned free of charge to nonpublic school students. In 2018, the Department of Education reported an estimated 225,000 students were enrolled across 2,270 eligible schools. In Table 40.4, the state appropriation for this program is part of line 18, representing $26.75 million in FY 2019.

Additionally, the state appropriates funding for services to students enrolled in nonprofit, nonpublic schools through disbursements to its 29 regional Intermediate Units. Services provided to eligible students include remedial reading and math, services for exceptional children, guidance counseling, psychological services, testing, and speech and hearing services. In 2018, the Department of Education reported an estimated 205,000 students enrolled across 1,940 schools were eligible for services. In Table 40.4, the state appropriation for this program is part of line 18, representing $87.95 million.

Approximately 3,242 public school children receive special education services through one of the 34 designated private schools approved by the Department of Education. These students are specially assigned to one of these schools because appropriate education is not available in the public schools. The resident district must provide funding for at least 40% of the approved tuition rate and the remaining is covered by the state. In Table 40.4, state appropriation for this program is line 5.

Four chartered schools[40] in Pennsylvania provide special education services to low incidence blind and deaf students. The schools include the Overbrook School for the Blind, Western Pennsylvania School for the Blind, Pennsylvania School for the Deaf, and Western Pennsylvania School for the Deaf. The resident school district must provide funding for at least 40% of the approved tuition rate and the remainder is covered by the state. In Table 40.4, the state appropriation for this program is part of line 16, representing $52.34 million in FY 2019.

OTHER GRANTS AND SUBSIDIES

The Commonwealth of Pennsylvania provides state funding for targeted and innovative professional development through the statewide Act 82 teacher evaluation system, Act 45 leadership training program, multi-measure evaluation system for professional development, and the Standards Aligned System (SAS). The SAS provides accessible information to schools and educators through its web-based resources to deliver standards-aligned instructional support. In Table 40.4, the state appropriation for teacher professional development funding is line 15.

Pennsylvania currently provides competitive grants to school districts and offers support related to school safety services. Distributed through the Office of Safe Schools in the Pennsylvania Department of Education, state grants are awarded pursuant to Section 1302-A of the Public School Code[41] and are targeted toward programs addressing school violence and improvements in school security. In Table 40.4, state appropriation for the Safe Schools Initiative is line 17.

Other grants and subsidies to school districts include the school food service reimbursement subsidy which provides funding for the School Breakfast Program and the National School Lunch Program. Distribution of funding for school food services is prescribed under Section 1337.1 of the Public School Code.[42] In Table 40.4, state appropriation for school food services is part of line 16, representing $30 million in FY 2019. Pennsylvania also provides funding to support library access to educational materials through the Public Library Subsidy, Library Services for Visually Impaired and Disabled, and Library Access appropriations. In Table 40.4, state appropriations for library programs are part of line 18, representing $60.11 million in FY 2019.

REVENUES

For FY 2017, total local revenues ($16.84 billion) in the Commonwealth represented 54.6% of total revenue ($30.84 billion), while property taxes ($13.05 billion) represented 42.4%. Property taxes comprised 77.5% of total local revenues, while the remaining share primarily came from local earned income taxes ($1.37 billion). State revenue to school districts totaled $11.3 billion for FY 2017, representing 36.7% of total revenue ($30.84 billion). State basic education funding ($5.89 billion) is the largest component of state revenue, representing 52.1% of total state revenue and 19.7% of total revenues during FY 2017. Tables 40.5 and 40.6 later in this chapter provide further detail including prior years.[43]

LOCAL REAL ESTATE TAXES

Special Session Act 1 of 2006, known as the Tax Payer Relief Act[44] as amended by Act 25 of 2011, impacted local revenues for school districts. The law first generated state revenues from casino gaming to provide allocations for property tax relief on homesteads throughout Pennsylvania. Additionally, Act 1, which created annual indices linked to inflation and adjusted for each school district by the wealth aid ratio, limited districts' ability to increase local property taxes by subjecting increases above the district's index to a public referendum. However, increases for certain expenditures specific under statute could be exempted from referendum if approved by the Pennsylvania Department of Education. Tax limitations on local property taxes were made pursuant to Section 333 of the Tax Payer Relief Act.[45]

In 2015, the median property tax rate in Pennsylvania was $2,223 per year for a home holding a median assessed value of $164,700. Tax rates are expressed in mills or $1 for each $1,000 of assessed property value. Each county in the state has its own method for determining assessed property value that includes county, municipal and school taxes. Therefore, a fair comparison for taxation among all counties is based on the effective tax rate or what percentage of a home's median value is spent annually on property taxes. Essentially, a $3,000 tax levied on a home with an assessed value of $200,000 produces an effective tax rate of 1.5%, or the property tax/assessed property value multiplied by 100.

Pennsylvania has the 39th highest effective tax rate in the U.S. at 1.51% of median assessed home value. The national average rate in 2014 was 1.29%, which was 22 basis points lower than Pennsylvania and higher than the average annual rates of 35 of the 50 states and the District of Columbia.

TAX CREDITS, DEDUCTIONS, AND EXEMPTIONS

Pennsylvania has two education tax credit programs known as the Educational Improvement Tax Credit (EITC)[46] and the Opportunity Scholarship Tax Credit (OSTC).[47] Tax credits under the EITC may be awarded to business firms making contributions to organizations certified by the Department of Community and Economic Development (DCED). A qualified scholarship organization provides tuition assistance in the form of scholarships to eligible students residing within the boundaries of a 'low-achieving school' to attend another public school outside the district or nonpublic school. A qualified educational improvement organization must contribute at least 80% of its annual EITC receipts as grants for innovative educational programs at a public school, charter school or private school approved under Section 1376 of the Public School Code.[48] A business firm making a one-time contribution is eligible for a tax credit of 75% of the contribution while two consecutive year contributions make the business firm eligible for a tax credit of 90% of the contribution. A statutory limit provides a maximum of $135 million in tax credits between the EITC and OSTC programs.

SUMMARY

Summary Table 40.4 illustrates total state spending on K–12 education which is comprised of numerous programs and formula distributions. In total, Pennsylvania appropriated $12.37 billion in grants and subsidies to the system of public education for FY 2019, a $451 million increase over FY

TABLE 40.4 Summary of State Appropriations General Fund: K–12 Grants/Subsidies ($ in thousands)

	Support of Public Schools	Page	FY 2018	FY 2019
1	Basic Education Funding	3	$5,995,079	$6,095,079
2	Ready to Learn Block Grant	4	$250,000	$268,000
3	Special Education	4	$1,121,815	$1,136,815
4	Early Intervention	5	$263,878	$285,500
5	Special Education–Approved Private Schools	9	$108,010	$111,089
6	Pre–K Counts	5	$172,284	$192,284
7	Head Start Supplemental Assistance	5	$54,178	$59,178
8	Career and Technical Education	5	$62,000	$92,000
9	Career and Technical Education Equipment Grant	6	$2,550	$2,500
10	Pupil Transportation	6	$549,907	$549,097
11	Nonpublic and Charter School Pupil Transportation	6	$80,009	$80,009
12	School Employees' Social Security	7	$499,500	$541,205
13	School Employees' Retirement	7	$2,264,000	$2,487,500
14	Authority Rentals and Sinking Fund Requirements	8	$29,703	$10,500
15	Teacher Professional Development	10	$5,959	$5,309
16	Other Support Grants and Subsidies to Public Schools	—	$145,243	$145,244
	Subtotal–Support of Public Schools		**$11,603,307**	**$12,063,510**
	Other Grants and Subsidies		FY 2018	FY 2019
17	Safe School Initiative	10	$8,527	$10,000
18	Other Grants and Subsidies	—	$217,123	$206,989
	Subtotal–Other Grants and Subsidies		**$255,650**	**$216,989**
	Total Grants & Subsidies		**$11,919,867**	**$12,370,491**

2018. These figures did not include general government operations which are funds appropriated to the Pennsylvania Department of Education for general operations of the Department of Education.

Table 40.5 shows that total school district revenues over the past seven fiscal years increased from $25.38 billion to $30.75 billion. More importantly, the breakdown of total expenditures by accounting object for FY 2016 and FY 2017, as illustrated in Table 40.6, shows which costs increased and decreased. Object 900, Other Uses of Funds, represents refinancing of old debt which comprised 46.5% of the overall year over year increase in total expenditures. Finally, Table 40.7 shows changes to school district expenditures by function across the years 2016–2017.

Pennsylvania

TABLE 40.5 Total Revenues by Source for all 500 Pennsylvania School Districts (in thousands)

Source	FY 2011	FY 2012	FY 2013	FY 2014	FY 2015	FY 2016	FY 2017
Local	$14,154,891	$14,496,636	$14,981,358	$15,361,453	$15,886,606	$16,309,685	$16,838,909
State	$8,670,492	$8,917,851	$9,152,394	$9,582,677	$10,022,410	$10,475,164	$11,310,533
Federal	$2,173,766	$1,048,442	$1,037,315	$812,525	$814,577	$774,735	$842,702
Other	$379,799	$567,636	$833,903	$461,070	$854,694	$934,474	$1,758,691
Total Revenue	$25,378,948	$25,030,565	$26,004,970	$26,217,725	$27,578,287	$28,494,058	$30,750,835
Total Expenses	$25,097,499	$24,761,443	$25,564,247	$26,128,265	$27,386,591	$28,308,905	$30,495,436

TABLE 40.6 Pennsylvania District Expenditures by Selected Objects FY 2017 ($ in thousands)

Object Code and Description		FY 2017	FY 2016	Increase $	Increase %	Share of Increase
100	Personnel Services–Salaries	$11,412,375	$11,179,007	$233,368	2.09%	10.7%
200	Personnel Services–Employee Benefits	$7,070,876	$6,509,500	$561,375	8.62%	25.7%
	Social Security Contributions	*$851,934*	*$837,306*	*$14,628*	*1.75%*	*0.7%*
	Retirement Contributions	*$3,376,829*	*$2,847,895*	*$528,933*	*18.57%*	*24.2%*
300	Purchased Prof. and Technical Services	$1,722,366	$1,606,767	$115,599	7.19%	5.3%
400	Purchased Property Services	$537,287	$598,883	($61,597)	-10.29%	-2.8%
500	Other Purchased Services	$3,969,958	$3,792,855	$177,103	4.67%	8.1%
	Charter School Tuition	*$1,654,993*	*$1,549,444*	*$105,549*	*6.81%*	*4.8%*
600	Supplies	$927,515	$780,824	$146,692	18.79%	6.7%
700	Property	$239,045	$275,118	($36,073)	-13.11%	-1.6%
800	Other Objects	$923,229	$889,000	$34,230	3.85%	1.6%
900	Other Uses of Funds	$3,692,785	$2,676,951	$1,015,834	37.95%	46.5%
	Total Expenditures	$30,495,436	$28,308,905	$2,186,530	7.72%	100.0%

TABLE 40.7 Pennsylvania District Expenditures by Selected Functions FY 2017 ($ in thousands)

Function Code and Description		FY 2017	FY 2016	Increase $	Increase %	Share of Increase
1000	Instruction	$17,446,974	$16,640,401	$806,573	4.85%	36.9%
	Regular Education Programs (1100)	$11,970,421	$11,474,087	$496,334	4.33%	22.7%
	Special Education Programs (1200)	$4,373,778	$4,099,293	$274,485	6.70%	12.6%
	Vocational Education Programs (1300)	$645,300	$635,517	$9,783	1.54%	0.4%
2000	Support Services	$8,042,999	$7,710,802	$332,197	4.31%	15.2%
	Instructional Support Staff (2200)	$833,416	$757,513	$75,903	10.02%	3.5%
	Administrative (2300)	$1,572,942	$1,526,115	$46,827	3.07%	2.1%
	O&M Facility Services (2600)	$2,180,292	$2,120,079	$60,213	2.84%	2.8%
	Safety/Security (2660)	$126,605	$117,979	$8,626	7.31%	0.4%
	Student Transportation (2700)	$1,446,592	$1,412,537	$34,055	2.41%	1.6%
3000	Non-Instructional Services	$506,738	$483,728	$23,010	4.76%	1.1%
	Student Activities (3200)	$461,041	$439,539	$21,501	4.89%	1.0%
4000	Facilities Acquisition, Construction and Improvement Services	$63,888	$73,101	–$9,212	–12.60%	–0.42%
5000	Other Exp. & Finance Uses	$4,434,836	$3,400,873	$1,033,963	30.40%	47.3%
	Refunded Bonds (5120)	$1,577,148	$838,898	$738,250	88.00%[1]	33.8%
	Capital Projects (5230)	$478,075	$326,913	$151,162	46.24%	6.9%
	Debt Service Fund Transfers (5240)	$453,001	$495,111	($42,109)	–8.51%	–1.9%
	Total Expenditures	$30,495,436	$28,308,905	$2,186,530	7.72%	100.0%

NOTES

1. Pa. Const. Art. III, § 14.
2. Louise Walsh and Matthew Walsh, *History and Organization of Education in Pennsylvania* (1930). Retrieved from https://hdl.handle.net/2027/mdp.39015008840095 p. 228
3. *The School Laws of Pennsylvania* (Collection). Retrieved from https://catalog.hathitrust.org/Record/007823490. https://catalog.hathitrust.org/Record/007823490
4. Janice Bissett & Arnold Hillman, *The History of School Funding in Pennsylvania 1682–2013* (2013). Retrieved from https://slidex.tips/downloadFile/the-history-of-school-funding-in-pennsylvania
5. https://babel.hathitrust.org/cgi/pt?id=pst.000062684637;view=1up;seq=81
6. *The School Laws of Pennsylvania* (1899). Retrieved from https://hdl.handle.net/2027/pst.000068060183?urlappend=%3Bseq=171
7. *The School Laws of Pennsylvania* (1913). Retrieved from https://babel.hathitrust.org/cgi/pt?id=pst.000068060244;view=1up;seq=123
8. Ibid p. 117.
9. *Statistics of the Public Schools* (1919). Retrieved from https://babel.hathitrust.org/cgi/pt?id=pst.000011821519;view=1up;seq=5
10. *The School Laws of Pennsylvania* (1923). Retrieved from https://babel.hathitrust.org/cgi/pt?id=pst.000068060251
11. For a complete legislative history of funding schools, see Janice Bissett & Arnold Hillman, *The History of School Funding in Pennsylvania 1682–2013* (2013). Retrieved from https://slidex.tips/downloadFile/the-history-of-school-funding-in-pennsylvania.
12. Janice Bissett & Arnold Hillman, *The History of School Funding in Pennsylvania 1682–2013* (2013). Retrieved from https://slidex.tips/downloadFile/the-history-of-school-funding-in-pennsylvania; Louise Walsh & Matthew Walsh, *History and Organization of Education in Pennsylvania* (1930), retrieved from: https://hdl.handle.net/2027/mdp.39015008840095; and Michelle J. Atherton, *How Pennsylvania Funds Public Schools: The Story of the State Share* (2014). Retrieved from http://www.cla.temple.edu/corp/files/2012/12/State-Share-Issue-Memo.pdf
13. William T. Hartman and Timothy J. Shrom, *Hard Choices Still Ahead: The Financial Future of Pennsylvania School Districts* (2017). Retrieved from http://www.cla.temple.edu/corp/files/2017/03/Fiscal-Outlook-2017-Update-Policy-Brief.pdf.
14. *William Penn School District v. Pennsylvania Department of Education*, 170 A.3d 414 (Pa. 2017).
15. Christine Kiracofe and Andrew L. Armagost, *Political Question Doctrine in the Keystone State: A Legal Analysis of Pennsylvania School Funding In Light of William Penn School District v. Pennsylvania Department of Education* (2017).
16. *William Penn School District, et al. v. Pennsylvania Department of Education et al.* (587 M.D. 2014).
17. Act 14 of 1949 (March 10, P.L. 30).
18. 22 Pa. Code § § 1—741.

19. Source data at http://www.education.pa.gov/Teachers%20-%20Administrators/School%20Finances/Finances/Pages/default.aspx.
20. 24 P.S. § 25-2502.53.
21. 24 P.S. § 25-2599.6.
22. 24 P.S. § 25-2509.5.
23. 24 P.S. § 15-1514-D.
24. 24 P.S. § § 15-1502-D — 15-1503-D.
25. 24 P.S. § 25-2502.8.
26. 24 P.S. § 25-2541.
27. 24 P.S. § 25-2509.3.
28. Source data available online at http://www.education.pa.gov/Teachers%20-%20Administrators/School%20Finances/Finances/AFR%20Data%20Summary/Pages/AFR-Data-Detailed-.aspx#.VZwC6mXD-Uk
29. 24 P.S. § 83-8326.
30. Actual and projected calculations from PSERS Comprehensive Annual Financial Reports. Retrieved from http://www.psers.pa.gov/FPP/Publications/General/Pages/CAFR.aspx
31. 24 P.S. § 83-8327.
32. Keystone Pension Report, Fall 2012. Retrieved from http://archive.pasbo.org/26Nov2012_Budget_PensionReport.pdf
33. Pennsylvania Association of School Business Officials Update on Pension Reform. Retrieved from https://www.pasbo.org/pension
34. 24 P.S. § § 25-2571 — 25-2580
35. *Foreman v. Chester-Upland School District*, 941 A.2d 108 (Commonwealth Court of Pennsylvania, January 18, 2008).
36. 24 P.S. § 17-1725-A.
37. 24 P.S. § 17-1725-A (a) (2).
38. 24 P.S. § 17-1725-A (a) (3).
39. Senate Bill 806.
40. Chartered schools are not the same as charter schools as established pursuant to the Article XVII of the Public School Code relating to cyber charter or brick and mortar charter schools.
41. 24 P.S. § 13-1302-A (c).
42. 24 P.S. § 13-1337.1.
43. Source data available online at http://www.education.pa.gov/Teachers%20-%20Administrators/School%20Finances/Finances/AFR%20Data%20Summary/Pages/AFR-Data-Detailed-.aspx#.VZwC6mXD-Uk
44. Act 1 of 2006, Special Session 1 (June 27, P.L. 1873).
45. § 333.
46. https://dced.pa.gov/programs/educational-improvement-tax-credit-program-eitc/
47. https://dced.pa.gov/programs/opportunity-scholarship-tax-credit-program-ostc/
48. 24 P.S. § 13-1326.
49. The Commonwealth paid multiple prior year funds owed for school construction reimbursement (PlanCON) within the single FY 2017, resulting in substantially higher amounts during this fiscal year for Refunded Bonds and Capital Projects.

CHAPTER 41

Rhode Island

Ken Wagner, Ph.D.
Commissioner
Rhode Island Department of Education

GENERAL BACKGROUND[1]

Rhode Island became a state in 1790, and the first state constitution was adopted in 1843. The Rhode Island constitution provides for public education:

> The diffusion of knowledge, as well as of virtue among the people, being essential to the preservation of their rights and liberties, it shall be the duty of the general assembly to promote public schools and public libraries, and to adopt all means which it may deem necessary and proper to secure to the people the advances and opportunities of education and public library services.[2]
>
> The general assembly shall make all necessary provisions by law for carrying this article into effect. It shall not divert said money or fund from the aforesaid uses, nor borrow, appropriate, or use the same, or any part thereof, for any other purpose, under any pretence whatsoever.[3]

Beginning in the 1960s, legislative engagement in providing state aid to Rhode Island public schools focused on the 'minimum guarantee,' a required minimum level the state provides for school revenue. In 1960, the Rhode Island General Assembly enacted the Foundation Level Support Act, with a guaranteed minimum state aid of 25% and simultaneously established the School Housing Act to support school construction. In 1964, the minimum guarantee was legislatively increased to 30% of revenue available to school districts. The 1967 Thibeault Commission used median family income, rather than local property values, to adjust district wealth in calculating state aid, believed to better reflect a district's current fiscal conditions. In 1983, the General Assembly decreased the minimum guarantee to 28%. In 1985, the General Assembly passed the Omnibus Property Tax Relief and Replacement Act, with the accompanying goal of increasing the state's share to 50% of district revenue.

Public school spending in Rhode Island has frequently exceeded the national average. In Fiscal Year 1991, Rhode Island was ranked eighth in per-student spending. By FY 2008, spending for schools on a per-pupil basis in Rhode Island was about 33% more than the national average ($14,459 vs. $10,532). In that same year, Rhode Island was ranked sixth in the nation in per-pupil spending, trailing only Arkansas, Connecticut, New Jersey, New York, and Washington D.C.

In 2010, Rhode Island enacted an education funding formula effective in FY 2012. In 2016, the state legislature made adjustments to the 2010 formula. Those changes related to adopting the principle that the money should follow the student, a change that resulted in some local education agencies (LEAs) receiving increases in state aid to education and others receiving less funding. Changes were scheduled for multi-year transition. That transition ended for some school districts in FY 2018, with full implementation by FY 2021.

Rhode Island's school finance formula now includes a core instruction amount for all students. This core funds several academic components; provides a poverty factor adjustment known as the 'student success factor;' and provides a state share ratio which is calculated using municipal property values, median family income, and student poverty status. The formula also includes categorical funding to support high cost programs: career and technical education, early childhood programs, high cost special education, English learners, non-public and regional student transportation, and a temporary bonus for regional school districts. Also, there is a categorical fund with a statutory sunset provision to support communities that favor charter and state schools. Stabilization funds are provided for three state schools: Davies Career and Technical School, the Metropolitan Career and Technical Center, and the Central Falls School Department—all of which are intended to stabilize these state-operated LEAs due to the loss of education aid.

In addition to state aid, municipalities also contribute to local school departments. Monies are determined by local control. Charter schools, as well as state-operated career and tech schools, do not receive direct municipality support; rather, the local/municipal funds received by such schools are determined by a local share calculation which is calculated by the Rhode Island Department of Education (RIDE). As a result, per-pupil funding for charter school or state-operated career and tech school students is the same as a student attending a district public school.

BASIC FUNDING PROGRAM[4]

Foundation education aid for each school district in Rhode Island is the sum of the core instruction per-pupil amount and the amount needed to support high need students (student success factor), multiplied by the district state share ratio. The core instruction amount is the accumulation of various costs, as compiled by the National Center for Education Statistics (NCES) for a select group of states.

The core instruction amount is based on cost studies from states deemed by researchers to be best practice financial models. In order to be informed, objective, and geographically sensitive, the formula uses an average cost of four New England states to provide a balanced perspective on what Rhode Island should be spending to provide high-quality education. The cost studies relied upon were a snapshot in time during the formula development process.

Rhode Island requires that the core instruction calculation must be completed by July to be used in the funding formula calculation. The formula calculation is a key component of state budget targets used for the agency's budget preparation. Agency budget estimates are submitted to the State Budget Office in July to create financial budget targets for the following fiscal year budget request. For example, estimates were due to the state budget office in July 2017 for budget targets used in the budget request that began July 2018 (i.e., FY 2019).

Types of LEA expenditures included in the core instruction component are as follows: face-to-face teaching and classroom materials; pupil, teacher and program support; and leadership, administration and school business operations and business support services. This includes a wide array of expenses, including but not limited to the following categories and subsets:

Face-to-face Teaching and Classroom Materials:

- Teachers, including full and part-time teachers for programs, teacher assistants, and substitute teachers;
- All fringe benefits except teacher retirement;
- All purchased services, including contracted technical and professional services;
- Instructional supplies and textbooks;
- Dues, fees, and professional memberships.

Pupil, Teacher, and Program Support:

- Social workers, guidance counselors, nurses, psychologists, occupational, physical and speech pathologies, audiology;
- All fringe benefits except retirement for this category;

- Instructional support services including library and media, computer lab staff, curriculum coordinators, professional development, and PD staff;
- Purchased services, including contracted labor and equipment for any of the included salaried categories;
- Supplies, books, periodicals, curricular books, films, slides, tapes, video tapes, television programs, and reference books not in the classroom;
- Dues and fees for professional membership in organizations.

Leadership:

- General administration, including salaries for superintendent and staff, school board and negotiations;
- All fringe benefits except retirement in this category;
- Purchased services, including expenditure for legal firms, election services, staff relations, and negotiation services;
- Supplies, including books, periodicals, general supplies, paper, and printing materials for the board and budget;
- Dues and fees for membership to professional organizations;
- Salaries for school principals and staff and department chairs;
- All fringe benefits except retirement for staff in this category;
- Purchased services, including consultants, school scheduling firms and administrative staff inservice;
- School administration, including supplies, books, periodicals and general supplies; dues and fees for professional organizations and miscellaneous expenditures for goods and services.

Items not in the core instruction foundation amount:

- Teacher retirement as part of a separate state funding mechanism;
- Food services, transportation, safety, building upkeep, utilities and maintenance, budgeted contingencies, debt service, capital projects, retiree benefits, out-of-district tuition and transportation, nonpublic textbooks, enterprise/community service, and claims and settlement;
- Expenditures funded by federal funds.

Core Instruction Calculation

Calculating the core instruction amount for school aid purposes in Rhode Island uses audited expenditure data for the region, including Connecticut, Massachusetts, New Hampshire, and Rhode Island. Information is drawn from the NCES government database. NCES releases expenditure data for public schools throughout the nation at a detailed level. The core instruction amount accounts for costs having the greatest impact on a student's ability to learn, including instruction, instruction support, some operating costs, and leadership costs. The average cost for core instruction expenditure categories for the four states is adjusted by the Consumer Price Index (CPI) to make the calculation more relevant to current costs. The calculated amount is called the 'core instruction amount.' The included costs are comprehensive and based on real expenditure data, including salaries, supplies, curriculum development, professional development, professional dues and fees, all classroom supports, all student-centered services, a portion of benefits, and all leadership costs including staff. The formula requires the core instruction amount to be updated annually.

The formula does not treat grade levels differently. Because NCES data already account for costs of delivering services at all grade levels, this formula uses averaging that spreads costs across all grade spans and all types of students in the New England region. Once a distribution is determined through the state funding formula, decisions on how funds are spent are maintained at the local level. Therefore, LEAs may choose to allocate funds differently across grade levels.

State Share

Rhode Island requires that the state and local school district share in the cost of educational programs. The state share is a component of the funding formula designed to provide state aid to municipal school departments based on the municipality's ability to provide support. Foundation education aid for each district is the sum of the per-pupil amount and the amount to support high need students (student success factor), multiplied by the district state share ratio.

Determining the state's share follows a pattern of key data reporting periods involving:

- In August of each year, the Rhode Island Department of Education (RIDE) receives Equalized Weighted Assessed Valuation[5] (EWAV) data;
- Each August 15, RIDE receives June 30 resident average daily membership (RADM) data, by district and statewide;
- On August 31, the state share ratio calculation is completed by RIDE;
- The methodology for the calculation requires:
  - Receive EWAV data;

- Obtain student enrollment and poverty data;
- Determine the State Share Ratio for each Community (SSRC), which may not be less than zero. i.e.,

$$SSRC = \frac{\text{District EWAV/District RADM}}{1 - (0.475 \times \text{State EWAV/State RADM})}$$

insert data into equation below

$$SSRC^2 + \%\underline{PK6POVERTY}^2$$
$$\text{State Share Ratio (SSR)} = \ldots /\text{---------}$$

Two examples of formula operation are as follows:

- Community 1 has a state share ratio of 70%; the amount of per-pupil aid Community 1 will receive is the core instruction per-pupil amount, plus the student success factor times the share ratio of 70%;
- Community 2 is better able to provide financial support for schools, causing its share ratio to be 55%. The amount of per-pupil aid Community 2 will receive is the core instruction per-pupil amount, plus the student success factor times the share ratio of 55%.

The state share ratio is a combination of two factors. The first factor is community property values, adjusted for median family income as provided by the Division of Municipal Finance at the Rhode Island Department of Revenue. This represents the community's ability to generate tax revenue per child attending a public school vs. the state average. The second factor is the percent of children in prekindergarten through sixth grade who meet the poverty criteria. These two factors represent two policy goals when determining where the state should distribute additional funds, i.e., what is the local ability to generate revenue for schools, and where are the concentrated pockets of need located.

These two factors combine into a single state share ratio, utilizing a mathematical average known as the quadratic mean. The practical effect of using this calculation is the larger number receives greater weight in a quadratic mean than a typical mean. In districts where the ability to generate tax revenue is high but the child poverty concentration is greater, the quadratic mean is closer to the value of poverty concentration.

There are differences in local tax burden for communities with the same adjusted assessed property values and different levels of poverty. Including student poverty in the state share ratio is a way to account for additional local burden that exists because of high concentrations of poverty. Without a poverty component, two communities with the same adjusted assessed property value could have drastically different expectations for local revenue generation. While including a poverty component in a straight mean helps reduce the difference, the calculation is more effective at equalizing the local burden in areas with concentrated poverty vs. those with less concentrated poverty.

Student Data in Formula

March 15 of each year is a key date for estimating student data for the budget year two years hence in the formula. As a more specific example, March 2016 data was used to estimate the 2017–18 budget allocation. This is because the state budget process requires agency budget estimates to be submitted to the state budget office one year prior to the start of the proposed budget year. Additionally, June 30 end-of-year resident average daily membership (RADM) is a component of the state share ratio calculation. Although this data is integral to calculation of the state share ratio for the funding formula, it is not the enrollment data used to determine education aid. Student data categories include (1) enrolled in an alternate learning program; (2) enrolled in a state-funded preschool classroom; (3) enrolled in a high school equivalency (GED) program; (4) home schooled; (5) enrolled in a transition program; (6) enrolled in an outplacement program; (7) enrolled in a public or state-operated school; and (8) enrolled in a private school with an IEP or service plan.

Student data is reported by LEAs through their student information systems to the RIDE Office of Data Analysis and Technology Services (OATS). Student data is compiled by OATS and submitted to the Finance Office for funding formula purposes. Prior to finalizing data and related calculations, OATS and the Finance Office verify the data. Material variances are investigated by RIDE prior to dissemination of formula calculations. LEAs are active participants in the review and finalization of student data.

For charter schools, a report on October 1 enrollments is required for any charter school having a 10% or greater change from the March data used to finalize state funding calculations. This adjustment is included to mitigate fluctuations between projected and actual enrollments of new and expanded charter schools.

Calculation of Formula Aid

The Rhode Island school funding formula is calculated as shown in Figure 41.1.

> Core Instruction Funding = Core Instruction Amount x PK–12 ADM
>
> Student Success Factor Funding = Core Instruction Amount x 40% x Poverty ADM
>
> =
>
> Total Foundation x State Share = State Formula funding

Figure 41.1 State Aid Formula Rhode Island 2018.

Funding for public schools of choice is calculated by the sending district using the same calculation, so that aid for each sending community is accumulated to determine the school's appropriation.

CATEGORICAL FUNDS

The funding formula includes several categorical aid programs that provide funding for costs beyond those covered in the primary aid formula. Unlike the primary aid scheme, these categorical funds are explicitly subject to annual appropriation. The original categorical funds from the FY 2010 legislation support high cost special education students, regional school and non-public school transportation (excluding special education), regional school and non-public school transportation, career and technical education, early childhood preschool programs, regional school districts, and Central Falls stabilization funding. In FY 2016, additional categorical funds were added, including English learner funds, PSOC density funding, and an expansion of stabilization funding for Davies and the Met Center, which are the remaining state schools funded in part by the funding formula. For all these funds, when the annual budget appropriation is insufficient to cover all statewide costs, the funds are prorated among the LEAs with eligible costs.

Within these categories are programs and methods for funding distribution. More specifically in bullet form:

- *High Cost Special Education.* This funding pays for all per-pupil special education costs above five times the sum of the basic core plus the student success amounts. The Office of Statewide Efficiencies at RIDE annually collects data where LEAs report per-pupil costs with special education costs net of third party reimbursements. RIDE reimburses LEAs only for the per-pupil amounts over the threshold.

- *Career and Technical Education* (CTE). This funding is for the state to pay a portion of per-pupil costs for high cost programs, for start-up costs, and for new or transformed programs. The amount dedicated to the high cost reimbursement is determined annually based on the career and technical education needs throughout the state. The high cost reimbursement is limited to RIDE-approved programs. For new and transformed programs, RIDE conducts an application process. High cost reimbursements are based on Uniform Chart of Accounts (UCOA) expenditure data for RIDE-approved CTE programs as compiled by the Office of Statewide Efficiencies. These per-pupil expenditures are a three-year average by program category. Every eligible program is reimbursed the per-pupil amount within each CTE category, regardless of actual expenditures.
- *Transportation.* This funding is for the state to pay 50% of transportation costs for regional school districts. The state also assumes costs for non-public out-of-district transportation for LEAs that participate in the statewide transportation system. The non-public out-of-district reimbursement is only for students who are transported to private and parochial schools—special education is not included. LEAs receive reimbursement for costs in the form of a credit against their invoices to the statewide transportation system. In the case of regional school districts, the state pays its portion as aid to the district. Regional transportation payments result from UCOA expenditure data; non-public out-of-district payments result from student utilization by district.
- *English Learners.* English Learners (EL) funding is for the state to pay for a portion of the per-pupil costs for all EL students who are in initial levels of the EL process. Based on the Assessing Comprehension and Communication in English State to State (ACCESS) annual proficiency assessment, students in the initial three categories (entering, emerging, and developing) are aid-eligible. The per-pupil aid amount is 10% of the core instruction amount multiplied by the applicable LEA state share ratio. To receive funding, LEAs must submit a signed set of assurances and, if the allocation exceeds $10,000 a detailed spending plan is sent to RIDE's Office of Student Community and Academic Support (OSCAS). These funds must be used to provide high quality, research-based services and may not be used for activities the district is currently funding.
- *Early Childhood.* This funding is to provide prekindergarten funding to LEAs and non-profits to run high quality voluntary pre-K classrooms. Funds are awarded on a competitive basis through an annual request for proposals (RFP) process administered by RIDE. Successful awards are funded for a three-year cycle subject to funds

availability and annual performance reviews. To be eligible, the community or individual elementary school must have at least 50% of students meeting poverty status.
- *Regional Bonus.* This funding seeks to remove financial barriers to LEAs combining and regionalizing by providing funds for two years to offset any additional costs incurred as a result of consolidation. Funding is calculated as a percentage of the aid received in the year an LEA regionalizes. In the first year following regionalization, the district receives a bonus of 2% of the amount it receives through the funding formula exclusive of categorical funds; in the second year, a 1% bonus follows.
- *Density Aid.* This funding is direct state aid available through FY 2019 to school districts having at least 5% of student populations enrolled in public schools of choice. The amount of aid is decreased annually from 2017 through 2019.
- *Stabilization Funds.* Central Falls, Davies, and the Met Center stabilization funds were established to ensure that appropriate funding is available. Additional support for Central Falls relates to concerns regarding the city's capacity to meet the local share. Additional support for Davies and the Met Center relates to costs of running stand-alone high cost schools offering both academic and career and technical coursework. Stabilization funds are determined on a case by case basis.

Other Aid Payments

There is a handful of education aid payments outside the aid formula that are not detailed in this chapter. These include Group Home Aid, E-Rate, Non-Public Textbook Aid, School Breakfast Aid, and Aid to the Recovery High School.

PUBLIC SCHOOLS OF CHOICE

As indicated, Rhode Island's school finance plan uses a 'money follows the student' method of distribution. This applies to public schools of choice (PSOC) as well. The allocation of municipal funds to municipal LEAs is strictly a local decision.

Key data reporting periods include the following: (1) LEAs are required to submit all UCOA data to RIDE and the Office of Statewide Efficiencies in December of each year for the fiscal year ending June 30 of the prior year. Student enrollment data are likewise reported on June 30 in the form of average daily membership, which becomes a component of the local share calculation. Local payment rates are then calculated by RIDE. Payments to PSOCs are calculated as shown in Figure 41.2.

---

1. Calculate the local payment rate (Step 1).
   a. The local per-pupil amount is calculated by dividing each sending district's local property tax appropriation to education, net of debt services and capital projects based on enrollment data for all public school students residing in the community. This calculation includes local students attending district public schools and PSOCs. End of year data is used for the budget year two years hence.

   Step 1 Example

   Local Tax Appropriation to Education ÷ Local Public School Students = X

2. Adjust the local payment rate for differences in certain financial obligations (Step 2). The local payment rate is adjusted for the greater of the following two reduction options:
   a. 7% of the local payment rate; or
   b. The per-pupil value of the district's statutorily defined expenditure categories minus the average expenses incurred by all PSOCs for those same categories of expenses. Expenditure categories are non-public textbook and transportation, retiree health benefits, out-of-district special education tuition and transportation, services for students ages 18–21, preschool screening and intervention, career and technical education tuition and transportation, debt service, and rent.

   Step 2 Example

   $$\text{Greater of Option (a) (7\% of } X\text{)}$$
   $$X - \text{ or } = \text{Local Payment Rate}$$
   $$\text{Option (b)}^{**}$$

   (June 30, 2016 data)   (FY 2018)

   ** Local payment rates to mayoral academy charter schools for districts qualifying for option (b) can be further reduced by an amount equal to the per-pupil value of teacher retirement costs attributable to the unfunded liability as calculated by the state's actuary. Membership in the Rhode Island State Employees Retirement System is not required for teachers employed by the mayoral academies.

3. Central Falls local payment rate.
   Due to the state's takeover of the school district on July 1, 1991, Central Falls is the only municipal LEA that does not receive municipal tax support for annual operating expenditures. RIDE calculates the Central Falls School District local payment rate as follows:
   a. Determine expenditures for UCOA codes not included in the core per-pupil; these are Operations (Transportation, Food Service, Safety, Building Upkeep, Utilities, Maintenance, Data Processing, and Business Operations), Out-of-District Obligations—tuition, Transportation, Textbooks, Debt Service and Capital Projects, Retiree Benefits, Enterprise and Community Service Operations, and Claims and Settlements.
   b. Determine what the local share of the core costs would be by subtracting Central Fall's state share of the funding formula from the total foundation aid.
   c. Combine the results of steps a and b and include as the local tax appropriation to education in Step 1 of the local payment rate calculation.

Figure 41.2 State Aid Formula Public Schools of Choice 2018.

Finally, local payment rates are calculated by RIDE and publicly released. PSOCs invoice the sending school districts on a quarterly basis using the actual enrollment on the first day of each quarter multiplied by 25% of the local payment rate. In accordance with statutes, the first local district payment is based on August 15 enrollment, while the remaining quarterly payments are invoiced using October 1, January 1, and April 1 enrollments. Any disputes unresolved within 90 days are sent to the Commissioner of Education who is authorized to withhold from state education aid the amount of delinquency.

CONCLUSION

State aid to Rhode Island schools in FY 2018 is graphically illustrated in Figures 41.3, 41.4, and 41.5. The flow chart in Figure 41.3 represents the state's share of aid as described in this chapter. Figure 41.4 does the same for categorical funds, and finally Figure 41.5 represents the state's involvement in public schools of choice.

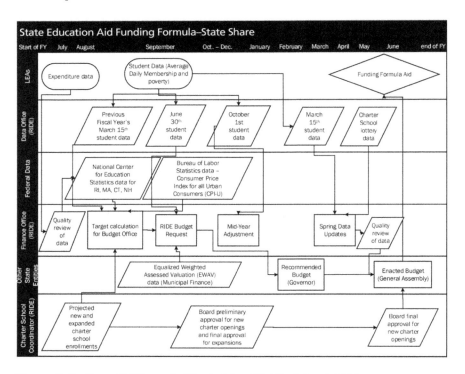

Figure 41.3   State Aid Formula Rhode Island Public Schools 2018.

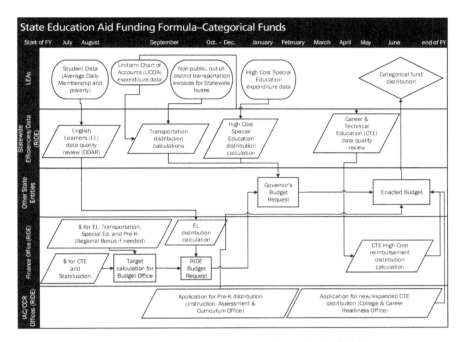

Figure 41.4 Categorical Funds Rhode Island Public Schools 2018.

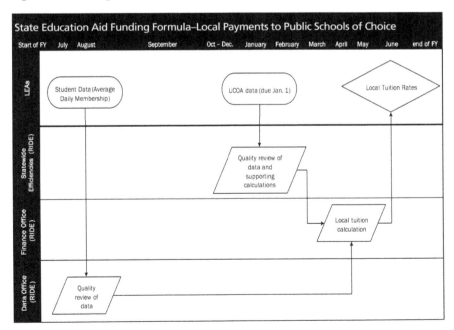

Figure 41.5 State Aid Formula Rhode Island Public Schools 2018.

NOTES

1. Portions of this general background section and the general outline of the history borrow and condense from Kenneth K. Wong. "The Design of the Rhode Island School Funding Formula: Toward a Coherent System of Allocating State Aid to Public Schools." Washington, DC: Center for American Progress (2011). Retrieved from https://files.eric.ed.gov/fulltext/ED535993.pdf and from Ken Wagner, "Funding Formula Reference Guide." Rhode Island Department of Education (2018).
2. R.I. Const. art. XII, §§ 1.
3. R.I. Const. art. XII, § 4.
4. The remainder of this chapter is taken from Ken Wagner, "Funding Formula Reference Guide." Rhode Island Department of Education. (2018). With author permission.
5. EWAV is a component of the state share ratio calculated by the Rhode Island Department of Revenue. EWAV is calculated in the following manner: The total assessed valuations of real and tangible property for each municipality, as of December 31 of the third preceding year, adjusted to bring the property valuation to market value. This value is adjusted by the ratio that compares the median family income of a city or town to the statewide median family income, as reported in the latest available federal census data. The EWAV calculation takes into consideration both the property values of a community and the income of its residents.

CHAPTER 42

South Carolina

Henry Tran, MPA, Ph.D.
University of South Carolina

Mazen Aziz, Ph.D. candidate
University of South Carolina

GENERAL BACKGROUND

The Colonial Period

To better understand South Carolina's education funding, it is important to review its historical roots dating back to the colonial period. Arriving from England, the first settlers of South Carolina held the belief that education was a private and voluntary matter. The affluent among them paid to have their children enrolled in private/religious schooling or educated by private tutors.[1] Limited public support existed during this time period for the children of non-affluent families of the colony. In fact, many of them were resistant to local taxes to fund public education as they saw education as a luxury for the wealthy and many farmers needed their children for farm labor.[2] The first legislative action taken toward establishing free public schools in South Carolina was "An act for the Founding and Erecting of a Free school for the use of the Inhabitants of South Carolina." As a result of this act in 1710, South Carolina's first free public school was established in Charleston.[3] These common schools were funded by colonial assembly-approved dollars and were established to provide elementary (and some secondary) education to a small number of white children whose families

---

Funding Public Schools in the United States and Indian Country, pages 613–631
Copyright © 2019 by Information Age Publishing
All rights of reproduction in any form reserved.

could not afford private schooling. These were often one-room schools. Since the inception of free schools, there existed inequitable school funding, as the free schools that were initially established were primarily located in the wealthier counties in the low country.

The 1800s

In the 1800s, citizens of the state saw the passing of over 750 Acts and Joint resolutions by the South Carolina General Assembly; among the most important was the new school law of 1811 that was the first bill to establish 'free schools' throughout the state of South Carolina.[4] Its aim was to place at least one public school in each of the state's 44 election districts. The bill provided each district with $300 per state representative.[5] Still, by the 1830s, South Carolina remained the only southern state to not establish a permanent public school fund prior to the Civil War.[6] Yet the trend for public school was growing, and by 1841 the South Carolina legislature's Report and Resolutions of the General Assembly reported that the state had 869 free schools and 9,187 students enrolled across various districts and parishes. Finally, the completely revised South Carolina state constitution of 1868 established the Office of Superintendent of Education and the enactment of a new school tax, along with a poll tax, to pay for free public schools.[7] In the following year, the South Carolina joint assembly passed a resolution appropriating $25,000 for the support of public schools. These funds were appropriated based on the number of students.[8] In 1870, a statewide comprehensive 'School Law' was passed, which established a State Board of Education led by a state Superintendent of Education, with County Commissioners, Board of Examiners, and School Trustees. The law outlined roles and responsibilities and appropriated $50,000 for the purpose of teacher pay, basing the pay on 5¢ per day per student's attendance.[9] The legislature appropriated $7,000 for the establishment of a uniform system of school records and blank forms to be used by offices and teachers of the free common schools within the state, enacted a school tax for the support and maintenance of all free common schools on all taxable property,[10] amended acts to increase teacher salary based on certification,[11] and levied poll taxes on each man between the ages of 21–65 for the general public school funds.[12] By the end of the century, the legislature reported that the state had 281,801 students enrolled in public schools across the state.

The 1900s

In the 1900s, there was increasing acknowledgment of race and gender disparities in both per-pupil expenditures and teacher pay. Average per-pupil expenditures in white schools was $14.94 compared to $1.86 for black schools. Average annual pay for black male teachers was $133 and $107 for black female teachers compared to $610 and $322 for their white counterparts in the 1913–14 academic year. The 1920s ushered in adult education classes as the state came to terms with low literacy test scores from World War II military recruits. The economic depression of the 1930s brought a period of reduced appropriations, salary cuts, divestment in capital programs, and reduced school terms. The aforementioned disparities continued in the 1940s as per-pupil spending for white schools was over double the per pupil spending for black schools; specifically, $111 compared to $50. Pay for white teachers was on average $643 higher than pay for black teachers; $2,057 compared to $1,414 respectively. Moreover, white schools' property values were, on average, over five times higher than that of black schools; $68.4 million compared to $12.9 million. Finally, transportation spending for whites was $2.4 million compared to $184,000 for blacks. In the 1950s and 60s, within the timeframe of the landmark U.S Supreme Court's *Brown vs. Board of Education of Topeka* decision, the state of South Carolina invested $100 million to build 200 black and 70 white schools, improved 250 existing ones for children from both races, and offered school transportation for black students all in an effort to avoid desegregation. In fact, politician James F. Byrne pushed for and helped enact the state's first sales tax (3¢ tax) passed in 1951 in order to help black schools better meet the requirements of 'separate but equal' with their white counterparts.[13] By the early 1970s, state spending on schools rose to $300 million as sales tax assumed most of the revenue-generating burden relative to property taxes and as federal desegregation support rolled in through legislation such as the Elementary and Secondary Education Act (ESEA) of 1965. This decade culminated in the passing of the state's foundational school funding support mechanism, the Education Finance Act (EFA) of 1977, which added $100,000,000 into the state's educational system over a five-year period and tied funding to a defined standard. The decade also saw the passing of the Education Improvement Act (EIA) of 1984 which provided an additional $217 million in funding through a 1¢ increase in sales tax.

The 2000s

In the 1990s and 2000s, there was an increasing emphasis on accountability, efficiency, and teacher quality. In the late '90s, for instance, The Education Accountability Act of 1998 was enacted to establish a comprehensive state performance-based accountability system that included the promotion of school performance incentives, accreditation, policy and standards reform, state assessment, the provision of resources, the availability of school and district performance information to the public (e.g., school and district report cards), professional development support and improvements to the evaluation system.[14]

During this time frame, the South Carolina Center for Teacher Recruitment (which began operation in the 1980s) evolved into the Center for Education Recruitment, Retention, and Advancement (CERRA) to address the ongoing teacher shortage problem. There was also increasing recognition of the inequality promoted by variation in conditions and education opportunities experienced by students across the state which culminated with the state's school finance lawsuit *Abbeville v. State of South Carolina*.[15] In the suit, the majority of the state's most rural, underperforming and impoverished districts sued the state for inadequate funding.[16] After 21 years, the state supreme court finally ruled for the plaintiff districts, but the case ultimately was dismissed in 2017 after the court saw changes in the justices.[17]

BASIC SUPPORT PROGRAM

The Education Finance Act

The basic support program for education in South Carolina is the Education Finance Act (EFA). The EFA was enacted in 1977 and represents the state's foundation education funding program for school and district operations. Per the Act, an average 70% of the cost of the foundation program is funded by the state, while the remaining 30% is funded by local school districts. However, each district's contribution differs as a result of what districts are expected to leverage from local property tax wealth (i.e., defined by each district's index of taxpaying ability) and their weighted pupil units (see Table 42.1 later), with subsequent state support varying correspondingly. Districts with lower tax-generating ability receive more state support, while districts with higher taxing ability receive less. The formula determines a per-pupil allocation known as the base student cost (BSC). Unfortunately, since the Great Recession of 2018 the BSC has not been fully funded by the state.[18] This pattern can be seen in Figure 42.1.

For Fiscal Year 2018, the BSC was $2,425 per pupil, with total pupil count projected at 721,401. Average state per-pupil funding was projected at $6,120, of which $2,339 came from the EFA, $1,294 from federal sources, and $5,726 from local sources. This provided an average total funding of $13,140 excluding revenue from local bond issues.[19] Beyond the EFA, districts also received funds from other sources, including the EIA of 1984 providing categorical funding for specific programs or initiatives designed to improve student achievement.[20]

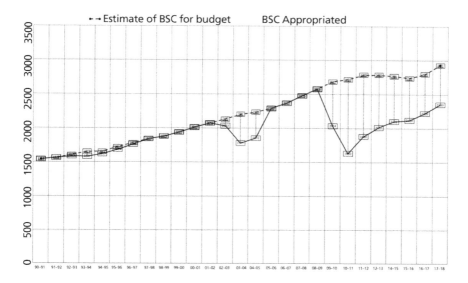

Figure 42.1 Base Student Cost Estimate Provided for the Budget and the BSC Appropriated FY 1991–2017. *Source:* Tran (2018). Taking the Mystery Out of South Carolina School Finance. 2nd Edition. ICPEL Publications. Ypsilanti, Michigan.

Earmarked State Revenue

South Carolina allocated 46% of its state general fund, just over $3.8 billion, for education in FY 2019. Specifically, the state appropriated $3,106,702,318 (37.8% of general fund appropriation) for K–12 educational expenditures and earmarked $836,987,000 from a 1¢ sales tax for the same purpose. Higher education was appropriated $665,705,579 (8.1%). Lastly, $17,018,330 of the total $476,021,493 revenue generated by the South Carolina Education Lottery was earmarked for K–12 education.[21]

Local School Revenue

Known as 'State Aid to Subdivisions,' the state of South Carolina collected 11 local taxes, ranging from income tax to alcohol tax, on behalf of local governments from the early- to mid-1900s. These funds were collected locally but routed to the state treasurer to be processed to local governments on calculations for each tax. No uniform collection method existed for these 11 taxes, as some would be diverted to the state's general fund when the state was in need while the rest would be redistributed based on statutory formulas.

Inconsistent tax formulas, flattening taxes, and revenue stagnation as compared to the overall economies in the 1980s greatly restricted local governments from effectively planning for expenditure and budgetary needs. Responding to this crisis, the state General Assembly relying on suggestions from the South Carolina Advisory Commission on Intergovernmental Relations (SC ACIR), proposed the establishment of a 'Local Government Fund.' Revenue from a simplified list of seven taxes (banks, beer, wine, gasoline, motor transport, alcohol mini-bottle, and income tax) would directly go to the state's general fund. Instead of direct funding from these sources, local governments would receive 4.5% of the previous year's (i.e., 1991) revenue from the same sources. Per the new law, these funds would be set aside before any other spending commitments were made to ensure consistent revenue streams for local governments. The share was also split 83.28% for county and 16.72% for municipal governments, and the funds would be distributed quarterly by the state treasurer to cities and counties. These distributions were based on per-capita basis based on the last census figures, i.e., each city/town would receive funds based on its percent of municipal population.[22] The local per-pupil revenue for the state was $5,869 in FY 2018.[23]

Finally, the level of discretion for school districts to set local tax rates varies across the state of South Carolina. Specifically, of the 82 public school districts in South Carolina, slightly more than 40% have authority to set millage rates within parameters established by the state, referenda or some other official body. Approximately 27% of districts are fiscally independent (i.e., they can set their own rates), while another 27% must secure approval by the county government to establish millage for current operations and debt services.[24] Districts without complete fiscal authority to set their own tax rates may request additional millage from some other governing body such as the county council, referendum or county legislation delegation. Most districts have two tax rates, one for school operations and another for debt service.

SPECIAL EDUCATION

The South Carolina Department of Education is required by the Individuals with Disabilities Education Act[25] (IDEA) and Education Department General Administration Regulation (EDGAR) to monitor local education agencies, charter schools, and state-operated programs to ensure fiscal compliance with state and federal laws, regulations, policies and procedures that govern the provision of special education and related services to appropriately identified children.[26] Funding for special education is included in the state's primary funding formula, is weighted per-pupil for students who are more expensive to educate, and is based on the cumulative 135-day average daily membership of each school district by program classification.[27] The weights were provided in Table 42.1. In addition, the state legislature created an ongoing voucher program known as 'Exceptional SC' that provides

TABLE 42.1 South Carolina EFA Weights 2018

Classification	Weightings
K–12	1.00
Educable Mentally Handicapped	1.74
Learning Disabilities[a]	1.74
Trainable Mentally Handicapped[b]	2.04
Emotionally Handicapped	2.04
Orthopedically Handicapped[c]	2.04
Visually Handicapped	2.57
Hearing Handicapped	2.57
Autism-Pupils with Autism	2.57
Speech Handicapped	1.90
Homebound	1.00
Vocational/Career (Grades 9–12)	1.29
Poverty (LUNCH/Medicaid)	Add-on weight: .20
Limited English Proficiency	Add-on weight: .20
Young Adult Education	Add-on weight: .20
Academic Assistance (student scoring "not met" on state assessment and *not* in poverty)	Add-on weight: .15
Dual Credit Enrollment	Add-on weight: .15
Gifted and Talented (artistic, academic, AP and IB)	Add-on weight: .15

Source: https://ed.sc.gov/finance/financial-services/manual-handbooks-and-guidelines/funding-manuals/fy-2017-2018-funding-manual/
[a] Includes developmentally delayed and other health impaired
[b] Includes profoundly mentally handicapped
[c] Includes traumatic brain injury

educational tuition scholarships for students with special needs in the state. The program is funded by tax-deductible donations. As of 2018, the maximum amount of credit that could be requested for qualifying students was $11,000 or the cost of tuition (whichever is less). South Carolina parental refundable tax credits may not exceed $2 million for the current year.[28]

COMPENSATORY EDUCATION[29]

Many compensatory education programs in South Carolina are funded by EIA funds. The state allocates EIA funds per pupil on the previous year's 135-day ADM. Table 42.2 displays the variation in per-pupil funding by poverty index ranges. Categorical programs funded by EIA include:

Reading coaches. These programs serve elementary school students. Allocation of funding is two-tiered. If the percentage of students not meeting performance expectations on state assessments is 20% or greater, the district receives either up to $62,730 or the actual salary/benefits cost of a coach, whichever is less. If the percentage of students scoring 'not met' on state assessment criteria is less than 20%, the district receives either up to $31,365 or 50% of the actual cost of the salary/benefits of a coach;

Student at risk of school failure. Two factors influence allocation of funds to school districts. The first is poverty rate per the add-on weight. The second is the prior fiscal year's number of weighted pupil units in need of academic assistance (i.e., those who failed high school assessment programs and scored 'not met' for reading and math test performance criteria in grades 3–9). The state requires that at least 85% of these funds must be spent on instruction.

GIFTED AND TALENTED EDUCATION

Funding for personalized instruction for gifted and talented pupils is weighted in the EIA at 0.15 in South Carolina. The state classifies gifted and talented students as "students who are classified as academically or artistically gifted and talented or who are enrolled in Advanced Placement (AP) and International Baccalaureate (IB) courses in high school."[30] The state

TABLE 42.2 South Carolina EIA Per-Pupil Poverty Funding

Poverty Index	Dollar per ADM
> 75%	$35
75–85%	$50
< 85% Or schools with no defined poverty index	$70

further specifies that districts should set aside 12% of their funds for use by these students. The state also specifies that the Department of Education can expend up to $500,000 of its EIA funding for the support of gifted and talented teacher endorsements and professional developments.[31]

BILINGUAL EDUCATION

Title III is part of the ESEA of 1965, and its purpose is to help English learners attain English language proficiency to meet academic standards. The South Carolina Department of Education oversees language instruction for limited English proficient and immigrant students through Title III. It does so by administering grants, recommending policy, promoting best practices, strengthening collaboration between federal, state and local programs, and monitoring funded programs for accountability.[32] The state funds bilingual education through its primary funding formula.[33] The limited English proficiency classification is weighted at .20.[34]

FUNDING CHARTER SCHOOLS

Charter schools became an option in South Carolina in 1996 as a result of the South Carolina Charter Schools Act of 1996.[35] Charter schools can be authorized by a traditional school district, the South Carolina Public Charter School District (SCPCSD) that was created in 2006, or a higher education institution. Charter schools in the SCPCSD or an institution of higher education receive state revenue from both EFA and EIA funds, but not from local tax revenue. Approximately 13% of EIA funds (i.e., $100,556,551) in FY 2018 went to the SCPCSD.[36]

Because local money does not follow the child in South Carolina, dollars are appropriated through an annual budget proviso for charter school funding. The schools chartered by SCPCSD and higher education institutions receive $3,600 per weighted pupil for students in physical schools and $1,900 per student for those enrolled in virtual charter schools.[37] They must make annual budget requests to the legislature to receive funding from the General Assembly. Locally sponsored charter schools are able to benefit from local funds and receive funding according to the same formula as local school districts. However, neither locally sponsored charters nor those sponsored by the SCPCSD receive transportation or facility funds except for conversion charters and a few that negotiated with a district board. In contrast, traditional public schools receive the benefits of all the

TABLE 42.3 SCPCSD Revenue from FY 2016–17 to 2018–19

Agency	FY 2017	FY 2018 estimated	FY 2019 estimated
Pupils	$21,280	$25,573	$27,966
Federal Revenue per Pupil	$595	$611	$688
State Revenue per Pupil	$8,369	$8,349	$8,474
Local Revenue per Pupil	$1,057	$919	$885
Total Revenue per Pupil	**$10,021**	**$9,879**	**$10,047**

Source: http://rfa.sc.gov/files/Revenue%20Per%20Pupil%20Report%20by%20District%20FY%202018-19%20for%20web_0.pdf
Note: Estimates are based on historical growth rates.

aforementioned funds. Table 43.3 displays revenue information for the SCPCSD for FY 2017–2019.

Charter schools have access to tax-exempt financing of facilities through the South Carolina Jobs-Economic Development Authority. In addition, the state Department of Education must make available, upon request from an existing charter school or charter school applicant, a list of vacant and unused portions of buildings that are owned by school districts in the state and that may be suitable for the operation of a charter school. The owner of a building on the list is not required to sell or lease the building or a portion of the building to a charter school; however, if a school district declares a building surplus and chooses to sell or lease, a charter school's board of directors or a charter committee operating or applying within the district must be given the first refusal to purchase or lease the building under the same or better terms and conditions as would be offered to the public. Charter schools are exempt from state and local taxation, except the sales tax, on earnings and property whether owned or leased. Charter schools also have access to low interest loans through the Charter School Facility Revolving Loan Program for costs related to the construction, purchase, renovation and maintenance of charter school facilities.[38]

STATE AID FOR PRIVATE K–12 SCHOOLS

Although public funding of private schools is prohibited by South Carolina's constitution[39] and no financial assistance is available for private school attendance,[40] private schools catering to the needs of high-poverty students are eligible to compete for the 21st Century Community Learning Centers Programs (Title IV, 21st Century Schools). These funds are assigned to state education agencies, which then award the funds on a competitive basis to eligible organizations.[41]

EARLY CHILDHOOD EDUCATION

The Early Childhood Development and Academic Assistance Act of 1993 (Act 135) designated funds appropriated for half-day programs for four-year-olds based on the number of kindergarten children eligible for free and reduced lunch under the federal free lunch program, with stipulation that no district receive less than 90% of the amount it received in the prior fiscal year. Early Childhood Assistance also received a .26 add-on weight in the state's EFA appropriation formula. In FY 2018, 6% of EIA funds (i.e., $49,838,283) was allocated to 4K public schools.[42] Of the funds appropriated, $300,000 was designated to the state's Education Oversight Committee to conduct an annual evaluation of the South Carolina Child Development Education Program. The program was introduced as a pilot in the annual budget proviso in 2006 for children in the *Abbeville* plaintiff school district, and the program was codified by law in 2014.[43] Funds were first provided for eligible children in the plaintiff trial districts, then to the remaining plaintiff districts, and finally to eligible children in districts with a poverty index ≥ 90%.[44]

The state also authorized up to $800,000 for 4K Early Literacy Competencies Assessment and for professional development toward analysis of early literacy and language development in public funded prekindergarten, and up to $2,000,000 in half-day program funding for four-year-olds and assessments to administer the Kindergarten Readiness Assessment for kindergarteners entering public school. In addition, during the current fiscal year the South Carolina Office of First Steps to School Readiness is authorized to spend up to $75,000 in four-year-old kindergarten carry-forward funds to purchase electronic devices for the administration of required school readiness assessments to children enrolled in the full-day 4K program in private centers; one device may be purchased for every ten centers serving children in the program.

Finally, the state funds public and private providers of South Carolina's Early Reading Development and Education Program at the instructional cost of $4,422 per student. Private transportation of children to and from school is also a category of eligibility for a $563 per child reimbursement.[45]

OTHER CATEGORICAL PROGRAMS

Categorical or unrestricted funds in South Carolina are allocated for specific purposes. These funds come from both state and federal governments. Funds are allocated by ADA and are reserved for legislative spending priorities.[46] The state allocated 74% of its education budget for the funding of categorical programs in FY 2014.[47] Many categorical programs are offered through EIA (e.g., technology support, professional development, job preparation programs, teacher salary increase) tied to funding in an effort to improve the quality of South Carolina's public education system. These funds are distributed without regard to wealth of districts.

TAX CREDITS, DEDUCTIONS, AND EXEMPTIONS

There are numerous exemptions for primary residence property tax in South Carolina, including a school tax credit for Act 388's school operating cost exemption and the Homestead Exemption for individuals who have lived in the state for a year and who are 65 or older, totally disabled, or legally blind. It also excludes the first $50,000 from the fair market value of the primary residential property and property tax exemption (including up to one acre of land) for widows and widowers of certain military veterans, noncommissioned members of the armed forces or law enforcement who passed away or became permanently disabled in the line of duty and for paraplegics and hemiplegics. Regardless of the justification and rationale behind each of these exemptions, the net result is less revenue for schools.[48] To make up for lost revenue from school operating tax exemptions, the state levied a 1¢ sales tax, but unfortunately due to the swapping of a relatively stable property tax revenue for a more volatile sales tax revenue, especially during the recession period, the overall result was a net loss in revenue for school districts. Because Act 388 traded property tax revenue for sales tax revenue, any exemption in sales tax unduly hurts revenue for schools. For example, under the Sales and Use Tax Law,[49] several categories of exemptions are identified that include government, business, agricultural general public good, alternative energy and of course education-related exemptions. Items comprising these categories range from coal to manufacturers, livestock, hearing aids, and so forth.[50] Table 42.4 lists these exemptions, code section and descriptions.

TRANSPORTATION

South Carolina's Department of Education owned and operated one of the largest school transportation fleets (5,582 buses) in the nation in the year 2018.[51] Pupil transportation is a large expense in South Carolina, constituting 5% of EIA funding or $41,198,813 in FY 2018.[52] Although South Carolina uses a weighted system to adjust for students who are costlier to educate when distributing EFA funding to school districts, no weighting exists for rural, low population density districts with higher transportation costs.[53]

TABLE 42.4	Educational Exemption Categories
Code Section	Description
12-36-2120(3)	Textbooks, books, magazines, periodicals, newspapers and access to online information used in a course of study or for use in a school or public library. These items may be in printed form or in alternative forms such as microfilm or CD ROM. Certain communication services and equipment subject to tax under South Carolina Code §§12-36-910(B)(3) and 12-36-1310(B)(3) are not exempt.
12-36-2120(8)	Newspapers, newsprint paper and South Carolina Department of Agriculture Market Bulletin.
12-36-2120(10)(a)	Meals or food used in furnishing meals to students in schools (not for profit).
12-36-2120(26)	Television, radio and cable TV supplies, equipment, machinery, and electricity.
12-36-2120(27)	Zoo plants and animals.
Temporary Proviso 117.37, year 2016–2017	Purchases of tangible personal property during the state fiscal year for use in private primary and secondary schools, (Act 284 of 2016) including kindergarten and early childhood education programs, are exempt from the use tax if the school is exempt from income taxes under Internal Revenue Code §501(c)(3)45.

Source: https://dor.sc.gov/resources-site/lawandpolicy/Documents/SC_Sales_and_Use_Tax_Manual_2017.pdf

CAPITAL OUTLAY AND DEBT SERVICE

South Carolina's constitutional provisions usually limit annual debt service of general obligation debt to 5% of the general state revenue from the previous fiscal year. There are five classes of bonds subject to this limit, including school bonds (constructing, improving, equipping, renovating and repairing school buildings or other school facilities and/or for land to construct facilities) and the state's School Facilities bonds (to assist districts in providing educational facilities).[54] Public School Facilities Assistance Act of 1996 funds are used for permanent school instructional facilities and fixed equipment (e.g., cost of construction, improvement, enlargement and renovation of school facilities).

South Carolina's Capital Reserve Fund (CRF) equates to 2% of the state's general fund revenue ($145,420,836 for FY 2018) and can be used for capital improvements or nonrecurring projects if there is no year-end deficit.[55] The state allocates reimbursements to school districts for approved capital projects based on the needs and financial abilities of the school district. Funding can come from general funds, EIA, the Education Lottery and funds from Children's Education Endowment Funds.[56]

In FY 2018, $55,828,859 was appropriated in nonrecurring facility upgrade funds for any school district that was a plaintiff in the *Abbeville* lawsuit or for districts with a poverty index of ≥ 80%.[57] Funding originated from EIA capital funds ($4.8 million), revolving student loan fund transfers ($16 million), and EIA prior year cash balance ($35 million). Fundable capital improvement project requests needed to address health and safety, technology, career and technology career education programs, or deferred maintenance needs.

TEACHER RETIREMENT

The South Carolina Retirement System (SCRS) was established in July 1945 as a defined benefit plan providing retirement and other related benefits for teachers and state employees. In 1987, the state introduced a defined contribution plan, known as the State Optional Retirement System (PORS), for members not participating in SCRS. Funding for retirement benefits derive from the balance of investment income, as well as employee and employer contributions.[58] Beginning in academic year 1998–99, school district employer contribution to state retirement (as well as funds for group life insurance, social security and health insurance) was allocated monthly to school districts in accord with the EFA.[59] Retirement benefit amount is based on an individual's years of service, age and compensation.

Act 13 of 2017 increased the employer contribution rate to 2% as of July 2017 to generate $73.6 million for the state) and 1% annually (i.e., $36.8 million) thereafter for five years, while employee contributions increased to a newly capped 9% for SCRS and 9.75% for PORS. In FY 2018, $34.2 million was appropriated from the General Fund to fund the initial 1% employer contribution increase for General Fund and school district employees and another $4.2 million appropriated in EIA to cover the 1% employer contribution increase. Finally, $118.1 million was funded to South Carolina's Public Employee Benefit Authority (PEBA) from the General Fund to help stabilize the pension by covering the second 1% employer contribution increase.[60]

South Carolina's retirement system has looming unfunded liabilities that amount to over $18 billion. Given these financial liabilities, in 2012 the state legislature decided to set an expiration date for the Teacher Employee Retirement Incentive Program (TERI). This deferred retirement program was introduced in 2000 to attract teachers to stay on the job. Specifically, TERI allowed retired workers to work up to five additional years in their school district after retirement and to continue accumulating pension benefits. According to PEBA, TERI is associated with almost $2 billion of the pension debt. The determined end date for TERI was June 30, 2018. To address the remaining financial liabilities, the state is expected to reform the pension system in the near future.

STATE GENERAL FUND EDUCATIONAL EXPENDITURE

Table 42.5 summarizes the state of South Carolina's educational expenditures for FY 2015, 2016, 2017, 2018, and 2019. Expenditures increased by $605,343,610 from FY 2015 to FY 2019, with the greatest dollar increase occurring in aid to school district expenditures, followed by operations and support. A slight decrease for the same time period occurred for superintendent of education and employee benefits expenditures. The state began investing in the school readiness program in FY 2018 and more than doubled funding for the program the following fiscal year.

TABLE 42.5 General Fund K12 Expenditures by the South Carolina Department of Education

Agency	FY 2014–15	FY 2015–16	FY 2016–17	FY 2017–18	FY 2018–19
Superintendent of Education Total	$1,552,980	$1,474,194	$1,474,194	$1,514,206	$1,514,206
Board of Education Total	$58,034	$58,034	$58,034	$58,034	$58,034
Accountability Total	$2,717,975	$2,959,093	$3,287,894	$3,382,771	$3,382,771
Chief Information Office Total	$1,974,600	$1,963,386	$3,633,042	$3,685,477	$3,685,477
School Effectiveness Total	$5,252,306	$8,442,533	$10,500,533	$10,675,729	$10,675,729
Chief Finance Office Total	$1,686,447	$2,074,858	$2,074,858	$2,285,479	$2,559,370
Operation and Support Total	$110,359,097	$118,295,981	$140,920,981	$108,688,927	$130,855,545
Governors School Science & Math Total	$9,291,069	$10,618,390	$12,013,748	$12,533,077	$12,749,154
Aid to School Districts Total	$2,300,147,698	$2,435,738,111	$2,680,523,110	$2,770,777,782	$2,863,313,227
Gov School for Arts & Humanities Total	$7,349,239	$7,689,270	$7,797,248	$8,199,722	$8,357,832
Employee Benefits	$9,525,537	$10,134,207	$10,719,319	$11,012,709	$6,521,510
First Steps to School Readiness Total	$ –	$ –	$ –	$6,521,510	$11,585,737
SC Department of Education	$2,449,914,982	$2,599,448,057	$2,873,002,961	$2,939,335,423	$3,055,258,592

Source: https://www.scstatehouse.gov/budget.php

NOTES

1. http://www.carolana.com/SC/Education/History_of_South_Carolina_Schools_Virginia_B_Bartels.pdf
2. H. Tran (2018). *Taking the Mystery Out of South Carolina School Finance*. 2nd Edition. ICPEL Publications. Ypsilanti, Michigan.
3. C. Meriwether and E. McCrady (2010). *History of Higher Education in South Carolina: With a Sketch of the Free School System.* Nabu Press. Charleston, South Carolina.
4. http://www.carolana.com/SC/Education/sc_education_1800s.html
5. The Statutes at Large of South Carolina–Volume V, pp. 639–641.
6. B. W. Eelman (2008). *Entrepreneurs in the Southern Upcountry: Commercial Culture in Spartanburg, South Carolina*, 18450 1880. University of Georgia Press.
7. http://www.carolana.com/SC/Legislators/Documents/Reports_and_Resolutions_of_the_General_Assembly_of_South_Carolina_1841.pdf
8. http://www.carolana.com/SC/Legislators/Documents/Acts_and_Joint_Resolutions_of_the_General_Assembly_of_the_State_of_South_Carolina_1868_1869.pdf
9. http://www.carolana.com/SC/Legislators/Documents/Acts_and_Joint_Resolutions_of_the_General_Assembly_of_the_State_of_South_Carolina_1869_1870.pdf
10. http://www.carolana.com/SC/Legislators/Documents/Acts_and_Joint_Resolutions_of_the_General_Assembly_of_the_State_of_South_Carolina_1871_1872.pdf
11. http://www.carolana.com/SC/Legislators/Documents/Acts_and_Joint_Resolutions_of_the_General_Assembly_of_the_State_of_South_Carolina_1890.pdf
12. http://www.carolana.com/SC/Legislators/Documents/Acts_and_Joint_Resolutions_of_the_General_Assembly_of_the_State_of_South_Carolina_1900.pdf
13. http://ldhi.library.cofc.edu/exhibits/show/history_burke_high_school/origins_public_education
14. Ibid. Tran (2018).
15. 515 S.E.2d 535 (1999).
16. http://www.carolana.com/SC/Education/History_of_South_Carolina_Schools_Virginia_B_Bartels.pdf
17. Ibid, Tran (2018).
18. SC Revenue and Fiscal Affairs Office, Figure 189D. Retrieved from http://rfa.sc.gov/files/Funding%20for%20Public%20Education%20-%20Trends%20and%20Observations%208-30-17.pdf)
19. 2017–18 Appropriation Act, 1B, 1.3.
20. Ibid. Tran (2018).
21. https://www.admin.sc.gov/budget/frequently%20asked%20questions
22. http://www.masc.sc/pages/resources/history-of-the-local-government-fund.aspx
23. http://rfa.sc.gov/files/Revenue%20Per%20Pupil%20Report%20for%20web%20FY%202017-18.pdf

24. Ibid. Tran (2018).
25. PL 108-446 (2004).
26. https://ed.sc.gov/districts-schools/special-education-services/fiscal-and-grants-management-fgm/fiscal-monitoring/
27. http://ecs.force.com/mbdata/mbquest3D?rep=SD10
28. https://dor.sc.gov/exceptional-sc
29. https://ed.sc.gov/finance/financial-services/manual-handbooks-and-guidelines/funding-manuals/fy-2017-2018-funding-manual/
30. https://www.scstatehouse.gov/query.php?search=DOC&searchtext=1.66&category=BUDGET&year=2018&version_id=7&return_page=&version_title=Appropriation%20Act&conid=10285689&result_pos=0&keyval=38813&numrows=50
31. https://www.scstatehouse.gov/sess122_2017-2018/appropriations2017/wmp1b.htm
32. https://ed.sc.gov/policy/federal-education-programs/esea-title-iii/
33. http://www.ecs.org/clearinghouse/01/16/94/11694.pdf
34. https://www.admin.sc.gov/files/H630%20-%20Dept%20of%20Education%20Revised%201-30-18.pdf
35. S.C. Code Ann. § 59-40-10.
36. Revenue and Fiscal Affairs Office. Retrieved from: http://rfa.sc.gov/files/Funding%20for%20Public%20Education%20-%20Trends%20and%20Observations%208-30-17.pdf
37. General Appropriations Act for 2017-2018, Proviso 1A.22.
38. S.C. Code Ann. § 59-40-175.
39. S.C Const. Art. 11, Sec. 7.
40. https://www2.ed.gov/admins/comm/choice/regprivschl/regprivschl.pdf
41. https://ed.sc.gov/finance/financial-services/manual-handbooks-and-guidelines/funding-manuals/fy-2017-2018-funding-manual/
42. South Carolina Revenue and Fiscal Affairs Office, 2017. Retrieved from http://rfa.sc.gov/files/Budget%20Impact%20of%20South%20Carolina%20Pension%20Reform%20-%20First%20Monday%20Club%208-7-17.pdf; http://scasbo.net/wp-content/uploads/2014/10/Capital-Improvement-Funding.pptx
43. South Carolina Department of Education. Retrieved from https://ed.sc.gov/instruction/early-learning-and-literacy/cdep/cdep-resources-and-forms1/
44. Act 284, Read to Succeed, 59-156-110.
45. General Appropriations Act for 2017-2018, Proviso 1A.30.
46. https://sites.google.com/a/acsd.k12.ca.us/categorical-state-federal-projects/home/funding-descriptions
47. https://www.urban.org/sites/default/files/publication/94961/making-sense-of-state-school-funding-policy_0.pdf
48. Ibid. Tran (2018).
49. Chapter 36 of Title 12.
50. https://dor.sc.gov/resources-site/lawandpolicy/Documents/SandU_9.pdf
51. https://ed.sc.gov/districts-schools/transportation/general-information/contacts/
52. https://www.scstatehouse.gov/sess122_2017-2018/appropriations2018/gbud1819.pdf

53. https://ed.sc.gov/data/reports/legislative/legislative-reports/special-one-time-reports/2017-updating-base-student-cost/
54. South Carolina State Treasury, 2017. Retrieved from https://treasurer.sc.gov/media/67433/june-2017-state-debt-report.pdf
55. Retrieved from http://www.admin.sc.gov/budget/frequently%20asked%20questions
56. 2017–18 Appropriation Act – Department of Education. Proviso, 1A.14.
57. Proviso 1A.50.
58. South Carolina Public Employee Benefit Authority; S.C. Code Ann. § 1-11-710(A)(2).
59. SC Code § 59-21-160.
60. South Carolina Revenue and Fiscal Affairs Office, 2017. Retrieved from http://rfa.sc.gov/files/Budget%20Impact%20of%20South%20Carolina%20Pension%20Reform%20-%20First%20Monday%20Club%208-7-17.pdf

CHAPTER 43

South Dakota

Wade Pogany, Ph.D.
Executive Director
Associated School Boards of South Dakota

Matt Flett
Chief Finance Officer
Associated School Boards of South Dakota

Tyler Pickner
Director of Communications
Associated School Boards of South Dakota

GENERAL BACKGROUND

In recent years the distribution of state funds in South Dakota's school finance system has evolved, but funding sources have remained relatively consistent. The two primary funding sources for the state's 149 public school districts are local property taxes and state funding through the state aid formula. In addition, schools receive funding from federal sources, local bonds issues, and other areas subsequently outlined.[1]

Prior to 1995, the South Dakota legislature funded school districts through an expenditure-driven formula. The more a district spent, the more state funding it received. The funding formula was revised by the state legislature in 1995 and implemented in January 1997.

The revised funding formula funded school districts based on a calculation that included a per-student allocation (PSA), a district's enrollment, and the amount of local property taxes levied within the district.[2] State law on school finance delineated the revised calculation which required several steps to determine the PSA.[3] The formula establishes a district's 'local need,' which is the amount required to fund the district with local property taxes and state aid. If a district is designated a small district—enrollment under 600 students—a small school factor adjustment is also applied. The district's 'local effort'—the total amount of local property taxes levied—is calculated as well. Finally, the local effort is subtracted from the district's local need to arrive at the amount of state aid allocated to the district.[4]

The revised funding formula established a foundational system whereby some equity exists based on the ability of a school district to raise property taxes (local effort) compared to its ability to fund the expenses of the district (local need). Districts with less property tax wealth receive more state funding due to diminished ability to raise necessary funding. Thus, a state aid foundational structure was established.

The key factor in the revised funding formula was the legislature establishing the PSA at $3,350 per student for Fiscal Year 1998. The PSA grew to $4,877 per student by FY 2016 based on legislative appropriation.

In the revised funding formula, state aid is the largest source of revenue for local school districts. Local property taxes are generally the next major source of revenue; other lesser sources of revenue include county fines, federal grants, school district gross receipts and bank franchise taxes.[5] School districts also receive funds for education-related purposes such as capital outlay and pension funds collected through local revenue and special education funds from federal, state and local sources. A district may also be eligible for a sparsity factor benefit based on enrollment size and distance criteria.[6]

STATE AID STUDY IN 2015

Growing Teacher Shortage

For decades, South Dakota teacher salaries ranked last in the nation.[7] Data gathered by the School Administrators of South Dakota and the Associated School Boards pointed to the fact that low pay was a contributing factor in a growing teacher shortage in South Dakota[8] (see Figure 43.1). Spurred by increasing concerns about teacher shortages,[9] the governor established a Blue Ribbon Task Force in February 2015, with the task of reevaluating the K–12 education funding system.[10] The 26-member task force included legislators, school board members, administrators, teachers, members of the governor's staff and state Department of Education staff, who were tasked with collecting and analyzing data, gathering input

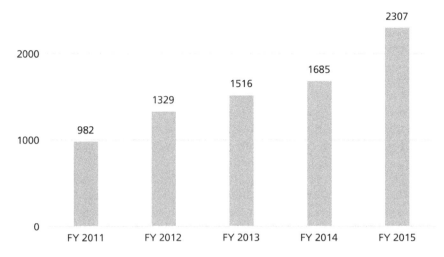

Figure 43.1 Open Teacher Positions in South Dakota 2011–2015. *Source:* South Dakota Teacher Placement Center (2015).

from stakeholders and the public, and producing a recommendation for changes needed to address the issue.

The Task Force was led by two legislators involved in education. The goal was to operationalize recommendations from the task force during the 2016 legislative session.[11]

Blue Ribbon Task Force Summary

According to the Executive Summary of Task Force findings, the committee, as a general understanding, concluded:

1. Schools matter to a community;
2. The most important factor to student success is the presence of a highly qualified teacher;
3. All students should have equal access to learning opportunities;
4. South Dakota faces a teacher shortage;
5. No one plan will fit the needs of all districts and funding equity is essential; and
6. Citizens expect that tax dollars are used in a cost-effective manner.

Additionally, any sustainable solution for the issues will require significant ongoing revenue.[12]

Major Findings of the Task Force

As it related to the many aspects of the state's school funding system and the teacher shortage, the Task Force found:

- *State funding priorities indicated a 149% increase* in state dollars for K–12 education since FY 1996. However, other state funding needs also increased, such as Medicaid which grew by 279%. The share of the state's general fund budget for education decreased even though the amount of money given to schools through the current per student allocation increased;
- *South Dakota's average teacher salary in 2013–14 was $40,023.* South Dakota's salary ranked last among the fifty states and the District of Columbia. Even adjusted by a comparable wage index, South Dakota's salaries lagged behind the regional average (of Nebraska, North Dakota, Montana, Iowa, Minnesota, and Wyoming) by $11,888 and $8,643 behind the next lowest neighbor (North Dakota);
- *Teacher turnover is not exclusively related to salaries,* but in South Dakota it is a significant factor;
- *The incoming pipeline of teachers* could not meet the projected needs of districts when looking ahead five years;
- *The current funding formula* was based on a per-student allocation (PSA) derived from a set amount of money available and not the specific needs of a district;
- *Capital outlay tax collections increased by 116.6%* or 9% a year from 2003–2015. At the same time, the PSA increased by 25.4% or 2% a year. In actual dollars, the capital outlay increase was $82.3 million to $178.3 million. In South Dakota, capital outlay per student spending exceeded the national average by $405 per student;
- *Administrator costs as a percentage of total expenditures* were comparable to surrounding states. Slightly higher than the national average, South Dakota's percentage was lower than North Dakota and Montana and nearly the same as Iowa. The number of South Dakota school administrators per student was among the lowest in the region and in line with the national average;
- *Reserve fund balances, on average, in South Dakota tended to be larger* than typical nationally;
- *Public input yielded qualitative data* that developed into clear themes:
  - Citizens seek bold, urgent, meaningful action as they perceive a current or looming crisis in education;
  - New revenue and equitable funding for salaries and benefits are essential in order to retain and recruit high quality teachers;

- Cost-saving measures of increasing efficiencies, cutting non-essentials, relying on more technology, sharing services, and partnering with the business community is imperative;
- Constituents seek stable, consistent, and equitable funding mechanisms for a long-term solution;
- Students need a variety of learning experiences in order to prepare them for careers as productive and contributing citizens;
- Education needs to be marketed as an investment in the future of South Dakota;
- Positive public perception about the value of education and its role in building strong communities and robust economies is essential.[13]

Task Force Recommendations

Based on the data generated and findings of the Task Force, recommendations were made to address the funding issues; most significant among the recommendations was a move to overhaul the state aid funding formula, based primarily on average teacher salaries rather a Per Student Allocation; thus, creating a significantly different state funding model. With an aim to improve teacher salaries, the governor agreed with the recommendations.

Recommendations for the New Funding Formula for State Aid included:[14]

- *Adopt a new formula based on a statewide target for statewide average teacher salary* of $48,000 and maintain the average statewide student-to-teacher ratio at approximately 14:1;
- *Replace current small school adjustment with a sliding scale*, depending on school enrollment, for the target student-to-teacher ratio;
- *Retain the current statutory minimum inflation factor* of 3% or inflation, whichever is less in the new formula;
- *Reevaluate teacher salaries every three years* to assure South Dakota remains competitive with surrounding states;
- *No change to the Limited English Proficiency* adjustment;
- *No change to the sparsity* factor.

Recommendations for new funding for teacher salaries included:

- *At least $75 million* in new ongoing funding for teacher salaries;
- *Use existing funds* to the greatest extent possible;
- *Increase the state sales and use tax* for additional ongoing revenue.

Recommendations to ensure accountability in the school funding system included:

- *Adopt mechanisms to monitor* the implementation of the new formula;

- *Develop benchmarks,* in particular for average teacher salaries, to ensure goals are met.[15]

Other school finance mechanisms were also studied by the Task Force, and changes were further recommended. Recommendations for additional adjustments included:

- *Reinstate statutory caps* on school district general fund reserves;
- *Develop a tiered reserve caps system* based on school enrollments;
- *Dollar-by-dollar reduction* in state aid payment for districts exceeding reserve fund cap;
- *Phase in the caps* over a three-year period;
- *Establish an oversight committee* to help districts with phase-in strategies for reserve caps, and assist when unique circumstances arise that may make the caps unrealistic;
- *Eliminate the pension levy.* The general education levies should be increased by 0.263 mills which would raise the same amount that the pension levy currently raises;
- *Equalize 'other revenue'* to establish greater equity by equalizing future growth in other revenue sources.[16]

Recommendations for adjustments to the funding system on a phased-in approach included:

- *Fully implement all recommendations* by the end of three years;
- *With a phased-in approach,* two points must be considered:
  - $75 million in new funding for teacher salaries was intended as a supplement to the current appropriations for schools. If the new funding were phased in over a period of years, it should be in addition to the inflationary increases required under current law;
  - Target teacher salary of $48,000 was chosen based on the most recent available data. If the reforms were phased in over period of years, the target salary must be increased in order to remain competitive with surrounding states.[17]

Funding Formula Revised in 2016

Based on the Blue Ribbon Task Force recommendations, the governor proposed that the legislature implement the funding system adjustments. These included House Bill 1182, Senate Bill 131, and Senate Bill 133.

The three bills were passed by the legislature during the 2016 session. Provisions from HB 1182, which included a half-cent increase in state sales tax, took effect June 1, 2016. The added half-cent provided an additional $67 million for K–12 education, $36 million for property tax relief, and $3 million for technical institutes. Provisions established in SB 131 and 133 took effect July 1, 2016.[18]

With legislation passed, the new state aid funding system for K–12 education in South Dakota took shape.

General Fund

The revised funding formula was based on a target statewide average salary of $48,500 (increased by CPI for FY 2018 to $48,645.50). The new formula worked as follows:

- For each district, calculate a target student-to-teacher ratio based on a sliding scale by student enrollment:
  - The district's target number of teachers was calculated by dividing the district's fall enrollment by the target student-to-teacher ratio;
  - The district's total instructional need was calculated by multiplying the district's target number of teachers by the statewide target for average teacher salary, and by increasing that total by 29% for benefits;
  - The total instructional need was increased by a calculated overhead rate (FY 2018 = 31.04%) to cover non-instructional costs. This category included operating costs as well as salaries and benefits of non-instructional staff such as administrators, guidance counselors, librarians, and school nurses;

These steps calculated the district's total need for state aid (see recent state aid history in Figure 43.2). At this point, local effort was applied against total need, with the state providing any necessary funds to achieve the total need.

Target Teacher Ratio Factor

The law provided the following sliding scale for the target ratio, based on student enrollment: Less than 200 (12 students to 1 teacher); between 200–600 (sliding scale between 12:1 and 15:1); and greater than 600 (15:1). The sliding scale retained the same enrollment thresholds as the small school factor of the previous funding formula. The formula did not require school districts to strictly meet the target ratio or to use a certain level of funding for benefits and overhead costs; those standards were merely used to calculate total need, and districts retained local control on how to use the dollars received.

Calculating the Number of Students

South Dakota's new state aid formula used fall enrollment count, which is school district enrollment on the last Friday of September. This number

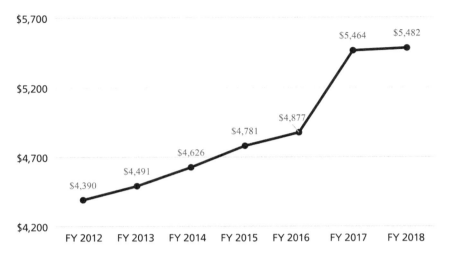

Figure 43.2 Overall State Funding per Student FY 2012–2018. *Source:* South Dakota Department of Education. 10 Year History of Per Student Allocations & Levies: http://doe.sd.gov/legislature/documents/18-10Year.pdf

included students tuitioned out of the district and students enrolled less than full-time, but it did not include students for whom a district received tuition.

Funding for Local Need

Money to pay for local need in the new formula was raised through both local and state taxes. Taxes funding local need were divided between money raised through school district taxes, called 'local effort' and money from the state's budget raised with state taxes, called 'state aid.'

Determining Local Effort

In the new formula, a school district's local effort was the amount of money raised by applying the maximum local property tax levies against the value of taxable property. The South Dakota Department of Revenue calculated the value of a school district's taxable property on which local effort would be raised through local property taxes. For taxes payable in 2018, school districts could levy a maximum of $1.507 per thousand for agricultural property; $3.372 per thousand for owner-occupied property; and $6.978 per thousand for non-agricultural property. The level of general education tax levy for school purposes was capped in law, but school boards could opt out of the maximums if two-thirds of the board supported it. This decision may be referred to a public vote, if 5% of the electorate advanced a petition against the opt out.

Other Revenues Counted as Local Effort

Other revenues were funding sources that school districts receive that, in the past, were counted outside the formula and therefore not equalized across all districts. In FY18, a calculation of local effort based on the phase-in of 'other revenue' equalization was implemented. These other revenues included utility taxes (rural electric and telephone); revenue in lieu of taxes (local and county); county apportionment; bank franchise tax; and wind farm taxes. Each school district was assigned a hold-harmless base amount based on the greatest of its previous three years collections – FY 2013, 2014 and 2015, that would be stepped down over five years at 20% per year. Each year any other revenue collected beyond the hold-harmless base would be counted as local effort and therefore equalized across districts through the funding formula. At that point, these revenue sources would be treated in the same way as local property taxes.

This new money did not offset state or local funding and did not take any funds away from the state's education system. The state's share of funding ratio was adjusted so that the state's dollar amount contribution was not reduced and local property taxes were not impacted.

Determining State Aid

In the new formula, the amount of state aid provided to school districts is calculated by taking the total 'local need' minus 'local effort'. A hypothetical school district example is as follows:

Local Need:	$2,634,000
Local Effort – Prop Taxes:	–$1,081,284
Local Effort – Other Revenue:	–$52,000
State Aid =	$1,500,716

For districts with very high levels of other revenue, the law allows an optional alternative to phase into the revised formula by permitting them to opt out of the revised formula, keep their current funding which would remain frozen at the FY 2016 amount per student generated through the previous formula, plus revenues from other identified revenues to be equalized. When the inflationary increases to the revised formula catch up with that school district, they may opt into the updated funding system. Figure 43.3 depicts total state aid expenditures over the last ten years, giving a view of growth under state aid formulas.

General Fund Cash Balance Caps

Included with the new funding formula legislation were other components with delayed implementation dates. Effective FY 2019, districts may be penalized if they exceed an allowable percentage of cash based on a

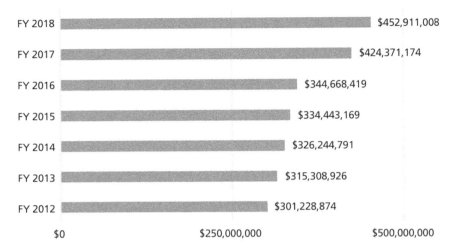

Figure 43.3 Total State Aid Expenditures FY 2012–2018. *Source:* South Dakota Department of Education. 10 Year History of Per Student Allocations & Levies: http://doe.sd.gov/legislature/documents/18-10Year.pdf

monthly report of cash balances in their general funds in the prior fiscal year. The percentage general fund cash balance cap is calculated by dividing the lowest monthly cash balance of the previous 12 months by total general fund expenditures. The purpose of this mechanism is to ascertain the general fund cash balance level that, over the course of a year, is never used. Districts' general fund cash balance allowances are based on student counts: Less than 200 students (capped at 40%); between 200–600 students (capped at 30%); and greater than 600 students (capped at 25%). Once in effect, a district exceeding the general fund cash balance cap would have its state aid reduced dollar-for-dollar. The governor appointed a five-member oversight board to consider districts' requests to waive general fund cash balance caps in special circumstances.

Sparsity Factor

The new formula recognized the unique challenges faced by extremely rural isolated school districts. Those meeting the definition of 'sparse' receive additional money outside the formula. These districts are eligible for additional state dollars not to exceed $110,000 per district. If the total appropriation for sparsity is less than the calculated amount for each district, the dollars available are prorated to each district. The criteria for meeting the definition of 'sparse' include state aid fall enrollment less than 500; state aid fall enrollment per square mile of 0.5 or less; school district area of 400 square miles or more; distance of at least 15 miles between a district's secondary attendance center and that of an adjoining district; operation of a secondary attendance center; and levying at the maximum for general fund purposes. Calculation of this additional aid is outlined in SDCL 13-13-79.[19]

OTHER REVENUE SOURCES

The state aid formula is not the only source of revenue for South Dakota schools. It is only one of more than 50 sources of revenue that local schools can use for educating students. Some of the other revenue sources for general education include federal grants, rental income, investment income, admissions, and contributions and donations.

Schools also have other specialized funds to pay for certain education projects, including revenue collected from local taxpayers for capital outlay and bond redemption over and above the per-student allocation, as well as federal, state and local funds for special education over and above the per-student allocation for special education students.

PENSION FUND LEVY ABOLISHED

In years prior to the new school aid formula, South Dakota school districts could assess up to 0.3 mills for a pension levy for a separate pension fund. The revised school funding system merged pension levies into the general education levy beginning FY 2021, providing districts with time to spend down these funds without initially counting against reserve fund caps. Because each class of property paid the same pension mill levy rate, the shift to a general education levy was even across the classes. Statewide application made the adjustment revenue neutral to taxpayers. The revised formula also included a benefits rate for schools to cover the pension-related benefits costs.

CAPITAL OUTLAY FUNDS

The revised funding system made four changes to South Dakota's school capital outlay levy provisions. First, it repealed the sunset clause of capital outlay flexibility and made it permanent. This broadened capital outlay flexibility so collections can be used for any general fund purpose at the current level of 45% of the capital outlay property tax revenue. It also required funds used for flexibility be transferred to the general fund instead of expended out of the Capital Outlay fund. Second, it required districts make annual capital outlay requests in the form of a dollar amount, not a mill levy rate. It thereby limited future growth in capital outlay collections by capping the maximum dollar amount that can be collected to increasing annually by 3% or inflation, whichever is less, plus new construction. Third, it imposed an alternative maximum on capital outlay collections on a per student basis at $2,800 per student, which is double the approximate state average of $1,400 per student. In future years this would inflate at the same rate as the formula CPI or 3%, whichever is less. This alternative maximum takes effect in FY 2021, with a special provision for districts with certain capital outlay debt obligations. And fourth, the revised funding system did not mandate that any current capital outlay funds be shifted to general education purposes; further, the adjustments had no effect on the general education levies.

CONCLUSION

The past few years brought significant changes to how South Dakota funds school districts. These various changes affected every school district differently. Some districts were impacted by changes to the 'other revenue' equalization, while others were impacted by fund balance caps or by the new ratio in the funding formula. All changes were balanced with the agreement that significant state aid funding would be provided through the increased sales tax, which was South Dakota's first permanent increase since 1968,

Figure 43.4 Average South Dakota Teacher Salary FY 2014–2019. *Source:* South Dakota Department of Education, South Dakota Legislative Research Council and National Education Association.

making the debate and decision to increase state revenues through a half-penny sales tax truly historic.

Reform largely began around the issue of teacher salaries. Figure 43.4 tracks average salaries across FY 2014–2019, showing desirable growth. Progress has come from the commitment and investment made by everyone involved in the Blue Ribbon Task Force and the subsequent efforts to get legislation passed, as teacher pay in South Dakota recently leaped out of last place in the nation for the time since 1985. With that accomplishment, there remains a need to commit to sticking to the philosophy and goals of the Blue Ribbon Task Force.

NOTES

1. SC *Davis v. State of South Dakota* 2011 (51).
2. SDCL 13-15-2 and 13-10-6; SC *Davis vs. State of South Dakota* 2011 (51).
3. SDCL 13-13-10.1.
4. SDCL 13-13-10.1(6).
5. S.D. Constitution Article VII (3).
6. SDCL 13-13-78-79.
7. NEA Teacher Salary Rankings. Retrieved from http://www.nea.org/assets/docs/2017_Rankings_and_Estimates_Report-FINAL-SECURED.pdf
8. Low Pay Spells Teacher Shortage in South Dakota, *Argus Leader*, Sept. 17, 2014.
9. Associated School Boards of SD online blog post, June, 28, 2015).
10. Associated School Boards SD online blog, Feb. 6, 2015. Retrieved from http://asbsd.org/index.php/gov-announces-task-force-for-k12/)
11. State of South Dakota Blue Ribbon Task Force Final Report. Retrieved from http://blueribbon.sd.gov/
12. Ibid.
13. Ibid.
14. Associated School Boards of SD blog post Dec. 8, 2015.)
15. State of South Dakota Blue Ribbon Task Force Final Report. Retrieved from http://blueribbon.sd.gov/
16. Ibid.
17. Ibid.
18. South Dakota Legislative Research Council, archived bills, 2016. Retrieved from http://www.sdlegislature.gov/Legislative_Session/Bills/Bill.aspx?Session=2016
19. South Dakota Department of Education–Issue Brief – March 2017. State Aid to K–12 General Education Funding Formula. Retrieved from http://doe.sd.gov/ofm/documents/17-SAbrief2.pdf

CHAPTER 44

Tennessee

Lisa G. Driscoll, Ph.D.
*Associate Professor
University of Tennessee*

GENERAL BACKGROUND

Tennessee drafted its first constitution in 1796, which was accepted immediately by Congress, conferring statehood for Tennessee to become the 16th state in the Union. Most provisions in the Tennessee constitution were drawn from the North Carolina and Pennsylvania constitutions. Unlike North Carolina's constitution, there was no provision for a system of publicly funded common schools in Tennessee. Private academies thus were established in Tennessee during this period.[1]

In 1806, the U.S. Congress passed the Cession Act[2] which was intended to officially establish public education in the state. It provided 100,000 acres to establish a public academy (i.e., common school) in each of the 27 counties in the state. Over the next decade there were numerous attempts by the General Assembly to establish a dedicated stream of adequate funding and supervision for these schools. However, funding was not forthcoming as these attempts did not prevail, and only four common schools were established. Meanwhile, the private academies attracted students and benefactors which bolstered their reputations and favor among influential persons. In 1929, the legislature authorized local taxation to support public schools.

Establishing and funding a system of common schools seemed thwarted even by acts that were designed to provide impetus to the cause. In 1815, a statute was passed levying taxes on property and polls to educate "those poor orphans who have no property to support them and educate them, and whose fathers were killed or have died in the service of their country in the war."[3] Tax proceeds were used to fund education in both common schools and private academies. This indistinct appropriation blurred the concept that public monies should indiscriminately support education in schools that were open to all.

In 1835, a new constitution was adopted which contained an education article[4] declaring the centrality of public education to the republic and assigned a 'duty' to the General Assembly for the establishment and appropriation of a perpetual common school fund:

> It shall be the duty of the General Assembly in all future periods of this government, to cherish literature and science. And the fund called the common school fund, and all the lands and proceeds thereof, dividends, stocks, and other property of every description whatever, heretofore by law appropriated by the General Assembly of this State for the use of common schools, and all such as shall hereafter be appropriated, shall remain a perpetual fund, the principal of which shall never be diminished by legislative appropriation, and the interest thereof shall be inviolably appropriated to the support and encouragement of common schools throughout the State, and for the equal benefit of all the people thereof.[5]

This constitution was remarkable in that a 'duty' was conferred to establish state funding for public schools 'for the equal benefit of all.' Into the future these words would suggest to the courts that the legislature intended to establish a state-supported uniform system of public education. During the session of 1839–40, the General Assembly passed "An act to establish a System of Common Schools in Tennessee."[6]

By 1853, after numerous attempts to fund common schools and to establish an organizational structure across the state, the governor advanced that inadequacy of school funding was to blame and vowed to increase the school fund using tax revenue. In 1854, the legislature levied both a property tax and a poll tax for the support of common schools. Funds were to be distributed to the counties based on 'scholastic population' (the number of school-age children in a district).[7] The cities of Nashville (1852) and Memphis (1858) established public school systems, but rural areas with small numbers of children did not establish such schools.

Tennessee seceded from the Union in 1861, and most schools were closed during the Civil War due to the reversion of education funds to the Confederate cause. Once the Civil War ended, a new constitution was written in 1870, although it was basically the same as the document of 1835. One change to the earlier constitution was that, "... State taxes, derived hereafter from polls, shall be appropriated to educational purposes, in such manner as the General Assembly shall from time to time direct by law."[8] This change has been interpreted by Tennessee courts as the state's intent to establish a 'uniform' system of education, even though the same section was also amended to "... no school established or aided under this section shall allow white and negro children to be received as scholars together in the same school."[9]

As the trend for taxpayer-funded secondary schools was gaining momentum throughout the U.S., especially in urban areas, in 1885 the Tennessee General Assembly provided for "municipal corporations to levy additional taxes and to establish graded high schools."[10] Through the Tennessee Private Acts,[11] process private academies (which included high school grades) could establish themselves as special school districts with separate and established boundaries within the county or municipality in which they were located. These special districts could levy property taxes and receive local and state funding. Over the next 40 years numerous special school districts were established through Private Acts. By 1899, the General Assembly required each county to establish a high school and to levy special taxes in lieu of the general fund to fund these schools. By 2018, 14 special school districts established during this period were still in operation.

Tennessee passed the General Education Act of 1909 which unified the state system and increased funding, largely to schools serving white children. Several private philanthropic organizations supported the improvement of education for black children, including the Julius Rosenwald Fund. A compulsory education law was passed in 1913 which necessitated additional funding. In 1947, the legislature levied a statewide sales tax, of which 80% of the revenue was planned for the public schools.

The 1870 Tennessee constitution was not amended in any significant manner until 1953. The poll tax, an addition to the 1870 constitution whose proceeds funded education statewide, was rescinded in 1953. Yet, the provisions that supported racially segregated schools remained. With the U.S. Supreme Court decision in *Brown v. Board of Education*[12] the following year, the segregation provisions were immediately unconstitutional. Another 14 years would pass before the references supporting segregated education were removed.

The 1977 convention approved a completely rewritten and abbreviated education clause that replaced detailed and operational language with exhortatory prose. The changes served to dilute the 'duty' to establish and fund the common schools as noted in earlier constitutions. The new clause read:

> The state of Tennessee recognizes the inherent value of education and encourages its support. The General Assembly shall provide for the maintenance, support, and eligibility standards of a system of free public schools. The General Assembly may establish and support such postsecondary institutions, including public institutions of higher learning, as it determines.[13]

As of 2018, the 1977 the education clause in the Tennessee constitution remained unchanged.

TENNESSEE FOUNDATION PROGRAM

After repeated attempts to address public school funding inequity in Tennessee, the legislature established the Foundation Program (TFP) in 1977 for equalizing resources. The TFP was a minimum foundation program that attempted to equalize funding by taking vertical (weighting expensive students and programs) and horizontal equity. Teacher qualifications were also considered in order to compensate districts for the added costs of more experienced teachers. A two-year study[14] of the Tennessee Foundation Program, the state tax system, and equity issues determined that although the program was capable of equalizing funding for school districts, the fact that it was underfunded by the General Assembly hindered its effectiveness. The study made several recommendations, though none were implemented. The state funded 92.5% of costs and local districts funded 7.5%; however, by 1988 chronic underfunding plagued the realization of fiscal equity among school districts.

SELECTED LITIGATION 1988–PRESENT

Tennessee Small School Systems, an unincorporated association of 77 rural small school districts, filed suit in 1988 against the state of Tennessee.[15] Suit was filed in the Davidson County Chancery Court and sought the current funding formula (the TFP) declared unconstitutional because it caused inequitable amounts of funding to be distributed to local school districts. Large school districts were allowed to intervene and join the defense. The case was unusual in that school finance litigation after 1989 tended to be based on adequacy arguments as opposed to fiscal equity arguments drawn from state education clauses. In 1991, the Chancery Court decided that the public education funding system violated the equal protection clause of the Tennessee constitution. The state appealed to the Tennessee Court of Appeals, which reversed the trial court. The Small Schools appealed the case to the Tennessee supreme court.[16]

While the suit was pending, the General Assembly passed the Educational Improvement Act[17] (EIA) of 1992 which contained a new funding formula known as the Basic Education Program (BEP). The EIA was a major legislative effort to improve K–12 public education. There were 88 sections in the EIA that forced sweeping changes in the funding, administration, and value-added accountability of public education. The EIA laid the foundation to conduct annual statewide assessments of all students and to adopt a value-added performance model for schools and districts.

The primary purpose of the EIA was to address fiscal equity by establishment of the BEP[18] funding formula. The BEP defined a cost basis for a basic program of education, set the state and local shares, and addressed differences in the ability to pay for basic education among districts.[19] The governor signed the EIA into law in March 1992, although no funding was appropriated pending outcome of the lawsuit.

In an opinion filed in March 1993, the Tennessee supreme court unanimously affirmed the trial court's decision that the current system of finance was inequitable and thus violated the Tennessee constitution on equal protection grounds. The case was remanded to the trial court to draft an order to correct funding inequities. When the chancery court judge denied plaintiffs' motion to immediately fully fund the BEP by omitting salary costs of teachers and other personnel,[20] plaintiffs appealed to the state supreme court a second time, whereon the court decided that salary costs were an essential component to equalize educational opportunity. The state legislature then passed the Salary Equity Plan in 1995.

Finally, in a third appeal to the Tennessee supreme court from the chancery court regarding whether the state's newest plan equalized teacher salaries in accord with the BEP plan, the court decided in favor of plaintiffs in that the Plan failed to achieve substantially equal opportunity.[21] In 2005, the legislature amended the BEP to include teacher and other personnel salary components.

In 2015, two separate suits were filed[22] by three of state's largest school districts, claiming that the state was failing to meet its obligation for free, adequate, and equitable educational opportunities. In 2016, the state of Tennessee launched a website providing greater transparency about how public schools are funded and "...to outline the basics of the BEP, allow users to download the BEP Calculator and see the BEP calculation, and provide some quick facts and statistics about school funding."[23] The site featured explanations, infographic handouts, reports, errata notices, and macro-driven Excel models for Fiscal Years 2017, 2018 and 2019 BEP funding by district.

BASIC SUPPORT PROGRAM

The Basic Education Program (BEP) is the funding formula for K–12 public schools in Tennessee. The formula was established as part of the EIA in 1992. Since Tennessee's constitution requires substantially equal educational opportunity for all students and since not all local governments are able to raise the same amounts of revenue per pupil considering how their disparate tax bases would necessitate widely variable rates of property taxes, the BEP's purpose was to determine the 'basic' cost of education in each county and to allocate minimum state and local shares of funding to pay for it. Tennessee requires no minimum rate of local taxation to raise local school funds, although the BEP as a minimum foundation program requires a minimum dollar amount of local funding share. The BEP formula was the first time that a local government's ability to pay for education was considered in Tennessee state appropriations. The BEP was phased in FY 1992–FY 1998 as part of the EIA. Since inception, the formula has undergone multiple updates to its cost of education calculation and its fiscal capacity calculation.

In 2005, the mayors of the four largest counties in Tennessee (in terms of average daily membership [ADM]) encouraged the governor to revisit the BEP cost model and to include components for English Language Learner (ELL) and At-Risk students and to change the way fiscal capacity is calculated. These discussions led to a 2007 proposal leading to BEP 2.0.[24] In BEP 2.0 the ELL and At-Risk components were added, thus increasing funding for districts with these students. A redesigned county fiscal capacity formula was also developed by the University of Tennessee's Center for Business and Economic Research[25] (CBER).[26] Other initiatives for BEP 2.0 included changes to the state's share of instructional salary components, which was increased from 65% to 70%, with an eventual percentage of 75%. Other component percentages remained the same.

In April 2016, the Tennessee legislature unanimously passed the BEP Enhancement Act which was part of the governor's budget. The Act addressed the BEP Review Committee's recommendations that improved teacher salaries and health insurance costs ($134 million) by increasing the salary unit cost in the BEP and doubled the state's investment in education technology (from $20 million to $40 million). As part of the governor's continued BEP enhancements, the 2017 legislature raised the funding level for ELL from 1:30 (teachers) and 1:300 (translators) to 1:20 and 1:200 respectively, increasing state expenditures by $16.9 million.

The BEP is a school funding program based primarily on inputs based on the cost of various resources such as teachers, administrators, textbooks, instructional equipment, transportation to school and so on, for a specified unit of students in ADM. In recent years, funding for districts has been tightly linked to accountability provisions including the continuing employment of teachers, specific evidence-based strategies to raise academic achievement, and equal opportunity for all students, especially the most challenged students, to reach specified outcomes. Figure 44.1 provides a visual overview of the relationship among cost components, county fiscal capacity, and the local share of funding. Later, Tables 44.1 through 44.4 provide line item detail on selected graphic components of Figure 44.1.

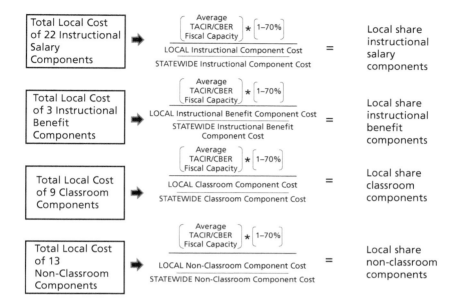

Figure 44.1 Overview of the Tennessee Basic Education Formula. *Note:* See Tables 44.1 through 44.4 later for definitions of components in left column of Figure 44.1.

BEP CALCULATION: STATE AND STATUTORY REQUIRED LOCAL SHARE

As seen in Figure 44.1, the BEP incorporates two sets of calculations, i.e., determining Local [County] Fiscal Capacity; and determining the Total Local Cost of a 'Basic' Education Program Component. Figure 44.2 shows how both sets of calculations (fiscal capacity and the cost of a basic education program) contribute to determining the Local Share.

Determining Local (County) Fiscal Capacity

Fiscal capacity is defined as the ability to pay for services through own-source revenue. BEP fiscal capacity refers to the ability of a county to pay for the Local Cost of Education (all four components) out of the revenue from its tax bases (usually property taxes and sales taxes).

At initial implementation, fiscal capacity for the BEP was determined solely by the Tennessee Advisory Commission on Intergovernmental Relations (TACIR) formula. In 2007, the BEP underwent a major change referred to as BEP 2.0. The change involved the development and addition

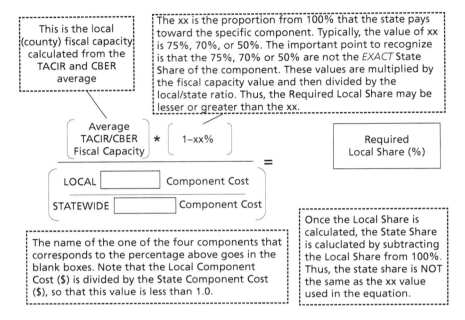

Figure 44.2 Relationship of Tennessee County Fiscal Capacity to the Cost of Education for Public School District(s) Within the County.

of the CBER fiscal capacity calculation. In 2016, the Tennessee General Assembly passed the BEP Enhancement Act[27] which resulted in the TACIR Index and the CBER Index weighted the same in the equalization formula. The BEP 2.0 used the average of both indices for each county to arrive at a final relative fiscal capacity for each county.

The TACIR Index

The TACIR Index estimates relative fiscal capacity at the county level by employing a statistical regression procedure. Using a county's three-year average of historical local revenue per pupil as a dependent variable, the regression procedure estimates the linear relationship among five other independent variables: (1) the three-year average per-pupil sales tax base; (2) the three-year average per-pupil property tax base; (3) the three-year average per-capita personal income; (4) the ratio of residential and farm property assessment to total assessment; and (5) the ratio of average daily membership to total population.

The regression model estimates the weighted average influence of each independent variable on predicting the historical revenue. Using the product of the estimated coefficients multiplied by a county's values for the independent values and added to the value of the intercept, a per-pupil estimate

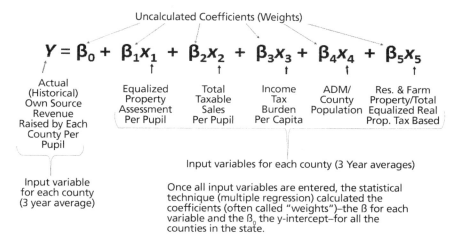

Figure 44.3 TACIR Fiscal Capacity Linear Regression Equation.

of fiscal capacity is predicted. After an aggregate of all county fiscal capacities is calculated, each county's fiscal capacity index becomes the county's percentage share of the total. Figure 44.3 provides a visual representation of the TACIR linear regression equation.

The CBER Index

The CBER Index is based on two factors, i.e., the property tax base and the sales tax base. The rationale for this formula is to employ variables that can be measured in a tangible way. There are six variables in the calculation used to find each county's fiscal capacity as a percentage of the entire state. These are: (1) county sales tax base[28]—the total of sales tax receipts in the county; (2) statewide local sales tax base—the total of sales tax receipts in the state; (3) statewide revenue from sales tax spent on education; (4) county property tax base—the equalized property tax base, including value of payments in lieu of taxes based on agreements with industrial development boards; (5) statewide property tax base; and (6) statewide property tax revenue spent on education. Figure 44.4 illustrates calculation of the CBER Index.

Each county's resultant sales tax base is calculated as the average of total county sales over three calendar years. The total county sales variable is comprised of building materials; general merchandise; food stores; autos, boats, and aircraft; gas products and service stations; apparel and accessories; furniture and home décor; eating and drinking; and other retail.[29] Each county's resultant county property tax base is calculated as the average of the equalized sum of total real property, total personal property, and public utility assessment over three calendar years.[30] A three-year estimate of industrial development board payments in lieu of taxes is added to the above.

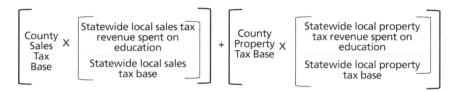

Figure 44.4 Calculation of CBER County Fiscal Capacity in Dollars, FY 2019. *Source:* Adapted from the Office of Research and Education Accountability. Legislative Brief: *Fiscal Year 2017–18 Verification of the Basic Education Program (BEP) Calculation.* (Tennessee Comptroller of the Treasury 18). https://gallery.mailchimp.com/48f2c0191ce31ce7af2dd9ffb/files/2cb9c6b8-df60-49a6-b429-8e831a2c8270/FY_18_BEP_varification_full_report.pdf

Determining the Total Local Cost of a 'Basic' Education's Program Components

There are 45 different cost components, divided among four different component categories, that contribute to the district cost determination: (1) Instructional Salary Category (22 components—see Table 44.1); (2) Instructional Benefit Category (3 components—see Table 44.2); (3) Classroom Category (13 components—see Table 44.3); and (4) Non-Classroom Category (9 components—see Table 44.4). Each of these components in

TABLE 44.1 Instructional Salary Category Components (22), Basic Education Program FY 2019

	Component	Funding Level Ratio	Salary FY 2019
1	Regular Education	1 per 20 ADM K–3 1 per 25 ADM 4–6 1 per 25 ADM 7–9 1 per 26.5 ADM 10–12	$47,150
2	Career & Technical Education (CTE)	1 per 20 career & technical education FTE ADM	$47,150
3	Special Education (Number of Students Identified and Served = I & S)	Caseload Allocations 1 per Option 1 91.0 1 per Options 2 and 3 58.5 1 per Options 4,5, and 6 16.5 1 per options 7, 8, 9, and 10 8.5	$47,150
4	Elementary Guidance	1 per 500 ADM K–6	$47,150
5	Secondary Guidance	1 per 350 ADM 7–12 (including CTE)	$47,150
6	Elementary Art	1 per 525 ADM K–6	$47,150
7	Elementary Music	1 per 525 ADM K–6	$47,150

(continued)

TABLE 44.1 Instructional Salary Category Components (22), Basic Education Program FY 2019 (continued)

	Component	Funding Level Ratio	Salary FY 2019
8	Elementary Physical Education	1 per 350 ADM K–4 1 per 265 ADM 5–6	$47,150
9	Elementary Librarians (K–8)	0.5 per school, 265 1 per school 265–439 1 per school 440–659 (+ .5 assistant) 1 per school > 660 (+ assistant)	$47,150 Asst. = $23,500
10	Secondary Librarians	0.5 per school, 300 1 per school 300–999 2 per school 1,000–1,499 2 per school > 1,500 (+ 1 per added 750)	$47,150 Asst. = $23,500
11	ELL Instructors	1 per 20 EL Stuents I & S	$47,150
12	ELL Translators	1 per 200 EL Students I & S	$47,150
13	Principals	No allocation < 100 (Elem. Only) 0.5 per school < 225 1 per school > 225	$47,150
14	Assistant Principals – Elementary	0.5 per school 660–879 1 per school 800–1,099 1.5 per school 1,100–1,249 2 per school > 1,320	$47,150
15	Assistant Principals – Secondary	0.5 per school 300–649 1 per school 650–999 1.5 per school 1,000–1,249 2 per school > 1,250 (+1 per added 1,000)	$47,150
16	Systemwide Instructional Supervisors	1 per < 500 total ADM 2 per 500–999 total ADM 3 per 1,000–1,999 total ADM 3 per > 2,000 total ADM (+1 per added 1,000)	$47,150
17	Special Education Supervisors	1 per 750 special education I & S	$47,150
18	Career & Technical Supervisors	1 per 1,000 CTE FTEADM	$47,150
19	Special Education Assessment Personnel	1 per 600 special education I & S	$47,150
20	Social Workers	1 per 2,000 total ADM	$47,150
21	Psychologists	1 per 2,500 total ADM	$47,150
22	Response to Instruction and Intervention (RTI)	1 per 2,750 total ADM	$47,150

Source: Office of Research and Education Accountability, The Basic Education Program: *BEP Calculator Fiscal Year 2018–19.* (Tennessee Comptroller of the Treasury 2018). Retrieved from https://www.comptroller.tn.gov/OREA/bep

TABLE 44.2 Instructional Benefit Category Components (3), Basic Education Program FY 2019

	Component	Funding Level Ratio	Salary FY 2019
1	Staff Insurance	$7,038.78 for each BEP position	N/A
2	Staff Benefits	7.65% of BEP salary for FICA and Medicare–(BEP positions only)	Supt salary = $112,900 Cert. Personnel = $47,150 Lib/Inst Asst = $23,500
3	Staff Retirement	10.46% of BEP salary per licensed position OR 7.75% of BEP salary per classified position for Tennessee Cons. Retire. System (TCRS)	Supt Salary = $112,900 Cert Personnel = $47,150 Lib/Inst Asst. = $23,500

Source: Office of Research and Education Accountability, The Basic Education Program: *BEP Calculator Fiscal Year 2018–19.* (Tennessee Comptroller of the Treasury 2018). Retrieved from https://www.comptroller.tn.gov/OREA/bep

each category has a 'funding level' set by the Tennessee legislature. Some funding levels apply to the district as a whole, and some funding levels apply to individual schools. Either way, it is evident that the two major cost drivers in the BEP are the number of students in ADM which determines the number of BEP funded positions or funding level and the salary dollar cost assigned to each component or subcomponent funding level.[31] Importantly, these are the same categories established earlier in Figure 44.1.

Once the Total Local Cost of a group of components is estimated, these Local Costs are aggregated using the Total Local Cost for each school district in the BEP calculation within each component category to form the Statewide Component Cost for that category. The variables are next entered into an equation that calculates the required local share of costs:

- Average of TACIR and CBER fiscal capacity calculations:
  - if a school district is equal to the average state fiscal capacity, the value is 1.0
  - if a school district is above average state fiscal capacity, the value is above 1.0
  - if a school district is below average state fiscal capacity, the value is below 1.0
- A ratio of the Total Local Component Cost to the Aggregated Statewide Component Cost (this number is less than 1.0 as no school district is equal or greater than the state aggregate)
- The percentage of the state share subtracted from 100% (or 1.0)
  - 70% of the Instructional Salary Component = state share
  - 70% of the Instructional Benefit Component = state share
  - 75% of the Classroom Component = state share
  - 50% of the Non-Classroom Component = state share

TABLE 44.3 Classroom Category Components (13), Basic Education Program FY 2019

	Component	Funding Level Ratio
1	K–12 At-Risk	$885.75 per identified at-risk ADM. Funded at 100% At-Risk.
2	Duty-Free Lunch	$12.25 per total ADM
3	Textbooks	$77.50 per total ADM
4	Classroom Materials & Supplies	$80.75 per regular ADM $157.75 per career & technical ed. FTEADM $36.50 per special ed I & S $47.15 per Academic exit exam (12th grade) $18.00 per Technical exit exam (1/4 CTE)
5	Instructional Equipment	$64.25 per regular ADM $99.75 per career & technical ed FTEADM $13.25 per special ed I & S
6	Classroom Related Travel	$14.50 per regular ADM $50.50 per career & technical ed FTEADM $17.25 per special ed I & S
7	Career & Technical Center Transportation	For participating systems to transport students to CTE center attended part of the day
8	Technology	$41.32 per funded ADM $40 M distributed on ADM basis
9	Nurses	1 per 3,000 total ADM (minimum per system)
10	Instructional Assistants	1 per 75 ADM K–6
11	Special Education Assistants	1 per 60 special ed I & S in Options 5, 7 and 8
12	Substitute Teachers	$61.75 per total ADM
13	Alternative Schools	$3.75 per total ADM K–12 plus $33.25 per ADM 7–12 (including CTE)

Source: Office of Research and Education Accountability, The Basic Education Program: BEP Calculator Fiscal Year 2018-19. (Tennessee Comptroller of the Treasury 2018). Retrieved from https://www.comptroller.tn.gov/OREA/bep

On a district level, these percentages of state (or local) shares of funding may be higher than statewide percentages based on aggregate costs. The BEP thus incorporates a state share and a local share of costs. Tennessee law requires that districts appropriate at least the minimum funds to meet their local share of BEP cost.[32]

In FY 2019, the total cost of education as determined by the BEP was $7.16 billion. State share of these costs was approximately $4.81 billion, over 25% of the state's General Fund appropriation. Combined required local match from all districts was $2.45 billion.

At the state level, revenue is primarily derived from sales and use tax. The state does not tax personal earned income, social security, or other

TABLE 44.4 Non-Classroom Category (9 components)	
Component	Funding Level Ratio
1 Superintendent	1 per county
2 System Secretarial Support	2 per system < 500 3 per system 1,251–1,999 3 per system 1,999 and above, plus 1 each for additional 1,000 ADM
3 Technology Coordinators	1 per system with one additional for each 6,400 ADM
4 School Secretaries	.5 per school < 225 1 per school 225–374 1 per 375 per school > 375 (plus 1 per each additional 375)
5 Maintenance & Operations	100 square feet per total K–4 ADM 110 square feet per total 5–8 ADM 130 square feet per total 9–12 ADM Total square foot × $3.44/square foot
6 Non-Instructional Equipment	$26.50 per total ADM
7 Pupil Transportation	Allocated to systems that provide transportation. Formula established by Commissioner of Education. Based on number of pupils transported, miles transported, and density of pupils per route mile.
8 Staff Benefits and Insurance	$6,569.53 per BEP position for insurance OR $9,854.29 per superintendent and technology coordinator; PLUS 7.65% of BEP salary for FICA and Medicare. Add 10.46% of BEP salary for superintendent and technology coordinator OR 7.75% of BEP salary per classified position for TCRS. Sch Sec. = $33,000; System Sec. = $42,200
9 Capital Outlay	100 square foot per total K–4 ADM × $139.41/ square foot 110 square foot per total 5–8 ADM × 140.00/ square foot 130 square foot per total 9–12 × 147.84/ square foot Add equipment: 10% of square foot cost Add Architect's fee (7% of square foot cost) Add debt service (20 years @ 6.00%) Divide total by 40 years = annual amount

Source: Office of Research and Education Accountability, The Basic Education Program: *BEP Calculator Fiscal Year 2018–19.* (Tennessee Comptroller of the Treasury 2018). Retrieved from https://www.comptroller.tn.gov/OREA/bep

pensions. At county or municipal levels, revenue is generated through real property taxes and local-option sales and use taxes. Fourteen special school districts, as designated by a private act of the General Assembly, are allowed to levy taxes on their jurisdictions.

TENNESSEE PUBLIC SCHOOL DISTRICTS

Tennessee has exhibited a steady increase in public school ADM over the last several years. ADM in schools and districts is the basis for funding levels,

TABLE 44.5 Pupils in Tennessee Public Schools, Average Daily Membership, K–12

2009–10	2010–11	2011–12	2012–13	2013–14	2014–15	2015–16	2016–17
948,508	949,354	950,547	956,973	958,280	959,536	960,959	963,294

Source: Tennessee Department of Education.

which determines the number of instructional, administrative and support personnel funded by the BEP. Table 44.5 indicates ADM data for Tennessee public schools across the years 2010–2017.

Tennessee has two types of school districts, i.e., regular (counties and municipalities) and special school districts. In the early years of public education in Tennessee, counties and cities established public school districts. Distance from school, poor roads, and lack of efficient transportation were hurdles to school attendance in rural areas. Therefore, public schools were located only a mile or two apart; were smaller in structure; and enrolled fewer students. Many counties had at least a hundred one-room schools, and other counties had fewer than ten schools. It was not until the 1940s that transportation became available in many locations.

In the 1960s, Tennessee encouraged consolidation of city school districts into county units. In the past 50 years, 14 school districts closed or consolidated in Tennessee. Notable closures were Knox City consolidating to Knox County (1987), Chattanooga to Hamilton County (1994), and Davidson County consolidating with Metro Nashville (1962). In FY 2018, the BEP provided equalized funding for 139 regular county and city school districts. These districts were geographically the same with county boundaries. County commissioners are their governing body, with taxing authority for regular school districts.

SPECIAL SCHOOL DISTRICTS

Tennessee's special school districts were created either by being granted a charter or by private act of the General Assembly. In 2018, there were 14 special school districts.[33] These school districts are funded by a prorated appropriation of the county-calculated BEP, the county property and sales tax, and a special school tax levied across their attendance zone. In FY 2018, the BEP provided funding for 14 special school districts.

COMPENSATORY EDUCATION

Tennessee's compensatory education framework includes the Response to Intervention (RTI) Program. In 2013, the State Board of Education adopted new guidelines and standards for special education at the recommendation of the RTI Task Force and the Tennessee Department of Education. These new guidelines sought to enhance alignment of state law to the updated IDA by revising the approved methods of identifying students with specific learning disabilities. The enacted guidelines removed the discrepancy method and adopted RTI as the new state criteria. As of July 2014, RTI2 became the sole criteria by which a student may be identified as having a specific learning disability in Tennessee.[34]

The RTI2 program started in FY 2015 as an unfunded statewide program to address what appeared to be over-identification of males and minorities in special education following on a steady increase in students identified and served in nearly every program from 2009–10 and 2014–15 academic years. In the 2014–15 academic year, enrollment in many disability categories decreased. However, students in the following categories increased substantially over the time period: Intellectually Disabled, Autism, Health Impaired, and Developmentally Delayed. But for the first time in FY 2019, the Tennessee budget contained a line item of $13.3 million in recurring funds for RTI.[35] RTI was assigned as a BEP component at the funding level of one position for every 2,750 students in ADM, with a minimum of one position for each district (see item 22 under the Instructional Salary components table). Table 44.6 provides enrollments for special education programs in Tennessee.

CAREER AND TECHNICAL EDUCATION

Career and Technical Education (CTE) in Tennessee is funded by both federal and state funding. For FY 2018, Tennessee was allocated $25.4 million in federal funding,[36] of which $16.5 million was dedicated to secondary programs in school districts. In the 2018–19 school year, 21 new certificates were added to programs public schools can offer. CTE programs are integral to the state's efforts to achieve 55% of Tennesseans with a college degree.

Tennessee CTE funds are allocated to eligible school districts based on ADM through the BEP at the Funding Level of one teacher per 20 career and technical education FTEADM 1 and supervisors per 1,000 CTE FTEADM. Other funding is allocated based on the District Plan required by the U.S. Department of Education. In 2017, there were 37,000 students enrolled in CTE programs, an increase of over 10,000 from 2015.

GIFTED AND TALENTED EDUCATION

Intellectually Gifted is a state-specific disability in special education in Tennessee; the state therefore treats gifted pupils as a subgroup with disabilities

TABLE 44.6 Tennessee Children Aged 3–21 With a Disability Receiving Special Education Services

	2009–10	2010–11	2011–12	2012–13	2013–14	2014–15	2015–16	2016–17
Learning Disabled	43,184	43,337	44,699	47,040	48,573	47,895	44,422	41,801
Intellectually Disabled	7,927	7,582	7,451	7,519	7,444	7,640	7,878	8,108
Speech/Language Impaired	33,802	32,925	33,886	33,314	33,167	32,884	33,048	32,571
Emotionally Disturbed	3,446	3,371	3,107	3,299	3,122	3,082	3,088	3,100
Autism	5,419	5,944	6,736	7,317	7,984	8,639	9,393	10,402
Health Impaired	12,327	12,824	13,666	14,630	15,150	15,399	15,964	16,795
Hearing/Physically Impaired	818	808	763	737	695	646	644	597
Hearing Impaired or Deaf	1,533	1,502	1,302	1,496	1,262	1,238	1,166	1,145
Visually Impaired of Blind	744	728	647	688	614	602	554	558
Deaf/Blind	9	10	8	11	9	12	10	10
Multi-Disabilities	2,197	2,164	2,135	2,214	2,097	2,121	2,050	2,047
Developmentally Delayed	7,391	7,929	8,448	8,814	9,043	9,403	9,987	10,597
Traumatic Brain Injury	305	292	307	328	334	334	341	361
Total	119,102	119,416	123,155	127,407	129,494	129,905	128,545	129,092

Source: Tennessee Department of Education. Data and Research. *Annual Statistical Reports* for each respective fiscal year, 2010 through 2017. Retrieved from https://www.tn.gov/education/data/department-reports.html

and includes them in counts of special education students. Tennessee is the only state that provides an individualized education program for gifted students. About 19,000 students were identified as intellectually gifted in Tennessee for FY 2018.

ENGLISH LANGUAGE LEARNERS

Tennessee provides additional funding as an Instructional Salary Component in the BEP (a funding level of one teacher to 20 students for ELL and one teacher to 200 students for a translator). Approximately 5.3% or 53,000 students were classified as ELL in FY 2017.

CHARTER SCHOOLS

The General Assembly of Tennessee authorized public charter schools as part of the state program of public education through the Tennessee Public Charter Schools Act of 2002. Charter schools are public schools operated by independent nonprofit governing bodies that must include parents. By this Act, all federal and state statutes as well as rules and regulations pertaining to the public school were applied to charter schools, including meeting the same performance standards and requirements adopted by the state board of education.

Public charter school enrollment increased from 4,844 (FY 2010) to over 35,000 (FY 2017).[37] Most charter schools are in Shelby County and the Metro Nashville School Districts. Knox County operates one charter school.

The statute governing public charter school funding is T.C.A. 49-13-112 which states:

> A local board of education shall allocate to the charter school an amount equal to the per student state and local funds received by the LEA and all appropriate allocations under federal law or regulation, including, but not limited to Title I and ESEA funds."

Under these conditions, the money follows the child from the district to the charter school in the same district. Charter school ADM is included in the school district's ADM for BEP calculation. Therefore, according to the Tennessee Department of Education, charter schools are entitled to the per-pupil amount equal to the total state and local revenue divided by the total district ADM. That amount should be allocated for each student in the school. Charter school ADM is not derived from the district's weighted average of the previous year, but instead is a weighted average of the actual number of students enrolled in the charter school for the current year.

VIRTUAL EDUCATION

In 2008, the Tennessee General Assembly passed a law authorizing school district use of BEP funds in implementing and operating virtual education programs.[38] Districts could implement virtual schools utilizing staff from their own district, or they could contract with a private provider for virtual school services. Students enrolled in any public school district in the state can attend a virtual school in any district. The money follows the student to the school district with the virtual school.

FOOD SERVICES

All Tennessee public school districts participate in the USDA's National School Lunch Program offering eligible students free or reduced lunch. Half of all school districts in Tennessee qualify for a Community Eligibility Provision that expands free meal coverage to the entire school. The number of economically disadvantaged students in Tennessee for FY 2017 was 347,000 (34.7%) of all students.[39]

GENERAL TRANSPORTATION

All regular education students in grades K–12 attending school in their attendance zone and living more than 1.25 miles from school (1.5 miles for high schools) are eligible for bus transportation. The BEP uses a statistical model of linear regression to estimate the impacts of four different factors on each school district's transportation spending over three years prior to the BEP-funding year. Those four factors are: (1) students transported per ADM based on a three-year rolling average; (2) special education students transported per ADM based on a three-year rolling average; (3) miles driven per ADM (based on a three-year rolling average; and (4) whether the school district is a county, city, or special district.

The funding model estimates average statewide effects (coefficients) of these factors on transportation expenditures and multiplies those estimated effects by each school district's respective factors to calculate the estimated cost to the school district of providing transportation services in past years. The BEP then adjusts these amounts by an inflation measure to calculate the actual dollar amount of transportation spending generated for each LEA.

SCHOOL FACILITIES

The Tennessee State School Bond Authority was established to issue bonds as part of a federal program to finance loans to qualifying K–12 schools in the state. The governing body consists of designated state officials, with the governor serving as chair. The authority may fix and collect charges and rentals, issue revenue bonds, and accept gifts, grants, or loans.

CAPITAL OUTLAY/DEBT SERVICE

Capital outlay and debt service are addressed through the BEP formula.

OTHER STATE AIDS

The state of Tennessee provides Driver's Education Funding. Revenues are derived through traffic fines and other sources. Currently, approximately $1.4 million is annually available. Other state aids include a Teacher Supply Funding per Teacher category in the amount of $200. Unspent funds can be carried over to the next year

LOCAL SCHOOL REVENUE

Local school revenue is comprised of the property tax and the local option sales tax.

SUMMARY

In the last decade, Tennessee's governors and legislatures have funded public education as a priority. Funding has increased to develop initiatives for student success and for attracting and retaining high quality teachers.

NOTES

1. Among the earliest academies were: Martin Academy (Greenville, 1783), Davidson Academy (Nashville, 1785), Blount College (Knoxville, 1794) and Greenville College (Greenville, 1795). See, Arthur P. Whitaker, "The Public School System of Tennessee, 1834–1860," in *Tennessee Historical Magazine*, 11 (1916). Retrieved from https://www.jstor.org/stable/42637961

2. The Act was an agreement among the federal government, Tennessee and North Carolina authorizing Tennessee to "issue grants,... perfect titles ... and to settle claims" concerning vacant and unappropriated lands within the state. The public school lands can be divided into three groups: the lands set aside for the common schools, the lands set aside for the academies, and the lands set aside for colleges.
3. See John Haywood and Robert L. Cobbs, *The Statute Laws of the State of Tennessee of a Public and General Nature.* Vol 1. (1831), 175-76.
4. TENN. CONST. of 1835, art. XI, §10. The fund was largely to receive its revenue from the sale of public lands and from interest on some state deposits. *See* Robert H. White, Development of the Tennessee State Educational Organization, 1796–1929, (1929).
5. TENN. CONST. of 1835, art. XI, §10.
6. Acts of 1887–8. Ch. 148.
7. "Scholastic population" refers the school census. See, Tennessee Secretary of State. School Census Records. Retrieved from https://sos.tn.gov/products/tsla/school-census-records
8. TENN. CONST. of 1870 art XI, § 12.
9. TENN. CONST. of 1870 art XI, § 12.
10. The Annual Report of the State Superintendent of Public Instruction for Tennessee for the Scholastic Year Ending June 30, 1891, p. 37.
11. A bill introduced and passed by the Tennessee General Assembly may be classified as either a Public Act or a Private Act. Private Acts do not amend the Tennessee Code and affect only one "locality." Private Acts need only approval of their local legislative delegation but may be referred to committee and the entire legislative body. Private Acts are published in bound volumes entitled Tennessee Private Acts. There are numerous Tennessee statutes that address the funding of special school districts. For an overview through March 2012, see, Office of Research and Education Accountability. *Statutory Options for School District Mergers: Report Addressing House Resolution 30, 2011.* (Tennessee Comptroller of the Treasury 2012). Retrieved from https://www.comptroller.tn.gov/Repository/RE/MemphisSchoolConsolidation.pdf
12. 347 U.S. 483 (1954).
13. TENN. CONST. of 1977, art. XI, § 12.
14. The Tennessee School Finance Equity Study. State Equalization Plan for Financing the Public Schools in Tennessee. (1979). This study was commissioned by the Joint Legislative Committee on Elementary and Secondary Finance established by the General Assembly in 1976.
15. *Tennessee Small School Systems, et al. v. McWherter (I),* 851 S.W. 2d 139 (Tenn. 1993).(Small Schools I).
16. S.C. No 01-S01-9209-CH-00101, Supreme Court of Tennessee, at Nashville, 851 S.W.2d 139; 1993 Tenn., March 22, 1993, Filed.
17. Education Improvement Act, Tennessee Public Acts and Resolutions, chapter 535 (1992).
18. Tenn. Code Ann. § 49-3-351.
19. EIA §§2-3.

20. The BEP in its original form as proposed by the State Board of Education included teachers and other salaries as one of the components, but the plan as enacted by the legislature did not.
21. *Tennessee Small School Systems v. McWherter*, 91 S.W. 3d 232 (Tenn. 2002). (Small Schools III).
22. *Hamilton County Board of Education v. Haslam* was filed in March 2015. Seven school districts alleged the state had not fully funded the Basic Education Program by underestimating teacher salaries and benefits, wherein Average Daily Membership (ADM) drove the total funding amount for K–12 education. In addition, the suit alleged that classroom costs were not fully funded. A second suit was filed against the state in September, 2015, *Shelby County Board of Education v. Haslam*, which alleged the state had failed to provide adequate funding to meet the needs of the large numbers of students in Memphis who are immigrants, students with disabilities and students from poverty backgrounds who have extensive needs for additional services, and thus, denied these students their rights to an adequate free public education and to an equal opportunity. The district claimed it lacked necessary funds to offer prekindergarten services, to adequately fund CTE programs, extracurricular activities, music, art, and mandatory foreign language education, and that students must pay fees to access these programs. After having its own lawsuit dismissed, Metro Nashville [Public Schools] Board of Education joined the Shelby County [Public Schools] Board of Education lawsuit in October 2017. The case was scheduled for trial in spring 2019.
23. Office of Research and Education Accountability. The Basic Education Program (BEP). (Tennessee Comptroller of the Treasury 2018). Retrieved from https://www.comptroller.tn.gov/OREA/bep
24. Although the amendments to the BEP in 2007 refer to it as renamed 'BEP 2.0,' the funding program was and is currently referred to as the BEP–even on official documents, websites, and in Tennessee statutes. Other than this paragraph, this chapter follows that convention of referring to all BEP information as the BEP.
25. The Center for Business and Economic Research name was changed in 2016 to the Boyd Center for Business and Economic Research., although the acronym for center remains CBER.
26. Originally, the CBER fiscal capacity formula was scheduled to replace the original TACIR formula, but because each of the formulas produced different state and local share proportions, it was decided to use both formulas and take the average of the fiscal capacities produced by each.
27. 2016 Appropriations Act (Public Chapter No. 1020).
28. According to the CBER, tax base is related to but not the same as actual revenue collected. A county's sales tax base is the value of all taxable purchases made in the county. CBER calculates sales tax base by dividing all county revenue from the local option sales tax rate. The property tax base is the assessed value of all property in the county, rather than actual property tax collected. The statewide tax base is the sum of all counties' tax bases.
29. Data are available at Tennessee Department of Revenue. Collections Spreadsheets by Fiscal Year and Monthly Collections Spreadsheets. Retrieved

from https://www.tn.gov/revenue/tax-resources/statistics-and-collections/collections-spreadsheets-by-fiscal-year.html
30. See, Tennessee Comptroller of the Treasury. Property Assessment. Assessment Information. Tax Aggregate Reports. Retrieved from https://www.tn.gov/revenue/tax-resources/statistics-and-collections/collections-spreadsheets-by-fiscal-year.html
31. An overview, although the numerical values are for FY16, is presented in the *Tennessee Basic Education Program Handbook for Computation* produced by the Tennessee Department of Education. Office of Local Finance. Retrieved from https://www.tn.gov/content/dam/tn/stateboardofeducation/documents/BEPHandbook_revised_July_2016.pdf
32. T.C.A. 49-3-356. State and local contributions to BEPs funds.
33. School districts that receive BEP funding are Bradford Special School District, Franklin Special School District, Gibson County Special School District, Hollow Rock-Bruceton Special School District, Huntingdon Special School District, Lebanon Special School District, McKenzie Special School District, Milan Special School District, Oneida Special School District, Paris Special School District, Richard City Special School District, South Carroll Special School District, Trenton Special School District, and West Carroll Special School District.
34. Tennessee Department of Education, Special Education Guidelines and Standards (2013).
35. Budget Overview, 2018–19. Retrieved from https://www.tn.gov/content/dam/tn/finance/budget/documents/overviewspresentations/19AdReq16.pdf
36. U.S. Department of Education. Office of Career, Technical and Adult Education. Retrieved from https://s3.amazonaws.com/PCRN/docs/Estimated_FY2018_Perkins_State_Allocations.pdf
37. Tennessee Department of Education. Office of Research and Policy. (March 2015). *Charter Schools 2015 Annual Report.* Retrieved from https://www.tn.gov/content/dam/tn/education/nonpublic/chtr_sch/chtr_sch_annual_report.pdf and the U.S. Department of Education. National Center for Education Statistics. Common Core of Data (CCD). (2017). *Table 216.90 Public Elementary and secondary charter schools by state: Selected Years 2001 through 2015–16.* https://nces.ed.gov/programs/digest/d17/tables/dt17_216.90.asp
38. Tenn. Code Ann. 49-16-103. Use of funds. [in Virtual education]
39. Tennessee State Report Card. 2016–17. Retrieved from https://www.tn.gov/education/data/report-card.html

CHAPTER 45

Texas

Lynn M. Moak, Ph.D.
Partner
Moak, Casey & Associates

Mary P. McKeown-Moak, Ph.D.
Consultant
Moak, Casey & Associates

GENERAL BACKGROUND

"The history of public school finance in Texas has been one of slow development marked by periodic neglect, intermittent crisis, and sporadic reform."[1] Almost 200 years ago, Texas began providing support for schools in 1827 when the Mexican state of Coahuila y Texas provided land grants and municipal funds for educational purposes.[2] After Texas gained its independence from Mexico, the Education Act of 1839 furthered land grants that today form the basis of County Permanent School Funds, and the Constitution of 1845 provided the first state funding of free schools with a minimum of 1/10 of the revenue from a state property tax to fund schools. The following year, several cities obtained the right to establish local taxes to support schools.[3] The School Law of 1854 provided a permanent endowment fund distributed on a per-capita basis which operated as a voucher system, with funds following the student to whatever school parents chose.[4] The Constitution of 1876 established the basic funding for schools: a flat, per capita amount from the Available School Fund consisting of income from the Permanent School Fund, a maximum of 1/4 general revenue and a poll tax of $1 on all males aged 21 to 60.[5] The Texas constitution states "A general diffusion of knowledge being essential to the preservation of the liberties and rights of the people, it shall be the duty of the Legislature of the State to establish and make suitable provision for the support and maintenance of an efficient system of public free schools."[6] Following the actions in the 1870s, funding issues were largely neglected until 1915. Between 1915 and 1949, funding for rural high schools, textbooks, and equity for rural schools were added. In 1949, the legislature adopted a minimum foundation program that used a complicated economic index to determine the local share, with the state providing 80% of funds.[7]

For the last 50 years, Texas school funding has been challenged in court many times and has gone from rulings that the system was constitutional but chaotic and unjust,[8] to unconstitutional,[9] to constitutional,[10] to unconstitutional,[11] and back to constitutional but flawed and imperfect.[12] In 1968, *Rodriguez v. San Antonio ISD* was filed in federal court, asserting that the state's school finance system discriminated against students in poor districts. In late 1971, a U.S. District Court held the state's finance method unconstitutional, but in 1973 the U.S. Supreme Court reversed the lower court's findings, declaring the system constitutional but unjust[13] since large differences in property wealth led to large differences in per-pupil funding. After *Rodriguez,* all filings were in the state's courts rather than federal courts.

In 1984, House Bill (HB) 72 made changes to the finance system, some of which are still in effect: a guaranteed yield program, a price differential index, FTE count of students, equalization aid, and a form of hold-harmless for districts losing state funds. In 1989, increasing the basic allotment, changing special education weights, replacing the price differential index with a cost-of-education index, and adding a second tier based on tax effort and a guaranteed yield were added. In 1990, Senate Bill (SB) 1 made substantial changes to address the court's findings in the *Edgewood* case, including a five-year phase-in of reform; 95% of students would be in a wealth-neutral system; increased the local share of the Foundation School Program (FSP); increased the guaranteed yield in the power-equalized second tier system; raised the tax rate the state would match; and other efficiency reforms. In 1993 after voters rejected a constitutional amendment to authorize tax base sharing at the county level, SB 7 required that districts above a specified level of wealth per student[14] engage in tax rate reduction or 'recapture' by choosing one of five options to limit access to property value above the equalized wealth level of $280,000 per weighted student (WADA).[15] [16] At that time, 104 school districts had property wealth above $280,000 per WADA.[17] Those wealthy districts were given five years to choose among available options and were protected by a hold-harmless. By 2018, 191 school districts were subject to recapture, and over $2.07 billion was projected to be recaptured.[18] Only two options for recaptured funds, both of which require voter approval, have been used in the last 25 years: pay the state, or pay another school district. SB 7 made other changes, including adding a new special education weight for mainstreamed students, reducing the basic allotment, increasing the local fund requirement for Tier 1, and eliminating proration when state appropriations were insufficient to fund the formula by creating a 'settle-up' process near the end of the year. SB 7 was challenged as unconstitutional by several groups, and the court declared funding to be constitutional and further addressed the concept of adequacy by linking the constitutional provision for a general diffusion of knowledge to the goals for public education in Chapter 4 of the Texas Education Code.

Numerous changes to the finance system were made between 1995 and 2014. In 1999, the temporary hold-harmless for wealthy districts was made permanent, and by 2017–18, 26 of the original districts were still held harmless. Among the most notable of other changes to the law were the addition of a facilities grant program and reduction or compression of tax rates to provide tax relief. School districts that lost property tax revenues due to the 2006 compression of tax rates were held harmless through 'Additional State Aid for Tax Reduction' (ASATR, which was in effect until 2017). For 2018 and 2019, financial hardship grants were being made to 127 school districts to continue the hold-harmless under the tax compression hold-harmless.

In 2014 in *Texas Taxpayer & Student Fairness Coalition et.al. v Scott*,[19] the district court ruled that the finance system was unconstitutional. On appeal, the Texas supreme court ruled in 2016 that the school finance system, although flawed and imperfect, was constitutional, and further that the legislature was responsible for designing the system. Unless the legislature made arbitrary or unreasonable choices, the court would defer to the legislature. In response, a School Finance Commission was established which is studying the system and will issue a report in time for the 2019 legislative session.

Not many changes were made during the 2017 session, as the state legislature focused on bathrooms and voucher programs, neither of which passed. One important change was that charter schools were made eligible for facilities funding. And, 15% ($236 million) of the estimated $1.58 billion to be spent on prekindergarten programs must be spent for 'high quality' prekindergarten programs as defined in the Texas Education Code.[20] Moreover, there are so many 'fine tuning' adjustments or exceptions to the formulas or calculations that make intimate knowledge of the entire finance system a necessity for calculating the correct amount of a district's state funding.

To summarize Texas court rulings on the school finance system, in 1989 and 1991 in *Edgewood I* and *II*, the system was ruled unconstitutional on equity grounds. In 1993, in *Edgewood III*, the system was ruled unconstitutional on statewide property tax grounds, but in 1995, in *Edgewood IV*, the supreme court ruled the system constitutional. In 2005, in *West Orange Cove*, the system was ruled unconstitutional again on statewide property tax grounds. In 2011, in *Texas Taxpayers*, the system was again ruled unconstitutional on equity grounds, but did not make a decision on adequacy. In 2016, the state supreme court determined that the legislature had failed to make the system whole, but the legislature had not failed so badly that the system was unconstitutional, thereby taking the courts out of school finance.

REVENUE

Texas has not been immune to general fluctuations in the U.S. economy. In 2011, declines in state revenues required deep cuts to state government funding, and state aid to school districts was reduced by about $4 billion. Some of those reductions were made up in the 2014–16 biennium, but total state appropriations remain below prior levels. This is partly due to increasing property values which reduces the amounts needed for state funding as calculated in the total FSP Tier 1 and Tier 2 allotments as explained later.

In the 2017–18 school year, total Texas funding for public education was estimated at $61 billion, comprised of $32.2 billion (53%) in property taxes, $23.6 billion (39%) in state aid, and $5.2 billion (8%) in federal resources. In the 2018–19 school year, property tax revenues were projected to provide 56% of revenue, while state aid dropped to 35%.[21] Public education educated 5.4 million students enrolled in 1,231 school districts and charter schools. School districts varied in size from seven students in ADA to 194,000 students. Approximately 875 school districts, with about 20% of the state's total ADA, enrolled fewer than 5,000 students, and 679 of those districts enrolled fewer than 1,600 students.

Funding totals included not only aid for school districts, but also funding for the 20 Regional Education Service Centers, the State School for the Blind, State School for the Deaf, the Texas Education Agency operations, and state payments of about $2.6 billion to the Teacher Retirement System (TRS) on behalf of public education employees. Contributions to TRS were made by the state, school districts, and the employee.

The majority of state funds are distributed to school districts and charter schools through the FSP. For 2017–18, $21.5 billion of state funds were appropriated for school operations and facilities. The FSP, the Property Tax Relief Fund, the Technology and Instructional Materials Fund, the General Revenue Fund, and the Available School Fund combine to provide state aid, most of which is formula-driven. In addition, the Permanent School Fund, which is an endowment fund created in the 1800s, provides investment income deposited in the Available School Fund.

Federal funds generally are used for the school lunch program, title programs, and special education. Some federal funding is received for career and technical education, migrant education, and special grants. For 2018–19, federal funds were projected to total $5.3 billion (9%) of total school revenues.

Local tax revenues for schools are paid by individual and business property owners on the taxable value of their property, after adjustments and certain exemptions. School districts are authorized to tax up to $1.17 per $100 in property value for maintenance and operations, and up to $0.50 on voter-authorized bonds approved by the state's attorney general. If property value declines after the bond issue, the rate is permitted to rise above $0.50 to make debt service payments. In 2017–18, school districts collected $25.5 billion in property taxes for maintenance and operations, and $6.7 billion for facilities.

BASIC SUPPORT PROGRAM

The Texas school finance system is based on a complex series of formula adjustments that begin with consideration for economy of scale (size) effects and a unique cost index developed in 1990 for each traditional independent school district (ISD). These factors then are applied to a tax rate level modified basic allotment to create the base funding level known as the 'adjusted allotment' that is then modified for special programs and adjustments. All charter schools have the same basic allotment and adjusted allotment funding level based on state ISD average basic allotment and adjusted allotment. The simple unweighted state average of each adjusted allotment is summed and divided by the count of districts to create a charter level adjusted allotment for all charter schools. After this stage, the adjusted allotment for a charter school is supplemented by the same adjustments used for ISDs.

School districts and charter schools are funded by a two-tier funding system based on the average daily attendance of students. The basic funding formula is called the 'Foundation School Program (FSP).'[22] Legislatively adopted state policy calls for the system to provide both adequacy and equity for the public schools. Traditional public school district funding is a shared responsibility between taxpayers and the state. The FSP has four basic variables: the number of students, the types of students, the property values in the district, and the tax rate applied to that property value. Each school district and each open-enrollment charter school is guaranteed a basic revenue level, with additional revenue allotted for pupils participating in special education, career and technology education, bilingual education, compensatory education and/or gifted and talented programs, and for the size of the district based on a series of weights or special allotments.

Although funding is allocated based on the type of student, the state grants school districts the flexibility to expend dollars to best meet overall student needs, within the maintenance of effort provisions for federal funds and within the rules of §29 and §42 of the Texas Education Code.

Tier I

For public school districts, Tier 1 of the formula is a basic foundation program, with a basic allotment per pupil and a series of weights for student and district characteristics. Each district that receives transportation assistance also receives an amount for transportation, for new instructional facilities, for high schools, virtual education, staff salary adjustments for auxiliary employees, and for any homestead exemptions. The total cost is shared between the state and the school district. The district's share is determined by applying a maintenance and operations (M&O) tax rate to the district's taxable property value for the prior year, and then the state pays any amounts between the total cost and the district share. More wealthy districts pay larger shares of their total entitlement, while the district's share remains the same, regardless of how many fewer or additional students there may be. The wealthiest districts pay most of the full cost of Tier 1 and an additional amount to meet equity standards through the recapture provisions of Chapter 41, TEC.

The basic allotment is an amount that every school district is guaranteed to receive from the combination of state and local funds (as described above) for each student in Average Daily Attendance (ADA). ADA is defined clearly in the Texas Education Agency's (TEA) Student Attendance Accounting Manual; attendance records are turned in for every child by six-week period, with certain exceptions for migrant students. The count is taken at 10:00 a.m. each day. The basic allotment was $5,140 per ADA for Fiscal Years 2018 and 2019 for those districts with a compressed M&O tax effort of $1.00 per $100 of taxable value (or one mill) in 2016 as certified by the Comptroller. Districts with lower tax effort are provided a reduced basic allotment.

The basic allotment for each traditional school district is adjusted for certain district characteristics to determine the Adjusted Allotment (AA), which is then used in the formulas. The basic allotment is multiplied by a 'Cost of Education Index' (CEI). Each ISD is assigned a CEI that is designed to recognize cost differences beyond the control of the school district, and includes variables for the average beginning salary of teachers in contiguous districts, the number of economically disadvantaged students in the district, the size of the district, and whether the district is in a rural county. CEIs range from 1.02 to 1.20. The CEI has not been recalculated since 1991 and is applied to 71% of the basic allotment.

In addition, to recognize that small or mid-sized districts cannot take advantage of economies of scale, a small size adjustment is added for districts with less than 1,600 ADA. In FY 2018, 679 school districts enrolling less than 10% of all the state's students qualified for the small district adjustment. Also, small districts with over 300 square miles in area receive a 37% larger increase. Beginning in 2019, the adjustment for districts with less than 300 square miles is set to increase over five years until the two adjustments for square miles are equal. Currently, 66 low enrollment districts (less than 130 students) also receive the sparsity adjustment. A mid-size adjustment is added for districts with between 1,601 and 5,000 ADA; 194 districts enrolling 12% of the state's students currently qualify for the mid-size adjustment.

In Tier I, the AA is the greater of the adjusted basic allotment (includes the CEI adjustment), the adjusted basic allotment modified for a small district, or the adjusted basic allotment modified for a mid-size district. For FY 2018, the AA varied by school district (depending on the characteristics of the district) from $4,631 to $9,008 and averaged $6,519.[23]

All charter schools have the same basic allotment and adjusted allotment funding level based on state ISD average basic allotment and adjusted allotment. The simple unweighted state average of each adjusted allotment is summed and divided by the count of districts to create a charter level adjusted allotment for all charter schools ($6,508 for FY 2018). After this stage, the allotment for a charter school is supplemented by the same adjustments used for ISDs. The formula for charter schools is substantially different from the formula for districts, in that amounts are based on state average allotments, not an allotment based on the individual characteristics of the charter. In particular, the basic allotment, the adjusted basic allotment, and the adjusted allotment amount are all set to state averages that were determined using a district-level analysis (all district amounts are summed and then divided by the number of districts). Additionally, Tier 2 funding (see next section) uses uniform measures of tax rates derived from similar averaging of the observed tax rates in each ISD. Use of the unweighted averages for the charter schools effectively treats charters schools as if they were all small districts with less than 1,600 students.

To calculate the Tier I entitlement, the adjusted allotment is multiplied by the number of students in each category of the student population and by the weight for that category of students. These amounts are then summed, together with amounts for transportation. From that total is subtracted the school district's share for Tier I. The ISD share is determined by applying the district's compressed M&O rate to the taxable value for the prior year and dividing by 100. If the school district's share exceeds the total for Tier I, the school district must remit the overage to the state as recapture or

'Robin Hood' funds. Then, amounts for supplemental salary adjustments, additional aid for homestead exemptions, and any hold-harmless amounts are added to determine the Tier I state aid. If the district is a recapture district, then the amount calculated for the Available School Fund distribution of $207 per ADA is added to the total state funds. Weights, number of students or staff, and total amount generated for each category are shown in Table 45.1. Most weights have not been changed for over 30 years.

Tier 2

Tier 2 is the guaranteed yield portion of funding and is used by districts to supplement revenue received in Tier 1. School districts may tax above the compressed tax rate of $1.00, up to a statutory cap of $1.17. If the ISD's compressed rate is less than $1.00, then the district has more discretion. The first $0.04 may be taxed without voter approval, but the remaining $0.13 requires voter approval unless the district is in an area designated as 'disaster'. By 2018, all school districts had levied the $0.04 not needing voter approval, and 773 districts had voter approval to levy some or all the remaining $0.13. The state equalizes revenue raised by each penny above the compressed rate, so that every ISD is guaranteed a minimum amount of state and local revenue per WADA per penny of enrichment tax.

However, WADA is not 'weighted average daily attendance' as conventionally defined, but rather a number calculated by dividing the total cost of Tier 1, with some deductions (the transportation allowance, the high school allowance, the new instructional facilities allotment, and 50% of the CEI adjustment), by the basic allotment. WADA is supposed to represent the number of students for which a district receives funding after adjusting for special needs. WADA calculated for charters is not the equivalent of WADA calculated for ISDs, largely due to the significant role of the small school allotments and the CEI. In FY 2018, there were 5,061,065 students in ADA, and 6,894,991 in WADA, including charter school students.

There are two parts to Tier 2: Level 1 'Golden Pennies' and Level 2 'Copper Pennies.' Level 1 local funds are not subject to recapture, but Level 2 local funds are subject to recapture. In Level 1, for each of the first six pennies above the compressed rate, the state supplements the amount generated to reach the amount per WADA generated by Austin ISD, which was estimated in the General Appropriations Bill to be $99.41 in FY 2018 and $106.28 in FY 2019. For example, if a district's taxable value generates $40.00 per penny per WADA, the state supplements those funds by $59.41 per penny per WADA. In FY 2018, TEA estimated that property values per WADA varied from $17,674 to $8,190,567.[24] These six pennies were *not* subject to recapture. The remaining pennies up to the statutory cap of $1.17

TABLE 45.1 Weights and Allotments in the 2017–18 Texas School Finance Formulas

Type of Student/ Program	Definition	Weight/Amount	Number of Students/Staff	Total Amount
Regular program	ADA students enrolled in regular program, not including special education (except for mainstream) or career/technology	1.00	4,749,683	$26,756,364,736
Special Education	12 weights from 1.1 to 5.0 based on FTE	1.1–5.0	121,712	$3,020,609,862
Career & Technology	FTE enrolled in grades 9–12 or disabled students in grades 7–12	1.35	285,715	$2,219,609,862
Advanced Career & Technology Education	FTE Students who take 2 or more advanced career or technology courses	$50 per ADA	4	$200
Bilingual	ADA Students with limited English proficiency	0.10 add on	899,166	$516,668,746
Compensatory Education	ADA Economically disadvantaged, at risk	0.20 add on	3,470,460	$4,009,651,368
Compensatory Education–Pregnant	ADA Pregnant students at risk of dropping out	2.41	943	$13,000,000
Gifted and Talented	ADA Students performing at a high level. Capped at 5% of a district's ADA	0.12 add-on	237,541	$162,135,150
High School Students	ADA Students in grades 9–12	$275 per ADA	1,433,588	$393,616,080
New Instructional Facility Equipment	ADA Students attending a newly built campus	$1,000 per ADA	23,750	$23,750,000
Staff Allotment	Full-time and part-time employees who are not administrators or subject to the minimum salary schedule	$500 per full-time and $250 per part-time	278,451 full-time and 21,971 part-time	$144,718,250
Transportation	$.68–$1.43 per mile of approved bus route based on number of students per square mile	$0.68–$1.43 per bus route mile	N/A	$376,145,451
Technology and Instructional Materials	Funding for instructional materials and technology	% of statewide ADA	5,061,065	$1.09 billion for the biennium
Available School Fund	Earnings from Permanent School Fund based on prior year ADA	$206.566 per ADA	4,969,638	$1,026,913,884

Source: Texas Education Agency 2017–18 Statewide Summary of Finance updated May 11, 2018. Includes charter schools.

are equalized in Tier 2, Level 2, the so-called Copper Pennies, up to the level of $31.95 per WADA. Revenues generated by local taxes in excess of $31.95 per WADA are subject to recapture.

Table 45.2 displays the calculation of the Foundation School Program allocations for a property-poor school district while Table 45.3 displays calculation for a property-wealthy or Chapter 41 school district. In addition to the adjustments shown in these examples, there are many other adjustments that may be made in the calculation of a district's allocation from the FSP, including hold-harmless provisions that are in effect for certain school districts. Calculation of a district's entitlement is a very complicated process requiring extensive knowledge of the many different rules governing Texas school funding.

CAREER AND TECHNOLOGY

Districts receive an add-on weight of 0.35 for each full-time equivalent student (FTE) in grades 9–12, or in grades 7–12 if the student is disabled, where FTE is defined as 30 hours of contact per week between a student and school personnel. These students are not included in the regular program count; there were an estimated 286,031 FTE in FY 2018 and a total program allotment of $2,219,650,535. In addition, for students taking two or more advanced career and technology courses for a total of three credits, or an advanced course as part of tech-prep program, a district would receive $50. Only four ADA pupils were estimated to be enrolled in the advanced program for FY 2018 at a total allotment of $200. Expenditures of the funds must be made under the rules in §42.154 and Subchapter F of §29 of the TEC.

SPECIAL EDUCATION

Districts receive additional funding to provide services for special education. Special education pupils are those students aged 3 to 21 with disabilities or a special condition. The allotment is based on a set of 12 different weights depending not on the special education condition but on the method of serving the student. The weights are multiplied by the FTE student count, where FTE is defined as 30 hours of contact per week between a student and school personnel. Weights vary from 1.1 to 5.0; 121,742 FTE were included in FY 2018 at a program amount of over $3 billion. Special education students are not included in the count of regular students, except for mainstreamed students. Uses of the funds must be made under the rules in §42.151 and Subchapter A of §29 of the TEC.

TABLE 45.2 Calculation of State and Local Revenues for a Property Poor District for 2017–18

	# Students	Type of Student	Weight	Total
$5,651	42,859	Regular Program ADA	1.00	$242,196,209
$5,651	2,153	Special Ed mainstream FTE	1.10	$13,383,263
$5,651	2	Special Ed Vocational Adj. Class FTE	2.30	$25,995
$5,651	25	Special Ed Off Home Campus FTE	2.70	$381,442
$5,651	400	Special Ed Resource Room FTE	3.00	$6,781,200
$5,651	458	Special Ed Self Contained FTE	3.00	$7,764,474
$5,651	10	Special Ed Hospital Class FTE	3.00	$169,530
$5,651	25	Special Ed Residential Care FTE	4.00	$565,100
$5,651	92	Special Ed Speech Therapy FTE	5.00	$2,599,460
$5,651	4	Special Ed Homebound FTE	5.00	$113,020
$5,651	2,314	Career and Technology FTE	1.35	$17,653,159
$5,651	50,755	Compensatory Education Prior year free & reduced lunch count	0.20	$57,363,301
$5,651	12	Compensatory Ed Pregnant ADA	2.41	$163,427
$5,651	2,309	Gifted and Talented ADA	0.12	$1,565,779
$5,651	7,755	Bilingual ADA	0.10	$4,382,350
$5,651	0	PEG ADA	0.10	$—
$275	11,562	High School ADA		$3,179,550
$—	0	ADA attending new high school		$—
$50	0	ADA taking advanced Career & Tech		$—
$400	0	ADA successfully completing virtual course		$—
$80	0	Students from district taking virtual course		$—
		Transportation Allotment		$2,517,648
Tier 1 Total				$360,804,907

(*continued*)

TABLE 45.2 Calculation of State and Local Revenues for a Property Poor District for 2017–18

School District's Share Tier 1	$1.00 × 16,028,720,310/100		$(160,287,203)
State Share, Tier 1			$200,517,704
Supplemental Staff Salary	$500 × 3,343 $250 × 0		$1,671,500
Additional State Aid for Tax Reduction			$—
State Aid, Tier 1 (financed partly by ASF Distribution of $206.566 × 46,431)			$202,189,204
Tier 2			
M&O Rate = $1.17	Golden Pennies = $0.06 Copper Pennies = $0.11		WADA = 65,960
	Wealth per WADA = $209,723		
Tier 2 Guarantee	($99.41 × 6 × 65,960) + ($31.95 × 11 × 65,960)		$62,524,144
Less Local Revenue	16,028,720,312 / 100 × $0.17		$(27,248,824)
State Aid, Tier 2			$35,275,320
Instructional Materials Allotment			
Instructional Materials Allotment	$9,900,300		$9,900,300

	Tier 1	Instructional Materials Allotment	Tier 2	Total	
State	$202,189,204	$9,900,300	$35,275,320	$247,364,824	57%
Local	$160,287,203	$—	$27,248,824	$187,536,027	43%
Total	**$362,476,407**	**$9,900,300**	**$62,524,144**	**$434,900,851**	
		State and Local Revenue per WADA		$6,593	

Source: Pace, S. op. cit. p. 22

TABLE 45.3 Calculation of State and Local Revenues for a Property Wealthy District for 2017–18

	# Students	Type of Student	Weight	Total
$5,651	4,409	Regular Program ADA	1.00	$24,302,408
$5,651	97	Special Ed mainstream FTE	1.10	$588,130
$5,651	6	Special Ed Vocational Adj. Class FTE	2.30	$76,065
$5,651	5	Special Ed Off Home Campus FTE	2.70	$74,412
$5,651	61	Special Ed Resource Room FTE	3.00	$1,008,696
$5,651	14	Special Ed Self Contained FTE	3.00	$231,504
$5,651	0	Special Ed Hospital Class FTE	3.00	$—
$5,651	0	Special Ed Residential Care FTE	4.00	$—
$5,651	8	Special Ed Speech Therapy FTE	5.00	$220,480
$5,651	0	Special Ed Homebound FTE	5.00	$—
$5,651	97	Career and Technology FTE	1.35	$721,796
$5,651	1,101	Compensatory Education Prior year free & reduced lunch count	0.20	$1,213,742
$5,651	0	Compensatory Ed Pregnant ADA	2.41	$—
$5,651	230	Gifted and Talented ADA	0.12	$152,131
$5,651	239	Bilingual ADA	0.10	$131,737
$5,651	0	PEG ADA	0.10	$—
$275	1,484	High School ADA		$408,100
$—	0	ADA attending new high school		$—
$50	0	ADA taking advanced Career & Tech		$—
$400	0	ADA successfully completing virtual ed course		$—
$80	0	Students from district taking virtual course		$—
		Transportation Allotment		$188,875
Tier 1 Total				$29,318,076

(continued)

TABLE 45.3 Calculation of State and Local Revenues for a Property Wealthy District for 2017–18

School District's Share Tier 1	$1.00 × 6,476,546,388/100		$(64,765,464)	
State Share, Tier 1	Recaptured local revenue		$(35,447,388)	
Supplemental Staff Salary	$500 × 194 $250 × 30		$104,500	
Additional State Aid for Tax Reduction			$481,174	
State Aid, Tier 1 (financed partly by ASF Distribution of $206.566 × 4,617 = $955,719)			$1,541,393	
Tier 2				
M&O Rate = $1.06	"Golden Pennies" = $0.06 "Copper Pennies" = $0.00		WADA = 5,439	
	Wealth per WADA = $1,190,760			
Tier 2 Guarantee	($99.41 × 6 × 5,439)		$3,244,146	
Less Local Revenue	6,476,546,388 / 100 × $0.06 (not recaptured)		$(3,885,928)	
State Aid, Tier 2			$—	
			$909,413	
Instructional Materials Allotment				
	Tier 1	Instructional Materials Allotment	Tier 2	Total
State	$1,541,393	$909,413	$—	$2,450,806	7%
Local	$29,318,076	$—	$3,885,928	$33,204,004	93%
Total	$30,859,469	$909,413	$3,885,928	$35,654,810	
		State and Local Revenue per WADA	$6,555		

Source: Pace, S. op. cit. p. 23

COMPENSATORY EDUCATION

Districts receive a .20 add-on weight to the regular program funding for services to students who are performing below grade level or who are at risk of dropping out of school. Funding is based on the number of students eligible for the federal free and reduced meal program in the prior year. Approximately 3.5 million students met the eligibility criteria for the 2017–18 school year, and more than $4.0 billion was allotted. School districts received an additional weight of 2.41 for the 943 students who were at risk of dropping out of school due to pregnancy, an allocation of $13 million. Expenditures of the funds must be made under the rules in §42.152 and Subchapter C of §29 of the TEC.

BILINGUAL

Districts receive an add-on weight of 0.10 for students who have limited English proficiency, students whose primary language is not English, and those whose language skills are such that the student has difficulty performing ordinary class work at an acceptable level in English, and who are in a bilingual program. In FY 2018, there were an estimated 899,166 students classified as bilingual, ESL, or limited English proficient, generating allotments of $516,668,746. Expenditures of the funds must be made under the rules in §42.153 and Subchapter B of §29 of the TEC.

GIFTED AND TALENTED

In addition to regular program funding, districts receive a 0.12 add-on weight for students who perform at a high level of accomplishment, or show the potential to achieve. The number of students is capped at 5% of a district's ADA. For 2017–18, an estimated 237,541 students were included in Gifted and Talented programs, for an estimated total allotment of $162,135,150. Expenditures of the funds must be made under the rules in §42.156 and Subchapter D of §29 of the TEC.

HIGH SCHOOL

Districts receive an additional $275 per ADA for students enrolled in grades 9–12. An estimated 1,433,584 students were enrolled in high school in 2017–18, resulting in an allotment of $393,616,080.

STUDENTS IN NEW INSTRUCTIONAL FACILITIES

Districts receive an additional $1,000 per ADA for every student attending a newly built campus in the campus' first year of operation, and for additional students attending in the second year. The total statewide appropriation for this purpose is limited by statute to $25 million. The legislature appropriated $23,750,000 for the 2017–18 school year for the estimated 23,750 students in new instructional facilities.

TRANSPORTATION

Districts receive funding for school transportation on a density formula that allocates between $0.68 and $1.43 per mile of approved bus routes, based on the number of students per square mile. To be eligible for transportation, a student must live more than two miles from campus unless there is a safety issue. Reimbursement rates have not changed since 1983, despite large increases in the cost of transportation. For 2017–18, the transportation allotment totaled $376,145,451. Only 59 of the 1,018 districts do not provide transportation services, although some districts participate in a county-wide transportation district. For the remaining districts, state law permits the district to charge a reasonable fee for transporting a student to and from school if the district does not receive a transportation allowance and does not participate in a county transportation system that does receive an allotment.

STAFF ALLOTMENT

In the 2017–18 school year, each district received $500 for each full-time employee and $250 for each part-time employee who is not an administrator or subject to a minimum salary schedule, which includes mostly auxiliary employees. These funds were intended to supplement salaries, and were fully funded by the state. An estimated $144,718,250 was provided for 278,451 full-time and 21,971 part-time employees. This allocation is a remnant of a much larger 2001 program for health insurance.

TECHNOLOGY AND INSTRUCTIONAL MATERIALS

Since 2011, 50% of the distribution from the Permanent School Fund to the Available School Fund must be deposited into the Technology and Instructional Materials Fund to be distributed by the Commissioner to school districts in the form of a technology and instructional materials allotment. The Commissioner creates an account for each school district and charter school into which funds are deposited at the beginning of the biennium, allocated based on the percentage of statewide ADA in the district or charter school. Funds may be withdrawn as needed during the biennium, and some districts withdraw the funds at the beginning of the two-year period. For the 2017–19 biennium, school districts and charter schools allocated about $1.09 billion. The Instructional Materials Allotment is added to the state revenue AFTER calculations of the amounts for Tier I and Tier 2.

AVAILABLE SCHOOL FUND

As indicated earlier, the Texas constitution requires that earnings from the Permanent School Fund be distributed to districts on a per-student basis. For 2017–18, approximately $1,026,913,884 from the Available School Fund (ASF) was distributed to school districts based on a rate of $206.566 for each of the 4,969,638 students in ADA in the prior year. For school districts that receive state funding from the Foundation School Program (FSP), the ASF distribution replaces FSP aid on a dollar for dollar basis. If a district has local funds recaptured, then the ASP calculation is added to the staff salary allotment and other special allotments such as aid for homestead exemptions to determine total Tier I state aid.

SCHOOL FACILITIES

Texas school districts may issue bonds to pay for the purchase of property, construction, acquisition, and equipment of a building or for purchase of school buses. Voters authorize the school district to adopt the tax rate needed to repay the principal and interest on a bond before bonds are issued. Texas school districts can adopt interest and sinking (I&S) tax rates up to $0.50 to generate revenue used to fund the annual debt service payments associated with bonds. Districts may go beyond the 50¢ limit if the property tax base declines after the tax rate is approved by the voters. Almost all Texas school district debt is guaranteed under the Permanent School Fund, which impacts the bond rating favorably. The state assists school districts to pay for facilities through two programs, the Instructional Facilities Allotment (IFA) and the Existing Debt Allotment (EDA). Funding formulas for facilities are similar to Tier II of the FSP because they work on a guaranteed yield per penny of tax effort per student. However, facilities funding formulas use ADA instead of the WADA used in Tier II, and facilities funds are not subject to recapture. Formulas have not been changed since 1999.

Both of the formulas or allotments are guaranteed yield programs that assist school districts with debt payments on bonds. The IFA was authorized in 1997 to assist with new instructional facilities. The state guarantees $35 per student in ADA for each penny levied for these facilities, and districts must apply to the TEA for funds. After TEA receives all requests, applying districts are ranked from lowest property wealth per ADA to the highest, and applications are funded in that order. State funding is limited to the lesser of the actual debt payment, or the greater of $250 per student or $100,000. Funding has not been sufficient to fully fund all requests, and only property-poor districts generally receive this aid.

The EDA was authorized in 1999 to assist districts with debt payments on bonds for which the district had made payments in the last year of the previous biennium and for which the district does not receive aid through the IFA. EDA funds may be used for both instructional and non-instructional facilities. As with the IFA, the state guarantees $35 per student in ADA in combined state and local revenue for each penny levied for these facilities up to $0.29. Beginning in 2018–19, the guarantee increases to the *lesser of* $40 per ADA per penny on interest and sinking fund taxes levied by school districts to pay the principal of and interest on eligible bonds, *or* an amount that would result in a $60 million increase in state aid from the previous yield of $35. The yield for the 2017–2018 school year is estimated to be less than $37.[25] Charter schools with an acceptable accountability rating became eligible in 2018–19 for facilities funding; their allotment is calculated using the state average debt service tax rate for school districts (estimated at 19.9¢) or a rate that delivers $60 million in additional funding (6.9¢) multiplied by the estimated EDA guaranteed yield ($37) multiplied by the charter school's ADA. The funding is to be allocated 50% to charter schools and 50% to ISDs. Charter schools were allowed to have bond debt guaranteed by the PSF beginning in 2018; this is a very controversial provision because charter schools enroll about 10% of the state's ADA.

In 2017–18, 398 school districts received funding totaling $636 million from either EDA or IFA.

SUMMARY

In 2017–18, 1,231 public school districts and charter schools provided educational services to 5.4 million enrolled students. School districts varied in size from 7 to 194,000 enrolled students, although approximately 875 school districts with about 20% of the state's total ADA enrolled fewer than 5,000 students, and 679 districts enrolled fewer than 1,600 students. Total funding for public education was estimated at $61 billion, with 53% of that funding coming from local property tax revenues, 39% from state aid, and 8% from federal funding. Total funding for public education for the

2017–19 biennium totaled $105.72 billion and was comprised of $59.5 billion (51%) local property tax revenues, $45.85 billion (40%) state revenues, and $10.4 billion (9%) federal revenues. Most state funding was distributed by a two-tiered funding formula where Tier 1 is a foundation program with recapture, while Tier 2A is guaranteed yield funding with no recapture, and Tier 2B is guaranteed yield funding with recapture.

NOTES

1. Stephen B. Thomas and B.D. Walker. (1982). "Texas School Finance," *Journal of Education Finance* p. 223–24, Vol. 8, No. 2, pp. 223–281.
2. Billy D. Walker and W. Kirby. (1986). *The Basics of Texas Public School Finance.* Austin, TX: Texas Association of School Boards.
3. Daniel T. Casey. *The Basics of Texas Public School Finance, Sixth Edition.* 1996. Austin, TX: Texas Association of School Boards.
4. Thomas and Walker (1982) p. 228.
5. Texas *State Constitution of 1876,* Article VII, Section 3.
6. Texas *State Constitution of 1876,* Article VII, Section 1.
7. Ibid Casey (1996) p. 11.
8. *San Antonio ISD v Rodriguez,* 411 U.S. 1 (1973).
9. *Edgewood ISD v Bynum* (1984); *Edgewood v Kirby* (1990); *Carrolton Farmers Branch ISD v Edgewood ISD* (1991).
10. *Edgewood ISD v Meno* (1993).
11. *West Orange Cove v Neeley* (2001); *Texas Taxpayer & Student Fairness Coalition et.al. v Scott* (2011).
12. Ruling of the Texas Supreme Court in *Texas Taxpayer & Student Fairness Coalition et.al. v Scott* (2014).
13. *San Antonio ISD v Rodriguez,* 411 U.S. 1 (1973).
14. Districts above the wealth level are called "Chapter 41" districts. In 2018, the Texas Education Agency report that there were 191 Chapter 41 districts, 26 of which are hold harmless districts.
15. Sheryl Pace (2018). *An Introduction to School Finance in Texas, Fourth Edition.* Austin, Texas: Texas Taxpayer and Research Foundation.
16. It is important to note that the weighted student or WADA is not "weighted average daily attendance" as defined in most school finance formulas; for a more complete explanation, see later in the chapter.
17. Ibid. p. 18.
18. Texas Education Agency, Cost of Recapture (n.d.).
19. *Texas Taxpayer & Student Fairness Coalition et.al. v Scott* (2014).
20. (TEC) §29.167-29.171.
21. Ibid.
22. Chapter 42, Texas Education Code (TEC).
23. Ibid, Pace (2018).
24. Ibid, Texas Education Agency (n.d.)..
25. TEA, Texas Public School Finance Overview Presentation, December 2017.

CHAPTER 46

Utah

W. Bryan Bowles, Ed.D.
Associate Clinical Professor
Brigham Young University

Robert W. Smith
Assistant Superintendent
Alpine School District

GENERAL BACKGROUND

Utah's public school finance plan is a modified foundation program, known as the Minimum School Program (MSP).[1] The foundation grant guaranteeing each student a minimum level of fiscal support is only one component of the MSP. The value of the foundation grant, named the Weighted Pupil Unit (WPU), is set each year by the legislature. School districts are required to tax local wealth (assessed valuation) using the program's Basic Tax Rate which is also set by the legislature. The difference between what can be raised locally by the Basic Tax Rate and the amount guaranteed by the state is paid from revenue generated by the state's Uniform School Fund—primarily personal income tax constitutionally earmarked for this purpose. Wealthy districts, using the Basic Tax Rate, are capable of raising revenue greater than the value of the foundation grant, with these monies subject to recapture. Recapture funds become revenue to the Uniform School Fund in the following year. Revenue to the foundation grant is heavily supported by the state, which pays about 80% of total. On average, local school district revenue accounts for $652 (19%) of the $3,395 guarantee by the state per WPU. Such an active effort on the part of the state accounts for the high degree of fiscal equity evident in the state's school finance plan.

Funding Public Schools in the United States and Indian Country, pages 691–715
Copyright © 2019 by Information Age Publishing
All rights of reproduction in any form reserved.

Consistent with the basic structure of a foundation plan, Utah's 41 school districts are able to levy additional taxes (five primary levies) against the value of local property which varies from $170,665 to $2,860,931 per pupil as seen in Figure 46.1. Local tax rates are limited, and several are equalized to some minimum level by the state's finance formula. Additionally,

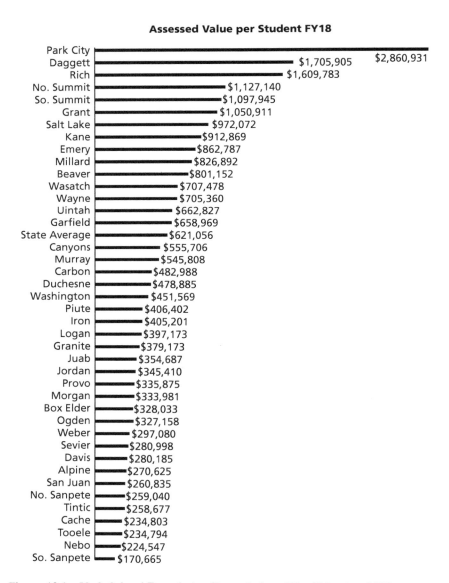

Figure 46.1 Utah School Foundation Formula Local Tax Valuation 2018.

the state contributes significantly to support special services such as special education, applied technology, at-risk programs, class size reduction, and adult education programs. The foundation grant ensures that Utah's 660,028 pupils (projected Fiscal Year 2020, an increase of 1.18% over the prior year) receive some minimum level of fiscal support. The foundation grant, however, only accounts for about 14% of the state's total MSP. In 2018, Utah's state budget appropriated $5.2 billion for public schools, or approximately 31% of Utah's $16.8 billion total operating state budget (up 3.8% from previous year).

Clear principles guide Utah's public school finance statutes:

- All children are entitled to reasonably equal educational opportunities, regardless of place of residence;
- Establishment of a school system is primarily a state function — school districts should pay a portion;
- Each locality should be empowered to provide educational facilities and opportunities beyond the minimum program.

UTAH'S SCHOOL FINANCE PLAN

Prior to statehood in 1896, education in Utah was a local issue with 'ward houses' of The Church of Jesus Christ of Latter-day Saints. Ward houses often served as both church and school. School revenue came in the form of charity, donations, and tuition. A school consolidation movement began about 1890, and with it came the move toward Utah's first real public school system. Beginning with statehood in 1896, Utah's constitution provided for a permanent state school fund and a uniform school fund.[2] The constitution also provided that "all revenue from...a tax on income shall be used to support the systems of public education and higher education."[3]

Utah's 224 school districts were legislatively consolidated to 40 by 1915. In 2009, the Jordan School District split into the Jordan School District and the Canyons School District, so that Utah now has 41 school districts ranging from large urban districts to small rural districts.

The basic school funding mechanism, a foundation aid program, was first established in 1921. State participation was based on state income taxes and local ad valorem property taxes. An equalization component was added in 1931 based on weighted pupil counts and cost differentials. Utah's foundation plan was formalized by 1948, earmarking income taxes for schools. The foundation program was accounted for in the Uniform School Fund. Additionally, a uniform accounting system was established, uniform tax rates were set, and equalization of tax support was guaranteed. State aid for school buildings became part of the funding mechanism at the time.

Federal impact aid, an increased role for property taxes, and locally voted leeway were all added to the funding plan. These components of the funding plan are still largely in place today.

Major school finance reform in 1973 led to improved statewide tax equalization (limited power equalization), along with conversion to weighted pupil units (WPU) promoting vertical equalization. Numerous categorical programs were introduced to the formula, dealing with special services and programs not previously addressed in the funding plan.

Another major reform of Utah's school finance program occurred in 1989. Budgetary and formula changes were implemented, including the establishment of a Capital Outlay Equalization Program and a Capital Foundation Program in 1993. In 2012, House Bill 301 modified the tax rates each school district could levy and established two levels of board levy, depending on current rates assessed. This rate consolidation action created board levy equity issues among the 41 school districts until it was changed in 2018 by HB 293 which established a single board levy cap of .002500.

In 2006, the governor implemented large cuts to the state's individual income taxes. These tax cuts, combined with the effects of the Great Recession, significantly reduced Utah's tax burden, but also decreased amounts of money generated for public schools. And, while a majority of other states raised taxes to make up for revenue declines caused by the recession, Utah avoided such a move by opting for further budget reduction. Additionally, Utah made consistent cuts to the minimum property tax rate, a critical source of education funding, claiming tax relief for businesses and homeowners.

Overall, though, Utah's economy has generally helped public schools. The state's economy was described in the 1998 Economic Report of the Governor's Office of Planning and Budget as the longest sustained economic expansion in the state's history. At the time, Utah's overall economy, the Gross State Product, had grown on average at a rate of over 8% per year after adjusting for inflation. Growth in new jobs had exceeded 3.0% for the last ten consecutive years, with Utah's per-capita income moving from 49th rank among states to 44th during the expansion period. Currently, Utah ranks 39th in per-capita income. These growth rates may have peaked, however, and legislative concern about the state's fiscal future is evident in conservative proposed increases for state funding.

Utah's unique demographic makeup strongly influences public school finance. Utah's high birth rates and young population (31% is under age 18) presents clear funding challenges because Utah has more children to educate and fewer working adults paying into the public education system. As a result, in 2018 Utah spent just $6,575 per pupil per year, a number that is lowest in the nation and more than $4,800 below the national average.

Minimum School Program

The structure for public school funding in Utah, known as the MSP, was created in the early 1970s due to nationwide funding equity conversations. Following broad study and conversation, the MSP framework was put in place by the legislature, with initial funding distributed in 1974. After the MSP was in place for a period of time, a comprehensive review was requested and completed in 1990. Following after, significant changes were made:

- 1998–Utah Charter Schools Act (HB 145S1);
- 2011–School District Property Tax Revisions (HB 301);
- 2015–Property Tax Equalization Amendments (SB 97S3);
- 2016–School Funding Amendments (SB 38S4); and
- 2018 Tax Rebalancing Provisions (HB 293S5).

Equitable funding for all children is one of the primary considerations of Utah's funding model. The legislature recognizes that "all children of the state are entitled to reasonably equal educational opportunities regardless of their place of residence in the state and of the economic situation of their respective school districts or other agencies."[4] In addition, statutes require a secondary consideration regarding reciprocal accountability between the state of Utah and each Local Education Agency (LEA) and the appropriate funding balance so each has 'skin in the game.' Finally, statutes empower each locality to provide educational facilities and opportunities beyond the minimum program. These three guiding principles have kept Utah at the forefront of equitable funding for students in the nation and have encouraged citizens and educational entities to avoid legal challenges to school funding.

Utah's MSP is comprised of the following four core areas: (1) Basic School Program; (2) Related to Basic Programs; (3) Voted and Board Levy Programs; and (4) One-Time Programs. Each is explained next.

Basic School Program

The Basic School Program equalizes funding and distributes dollars to LEAs based on the number of Weighted Pupil Units (WPUs) the LEA generates and the dollar value of the WPU set by the legislature. The WPU value for FY 2019 is $3,395, an increase of $84 (2.54%) over FY 2018. A WPU is generated when a student is in membership for 180 days and 990 clock hours during the prior school year.

Utah law defines WPUs for each program and is different between school districts and charter schools as follows:

District school students		Charter school students	
Kindergarten:	.55 WPUs	Kindergarten:	.55 WPUs
Grades 1 – 12:	1.0 WPUs	Grades 1–6:	.90 WPUs
Special Education:	1.53 WPUs	Grades 7–8:	.99 WPUs
		Grades 9–12:	1.2 WPUs
		Special Education:	1.53 WPUs

LEAs generate dollars based on prior year WPUs plus growth in the current year in the following areas:

- Kindergarten WPUs
- 1–12 Student WPUs

These dollars are unrestricted and comprise a significant part of most LEA budgets. For example, when analyzing FY 2019 state revenue, unrestricted resources in the Basic Program accounted for 56.5% of revenues in this category for the Alpine School District, the largest LEA in Utah serving ~80,000 students.

Also in the Basic Program are revenues that are restricted to use in specific areas. Restrictions include Special Education WPUs, Career and Technical Education (CTE) WPUs, and Class Size Reduction K–8 WPUs. Unrestricted and restricted portions of the Basic Program resources are primarily used for classroom instruction.

Related to Basic Programs

Related to Basic Programs are non-WPU driven programs, often referred to as 'below-the-line.' Such programs are intended by the legislature to complement or enhance the Basic Program and are subject to annual appropriation. The following are a few major areas related to Basic Programs and their allocation methodology:

- *Enhancement for At-Risk*: Base amount + per-student amount;
- *School Land Trust*: Base amount + per-student amount;
- *Flexible allocation*: per-student amount / WPU;
- *Charter school local replacement*: per-student amount / WPU;
- *Pupil transportation to and from school*: qualification criteria comprised of number of miles and minutes driven;
- *Youth in Custody*: qualification criteria;
- *Teacher Salary Supplement*: grant based;
- *Critical languages and dual immersion*: grant based.

Voted and Board Local Levy Programs

As equalization is a primary tenet of Utah's funding priorities, this source recognizes that regardless of where a student lives, the local tax generated will be vastly different and, therefore, additional state resources are provided to improve funding equity per student across the state. The FY 2018 state support of voted and board local levy programs totaled $172 million statewide. State support for FY 2019 for voted and board local levy guarantee programs was estimated at $221 million statewide.

These guaranteed programs establish a minimum revenue amount that is generated for each WPU a school district qualifies to receive, multiplied by tax increments the district levies up to a maximum 20 increments[5] in the voted and board levy programs multiplied by a dollar value set by the legislature. The estimated guarantee value for FY 2019 was $43.10. As an example, District 15 levies 20 increments, has 1,000 WPUs, and the guarantee is $43.10: the district's voted and board local levy program thus guarantees $862,000. If the local property tax only generated $562,000 in revenue, the state would contribute the additional $300,000 to the LEA.

One-Time Programs

The Utah legislature annually supports many one-time programs. These programs are used for specific or special needs and are not expected to continue long-term. Allocations may include resources for Teacher Supplies and Materials, Digital Teaching and Learning grants, and more.[6]

PUPIL TRANSPORTATION

The state of Utah provides funding to school districts to transport pupils if they meet qualifying criteria. Funding is in accordance with the prior year's eligible transportation as legally reported by LEAs. Prior year costs include allowance per mile for approved routes, allowance per minute for approved routes, and a minimum amount for each district. State law notes that the state will "...contribute 85% of approved transportation costs, subject to budget constraints." [7] Costs of equipment and administration are also considered in the funding model. Spending on transportation among districts typically ranges from $277 per pupil to $1,500.

In order to qualify for transportation, a student must live at least 1.5 miles (elementary) or 2.0 miles (secondary) from school. The qualifying distance must be calculated using the most direct route, road, trail or path to the nearest entrance on school property. The district must have at least ten qualifying students for a regular route to be eligible or five qualifying special education students (wheelchair students count as 5). The state also provides reimbursement or 'fee in lieu of transportation' for parents of eligible students as an alternative to busing or when the cost of busing exceeds the reimbursement.

Funds received by LEAs for pupil transportation are restricted by program and are only used for transportation expenses. All school districts subsidize transportation costs with local resources. This funding reality is particularly challenging for rural districts having have significant geographic challenges and isolated student populations.

FOOD SERVICES

All Utah school districts provide full food service programs following state and federal guidelines. Districts provide food services through private vendors, district cooperatives, and in-house departments. Individual districts, by local school board approval, set lunch prices without expectation for consistency throughout the state. About 50–55% of the cost is paid by federal funding. The state of Utah contributes 15–20% of costs on a reimbursement basis through revenue generated from taxes on alcohol. The remaining amount (25–35%) is local revenue generated by lunch sales.

CAPITAL OUTLAY

Funding for capital projects, new school construction and renovation or replacement, including maintenance and repair of facilities, is primarily funded at the local level. Boards of education approve capital improvement plans.

Each school district may levy a tax for capital or technology projects up to a maximum .003 mills per calendar year. Since funds generated in each district vary due to relative wealth and assessed property value per student and with some districts experiencing intense pressure for capital dollars due to rapid growth, the legislature enacted two programs to mitigate the impact of growth, with some equalization of revenue based on local tax effort.

The first capital outlay program is a foundational program, establishing an effort or floor of at least .002400 per dollar of taxable value to qualify for full funding. Should a district levy a combined rate less than the floor, the amount of funding is proportional. The guaranteed amount is based on ADM and assessed value per ADM and distributes the full amount in one lump sum payment to districts based on legislative appropriation. These resources find their way to low wealth districts as well as those having large ADM populations. The FY 2019 foundation guarantee was $27.6 million.

The second capital outlay program is an enrollment growth program recognizing the additional pressure that fast growing districts and taxpayers feel to keep up with the need for construction of new facilities. In order to receive funding in this program, districts must qualify for funding in the capital foundation program mentioned above and have enrollment growth in the past three years. Legislatively appropriated resources are distributed to those districts having an average net increase in enrollment over the prior three years. The FY 2019 enrollment growth program allocation was $5.6 million.

The final capital outlay funding mechanism is found in the statutory school building revolving account. This account was set up to allow short-term loans for school districts and charter schools for construction and renovation of school buildings. The state Superintendent for Public Instruction administers the program, sets amounts of loans, interest rates, and terms of repayment based on an appointed committee's recommendations. Repayment terms are up to five years.

TEACHER RETIREMENT

The Utah Retirement System (URS) was created in 1986 as the state of Utah transitioned from a contributory program to a non-contributory program. Education employers who elected to participate may not withdraw from the system.[8] Employees participating in the contributory program prior to July 1986 received the option to continue participation.

The URS non-contributory program provides defined benefits for eligible employees according to the framework of benefits outlined in state law. Education employees meeting eligibility requirements and who were hired prior to July 1, 2011 are considered members of Tier I benefits. A basic outline of Tier I non-contributory benefits is as follows:

- Unreduced retirement benefits at 30 years of service;
- 2% benefit per year of service;
- Retirement calculated on highest three years of salary average;
- Continuation of service credit if disabled and employer has a qualifying plan.

For example, if a public school teacher accumulated 30 years eligible service with a three-year average salary of $75,000, the retirement benefit would be ~$45,000 per year or 60% of the three-year average salary.

Responding to changes in governmental accounting standards and the impact of the Great Recession, the Utah legislature modified retirement benefits for eligible education employees hired after July 1, 2011, creating a Tier II benefit program. In the Tier II program, eligible employees may choose to participate in a non-contributory program (with reduced benefits as compared to Tier I employees) or a contributory defined contribution program. If no employee election is made, the default is the non-contributory program. A basic outline of Tier II non-contributory system benefits is as follows:

- Unreduced retirement benefits at 35 years of service;
- 1.5% benefit per year of service;
- Retirement calculated on highest five-year salary average;
- Continuation of service credit if disabled and employer has qualifying plan.

For example, if a public school teacher had 35 years eligible service with a five-year average salary of $75,000, the retirement benefit would be ~$39,375 per year or 52.5% of the five-year average salary.

The contributory benefit option for Tier II employees is similar to a 401K program where the employer deposits a required contribution, currently 10% of the employee's salary, into a 401K.

Additional 401K contributions are made by Utah's education entities. Employers contribute an additional 1.5% into employees' 401K without requiring a match from employees. Currently, a few employers choose to contribute a higher percentage than the standard 1.5%.

Education entities also have the option to provide local retirement incentives, including cash payment or insurance eligibility. With accounting changes made by the Governmental Accounting Standards Board (GASB) in 2007, most retired insurance benefits were eliminated in lieu of complying with accounting and trust requirements.

SPECIAL EDUCATION

FY 2019 funding for pupils receiving special education services in Utah totaled slightly over $111.5 million. Funding is provided in the following major categories: Add-On–additional WPUs provided to add on to the regular program; Self-Contained–additional WPUs provided based on the ADA in self-contained programs; and Pre-school–WPUs provided based on actual enrollment of preschool students qualifying as SPED. Additional resources are provided for students who require intensive services and specialized care-giving.

GIFTED AND TALENTED

Funding for Utah's Gifted and Talented programs has been subsumed under the category of Enhancement for Accelerated Learning programs. This funding category includes traditional Gifted and Talented programs, the state's Advanced Placement program, its Concurrent Enrollment program, and its International Baccalaureate program.

Funding for Gifted and Talented programs (about 20% of the Accelerated Learning budget) is distributed on a per-pupil basis. Each district receives its share, depending on the district's proportional share of the state's total K–12 and Small Schools WPUs. Funding for the state's Advanced Placement program is based on tests and hours completed. Funding for Concurrent Enrollment programs is based on the hours of higher education courses completed by students. The largest share of the budget in this category goes to Concurrent Enrollment (64%) which allows students to earn college credit concurrently while earning high school credit. This idea, wildly popular in Utah, requires a certified teacher with a masters degree to teach 'college' content in what is otherwise a high school course. Funding for this program compensates teachers, provides money for additional supplies and materials, and reimburses some costs of the administrative work of both districts and colleges participating in the program.

Districts differ widely in their use of these funds to aid in educating gifted and talented students. One growing concern associated with these popular programs is that, with increased funding, the demand for more accountability is also likely to increase.

BILINGUAL EDUCATION

Funding for bilingual education in Utah is found in the Basic Program and in the Enhancement for At-Risk Students Program, which is allocated by formula to LEAs.[9] The composite of program funding is used to provide special help and instruction for students with limited knowledge of English, among other program objectives. This is considered a special purpose district option program under the overall MSP. Funding can come from a combination of general discretionary state and local sources.

CHARTER SCHOOL FUNDING

Charter schools were initially authorized in Utah during the 1998 legislative session. The intended purpose of these new schools was to innovate, encourage parental involvement, find ways to educate for less resources, and provide choice for students and parents. The first charter school was authorized in 2000 and began operation shortly thereafter. Nearly 20 years later, Utah enrolls 75,567 students in its 134 Utah Charter Schools (11.6% of total students). The WPU generated for students in charter schools is slightly different than the allocation for students in district schools and was addressed earlier in this chapter. Legislators continue to look for ways to provide equitable opportunities for all students, as shown in multiple pieces of legislation over the years like SB 38 and HB 293S5 in the last two legislative sessions.

STATE AID FOR PRIVATE K–12 SCHOOLS

Utah does not provide aid for private K–12 schools.

EARLY CHILDHOOD EDUCATION

Utah has never appropriated state monies to support traditional preschool programs. In lieu of traditional programs, the legislature has supported an online program named UPSTART.[10] During the 2018 legislative session, lawmakers approved funding that provided roughly $11.5 million in mostly federal money to expand public preschool through private programs, public schools, and online technology. The bill allowed up to $2 million to expand UPSTART, with that funding bringing UPSTART to $8.7 million (up from $4.7 million in 2015). Parents who apply to participate are selected on a first-come-first-served basis until the appropriation runs out each fiscal year. UPSTART was set to serve up to 10,000 students in the 2018–2019 school year. The program has grown quickly since its inception in 2008, bolstered by external evaluations showing early literacy gains among children. During the 2018 legislative session, lawmakers appropriated an additional $1.5 million for UPSTART service which the governor vetoed, arguing that the program is fraught with many unanswered questions.

LOCAL SCHOOL REVENUE, PROPERTY TAX, AND EXEMPTIONS

The Utah legislature has recognized the importance of balancing taxation stewardship between state and local levels. As such, the legislature has empowered local school boards with taxation in the following areas:

- *Basic State Levy:* 53F-2-3-1 rate set by the legislature is .001666 for FY 2019. This levy is a component of the fully equalized funding mechanism in Utah known as the Weighted Pupil Unit, which guarantees a fixed dollar amount per student, currently $3,395 for FY 2019 regardless of the local tax generated by this levy in each school district. In order to participate in the guarantee, each school district

must levy this tax rate. The state adds income tax revenue to local revenue in order to guarantee the amount guaranteed per student.
- *Board Local Levy*: 53F-2-602 statutory limit is .002500. This rate affords a local education entity to provide educational services beyond the minimum school program as noted in statute. A local board has authority to set this rate annually, subject to the provisions of statute.
- *Voted Local Levy*: 53F-2-601 statutory limit is .002000. LEAs may take to voters a proposition to raise local property tax for specific purposes subject to the limits in statute. If approved by a majority of those voting in the local jurisdiction election, the LEA may levy the tax the following fiscal year.
- *Capital Local Levy*: 53F-8-303 statutory limit is .003000. LEAs may take a proposition to voters to raise local property taxes for capital construction, maintenance of facilities, and more. Currently, no LEAs in Utah use this financing option.
- *Debt Service Levy:* 53F-8-401, 405 and 11-14-19 delineate that the purpose of this levy is for payment of principal and interest on general obligation bonds. By a simple majority of voters, LEAs must pass a voter resolution authorizing the tax. If approved, the LEA may levy a tax sufficient to make the principal and interest payments on the outstanding debt. LEAs are subject to legal debt margin requirements in statute, which limits debt to 4% of the LEA's fair market value, which is all taxable property within the LEA's boundaries.

When calculating property tax, the Utah legislature provides an exemption to encourage primary home ownership and community stability. The primary home exemption is 45% of the primary home's assessed value. Property taxes are set as of the lien date, which is January 1st each year. Property taxes are due by November 30 each year.

Another factor in Utah is the requirement for Truth in Taxation, which limits taxing entities to tax rate assessments that generate no more than the same budgeted revenue from one year to the next. Once the certified rate is set, new commercial or residential construction (growth) yields additional marginal revenues for the LEA. In reaction to that growth, the certified rate reduces in order to maintain the same budgeted revenue. If an LEA wants to exceed its certified rate, it must follow the requirements found in Utah Code 59-2-19 notice and public hearing requirements for certain tax increases. The effect of this legislation causes tax rates to go down over time as property values increase. Statute intends that LEAs are accountable to local taxpayers for adjustments to tax rates that yield additional revenues.

OTHER CATEGORIES

Necessarily Existent Small Schools

In Utah, several small schools are located in sparsely populated rural areas of the state where distance precludes the opportunity to combine students into larger schools. Because of diseconomies of scale, these schools are compensated by the state through its Necessarily Existent Small Schools program (NESS). Funds are intended for specific schools meeting specific criteria. The laws and board rules regulating this account are complicated and require schools to complete an annual funding application. Recent current appropriation increased by $1,209,000 to $31,501,000.

BEVERLY TAYLOR SORENSON ARTS LEARNING PROGRAM

The Beverley Taylor Sorenson Arts Learning Program (BTSALP) provides arts-integrated instruction to elementary students. State funding provides matching funds for school-based arts specialists in participating schools and arts specialists in seven state universities. According to the BTSALP directors, the program currently resides in 300 Utah elementary schools in 31 (76%) school districts including over 30 charter schools and serves approximately 202,800 pupils. The state allocation increased by $1,000,000 in 2018 to $9,880,000. An additional $120,000 was appropriated for state board of education administrative costs.

K–3 READING IMPROVEMENT PROGRAM

The K–3 Reading Improvement Program was created during the 2004 general legislative session. The program was a project supported by a recent governor who supported the goal of all Utah students reading at or above grade level by the time they complete the third grade. Monies have been appropriated annually since 2004. Three programs comprise the K–3 Reading Improvement Program: Base Level, Guarantee Program, and Low Income Students Program. School districts and charter schools must submit a state board-approved plan for reading proficiency improvement prior to using the program funds.[11] The Utah State Office of Education drafted a framework for instruction and intervention to ensure that all students progress at an appropriate and successful rate, mitigating the cycle of reading failure. Formulas for each of the three funding programs include:

- *Base Level*: a base amount as determined by fall enrollment;
- *Guarantee Program*: $21 per WPU minus the amount raised by a local tax levy of 0.000056 or matching funds provided by the district or charter school;
- *Low Income Program*: $21 per WPU minus the amount raised by a local tax levy of 0.000065 or matching funds provided by the district or charter school.

State statute allows the state board of education to use no more than $7.5 million for computer-assisted instructional learning and assessment programs. The 2018 legislature appropriated $15,000,000 for this program.

UTAH SCHOOLS NOW

Currently, a citizen's initiative known as Proposition 1 (Our Schools Now) is promoting increased funding for schools and roads through a 10¢ increase in the motor fuel tax. The initiative is led by a coalition of business leaders and education associations. If successful, this non-binding resolution would provide an estimated infusion of $150 million annually on a per-pupil basis to each school in the state. The initiative would also provide resources to higher education and to counties and cities for roads.

FY19 MSP LEGISLATIVE ESTIMATES

FY 2019 allocations are shown in Table 46.1. For FY 2019, estimates project the total MSP at $4.4 billion, with $2.9 billion in funding for various WPU categorical programs; another $780.6 million for below-the-line categorical programs; and $670.4 million for the state guarantee and local funds for voted and board leeway programs. Between local, state, and federal sources, Utah's public schools can expect to receive approximately $6 billion per year: 8% federal, 37% local, and 55% state.

TABLE 46.1 Utah MSP Program Budget Detail

Section 1: Minimum School Program- Summary of Total Revenue Sources and Expenditures

Total Revenue Sources	FY 2018 Revised Amount	FY 2019 Appropriated Amount
A. General State Revenue		
1. Education Fund	3,110,558,400	3,205,197,000
a. Education Fund, One-Time	(1,131,500)	(9,708,600)
B. Restricted State Revenue		
1. Uniform School Fund	27,500,000	27,500,000
a. Uniform School Fund, One-Time	3,500,000	10,000,000
2. USF Restricted—Trust Distribution Account	64,252,300	74,000,000
3. EF Restricted—Minimum Basic Growth Account	56,250,000	56,250,000
4. EF Restricted—Charter School Levy Account[f]	22,100,000	23,839,600
5. EF Restricted—Teacher and Student Success Account[g]	0	0
6. EF Restricted—Local Levy Growth Account[g]	0	36,117,300
Subtotal State Revenues:	*$3,283,029,200*	*$3,423,195,300*
C. Local Property Tax Revenue		
1. Minimum Basic Tax Rate		
a. Basic Levy	324,041,300	333,073,800
b. Basic Levy Increment Rate	75,000,000	75,000,000
2. Equity Pupil Tax Rate[b]	0	36,117,300
3. WPU Value Rate	0	18,650,000
4. Voted Local Levy	299,360,200	324,424,900
5. Board Local Levy	100,416,300	109,864,100
a. Early Literacy Program	15,000,000	15,000,000
Subtotal Local Revenues:	*$813,817,800*	*$$912,130,100*

(continued)

TABLE 46.1 Utah MSP Program Budget Detail (continued)

	FY 2018 Revised	FY 2019 Appropriated
D. Transfer to Education Fund	(12,500,000)	0
E. Beginning Nonlapsing Balances	32,500,700	48,854,100
F. Closing Nonlapsing Balances	(20,000,700)	(48,854,100)
Total Revenues:	**$4,096,847,000**	**$4,335,325,400**
Total Expenditures by Program		
A. Basic School Program	2,857,024,700	2,949,399,100
B. Related to Basic School Program	653,005,700	780,679,500
C. Voted and Board Local Levy Programs	586,816,600	670,396,800
Total Expenditures:	**$4,096,847,000**	**$4,400,475,400**
Section 2: Minimum School Program–Detail of Revenue Sources & Expenditures by Program		
Table A: Basic School Program (Weighted Pupil Unit Programs)		
WPU Value:	*$3,311*	*$3,395*
Basic Tax Rate:	*0.001568*	*0.001669*
Revenue Sources	Amount	Amount
A. State Revenue		
1. Education Fund	2,422,483,400	2,459,066,600
a. Education Fund, One-Time	4,500,000	(10,008,600)
B. Restricted State Revenue		
1. Uniform School Fund	27,500,000	27,500,000
a. Uniform School Fund, One-Time	3,500,000	10,000,000
Subtotal–State Revenues:	*$2,457,983,400*	*$2,486,558,000*
C. Local Property Tax Revenue		
1. Minimum Basic Tax Rate		
a. Basic Levy	324,041,300	333,073,800

(continued)

TABLE 46.1 Utah MSP Program Budget Detail (continued)

	FY 2018 Revised		FY 2019 Appropriated	
b. Basic Levy Increment Rate		75,000,000		75,000,000
2. Equity Pupil Tax Rate[g]				36,117,300
3. WPU Value Rate[g]				18,650,0000
Subtotal–Local Property Tax Revenues		**$399,041,300**		**$462,841,100**
D. Transfer Education Fund[d]		(5,328,800)		0
E. Beginning Nonlapsing Balances[d]		16,371,500		25,487,700
F. Closing Nonlapsing Balances		(11,042,700)		(25,487,700)
Total Revenues:		**$285,024,700**		
Expenditures by Categorical Program	WPUs	Amount	WPUs	Amount
A. Regular Basic School Program				
1. Kindergarten	27,099	89,724,899	26,383	89,570,300
2. Grades 1–12[d]	587,693	1,953,851,500	593,523	2,015,010,600
3. Foreign Exchange Students	328	1,086,000	328	1,113,600
4. Necessarily Existent Small Schools	9,514	31,501,000	9,588	32,551,300
5. Professional Staff	55,808	184,780,300	55,545	188,575,300
6. Administrative Cost	1,565	5,181,700	1,505	5,109,500
Subtotal–Regular Basic School Program:	**682,007**	**2,266,125,300**	**686,872**	**2,331,930,600**
Section 1: Minimum School Program–Summary of Total Revenue Sources and Expenditures				
B. Restricted Basic School Program				
1. Special Education–Regular–Add-on WPUs[a,c]	80,250	265,707,700	82,342	279,978,300
2. Special Education–Regular–Self-Contained	13,944	46,168,600	13,970	47,428,200
3. Special Education–Pre-School	10,777	35,682,600	11,052	37,521,500
4. Special Education–Extended Year Program	439	1,453,500	447	1,517,600

(continued)

TABLE 46.1 Utah MSP Program Budget Detail (continued)

	FY 2018 Revised	FY 2019 Appropriated
5. Special Education–Impact Aid[b]	1,988	6,584,100	2,015	6,840,900
6. Special Education–Intensive Services	769	2,546,200	778	2,641,300
7. Special Education–Extended Year for Special Educators	909	3,009,700	909	3,086,100
8. Career & Technical Education–District Add-on[b]	28,480	94,297,300	28,821	97,847,300
9. Class Size Reduction	40,909	135,449,700	41,416	140,607,300
Subtotal- Restricted Basic School Program:	*178,465*	*590,899,400*	*181,750*	*617,468,500*
Total Expenditures:	**860,472**	**2,857,024,700**	**868,622**	**2,949,399,100**

The Line

Table B: Related to Basic School Program (Below-the-Line)

Revenue Sources	Amount	Amount
A. State Revenue		
1. Education Fund		
a. Education Fund, One-Time		
B. Restricted State Revenue		
1. USF Restricted–Trust Distribution Account		
2. EF Restricted–Teacher and Student Success Account[g]		
a. Teacher and Student Success Account, One-Time		
3. EF Restricted–Charter School Levy Account		
Subtotal State Revenues:	*653,005,700*	*780,679,500*
C. Transfer to Education Fund[d]	(7,171,200)	0
D. Beginning Nonlapsing Balances[d]	16,129,200	23,366,400
E. Closing Nonlapsing Balances	(8,958,000)	(23,366,400)
Total Revenues:	**653,005,700**	**780,679,500**

(continued)

TABLE 46.1 Utah MSP Program Budget Detail (continued)

Expenditures by Categorical Program	FY 2018 Revised		FY 2019 Appropriated	
	Changes	Funding	Changes	Amount
A. Relate to Basic Programs				
1. Pupil Transportation–To & From School[f]	0	83,730,200	7,606,000	91,336,200
2. Pupil Transportation–Grants for Unsafe Routes[b]	0	500,000	(500,000)	0
3. Pupil Transportation–Guarantee Transportation Levy	0	500,000	0	500,000
4. Pupil Transportation–Rural School Reimbursement	0	0	500,000	500,000
5. Flexible Allocation–WPU Distribution[c-g]	0	7,788,000	65,150,000	72,938,000
6. Charter School Local Replacement	0	170,579,200	7,946,800	178,526,000
7. Charter School Administrative Costs	0	7,825,600	155,000	7,980,600
Subtotal- Related to Basic Programs	*0*	*270,923,000*	*80,857,800*	*351,780,800*
B. Focus Population				
1. Enhancement for At-Risk Students	0	28,034,800	10,339,900	38,374,500
2. Youth-in-Custody[b,c]	0	22,716,200	195,900	24,712,100
3. Adult Education[b,e]	0	11,159,000	2,333,100	13,942,100
4. Enhancement for Accelerated Students	0	5,032,400	186,700	5,219,100
5. Centennial Scholarship Program	0	250,000	0	250,000
6. Concurrent Enrollment	0	10,784,300	400,100	11,184,400
7. Title| Schools in Improvement-Paraeducators	0	300,000	0	300,000
8. Early Literacy Program	0	15,000,000	0	15,000,000
9. Early Intervention	0	7,500,000	0	7,500,000
10. Early Graduation from Competency-Based Education	0	55,700	0	55,700
Subtotal–Focus Populations:	*0*	*199,832,200*	*15,255,700*	*116,087,900*

(continued)

TABLE 46.1 Utah MSP Program Budget Detail (continued)

	FY 2018 Revised		FY 2019 Appropriated
C. Educator Supports			
1. Educator Salary Adjustments	2,556,100	173,645,500	2,556,100	173,645,500
2. Teacher Salary Supplement	0	6,799,900	7,475,000	14,274,900
3. Teacher Supplies & Materials	0	5,000,000	500,000	5,500,000
4. Effective Teachers in High Poverty Schools	0	250,000	0	250,000
5. Elementary School Counselor Program	0	0	2,100,000	2,100,000
Subtotal–Educator Supports:	*2,556,100*	*185,695,400*	*12,631,100*	*195,770,400*
D. Statewide Initiatives				
1. School LAND Trust Program[c]	13,852,300	64,252,300	23,600,000	74,000,000
2. School Library Books & Electronic Resources	0	850,000	0	850,000
3. Matching Fund for School Nurses	0	1,002,000	0	1,002,000
4. Dual Immersion[b]	0	3,556,000 6,200,000	700,000	4,256,000
5. Year-Round Math & Science (USTAR Centers)	0	9,880,000	0	6,200,000
6. Beverly Taylor Sorenson Arts Learning Program[b]	0	9,664,800	1,000,000	10,880,000
7. Digital Teaching & Learning Program[b]	(187,600)	9,664,800	10,000,000	19,852,400
8. Civics Education–State Capital Field Trips	0	150,000	(150,000)	0
Subtotal–Other Programs:	*13,644,700*	*95,555,100*	*35,150,000*	*117,040,400*
Total Expenditures:	**16,220,800**	**653,005,700**	**143,894,600**	**780,679,500**

(continued)

TABLE 46.1 Utah MSP Program Budget Detail (continued)

	FY 2018 Revised		FY 2019 Appropriated	
Table C: Voted & Board Local Levy Programs				
Revenue Sources		Amount		Amount
A. State Revenue				
1. Education Fund		123,790,100		128,740,500
a. Education Fund, On-Time[d]		(8,000,000)		
B. Restricted State Revenue				
1. EFR- Minimum Basic Growth Account		56,250,000		56,250,000
2. EFR- Local Levy Growth Account				36,117,300
Subtotal State Revenues:		*172,040,100*		*221,107,800*
C. Local Property Tax Revenue				
1. Voted Local Levy		299,360,200		324,424,900
2. Board Local Levy		100,416,300		109,864,100
a. Reading Improvement Program		15,000,000		15,000,000
Subtotal–Local Property Tax Revenues:		*414,776,500*		*449,289,000*
Total Revenues:		**586,816,600**		**670,396,800**
Expenditures by Categorical Program	Changes	Amount	Changes	Amount
Guarantee Rate (per 0.001 Tax Rate per WPU):		*39.68*		*43.10*
A. Voted and Board Local Levy Programs				
1. Voted Local Levy Program[d,g]	(4,000,000)	441,275,000	49,897,900	495,172,900
2. Board Local Levy Program[d,g]	(4,000,000)	130,541,600	25,682,300	160,223,900
3. Board Local Levy–Early Literacy Program	0	15,000,000	0	15,000,000
Total Minimum School Expenditures:		**4,096,847,000**		**4,400,475,400**

(continued)

TABLE 46.1 Utah MSP Program Budget Detail (continued)

	FY 2018 Revised		FY 2019 Appropriated	
Section 3: School Building Programs–Total Revenues & Expenditures (Not Included in MSP Totals Above)				
Revenue Sources	Amount		Amount	
A. State Revenue				
1. Education Fund	14,499,700		14,499,700	
B. Restricted State Revenue				
2. EFR–Minimum Basic Growth Account	18,750,000		18,750,000	
Total Revenues:	33,249,700		33,249,700	
Expenditures by Categorical Program	Amount	Changes	Amount	Changes
A. Capital Outlay Programs				
1. Foundation	27,610,900		27,610,900	
2. Enrollment Growth	5,638,800		5,638,800	
Total Expenditures:	33,249,700		33,249,700	

Notes:

[a] Includes $435,800 ongoing and $8,600 one time to implement HB 317, Special Education Amendments (2018 GS).

[b] Administrative funding for certain MSP Categorical programs can be found in the "MSP Categorical Program Administration" line item in the State Board of Education's Budget. Adding program and administration funding will provide the full-cost for the program.

[c] Includes one-time funding appropriated by the Legislature as a supplemental in FY 2018 or FY 2019, as follows: Special Education Add-on ($8,600). Flexible Allocation $65,150,00, At-Risk Students $300,000, Educator Salary Adjustments $2,556,100 (FY18), and School LAND Trust $13,852,300 (FY18)

[d] Transferred a total of $8.0 million one-time from the Voted & Board Local Levy Programs to the Basic School Program—Grades 1–12 in FY 2018 to provide the State Board of Education flexibility to maintain categorical program funding levels as authorized under 53F-2-205.

[e] The Legislature consolidated the "Education Contracts" line-item into two MSP Categorical programs. The Youth Center, which provides education services to students at the State Hospital, was combined into the Youth- In Custody program. Funding for Corrections Education, which provides education services to adults in state prisons, was combined into the Adult Education program. The Adult Education statute was changed to incorporate the corrections education program.

(continued)

TABLE 46.1 Utah MSP Program Budget Detail (continued)

	FY 2018 Revised	FY 2019 Appropriated

f Includes funding for student transportation at the Utah Schools for the Deaf and the Blind.

g HB 293, Tax Rebalancing revisions (2018 GS) increased local property tax revenue generated to support the Basic School Program. The bill created Equity Pupil Rate and the WPU Value Rate. The bill was also created two restricted accounts the local levy growth account and the Teacher and Student Success account. Increased local revenue supporting WPU's in the Basic School Program reduces the state cost for the program. The state fund "savings" generated through the increased property taxes was transferred to the two restricted funds to support education programs.

h Funding for the Pupil Transportation- Grants for Unsafe Routes program was transferred to the Pupil Transportation- To & From School Program. The corresponding statute was repealed in Senate Bill 2 (2018 General Session).

i The Legislature provided the State Board of Education authority to use up to $5.0 million of the nonlapsing balances in the Basic School Program to begin work on improving Board information technology systems. Authority was also provided to the Board to use up to $1.7 million to acquire analytical software for the Early Intervention Reading Software program. This authority can be found in HB 3, Appropriations Adjustments (2018 GS).

NOTES

1. Title 53A, Chapter 17a Utah Code. Retrieved from https://le.utah.gov/lfa/reports/cobi2013/agcy_401.htm
2. Utah Constitution, Article X, Section 5.
3. Art XIII, Section 5(5).
4. Utah statute, 53F-2-103.
5. HB 293 FY 2018 Session.
6. Utah State Board of Education. Legislative Update (2018). Retrieved from https://schools.utah.gov/file/2500950b-a97a-48ee-8cec-e85f6e9604a3
7. 53F-2-402 3(b).
8. UCA 49-13-202(1).
9. Utah Code 53F-2-410.
10. Utah Code 53F-4-402. UPSTART = Utah Preparing Students Today for a Rewarding Tomorrow, administered by a private vendor.
11. USOE Finance & Statistics, MSP Descriptions, November 2006.

CHAPTER 47

Vermont

Susan B. Holson
Director of Education Services
Vermont School Boards Association

Nicole Mace
Executive Director
Vermont School Boards Association

GENERAL BACKGROUND

In 1997, the Vermont supreme court held "Yesterday's bare essentials are no longer sufficient to prepare a student to live in today's global marketplace. To keep a democracy competitive and thriving, students must be afforded equal access to all that our educational system has to offer. In the funding of what our Constitution places at the core of a successful democracy, the children of Vermont are entitled to a reasonably equal share."[1]

Vermont's founding fathers identified the importance of public education in the state's original constitution of 1777, declaring, "A school or schools shall be established in each town, by the legislature, for the convenient instruction of youth, with such salaries to the masters, paid by each town, making proper use of school lands in each town, thereby to enable them to instruct youth at low prices. One grammar school in each county, and one university in this State, ought to be established by direction of the General Assembly."[2]

In 1890, the state of Vermont enacted a statewide property tax designed to equalize great disparities in school districts' ability to fund adequate instruction. At the same time, laws were passed aimed at consolidating the state's thousands of local school districts and improving teacher training. With passage of a law in 1892 mandating town schools, Vermont went from a system with more than 2,500 school districts to one with fewer than 300.[3] The statewide property tax was replaced with a statewide income tax in 1931, and education funding reverted to local property taxes.[4]

By the 1990s, Vermont funded public education through a combination of local property tax assessments and state aid, known as the Foundation Plan. Under the Plan, the state annually set a foundation tax rate, which the state considered to be a reasonable rate of local property taxation necessary to enable each district to raise enough funds to provide at least a minimum quality education program. The amount needed for a minimum quality program was known as the 'foundation cost.' State aid was then calculated to make up the difference between the foundation cost for all students in a district and the amount the district could actually raise at the foundation tax rate. Under the Plan, the foundation tax rate was not a minimum or maximum rate imposed on school districts. Rather, it was a rate used to calculate the amount of state aid that would be necessary to equalize disparities among districts' taxable property wealth.[5]

The Foundation Plan led to significant disparities in resources available to property-rich districts vs. property-poor districts. In 1997, a group of plaintiffs sued the state of Vermont and the Vermont supreme court responded with the *Brigham* decision. Plaintiffs alleged that Vermont's education financing system violated the state constitution by:

- *depriving students* residing in property-poor school districts of their right to the same educational opportunities as students in wealthier school districts;
- *compelling property owners* in property-poor school districts to contribute an unjust proportion of tax dollars to fund education; and
- *depriving property-poor school districts* of the ability to raise sufficient money to provide educational opportunities equal to those in wealthier school districts and compelling the districts to impose disproportionately high tax rates.[6]

In finding the system unconstitutional, the court said, "The distribution of a resource as precious as educational opportunity may not have as its determining force the mere fortuity of a child's residence. It requires no particular constitutional expertise to recognize the capriciousness of such a system."[7] The court found that the funding system "with its substantial dependence on local property taxes and resultant wide disparities in revenues available to local school districts, deprive[d] children of an equal educational opportunity"[8] in violation of Chapter II, §68 and Chapter I,

Article 7 of the Vermont constitution. The court did not specify a remedy for the violation, leaving the question of how to ensure equal access to education funding to the General Assembly. The court was clear, however, that the General Assembly could not delegate that responsibility to local school boards, stating "The state may delegate to local towns and cities the authority to finance and administer the schools within their borders; it cannot, however, abdicate the basic responsibility for education by passing it on to local governments, which are themselves creations of the state."[9]

The General Assembly responded to the *Brigham* ruling by passing Act 60 in 1997 and Act 68 in 2003. The funding formula has been modified and tweaked over time, but the essential elements have remained constant for more than two decades. In 2012, an independent study found the funding system to be "working well and meeting the goals established in Acts 60 and 68...The state has designed an equitable system. We found virtually no relationship between wealth (measured by both district property wealth and personal income) and spending levels."[10]

ENSURING EQUAL ACCESS

Act 60 of 1997, titled An Act Relating to Equal Educational Opportunity,[11] and its companion Act 68 of 2003 An Act Relating to Education Funding,[12] attempted to strike a balance between local control over education spending and equal opportunity for all of Vermont's students. Act 60 defined, and Act 68 refined, the mechanisms for establishing school budgets and distributing funds to cover education expenses. Act 60 was the first attempt to equalize many factors including student population or school size, local market value of property, and student needs.[13]

The fundamental feature of Acts 60 and 68 was that communities spending the same amount per equalized pupil should have the same residential tax rate, regardless of how much property value existed in the community. Likewise, the nonresidential tax rate should be the same statewide irrespective of the community in which the property is located and the amount spent on education. Local communities should determine how much they want to spend per equalized student, and the state should set statewide residential and nonresidential property tax rates in order to raise enough revenue to fund the budgets that are approved at the local level.

The Education Fund

In Vermont, local school boards adopt budgets annually, which are approved by district voters each spring. The amount funded by the state, or 'education spending,' is the total voter-approved expenditure budget less any revenue from federal, state, or local sources, such as grants, special education funding, or surplus/reserve funds.[14] The state pays for PreK–12 education expenses through the Education Fund. The Fund is comprised of property taxes from both residential and non-residential sources, which are treated as state revenues. Non-property tax sources include state lottery revenue, sales and use taxes, and portions of meals and rooms taxes, purchase and use tax, and Medicaid reimbursements. The state's Joint Fiscal Office projected Fiscal Year 2019 Education Fund revenue sources to be distributed as seen in Figure 47.1.[15]

Education payments to school districts were projected to account for 83.6% of Education Fund appropriations for FY 2019.[16] Remaining funds were to be allocated for special education aid, state-placed students, transportation aid, technical education aid, small school support, Essential Early Education aid, Flexible Pathways, and the normal cost of teacher pensions.

Equalizing Access to Educational Resources

Several features of the Vermont school funding system are intended to ensure equitable collection and redistribution of education funds statewide.

Equalized Pupils

Residential tax rates are a function of education spending per equalized pupil. The formula is designed to account for differences in student population among communities by adding 'weights' to certain categories

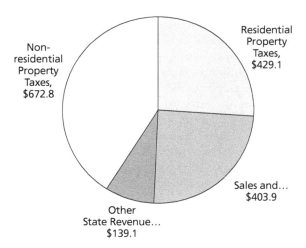

Figure 47.1 Vermont Projected FY 2019 Education Fund Sources (in millions).

of students. Vermont statute[17] recognizes four such categories (current weighting factors in parentheses):

- *prekindergarten* children, including those receiving essential early education services (0.46);
- *secondary* students, grades 7 through 12 (1.13);
- *students from economically deprived* backgrounds (1.25 by formula); and
- *students for whom English* is not their primary language (1.20).[18]

The intended end result is that the cost of an equalized pupil from any school district can be compared to the cost of an equalized pupil from any other district.[19] Special education is not a factor in equalized pupil calculation since there is a separate funding mechanism for special education students.[20]

Common Level of Appraisal

Another method of equalizing Education Fund revenue in Vermont is a calculation called the Common Level of Appraisal (CLA), which is a market correction factor to assure all towns' grand lists reflect fair market value. The Department of Taxes defines grand list as:

> 1% of the listed value established by the local assessing officials, and the value used to determine municipal taxes for a municipality. It includes any business personal property taxable at the local level and excludes locally voted exemptions. Properties subject to local stabilization agreements are included at their stabilized values. The education grand list is 1% of the education property values per 32 VSA§ 5404. It is the value to be used to determine the State Education Tax and the Local Share Tax and generally doesn't include inventory or business personal property. It includes the value of properties exempted by local vote (if not "grandfathered") as well as the full value of properties subject to local stabilization agreements as defined in 32 VSA § 5401(5).[21]

The CLA for every Vermont town is the primary result of an equalization study performed by the Tax Department every year. The equalization study compares the ratio of the grand list listed value to the sale price for all the arms-length sales in the town over the prior three-year period. The study considers sales price as the best measurement of fair market value. If grand list values are generally less than sale prices for the recent sales, the town will end up with a CLA of less than 100%. If grand list values are generally more than sale prices for the recent sales, the town will end up with a CLA of more than 100%. Once the CLA is determined, it is used to adjust the homestead and nonresidential education tax rates. The CLA does not change taxpayer property values, only the education tax rate in a town, i.e., an example of *indirect* equalization.[22]

Small School Grants

Vermont has many rural school districts and small schools. Recognizing that small schools lack the ability to achieve economies of scale and are therefore likely to have higher spending per pupil, Act 60 included small school grants for qualifying districts. A small school grant brings revenue to a district, allowing it to reduce education spending per equalized pupil. This in turn leads to lower tax rates than would otherwise be necessary to support a school district's budget. Vermont statute[23] provides small school support grants to districts operating at least one school if the two-year average enrollment is less than 100 or if the average grade size is 20 or fewer. Districts receiving a support grant are also eligible for a small schools financial stability grant if there was a 10% decrease in the two-year average enrollment in any one year.[24] The 2015 legislature[25] altered eligibility requirements for schools that demonstrate geographical isolation from "the nearest school with excess capacity," or demonstrate "academic excellence and operational efficiency."[26] This change took effect July 1, 2019.

Dollar Equivalent Yields

The base rate for statewide property taxes is $1.00 per $100,000 of property value. According to statute,[27] the legislature is required to set yields to generate enough property tax revenue to support the anticipated statewide education spending after all other education fund revenue sources are accounted. The 'dollar equivalent yields' are the amounts of per-pupil spending that could be supported each year by a fixed homestead base tax rate of $1.00 for taxpayers who pay based on the value of their property or by a fixed applicable income percentage of 2% for taxpayers who receive an income sensitivity adjustment. The Commissioner of Taxes proposes each dollar equivalent yield for the following fiscal year on or before December 1, but the General Assembly establishes each dollar equivalent yield after voters approve budgets in the spring.[28]

Calculating Residential and Non-Residential Rates

Acts 60 and 68 differentiated between homestead (residential) property and nonresidential property and assessed each type of property differently.

Residential Rates

A 'homestead' is the principal dwelling and parcel of land surrounding the dwelling, owned and occupied by the resident as the person's domicile.

In order to qualify for the homestead tax assessment, residents must file an annual homestead declaration with the state. Revenues generated by the homestead portion of education property taxes were estimated at $429.1 million for FY 2019. Residents' homestead taxes are calculated in one of two ways. In both instances, tax rates reflect local spending decisions:

- *Rates Based on Property Value:* The standard calculation for determining a household's education tax is based on the homestead's assessed value modified by the district's budgeted spending per equalized pupil, the municipality's common level of appraisal, and the property dollar equivalent yield established annually by legislature. The base tax rate was frozen at $1.00 per $100,000 of assessed value in FY 2017. The Property Dollar Equivalent Yield was set at $10,220 for FY 2019. Thus, the base calculation for a homestead is as follows:

    Spending per Pupil = Total Budgeted Education Spending – Local Revenues (federal, state grants, local sources) / Equalized Pupils

    Property Tax Rate = Spending per Pupil/Property Yield
    Homestead Property Tax Calculation
    = (Property Tax Rate/CLA) × (Assessed Value/100)

- *Rates Based on Income:* For homesteads with household income below a threshold, education taxes may receive an adjustment. In FY 2019, households with income below $140,000 had opportunity to take advantage of tax adjustments modified by the income dollar equivalent yield established by the state legislature. As outlined in 32 V.S.A. §6066, adjustments are reflected in the following year's property tax bill. Three levels of income qualify for some adjustment:

    Under $47,000
    $47,000–$90,000
    $90,000–$140,000

The base rate for calculating income-based education tax adjustments is 2% of household income. Starting with calculation of homestead property taxes above, income-based taxes then consider budgeted spending per equalized pupil, the CLA, and an income yield, which is generally higher than the property dollar equivalent yield. Over 70% of Vermonters paid education taxes based on income in FY 2018.[29] The FY 2019 income yield was set by the legislature at $12,380. The calculation for income-based taxes is:

Spending per Pupil = Total Budgeted Education Spending
− Local Revenues (federal and state grants and local sources)/
Equalized Pupils

Income Tax rate = (Spending per Pupil/Income Yield) × 2%
Income-Based Tax Calculation: Homestead Property Tax
− (Income Tax Rate × Household Income)

Nonresidential Rates

Nonresidential property includes all taxable real property that does not qualify as a homestead, including commercial and industrial property, rental housing, and second homes. The nonresidential rate is uniform statewide and does not depend on spending per equalized pupil in the town in which it is located. The only adjustment is the CLA for the municipality. For FY 2019, the nonresidential rate was established by legislature at $1.58 per assessed value/$100.

SPECIAL EDUCATION

Vermont special education and related services for students with disabilities are largely funded by state categorical grants and local education funds. Only 6% of total funding comes from federal grants. In recent years, approximately 60% of remaining costs have been funded by state appropriation, with the remainder funded through local education budgets.[30]

Vermont's current formula relies on multiple funding mechanisms to distribute special education funds to localities, consisting of three integrated parts:

- *The state operates a block grant* that is linked to schools' enrollment, which is calculated using average special education teacher salaries.[31] For supervisory unions or districts with 1,500 or more students, additional funding is provided for administrative costs;
- *The state operates an extraordinary services reimbursement program* to assist localities with paying for the costs of high-need or high-cost students with disabilities. Such students may be unevenly distributed across localities within the state and can pose disproportionate spending pressures on localities, particularly for small school districts with more limited financial capacity. This mechanism provides funding on top of the standard mainstream block grant to supervisory unions or districts in instances where more than $50,000 is spent for special education and related services for a student in a particular school year. The state reimburses 90% of funds spent in

excess of the $50,000 threshold, as well as approximately 60% of allowable spending up to $50,000. For FY 2016, 564 students with IEPs statewide were eligible for extraordinary services reimbursements from the state;

- *The state reimburses localities for allowable special education expenditures* (as identified by the State Board of Education) not already paid with federal aid, the state's mainstream block grant or extraordinary services reimbursement, and other state funding sources. The state's reimbursement percentage is adjusted annually to achieve a 60% state share of spending across all three funding components. For FY 2016, the percentage of costs reimbursed by the state was about 57%.[32]

Act 173 of 2018 changed the funding model for special education from a reimbursement model to a census-based model and expanded supports for all students who struggle.[33] It was created to enhance the effectiveness, availability, and equity of services provided to all students who require additional support in Vermont's schools. Students defined as needing extra support include students who:

- Have an individualized education program (IEP);
- Have a Section 504 plan under the Rehabilitation Act of 1973;
- Are not on an IEP or Section 504 plan but whose abilities to learn are negatively impacted by a disability or by social, emotional, or behavioral needs;
- Have a primary language other than English;
- Read below grade level.

Act 173 was designed to be phased in over time. When the new system is fully realized in FY 2021, the mainstream block grant and special education expenditure reimbursement will be replaced with a census-based grant. The state will establish a per-student amount, and supervisory unions and supervisory districts (SU/SD) will receive a grant equal to the per-student amount factored by its three-year average student count. Funds will be used for services outlined in IEPs and will ensure compliance with IDEA fiscal requirements. However, if funds are still available after those requirements are met SU/SDs can use the funds to provide other services to students such as Multi-Tiered System of Supports (MTSS) and other preventative services that were not allowable for reimbursement under the reimbursement model. All remaining costs will be the obligation of the SU/SD. Extraordinary cost relief will be available at 95% of the cost for a student with high individual costs using a new threshold of $60,000 adjusted annually for inflation.

SUMMARY

In FY 2018, Vermont spent $1.621 billion to educate 89,254 publicly funded PreK–12 students.[34] Current funding mechanisms, as well as those being considered in the near future, prioritize equal opportunity for all children in the state regardless of socio-economic or geographic circumstance. Declining student population will continue to challenge educators and lawmakers as they work together to balance equity, efficiency, and quality.

NOTES

1. *Brigham v. State of Vermont* 166 Vt. 246; 692 A.2d 384 (1997).
2. J. Fay, (1777, July 8). 1777 Constitution. Retrieved from Vermont Secretary of State https://www.sec.state.vt.us/archives-records/state-archives/government-history/vermont-constitutions/1777-constitution.aspx
3. D. Cyprian (2011). *A Brief History of Public School Organization in Vermont*. Montpelier: Vermont School Boards Association et. al.
4. J.A. Sautter, J. A. (2008). Equity in History: Vermont's Education Revolution of the Early 1890s. *Vermont History Journal*, 1.
5. D. Russo-Savage, P. Griffin, and R. Wasserman (2015). *Brigham v. State, 166 Vt. 246 (1997) Memorandum*. Montpelier: State of Vermont Office of Legislative Council.
6. Russo-Savage et al (2015).
7. *Brigham* at 265.
8. Ibid, p. 249.
9. Ibid. p. 264.
10. Lawrence O. Picus and Associates. (2012). *An Evaluation of Vermont's Education Finance System*.
11. http://www.leg.state.vt.us/docs/1998/acts/act060.htm
12. http://www.leg.state.vt.us/docs/legdoc.cfm?URL=/docs/2004/acts/ACT068.HTM
13. S. Holson. (2017). *Making Sense of Vermont's Education Funding System* [Motion Picture].
14. Vermont Department of Education, Finance & Administration. (2016). *Vermont's Education Funding System*. Montpelier: Vermont Department of Education.
15. Vermont Joint Fiscal Office. (2018, June 26). *Education Fund Outlook*. Retrieved from Vermont General Assembly http://www.leg.state.vt.us/jfo/education/EF_Outlook_H.16_June_2018.pdf
16. Ibid.
17. 16 V.S.A. §§ 4010.
18. R. Holcombe (2017). *Evaluation of the Accuracy of the Secondary Weight for the Equalized Pupil Count*. Montpelier: Vermont Agency of Education.
19. B. James (2017, February 9). *Equalized Pupils 101*. Retrieved from Vermont General Assembly https://legislature.vermont.gov/assets/Documents/2018/WorkGroups/Senate%20Education/Bills/S.122/17-0761%20Act%2046%20

Committee%20Bill%20Documents/W~Brad%20James~Equalized%20Pupil%20Overview~2-9-2017.pdf
20. Ibid.
21. *Tax Glossary.* (2018, September 19). Retrieved from State of Vermont: http://tax.vermont.gov/home/tax-learning-center/glossary
22. Vermont Department of Taxes. (2018, September 17). *Education Tax Rate FAQs*; see also retrieved from Vermont Deparment of Taxes: http://tax.vermont.gov/property-owners/understanding-property-taxes/education-tax-rates/faqs
23. 16 V.S.A. § 4015.
24. *Small School Grants.* (2018, September 20). Retrieved from State of Vermont Agency of Educatoon http://education.vermont.gov/data-and-reporting/financial-reports/small-school-grants
25. Section 20 of Act 46 of 2015.
26. Huling, K. (2018). *Determining Eligibility for Small Schools Grants*. Barre: Vermont State Board of Education.
27. 32 V.S.A. § 5402b.
28. Mace, N. (2015). *2015 Legislative Report: Final Report*. Montpelier: Vermont School Boards Associaiton et. al.
29. D.O. Review (2018). *Annual Report Based on 2017 Grand List Data*. Montpelier: Vermont Department of Taxes.
30. T. Kolby and K. Killeen (2018). *Study of Vermont State Funding for Special Education*. Burlington: University of Vermont Education and Social Services.
31. 16 VSA Section 2961.
32. Kolby and Killeen (2018).
33. (Bouchey, Fowler, & Byrne, 2018)
34. Vermont Agency of Education. (2018). *FY 2019 Budget Book*. Montpelier: Vermont Agency of Education.

CHAPTER 48

Virginia

William Owings, Ed.D.
Professor
Old Dominion University

Leslie S. Kaplan, Ed.D.
Education Researcher and Writer

GENERAL BACKGROUND

The nation's founders believed education was essential to maintaining their new experiment in government. Rousseau noted in 1758 that "public education...is one of the fundamental rules of a popular or legitimate government."[1] In the 1830s, when de Tocqueville visited the United States, he reported that even the roughhewn pioneer "with the Bible, an axe, and a file of newspapers" was educated.[2]

The evolution of education in the new republic, however, varied among different regions. Virginia, as Cubberley wrote, fell into the category of *pauper and parochial* school conditions.[3] In the colonial years, with Governors Thomas Jefferson, James Monroe, George Cabell, and John Tyler as the exceptions, the Commonwealth of Virginia was slow to support free public schools. This was also true of many other southern states. In 1810, the Virginia General Assembly, under Governor Tyler's leadership, established the Virginia Literary Fund to provide public education funding for the poor.[4] The bill stated:

> Be it enacted: That all escheats, confiscations, fines, penalties and forfeitures, and all rights in personal property accruing to the Commonwealth, as der-

elict, and having no rightful proprietor, be, and the same are hereby appropriated to the encouragement of learning. That the aforesaid fund shall be appropriated to the sole benefit of a school or schools, to be kept in each and every county within this Commonwealth.[5]

The Literary Funds were to be used only for public schools. Nonetheless, government officials often redirected those resources for other purposes. One early diversion helped to establish the University of Virginia.[6]

After the Civil War, in 1867 Virginia assembled a constitutional convention. A new constitution, effective in 1870, required a compulsory universal free system of public education to be funded by the Commonwealth by the Literary Fund and a statewide property tax.[7] The first Superintendent of Public Instruction was appointed in the same year. Separate and unequally funded schools became available for Black and White students.

In 1902, a new Virginia state constitution was enacted. It called for establishment and maintenance of an efficient system of free public schools. One change in the new constitution reduced the distribution of funds based on the number of children in each school division[8] from 5–21 to 7–20 years of age.

In 1972, Virginia legislators ratified a new constitution which required a more comprehensive system for managing and funding public schools. Its name is still used today—Standards of Quality (SOQ). The SOQ required that the General Assembly "shall provide for a free system of public elementary and secondary schools for all children throughout the Commonwealth, and shall seek to ensure[9] that an educational program of high quality is established and continually maintained."[10] It laid out the basic foundation formula for a floor level of services and minimum required local effort and state support for school divisions to provide.

BASIC SUPPORT PROGRAM

Virginia has a biennial budget system. The budget is enacted into law in even-numbered years, and amendments are enacted in odd-numbered years.

The SOQ program required the Commonwealth to change its school funding formula to include a calculation for determining a locality's wealth—i.e., fiscal capacity. Using a mixture of true value of property (weighted at .5), local adjusted gross income (weighted at .4), and local taxable retail sales (weighted at .1), the state determines local fiscal capacity on a range from 0 to 1.0 as shown in Figure 48.1. The top capacity level is capped at 0.80 while the lowest capacity school division is currently set at .1754. This value is referred to as the Local Composite Index (LCI) which determines the Local Required Effort (LRE). This value tends to equalize

ADM Component =

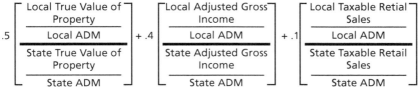

Population Component =

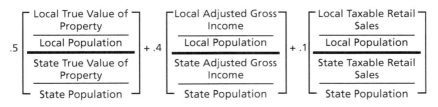

Local Composite Index =
((.6667 x ADM Component) + (.333 x Population Component)) x 0.45
(average local share)

Figure 48.1 Local Composite Index Calculation. *Source:* Dickey, K. C. (2013, July). Overview of K–12 education funding in Virginia (Direct Aid to Public Education Budget). Richmond, VA: Virginia Department of Education, page 16. Retrieved from https://www.nvic.org/cmstemplates/nvic/pdf/state-legislature/soq-funding-presentation-3.pdf

for variance in local fiscal capacity, as less wealthy school divisions receive more state aid while wealthier school divisions receive less aid.

Using the formula in Figure 48.1, a school division with an LCI of .3511 would be responsible for funding 35.11% of SOQ costs—i.e., the school division's LRE. In turn, the state would fund 64.89% of SOQ costs. The SOQ funding level is considered to be a low bar, as all school divisions in Virginia typically exceed the local required SOQ funding level of effort. In FY 2017, the average local expenditure in excess of LRE was 81.39%.[11]

SOQ funding is the largest category of Virginia's Direct Aid budget to school divisions, averaging about 90% of state funding.[12] Additional funding is appropriated in five other categories including:

- Incentive Programs;
- Categorical Programs;
- Lottery Proceeds Fund;

- Supplemental Education Programs;
- Federal Funds.

OTHER FUNDING CATEGORIES[13]

Incentive Programs

Virginia's school aid plan does not require incentive programs, leaving them voluntary for localities. Examples of incentive programs include Governor's Schools, additional special education programs, and compensation supplements in the Commonwealth's higher cost of living areas. Participating school divisions must agree to ensure they will offer the specific program and meet all established requirements. This category generally accounts for 2–3% of total state funding.

Categorical Programs

Categorical programs provide funding beyond that in the SOQ required by state or federal regulations. These programs target specific student populations such as adult education and literacy, Virtual Virginia (on-line courses for students enrolled in public schools), required services for students identified as eligible for special education services, and the school lunch program's state match. This category generally accounts for approximately 1% of total state funding.

Lottery Proceed Funds

Lottery Proceed Funds are designed for 20 programs formerly funded with general funds. Virginia's lottery began in 1987 to aid public education. But rather than supplement state education funding, the lottery funds supplanted it. Lottery revenue funds four SOQ accounts: Textbooks, English Language Learners (ESL), Early Reading Intervention, and the Standards of Learning (SOL—academic competencies required for state accountability testing) for Algebra Readiness. Most funding requires a local match, and some funding is equalized based on student eligibility for free or reduced price lunch rates. The Virginia Preschool Initiative, Early Reading Intervention, and K–3 Class Size Reduction programs also receive funding. This category generally accounts for 7–8% of total state funding.

Supplemental Education Funds

Supplemental Education Funds provide monies for specific purposes that the Act spells out. This small percentage of state funding (less than 1%), goes to the Virginia Teaching Scholarship Loan program and National Board Certification teacher bonuses. Funding is not available to all school divisions in the Commonwealth—eligibility is restricted to language in the Act.

Federal Funding

Typically, federal funding for schools in the state of Virginia comes through the Elementary and Secondary Education Act[14] (ESEA—now ESSA), Individuals with Disabilities Education Act[15] (IDEA), Carl Perkins Act,[16] Adult Education and Family Literacy Act,[17] and the School Nutrition Act.[18] Funds are paid on a reimbursement basis to school divisions based on a formula.

GENERAL TRANSPORTATION

Each school day, more than 15,000 school buses transport almost 1 million students in the state of Virginia.[19] The state allows reimbursement for school division transportation expenses, including allowed mileage and school bus purchases under the Direct Aid Budget. School divisions are eligible for percentage reimbursement of allowable charges based on the LCI.

SCHOOL FACILITIES

By legislative requirement, responsibility for constructing, furnishing, and equipping public schools in Virginia is the responsibility of local school divisions. School facilities can be financed using (1) cash, (2) bonds, or (3) bank loans. Bonds are the most frequently used vehicle. Virginia's constitution limits cities and towns when issuing bonds or other interest-bearing obligations to 10% of local assessed real estate value.[20] Counties wishing to sell bonds are required to hold a referendum for voter approval.[21]

General obligation bonds are secured by the full faith and credit of the issuer, with taxing power by one of four methods. First, direct local government borrowing occurs when the locality issues and sells bonds in the public or private market. Second, financing can come through the Literary Fund Direct Loan program which is administered through the Virginia Department of Education. This mechanism funds individual projects up to $7.5 million, with a cap of $20 million to any locality. Third, financing can come from the Virginia Public School Authority (VPSA), a pooled bond program administered by VSPA. Fourth, funding can come through Subject to Appropriation Bonds, usually issued through a Local Industrial Development Authority (IDA) or Local Economic Development Authority (EDA). The IDA or EDA borrows the required funds to build the school and then leases the school back to the school division. This fourth method is usually more expensive than the first three methods.

After construction is completed, building maintenance is funded through SOQ dollars according to the LCI. Additional information on school facility funding can be found at the following location.[22]

CAREER AND TECHNICAL EDUCATION

Virginia's Career and Technical Education (CTE) program is funded through state appropriations to school divisions by SOQ funding and supplemented by federal funds through the Carl Perkins Career and Technical Education Act.

SPECIAL EDUCATION

The state of Virginia allocates funds for special education using a staff-based formula. For each child counted in the school division's average daily membership (ADM), the state pays an amount—called the *special education add-on*—to assist in the cost of implementing the state's special education program standards. The state calculates the per-child special education add-on amount by determining the theoretical number of teachers and classroom aides needed to meet the SOQ for special education at each school site. This theoretical number is based on information supplied on the December 1 Count of Children Receiving Special Education and Related Services. The state then determines its share of these theoretical costs according to the school division's LCI. The state pays these funds into each local school division's general fund.[23] All disbursements are subject to availability of funds.

The state of Virginia provides additional funds to support costs of providing special education in local school divisions for homebound instruction, children with disabilities enrolled in public regional special education programs, children with disabilities receiving special education and related services in regional or local jails, and children with disabilities whose IEPs specify private day or private residential placement. The state also reimburses costs for educating children with disabilities who have been placed in Code of Virginia-licensed foster care or other custodial care, orphanages or children's homes, or child-care institution or group homes. Tuition for institutional placements is funded through an interagency pool which exists under the Comprehensive Services Act to pay the state's share of these costs. Payment is in the form of percentage reimbursement based on the LCI for actual costs incurred for services purchased.[24] Likewise, state and federal funds support education of children with disabilities at state mental health facilities, state training centers for people with intellectual disabilities, and state specialized children's hospitals. Once the school division receives state approval, the school division spends the monies and the state reimburses approved expenditures.

Currently, the state of Virginia is in process of transitioning from the existing model of funding special education regional programs to a new model meant to provide a more equitable distribution of funds to all 132 Virginia school divisions for students with intensive support needs.[25] In perspective, for Fiscal Years 2018–2020, Virginia's budgets are $382.4 million, $397.7 million, and $398.5 million respectively (based on Chapter 2 budget).[26] For the school year 2018–2019, Virginia's state total for IDEA Part B (Section 611) special education flow-through funding was $263,163,370 million,[27] and the state's total for Part B (Section 619) preschool subgrants was $6,733,264.[28]

The local school division also pays a proportionate share of its federal special education funds for special education and related services costs for children ages 3–21 with disabilities whose parents homeschool or place them in private elementary or secondary schools, including religious schools, located within the school division. These costs may include direct and consultative services, equipment or materials for training for private school teachers, and other private school personnel.[29]

Eligibility for federal funds for preschool and K–12 special education programs depends partly on the school division's maintenance of fiscal effort: i.e., the locality must use federal funds to supplement, but not supplant, state and local special education and related services expenditures.[30] A formula considering historical federal funding, total school enrollment, and the locality's poverty level determines amounts each division receives. School divisions may also seek federal Medicaid reimbursement for certain students and services by applying to the Department of Medical Assistance Services to be an approved provider.[31]

If the Virginia Department of Education (VDOE) determines that a school division is adequately providing a free and appropriate public education to all children with disabilities living in the area the division serves using state and local funds, the VDOE may reallocate unused funds under Part B to other school divisions in the state that are not adequately providing special education and related services.

VIRTUAL EDUCATION

The Code of Virginia allows school divisions to offer online instruction to students in multiple divisions using a private organization, educational institution, or nonprofit virtual school organization that meets Board of Education approved criteria to operate as a multi-division online provider (MOP). Multi-division online providers may be private or non-profit organizations or may be run by local school boards. MOPs must hold accreditation from a Board of Education-approved agency in addition to meeting Board criteria.[32] Local school divisions wishing to provide an online learning option can contract with approved providers or may offer their own fully online or blended learning programs. Some school divisions may become multi-division online providers.

Adding to the identified options, since 2002 the VDOE has also offered Virtual Virginia (VVa), an online K–12 program for public school pupils. Students receive instruction via the Internet through a secure web environment; students may participate at school or at home. The VDOE may contract with one or more local school boards that have created online courses to make one or more such courses available to other school divisions through the VVa.

The state of Virginia funds online supplemental and statewide online learning programs using a fixed annual appropriation that sets a limit to the number of students served.[33] In FY 2019, Virginia allocated $5.4 million for the VVa.[34] While VVa charges no fee for in-state public school students who enroll in the standard core, world language, electives or those participating in the Early College Scholars (ECS) program, non-ECS Virginia public school students enrolled in AP courses pay $375 multiplied by the LCI. Similarly, Virginia's private and homeschooled students pay $499 per full-credit course and $299 per half-credit course. Students pay for textbooks, fees, and other materials.[35] VVa also charges enrollment fees for all VVa summer school students at $375 per course.[36]

Likewise, school divisions making these courses available online to other school divisions may charge a per-course or per-student fee to defray costs of developing courses and providing instruction using teachers employed by the local school board. The VDOE must approve such fee schedules before the school board offers the course through VVa.[37]

FOOD SERVICES

By law, food service operations must be self-supporting in Virginia. Other local or state categorical funds cannot be used to supplement food service budgets.

Sale of meals, free and reduced price meal reimbursements, and donations from various federal, state or local sources must fund the entire budget.

CHARTER SCHOOLS

All charter schools in Virginia are nonsectarian alternative public schools, located within a school division and under the authority of a local school board.[38] A public charter school may be created as a new school or established by converting all or part of an existing school. No public charter can be created by converting a private school or nonpublic home-based educational program. Enrollment is open to children residing in the relevant school division (or divisions for regional public charter schools) using a lottery process on a space-available basis. Public charter students are included in the division's ADM. Charters may be approved/renewed for a period not exceeding five years. At present, Virginia has eight public charter schools in operation.

The limited number of authorized charter schools may be related to Virginia's clear and accountable public charter school laws. Before a public charter application (or renewal) can be submitted for review, the state Board of Education must review, comment, and decide whether the proposed application meets the Board's approval criteria. The Board examines applications for feasibility, curriculum, fiscal soundness, and other objective criteria consistent with existing state laws. As part of the application, the public charter must report on academic and other progress. It must also provide a concise and clear financial statement on Board-prescribed forms disclosing the costs of administration, instruction, and other spending categories. This practice enables the Board and the public to compare costs with other schools or similar organizations. Failure to make reasonable progress toward achievement of content standards or student performance and/or failure to meet generally accepted standards of fiscal management may lead to the charter's revocation.[39]

The local school board contracts with each public charter school through an agreement stating the conditions for funding the charter, including funding for educational programs and services (e.g., food service, custodial and maintenance, curriculum, media and library services, warehousing) to be provided. Per-pupil funding provided to the charter school is negotiated in the charter agreement and must be commensurate with the average school-based costs of educating students in existing schools in the division (or divisions) unless the cost of operating the charter school is less than the average school-based cost. Funding and service agreements may not provide financial incentive – or constitute financial disincentive – to establish a public charter school. Public charters also receive a proportionate share of state and federal resources allocated to students with disabilities and school personnel assigned to special education programs under other federal or state categorial aid for eligible students. Any educational and related fees collected from students enrolled at a public charter school are credited to the public charter's account established by the relevant local school board. Finally, a public charter school's management committee (composed of parents of students enrolled in the school, teachers, and administrators working in the school, and community sponsors' representatives) is authorized to accept gifts, donations, or grants made to the charter and to spend funds in accordance with the donor's prescribed conditions as long as the conditions are in accord with law or the charter agreement.

Importantly, a management committee administers the charter school in a manner in which the charter and the local school board agree. Public charters are subject to the SOQ and all standards of learning and standards of accreditation requirements. Any services for which a public charter school contracts with a school division—such as for building and grounds, maintenance and operations, or performance of any required service—cannot exceed the division's cost to provide such services. Under no circumstance may a public charter school charge tuition or be required to pay rent for space.

In 2007 and as amended in 2016, the state of Virginia created in the state treasury a special non-reverting fund named the Public Charter School Fund. This fund is to be credited with any gifts, grants, bequests, or donations from public or private sources and paid into the state treasury to support public charters. At the end of each year, any monies remaining in the fund, including interest, is meant to not revert to the general fund. Rather, these monies remain in the Charter Fund for the purpose of supporting public charter schools. The state Comptroller, upon written request from the Superintendent of Public Instruction, is the only person who can expend and disburse these funds. The state Board of Education established criteria for making distributions from the fund, with guidelines governing it as necessary and appropriate.[40]

Accountability is a watchword for Virginia's public charter schools. In 2016, the General Assembly passed a law amending charter applications, adding a section on applicability of other laws, regulations, policies and procedures for civil rights, health and safety, and student assessment and accountability. The revision required the charter contract to address academic and operational performance expectations, indicators, measures, and metrics based on a performance framework with annual performance targets. The performance framework must include indicators, measures, and metrics of student academic proficiency; student academic growth; achievement gaps in both proficiency and growth (disaggregated) between major student subgroups;[41] attendance; recurrent annual enrollment;

postsecondary education readiness of high school students; fiscal performance and sustainability; and management committee performance and stewardship, including compliance with all applicable laws, regulations, and terms of the charter contract. An executed charter school contract must be approved in an open meeting of the local school board before a charter school can begin. Moreover, public charter management committees are subject to and must comply with the Virginia's Freedom of Information Act.[42]

STATE FUNDING FOR NON-PUBLIC SCHOOLS

Virginia has not engaged in public funding for non-public schools to any extent other than required by law—mainly in testing students for special education eligibility. Additionally, school divisions pay a proportionate share of federal special education funds for children ages 3–21 with disabilities whose parents homeschool or place them in private elementary or secondary schools, including religious schools, located in the school division. Recent state legislative attempts to enable parents to use state funds to pay for private schools or home schooling have not been successful.[43]

VIRGINIA RETIREMENT SYSTEM[44]

Virginia has three basic retirement plans for public school employees named Plan 1, Plan 2, and the Hybrid plan. The plan to which employees belong depends on date of hire. Plans 1 and 2 are defined benefit plans. The Hybrid plan is a mixture of defined contribution and defined benefit. Each plan provides a successively lower retirement benefit for employees.

Those in Plan 1 were hired or rehired before July 1, 2010 and must have at least five years' creditable service as of January 1, 2013 and must not have not taken a refund. The account accrues at 4% interest, compounded annually. The retirement benefit is based on the average of the employee's 36 consecutive months of highest compensation, years of service, and a multiplier of 1.7. An unreduced benefit requires the employee to be at least 50 years of age with at least 30 years of creditable service or age 65 with at least 60 months of credit. Employees must contribute 5% of compensation on a pre-tax salary reduction basis.

A hypothetical retirement Plan 1 employee's benefit could be calculated as follows. Assume the highest three-year average salary of $100,000 over a 30-year career with the multiplier at 1.7. Thus, 30 years multiplied by 1.7 equals 51% of the average salary or $51,000. If another hypothetical employee had the same final average salary with 40 years' service, 40 multiplied by 1.7 equals 68% of salary or $68,000 per year. A $4.00 per year health insurance credit is available for those with at least 15 years of service, along with a benefit reducing the life insurance plan to 25% of the original benefit over time.

Those in Plan 2 were hired or rehired before July 1, 2010 and did not have at least five years of creditable service as of January 1, 2013 and had not taken refunds. The account accrues at 4% interest compounded. The retirement benefit is based on the average of the employee's 60 consecutive months of highest compensation, years of service, and a multiplier of 1.65. An unreduced benefit requires the employee to be of normal Social Security retirement age with at least 60 months service credit or when the person's age in years and service in years equals 90. Employees contribute 5% of compensation on a pre-tax salary-reduction basis.

A hypothetical retirement Plan 2 employee benefit calculates as follows. Assume the highest five-year average salary of $100,000 over a 30-year career at age 60 (30 + 60 = 90) with a multiplier of 1.65. Thirty years multiplied by 1.65 equals 49.5% of average salary, or $49,500. If another hypothetical employee had the same final average salary with 40 years' service, 40 multiplied by 1.65 equals 66% of the salary or $66,000 per year. A $4.00 per year health insurance credit is available for those with at least 15 years' service along with a benefit-reducing life insurance plan.

Those in the Hybrid Plan were hired on or after January 1, 2014. The employee contributes a mandatory 4% of creditable compensation to the plan. Employees contribute on a pre-tax salary reduction basis. The employer pays to the defined benefit component of the plan at the same rate (4%), less employer contributions to the defined contribution component of the retirement plan. Employees contribute 1% of creditable compensation to the 401(a) (Hybrid Plan defined contribution) account with an employer match. Beginning January 1, 2016 school divisions could elect to offer Hybrid Plan employees an employer-sponsored 403(b) option for employee's voluntary contributions. Employees could contribute up to 4% of compensation, with employers matching up to 2.5% of compensation.

A hypothetical retirement Hybrid Plan employee benefit calculates as follows. Assume the highest five-year average salary of $100,000 over a 30-year career at age 60 (30 + 60 = 90), with a multiplier of 1.0. Thirty years multiplied by 1.0 equals 30% of average salary, or $30,000. If another hypothetical employee had the same final average salary with 40 years' service, 40 multiplied by 1.0 equals 40% of salary or $40,000 per year. On top of this benefit is the defined contribution plan. This component requires an employee/employer contribution of 1% with a voluntary employee contribution of 0–4% and an employer match of 0–2.5%. This portion of the calculation would vary from person to person depending on the individual's voluntary contributions. The same $4.00 per year health insurance credit is available for those with at least 15 years' service along with a benefit-reducing life insurance plan as for those in Plan 1 or Plan 2.

REVENUE

Revenue for Virginia's public schools mainly comes from local taxes, state sales tax, state taxes, and federal funds. Table 48.1 shows amounts and percentages from each source. Local taxes are the primary source of revenue for public schools. The major source of funds comes from local property taxes on real estate and public service corporations. Other local taxes come from optional local sales, motel and hotel rooms, personal property, business licenses, utility, motor vehicle licenses, and others. In FY 2017, local funds accounted for 51.34% of total public school funding.

State sales tax rates vary in Virginia. Rates are higher in three regions—Hampton Roads, Northern Virginia, and the Historic Triangle areas. Table 48.2 shows those rates. There is a general sales tax rate and an additional rate for food for home consumption. A dedicated 1¢ state sales tax is considered local revenue and is apportioned among localities based on census count. State sales tax revenue accounts for 8.67% of Virginia's public school budgets.

State taxes account for the second largest source of revenue for public schools. Virginia has been considered a low tax state for many years.

TABLE 48.1 Revenue and Expenditure by Source, Percentage for Virginia Public Schools, FY 2017

Source	Revenue/Expenditure	Percent
Local	$8,024,690,150	51.34
State	$5,132,518,582	32.83
Sales Tax	$1,354,566,067	8.67
Federal	$1,118,654,107	7.16
Total	$15,630,428,907	100.00

Source: Table 15 of the Superintendent's Annual Report for Virginia, FY 2017. Retrieved from http://www.doe.virginia.gov/statistics_reports/supts_annual_report/2016-17/index.shtml

TABLE 48.2 Virginia Sales Tax Rates

	Hampton Roads	Northern Virginia	Historic Triangle	Everywhere Else
General Sales Tax Rate	6.0%	6.0%	7.0%	5.3%
Food for Home Consumption	2.5%	2.5%	2.5%	2.5%

Source: https://tax.virginia.gov/retail-sales-and-use-tax

According to one review, in 2012 Virginia ranked eighth in per-capita income among all states and ranked among the lowest in state fiscal effort for public schools.[45] Education Week's *Quality Counts 2018* gave Virginia a grade of C for state education spending on education and total taxable resources.[46] A third study showed Virginia ranking at 34th in the U.S. on fiscal effort for public schools in 2016.[47] And despite Virginia's extensive military and government presence, federal funding typically accounts for less than 10% of public school funding.

SUMMARY

Table 48.3 shows the operating budget and the capital budget for Virginia for both years of the biennium. Education accounts for just over 34% of an almost $57 billion operating budget and just over 21% of the $1.22 billion capital budget for FY 2019.[48] FY 2020 is set for amendment during the next budget cycle.

The number of students in Virginia's public schools fell by 9,465 headcount from the beginning of the 2017–2018 school year until year end.[49] This could signal a reduction in funding for the coming education budget cycle.

TABLE 48.3 Virginia's Operating and Capital Budget for the 2018–2020 Biennium

Operating Budget for the 2018–2020 Biennium	Dollars	
	FY 2019	FY 2020
Education	$19,437,284,736	$19,711,193,513
Health and Human Resources	$16,788,153,180	$18,507,494,586
Transportation	$7,458,893,989	$7,035,705,622
Administration	$4,071,420,947	$4,177,894,413
Public Safety	$3,138,811,641	$3,177,187,297
Finance	$2,626,205,010	$2,679,216,778
Independent Agencies	$987,724,150	$973,655,640
Commerce and Trade	$925,805,985	$923,967,289
Judicial	$529,358,799	$538,749,664
Natural Resources	$430,206,909	$390,302,417
Central Appropriations	$202,537,045	$410,047,561
Agriculture and Forestry	$111,373,547	$111,152,547
Legislative	$96,276,428	$96,176,428
Veterans and Defense Affairs	$87,838,961	$101,196,772
Executive Officers	$71,694,622	$70,901,065
Total Operating Budget	$56,963,585,949	$58,904,841,592
Capital Budget		
Central Appropriations	$498,303,936	$128,566,436
Transportation	$416,000,000	$85,000,000
Education	$259,707,000	$3,100,000
Natural Resources	$14,620,000	$10,400,000
Administration	$13,600,000	$0
Everything Else	$18,150,000	$0
Total Capital Budget	$1,220,380,936	$227,066,436

Source: Virginia General Assembly (n.d.), DPB Home Page, Chapter 2, 2018–2020. Virginia's Budget, Richmond, VA: Author. Retrieved from http://publicreports.dpb.virginia.gov/rdPage.aspx?rdReport=BDOCFinal_FrontPage&Biennium=2018-2020&BudgetRound=Initial

NOTES

1. Jean Jacques Rousseau, "A Discourse of Political Economy, 1758" in *The Social Contract and Discourses,* translation and introduction by G. D. H. Cole (London: J. M. Dent & Sons, 1973), p.149.

2. A. de Toqueville. *Democracy in America.* (1835/2000). (trans. By H.C. Mansfield and D. Winthrop). Chicago, IL: University of Chicago Press (2002) p. 180.
3. E. Cubberley. *Public Education in the United States: A Study and Interpretation of American Educational History.* Cambridge, MA: Houghton Mifflin (1947) pp. 97–105.
4. *Constitution of Virginia, (1971),* Article VIII, §8 and *Code of Virginia (1950),* §§22.1-142 to 22.1-161.
5. Commonwealth of Virginia. General Assembly. House of Delegates (1810). *Journal of the House of Delegates of the Commonwealth of Virginia.* Richmond, VA: Author, Feb. 2, 1810, Chap.14, p. 5.
6. *Acts of Virginia Assembly of the Commonwealth of Virginia, (1818).*
7. *Constitution of Virginia, (1869),* Article VIII, §§1-12.
8. Virginia school districts are referred to as school divisions.
9. Also known as "try to, but this is not required."
10. *Constitution of Virginia (1971).* Article VIII §1.
11. S. Constantino. Division of Legislative Automated Systems report. Richmond, VA; Virginia Department of Education (2018, January 10). Retrieved from https://rga.lis.virginia.gov/Published/2018/RD43/PDF
12. Virginia Education Association. Funding K–12 Education in the Commonwealth. School Finance 101. Richmond VA: Author. (2009, July). Retrieved from http://www.veanea.org/assets/document/finance-2010-04.pdf
13. Dickey (2013). Retrieved from https://www.nvic.org/cmstemplates/nvic/pdf/state-legislature/soq-funding-presentation-3.pdf
14. P.L. 89-10 (1965) as amended through *Every Child Succeeds Act* [ESSA] P.L. 114-95 (2015).
15. P.L. 94-142 (1975) as amended et seq.
16. P.L. 115-224 (2018).
17. PL 113-128 (2014).
18. P.L. 111-296 (2010).
19. Virginia Department of Education (n.d.) Pupil Transportation. Richmond, VA: Author. Retrieved from http://www.doe.virginia.gov/support/transportation/index.shtml
20. Virginia Constitution, Article VII, §10(a). Debt.
21. *Code of Virginia,* §15.2-2611. Holding of election; order authorizing bonds; authority of governing body.
22. http://www.doe.virginia.gov/support/facility_construction/literary_fund_loans/funding_options.pdf
23. Virginia Department of Education (n.d.). How Special Education Programs are Funded in Virginia's Schools. Richmond, VA: Author. Retrieved from http://www.doe.virginia.gov/special_ed/grants_funding/how_speced_funded.pdf
24. Ibid.
25. Superintendent's Memo #343-18 (2018, December 21). Update on Virginia Department of Education Study of Special Education Regional Programs. Retrieved from http://www.doe.virginia.gov/administrators/superintendents_memos/2018/index.shtml

26. Virginia Department of Education (2018, September 19). *Overview of Virginia K–12 Funding Formulas and Formal Approaches to Recognize Student Need.* p. 18. Retrieved from www.pen.k12.va.us/boe/ . . . /2018/ . . . /overview-of-virginia-k12-funding-formulas.pptx
27. Virginia Department of Education (2018). Division of Special Education and Student Services Grants and Funding. IDEA Part B (Section 611)—Flow-Through funding, 2018–2019. Retrieved from http://www.doe.virginia.gov/special_ed/grants_funding/index.shtml
28. Virginia Department of Education (2018). Division of Special Education and Student Services Grants and Funding. IDEA Part B (Section 619), Preschool subgrants awards. Retrieved from http://www.doe.virginia.gov/special_ed/grants_funding/index.shtml
29. Superintendent's Memo 309-18, Superintendent's Memo 309-18, Attachment A, and Guidance document (2018). Retrieved from http://www.doe.virginia.gov/special_ed/grants_funding/index.shtml#fed
30. Virginia Department of Education, Division of Special Education and Student Services (2010, January 25). Regulations Governing Special Education Programs for Children with Disabilities in Virginia. Part IV. Funding. Richmond, VA: Author. Retrieved from http://www.doe.virginia.gov/special_ed/regulations/state/regs_speced_disability_va.pdf
31. Virginia Department of Education (n.d.). How Special Education Programs are Funded in Virginia's Schools. Richmond, VA: Author. Retrieved from http://www.doe.virginia.gov/special_ed/grants_funding/how_speced_funded.pdf
32. Virginia Department of Education. (n.d.). Virtual School Programs (Multi-Division Online Providers). Retrieved from http://www.doe.virginia.gov/instruction/virtual_learning/virtual_schools/index.shtml
33. S. Patrick, J. Myers, J. Silverstein, A. Brown & J. Watson. *Performance-based Funding & Online Learning: Maximizing Resources for Student Success.* Vienna, VA: International Association for K–12 Online Learning (2015). Retrieved from http://qa.inacol.org/wp-content/uploads/2015/03/iNACOL-Performance-Based-Funding-and-Online-Learning.pdf; see also A. Powell, *Costs and Funding for Virtual Schools.* International Association for K–12 Online Learning. (n.d.). Retrieved from http://sfc.virginia.gov/pdf/committee_meeting_presentations/2011%20Interim/September_22/092211_No2.pdf
34. Virginia Department of Education (2018, September 19). *Overview of Virginia K–12 Funding Formulas and Formal Approaches to Recognize Student Need.* p. 22. Retrieved from www.pen.k12.va.us/boe/ . . . /2018/ . . . /overview-of-virginia-k12-funding-formulas.pptx
35. Virtual Virginia Fees and Billing. Richmond, VA: Virginia Department of Education (2018). Retrieved from https://www.virtualvirginia.org/about/fees-and-billing/
36. Virtual Virginia. Summer Session 2018. Richmond, VA: Virginia Department of Education. Retrieved from https://www.virtualvirginia.org/programs/summer/
37. Virginia House of Delegates (2018, January 10). House Bill No. 831. A bill to amend and reenact sec. 22.1-212.2 of the Code of Virginia, Relating to public

schools; Virtual Virginia' availability. Retrieved from https://lis.virginia.gov/cgi-bin/legp604.exe?181+ful+HB831
38. Virginia General Assembly (2016, July 1). Virginia's Charter School Laws. Code of Virginia. Retrieved from http://www.pen.k12.va.us/instruction/charter_schools/index.shtml
39. A public charter school applicant whose application was denied or a grantee whose charter was revoked or not renewed is entitled to petition the local school board for reconsideration. Before reconsideration, the applicant or grantee may seek technical assistance from the Superintendent of Public Instruction to address the reasons for the denial, revocation, or non-renewal.
40. Virginia Department of Education. (n.d.) Charter schools. Richmond, VA: Author. Retrieved from http://www.pen.k12.va.us/instruction/charter_schools/index.shtml
41. Student subgroups are based on gender, race, poverty status, special education status, English language learner status, and gifted status.
42. Virginia Department of Education. Charter Schools. Richmond, VA: Author (n.d.). Retrieved from http://www.pen.k12.va.us/instruction/charter_schools/index.shtml
43. House Bill 389, 2016.
44. All retirement plan information can be found at: https://www.varetire.org/members/index.asp
45. R.G. Salmon and M.D. Alexander. *Taking the Mystery Out of Virginia School Finance.* Ypsilanti, MI: National Council of Professors of Educational Administration (2014) p. 38–39.
46. Education Week. *Quality Counts 2018: Finance: Grading the States.* (2018, June 13) *37* (4), 20.
47. W. Owings and L. Kaplan. *American Public School Finance.* New York, NY: Routledge (2019 forthcoming).
48. Education includes both public and higher education.
49. Virginia Department of Education. Superintendent's Annual Report 2017–2018. Table 1, Membership. Richmond, VA: Author. Retrieved from http://www.doe.virginia.gov/statistics_reports/supts_annual_report/2017-18/index.shtml

CHAPTER 49

Washington

Staff Writer[1]

GENERAL BACKGROUND[2]

Washington's school finance system is driven by strong state constitutional provisions. Article IX §1 declares in forceful fashion:

> It is the paramount duty of the state to make ample provision for the education of all children residing within its borders, without distinction or preference on account of race, color, caste or sex.[3]

Article IX §2 goes on to mandate:

> The legislature shall provide for a general and uniform system of public schools. The public school system shall include common schools, and such high schools, normal schools, and technical schools as may hereafter be established. But the entire revenue derived from the common school fund and the state tax for common schools shall be exclusively applied to the support of the common schools.[4]

Notwithstanding, the state of Washington has experienced multiple lawsuits challenging the legislature's plan for funding public schools.[5] Modern reform progress in the state is generally marked as beginning in 1978 with the Washington supreme court's overturning the school finance system in *Seattle School District No. 1 v. State*,[6] a ruling that emphasized the specific language of 'paramount duty' and concluding that "... the constitution has created a 'duty' that is supreme, preeminent or dominant."[7] This represented a dramatic shift, as only four years earlier the same state high court had ruled in favor of the state in *Northshore School District v. Kinnear*.[8]

Funding Public Schools in the United States and Indian Country, pages 747–761
Copyright © 2019 by Information Age Publishing
All rights of reproduction in any form reserved.

Legislative action coincided with *Seattle I*, as the legislature passed the Basic Education Act[9] in which the state assumed responsibility for fully funding basic education along with substantially increased funding. Subsequent trial court litigation in *Seattle II*[10] found the legislation still flawed and added special education, bilingual, and remedial programs to the definition of basic education—a ruling that went uncontested by the state and with subsequent legislative formula revision to account for these modifications.

Other litigation followed,[11] with the most overarching state supreme court decision in 2012 in *McCleary v. State*.[12] Briefly said, *McCleary* examined fiscal adequacy arguments, finding that the state had failed to meet its paramount duty to amply fund schools because state monies fell short of actual costs of the basic education requirement. The legislature subsequently established a Joint Select Committee on Article IX Litigation, with the court ordering the committee to annually report on its progress toward the mandate to fully satisfy the court by 2018. Multiple legislative sessions followed, with the state supreme court finding the legislature in contempt on two occasions for failure to redress issues of class size and salaries. Legislative response was to establish an Education Funding Task Force in 2016 to gather market data after passing a reform bill.[13] The court's response acknowledged the time-consuming nature of the endeavor and that the legislature had committed to an implementation schedule. The court's most recent order came in late 2017,[14] concluding that the state had met its constitutional duty to fully fund basic education with regard to materials, supplies, and operating costs; pupil transportation; and categorical programs of basic education, including special education; the highly capable student program; the Transitional Bilingual Instruction Program; the Learning Assistance Program which provides remedial education; and the education of students in residential programs, juvenile detention, and adult correctional facilities.

BASIC SUPPORT PROGRAM

The effect of the 1977 Basic Education Act (BEA) has been at the heart of all recent disputes. The BEA defined a basic education for Washington children by establishing goals, minimum program hours, teacher contact hours, and a set of course offerings for school districts to provide. Intact today are seven of the original BEA programs known as General Apportionment; Special Education; pupil transportation; the Learning Assistance Program (LAP) for remediation assistance; the Transitional Bilingual Instruction Program (TBIP); the Highly Capable Program; and educational programs in juvenile detention centers and state institutions. The sum of these programs still form the state's principal definition of basic education.

As indicated, reform has impacted state fiscal support for Washington's school districts. Intervention by legislation particularly has occurred under Substitute House Bill (SHB) 2261[15] and SHB 2776[16] which collectively established a new funding formula and implemented K–3 class size reduction, changed pupil transportation, added all-day kindergarten, and increased Materials, Supplies, and Operating Costs (MSOC) funding. Other funding enhancements and reforms followed through Engrossed House Bill (EHB) 2242[17] which set in place for Fiscal Year 2018 increased funding for LAP, the Special Education Program, the Highly Capable Program, the TBIP, and reduced class sizes for career and technical education and skill centers. Upgrades were scheduled to continue for FY 2019, including additional funding enhancements for K–12 state salary and health benefits and state funding for professional learning days—all disputatious issues during the *McCleary* litigation.

Reforms flowing from litigation were comprehensive, including a framework for a new distribution formula for the basic education funding allocation based on state-defined prototypical schools and a new funding formula for pupil transportation. Changes were first effective in September 2011. SHB 2776 set targets and established a timeline to phase in enhancements to instructional programs, including all-day kindergarten, K–3 class size reduction to 17 students per teacher, and increased funding for MSOC. Those enhancements were to be fully implemented by the 2017–18 school year. The funding model required school district reporting of actual staffing and expenditures in order to permit comparison to the funding provided in the prototypical model. In addition, EHB 2242 provided new state common school tax revenues, increased state programming and funding for several K–12 basic education programs, reformed how local tax levy revenues were calculated[18] and their uses, and enacted other reforms to increase the transparency, accountability, and efficiency of school funding. In 2018, additional changes were made to K–12 funding through Engrossed Second Substitute Senate Bill (E2SSB) 6362,[19] including accelerating the schedule for increased state salary allocations for school employees to FY 2019, increasing the special education excess cost multiplier, adding a regionalization adjustment, and adding an experience factor to provide extra funding to school districts that met certain instructional staff requirements.

Operational Overview of the Program of Basic Education

As indicated, a basic education in Washington's school finance formula is comprised of (1) General Apportionment; (2) Special Education; (3) pupil transportation; (4) the Learning Assistance Program; (5) the Transitional Bilingual Instruction Program; (6) the Highly Capable Program; and (7) educational programs in juvenile detention centers and state institutions.

General Apportionment

The General Apportionment formula provides foundation state funding to school districts. Its purpose is to fund basic education along with several non-basic adjustments. The amount of formula aid received by each district varies based on legislative priority factors, with enrollment being the largest variable. Enrollment drives numbers of certificated, administrative, and classified staff and their associated salaries and benefits, as well as allocation of funds for other non-employee costs. On average, statewide allocation through the General Apportionment formula was estimated at $8,736 per pupil for FY 2019.

The General Apportionment formula is based on legislatively established prototypical school models, wherein a prototype proxies a level of resources needed to operate a school of a particular size containing particular student needs and grade levels. Per-pupil allocations are based on full-time equivalent (FTE) enrollment in each grade in the school district, adjusted for small schools and other factors. Funding is allocated to three primary groups: (1) *school* support; (2) *district-wide* support; and (3) *central administration* support. However, prototypes are not spending mandates, as local districts have discretionary authority in resource allocation except in categorical or dedicated programs. Prototype profiles are made available to the public, along with annual reports from local districts on resource utilization in those same categories so that citizens can make judgments about local resource effectiveness and efficiency by comparing local fiscal practice against the state's definition of a prototypical school.[20]

School-Level Support. A key allocation driver for a prototypical school is class size, expressed as the number of funded teachers. Table 49.1 shows the

TABLE 49.1 School Year 2018–19 Class Sizes

Grade	Class Size
Grades K–3	17
Grades 4–6	27
Grades 7–8	28.53
Grades 9–12	28.74
Career & Tech. Ed (CTE) 7–8	23
CTE 9–12	23
Skills Centers	20
Lab Science	19.98

Length of teacher day is assumed to be 5.6 hours in elementary school and 6.0 hours in middle and high school. Planning time is assumed to be 45 minutes per day in elementary school and 60 minutes in high school.
Source: Senate Committee Services, "A Citizen's Guide to Washington State K–12 Finance 2019." Olympia, WA (2019).

most recent legislative definition of the role of class size. The underlying calculation is:

(Enrollment/Class Size) × (1 + Planning Time Factor) = Teachers

Another key allocation driver in the school prototype model is other staff by organizational level. Table 49.2 shows the legislative definition for other staff types by elementary, middle, and high school levels. For example, the prototypical model assumes 400 students per elementary school. But if a school district has 800 elementary pupils, funding is doubled for staff positions based on pupil-teacher ratios.

District-Level Support. District-wide support is funded in the prototypical model since services need to be provided district-wide. Once again, funding is based on overall enrollment levels as seen in Table 49.3.

Central Administration Support. Administration costs directly associated with schools are included in the staffing levels seen in Table 49.2. Central administration receives an additional 5.3% of other staffing units generated by the formula. These staffing units include K–12 teachers, school-level staffing, and district-wide support; however, staffing for vocational programs, specialized classes, and categorical programs are excluded from the 5.3% add-on.

TABLE 49.2 School Year 2018–19 Staffing

Staffing	Elementary School	Middle School	High School
Prototypical School Size:			
Number of students	400	432	600
Staff per school:			
Principals/administrators	1.2530	1.3530	1.8800
Librarian/media specialist	0.6630	0.5190	0.5230
School nurses	0.0760	0.0600	0.0960
Social workers	0.0420	0.0060	0.0150
Psychologists	0.0170	0.0020	0.0070
Guidance counselors	0.4930	1.2160	2.5390
Instructional aides	0.8360	0.7000	0.6520
Office support and non-instructional aides	2.0120	2.3250	3.2690
Custodians	1.6570	1.9420	2.9650
Classified staff for student and staff safety	0.0790	0.0920	0.1410
Parent involvement coordinators	0.0825	0.0000	0.0000

Source: Senate Committee Services, "A Citizen's Guide to Washington State K–12 Finance 2019." Olympia, WA (2019).

TABLE 49.3 School Year 2018–19 District-Level Support

Number of Students	1,000
Classified Staff	Per 1,000 students
Technology	0.628
Facilities, maintenance, grounds	1.813
Warehouse, laborers, mechanics	0.332

Source: Senate Committee Services, "A Citizen's Guide to Washington State K–12 Finance. 2019" Olympia, WA (2019).

Non-Employee Costs. Finally, the General Apportionment formula includes an allocation for Materials, Supplies, and Operating Costs. The formula provides MSOC monies on a per-pupil basis, adjusted annually for inflation. The 2018 supplemental budget provided $1,267.80 per pupil for MSOC in school year 2018–19 for a total biennial cost of $2.7 billion. The 2018 supplemental budget also provided enhancements for grades 9–12 and for career and technical education and skill center programs for a total biennial cost of approximately $322 million. Table 49.4 provides detail on MSOC structure and costs.

Special Education Program

Special education is core to the Washington definition of a basic education program. Special education is based on the concept of excess costs

TABLE 49.4 School Years Budgeted Materials, Supplies, and Operating Costs (MSOC) 2017–18 and 2018–19

MSOC Component	Per-Pupil Allocation School Year 2017–18	Per-Pupil Allocation School Year 2018–19
Technology	$130.76	$133.24
Utilities and insurance	$355.30	$362.05
Curriculum and textbooks	$140.39	$143.06
Library materials	$20.00	$20.38
Other supplies	$278.05	$283.33
Instructional professional development for Certified and classified staff	$21.71	$22.12
Facilities maintenance	$176.01	$179.36
Security and central office	$121.94	$124.26
Total	**$1,244.16**	**$1,267.80**
Students in grades 9–12	$1,415.07	$1,441.96
Students in CTE & skill center programs	$1,472.01	$1,499.98

Source: Senate Committee Services, "A Citizen's Guide to Washington State K–12 Finance 2019." Olympia, WA (2019).

of educating students receiving services. The formula was implemented in 1995 and remained unchanged until the 2018 legislative session when the excess cost multiplier was increased from 0.9309 to 0.9609.

Excess funding is provided for birth through four-year-olds who are eligible and enrolled in special education. This category of qualified recipient receives 115% of the school district's average per-pupil General Apportionment allocation. Excess cost is also provided for five to 21-year-olds, with the excess cost allocation set at 96% of the district's average per-pupil General Apportionment allocation. In addition, the state's special education funding structure provides safety net funding for districts able to demonstrate extraordinary special education program costs beyond state and federal resources. The 2018 supplemental budget appropriated $67 million for this purpose.

The total 2018 supplemental budget for special education was $2.5 billion, with the estimated average additional special education per-pupil amount at $6,897 for FY 2018 and $8,749 for FY 2019.

Transportation

Also included in the Washington definition of a program of basic education is transportation services. A revised formula was adopted in 2011 and became fully implemented in FY 2015. Implementation was phased in to define transportation of students as to-and-from school as part basic education, with the new formula requiring funding to be calculated using a regression analysis of major cost factors including basic and special education student ridership counts, district geography, roadway miles, average distance to school, and other statistically significant coefficients. State funding for FY 2018's supplemental budget for pupil transportation was approximately $1 billion.

Included in the new transportation formula was state funding for school bus replacement using a depreciation schedule. The formula provides annual payments to school districts from point of purchase through scheduled end of service. State allocations are deposited to the district's transportation fund to be used only for purchase of new buses or for major repairs.

Learning Assistance Program

Also included in the Washington definition of a program of basic education is the Learning Assistance Program (LAP). LAP's purpose is to provide remediation assistance to students scoring below grade level in reading, math, and language arts. LAP allocations are based on students in poverty as measured by eligibility for free or reduced price lunch.

State law provides 2.3975 hours of LAP instruction per week, with associated parameters expecting class sizes of 15 students per certificated instructional staff. The LAP formula translated to additional funding of $671 million for the 2017–19 biennium. EHB 2242 also created a new program within LAP for 2018, establishing a high poverty, school-based LAP allocation for schools with at least 50% of students eligible for free or reduced meal service. The new program required 1.1 hours per week in extra instruction with a class size of 15 pupils, with strict accounting for distribution of funds to those schools that generated the allocation and with proof that funding did not supplant district expenditures for LAP for these same schools. Funding for the added program in the 2017–19 biennial budget was approximately $200 million.

Transitional Bilingual Instructional Education Program

Also included in Washington's definition of a program of basic education is the Transitional Bilingual Instructional Program (TBIP). TBIP was first legislatively created in 1979 to support students whose primary language is not English and whose English skills impede learning proficiency in English.

For students in grades K–6, assuming class sizes of 15 students, the TBIP formula provides 4.778 hours of bilingual instruction per week. New funding under EHB 2242 also provided funding for two additional hours of instruction per week in grades 7–12, thereby increasing the minimum allocation to a total of 6.778 hours with a class size of 15 students. Under these requirements and conditions, the TBIP formula provided additional funding of approximately $310 million in the FY 2018 supplemental budget. Funding for transitional support for up to two years after program exit is also provided to assist students who have met proficiency standards. Under current law, 3.0 hours of additional instruction are provided for students who exited the program in the immediate prior two years.

Highly Capable Program

The Highly Capable Program is also included in the state definition of a program of basic education. The program serves gifted students for up to 5% of a school district's basic education student enrollment. This allocation more than doubled in percentage amount (up from 2.314%) under EHB 2242.

The Highly Capable Program provides 2.1590 hours per week in qualified instruction, assuming class sizes of 15 students. This provision added approximately $45.7 million for the 2017–19 biennium.

Institutional Education Programs

Finally, also included in the Washington definition of a program of basic education are certain institutional education programs whereby the state funds a 220-day set of services for children in certain institutions. School districts, educational service districts, or others receive institutional education funds if they provide these educational programs. While amounts vary based on type and size of programs, the current state allocation was approximately $28 million for the 2017–19 biennium.

OTHER STATE FUNDING OUTSIDE THE BASIC SUPPORT PROGRAM

The state of Washington funds programs and activities beyond the legislative definition of basic education. Table 49.5 cumulatively identifies funding for both basic and extended programs for FY 2018. In sum, the state funds the basic areas of General Apportionment, Special Education, Transportation, Learning Assistance Program, Highly Capable Program, Transitional Bilingual Instructional Education, and Institutions *plus* the supplemental areas of compensation adjustments, levy equalization, statewide programs,

TABLE 49.5 Fiscal Year 2018 Basic and Non-Basic Education State Supports		
Basic Education Programs (in millions)		
General Apportionment	$14,989	65.7%
Special Education	$2,043	9.0%
Transportation	$1,038	4.6%
Learning Assistance	$672	2.9%
Bilingual	$46	0.1%
Institutions	$28	0.1%
Subtotal Basic Education Programs	**$19,126**	**83.8%**
Non-Basic Education Programs (in millions)		
Compensation Adjustments	$2,320	10.2%
Local Effort Assistance (Levy Equalization)	$877	3.8%
Education Reform	$291	1.3%
OSPI and Statewide Programs	$107	0.5%
Educational Service Districts	$18	0.1%
Food Service	$15	0.1%
Charter Schools	$56	0.2%
Charter School Commission	$1	0.0%
Subtotal Non-Basic Education Programs	**$3,685**	**16.2%**
Total State Funds[a] (in millions)	**$22,811**	**100.0%**

Source: Senate Committee Services, "A Citizen's Guide to Washington State K–12 Finance 2019." Olympia, WA (2019).

[a] State Funds include the General Fund-state, Opportunity Pathways Account, the Education Legacy Trust Account, the Pension Funding Stabilization Account, and the Dedicated McCleary Penalty Account, together known as Total Near General Fund.

educational service districts, food service, charter schools, and the charter school commission.

Program details and impacts are seen in Figure 49.1 which graphically visualizes spending by program for FY 2018. In brief, school funding reform in Washington has resulted in expenditure patterns as follows:

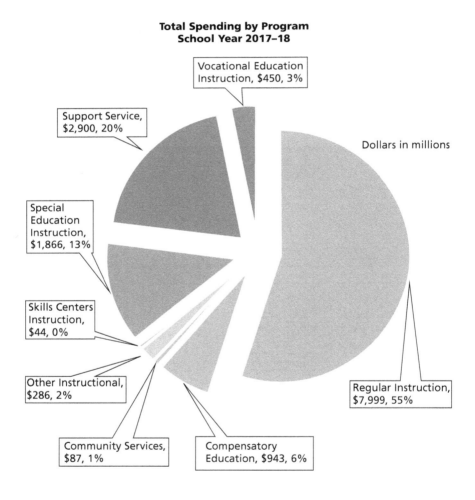

Source: OSPI F195/F196 SAFS Reports

Figure 49.1 Fiscal Year 2018 Program-Level Spending. *Source:* Senate Committee Services, "A Citizen's Guide to Washington State K–12 Finance 2019." Olympia, WA (2019).

- *Regular Instruction.* $8 billion in basic education expenditures, including alternative learning and dropout reengagement;
- *Special Education Instruction:* $1.9 billion in excess costs for special education and related services;
- *Support Services:* $2.9 billion for activities to accomplish objectives supporting the educational programs of school districts, including food services and transportation;
- *Compensatory Education Instruction:* $943 million on programs including federal remediation, Learning Assistance Program, and state institutions for juveniles;
- *Community Services:* $87 million on programs primarily benefiting communities, including public radio or television stations, childcare programs, and recreational programs;
- *Other Instructional Programs:* $286 million on programs including traffic safety, summer school, highly capable, targeted assistance for at-risk students, and youth training programs;
- *Skills Centers Instruction:* $44 million on operational costs for centers approved the Office of Superintendent of Public Instruction (OSPI);
- *Vocational Education Instruction:* $450 million, including the basic education allocation and enhanced allocations for MSOC and class-size reductions.

OTHER NOTABLE FEATURES

School Facilities

Although school capital construction was not held in *McCleary* to be part of the state's constitutional duty, the state of Washington provides financial assistance to school districts for new construction and remodeling of existing school buildings. State assistance is based on a state/local cost share and on the principle of equalizing the burden among school districts in order to minimize wealth effects.

Eligibility for state support for school facilities requires local voter approval of a bond levy or other funding for the local share of a capital project. State money follows, based on a formula comprised primarily of a set of space and cost standards and a matching ratio tied to local school district wealth. Unaided costs include site acquisitions, administrative buildings, stadiums/grandstands, most bus garages, and local sales tax. Costs eligible for state support include costs per-square-foot, architectural and engineering fees, construction management, value engineering studies, furniture and equipment, energy conservation reports, and inspection and testing.

Tax and Spending Limits

The full phase-in plan for the new Washington school finance system included tax limitations. In particular, districts' maintenance and operations (M&O) levies were restricted by EHB 2242 beginning in 2019 and beyond. EHB 2242 renamed M&O levies to be called 'enrichment' levies, a change also applied to transportation where such local levies were changed to be called ' transportation vehicle enrichment' levies. EHB 2242 established levy lids, so that a district's maximum enrichment levy is the lesser of $2,500 per pupil or a rate of $1.50 per $1,000 of assessed value and further permitting the cap to be adjusted by inflation beginning in 2020. Additionally starting in calendar year 2020, enrichment levies were subjected to a new requirement for pre-ballot approval by OSPI which is tasked with determining whether the district will spend enrichment levy revenues and other local revenues only for permitted enrichment activities.

Charter Schools

Charter schools have been part of Washington's landscape since 2012 when voters approved establishment of up to 40 charter schools. The measure stated that charter schools would be public common schools open to all children free of charge. Charter schools were held to the same basic education requirements under supervision of the OSPI. Under the act, charter schools must provide a basic education similar to that provided by traditional public schools, including instruction in academic learning requirements developed by the superintendent of public instruction. Finally, the 2012 authorization provided funding identical to other state public schools.

In 2015, the Washington supreme court ruled in *League of Women Voters*[21] that state tax monies could not be used in support of charter schools. The court held that charter schools are not 'common schools' under Article IX §§ 1–3 of the state constitution. The primary rationale rested on charter schools' lack of political accountability. In response, the legislature in 2016 shifted charter schools' funding source to the state lottery. This option came as a result of how the legislature in 2010 had passed E2SSB 6409[22] which set up the Washington Opportunity Pathways Account (WOPA) which, in part, was designated in support of early learning programs. In that same vein, in 2016 the legislature passed E2SSB 6194[23] shifting charter school funding to the WOPA, thereby avoiding direct expenditure of state general fund monies in support of charter schools.

Table 49.5 earlier identified state funding supports for Washington's charter schools in FY 2018.

CONCLUSION

Major school funding reform was realized over decades in the state of Washington. Like many states, reform was influenced by lengthy litigation. The nearby *McCleary* decision framed much of today's state funding system, so that Washington's funding profile as seen in Figure 49.2 is significantly changed from the pre-*McCleary* days.

Considered in tandem with Figure 49.1 earlier detailing FY 2018 spending outcomes, Figure 49.2 reveals and aligns spending patterns with revenue sources. Figure 49.2 illustrates today's reality in the state of Washington, showing a mix of funding sources:

- *State.* Approximately 71% ratio ($10.25 billion) in support of the seven programs currently defined as 'basic education': General Apportionment; Special Education; transportation; LAP; TBIP; the Highly Capable program; and educational programs in state institutions. The ratio includes other grants, allocations, and items funded from the state general fund and the education legacy trust account;
- *Local.* Approximately 17% ratio ($2.5 billion) derived primarily from local taxes which, beginning in calendar year 2019, were renamed 'enrichment levies;'
- *Federal.* Approximately 7% ratio ($1.04 billion) in support of the Individuals with Disabilities Education Act (IDEA), instructional as-

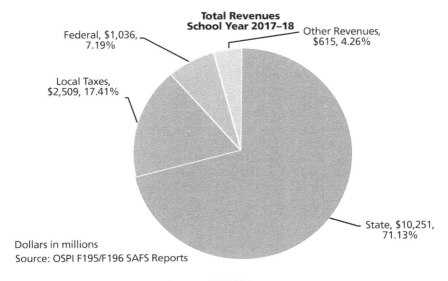

Figure 49.2 School Revenue Sources FY 2018.

sistance and other strategies aimed at high poverty schools, a variety of professional development activities, school lunch and nutrition, offsets to compensate for federal land ownership, and other smaller allocations and grants; and

- *Other Revenue and Reserves.* Approximately 4% ($615 million) derived from miscellaneous sources such as charges and fees for non-basic education programs, school lunch charges, revenue from other school districts, rental income, donations, and the use of reserves or fund balance.

NOTES

1. No state-based expert was available to author this chapter at time of publication. The chapter is drawn from sources as footnoted and represents the editorial staff's best interpretation of issues, trends and findings regarding the state of Washington. For additional information and updates and detail, contact the Office of Superintendent of Public Instruction.
2. By permission, much of this chapter follows and is condensed from the Senate Committee Services, "A Citizen's Guide to Washington State K–12 Finance. 2019." Olympia, WA (2019). Retrieved from http://leg.wa.gov/Senate/Committees/WM/Documents/Publications/BudgetGuides/2019/K–12%20Booklet_2019%20%28Final%29_ website%20version.pdf
3. Constitution of the State of Washington. Legislative Information Center (Revised 01-12-11), p. 36. Retrieved from http://leg.wa.gov/lawsandagencyrules/documents/12-2010-wastateconstitution.pdf
4. Ibid.
5. See chronology overview at SchoolFunding.Info (2019). Retrieved from http://schoolfunding.info/litigation-map/washington/#1485219774549-72fcfdc3-4082
6. 585 P.2d 71 (1978) known as *Seattle I.*
7. Ibid. p. 91.
8. 550 P.2d 178 (1974).
9. Ch. 359 Washington Laws, 1977 1st Ex. Sess. Retrieved from http://leg.wa.gov/CodeReviser/documents/sessionlaw/1977ex1c359.pdf
10. 647 P.2d 25 (1982).
11. See, e.g., *Federal Way School District No. 210 v. State of Washington,* 167 Wn.2d 514 (2009) mandating uniform content, certification, assessment, etc; *School Districts' Alliance for Adequate Funding of Special Education,* 244 P.3d 1 (2010) upholding the status quo; *League of Women Voters,* 355 P.3d 1131 (2015) disallowing public funds to charter schools; and *El Centro de la Raza v. Washington,* No. 94269-2 Slip Op. Filed October 25, 2018) holding that lottery money to support charter schools is permissible (as distinct from state appropriations).
12. 269 P.3d 227 (2012).
13. Engrossed House Bill (EHB) 2242 (Chapter 13, Laws of 2017, third special session).

14. *McCleary v. State of Washington,* Order Supreme Court No 84362-7. Filed November 15, 2017.
15. (Chapter 548, Laws of 2009).
16. (Chapter 236, Laws of 2010).
17. (Chapter 13, Laws of 2017, third special session).
18. EHB 2242 (see fn. 17 and text discussion above) mandated how the local share is calculated. Beginning in calendar year 2019, Local Effort Assistance (i.e., state aid) is to be calculated under a new formula that provides assistance for any school district unable to generate a local school tax levy of at least $1,500 per pupil when levying at a rate of $1.50 per $1,000 of assessed value. Beginning in calendar year 2020, the $1,500 per-pupil cap is to be increased by inflation.
19. (Chapter 266, Laws of 2018, regular session).
20. Available at the Office of Superintendent of Public Instruction. Retrieved from http://k12.wa.us/safs/INS/2776/Portal.asp.
21. *League of Women Voters v. State of Washington,* 355 P.3d 1131 (2015).
22. https://apps.leg.wa.gov/documents/billdocs/2009-10/Pdf/Bill%20Reports/Senate/6409-S2.E%20SBR%20APS%2010.pdf
23. http://lawfilesext.leg.wa.gov/biennium/2015-16/Pdf/Bill%20Reports/Senate/6194-S2.E%20SBR%20FBR%2016.pdf

CHAPTER 50

West Virginia

Keith A. Butcher[1]
Clinical Assistant Professor
University of Houston

GENERAL BACKGROUND

West Virginia became a state in 1863.[2] Article X of the state constitution stated, "The Legislature shall provide, as soon as practicable, for the establishment of a thorough and efficient system of free schools."[3] More particularly, the first two sections of Article X provided for establishment and funding of a system of free schools in clear terms:

> All money accruing to this State, being the proceeds of forfeited, delinquent, waste and unappropriated lands; and of lands heretofore sold for taxes and purchased by the State of Virginia, if hereafter redeemed, or sold to others than this State; all grants, devises or bequests that may be made to this State for the purposes of education, or where the purposes of such grants, devises or bequests are not specified; this State's just share of the Literary fund of Virginia, whether paid over or otherwise liquidated, and any sums of money, stocks or property which this State shall have the right to claim from the State of Virginia for educational purposes; the proceeds of the estates of all persons who may die without leaving a will or heir, and of all escheated lands; the proceeds of any taxes that may be levied on the revenues of any corporation hereafter created; all monies that may be paid as an equivalent for exemption from military duty, and such sums as may from time to time be appropriated by the Legislature for the purpose, shall be set apart as a separate fund, to be called the School Fund, and invested under such regulations as may be prescribed by law, in the interest bearing securities of the United States, or of this

State; and the interest thereof shall be annually applied to the support of free schools throughout the State, and to no other purpose whatever. By any portion of said interest remaining unexpended at the close of a fiscal year, shall be added to, and remain a part of, the capital of the School Fund.

The Legislature shall provide, as soon as practicable, for the establishment of a thorough and efficient system of free schools. They shall provide for the support of such schools by appropriating thereto the interest of the invested school fund; the net proceeds of all forfeitures, confiscations and fines accruing to this State under the laws thereof; and by general taxation on persons and property, or otherwise. They shall also provide for raising, in each township, by the authority of the people thereof, such a proportion of the amount required for the support of free schools therein as shall be prescribed by general laws.[4]

In 1933, the state legislature abolished the 398 original school districts and established county units of government. This action created 55 county school districts, each with five member boards of education.[5] A tax limitation amendment in 1934 established maximum tax rates on four classes of property.[6] The West Virginia Public School Support Plan (PSSP) was created in 1939. The PSSP was rewritten in 1971 and amended in 1973, 1981, and 1982 and has been revised almost every year since 1982.[7] In aggregate, the PSSP, among other areas, computes funding for schools in the areas of professional educators, service personnel, fixed charges, transportation, administration, other current expenses, and instructional programs.

In 1982, a circuit court in *Pauley v. Kelley*[8] found the system of school finance in West Virginia unconstitutional, stating that the system did not provide equitable and adequate funding for a thorough and efficient system of education. In addition to other deficiencies, the court found that:

> The inadequacies and inequalities in educational offerings in West Virginia are directly produced by the inadequacies and inequalities in the level of educational resources and expenditures among counties in West Virginia. The present system allocates funds according to factors such as the amount of a county's property wealth and its ability to pass excess and bond levies. These factors bear no relation to educational needs and costs of substantive educational offerings and results. Indeed, counties where children have the greatest educational needs attend school in counties which in most instances have the least taxable wealth per pupil and the fewest education resources.[9]

The court ordered the executive and legislative branches of government to develop a plan for an equitable quality system of education. The West Virginia supreme court approved a Master Plan for Public Education in 1984.[10] As a result of the Master Plan, the school aid formula was revised to provide more equitable funding distributions to counties. In 2003, the court closed the decades-long *Pauley* case, relinquishing jurisdiction.[11]

PUBLIC SCHOOL SUPPORT PROGRAM

State Share

The West Virginia Public School Support Plan (PSSP) is the established plan of fiscal support for public schools. The PSSP defines statutory responsibilities of both the state and the 55 county school districts. The state's responsibility is the total of allocated funding calculated under Steps 1–7 of the PSSP, less amounts calculated as the school district's local share. The basic foundation allowance of the PSSP provides funding to local districts for professional educator salaries (Step 1), service personnel salaries (Step 2), employee benefit costs (Step 3), transportation operating costs (Step 4), professional support personnel salaries (Step 5), general operating costs, substitute employee costs and allowances for faculty senates (Step 6), and instructional improvement, technology improvement funding, and advanced placement programs (Step 7). Additional allocations are provided for other programs, such as alternative education programs and increased enrollment. Although not part of the PSSP, the state provides appropriations for the education of exceptional children.

Total number of funded personnel (Steps 1 and 2) for each district is set by the net enrollment of each district. In addition, each district's state aid allowance for personnel depends on salary degree classifications (pay grade for service personnel) and actual years of experience of personnel employed in each district. In general, student transportation funding (Step 4) is determined by actual transportation expenditures incurred by districts. Funding for improvements to instructional programs (Step 7a) and funding for technology (Step 7b) is based on the previous year's allocation plus 10% and 20% of the increase in local shares for each purpose. District funding computations using enrollment and employment data are based on each district's second-month reported data from the preceding school year.

For the purposes of determining PSSP funding, school districts are separated into four groups based on student net enrollment per square mile as shown in Table 50.1.

In addition, for districts with less than 1,400 students, the PSSP determines an additional number of pupils to be added to the county's actual enrollment based on the following formula: i.e., determine the enrollment difference between the district's actual enrollment and 1,400; multiply the difference by the percent derived by dividing the district's student population density into the student population density of the district with the

TABLE 50.1 Student Net Enrollment per Square Mile PSSP	
District Type	Enrollment
Sparse	Less than 5 students per square mile
Low	5 to less than 10 students per square mile
Medium	10 to less than 20 students per square mile
High	20 or more students per square mile

Source: State of West Virginia Executive Summary of the Public School Support Program Based on the Final Computations for the 2018–19 Year, p. 1.

lowest density; and restrict the total net enrollment for each eligible district so that it does not exceed 1,400.

The total basic foundation program allowance is the sum of the following seven allowances (Step 1–Step 7), excluding the amounts for the West Virginia School Building Authority (SBA) and retirement, less the amount calculated for local share.

STEP 1 Foundation Allowance for Professional Educators

The PSSP provides each school district with funding for salaries of professional educators. This allowance includes the annual state minimum salary per degree classification and years of experience,[12] the state salary increment paid to each principal and assistant principal,[13] and a supplement equity amount established to assist the state in meeting its objective for establishing salary equity among the school districts.[14] The state has a funding ratio of allowable professional educators (PE) per 1,000 students as shown in Table 50.2. Each district is required to maintain a minimum number of professional instructional personnel (PI) or suffer a reduction to the Step 1 allowance. Districts with a net enrollment increase are exempt from the PI reduction requirement. Effective with Fiscal Year 2019 school year, the PI

TABLE 50.2 West Virginia Allowance for Professional Educators		
District Category	PE	PI
Sparse	72.75	91.07%
Low	72.60	91.18%
Medium	72.45	91.24%
High	72.30	91.29%

Source: State of West Virginia Executive Summary of the Public School Support Program Based on the Final Computations for the 2018–19 Year, p2.

requirement is based on a percentage of the lesser of the number of professional educators actually employed or the number funded.

STEP 2 Foundation Allowance for Service Personnel

The PSSP provides to each school district funding for salaries of service personnel (secretaries, cooks, bus drivers, mechanics, etc.). This allowance includes the annual state minimum salary per pay grade and years of experience[15] and a supplement equity amount established to assist the state in meeting its objective for establishing salary equity among school districts. The state has established a funding ratio of allowable service personnel (SP) per 1,000 students as shown in Table 50.3.

STEP 3a Foundation Allowance for Fixed Charges

The PSSP provides funding to districts to cover the employer's share of contributions for social security, unemployment compensation and workers' compensation.

STEP 3b Foundation Allowance for Retirement

Step 3 of the PSSP provides allowance to the teachers' retirement system. The allowance is calculated as the average retirement contribution rate of each county board, multiplied by the sum of the basic foundation allowance for salaries, i.e., all salary equity appropriations and such amounts as are paid by the school districts as salary supplements to the extent that such county supplements are equal to the amount distributed for salary equity among the school districts; and additional amounts estimated to be required to eliminate the unfunded liability by June 30, 2034, with such amount to be based on an annual actuarial report to be provided to the legislature.

TABLE 50.3 West Virginia Allowance for Service Personnel

District Category	SP
Sparse	45.68
Low	45.10
Medium	44.53
High	43.97

Source: State of West Virginia Executive Summary of the Public School Support Program Based on the Final Computations for the 2018–19 Year, p2.

STEP 4 Foundation Allowance for Transportation Costs

The PSSP provides each school district an allowance for student transportation. This allowance is defined as an amount for the operation, maintenance and contracted services of student transportation based on a percentage of each district's actual costs corresponding with their student population density. Table 50.4 details these allowances, not inclusive of salaries.

More particularly, West Virginia's transportation aid plan includes the following features:

- Allowance of 10% of actual expenditures for that portion of the bus fleet (12-year replacement cycle) that is using propane or compressed natural gas as an alternative fuel;
- Allowance of 10% of actual expenditures for operations, maintenance, and contracted services, exclusive of salaries, for that portion of the bus fleet used to transport students to and from multi-county vocational centers;
- Allowance equal to 100% of insurance premium costs on buses, buildings and equipment used in transportation;
- Allowance equal to 8.33% of the current replacement value of each school district's school bus fleet plus the remaining replacement value of buses purchased after July 1, 1999 that attain 180,000 miles;
- Aid paid to students in lieu of transportation, based on the state average amount paid per pupil.

Each district's student transportation allowance is limited to 1/3 above the computed state average allowance per mile multiplied by the total mileage for the district. This amount does not include allowance for the purchase of additional buses. Each school district is required to reserve 1/2 of 1% of its total transportation allowance for expenditure for trips related to academic classroom curriculum.

TABLE 50.4 West Virginia Allowance for Transportation Costs

District Category	Percent of Actual Expenditures
Sparse	95.0%
Low	92.5%
Medium	90.0%
High	87.5%

Source: State of West Virginia Executive Summary of the Public School Support Program Based on the Final Computations for the 2018–19 Year, p3.

STEP 5 Foundation Allowance for Professional Student Support Services

The PSSP defines professional student support personnel as school counselors and school nurses. Instead of establishing a funding ratio for student support personnel, each district receives the same allowance amount it received during the 2012–2013 year, as increased for any legislative pay increases for 2018–19 and moving forward. This funding level was restated for the 2016–17 year and thereafter. The number of student support personnel positions funded is computed by dividing the district's allowance by the district's average state-funded professional student support personnel salary.

STEP 6 Foundation Allowance for Other Current Expenses, Substitute Salary Costs and Faculty Senates

Step 6 of the PSSP provides an allowance to each school district for other current expenses, substitute salary costs and faculty senates.[16]

Step 6a School Operating Expenses

Actual operations and maintenance expenditures reported by each county are divided by the total reported square footage of school buildings in each county to determine a state average expenditure per square foot for operations and maintenance. The total reported square footage for school buildings in each county is divided by the total net enrollment for each county to calculate a state average square footage per student. Each county's net enrollment is multiplied by the state average expenditure per square foot and the state average square footage per student. Each county's total is then multiplied by 70.25% to determine the Step 6a allowance.

Step 6b Substitute Salary Costs of Professional Educators

The allowance for professional educator substitute salary costs is 2.5% of the computed allowance for salaries under Steps 1 and 5; distribution is made to each district proportionally based on the number of professional educators respectively authorized.

Step 6c Substitute Salary Costs of Service Personnel

The allowance for service personnel substitute salary costs is 2.5% of the computed allowance for salaries under Step 2; distribution is made to each district proportionally based on the number of service personnel allowed.

Step 6d Faculty Senate

Each district receives an allowance of $200 multiplied by the number of professional instructional and student support personnel employed at each school. School districts are required to forward the allowance to each school during the month of September of each year. Faculty Senate funds are to be used for academic materials, supplies, and equipment.

STEP 7 Foundation Allowance for Improvement of the Instructional Program

Step 7 of the PSSP provides allowances for improvement of instructional programs; improvement of instructional technology; advanced placement dual credit and International Baccalaureate programs; teacher and leader induction programs; and funding to meet debt service requirements on revenue bonds issued by the West Virginia School Building Authority.

Step 7a Improvement of Instructional Programs
The amount appropriated each year to school districts for the improvement of instructional programs is the amount appropriated for the preceding year, plus 10% of growth in local share. Step 7a funds are to be used to improve instructional programs in accordance to a plan developed by each county board and submitted to the state board for approval. The state distributes $150,000 to each school district as a base amount, with remaining funds allocated proportionally on the basis of the average of each district's average daily attendance for the preceding year and the district's second month enrollment.

Step 7b Improvement of Instructional Technology
The amount appropriated each year to school districts for the improvement of instructional technology is the amount appropriated for the preceding year, plus 20% of growth in the local share. Step 7b funds are designated to improve instructional technology according to the county and schools' strategic plans. The state distributes $30,000 to each school district as a base amount, with remaining funds allocated proportionally on the basis of the average of each district's average daily attendance for the preceding year and the district's second month enrollment.

Step 7c Advanced Placement, Dual Credit, and International Baccalaureate Programs
The PSSP provides an allowance for students enrolled in advanced placement, dual credit, and international baccalaureate courses. This allocation is based on 1% of the state average per-pupil state aid multiplied by the number of students enrolled in such courses in each district.

Step 7d Comprehensive Systems for Teacher and Leader Induction and Professional Growth

The amount appropriated through the PSSP for teacher and leader induction and professional growth programs is the amount appropriated in the immediately preceding school year, plus 20% of growth in local share. Funds are distributed to county boards of education in a manner established by the state board of education in accordance with factors outlined in statute.

Step 7e Debt Service

Step 7e provides to the West Virginia School Building Authority (SBA) the amount of funds required to meet debt service requirements on revenue bonds issued by the SBA prior to January 1, 1994.

Local Share

West Virginia defines local share as a computation of each school district's projected regular levy property tax collections for the year, i.e., "[T]he amount of revenue which the levies would produce if levied upon one hundred percent of the assessed value of each of the several classes of property contained in the report or revised report of the value made to it by the Tax Commissioner."[16] Projected excess levy tax collections are not included as part of the local share. Local share for each year is computed by multiplying the taxable assessed valuation of all property in the district for the current fiscal year as certified by the county assessor by 90% of the regular levy rates for the year as set by the legislature and then deducting 4% as an allowance for discounts, exonerations, delinquencies, and reducing the amount further by the amount that is to be paid to the Assessor's Valuation Fund. Table 50.5 provides the projected levy rates for calculating the local share.

The total local share calculated for each school district is subtracted from the total basic foundation allowance to determine the state's share to be appropriated. State code provides that the allocation for each school

TABLE 50.5 Projected Tax Levy Rates for West Virginia Local Share	
Property Class	Amount per $100 for Assessed Valuation
Class I Property	19.40¢
Class II Property	38.80¢
Class III Property	77.60¢
Class IV Property	77.60¢

Source: State of West Virginia Executive Summary of the Public School Support Program Based on the Final Computations for the 2018–19 Year, p6.

district is to be adjusted for certain circumstances where the calculated local share is not reflective of local funds available to the district, errors by the county assessor, or payments received in lieu or property taxes.[17]

Other Allowances

Other allowances are provided to school districts through the PSSP for county transfers, increased student enrollment, alternative education, Limited English Proficient students, and the Public Employees Insurance Fund.

County Transfers
According to the PSSP, allowance is provided for county school districts that agree to transfer students to another school district pursuant to an agreement approved by the state board if funds are appropriated. The allowance for the year in which the transfer occurs is to be 100% of amounts in the agreement, not to exceed the district's per-pupil state aid allocation. The allowance in the first year after the transfer occurs is to be 50% of the agreed amount, and the allowance for the second year is to be 25%. This allowance is reduced under certain circumstances.[18]

Increased Enrollment
Each school district which has an increase in net enrollment is to receive an allocation equal to the district's increase in net enrollment over the previous year, multiplied by each district's average per-pupil state aid.[19]

Alternative Education
The allowance provided by the PSSP for alternative education programs is $18 per enrolled student.[20]

Limited English Proficient Students
State statute does not require any specific amount of funding to be appropriated to districts for Limited English Proficient (LEP) students through the PSSP. Districts are required to apply for funds that are available in accordance with provisions contained in state board policy.[21]

Public Employees Insurance Fund
The total allowance provided through the PSSP for the Public Employees Insurance Fund is based on an average premium rate for all school district employees as established by the Public Employees Insurance Agency (PEIA) Finance Board, multiplied by the number of personnel allowed for funding under the Public School Support Program (PSSP).[22] The average

TABLE 50.6 Public School Support Program Summary			
PSSP Step	2016–2017	2017–2018	2018–2019
Step 1 Professional Educators	$856,017,057	$843,200,570	$876,075,903
Step 2 Service Personnel	$290,711,435	$286,915,321	$297,680,615
Step 3 Fixed Charges	$102,033,345	$100,484,631	$103,542,614
Step 4 Transportation	$74,729,928	$70,276,078	$73,375,145
Step 5 Professional Student Support Services	$36,952,999	$36,952,999	$38,686,260
Step 6 Other Current Expenses, Substitute Employee Salaries, and Faculty Senates	$152,089,960	$149,939,086	$149,651,626
Step 7 Improvement of Instructional Programs	$70,431,750	$70,442,043	$71,724,477
Total Basic Foundation Allowance	$1,582,966,474	$1,558,210,728	$1,610,736,640
Local Share	$(467,039,269)	$(454,486,958)	$(458,622,709)
Other Adjustments	$(2,527,044)	$(2,441,341)	$(1,694,701)
State Aid Allowance for County School Districts	$1,113,400,161	$1,101,282,429	$1,150,419,230
Teacher's Retirement System–PSSP	$388,098,000	$416,088,000	$426,359,190
Public Employees Insurance Agency	$241,429,043	$242,714,967	$232,810,116
School Building Authority (debt service on bonds prior to 1/194)	$23,421,520	$23,424,770	$23,420,520
Other Allowances (enrollment, alternative education ESL)	$12,332,030[a]	$7,722,171[b]	$7,875,447
Total Appropriation–PPSP	**$1,778,680,754**	**$1,791,232,337**	**$1,840,884,503**

Source: State of West Virginia Abbreviated Summary of the Public School Support Program Based on the Final Computations for the Years of 2016–2017, 2017–2018, and 2018–2019.
[a] The Other Allowances amount for 2016–2017 also includes funding for county transfers and Regional Education Service Agencies.
[b] The Other Allowances amount for 2017–2018 also includes funding for county transfers.

premium rate includes a proportionate share of retirees' subsidy established by the PEIA Finance Board.

Table 50.6 details selected step-based programs and appropriations relating to public school support engaged by the West Virginia legislature across FY 2017–2019. Nearly $2 billion is committed to total appropriation for use in the PPSP.

SCHOOL BUILDING AUTHORITY

The West Virginia School Building Authority (SBA) was created in 1989 by the state legislature to meet the educational planning and school construction needs of the state.²³ The legislature created a funding mechanism through the SBA to assist local boards of education in the construction and renovation of new and existing facilities. A board made up of citizens, state board of education members, and members of the construction trades industry governs the policies and procedures of the SBA. Each county school district must have a Comprehensive Educational Facilities Plan (CEFP) approved by the SBA and the state board of education. School projects from approved CEFPs are eligible for capital improvement funds from the SBA based on needs of the facilities in each district. County school districts work with SBA staff to evaluate the needs of facilities. The SBA is funded annually by the legislature using funding generated through general state revenue, lottery funds, and excess lottery funds. Construction funds are created through the annual sale of capital improvement bonds and general revenue.²⁴

PUBLIC EMPLOYEES INSURANCE AGENCY

The West Virginia Public Employees Insurance Agency (PEIA) was established in 1971 to provide insurance coverage to eligible employees. Benefits are available to all current employees of the state of West Virginia, including employees of various related state agencies and local governments. PEIA participants may elect health insurance coverage through a fully self-insured preferred provider benefit plan or through externally managed care organizations. Participants may also elect to purchase optional life insurance. PEIA relies almost solely on premiums paid directly by its participating employers and employees.²⁵

CONSOLIDATED PUBLIC RETIREMENT BOARD TEACHER'S RETIREMENT SYSTEM

The State Teachers Retirement System (TRS), a defined benefit, was established in 1941 to provide retirement benefits for teachers and school service personnel. In 2018, TRS had approximately 35,807 active members and 31,913 retired members. Active members contribute 6% of gross monthly salary to the retirement plan. For members enrolled prior to July 1, 1991, the employer contributes an additional 15% of the member's gross monthly salary to the plan. For members hired for the first time on or after July 1, 2005 or for members who transferred from the Teachers' Defined Contribution (TDC) System, the employer contributes an additional 7.5% of the member's gross monthly salary to the plan.²⁶

NOTES

1. This chapter is indebted to Amy Willard, Executive Director of the Office of School Finance, West Virginia Department of Education, for her review and comment. The chapter author previously served in numerous leadership roles in West Virginia, including faculty roles at Marshall University and Concord University, along with multiple roles in the West Virginia Department of Education.
2. https://www.history.com/this-day-in-history/west-virginia-enters-the-union
3. http://www.wvculture.org/history/statehood/constitution.html
4. Ibid.
5. WVC §18-1-3.
6. WVC, Article 10, Section 1. https://tax.wv.gov/Business/PropertyTax/Pages/PropertyTax.aspx
7. https://nces.ed.gov/edfin/pdf/StFinance/WestVir.pdf
8. Civil Action No. 75-1268 (1982).
9. http://www.wvculture.org/HiStory/education/recht01.html
10. http://www.wvencyclopedia.org/articles/19.
11. But follow West Virginia's litigation path, *Pauley v. Kelly,* 255 S.E.2d 859 (1979); *Pauley v. Bailey,* 324 S.E.2d 128 (1984); http://schoolfunding.info/litigation-map/west-virginia/#1485221530656-e269f3ce-26a7.
12. WVC §18A-4-2.
13. WVC §18A-4-3.
14. WVC §18A-4-5.
15. WVC §18A-4-8a.
16. WVC §18-9A-11(a).
17. WVC §18-9A-12.
18. WVC §18-9A-12
19. WVC §18-9A-14
20. WVC §18-9A-21
21. WVC §18-9A-22.
22. WVC §§5-16-18 and 18-9A-24.
23. WVC §18-9D.
24. https://sba.wv.gov/aboutus/Pages/default.aspx.
25. WVC §5-16-18
26. http://www.wvretirement.com/TRS.html

CHAPTER 51

Wisconsin

Faith E. Crampton
Crampton and Associates

GENERAL BACKGROUND

The state of Wisconsin educates 854,402 elementary and secondary students via 422 public school districts, 242 charter schools (44,300 student enrollment), and 218 voucher-recipient schools (10,218 voucher student enrollment). School districts can be identified by three configurations: (1) elementary and secondary grades combined (K–12); (2) elementary grades only; and (3) high school grades only. Intermediate configurations include 12 regionally-based cooperative educational service agencies (CESAs) and four county-based children with disabilities education boards (CCDEBs). All school districts are fiscally independent. In contrast, CESAs are fiscally dependent on their respective school district members while CCDEBs represent a mix, with three fiscally independent and one fiscally dependent.

The state provides 45.9% of school district revenues while local districts provide 46.6%. Federal aid represents 7.5%. In Fiscal Year 2017, the state distributed $5,444,353,300 in state aid to K–12 education. Of that, the state classified $4,600,928,00 as general or basic aid and $843,625,300 as categorical aid. Total state aid represented approximately 32% of the state's general fund, its single largest appropriation.

In Wisconsin, 39.5% of students are considered economically disadvantaged, defined as eligible for the federal free or reduced price meal program. Approximately 13.7% are classified as having a disability, and 5.4% are identified as English language learners. Although the high school graduation rate was 88.4% in 2015 (the latest year for which statewide data are available), fewer than half of high school students scored proficient or advanced on state tests in English language arts and mathematics.

BASIC SUPPORT PROGRAM

Equalization Aid

Wisconsin remains the only state in the nation to use a guaranteed tax base formula, referred to in Wisconsin as the 'equalization formula,' as its major form of basic or general aid. The major purpose of a guaranteed tax base formula is to provide taxpayer, not student, equity.[1] 'Equalization Aid' is computed via a complex three-tier guaranteed tax base formula where the first tier acts like a flat grant and the second tier as a foundation without a required minimum local tax rate, while the third tier most resembles a true guaranteed tax base approach. In addition, the third tier includes a 'negative aid' feature, which, on paper, acts like a recapture provision.

Five factors are used in the computation of Equalization Aid: (1) pupil membership; (2) shared cost; (3) equalized property valuation; (4) state-guaranteed property valuations; and (5) total amount of state funding available for distribution. Membership, shared cost, and equalized property valuation are based on school district data from the prior school year. Pupil membership, with some exceptions, refers to student enrollment. Shared cost is defined as school district expenditures that the state has deemed aidable through the equalization formula. Equalized valuation is the full market value of taxable property in the school district, while guaranteed valuations are the amount of property tax base support that the state guarantees for each student. There are three guaranteed property valuations used in the equalization formula that are applied to the three tiers.

Tier One Equalization Aid is also referred to as the 'Primary Aid' tier. Every school district whose equalized property valuation per pupil is below $1,930,000 receives Primary Aid up to $1,000 per student. Because only a handful of school districts have per-pupil property wealth exceeding this figure, virtually all districts receive this type of aid. Notably, a district's Primary Aid cannot be reduced by negative aid. This feature is generally referred to as the Primary Aid hold harmless.

Tier Two Equalization Aid is also referred to as the 'Secondary Aid' Tier. The second-tier computation provides Equalization Aid for shared cost between $1,000 per pupil and the state-determined secondary cost ceiling (also referred to as secondary shared cost) for those school districts having property values per pupil up to the secondary valuation. For FY 2017, the state set the secondary cost ceiling at $9,539 per pupil, and the secondary guaranteed property valuation at $1,146,821 per pupil.

Tier Three Equalization Aid is also referred to as the 'Tertiary Aid' tier. This tier considers shared costs per student above the secondary cost ceiling. In FY 2017, state aid on tertiary shared cost was calculated using the tertiary guaranteed property valuation per pupil of $558,546. The tertiary guarantee is set equal to the statewide average equalized property value per student. It is deliberately set at an amount lower than the secondary guarantee so that the state's share will be lower on costs above the secondary cost ceiling per pupil. If a school district's tertiary aid is a negative number, this amount is deducted from its secondary aid. If the sum of a district's secondary and tertiary aid is a negative number, this amount is not deducted from its primary aid amount.

Revenue Limits

General aid to school districts is subject to state-imposed revenue limits. See Tax and Spending Limits later in this chapter for a full description.

Per-Pupil Aid

Although statutorily defined as categorical aid,[2] Per-Pupil Aid is more appropriately classified as a form of basic or general aid. Under this state aid program, every school district in the state, regardless of property wealth, receives the same amount per pupil. Originally enacted in FY 2013, funding expanded rapidly from $50 per pupil to a budgeted amount of $450 per pupil in the 2017–2018 school year. Between 2013 and 2016, total state funding for this aid program more than tripled from $63,462,200 to $219,992,800. No other part of the state school funding system approximated this rate of growth during this time period. As a type of general purpose aid that acts as a flat grant,[3] it represents the most disequalizing form of state aid.

Special Adjustment Aid

This aid is provided to school districts as: (1) hold-harmless aid due to declining enrollments; or (2) incentive aid for school district consolidation. In the former, the state guarantees districts with declining enrollments 85% of their prior year's general aid. In the latter, for the first five years after consolidation, the state guarantees the new school district at least as much general aid as the separate districts received in the year prior to consolidation. In the sixth and seventh years, the consolidated district receives a revenue limit adjustment equal to 75% of the consolidation aid it received in the fifth year. In 2016–2017, there were 62 school districts receiving $17,548,000 in Special Adjustment Aid.

SCHOOL INFRASTRUCTURE

Bond Debt Programs

In Wisconsin, financing of school infrastructure, with few exceptions, is a local responsibility; that is, the state provides no substantive aid.[4] As a result, school districts must rely primarily on bonded indebtedness, subject to voter approval, to finance capital projects. State law prescribes how these referenda are to be conducted and limits a school district's total debt to 10% of its equalized property valuation.[5]

Legacy Programs

There are two relatively small, targeted legacy programs for debt service aid and state loans to school districts. These are known as SAGE Debt Service Aid and as Technology Infrastructure Financial Assistance.

SAGE Debt Service Aid

This is a legacy program for school districts, with the exception of the Milwaukee Public Schools, that passed a bond referendum, approved by the state Department of Public Instruction (DPI), prior to June 30, 2001. To be eligible, the referendum had to identify the amount of bonding attributable to increased classroom space needs resulting from participation in the SAGE program.[6] Such school districts are eligible for state aid equal to 20% of debt service costs associated with SAGE building costs.[7] In the 2015–2016 school year, the state distributed $133,700 in SAGE Debt Service Aid to ten school districts, and the same amount was estimated for 2016–2017.

Technology Infrastructure Financial Assistance

Technology Infrastructure Financial Assistance is also a legacy program. This program closed to new applications July 2003. Under this program, school districts and public libraries could apply for state loans to fund upgrades of electrical wiring and installation and upgrading of computer network wiring in buildings that were in existence on October 14, 1997. State bonds totaling $71,900,000 were issued for school district loans over the course of this program. In 2016–2017, debt service costs for financing of infrastructure loans to school districts was budgeted at $1,033,300.

Capital Expansion Funds and Long-Term Capital Improvement Trust Funds

Wisconsin state law authorizes school districts to create a Capital Expansion Fund to finance current and future capital expenditures related to buildings and sites.⁸ If a school district makes an expenditure from its Capital Expansion Fund, its shared cost is increased by an amount determined by dividing the expenditure by the number of years in which the district levied a property tax for the capital project. State law also gives school districts the option to create Long-Term Capital Improvement Trust Funds to finance projects included in a long-term capital improvement plan.⁹ The plan must be approved by the school board and cover at least a ten year period. School districts may not make expenditures from the fund in the first five years after its creation. State law specifies that a school district's shared cost includes any amount deposited into the fund, but does not include any amount expended from the fund.

BILINGUAL-BICULTURAL EDUCATION

Bilingual-Bicultural Aid

In Wisconsin, Bilingual-Bicultural Aid provides support to school district programs meant to improve English language comprehension, speaking, reading, and writing ability of limited English speaking (LEP) students. School districts receive reimbursement at a specified percentage rate for eligible costs incurred the previous school year.[10] The state requires special classes for LEP students at schools that enroll ten or more LEP students in a language group in grades K–3; or 20 or more in grades 4–8 or 9–12. For the 2015–2016 school year, the state provided $8,589,900 to 49 school districts for bilingual-bicultural education.

Tribal Language Revitalization Grants

This program supports instruction in one or more American Indian languages through grants to school districts and CESAs. Funding is provided from tribal gaming program revenue.[11] To be eligible, a school district or CESA, in conjunction with a tribal authority, must apply for a grant annually. In FY 2016, the state distributed $145,800 in grants to 11 school districts. For FY 2017, an increase to $222,800 was budgeted.

COMPENSATORY EDUCATION

Achievement Gap Reduction

Achievement Gap Reduction (AGR) is a grant program that replaced the Student Achievement Guarantee in Education (SAGE) program beginning

2015. AGR was phased in through the 2017–2018 school year. Although SAGE is probably best known as a student/teacher ratio reduction initiative that focused on schools with high percentages of low income students, it also funded other services.[12] To be a part of SAGE, eligible schools originally entered into a renewable five-year contract with the DPI. Only former SAGE schools are eligible to enter five-year contracts with DPI for the AGR program. Although a number of aspects of SAGE were preserved under AGR, such as student/teacher ratio reduction and professional development requirements, differences include articulation and assessment of pupil performance objectives, and provision of 1:1 student tutoring and instructional coaching. For the 2015–2016 school year, $109,184,500 was provided in grants to schools, or approximately $2,172 per pupil.

Head Start Supplement

Head Start is a state-administered grant program whereby grants are awarded to local Head Start providers, including but not limited to school districts and CESAs, to supplement federal funds that provide educational, health, nutritional, social, and other services to economically disadvantaged preschool children and their families. The purpose of state funds is to enable expansion of Head Start and Early Head Start programs to serve more families. Grants may be used as a match for federal funds only if state funds are used to secure additional federal support. In FY 2016, the state distributed $6,264,100 to 40 grantees. (*See also*, Early Childhood Education in this chapter).

High Poverty Aid

High Poverty Aid is distributed to school districts where 50% or more of their student enrollment qualifies for the federal free and reduced price lunch program. High Poverty Aid is subject to revenue limits for all eligible school districts except the Milwaukee Public Schools (MPS). For MPS, High Poverty Aid must be used to reduce the school property tax levied for the purpose of offsetting any state aid reduction attributable to the Milwaukee Parental Choice program. Normally, one would consider the purpose of such an aid program as compensatory, but, in the case of the Milwaukee Public Schools, its effect is to reduce local property taxes. In 2016–2017, the state provided a total of $16,830,000 in High Poverty Aid.

Integration Aid

Commonly referred to as 'Chapter 220' aid, this is a legacy program.[13] The goal of Chapter 220, enacted in 1975, was voluntary racial integration to achieve greater racial balance across and within Milwaukee area schools. Beginning with the 2016–2017 school year, this program was being phased out, ostensibly due to falling participation rates. A school district that receives students across district lines (interdistrict) is paid a state Integration Aid amount equal to the district's average net cost per pupil. The sending school district does not receive any Integration Aid, but it is eligible to count the student at .75 membership in Equalization Aid and revenue limit computations. A school district that transfers students within district lines (intradistrict) receives Integration Aid equal to an additional 25% of its Equalization Aid per student. For the 2016–2017 school year, state integration aid totaled $56,033,000 for 22,416 students.

GIFTED AND TALENTED EDUCATION

In Wisconsin, gifted and talented education is a grant-based program to provide qualified students with services and activities to assist them in development of their full potential.[14] Grants may be awarded to nonprofit organizations, CESAs, institutions within the University of Wisconsin system, and the Milwaukee Public Schools, either individually or as collaborative projects. Funding for the 2015–2016 school year was $209,000.

SPECIAL EDUCATION

Wisconsin provides funding for students with disabilities through three categorical aid programs: Special Education and School-Age Parents Aid; High Cost Special Education Aid; and Supplemental Special Education Aid.

Special Education and School-Age Parents Aid

This is the major state categorical aid program supporting special education in Wisconsin. School districts receive partial reimbursement for eligible costs, as defined by the state, which were incurred the prior school year.[15] In addition to school districts, CESAs, CCDEBs, and some types of charter schools are eligible for this type of aid. The Wisconsin Department of Public Instruction estimates that this aid program covers about 25% of eligible special education expenses at the local level. In 2015–2016, the state distributed $368,939,100 in Special Education and School-Age Parents Aid. In 2016–2017, it was estimated that the same amount was distributed. In 2015–2016, 421 school districts, 21 charter schools, 12 CESAs, and three CCDEBs received funding through this program.

High Cost Special Education Aid

This program provides state aid for students with disabilities who required more than $30,000 in expenditures on special education-related services in the prior school year, excluding certain reimbursements.[16] In addition to school districts, CCDEBs, CESAs, and some types of charter schools are eligible to receive this type of aid. The average reimbursement rate is 90% of each student's cost above $30,000. In 2015–2016, the state distributed $3,500,000 to 162 school districts. In 2016–2017, state funding for this aid program was expected to rise to $8,500,000.

Supplemental Special Education Aid

This state aid program is targeted to small school districts with high special education costs and below average ability to raise property tax revenues. Eligibility is based on a formula defined in state law.[17] To be eligible, a school district must meet three criteria: (1) its per-pupil revenue authority must be below the state average; (2) special education comprises more than 16% of the district's total costs; and (3) student enrollment, defined as membership for Equalization Aid, is below 2,000. Prior school year data are used to assess whether a school district meets these criteria. Under Wisconsin law, a school district may not receive both Supplemental Special Education Aid and High Cost Special Education Aid. In 2015–2016, the state distributed $1,050,000 to seven school districts. For the 2016–2017 school year, aid was expected to rise to $1,750,000.

Special Education Transition Grants

This is a one-year program to provide grants of up to $1,000 per pupil to school districts or independent charter schools for students who met the following three criteria: (1) attended school in the district or charter school in the 2014–2015 or 2015–2016 school years; (2) had an individualized education program (IEP); and (3) was enrolled in a higher education program or another postsecondary education or training program, or was competitively employed for at least 90 days. An appropriation of $100,000 was provided in 2016–2017 to fund the program.

County Children with Disabilities Education Boards

Those CCDEBs which are fiscally independent and fund the local share of their educational programs through the county property tax levy are eligible to receive state aid for students enrolled solely in CCDEB-operated programs and for costs incurred by CCDEBs for students jointly enrolled in school district and CCDEB programs.[18] Calculation of the level of state aid is somewhat complex and is dependent on a school district's level of Equalization Aid, shared costs, and/or net costs of the CCDEB's services. For the 2015–2016 school year, three CCDEBs received $4,0673,300.

NUTRITION PROGRAMS

In Wisconsin, student nutrition aid programs include school lunch, school breakfast, and school day milk. The state provides aid to school districts, charter schools, and private schools in order to: (1) partially match the federal contribution under the national school lunch program that provides free or reduced price meals to low income children; (2) provide a per-meal reimbursement of 15¢ for each school breakfast served under the federal program; and (3) fully reimburse the cost of milk for low income preK–5 students in schools that do not participate in the federal special milk program. For the 2015–2016 school year, state aid for the school lunch program was $4,218,100. For the school breakfast program, it was $2,510,500; and, for the school day milk program, it was $617,100. For 2016–2017, the same amounts were budgeted.

TRANSPORTATION

Pupil Transportation Aid

In Wisconsin, state aid partially reimburses school districts for the costs of transporting public and nonpublic school pupils.[19] Independent charter schools choosing to provide transportation are also eligible to receive aid. Public school districts are not required to transport charter school students. Aid is calculated based on the distance each student is transported as shown in Table 51.1. For the 2016–2017 school year, it was estimated that school districts and independent charter schools received $23,954,000 for having transported 486,555 public school pupils and 31,755 private school pupils in 2015–2016.

High-Cost Transportation Aid

This aid is provided to school districts with higher than average per-pupil transportation costs for the previous school year.[20] Eligibility rests on two

TABLE 51.1 Wisconsin Reimbursement Formula for Pupil Transportation

Distance (in miles)	Reimbursement Per Pupil ($)	
	Regular School Year	Summer School
0–2*	$15	$0
2–5	$35	$4
5–8	$55	$6
8–12	$110	$6
12 and over	$300	$6

Note: Limited to transportation in hazardous areas.

criteria: (1) per-pupil transportation cost, based on audited information from the previous fiscal year exceeding 150% of the statewide average per-pupil cost; and (2) pupil population density is 50 pupils per square mile or less. Aid is distributed to eligible districts based on the difference between the district's per-pupil transportation cost and the aid threshold of 150% of the statewide average. In 2015–2016 school year, $7,500,000 was appropriated.

Open Enrollment and Course Options Aid for Transportation

Under the state's open enrollment program, students may attend a public school outside their school district of residence within the state. Although parents are responsible for transporting their children to and from the school, exceptions are made for low income students and those with disabilities. Low income students, defined as those eligible for the federal free and reduced price lunch program, may apply to the state for reimbursement of transportation costs. The state then determines the reimbursement amount, which may not exceed the parent's actual costs or three times the statewide average per-pupil transportation costs, whichever is less. For students with disabilities, defined as those with an IEP, the nonresident district must provide transportation.

Under the state's course options program, any student in a public school may enroll in up to two courses at any time at other educational institutions, including public schools in a nonresident school district, the University of Wisconsin system, technical colleges, nonprofit institutions of higher education, tribal colleges, charter schools, and any state-approved nonprofit organization.[21] Although parents are generally responsible for transportation, they may apply for state reimbursement of transportation costs if they are unable to afford them. The state then calculates the amount of the reimbursement, giving preference to low income students, defined as those eligible for the federal free and reduced price lunch program. During the 2015–2016 school year, 2,392 students received open enrollment transportation aid while two received course options transportation aid, for a total of $434,200. The same amount was budgeted for 2016–2017.

Youth Options Aid for Transportation

The state Youth Options program provides 11th and 12th grade public school students the opportunity to enroll in one or more nonsectarian courses at a postsecondary institution for postsecondary credit. These include the University of Wisconsin campuses; Wisconsin technical colleges; participating private, nonprofit colleges; and tribal colleges. Funding is provided to reimburse parents of students who are unable to afford the cost of transportation between the high school and the postsecondary institution. Preference for reimbursement is given to low income students, defined as those who are eligible for the federal free and reduced price school lunch program. In order to be eligible for reimbursement of transportation costs, the postsecondary courses must be taken for high school credit. State aid for this program totaled $17,400 in the 2016–2017 school year.

PRIVATE AND PUBLIC SCHOOL CHOICE

Overview of Private School Choice

Wisconsin has a long history regarding the provision and funding of private school choice, beginning with the Milwaukee Parental Choice Program (MPCP) in 1989. More recent additions include the Racine Parental Choice Program (RPCP) and the Wisconsin Parental Choice Program (WPCP), the latter a statewide expansion. All are voucher programs. Student eligibility, which is established by state law, varies for each program and is a combination of student residence, income, and prior year attendance. Choice school teachers and administrators, unlike their counterparts in public schools, are not required to hold a state educational license if they hold, at minimum, a bachelor degree.

Participating private, nonprofit, religious, and nonsectarian schools receive a state aid payment for each eligible student on behalf of the parent or guardian. For the 2016–2017 school year, a voucher was valued at $7,323 for a K–8 pupil and $7,969 for a pupil enrolled in grades 9–12. In addition, Wisconsin has a Special Needs Scholarship, which is also a voucher program. A fifth program, referred to as a 'Private School Tuition Deduction,' subsidizes parents, regardless of wealth, who choose to send their children to private schools through the ability to deduct the cost of tuition from reported income on their annual state tax return. Finally, the state also authorizes Home-Based Private Education, commonly referred to as homeschooling.

Milwaukee Parental Choice Program (MPCP)
In the 2015–2016 school year (the latest year for audited data), 26,470 students redeemed vouchers at 177 private schools in Milwaukee, for an estimated $203,700,000 in state aid. This represented approximately 20% of students in the city.

Racine Parental Choice Program (RPCP)
The Racine Parental Choice Program was authorized by the state beginning in the 2011–2012 school year. It is available to students in the Racine Unified School District (RUSD). Located in southeastern Wisconsin, RUSD enrolls 19,455 K–12 students. In the 2015–2016 school year (the latest year for audited data), 2,057 students redeemed vouchers at 19 private schools within the borders of RUSD for an estimated $15,100,00 in state aid.

Wisconsin Parental Choice Program (WPCP)
The Wisconsin Parental Choice Program is a statewide voucher program which began with the 2013–2014 school year. In the 2015–2016 school year (the latest year for audited data), 2,483 students redeemed vouchers at 82 private schools across the state, excluding Milwaukee and Racine, for an estimated $18,400,00 in state aid.

Special Needs Scholarships
Enacted in 2015, this Wisconsin program allows a student with a disability, who meets certain eligibility requirements, to receive a state-funded scholarship to attend a participating private school.[22] In practice, these scholarships are vouchers. For the 2017–2018 school year, the maximum scholarship was $12,207 per student. See the section of this chapter addressing special education.

Private School Tuition Deduction
This Wisconsin state program allows parents of elementary and secondary students to deduct private school tuition from their taxable income as reported on their annual state tax return,[23] thus lowering their state tax liability. The maximum deduction is $4,000 per calendar year per K–8 student and $10,000 per student in grades 9–12. To qualify, a student must be claimed as a dependent for federal income tax purposes and be enrolled in

kindergarten or grades 1–12 of a private school, as defined in state law. See the section on *Tax Credits, Deductions, and Exemptions.*

Home-Based Private Education

Home-based private education refers to a program of educational instruction provided to a child by a parent, guardian, or person designated by the parent or guardian.[24] While the state provides no direct aid to those who homeschool, school districts may incur costs related to homeschooled students. For example, under Wisconsin state law, a homeschooled student may attend at no cost a maximum of two courses per semester in two school districts.[25] Second, the child may participate in interscholastic athletics and extracurricular activities on the same basis and to the same extent as students enrolled in the school district, again at no cost unless the district charges fees to resident students. Third, although school districts are not required to provide special education services to homeschooled students, district are required to identify and evaluate all children in the district who may have a disability. In 2016–2017, a total of 20,362 students were homeschooled, representing a little over 2% of all students statewide.

Overview of Charter Schools

In 1989, the state of Wisconsin enacted legislation permitting the establishment of charter schools. Charter schools are considered public schools, although they may be managed by private entities. The method by which the state funds charter schools depends upon the charter authorizer.[26] Charter schools may be authorized by one of two methods. First, they may be authorized by the school district in which they reside. In Wisconsin, these are referred to as 'instrumentality' charter schools, and there is no statewide cap on the number of instrumentality charter schools that may be established by school districts. Charter schools may also be authorized by other state-approved entities where there may be state-imposed limits on their numbers.[27] These are referred to as 'independent' charter schools. A third variation is virtual charter schools.

For an instrumentality charter school, the contract between the school district and the the charter school specifies the amount to be paid to the charter school. In contrast, independent charter schools receive state aid which, for the 2016–2017 school year, was $8,188 per student for an estimated annual total of $62,000,000 in state aid. It should be noted that, in some cases, the state may reduce school districts' Equalization Aid to generate sufficient revenues for state aid to independent charter schools. In addition, independent charter schools are eligible for state aid related to special education, transportation, and nutrition programs. Instrumentality charter schools are not eligible for such aid, but they may negotiate for the provision of such services in the contract with their authorizing school district.

Virtual charter schools are a subtype of instrumentality charter schools.[28] From their inception in Wisconsin in 2002, they have not been without controversy.[29] Virtual charter schools accept students from the school district within which they are chartered, students from other Wisconsin school districts, and out-of-state students. Funding for within-district students is negotiated with the school district, while funding for students from other school districts is provided through the Open Enrollment program described below. For out-of-state students, virtual charter schools are required to charge tuition equivalent to the cost of an open-enrolled student: $6,639 per pupil. In the 2015–2016 school year, 35 virtual charter schools, authorized by 30 school districts, enrolled approximately 6,300 students. Enrollments by school varied widely, from 1 to 994 students.

Open Enrollment

Open enrollment represents another form of public K–12 school choice in Wisconsin, specifically, interdistrict choice. Authorized by the state in 1998, this program allows parents to apply for children to attend public school in a district other than the one in which they reside. In addition, students may attend prekindergarten, four-year-old kindergarten, early childhood or school-operated child care programs outside their school district of residence if their school district of residence offers the same type of program that the student wishes to attend and the student is eligible to attend that program in his or her school district of residence.

Under the open enrollment program, resident school districts are allowed to count students who have transferred to another district in their pupil membership for revenue limits and general support purposes. Then, for each open-enrolled student, a uniform state-set amount is transferred from the resident school district to the nonresident district in the final state aid payment at the end of the school year. In 2015–2016, this amount was $6,639 per pupil for a statewide total of $303,200,000.[30]

EARLY CHILDHOOD EDUCATION

Four-Year-Old Kindergarten (K4) Grants

Wisconsin provides two-year grants to school districts that implement a K4 program. Eligible districts receive up to $3,000 per pupil the first year of the grant and up to $1,500 per pupil in the second year. Districts continuing in the grant program in their second year have priority for funding over districts new to the program. In the 2015–2016 school year, eight school districts received $1,350,000 in grants.

Head Start Supplement

See earlier full description under Compensatory Education.

TAX CREDITS, DEDUCTIONS, AND EXEMPTIONS

Private School Tuition Deduction

See earlier full description under Private School Choice.

TAX AND SPENDING LIMITS

Revenue Limits

As described earlier under Basic Support, general or basic aid to school districts is subject to state-imposed revenue limits. State categorical aid and federal aid are not limited. Also, any revenue that a school district receives from local non-property tax sources, e.g., student fees, ticket sales, or interest income, is exempt from revenue limits. In addition, special provisions apply to the treatment of property tax levies for debt service and for community service activities. Under Wisconsin law, there is a limit on the annual amount of revenue each school district can raise through the combination of general school aid, computer aid,[31] and local property tax levy.[32] In addition to Equalization Aid, Integration Aid, Special Adjustment Aids, and High Poverty Aid are included in the calculation of a district's revenue limit. A school district can exceed its revenue limit only by local voter approval of a referendum.

PUBLIC SCHOOL EMPLOYEE RETIREMENT

The Wisconsin public school employee retirement system is part of the larger public employee retirement system known as the the Wisconsin Retirement System (WRS), which is administered by the state's Department of Employee Trust Funds. The WRS is a defined benefit program where retiree annuities are adjusted annually based on investment returns to the trust funds.[33]

VIRTUAL EDUCATION

Virtual Charter Schools

See earlier full description under Private and Public School Choice.

OTHER

Alcohol and Other Drug Abuse

Alcohol and Other Drug Abuse (AODA) is a block grant-funded program designed to address alcohol and other drug abuse among school-age children and young people. Emphasis is placed on prevention and intervention through K–12 curriculum development, family involvement, drug abuse resistance education, and student-designed prevention or intervention projects.[34] Revenue from the penalty assessment surcharge funds these grants. In the 2015–2016 school year, grants totaling $1,207,100 were distributed to 40 school districts and three CESAs, which administered grants on behalf of consortia representing 24 additional school districts. For 2016–2017, the state budgeted $1,284,700.

Educator Effectiveness Grants

These grants reimburse school districts and independent charter schools for costs associated with the state-mandated educator effectiveness evaluation system.[35] Eligible costs include system development, training, software, support, resources, and refinement. Those using an approved alternative evaluation process are also eligible. An application is required on an annual basis to receive grant funding, which is set at $80 for each participating teacher, principal, or other licensed educator. In 2016–2017, the state distributed $5,746,000 in grants.

Educational Telecommunications Access Support

This program is part of Technology for Educational Achievement (TEACH) and is administered by the state Department of Administration. It provides Internet and two-way interactive video services through rate discounts and subsidized installation of data lines and video links. Eligible entities include school districts, private schools, CESAs, technical college districts, charter school sponsors, juvenile correctional facilities, private and tribal colleges, and public libraries. The program also provides grant funding to consortia of rural school districts for teacher training in technology. Funding for the entire program is provided through the segregated Universal Service Fund (USF), which in turn is funded by assessments on annual gross operating revenues from intrastate telecommunications providers. In 2015–2016, the state of Wisconsin distributed $8,499,100 to school districts for this program, and $10,105,100 was budgeted for 2016–2017.

Peer Review and Mentoring Grants

These grants are awarded annually on a competitive basis.[36] Under this program, CESAs, consortia of school districts, consortia of CESAs, or consortia of CESAs and school districts are eligible to apply for grants to provide peer review and mentoring for early career teachers. Grantees are required to provide matching funds, which may be in the form of money and/or in-kind services, and must be equivalent to at least 20% of the amount of the grant. Individual grants may not exceed $25,000 per applicant for the fiscal year. In 2015–2016, Wisconsin distributed $1,265,100. For 2016–2017, $1,606,700 was budgeted.

Robotics League Participation Grants

These grants provide funding for student participation in robotics competitions. In the 2016–2017 school year, grants of up to $5,000 were available to eligible teams consisting of students in grades 9–12 and at least one mentor. Grants may be awarded to public schools, independent charter schools, and home-based educational programs. Funds must be used to participate in a competition sponsored by a nonprofit organization that requires teams to design and operate robots. Eligible expenses include fees, kits, supplies, travel expenses, and a stipend for the team mentor. Teams must provide matching funds equal to the amount of the grant. In 2016–2017, a total of $250,000 was budgeted for grant awards

School Library Aid

This state aid is provided to school districts for the purchase of library books, instructional materials, and library-related computers and software. The funding source is income generated from the state's common school fund.[37] School districts receive a per-capita payment based on the share of the total number of children in the state between the ages of 4–20 residing in their respective districts. For the 2015–2016 school year, total state aid was $36,000,000.

Sparsity Aid

This program provides state aid to small school districts with low pupil density.[38] To qualify, a district must have 745 pupils or fewer, and fewer than ten pupils per square mile. Aid is calculated at $300 per pupil based on the previous school year's enrollment. For the 2016–2017 school year, total state aid was $17,674,000 with 141 (33%) of 422 school districts eligible to receive funding.

State Tuition Payments

These payments are provided to school districts that enroll students who reside in facilities as a result of action taken by a unit of local, state or federal government.[39] To receive payments, school districts must apply for reimbursement for eligible students they enrolled in the prior school year. For the 2015–2016 school year, 27 school districts received $8,224,500 in state tuition payments.

Supplemental Aid

This aid program provides state fiscal assistance to school districts with several unique characteristics: large geographical size, small student population, and small tax base due to a high percentage of exempt property. Specifically, a school district must meet three criteria: (1) enrollment below 500 pupils based on prior school year enrollment; (2) at least 200 square miles in area; and (3) at least 80% of real property in the school district exempt from property taxation, taxed as forest croplands, owned or held in trust by a federally recognized American Indian tribe, or owned by the federal government.[40] School districts that meet these criteria must apply annually for funding. In that sense, this type of funding more closely resembles a grant program although the state refers to it as categorical aid. The stated purpose is to supplement Equalization Aid.[41] Eligible school districts receive $350 per pupil based on prior year enrollment. In 2015–2016, the state distributed $73,500. For the 2016–2017 school year, $100,000 was budgeted.

NOTES

1. Faith E. Crampton, R. Craig Wood, and David C. Thompson, *Money & Schools*, 6th ed. (NY: Routledge, 2015).
2. Wis. Stat. §115.437 (2017).
3. Crampton, et al. 89, 92.
4. According to Crampton et al. (p. 252), school infrastructure may be defined as follows: "Different language has been used over the years to describe the physical environment of education. 'School plant' and 'facilities' have historically been used to describe school buildings while 'capital outlay' usually has referred to all aspects of paying for the permanent facility and major equipment needs of schools. In a broader and more recent context, the term 'infrastructure' has gained acceptance because it captures the full range of capital needs in a single word."
5. Wis. Stat. §120.115 (2017).
6. SAGE stands for Student Achievement Guarantee in Education. SAGE focused on improvement of academic achievement for low income students. One of the key components of the program was reduction of teacher/student ratios.
7. Wis. Stat. §255.505 (2017).
8. Wis. Stat. §120.10 (2017).
9. Wis. Stat. §120.137 (2017).
10. Wis. Stat. §115.995 (2017).
11. Wis. Stat. §115.745 (2017).
12. Other services included: (1) maintenance of an extended school day to provide educational, recreational, community, and social services to students as well all district residents; (2) provision of a rigorous academic curriculum to improve academic achievement; (3) creation of staff development and accountability programs to train new staff and encourage employee collaboration; and (4) development and administration of professional development plans and performance evaluations.
13. Wis. Stat. §121.85 (2017).
14. Wis. Stat. §118.35(4) (2017); Wis. Admin Code PI 13 (2017).
15. Wis. Stat. §115.76 (2017).
16. Wis. Stat. §115.881 (2017); Wis. Admin. Code PI 30 (2017).
17. Wis. Stat. §115.883 (2017).
18. The one fiscally dependent CCDEB receives revenues through contracts with participating school districts.
19. Wis. Stat. §121.58. Note that in Wisconsin school districts are required to provide transportation to private school students at no cost to the private school.
20. Wis. Stat. §121.59 (2017).
21. Note that beginning in the 2017–2018 school year, this program is now part of the state's Early College Credit Program. See, Wis. Stat. §118.55.
22. Wis. Stat. §115.7915 (2017); Wis. Admin. Code PI 49 (2017).
23. Wis. Stat. §71.05(6)(b)49 (2017).
24. Wis. Stat. §115.001 (2017).

25. Wis. Stat. §115.83(4) (2017). However, an instructional program provided to more than one family member does not constitute a home-based private educational program.
26. Wis. Stat. §118.40 (2017).
27. Prior to 2015, state-approved entities included the Milwaukee City Council, University of Wisconsin-Milwaukee (UWM), Milwaukee Area Technical College (MATC), and University of Wisconsin-Parkside. Subsequent to new legislation enacted in 2015, additional entities include: University of Wisconsin System's Office of Educational Opportunity; Gateway Technical College; College of Menominee Nation; and Lac Courte Oreilles Ojibwa.
28. Wis. Stat. §115.001(16) (2017).
29. See, *Johnson v. Burmaster*, 2008 WI App 4 (https://www.wicourts.gov/ca/opinion/DisplayDocument.html?content=html&seqNo=31069).
30. Starting with the 2016–2017 school year, 2015 open-enrolled students with disabilities receive a transfer amount of $12,000. See Wis. Stats. §115.76(5) (2017).
31. Computer Aid is state funding provided to local units of government, including school districts, equal to the amount of property tax that would otherwise have been paid on exempt equipment.
32. Wis. Stat. 120.90 (2017).
33. For more information, see, 'Fact Sheet,' State of Wisconsin Retirement System, December 7, 2017, http://etf.wi.gov/publications/et8901.pdf.
34. Wis. Stat. §115.36(3) (2017).
35. Wis. Stat. §115.415 (2017).
36. Wis. Stat. §115.405 (2017).
37. Common school fund income is derived primarily from interest payments on loans made from the fund to municipalities and school districts by the state Board of Commissioners of Public Lands. In addition, per the Wisconsin constitution, revenues from certain fines and forfeitures and sales of public lands are deposited in the common school fund.
38. Wis. Stat. §115.436 (2017).
39. Wis. Stat. §121.79 (2017).
40. Wis. Stat. §115.435 (2017).
41. Wis. Stat. §121.08 (2017).

CHAPTER 52

Wyoming

Brian Farmer
Executive Director
Wyoming School Boards Association

GENERAL BACKGROUND

Funding for public schools in Wyoming is unique. The system in place today is the result of years of litigation and the legislative development of a statewide system that is intended to be cost-based. The state is ultimately responsible for providing for the cost of education. Local resources are part of the equation, but the system is intended to provide equitable access to a 'basket of educational goods' regardless of a child's zip code.

History and Litigation

Over the years, public education in Wyoming was funded like most of the rest of the country—primarily by local property taxes. Local ad valorem taxes were responsible for a majority of the funding to the state's elementary and secondary public schools. Those funds were lightly supplemented with appropriations from the state's general fund and some federal funding. Trouble began to arise when school districts recognized that local taxes resulted in a system of 'haves and have-nots,' potentially violating the Wyoming constitution's promise of equal educational opportunity.[1] By the 1970s, mineral wealth had created a disparity as to what local taxes could generate. Due to the manner in which minerals were taxed, those jurisdictions with minerals realized a benefit to local revenues. Those jurisdictions lacking minerals generally did not produce as much revenue from ad valorem taxes. The discrepancy in levels of funding for education across the state was striking. In *Sweetwater County Planning Committee for Organization of School Districts v. Hinkle,*[2] two school districts fought over inclusion of the Bairoil school district in their consolidated district in order to enhance their tax bases. The court did not address the issue head-on, but reluctantly made suggestions to the legislature of ways to address the constitutional problem by a statewide financing system.

By 1980, the situation was worse and the disparate ability of local school districts to offer educational opportunities led to a challenge of the state's education finance system. In *Washakie County Sch. Dist. No. One v. Herschler,*[3] the Wyoming supreme court declared the entire school finance system unconstitutional. That decision concurred with *Hinkle* in holding that disparities were dramatic, and that a system based principally upon local property taxes whereby property-poor districts had less total revenue per student than property-rich districts failed to afford equal protection in violation of the state constitution. The court further declared education to be a fundamental right under the state constitution and that wealth-based classifications in regard to this right were subject to the strict scrutiny test. The court expressly held, "... whatever system is adopted by the legislature, it must not create a level of spending which is a function of wealth other than the wealth of the state as a whole."[4] The problem with the education finance system was that it resulted in disparate educational opportunities provided to children in different communities around the state. The court held that school funding must depend on state wealth and not local wealth, and it concluded that there could be no equality of quality until there was an equality of financing.

Following the *Washakie* decision, the Wyoming legislature went about redesigning the state's school finance system. A Foundation Program was devised to help equalize financial support to local school districts. The Foundation Program was financed by a mandated local 25 mill levy, a state 12 mill levy, and a county 6 mill levy. The state constitution was amended to allow the legislature to recapture revenues generated by the local 25 mill school levy when it exceeded the amount determined by formula as necessary for education financing. Those recapture funds were redistributed to areas of less local wealth through the Foundation Program. However, disparity still existed as local districts could impose up to six additional mills at their own option for use at the local level.

These changes led to a complex system of public education financing in which the state and local district shared the burden of funding education through the Foundation Program. The level of funding was a function of state and local property taxation, along with certain fines and fees. The local district would employ a statutory formula to determine necessary funding, called the foundation guarantee. The district would compute the amount of funding it would generate through local taxes, fines and fees. When local revenues were less than the foundation guarantee, the difference was paid to the district by the state as a foundation entitlement. If local revenue exceeded the foundation guarantee, the excess was recaptured by the state and rebated to the foundation fund for redistribution to the rest of the school districts in the state. The state also offered reimbursement for parts of the cost of certain 'add-ons' to the formula such as transportation expenditures and special education expenditures.

In the decade following *Washakie*, the legislative formula used to determine the foundation guarantee underwent several changes. In 1992, several districts again challenged the school finance system, alleging that changes to the system had increased and exacerbated the funding disparities identified in *Washakie*. Plaintiffs alleged wealth-driven disparities in the system so that irrational, arbitrary spending disparities continued to create unjustifiable disparity and denial of equal educational opportunity. Litigation again made its way through the system, eventually reaching the Wyoming supreme court in *Campbell County School Dist. v. State*.[5] Four Wyoming school districts initiated the litigation, claiming certain components of the school finance system were unconstitutional. A coalition of 25 school districts intervened as defendants aligned with the state, while one additional district and the Wyoming Education Association intervened as plaintiffs. Additional claims against the state school finance system were made and the issues were joined. The court found in favor of plaintiffs, again requiring changes to the school finance system in order to achieve equity.

The findings of the state supreme court in *Campbell I* were strongly in favor of plaintiffs. The court stated:

> To summarize, considering all of these various factors, the legislature must first design the best educational system by identifying the "proper" educational package each Wyoming student is entitled to have whether she lives in Laramie or in Sundance. The cost of that educational package must then be determined and the legislature must then take the necessary action to fund that package. Because education is one of the state's most important functions, lack of financial resources will not be an acceptable reason for failure to provide the best educational system. All other financial considerations must yield until education is funded.

> The state financed basket of quality educational goods and services available to all school-age youth must be nearly identical from district to district. If a local district then wants to enhance the content of that basket, the legislature can provide a mechanism by which it can be done. But first, before all else, the constitutional basket must be filled.[6]

The court provided a deadline of July 1, 1997 by which the legislature should accomplish its directive.

The legislature responded to *Campbell I* by immediately by hiring an external consultant with expertise in school finance to assist in developing a school financing system. The task was to develop a revenue distribution model which would assure adequate resources were distributed to provide a proper education for every Wyoming child based on the cost of that education. The consultant chose a block grant model to preserve as much local control as possible. The concept was that the model would produce the cost per average daily membership (ADM) and that cost would then be multiplied by an individual district's ADM to determine that district's allocation of funds. The consultant first helped to define the 'education basket of goods and services' which every child was to receive. The legislature codified this as a list of core knowledge and skill areas. The second step was to identify the instructional components necessary to deliver the basket of goods and services. The third step was to determine the cost of providing those components, and the final step was to make any needed adjustments to the model. The model was presented to the legislature in 1997.

Following the 1997 legislative session, various school districts and the Wyoming Education Association filed suit, challenging the constitutionality of the legislature's actions. Additional legislation was enacted in the 1998 session, and a special session was held later that year to address specific elements of education financing. In 1998, the legislature conducted the Wyoming Education Funding Adequacy Study in an effort to demonstrate funding was adequate. The issue moved through two trials at the lower court level, with the court ultimately concluding that the state had met its burden of proving that the revised school funding system was adequate to provide the basket of educational goods and services to Wyoming's students. A number of technical elements of the formula, however, remained a matter of dispute and in 2001 proceeded to the Wyoming supreme court in *State, et al., v. Campbell County School District, et al.*[7] The state high court again ruled in favor of plaintiffs and underscored the importance of equity in the school finance system. The court provided direction with regard to a number of elements of the financing formula and provided a deadline of July 1, 2002 by which the legislature should accomplish its directives. It is worth noting that the court acknowledged that much of the effort expended by the legislature took place in an environment of tax revenue shortfalls. Yet, the court held fast to its prior holding that education funding is a fundamental right of citizens and "lack of financial resources will not be an acceptable reason for failure to provide the best educational system."[8]

While prior cases dealt with the issue of school capital construction and the court held that the provision of adequate facilities was part of the responsibility of the state to provide for the education of Wyoming's school children, decisions tended to focus more on operations. In *State v. Campbell County School District*,[9] the state high court focused specifically on school facilities and capital construction. In this case, all parties agreed that the present method of financing capital construction was not constitutional and that capital construction financing cannot be based on local wealth but must be based upon the wealth of the state as a whole. The court held that inadequate funding for capital construction causes serious damage to school districts' ability to deliver a constitutional education to the children of the state. The court provided guidance with regard to the state's plan for addressing capital construction. The court held that the state is responsible for funding capital construction of facilities to the level deemed adequate by state standards; that the legislature is in control of the ultimate amount of spending as it exercises its responsibility of review and oversight of specific projects proposed by local school districts; that local school districts may supply revenue in excess of legislative spending; and that local bonded indebtedness is no longer required.

The final court case in the Wyoming school finance saga came in 2008 in *Campbell County School Dist. v. State*.[10] School districts and associations again challenged the constitutionality of the school finance system. The court held that the state had provided a constitutional system of school finance and that the court no longer retained jurisdiction over the matter. The court found that the state had made necessary changes to the operations components of the model. The court further found that the approach used by the state was cost-based and reasonably and accurately captured the cost of education. The court reiterated earlier rulings issued over a thirty-year period that it is the legislature's role to determine what should be included in an adequate education for Wyoming children, and then it is the legislature's responsibility to adequately fund the programs necessary to deliver that education. The court provided some guidance with regard to adjustments to the funding formula and capital construction. The court sought to close this chapter in school finance litigation and encouraged the parties to work together for the good of Wyoming's school children.

BASIC SUPPORT PROGRAM

Defining and Costing the Educational Program

The Wyoming legislature must first determine the 'proper' educational package each student is entitled to have. This is known as the 'basket of goods.' This was defined by the legislature as the Common Core of Knowledge and Common Core of Skills.[11] The Common Core of Knowledge and Common Core of Skills is implemented through content and performance standards by grade level as developed by the state board of education. The legislature further defined the educational program to include special needs programs, small class size, and instruction in state and federal constitutions. All basket components are implemented and enforced by rules and regulations of the state board of education, to be of sufficient quality to prepare students for future postsecondary education or employment opportunities and participation as citizens. State accountability and accreditation systems hold districts accountable for providing students equal access to a quality education.

The next step is to determine the cost of the proper educational package. The legislature has traditionally hired consultants to assist in determining the cost of education components. Together with the Wyoming Department of Education and the Wyoming Legislative Service Office, components of the model are costed out so that a determination of funding can be made.[12]

Once the proper educational package is defined and cost is determined, the final step is for the legislature to fund it. Funding is made as a block grant allocation, and spending is at the prerogative of the local school district.

School Foundation Program Block Grant

The starting point to understanding school finance in Wyoming today is to recognize that everything depends on a formula (funding model), adopted by the legislature. This formula determines how much money a school district receives for the education of students within the district. The system of finance is known as the School Foundation Program (SFP). Because education is ultimately the responsibility of the state, the total amount of funding a district receives is known as a guarantee. The SFP provides each district with the funding necessary to provide each student with an equal opportunity to receive a proper education. The cost-based SFP formula determines the amount of block grant resource provided to a district based on the characteristics of the schools, staff and students within the district, but the district determines how the funding is spent.

To determine the amount of the Foundation Program Guarantee a district is entitled to receive, one must start with the base resources of the funding model. Base resource funding represents funding generated at the school level by elementary school, middle school, and high school prototypes. There are additional prototypes for alternative schools and small schools (with an average daily membership of 49 or fewer students). Prototypes include the personnel, resources, supplies and materials, and additional components needed to provide for the education of students at the school. Prototypes are based on the average daily membership (ADM) of the schools. District level resources are then added to school-based resources. District resources include central office staff and supplies, maintenance and operations staff and supplies, and utilities. District prototype resources are also based on the ADM of the district.

Base resources are adjusted by further components of the funding model before the Foundation Program Guarantee is determined. Because cost of living across the state varies, a regional cost adjustment (RCA) is made to keep the formula cost-based. The theory is that the buying power of the components is to be equalized for those areas that are more costly to live in by adjusting for that higher cost of living. There is also to be an external cost adjustment (ECA) to account for costs of inflation, keeping the model current. The ECA is determined by the legislature. Four categories are evaluated: educational materials, energy, nonprofessional labor, and professional labor. There are also certain hold-harmless provisions that are intended to protect against unintended consequences for small districts or to phase in changes to the model. Districts are reimbursed for costs they have incurred for special education, transportation and certain other expenses. The Foundation Program Guarantee is the amount computed by multiplying base resources by the RCA and the RCA adjusted base resources by the ECA, then adding in any hold-harmless and reimbursements.

It is important to note that some funding for certain educational resources comes outside the block grant funding model. These resources are sometimes referred to as supplemental funding to the Foundation Program Guarantee. These include a number of grants and payments that may be made by a district. The legislature has agreed to pay for these components outside the block grant. These are not to be included in calculations of the Foundation Program Guarantee.

Funding the Block Grant

Once the Foundation Program Guarantee has been computed, the question is how to pay for it. Who is responsible for financing the educational program of the school district? The answer is that both the state and local jurisdiction (school district) may share in that responsibility. To determine district funding, it is necessary to subtract local resources from the Foundation Program Guarantee. If the Foundation Program Guarantee exceeds local resources, then the district is known as an entitlement district and the School Foundation Program Account makes a payment to the district. If local resources exceed the Foundation Program Guarantee, then the district is known as a recapture district and the School Foundation Program Account recaptures the excess revenue from the district.

Local resources are subtracted from the Foundation Program Guarantee to determine if a school district receives payment from the state as an entitlement district, or if the state is to recapture the excess revenue to be distributed to other districts across the state. State statutes determine which local resources (revenues) are to be included or excluded from the calculation. The following revenues are considered to be local resources: (1) revenue generated from a countywide 6 mill property tax; (2) the district's share of Taylor Grazing Act funds distributed to it during the previous year under federal law; (3) the district's share of railroad car company taxes distributed to it during the previous school year; (4) revenue generated from a 25 mill property tax within the school district; (5) revenue generated from motor vehicle licensing and registration, distributed in the same manner as property taxes; (6) any amount received by the district in the preceding year from the sale of real or personal property; (7) the district's share of fines and forfeitures distributed to it during the previous school year; (8) revenue generated from certain tuition received during the previous school year; (9) the district's share of forest reserve funds distributed to it during the previous year under federal law; (10) the district's share of interest and penalties on delinquent taxes distributed to it during the previous school year; (11) the district's funds exceeding the 15% allowable reserves; and (12) other revenue received by the district during the previous year that is not specifically excluded. The following revenues are specifically excluded from counting as local resources: (1) private contributions and gifts; (2) revenue dedicated to bond debts; (3) fees or charges for goods or services; (4) interest, capital gains or other earnings; (5) certain real property sales, particularly disposal of surplus buildings under the School Facilities Department; and (5) federal funds.

The state remains ultimately responsible for provision of the educational program. If the School Foundation Guarantee amount exceeds local resources, the state makes up the difference. The first payment is received by the school district by August 15 and installments are paid every month through May. If local resources exceed the School Foundation Guarantee amount, the excess is recaptured by the state. Recapture happens with two payments to the state: once in January and once in June. Districts that receive 20% or less of their funding from state revenue are eligible for advance payments.

Revenues Deposited to State Accounts

While the state's side of school finance is relatively complex, the major funds used for schools are the School Foundation Program and the School Capital Construction Account. The SFP account receives revenues generated from (1) a 12-mill statewide property tax; (2) Common School Land Income [interest, dividends, and net realized capital gains on the Common School Account, as well as revenue from non-depletable activities on Common School Account lands, including revenue streams such as grazing leases and oil or coal bonus payments]; (3) revenue transfers pursuant to spending policy; (4) revenue generated from federal mineral royalties distributed under federal law; (5) interest derived from property tax holdings by the county prior remitting it to the state and interest derived from the pooled earnings of the School Foundation Program; (6) recapture [monies paid by school districts with local resources exceeding their guarantee]; (7) revenue generated from motor vehicle licensing and registration, distributed in the same manner as property taxes; (8) revenue generated from railroad car company taxes, distributed in the same way as property taxes; and (9) any cash flow loans or augmentations directed by the legislature. The School Capital Construction Account receives revenues from federal mineral royalties, coal lease bonuses, and state mineral royalties/leases. The state spends just below 40% of its total budget on education.

Just over 48% of Wyoming is comprised of federal land acreage. As a mineral-rich state, much of that federal land is capable of producing minerals. Wyoming relies on taxation of mineral extraction from state and private lands. Since the state is unable to tax the federal government directly for extraction of minerals from federal lands, a mineral royalty is collected from the extractor in lieu of taxes. Of the first $200 million collected, nearly half (44.8%) goes to the School Foundation Program. A small amount (2.7%) goes to the School Capital Construction Account. One-third (33%) of the amount collected in excess of $200 million also goes to education.

The federal government controls much of the coal in the Powder River Basin. When that land is leased for mining of coal, the successful company must pay a bonus over time that is divided between state and federal governments. These bonuses are paid over a period of five years. Coal lease bonuses have been a great economic boon for the state of Wyoming, with over $1 billion collected between 2003 and 2009. These monies have largely gone to the construction of new schools (School Capital Construction Account). The state has largely been able to meet its obligation of providing adequate educational facilities for the delivery of the educational program through the use of these funds. However, with the diminution of coal in the U.S. energy market, new leases are rare, and the state likely will not be able to continue to rely on these funds far into the future.

It is important to understand that there are two production taxes on all Wyoming mineral production. Both taxes are assessed based on the taxable value of mineral production at the point of valuation. The point of valuation is the point where the production process (extraction) is complete, but before the mineral is processed or transported. The first of these taxes is a severance tax, assessed on the taxable value of the current year's production. The second tax is a county gross products tax—an ad valorem property tax based on the taxable value of the previous year's production. Mineral taxpayers are required to report and pay severance taxes monthly to the state based on the taxable value of the current period's production. Counties are responsible for billing and collecting the gross products tax directly from mineral taxpayers. Minerals are taxed in Wyoming after production, with the fair market value determined in February of the year following production. These ad valorem tax payments are then due in November (50%) of the year following production, and a final payment is due in May (50%) of the second year following production. With K–12 education receiving approximately 70% of the revenue from ad valorem property taxes levied on statewide assessed value, it is important to remember that a portion of the revenue comes from the gross products tax on minerals.

Visualizing Wyoming School Finance

The Wyoming School Foundation Program (SFP) provides a guaranteed level of funding to each school district. This guarantee serves as a block grant based on multiple factors, with the principal building block being pupil enrollment in the prior year. Other building blocks affecting the guarantee are special education and transportation along with the number, size and location of statutorily defined small schools.

Figures 52.1 through 52.3 provide a visual flowchart of how Wyoming funds the block grant in the SFP.[13] Figure 52.1 represents calculation of the SFP, wherein the model accounts for district-level resources and school-level resources to arrive at the estimated foundation guarantee. Resource categories are those attributed to an adequate and equitable equal educational opportunity. Expressed as four parts in Figure 52.1 the SFP solves for (1) base resources, (2) foundation guarantee, (3) supplemental funding to the foundation, and (4) determining foundation aid entitlement or recapture for each school district. Figure 52.1 includes a fifth outcome explaining the revenue sources feeding the SFP.

Figure 52.2 provides greater detail on calculating base resources in the SFP, particularly contributions to school resources and district resources—the sum of which comprises total base resources. Figure 52.2 also reveals calculation of the foundation guarantee, along with calculating foundation guarantee supplemental funding. The flowchart leads to Figure 52.3 which, as a final outcome, illustrates the overall operation of the SFP's decision tree which determines each school district's aid entitlement or recapture liability.

Finally, Figure 52.4 illustrates a sample impact on any given school district's state fiscal support.

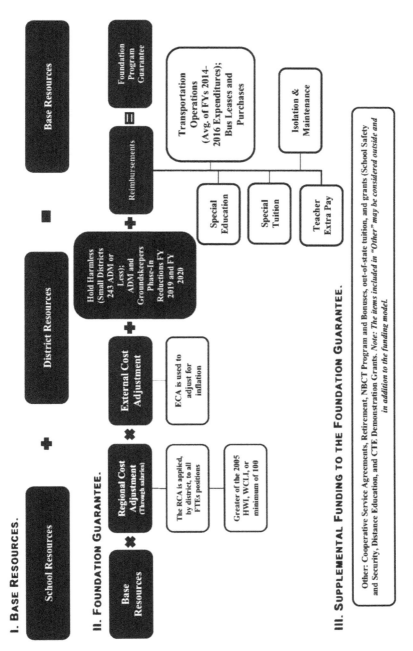

Figure 52.1a Wyoming School Foundation Program Block Grant 2018.

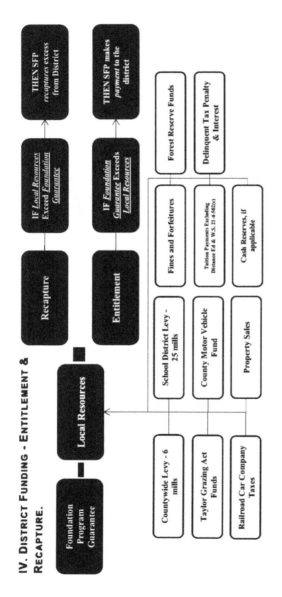

Figure 52.1b Wyoming School Foundation Program Block Grant 2018. *Source:* Wyoming LSO Budget and Fiscal Section. "State of Whyoming School Foundation Program Flow Chart." March (2018). https://wyoleg.gov/docs/SchoolFinance/SchoolFoundation-BlockGrantFlowChart.pdf By permission.

Calculating Base Resources

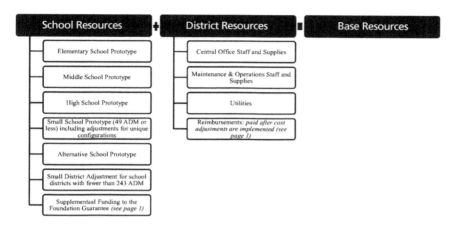

Calculating The Foundation Guarantee

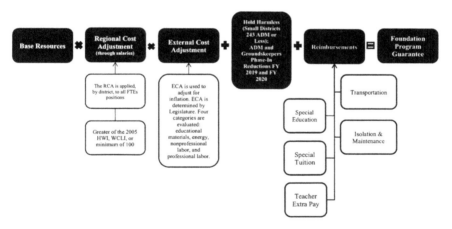

Figure 52.2a Selected Elements of the Wyoming Foundation Block Grant 2018.

Calculating Foundation Guarantee Supplemental Funding

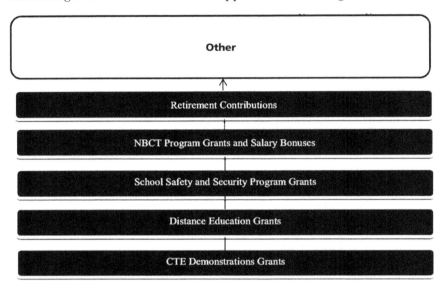

Figure 52.2b Selected Elements of the Wyoming Foundation Block Grant 2018. *Source:* Wyoming LSO Budget and Fiscal Section. "State of Wyoming School Foundation Program Flow Chart." March (2018). https://wyoleg.gov/docs/School-Finance/SchoolFoundationBlockGrantFlowChart.pdf By permission..

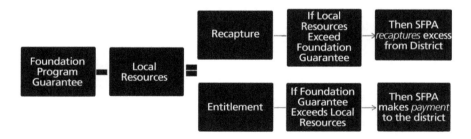

Figure 52.3 Calculating Wyoming Foundation Direct Entitlement and Recapture. *Source:* Wyoming LSO Budget and Fiscal Section. "State of Wyoming School Foundation Program Flow Chart." March (2018). https://wyoleg.gov/docs/School-Finance/SchoolFoundationBlockGrantFlowChart.pdf By permission.

Figure 52.4 Sample Impact of the Wyoming School Foundation Program on a School District 2018. *Source:* Wyoming Department of Education. "School Foundation, Final Statewide Payment Models Fiscal Year 2018." https://edu.wyoming.gov/beyond-the-classroom/school-programs/school-foundation/ Resourced from Direct Summary Tab FINAL_FY18_StatewidePayment_Model_6-20-18_protected_jc

OTHER SELECTED FUNDING PROVISIONS[14]

The following categories call out topics about school funding that are common to other chapters in this book. In the case of Wyoming, most are included in the School Foundation Plan (SFP). Reference is made to 'Tabs' in the state's extensive data worksheets. As an anchoring point, the School Resources Tab[15] in state spreadsheet form accumulates and illustrates the operation of these provisions.

Density or Sparsity

Density or sparsity in pupil enrollment is adjusted in the SFP based on ADM through calculations using pupil-teacher ratios generated through the SFP model. See Small District Adjustment Tab.[16]

Grade Level Differences

Grade level differences apply through the SFP by elementary, middle, and high school formula provisions for calculation. See SFC Building Tab.[17]

Capital Outlay and Debt Service

Capital outlay and debt service are supported in Wyoming through the School Facilities Division of the State Construction Department. Current effort is underway to alter the state's liability for school infrastructure costs given the state's large role in funding new construction for public schools. See SFC Building Data Tab.[18]

Transportation

The state of Wyoming reimburses 100% of pupil transportation costs. See Transportation Tab.[19]

Special Education

Special education is supported through calculation of the SFP. Calculation of fiscal support occurs through the special education worksheet of the statewide payment model. Adjustments are made on an ADM basis. See Special Education Tab.[20]

Compensatory Programs

Compensatory programs are supported through calculation of the SFP in the school-level resources sequence. See At-Risk Tab.[21]

English Language Learner/Bilingual Education

English language support programs are supported through calculation of the SFP in the school-level resources sequence. See School Resources Tab.[22]

Career and Technical Education

Career and technical education programs are supported through calculation of the SFP in the school-level resources sequence. See Voc Ed Tab.[23]

Preschool Programs

The state of Wyoming does not allocate specific funds for preschool programs. Local districts may use School Foundation Program monies in support of preschool programs.

Charter Schools

Charter schools in Wyoming are supported through calculation of the SFP. Calculation of fiscal support occurs through the Charter School Adjustments worksheet of the statewide payment model. Adjustments are made on an ADM basis. See Charter School Adjustment Tab.[24]

CONCLUSION

For Fiscal Year 2018, total State Foundation Program payments to Wyoming school districts totaled $858,211,428.71.[25] These amounts were distributed to 48 school districts serving 91,281.9 ADM pupils.[26] The 2018 Wyoming legislative session ended with education funding cuts in the amounts of approximately $8 million for FY 2019 and $19.3 million for FY 2020. The bulk of these cuts were aimed at changes to the funding formulas for ADM and school groundskeepers and the implementation of a cap on special education funding.[27] Major modifications to the SFA included: (1) limiting total statewide special education reimbursements for school years 2019–20 and 2020–21 to not exceed the amount to be reimbursed in school year 2018–19; (2) requiring school districts to participate in Department of Workforce Services' programs that reduce school district worker's compensation premiums; (3) restricting workers compensation extra-hazardous employment designation for special education assistants, teachers, and related service providers to only apply when the employee is working directly with eligible students; and (4) prohibiting school districts from entering into a new leases for school buses, although school districts would be eligible receive 100% reimbursement for a bus purchase in the year following the purchase.[28] More cuts loom, as the state senate has vowed to cut another $100 million from the education budget, while rejecting increases in revenue to improve the cash flow for the state budget.[29]

Today, the state of Wyoming anticipates a structural deficit between the anticipated expenditures for education (the School Foundation Program Account and the School Capital Construction Account) and the traditional sources of revenue used to fund education. The 64th Wyoming Legislature established the state's 'rainy day fund' (Legislative Stabilization Reserve Account) as a backstop to fill the deficit. However, with approximately $1.6 billion in reserve, the account is finite. The state is currently searching for revenue solutions to address the problem, and state-initiated cuts to education spending appear to have dropped below the constitutional floor of a cost-based education. This leaves open the threat of future litigation and would only be exacerbated by further cuts. The state continues to explore efficiencies to reduce the cost of education. It has also made some changes to spending policy and the flow of revenue within the complex fiscal system that have resulted in more money for education.

Like much of the rest of government operations in Wyoming, the fate of education finance appears to be tied to the mineral industry. When the energy economy is doing well, new schools will be built, and operations will be adequately funded. However, as the energy industry is subject to boom and bust cycles, proper education funding will be threatened along with the ups and downs of the energy industry. Much of the funding for K–12 education in Wyoming over the last few decades has been the beneficiary of a positive energy market. Recent threats to the extraction of coal, oil and natural gas in Wyoming point to a need to rethink how Wyoming funds education.

NOTES

1. Wyo. Const. Art. 7, §1. "The legislature shall provide for the establishment and maintenance of a complete and uniform system of public instruction, embracing free elementary schools of every needed kind and grade, a university with such technical and professional departments as the public good may require and the means of the state allow, and such other institutions as may be necessary."
2. 491 P.2d 1234, 1237 (Wyo. 1971).
3. 606 P.2d 310 (Wyo. 1980).
4. Ibid. p. 336.
5. 907 P.2d 1238 (Wyo. 1995), a.k.a. *Campbell I*.
6. Ibid. p. 1279.
7. 19 P.3d 518 (Wyo. 2001), a.k.a. *Campbell II*.
8. Ibid. 1279.
9. 32 P.3d 325 (Wyo. 2001), a.k.a. *Campbell III*.
10. Nos. 06-74, 06-75, 2008 WY 2, a.k.a. *Campbell IV*.
11. W.S. 21-9-101.
12. The most recent consultant hired by the Wyoming Legislature for this purpose was Augenblick, Palaich and Associates in 2017. The legislature did not adopt the recommendations of the 2018 Recalibration Report by APA. Thus, they have continued to rely on recommendations of a previous consultant, i.e., a report from Picus, Odden and Associates from 2015.
13. Graphics excerpted and condensed with permission from the Wyoming Legislative Service Office's extensive flowchart illustrating all elements of calculation (2018). Retrieved from https://wyoleg.gov/docs/SchoolFinance/SchoolFoundationBlockGrantFlowChart.pdf
14. This section draws partly on Deborah Verstegen, "Wyoming." *A Quick Glance at School Finance: A 50 State Survey of School Finance Policies 2018*. Retrieved from https://schoolfinancesdav.wordpress.com The section also relies on the Wyoming Department of Education's "The Wyoming Funding Model Guidebook and Technical Specifications." Retrieved from https://edu.wyoming.gov/beyond-the-classroom/school-programs/school-foundation/
15. Wyoming Department of Education, "School Foundation, Final Statewide Payment Models Fiscal Year 2018." Retrieved from https://edu.wyoming.gov/beyond-the-classroom/school-programs/school-foundation/ Resourced from FINAL_FY18_StatewidePayment_Model_6-20-18_protected_jc
16. Ibid.
17. Ibid.
18. Ibid.
19. Ibid.
20. Ibid.
21. Ibid.
22. Ibid.
23. Ibid.
24. Ibid.

25. Ibid, Tab Payments. See this tab for a total accumulation of payments to school districts.
26. Ibid, Tab ADM.
27. Wyoming Education Association. "Governor Mead Signs Bill Today Cutting Public Education." (Press release March 27, 2018). Retrieved from http://wyoea.org/files/2018/03/WEA_Press_Release_March27-18.pdf/
28. Wyoming Legislative Service Office. Memorandum: End of Session Summary." March 15, 2018. Retrieved from https://wyoleg.gov/docs/School Finance/SchoolFinanceEndofSessionSummarywithCharts.pdf
29. Wyoming Education Association. "December 2018 Legislative Update." (2018). Retrieved from http://view.email.nea.org/?qs=1e31d2a9fb43fd1a7dc3f822f6-b56bc27bd1b6a9ddc655e705d48d0f3debdcca3ec5733c6262d62a28fe1d0f9 047c4f3a7f06d397c7d36f244b681f553e6e51fc74884c07014b4012163d289f-57b1ef1

CPSIA information can be obtained
at www.ICGtesting.com
Printed in the USA
LVHW030008110519
617478LV00003B/3/P